Learn Java/J2EE core concepts and key areas

With

Java/J2EE Job Interview Companion

By

K.Arulkumaran
&
A.Sivayini

Technical Reviewers

Craig Malone
Stuart Watson
Arulazi Dhesiaseelan
Lara D'Albreo

Cover Design, Layout, & Editing

A.Sivayini

Acknowledgements

A. Sivayini
Mr. & Mrs. R. Kumaraswamipillai

Java/J2EE

Job Interview Companion

The author has made every effort in the preparation of this book to ensure the accuracy of the information. However, information in this is sold with warranty either expressed or implied. The author will not be held liable for any damages caused or alleged to be caused either directly or indirectly by this book.

Please e-mail feedback and corrections (technical, grammatical and / or spelling) to

java-interview@hotmail.com

First Edition (220 + Q & A): Dec. 2005
Second Edition (400 + Q & A): March 2008 (Batch 1)

Printed & Distributed in India by

Goel's Computer Hut

126 Budhwar Peth,
Pune – 411002.
Tel: +91 (020) 24451958/59
Fax: +91(020) 24451959
computhut@pn2.vsnl.net.in

O537

Outline

SECTION	DESCRIPTION
	What this book will do for you?
	Motivation for this book
	Key Areas index
SECTION 1	Interview questions and answers on: **Java** • Fundamentals • Swing • Applet • Performance and Memory issues • Personal and Behavioral/Situational • Behaving right in an interview • Key Points
SECTION 2	Interview questions and answers on: **Enterprise Java** • J2EE Overview • Servlet • JSP • JDBC / JTA • JNDI / LDAP • RMI • EJB • JMS • XML • SQL, Database, and O/R mapping • RUP & UML • Struts • Web and Application servers. • Best practices and performance considerations. • Testing and deployment. • Personal and Behavioral/Situational • Key Points
SECTION 3	Putting it all together section. **How would you go about...?** 1. How would you go about documenting your Java/J2EE application? 2. How would you go about designing a Java/J2EE application? 3. How would you go about identifying performance problems and/or memory leaks in your Java application? 4. How would you go about minimizing memory leaks in your Java/J2EE application? 5. How would you go about improving performance of your Java/J2EE application? 6. How would you go about identifying any potential thread-safety issues in your Java/J2EE application? 7. How would you go about identifying any potential transactional issues in your Java/J2EE

<table>
<tr><td colspan="2">

application?

8. How would you go about applying the Object Oriented (OO) design concepts in your Java/J2EE application?

9. How would you go about applying the UML diagrams in your Java/J2EE project?

10. How would you go about describing the software development processes you are familiar with?

11. How would you go about applying the design patterns in your Java/J2EE application?

12. How would you go about designing a Web application where the business tier is on a separate machine from the presentation tier. The business tier should talk to 2 different databases and your design should point out the different design patterns?

13. How would you go about determining the enterprise security requirements for your Java/J2EE application?

14. How would you go about describing the open source projects like JUnit (unit testing), Ant (build tool), CVS (version control system) and log4J (logging tool) which are integral part of most Java/J2EE projects?

15. How would you go about describing Service Oriented Architecture (**SOA**) and Web services?

</td></tr>
</table>

SECTION 4	**Emerging Technologies/Frameworks**
	• Test Driven Development (**TDD**).
	• Aspect Oriented Programming (**AOP**).
	• Inversion of Control (**IoC**) (Also known as **Dependency Injection**).
	• Annotations or attributes based programming (xdoclet etc).
	• Spring framework.
	• Hibernate framework.
	• EJB 3.0.
	• JavaServer Faces (**JSF**) framework.
SECTION 5	**Sample interview questions …**
	• **Java**
	• **Web Components**
	• **Enterprise**
	• **Design**
	• **General**
	GLOSSARY OF TERMS
	RESOURCES
	INDEX

Table of contents

What this book will do for you?

Have you got the time to read 10 or more books and articles to add value prior to the interview? This book has been written mainly from the perspective of **Java/J2EE job seekers** and **interviewers**. There are numerous books and articles on the market covering specific topics like Java, J2EE, EJB, Design Patterns, ANT, CVS, Multi-Threading, Servlets, JSP, emerging technologies like AOP (Aspect Oriented Programming), Test Driven Development (TDD), Dependency Injection DI (aka IoC – Inversion of Control) etc. But from an interview perspective it is not possible to brush up on all these books where each book usually has from 300 pages to 600 pages. The basic purpose of this book is to cover all the core concepts and key areas, which all Java/J2EE developers, designers and architects should be conversant with to perform well in their current jobs and to launch a successful career by doing well at interviews. The interviewer can also use this book to make sure that they hire the right candidate depending on their requirements. This book contains a wide range of topics relating to Java/J2EE development in a concise manner supplemented with diagrams, tables, sample codes and examples. This book is also appropriately categorized to enable you to choose the area of interest to you.

This book will assist all Java/J2EE practitioners to become better at what they do. Usually it takes years to understand all the core concepts and key areas when you rely only on your work experience. The best way to fast track this is to read appropriate technical information and proactively apply these in your work environment. It worked for me and hopefully it will work for you as well. I was also at one stage undecided whether to name this book "**Java/J2EE core concepts and key areas**" or "**Java/J2EE Job Interview Companion**". The reason I chose "**Java/J2EE Job Interview Companion**" is because the core concepts and key areas discussed in this book helped me to be successful in my interviews, helped me to survive and succeed at my work regardless what my job (junior developer, senior developer, technical lead, designer, contractor etc) was and also gave me thumbs up in code reviews. This book also has been set out as a handy reference guide and a roadmap for building enterprise Java applications.

Motivation for this book

I started using Java in 1999 when I was working as a junior developer. During those two years as a permanent employee, I pro-actively spent many hours studying the core concepts behind Java/J2EE in addition to my hands on practical experience. Two years later I decided to start contracting. Since I started contracting in 2001, my career had a much-needed boost in terms of contract rates, job satisfaction, responsibility etc. I moved from one contract to another with a view of expanding my skills and increasing my contract rates.

In the last 5 years of contracting, I have worked for 5 different organizations both medium and large on 8 different projects. For each contract I held, on average I attended 6-8 interviews with different companies. In most cases multiple job offers were made and consequently I was in a position to negotiate my contract rates and also to choose the job I liked based on the type of project, type of organization, technology used, etc. I have also sat for around 10 technical tests and a few preliminary phone interviews.

The success in the interviews did not come easily. I spent hours prior to each set of interviews wading through various books and articles as a preparation. The motivation for this book was to collate all this information into a single book, which will save me time prior to my interviews but also can benefit others in their interviews. What is in this book has helped me to go from **just a Java/J2EE job to a career in Java/J2EE** in a short time. It has also given me the job security that 'I can find a contract/permanent job opportunity even in the difficult job market'.

I am not suggesting that every one should go contracting but by performing well at the interviews you can be in a position to pick the permanent role you like and also be able to negotiate your salary package. Those of you who are already in good jobs can impress your team leaders, solution designers and/or architects for a possible promotion by demonstrating your understanding of the key areas discussed in this book. You can discuss with your senior team members about **performance issues, transactional issues, threading issues (concurrency issues)** and **memory issues**. In most of my previous contracts I was in a position to impress my team leads and architects by pinpointing some of the critical performance, memory, transactional and threading issues with the code and subsequently fixing them. Trust me it is not hard to impress someone if you understand the key areas.

For example:

- Struts action classes are not thread-safe (Refer **Q113** in Enterprise section).
- JSP variable declaration is not thread-safe (Refer **Q34** in Enterprise section).
- Valuable resources like database connections should be closed properly to avoid any memory and performance issues (Refer **Q45** in Enterprise section).
- Throwing an application exception will not rollback the transaction in EJB. (Refer **Q77** in Enterprise section).

The other key areas, which are vital to any software development, are a good understanding of some of **key design concepts, design patterns,** and a **modeling language** like **UML**. These key areas are really worthy of a mention in your resume and interviews.

For example:

- Know how to use inheritance, polymorphism and encapsulation (Refer **Q7**, **Q8**, **Q9**, and **Q10** in Java section.).
- Why use design patterns? (Refer **Q5** in Enterprise section).
- Why is UML important? (Refer **Q106** in Enterprise section).

If you happen to be in an interview with an organization facing serious issues with regards to their Java application relating to memory leaks, performance problems or a crashing JVM etc then you are likely to be asked questions on these topics. Refer **Q72 – Q74** in Java section and **Q123, Q125** in Enterprise section.

If you happen to be in an interview with an organization which is working on a pilot project using a different development methodology like agile methodology etc or has just started adopting a newer **development process** or **methodology** then you are likely to be asked questions on this key area.

If the team lead/architect of the organization you are being interviewed for feels that the current team is lacking skills in the key areas of **design concepts** and **design patterns** then you are likely to be asked questions on these key areas.

Another good reason why these key areas like transactional issues, design concepts, design patterns etc are vital are because solution designers, architects, team leads, and/or senior developers are usually responsible for conducting the technical interviews. These areas are their favorite topics because these are essential to any software development.

Some interviewers request you to write a small program during interview or prior to getting to the interview stage. This is to ascertain that you can code using object oriented concepts and design patterns. So I have included a **coding key area** to illustrate what you need to look for while coding.

- Apply OO concepts like inheritance, polymorphism and encapsulation: Refer **Q10** in Java section.
- Program to interfaces not to implementations: Refer **Q12, Q17** in Java section.
- Use of relevant design patterns: Refer **Q11, Q12** in How would you go about… section.
- Use of Java collections API and exceptions correctly: Refer **Q16** and **Q39** in Java section.
- Stay away from hard coding values: Refer **Q05** in Java section.

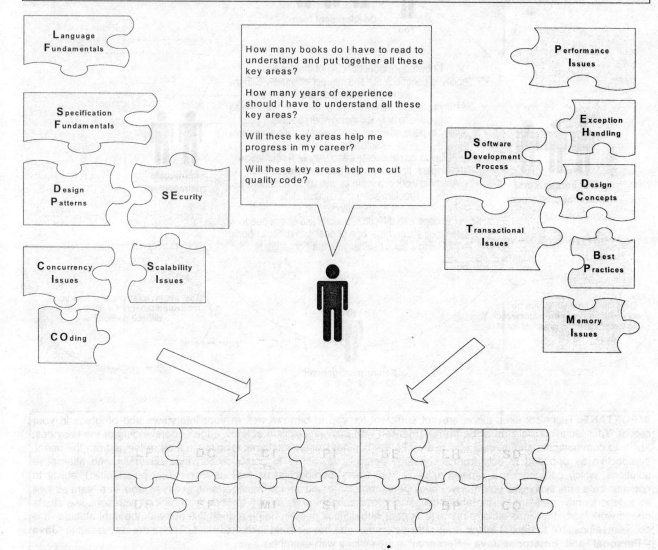

This book aims to solve the above dilemma.

My dad keeps telling me to find a permanent job (instead of contracting), which in his view provides better job security but I keep telling him that in my view in Information Technology the job security is achieved only by keeping your knowledge and skills sharp and up to date. The 8 contract positions I held over the last 5.5 years have given me broader experience in Java/J2EE and related technologies. It also kept me motivated since there was always something new to learn in each assignment, and not all companies will appreciate your skills and expertise until you decide to leave. Do the following statements sound familiar to you when you hand in your resignation or decide not to extend your contract after getting another job offer? "Can I tempt you to come back? What can I do to keep you here?" etc. You might even think why you waited so long. The best way to make an impression in any organizations is to understand and proactively apply and resolve the issues relating to the **Key Areas** discussed in this book. But **be a team player, be tactful** and **don't be critical of everything, do not act in a superior way** and **have a sense of humor.**

"Technical skills must be complemented with good business and interpersonal skills."

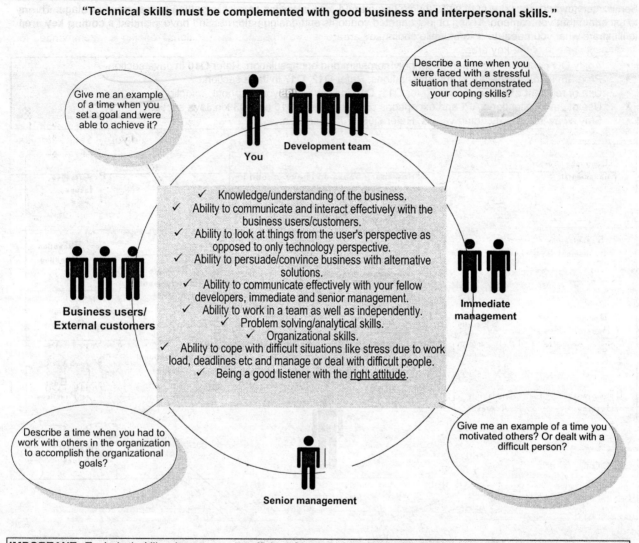

IMPORTANT: Technical skills alone are not sufficient for you to perform well in your interviews and progress in your career. Your technical skills **must be complemented** with business skills (i.e. knowledge/understanding of the business, ability to communicate and interact effectively with the business users/customers, ability to look at things from the users' perspective as opposed to only from technology perspective, ability to persuade/convince business with alternative solutions, which can provide a win/win solution from users' perspective as well as technology perspective), ability to communicate effectively with your fellow developers, immediate and senior management, ability to work in a team as well as independently, problem solving/analytical skills, organizational skills, ability to cope with difficult situations like stress due to work load, deadlines etc and manage or deal with difficult people, being a good listener with the right attitude (It is sometimes possible to have "**I know it all attitude**", when you have strong technical skills. These are discussed in "**Java – Personal**" and "**Enterprise Java – Personal**" sub-sections with examples.

Quick Read guide: It is recommended that you go through all the questions in all the sections (all it takes is to read a few questions & answers each day) but if you are pressed for time or would like to read it just before an interview then follow the steps shown below:

-- Read/Browse all questions marked as **"FAQ"** in all four sections.
-- Read/Browse **Key Points** in Java and Enterprise Java sections.

Key Areas Index

I have categorized the core concepts and issues into **14 key areas** as listed below. These key areas are vital for any good software development. This index will enable you to refer to the questions based on **key areas**. Also note that each question has an icon next to it to indicate which key area or areas it belongs to. Additional reading is recommended for beginners in each of the key areas.

Key Areas	icon	Question Numbers			
		Java section	**Enterprise Java section**	**How would you go about...?**	**Emerging Technologies / Frameworks**
Language Fundamentals	LF	Q1-Q6, Q12-Q16, Q18-Q24, Q26-Q33, Q35-Q38, Q41-Q50, Q53-Q71	-		Q10, Q15, Q17, Q19
Specification Fundamentals	SF	-	Q1, Q2, Q4, Q6, Q7-Q15, Q17-Q19, Q22, Q26-Q33, Q35-Q38, Q41, Q42, Q44, Q46-Q81, Q89-Q93, Q95-Q97, Q99, 102, Q110, Q112-Q115, Q118-Q119, Q121, Q126, Q127, Q128	Q15	
Design Concepts	DC	Q1, Q7-Q12, Q15, Q26, Q22, Q56	Q2, Q3, Q19, Q20, Q21, Q31, Q45, Q91, Q94, Q98, Q101, Q106, Q107, Q108, Q109, Q111	Q02, Q08, Q09, Q15	Q3 - Q13, Q13, Q14, Q16, Q17, Q18, Q20
Design Patterns	DP	Q12, Q16, Q24, Q36, Q51, Q52, Q58, Q63, Q75	Q5, Q5, Q22, Q24, Q25, Q41, Q83, Q84, Q85, Q86, Q87, Q88, Q110, Q111, Q116	Q11, Q12	Q9 - Q13
Transactional Issues	TI	-	Q43, Q71, Q72, Q73, Q74, Q75, Q77, Q78, Q79	Q7	
Concurrency Issues	CI	Q15, Q17, Q21, Q34, Q42, Q46, Q62	Q16, Q34, Q72, Q78, Q113	Q6	
Performance Issues	PI	Q15, Q17,Q20-Q26, Q46, Q62, Q72	Q10, Q16, Q43, Q45, Q46, Q72, Q83-Q88, Q93, Q97, Q98, Q100, Q102, Q123, Q125, Q128	Q3, Q5	
Memory Issues	MI	Q26, Q34, Q37,Q38, Q42, Q51, Q73, Q74	Q45, Q93	Q3, Q4	
Scalability Issues	SI	Q23, Q24	Q20, Q21, Q120, Q122		
Exception Handling	EH	Q39, Q40	Q76, Q77		
Security	SE	Q10, Q35, Q70	Q12, Q13, Q23, Q35, Q46, Q51, Q58, Q81, Q92	Q13	
Best Practices	BP	Q17, Q25, Q39, Q72, Q73	Q10, Q16, Q39, Q40, Q41, Q46, Q82, Q124, Q125	Q1, Q2	

Software Development Process	SD	-	Q103-Q109, Q129, Q130, Q132, Q136	Q1, Q9, Q10, Q14	Q1, Q2
Coding[1]	CO	Q05, Q10, Q12, Q14 – Q21, Q23, Q25, Q26, Q33, Q35, Q39, Q51, Q52, Q55	Q10, Q18, Q21, Q23, Q36, Q38, Q42, Q43, Q45, Q74, Q75, Q76, Q77, Q112, Q114, Q127, Q128	Q11, Q12	
Frequently Asked Questions	FAQ	Q1, Q6, Q7, Q9, Q10, Q12, Q13, Q14, Q15, Q16, Q18, Q20, Q21, Q22, Q23, Q27, Q28, Q29, Q30, Q31, Q32, Q36, Q37, Q43, Q45, Q46, Q48, Q51, Q52, Q55, Q58, Q60, Q62, Q63, Q64, Q67, Q68, Q69, Q70, Q71 Q72 – Q86	Q1, Q2, Q3, Q7, Q10, Q11, Q12, Q13, Q16, Q19, Q22, Q24, Q25, Q27, Q28, Q30, Q31, Q32, Q34, Q35, Q36, Q39, Q40, Q41, Q42, Q43, Q45, Q46, Q48, Q49, Q50, Q52, Q53, Q61, Q63, Q65, Q66, Q69, Q70, Q71, Q72, Q73, Q76, Q77, Q82, Q83, Q84, Q85, Q86, Q87, Q90, Q91, Q93, Q95, Q96, Q97, Q98, Q100, Q101, Q102, Q107, Q108, Q110, Q113, Q115, Q116, Q118, Q123, Q124, Q125, Q126, Q129, Q130, Q131, Q133, Q134, Q135, Q136.	Q1, Q2, Q3, Q4, Q5, Q6, Q7, Q8, Q9, Q10, Q12, Q15	Q1, Q6, Q7, Q9, Q10, Q11, Q15, Q16, Q17, Q18

[1] Some interviewers request you to write a small program during interview or prior to getting to the interview stage. This is to ascertain that you can code using object oriented concepts and design patterns. I have included a coding key area to illustrate what you need to look for while coding. Unlike other key areas, the CO is not always shown against the question but shown above the actual section of relevance within a question.

SECTION ONE

Java – Interview questions & answers

K
E
Y

A
R
E
A
S

- Language Fundamentals **LF**
- Design Concepts **DC**
- Design Patterns **DP**
- Concurrency Issues **CI**
- Performance Issues **PI**
- Memory Issues **MI**
- Exception Handling **EH**
- Security **SE**
- Scalability Issues **SI**
- Coding[1] **CO**

FAQ - **F**requently **A**sked **Q**uestions

---

[1] Unlike other key areas, the **CO** is not always shown against the question but shown above the actual content of relevance within a question.

Java – Fundamentals

Q 01: Give a few reasons for using Java? LF DC FAQ
A 01: Java is a fun language. Let's look at some of the reasons:

- Built-in support for multi-threading, socket communication, and memory management (automatic garbage collection).

- Object Oriented (OO).

- Better portability than other languages across operating systems.

- Supports Web based applications (Applet, Servlet, and JSP), distributed applications (sockets, RMI, EJB etc) and network protocols (HTTP, JRMP etc) with the help of extensive standardized APIs (Application Programming Interfaces).

Q 02: What is the main difference between the Java platform and the other software platforms? LF
A 02: Java platform is a software-only platform, which runs on top of other hardware-based platforms like UNIX, NT etc.

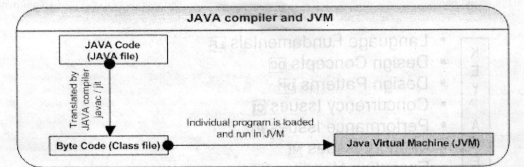

The Java platform has 2 components:

- Java Virtual Machine (**JVM**) – 'JVM' is a software that can be ported onto various hardware platforms. Byte codes are the machine language of the JVM.

- Java Application Programming Interface (**Java API**) – set of classes written using the Java language and run on the JVM.

Q 03: What is the difference between C++ and Java? LF
A 03: Both C++ and Java use similar syntax and are Object Oriented, but:

- Java does not support pointers. Pointers are inherently tricky to use and troublesome.

- Java does not support multiple inheritances because it causes more problems than it solves. Instead Java supports **multiple interface inheritance**, which allows an object to inherit many method signatures from different interfaces with the condition that the inheriting object must implement those inherited methods. The multiple interface inheritance also allows an object to behave **polymorphically** on those methods. [Refer **Q9** and **Q10** in Java section.]

- Java does not support destructors but adds a finalize() method. Finalize methods are invoked by the garbage collector prior to reclaiming the memory occupied by the object, which has the finalize() method. This means you do not know when the objects are going to be finalized. **Avoid using finalize() method to release non-memory resources** like file handles, sockets, database connections etc because Java has only a finite number of these resources and you do not know when the garbage collection is going to kick in to release these resources through the finalize() method.

- Java does not include structures or unions because the traditional data structures are implemented as an object oriented framework (Java Collections Framework – Refer **Q16**, **Q17** in Java section).

- All the code in Java program is encapsulated within classes therefore Java does not have global variables or functions.

- C++ requires explicit memory management, while Java includes automatic garbage collection. [Refer **Q37** in Java section].

Q 04: What are the usages of Java packages? `LF`

A 04: It helps resolve naming conflicts when different packages have classes with the same names. This also helps you organize files within your project. `For example:` **java.io** package do something related to I/O and **java.net** package do something to do with network and so on. If we tend to put all .java files into a single package, as the project gets bigger, then it would become a nightmare to manage all your files.

You can create a package as follows with **package** keyword, which is the first keyword in any Java program followed by **import** statements. The **java.lang** package is imported implicitly by default and all the other packages must be explicitly imported.

```
package com.xyz.client ;
import  java.io.File;
import  java.net.URL;
```

Java package helps you resolve the naming conflicts.

Q 05: Explain Java class loaders? If you have a class in a package, what do you need to do to run it? Explain dynamic class loading? `LF`

A 05: Class loaders are hierarchical. Classes are introduced into the JVM as they are referenced by name in a class that is **already running** in the JVM. So, how is the very first class loaded? The very first class is especially loaded with the help of *static main( )* method declared in your class. All the subsequently loaded classes are loaded by the classes, which are already loaded and running. A class loader creates a namespace. All JVMs include at least one class loader that is embedded within the JVM called the primordial (or bootstrap) class loader. Now let's look at non-primordial class loaders. The JVM has hooks in it to allow user defined class loaders to be used in place of primordial class loader. Let us look at the class loaders created by the JVM.

CLASS LOADER	reloadable?	Explanation
Bootstrap (**primordial**)	No	Loads JDK internal classes, *java.** packages. (as defined in the sun.boot.class.path system property, typically loads rt.jar and i18n.jar)
Extensions	No	Loads jar files from JDK extensions directory (as defined in the java.ext.dirs system property – usually lib/ext directory of the JRE)
System	No	Loads classes from system classpath (as defined by the java.class.path property, which is set by the **CLASSPATH** environment variable or –classpath or –cp command line options)

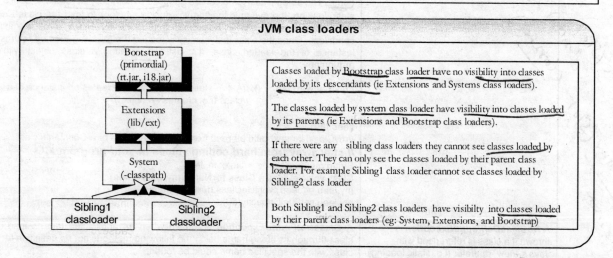

JVM class loaders

Classes loaded by Bootstrap class loader have no visibility into classes loaded by its descendants (ie Extensions and Systems class loaders).

The classes loaded by system class loader have visibility into classes loaded by its parents (ie Extensions and Bootstrap class loaders).

If there were any sibling class loaders they cannot see classes loaded by each other. They can only see the classes loaded by their parent class loader. For example Sibling1 class loader cannot see classes loaded by Sibling2 class loader

Both Sibling1 and Sibling2 class loaders have visibilty into classes loaded by their parent class loaders (eg: System, Extensions, and Bootstrap)

Class loaders are hierarchical and use a **delegation model** when loading a class. Class loaders request their parent to load the class first before attempting to load it themselves. When a class loader loads a class, the child class loaders in the hierarchy will never reload the class again. Hence **uniqueness** is maintained. Classes loaded

JVM has class loader known as Bootstrap

by a child class loader have **visibility** into classes loaded by its parents up the hierarchy but the reverse is not true as explained in the above diagram.

Q. What do you need to do to run a class with a main() method in a package?

Example: Say, you have a class named "Pet" in a project folder "c:\myProject" and package named com.xyz.client, will you be able to compile and run it as it is?

```
package com.xyz.client;

public class Pet {
    public static void main(String[] args) {
        System.out.println("I am found in the classpath");
    }
}
```

To run → c:\myProject> `java com.xyz.client.Pet`

The answer is no and you will get the following exception: "Exception in thread "main" java.lang.-NoClassDefFoundError: com/xyz/client/Pet". You need to set the classpath. How can you do that? One of the following ways:

1. Set the operating system **CLASSPATH** environment variable to have the project folder "c:\myProject". [Shown in the above diagram as the System –classpath class loader]
2. Set the operating system **CLASSPATH** environment variable to have a jar file "c:/myProject/client.jar", which has the *Pet.class* file in it. [Shown in the above diagram as the System –classpath class loader].
3. Run it with –cp or –classpath option as shown below:

```
c:\>java -cp  c:/myProject  com.xyz.client.Pet
            OR
c:\>java -classpath c:/myProject/client.jar  com.xyz.client.Pet
```

Important: Two objects loaded by different class loaders are never equal even if they carry the same values, which mean a class is uniquely identified in the context of the associated class loader. This applies to **singletons** too, where **each class loader will have its own singleton**. [Refer **Q51** in Java section for singleton design pattern]

Q. Explain static vs. dynamic class loading?

Static class loading	Dynamic class loading
Classes are statically loaded with Java's "new" operator.	Dynamic loading is a technique for programmatically invoking the functions of a class loader at run time. Let us look at how to load classes dynamically.

class MyClass {
   public static void main(String args[]) {
      Car c = **new** Car();
   }
	Class.forName (String *className*); //static method which returns a Class
	
	The above static method returns the class object associated with the class name. The string *className* can be supplied dynamically at run time. Unlike the static loading, the dynamic loading will decide whether to load the class *Car* or the class *Jeep* at runtime based on a properties file and/or other runtime conditions. Once the class is dynamically loaded the following method returns an instance of the loaded class. It's just like creating a class object with no arguments.
	
	class.newInstance (); //A non-static method, which creates an instance of a
	                    //class (i.e. creates an object).
	
	Jeep myJeep = null ;
	//myClassName should be read from a .properties file or a Constants class.
	// stay away from hard coding values in your program. CO
	String myClassName = "au.com.Jeep" ;
	Class vehicleClass = **Class.forName**(myClassName) ;
	myJeep = (Jeep) vehicleClass.**newInstance**();
	myJeep.setFuelCapacity(50);

A *NoClassDefFoundException* is thrown if a class is referenced with Java's "*new*" operator (i.e. static loading) but the runtime system cannot find the referenced class.	A *ClassNotFoundException* is thrown when an application tries to load in a class through its string name using the following methods but no definition for the class with the specified name could be found:
	
	  ▪ The forName(..) method in class - *Class*.
	  ▪ The findSystemClass(..) method in class - *ClassLoader*.
	  ▪ The loadClass(..) method in class - *ClassLoader*.

Q. What are "static initializers" or "static blocks with no function names"? When a class is loaded, all blocks that are declared static and don't have function name (i.e. static initializers) are executed even before the constructors are executed. As the name suggests they are typically used to initialize static fields. CO

```
public class StaticInitializer {
    public static final int A = 5;
    public static final int B; //note that it is not → public static final int B = null;
    //note that since B is final, it can be initialized only once.

    //Static initializer block, which is executed only once when the class is loaded.

    static {
        if(A == 5)
            B = 10;
        else
            B = 5;
    }

    public StaticInitializer(){}  //constructor is called only after static initializer block
}
```

The following code gives an **Output of** A=5, B=10.

```
public class Test {
    System.out.println("A =" + StaticInitializer.A + ", B =" + StaticInitializer.B);
}
```

Q 06: What is the difference between constructors and other regular methods? What happens if you do not provide a constructor? Can you call one constructor from another? How do you call the superclass's constructor? LF FAQ

A 06:

Constructors	Regular methods

Constructors must have the same name as the class name and cannot return a value. The constructors are called only once per creation of an object while regular methods can be called many times. E.g. for a Pet.class
 	
public Pet() {} // constructor
	Regular methods can have any name and can be called any number of times. E.g. for a Pet.class.
	
	public **void** Pet(){} // regular method has a void return type.
	
	Note: method name is shown starting with an uppercase to differentiate a constructor from a regular method. Better naming convention is to have a meaningful name starting with a lowercase like:
	
	public **void createPet**(){} // regular method has a void return type

Q. What happens if you do not provide a constructor? Java does not actually require an explicit constructor in the class description. If you do not include a constructor, the Java compiler will create a default constructor in the byte code with an empty argument. This default constructor is equivalent to the explicit "Pet(){}". If a class includes one or more explicit constructors like "public Pet(int id)" or "Pet(){}" etc, the java compiler does *not* create the default constructor "Pet(){}".

Q. Can you call one constructor from another? Yes, by using **this()** syntax. E.g.

```
public Pet(int id) {
    this.id = id;                    // "this" means this object
}
public Pet (int id, String type) {
    this(id);                        // calls constructor public Pet(int id)
    this.type = type;                // "this" means this object
}
```

Q. How to call the superclass constructor? If a class called "*SpecialPet*" extends your "*Pet*" class then you can use the keyword "**super**" to invoke the superclass's constructor. E.g.

```
public SpecialPet(int id) {
    super(id);                       //must be the very first statement in the constructor.
}
```

To call a regular method in the super class use: "**super**.myMethod( );". This can be called at any line. Some frameworks based on JUnit add their own initialization code, and not only do they need to remember to invoke their parent's setup() method, you, as a user, need to remember to invoke theirs after you wrote your initialization code:

```java
public class DBUnitTestCase extends TestCase {
  public void setUp() {
    super.setUp();
    // do my own initialization
  }
}

public void cleanUp() throws Throwable
{
    try {
      … // Do stuff here to clean up your object(s).
    }
    catch (Throwable t) {}
    finally{
        super.cleanUp(); //clean up your parent class. Unlike constructors
                   // super.regularMethod() can be called at any line.
    }
}
```

Q 07: What are the advantages of Object Oriented Programming Languages (OOPL)? DC FAQ

A 07: The Object Oriented Programming Languages directly represent the real life objects like *Car*, *Jeep*, *Account*, *Customer* etc. The features of the OO programming languages like **polymorphism, inheritance** and **encapsulation** make it powerful. [**Tip:** remember **pie** which, stands for **P**olymorphism, **I**nheritance and **E**ncapsulation are the **3 pillars** of OOPL]

Q 08: How does the Object Oriented approach improve software development? DC

A 08: The key benefits are:

- *Re-use* of previous work: using **implementation inheritance** and **object composition**.
- *Real mapping to the problem domain:* Objects map to real world and represent vehicles, customers, products etc: with **encapsulation**.
- *Modular Architecture:* Objects, systems, frameworks etc are the building blocks of larger systems.

The **increased quality** and **reduced development time** are the by-products of the key benefits discussed above. If 90% of the new application consists of proven existing components then only the remaining 10% of the code have to be tested from scratch.

Q 09: How do you express an *'is a'* relationship and a *'has a'* relationship or explain inheritance and composition? What is the difference between composition and aggregation? DC FAQ

A 09: The *'is a'* relationship is expressed with **inheritance** and *'has a'* relationship is expressed with **composition**. Both inheritance and composition allow you to place sub-objects inside your new class. Two of the main techniques for **code reuse** are **class inheritance** and **object composition**.

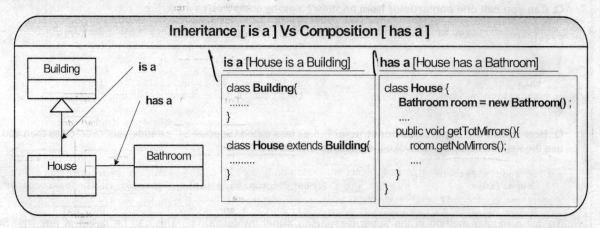

Inheritance [is a] Vs Composition [has a]

Inheritance is uni-directional. For example *House* **is a** *Building*. But *Building* is not a *House*. Inheritance uses **extends** key word. **Composition:** is used when *House* **has a** *Bathroom*. It is incorrect to say *House* is a

Bathroom. Composition simply means using instance variables that refer to other objects. The class *House* will have an instance variable, which refers to a *Bathroom* object.

Q. Which one to favor, composition or inheritance? The guide is that inheritance should be only used when *subclass* 'is a' *superclass*.

- Don't use inheritance just to get code reuse. If there is no 'is a' relationship then use composition for code reuse. Overuse of **implementation inheritance** (uses the "extends" key word) can break all the subclasses, if the superclass is modified.

- Do not use inheritance just to get polymorphism. If there is no 'is a' relationship and all you want is polymorphism then use **interface inheritance** with **composition,** which gives you **code reuse** (Refer **Q10** in Java section for interface inheritance).

What is the difference between aggregation and composition?

Aggregation	Composition
Aggregation is an association in which one class belongs to a collection. This is a part of a whole relationship where a part can exist without a whole. For example a line item is a whole and product is a part. If a line item is deleted then corresponding product need not be deleted. So **aggregation has a weaker relationship**.	Composition is an association in which one class belongs to a collection. This is a part of a whole relationship where a part cannot exist without a whole. If a whole is deleted then all parts are deleted. For example An order is a whole and line items are parts. If an order is deleted then all corresponding line items for that order should be deleted. So **composition has a stronger relationship**.

Q 10: What do you mean by polymorphism, inheritance, encapsulation, and dynamic binding? `DC` `SE` `FAQ`

A 10: *Polymorphism* – means the ability of a single variable of a given type to be used to reference objects of different types, and automatically call the method that is specific to the type of object the variable references. In a nutshell, polymorphism is a bottom-up method call. The benefit of polymorphism is that it is **very easy to add new classes of derived objects without breaking the calling code** (i.e. getTotArea() in the sample code shown below) that uses the polymorphic classes or interfaces. When you send a message to an object even though you don't know what specific type it is, and the right thing happens, that's called *polymorphism*. The process used by object-oriented programming languages to implement polymorphism is called *dynamic binding*. Let us look at some sample code to demonstrate polymorphism: `CO`

Sample code:

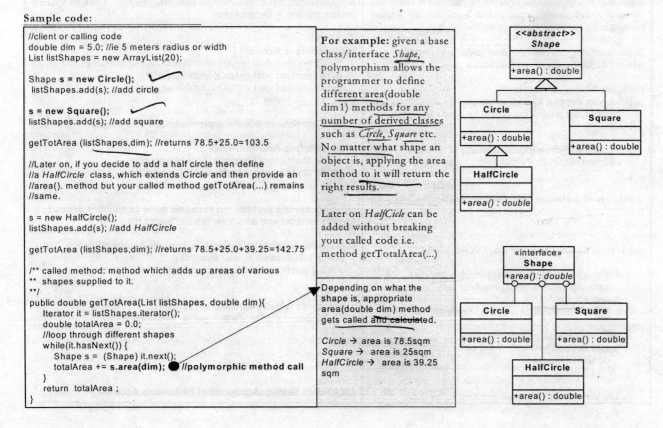

```
//client or calling code
double dim = 5.0; //ie 5 meters radius or width
List listShapes = new ArrayList(20);

Shape s = new Circle();
 listShapes.add(s); //add circle

s = new Square();
listShapes.add(s); //add square

getTotArea (listShapes,dim); //returns 78.5+25.0=103.5

//Later on, if you decide to add a half circle then define
//a HalfCircle class, which extends Circle and then provide an
//area(). method but your called method getTotArea(...) remains
//same.

s = new HalfCircle();
listShapes.add(s); //add HalfCircle

getTotArea (listShapes,dim); //returns 78.5+25.0+39.25=142.75

/** called method: method which adds up areas of various
** shapes supplied to it.
**/
public double getTotArea(List listShapes, double dim){
    Iterator it = listShapes.iterator();
    double totalArea = 0.0;
    //loop through different shapes
    while(it.hasNext()) {
        Shape s =  (Shape) it.next();
        totalArea += s.area(dim);  ● //polymorphic method call
    }
    return  totalArea ;
}
```

For example: given a base class/interface *Shape*, polymorphism allows the programmer to define different area(double dim1) methods for any number of derived classes such as *Circle*, *Square* etc. No matter what shape an object is, applying the area method to it will return the right results.

Later on *HalfCicle* can be added without breaking your called code i.e. method getTotalArea(...)

Depending on what the shape is, appropriate area(double dim) method gets called and calculated.

Circle → area is 78.5sqm
Square → area is 25sqm
HalfCircle → area is 39.25 sqm

Inheritance – is the inclusion of behavior (i.e. methods) and state (i.e. variables) of a base class in a derived class so that they are accessible in that derived class. The key benefit of Inheritance is that it provides the formal mechanism for **code reuse**. Any shared piece of business logic can be moved from the derived class into the base class as part of refactoring process to improve maintainability of your code by avoiding code duplication. The existing class is called the *superclass* and the derived class is called the *subclass*. **Inheritance** can also be defined as the process whereby one object acquires characteristics from one or more other objects the same way children acquire characteristics from their parents. **There are two types of inheritances:**

1. **Implementation inheritance** (aka class inheritance): You can extend an application's functionality by reusing functionality in the parent class by inheriting all or some of the operations already implemented. In Java, you can only inherit from one superclass. Implementation inheritance promotes reusability but improper use of class inheritance can cause programming nightmares by breaking encapsulation and making future changes a problem. With implementation inheritance, the subclass becomes tightly coupled with the superclass. This will make the design fragile because if you want to change the superclass, you must know all the details of the subclasses to avoid breaking them. So when using implementation inheritance, **make sure that the subclasses depend only on the behavior of the superclass**, **not on the actual implementation**. For example in the above diagram, the subclasses should only be concerned about the behavior known as area() but not how it is implemented.

2. **Interface inheritance** (aka type inheritance): This is also known as subtyping. Interfaces provide a mechanism for specifying a relationship between otherwise unrelated classes, typically by specifying a set of common methods each implementing class must contain. Interface inheritance promotes the design concept of **program to interfaces not to implementations**. This also reduces the coupling or implementation dependencies between systems. In Java, you can implement any number of interfaces. This is more flexible than implementation inheritance because it won't lock you into specific implementations which make subclasses difficult to maintain. So care should be taken not to break the implementing classes by modifying the interfaces.

Which one to use? Prefer interface inheritance to implementation inheritance because it promotes the design concept of **coding to an interface** and **reduces coupling**. Interface inheritance can achieve **code reuse** with the help of **object composition**. If you look at Gang of Four (GoF) design patterns, you can see that it favors interface inheritance to implementation inheritance. **CO**

Implementation inheritance	Interface inheritance with composition
Let's assume that savings account and term deposit account have a similar behavior in terms of depositing and withdrawing money, so we will get the super class to implement this behavior and get the subclasses to reuse this behavior. But saving account and term deposit account have specific behavior in calculating the interest.	Let's look at an **interface inheritance** code sample, which makes use of **composition** for reusability. In the following example the methods deposit(…) and withdraw(…) share the same piece of code in *AccountHelper* class. The method calculateInterest(…) has its specific implementation in its own class.
| Super class *Account* has **reusable code** as methods **deposit** (double amount) and **withdraw** (double amount). | ```java
public interface Account {
    public abstract double calculateInterest(double amount);
    public abstract void deposit(double amount);
    public abstract void withdraw(double amount);
}
``` |
| ```java
public abstract class Account {
    public void deposit (double amount) {
        System.out.println("depositing " + amount);
    }

    public void withdraw (double amount) {
        System.out.println ("withdrawing " + amount);
    }

    public abstract double calculateInterest(double amount);
}
``` | Code to interface so that the implementation can change.

```java
public interface AccountHelper {
    public abstract void deposit (double amount);
    public abstract void withdraw (double amount);
}
``` |
| ```java
public class SavingsAccount extends Account {

    public double calculateInterest (double amount) {
        // calculate interest for SavingsAccount
        return amount * 0.03;
    }

    public void deposit (double amount) {
        super.deposit (amount); // get code reuse
        // do something else
    }

    public void withdraw (double amount) {
``` | class **AccountHelperImpl** has **reusable code** as methods **deposit** (double amount) and **withdraw** (double amount).

```java
public class AccountHelperImpl implements AccountHelper {
    public void deposit(double amount) {
        System.out.println("depositing " + amount);
    }

    public void withdraw(double amount) {
        System.out.println("withdrawing " + amount);
    }
}
```

```java
public class SavingsAccountImpl implements Account {
``` |
```

```java
        super.withdraw (amount); // get code reuse
        // do something else
    }
}

public class TermDepositAccount extends Account {

    public double calculateInterest (double amount) {
        // calculate interest for SavingsAccount
        return amount * 0.05;
    }

    public void deposit(double amount) {
        super.deposit (amount); // get code reuse
        // do something else
    }

    public void withdraw(double amount) {
        super.withdraw (amount); // get code reuse
        // do something else
    }
}
```

```java
    // composed helper class (i.e. composition).
    AccountHelper helper = new AccountHelperImpl ();

    public double calculateInterest (double amount) {
        // calculate interest for SavingsAccount
        return amount * 0.03;
    }

    public void deposit (double amount) {
        helper.deposit( amount); // code reuse via composition
    }

    public void withdraw (double amount) {
        helper.withdraw (amount); // code reuse via composition
    }
}

public class TermDepositAccountImpl implements Account {

    // composed helper class (i.e. composition).
    AccountHelper helper = new AccountHelperImpl ();

    public double calculateInterest (double amount) {
        //calculate interest for SavingsAccount
        return amount * 0.05;
    }

    public void deposit (double amount) {
        helper.deposit (amount) ;  // code reuse via composition
    }

    public void withdraw (double amount) {
        helper.withdraw (amount) ;  // code reuse via composition
    }

}
```

The Test class:

```java
public class Test {
    public static void main(String[] args) {
        Account acc1 = new SavingsAccountImpl();
        acc1.deposit(50.0);

        Account acc2 = new TermDepositAccountImpl();
        acc2.deposit(25.0);

        acc1.withdraw(25);
        acc2.withdraw(10);

        double cal1 = acc1.calculateInterest(100.0);
        double cal2 = acc2.calculateInterest(100.0);

        System.out.println("Savings --> " + cal1);
        System.out.println("TermDeposit -->  " + cal2);
    }
}
```

Class inheritance is done statically at compile tim

The output:

```
depositing 50.0
depositing 25.0
withdrawing 25.0
withdrawing 10.0
Savings --> 3.0
TermDeposit --> 5.0
```

Q. Why would you prefer code reuse via composition over inheritance? Both the approaches make use of polymorphism and gives code reuse (in different ways) to achieve the same results but:

- The advantage of class inheritance is that it is done statically at compile-time and is easy to use. The disadvantage of class inheritance is that because it is static, implementation inherited from a parent class cannot be changed at runtime. In object composition, functionality is acquired dynamically at run-time by objects collecting references to other objects. The advantage of this approach is that implementations can be replaced at run-time. This is possible because objects are accessed only through their interfaces, so one object can be replaced with another just as long as they have the same type. For example: the composed class **AccountHelperImpl** can be replaced by another more efficient implementation as shown below if required:

```
public class EfficientAccountHelperImpl implements AccountHelper {
    public void deposit(double amount) {
        System.out.println("efficient depositing " + amount);
    }

    public void withdraw(double amount) {
        System.out.println("efficient withdrawing " + amount);
    }
}
```

- Another problem with class inheritance is that the subclass becomes dependent on the parent class implementation. This makes it harder to reuse the subclass, especially if part of the inherited implementation is no longer desirable and hence can break encapsulation. Also a change to a superclass can not only ripple down the inheritance hierarchy to subclasses, but can also ripple out to code that uses just the subclasses making the design fragile by tightly coupling the subclasses with the super class. But it is easier to change the interface/implementation of the composed class.

Due to the flexibility and power of object composition, **most design patterns emphasize object composition over inheritance whenever it is possible**. Many times, a design pattern shows a clever way of solving a common problem through the use of object composition rather then a standard, less flexible, inheritance based solution.

Encapsulation – refers to keeping all the related members (variables and methods) together in an object. Specifying member variables as private can hide the variables and methods. Objects should hide their inner workings from the outside view. Good **encapsulation improves code modularity by preventing objects interacting with each other in an unexpected way**, which in turn makes future development and refactoring efforts easy. CO

Sample code

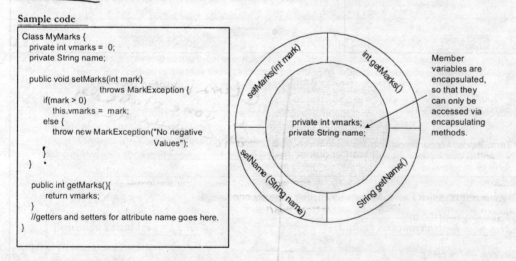

```
Class MyMarks {
    private int vmarks =  0;
    private String name;

    public void setMarks(int mark)
                    throws MarkException {
        if(mark > 0)
            this.vmarks =  mark;
        else {
            throw new MarkException("No negative
                            Values");
        }
    }

    public int getMarks(){
        return vmarks;
    }
    //getters and setters for attribute name goes here.
}
```

Member variables are encapsulated, so that they can only be accessed via encapsulating methods.

Being able to encapsulate members of a class is important for **security** and **integrity**. We can protect variables from unacceptable values. The sample code above describes how encapsulation can be used to protect the *MyMarks* object from having negative values. Any modification to member variable "*vmarks*" can only be carried out through the setter method *setMarks(int mark)*. This prevents the object "*MyMarks*" from having any negative values by throwing an exception.

Q 11: What is design by contract? Explain the *assertion* construct? DC

A 11: Design by contract specifies the obligations of a calling-method and called-method to each other. Design by contract is a valuable technique, which should be used to build well-defined interfaces. The strength of this programming methodology is that it gets the programmer to **think clearly about what a function does**, what pre and post conditions it must adhere to and also it **provides documentation for the caller**. Java uses the *assert* statement to implement pre- and post-conditions. Java's exceptions handling also support design by contract especially **checked exceptions** (Refer **Q39** in Java section for checked exceptions). In design by contract in addition to specifying programming code to carrying out intended operations of a method the programmer also specifies:

1. *Preconditions* – This is the part of the contract the **calling-method must agree to**. Preconditions specify the conditions that must be true before a called method can execute. Preconditions involve the system state and the arguments passed into the method at the time of its invocation. **If a precondition fails then there is a bug in the calling-method or calling software component.**

On public methods	On non-public methods
| Preconditions on *public* methods are enforced by explicit checks that throw particular, specified exceptions. You **should not use assertion to check the parameters of the public methods** but can use for the non-public methods. *Assert* is inappropriate because the method guarantees that it will always enforce the argument checks. It must check its arguments whether or not assertions are enabled. Further, assert construct does not throw an exception of a specified type. It can throw only an *AssertionError*.<br><br>```java
public void setRate(int rate) {
  if(rate <= 0 || rate > MAX_RATE){
    throw new IllegalArgumentException("Invalid rate → " + rate);
  }
  setCalculatedRate(rate);
}
``` | You can use assertion to check the parameters of the non-public methods.<br><br>```java
private void setCalculatedRate(int rate) {
  assert (rate > 0 && rate < MAX_RATE) : rate;
    //calculate the rate and set it.
}
```<br><br>Assertions can be disabled, so programs must not assume that assert construct will be always executed:<br><br>//**Wrong**:<br>//if assertion is disabled, "pilotJob" never gets removed<br>**assert** jobsAd.remove(pilotJob);<br><br>//**Correct**:<br>boolean pilotJobRemoved = jobsAd.remove(pilotJob);<br>**assert** pilotJobRemoved; |

2. *Postconditions* – This is the part of the contract the **called-method agrees to**. What must be true after a method completes successfully. Postconditions can be used with assertions in both public and non-public methods. The postconditions involve the old system state, the new system state, the method arguments and the method's return value. **If a postcondition fails then there is a bug in the called-method or called software component.**

```java
public double calcRate(int rate) {
   if(rate <= 0 || rate > MAX_RATE){
      throw new IllegalArgumentException("Invalid rate !!! ");
   }

   //logic to calculate the rate and set it goes here

   assert this.evaluate(result) < 0 : this; //message sent to AssertionError on failure
   return result;
}
```

3. *Class invariants* - what must be true about each instance of a class? A class invariant as an internal invariant that can specify the relationships among multiple attributes, and should be true before and after any method completes. **If an invariant fails then there could be a bug in either calling-method or called-method.** There is no particular mechanism for checking invariants but it is convenient to combine all the expressions required for checking invariants into a single internal method that can be called by assertions. For example if you have a class, which deals with negative integers then you define the **isNegative()** convenient internal method:

```java
class NegativeInteger {
   Integer value = new Integer (-1); //invariant

   //constructor
   public NegativeInteger(Integer int) {
       //constructor logic goes here
       assert isNegative();
   }

   // rest of the public and non-public methods goes here. public methods should call
   // assert isNegative(); prior to its return

   // convenient internal method for checking invariants.
   // Returns true if the integer value is negative

   private boolean isNegative(){
       return  value.intValue() < 0 ;
   }
}
```

The isNegative() method should be true <u>before and after any method completes</u>, each public method and constructor should contain the following assert statement immediately prior to its return.

```
assert isNegative();
```

Explain the assertion construct? The assertion statements have two forms as shown below:

```
assert Expression1;
assert Expression1 : Expression2;
```

Where:
- **Expression1** → is a boolean expression. If the *Expression1* evaluates to false, it throws an *AssertionError* without any detailed message.
- **Expression2** → if the *Expression1* evaluates to false throws an *AssertionError* with using the value of the *Expression2* as the error's detailed message.

Note: If you are using assertions (available from JDK1.4 onwards), you should supply the JVM argument to enable it by package name or class name.

java -ea[:packagename...|:classname] or **java -enableassertions**[:packagename...|:classname]
java –ea:Account

Q 12: What is the difference between an abstract class and an interface and when should you use them? LF DP DC FAQ

A 12: In design, you want the base class to present *only* an interface for its derived classes. This means, you don't want anyone to actually instantiate an object of the base class. You only **want to upcast to it** (implicit upcasting, which gives you polymorphic behavior), so that its interface can be used. This is accomplished by making that class *abstract* using the **abstract** keyword. If anyone tries to make an object of an **abstract** class, the compiler prevents it.

The **interface** keyword takes this concept of an **abstract** class a step further by preventing any method or function implementation at all. You can only declare a method or function but not provide the implementation. The class, which is implementing the interface, should provide the actual implementation. The **interface** is a very useful and commonly used aspect in OO design, as it provides the **separation of interface and implementation** and enables you to:

- Capture similarities among unrelated classes without artificially forcing a class relationship.
- Declare methods that one or more classes are expected to implement.
- Reveal an object's programming interface without revealing its actual implementation.
- Model multiple interface inheritance in Java, which provides some of the benefits of full on multiple inheritances, a feature that some object-oriented languages support that allow a class to have more than one superclass.

Abstract class	Interface
Have executable methods and abstract methods.	Have no implementation code. All methods are abstract.
Can only subclass one abstract class.	A class can implement any number of interfaces.

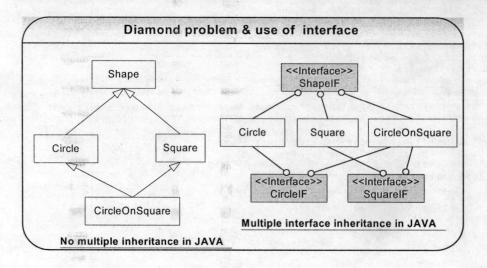

Q. When to use an abstract class?: In case where you want to use **implementation inheritance** then it is usually provided by an abstract base class. Abstract classes are excellent candidates inside of application frameworks. Abstract classes let you define some default behavior and force subclasses to provide any specific behavior. Care should be taken not to overuse implementation inheritance as discussed in **Q10** in Java section.

Q. When to use an interface?: For polymorphic interface inheritance, where the client wants to only deal with a type and does not care about the actual implementation use interfaces. If you need to change your design frequently, you should prefer using interface to abstract. **CO** Coding to an interface **reduces coupling** and interface inheritance can achieve **code reuse** with the help of **object composition**. **For example:** The Spring framework's dependency injection promotes code to an interface principle. Another justification for using interfaces is that they solve the **diamond problem** of traditional multiple inheritance as shown in the figure. Java does not support multiple inheritance. Java only supports **multiple interface inheritance**. Interface will solve all the ambiguities caused by this 'diamond problem'.

Design pattern: Strategy design pattern lets you swap new algorithms and processes into your program without altering the objects that use them. **Strategy design pattern:** Refer **Q11** in How would you go about… section.

Q 13: Why there are some interfaces with no defined methods (i.e. marker interfaces) in Java? **LF** **FAQ**

A 13: The interfaces with no defined methods act like markers. They just tell the compiler that the objects of the classes implementing the interfaces with no defined methods need to be treated differently. **Example** java.io.Serializable (Refer **Q23** in Java section), java.lang.Cloneable, java.util.EventListener etc. Marker interfaces are also known as "tag" interfaces since they tag all the derived classes into a category based on their purpose.

Q 14: When is a method said to be overloaded and when is a method said to be overridden? **LF** **CO** **FAQ**

A 14:

Method Overloading	Method Overriding

Overloading deals with multiple methods in the same class with the same name but different method signatures.
 	
class MyClass {
    public void **getInvestAmount**(int rate) {…}
 	
    public void **getInvestAmount**(int rate, long principal)
    { … }
}
 	
Both the above methods have the same method names but different method signatures, which mean the methods are overloaded.
	Overriding deals with two methods, one in the parent class and the other one in the child class and has the same name and signatures.
	
	class **BaseClass**{
	    public void **getInvestAmount**(int rate) {…}
	}
	
	class **MyClass extends BaseClass** {
	    public void **getInvestAmount**(int rate) {…}
	}
	
	Both the above methods have the same method names and the signatures but the method in the subclass *MyClass* overrides the method in the superclass *BaseClass*.

Overloading lets you define the **same operation in different ways for different data**.	Overriding lets you define the **same operation in different ways for different object types**.

Q 15: What is the main difference between an ArrayList and a Vector? What is the main difference between HashMap and Hashtable? What is the difference between a stack and a queue? **LF** **DC** **PI** **CI** **FAQ**

A 15:

Vector / Hashtable	ArrayList / HashMap
Original classes before the introduction of Collections API. *Vector* & *Hashtable* are synchronized. Any method that touches their contents is thread-safe.	So if you don't need a thread safe collection, use the *ArrayList* or *HashMap*. Why pay the price of synchronization unnecessarily at the expense of performance degradation.

Q. So which is better? As a general rule, prefer *ArrayList/HashMap* to *Vector/Hashtable*. If your application is a multithreaded application and **at least one of the threads either adds or deletes an entry into the collection** then use new Java *collections* API's external synchronization facility as shown below to **temporarily synchronize** your collections as needed: **CO**

```
Map myMap  = Collections.synchronizedMap (myMap);      // single lock for the entire map
List myList = Collections.synchronizedList (myList);   // single lock for the entire list
```

J2SE 5.0: If you are using J2SE5, you should use the new *"java.util.concurrent"* package for improved performance because the concurrent package collections are not governed by a single synchronized lock as shown above. The *"java.util.concurrent"* package collections like **ConcurrentHashMap** is threadsafe and at the same time safely permits any number of concurrent reads as well as tunable number of concurrent writes. The "java.util.concurrent" package also provides an efficient scalable thread-safe non-blocking FIFO queue like **ConcurrentLinkedQueue.**

J2SE 5.0: The *"java.util.concurrent"* package also has classes like **CopyOnWriteArrayList, CopyOnWrite-ArraySet,** which gives you thread safety with the added benefit of immutability to deal with data that changes infrequently. The **CopyOnWriteArrayList** behaves much like the ArrayList class, except that when the list is modified, instead of modifying the underlying array, a new array is created and the old array is discarded. This means that when a caller gets an iterator (i.e. `copyOnWriteArrayListRef.iterator()`), which internally holds a reference to the underlying CopyOnWriteArrayList object's array, which is immutable and therefore can be used for traversal without requiring either synchronization on the list `copyOnWriteArrayListRef` or need to clone() the `copyOnWriteArrayListRef` list before traversal (i.e. there is no risk of concurrent modification) and also offers better performance.

Array	List / Stack etc
Java arrays are even faster than using an *ArrayList/Vector* and perhaps therefore may be preferable if you know the size of your array upfront (because **arrays cannot grow as Lists do**).	*ArrayList/Vector* are specialized data structures that internally uses an array with some convenient methods like add(..), remove(...) etc so that they can grow and shrink from their initial size. ArrayList also supports index based searches with indexOf(Object obj) and lastIndexOf(Object obj) methods.
In an array, any item can be accessed.	These are more abstract than arrays and access is restricted. For example, a stack allows access to only last item inserted.

Queue<E> (added in J2SE 5.0)	Stack
First item to be inserted is the first one to be removed.	Allows access to only last item inserted.
This mechanism is called First In First Out (FIFO).	An item is inserted or removed from one end called the "top" of the stack. This is called Last In First Out (**LIFO**) mechanism.
Placing an item in the queue is called "enqueue or insertion" and removing an item from a queue is called "dequeue or deletion". Pre J2SE 5.0, you should write your own *Queue* class with enqueue() and dequeue() methods using an *ArrayList* or a *LinkedList* class. J2SE 5.0 has **a java.util.Queue<E>** interface.	Placing the data at the top is called "pushing" and removing an item from the top is called "popping". If you want to reverse "XYZ" → ZYX, then you can use a **java.util.Stack**

Q 16: Explain the Java Collections Framework? **LF** **DP** **FAQ**
A 16: The key interfaces used by the collections framework are *List, Set* and *Map*. The *List* and *Set* extends the *Collection* interface. Should not confuse the *Collection* interface with the **Collections** class which is a utility class.

Set (HashSet , TreeSet)	List (ArrayList, LinkedList, Vector etc)
A *Set* is a collection with <u>unique elements</u> and prevents duplication within the collection. *HashSet* and *TreeSet* are implementations of a *Set* interface. A TreeSet is an ordered HashSet, which implements the **SortedSet** interface.	A *List* is a collection with an <u>ordered sequence of elements</u> and <u>may contain duplicates</u>. *ArrayList, LinkedList* and *Vector* are implementations of a *List* interface. (i.e. an index based)

The Collections API also supports maps, but within a hierarchy distinct from the **Collection** interface. A **Map** is an object that maps keys to values, where the list of keys is itself a collection object. A map can contain duplicate values, but the keys in a map must be distinct. **HashMap, TreeMap** and **Hashtable** are implementations of a *Map* interface. A **TreeMap** is an ordered HashMap, which implements the **SortedMap** interface.

Q. How to implement collection ordering? *SortedSet* and *SortedMap* interfaces maintain sorted order. The classes, which implement the **Comparable** interface, impose <u>natural order</u>. By implementing **Comparable**, sorting an array of objects or a collection (List etc) is as simple as:

```
Arrays.sort(myArray);
Collections.sort(myCollection);      // do not confuse "Collections" utility class with the
                                     // "Collection" interface without an "s".
```

For classes that don't implement *Comparable* interface, or when one needs even more control over ordering based on multiple attributes, a **Comparator** interface should be used.

Comparable interface	Comparator interface
The "Comparable" allows itself to compare with another similar object (i.e. A class that implements *Comparable* becomes an object to be compared with). The method **compareTo()** is specified in the interface.	The Comparator is used to compare two different objects. The following method is specified in the **Comparator** interface. `public int compare(Object o1, Object o2)`

Many of the standard classes in the Java library like String, Integer, Date, File etc implement the **Comparable** interface to give the class a "Natural Ordering". For example String class uses the following methods:
 	
`public int compareTo(o)`
`public int compareToIgnoreCase(str)`
 	
You could also implement your own method in your own class as shown below:
 	
...imports
 	
public class Pet implements **Comparable** {
 	
  int petId;
  String petType;
 	
  public Pet(int argPetId, String argPetType) {
    petId = argPetId;
    this.petType = argPetType;
  }
 	
  public **int compareTo**(Object o) {
    Pet petAnother = (Pet)o;
 	
    //natural alphabetical ordering by type
    //if equal returns 0, if greater returns +ve int,
    //if less returns -ve int
    return this.petType.compareTo(petAnother.petType);
  }
 	
  public static void main(String[] args) {
    List list = new ArrayList();
    list.add(new Pet(2, "Dog"));
    list.add(new Pet(1, "Parrot"));
    list.add(new Pet(2, "Cat"));
 	
    Collections.sort(list); // sorts using compareTo method
 	
    for (**Iterator** iter = list.iterator(); iter.hasNext();) {
      Pet element = (Pet) iter.next();
      System.out.println(element);
    }
  }
 	
  public String toString() {
    return petType;
  }
 	
}
Output: Cat, Dog, Parrot
	You can have more control by writing your Comparator class. Let us write a Comparator for the Pet class shown on the left. For most cases natural ordering is fine as shown on the left but say we require a special scenario where we need to first sort by the "petId" and then by the "petType". We can achieve this by writing a "Comparator" class.
	
	...imports
	
	public class PetComparator implements **Comparator**, Serializable{
	
	  public int **compare**(Object o1, Object o2) {
	    int result = 0;
	
	    Pet pet = (Pet)o1;
	    Pet petAnother = (Pet)o2;
	
	    //use Integer class's natural ordering
	    Integer pId = new Integer(pet.getPetId());
	    Integer pAnotherId = new Integer(petAnother.getPetId());
	
	    result = pId.compareTo(pAnotherId);
	
	    //if ids are same compare by petType
	    if(result == 0) {
	      result= pet.getPetType().compareTo
	        (petAnother.getPetType());
	    }
	
	    return result;
	  }
	
	  public static void main(String[] args) {
	    List list = new ArrayList();
	    list.add(new Pet(2, "Dog"));
	    list.add(new Pet(1, "Parrot"));
	    list.add(new Pet(2, "Cat"));
	
	    Collections.sort(list, **new PetComparator()**);
	
	    for (Iterator iter = list.iterator(); iter.hasNext();){
	      Pet element = (Pet) iter.next();
	      System.out.println(element);
	    }
	  }
	}
	
	Output: Parrot, Cat, Dog.
	
	Note: some methods are not shown for brevity.

Important: The ordering imposed by a java.util.**Comparator** "myComp" on a set of elements "mySet" should be consistent with **equals()** method, which means for example:

```
if compare(o1,o2)  == 0    then    o1.equals(o2)    should be true.
if compare(o1,o2)  != 0    then    o1.equals(o2)    should be false.
```

If a comparator "myComp" on a set of elements "mySet" is inconsistent with **equals()** method, then SortedSet or SortedMap will behave strangely and is hard to debug. For example if you add two objects o1, o2 to a **TreeSet** (implements **SortedSet**) such that o1.equals(o2) == true and compare(o1,o2) != 0 the second add operation will return false and will not be added to your set because o1 and o2 are equivalent from the TreeSet's perspective. **TIP:** It is always a good practice and highly recommended to keep the Java API documentation handy and refer to it as required while coding. Please refer to **java.util.Comparator** interface API for further details.

Design pattern: **Q. What is an Iterator?** An Iterator is a use once object to access the objects stored in a collection. **Iterator design pattern** (aka Cursor) is used, which is a behavioral design pattern that provides a way to access elements of a collection sequentially without exposing its internal representation.

Q. Why do you get a ConcurrentModificationException when using an iterator? **CO**

Problem: The java.util Collection classes are fail-fast, which means that if one thread changes a collection while another thread is traversing it through with an iterator the iterator.hasNext() or iterator.next() call will throw **ConcurrentModificationException.** Even the synchronized collection wrapper classes *SynchronizedMap* and *SynchronizedList* are only conditionally thread-safe, which means all individual operations are thread-safe but compound operations where flow of control depends on the results of previous operations may be subject to threading issues.

```
Collection<String> myCollection = new ArrayList<String>(10);

myCollection.add("123");
myCollection.add("456");
myCollection.add("789");

for (Iterator it = myCollection.iterator(); it.hasNext();) {
    String myObject = (String)it.next();
    System.out.println(myObject);
    if (someConditionIsTrue) {
        myCollection.remove(myObject);   //can throw ConcurrentModificationException in single as
                                         //well as multi-thread access situations.
    }
}
```

Solutions 1-3: for multi-thread access situation:

Solution 1: You can convert your list to an array with list.toArray() and iterate on the array. This approach is not recommended if the list is large.

Solution 2: You can lock the entire list while iterating by wrapping your code within a synchronized block. This approach adversely affects scalability of your application if it is highly concurrent.

Solution 3: If you are using JDK 1.5 then you can use the *ConcurrentHashMap* and *CopyOnWriteArrayList* classes, which provide much better scalability and the iterator returned by ConcurrentHashMap.iterator() will not throw *ConcurrentModificationException* while preserving thread-safety.

Solution 4: for single-thread access situation:

Use:
```
    it.remove();       // removes the current object via the Iterator "it" which has a reference to
                       // your underlying collection "myCollection". Also can use solutions 1-3.
```

Avoid:
```
    myCollection.remove(myObject); // avoid by-passing the Iterator. When it.next() is called, can throw  the exception
                                   // ConcurrentModificationException
```

Note: If you had used any Object to Relational (OR) mapping frameworks like Hibernate, you may have encountered this exception "ConcurrentModificationException" when you tried to remove an object from a collection such as a java.util Set with the intention of deleting that object from the underlying database. This exception is not caused by Hibernate but rather caused by your java.util.Iterator (i.e. due to your `it.next()` call). You can use one of the solutions given above.

Q. What is a list iterator?

The java.util.**ListIterator** is an iterator for lists that allows the programmer to traverse the list in either direction (i.e. forward and or backward) and modify the list during iteration.

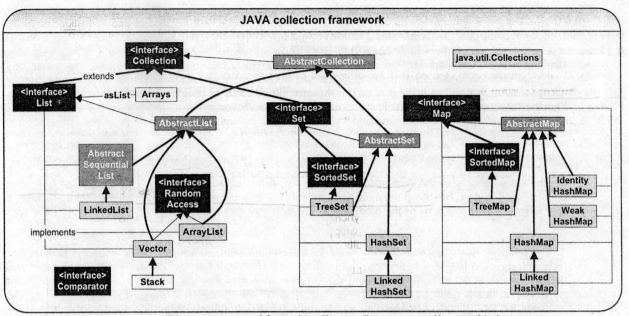

(Diagram sourced from: http://www.wilsonmar.com/1arrays.htm)

What are the benefits of the Java Collections Framework? Collections framework provides flexibility, performance, and robustness.

- **Polymorphic algorithms** – sorting, shuffling, reversing, binary search etc.
- **Set algebra** - such as finding subsets, intersections, and unions between objects.
- **Performance** - collections have much better performance compared to the older *Vector* and *Hashtable* classes with the elimination of synchronization overheads.
- **Thread-safety** - when synchronization is required, wrapper implementations are provided for temporarily synchronizing existing collection objects. For J2SE 5.0 use *java.util.concurrent* package.
- **Immutability** - when immutability is required wrapper implementations are provided for making a collection immutable.
- **Extensibility** - interfaces and abstract classes provide an excellent starting point for adding functionality and features to create specialized object collections.

Q. What are static factory methods? CO

Some of the above mentioned features like searching, sorting, shuffling, immutability etc are achieved with *java.util.Collections* class and *java.util.Arrays* utility classes. The great majority of these implementations are provided via **static factory methods** in a single, non-instantiable (i.e. private constrctor) class. Speaking of **static factory methods,** they are an alternative to creating objects through constructors. Unlike constructors, static factory methods are not required to create a new object (i.e. a duplicate object) each time they are invoked (e.g. immutable instances can be cached) and also they have a more meaningful names like valueOf, instanceOf, asList etc. **For example:**

Instead of:
```
String[] myArray = {"Java", "J2EE", "XML", "JNDI"};
for (int i = 0; i < myArray.length; i++) {
    System.out.println(myArray[i]);
}
```

You can use:
```
String[] myArray = {"Java", "J2EE", "XML", "JNDI"};
System.out.println(Arrays.asList(myArray)); //factory method Arrays.asList(…)
```

For example: The following static factory method (an alternative to a constructor) example converts a **boolean** primitive value to a **Boolean** wrapper object.

```
public static Boolean valueOf(boolean b) {
    return (b ? Boolean.TRUE : Boolean.FALSE)
}
```

Q 17: What are some of the best practices relating to Java collection? `BP` `PI` `CI`

A 17:

- Use ArrayList, HashMap etc as opposed to Vector, Hashtable etc, where possible to avoid any synchronization overhead. Even better is to use just arrays where possible. If multiple threads concurrently access a collection and **at least one of the threads either adds or deletes an entry into the collection**, then the collection must be externally synchronized. This is achieved by:

```
Map    myMap   = Collections.synchronizedMap (myMap); //conditional thread-safety
List   myList  = Collections.synchronizedList (myList); //conditional thread-safety
// use java.util.concurrent package for J2SE 5.0 Refer Q16 in Java section under ConcurrentModificationException
```

- Set the initial capacity of a collection appropriately (e.g. ArrayList, HashMap etc). This is because *Collection* classes like ArrayList, HashMap etc must grow periodically to accommodate new elements. But if you have a very large array, and you know the size in advance then you can speed things up by setting the initial size appropriately.

  For example: HashMaps/Hashtables need to be created with sufficiently large capacity to minimize **rehashing** (which happens every time the table grows). HashMap has two parameters initial capacity and load factor that affect its performance and space requirements. Higher load factor values (default load factor of 0.75 provides a good trade off between performance and space) will reduce the space cost but will increase the lookup cost of myMap.get(...) and myMap.put(...) methods. When the number of entries in the HashMap exceeds the **current capacity * loadfactor** then the capacity of the HashMap is roughly doubled by calling the rehash function. It is also very important not to set the initial capacity too high or load factor too low if iteration performance or reduction in space is important.

- **Program in terms of interface not implementation:** `CO` For example you might decide a LinkedList is the best choice for some application, but then later decide ArrayList might be a better choice for performance reason. `CO`

  Use:
  ```
  List list = new ArrayList(100); // program in terms of interface & set the initial capacity.
  ```
  Instead of:
  ```
  ArrayList list = new ArrayList();
  ```

- **Return zero length collections or arrays as opposed to returning null:** `CO` Returning null instead of zero length collection (use *Collections.EMPTY_SET*, *Collections.EMPTY_LIST*, *Collections.EMPTY_MAP*) is more error prone, since the programmer writing the calling method might forget to handle a return value of null.

- **Immutable objects should be used as keys for the HashMap:** `CO` Generally you use a java.lang.Integer or a java.lang.String class as the key, which are immutable Java objects. If you define your own key class then it is a best practice to make the key class an immutable object (i.e. do not provide any `setXXX() methods etc`). If a programmer wants to insert a new key then he/she will always have to instantiate a new object (i.e. cannot mutate the existing key because immutable key object class has no setter methods).   Refer **Q20** in Java section under "**Q. Why is it a best practice to implement the user defined key class as an immutable object?**"

- **Encapsulate collections:** `CO` In general collections are not immutable objects. So care should be taken not to unintentionally expose the collection fields to the caller.

Avoid where possible	Better approach

The following code snippet exposes the Set "setCars" directly to the caller. This approach is riskier because the variable "cars" can be modified unintentionally.
 	
public class CarYard{
  //...
  private Set<Car> cars = new HashSet<Car>();
 	
  //exposes the cars to the caller
  public Set<Car> getCars() {
    return cars;
  }
 	
  //exposes the cars to the caller
  public void setCars(Set<Car> cars) {
	This approach prevents the caller from directly using the underlying variable "cars".
	
	public class CarYard{
	
	  private Set<Car> cars = new HashSet<Car>();
	  //...
	  public void **addCar**(Car car) {
	    cars.add(car);
	  }
	
	  public void **removeCar**(Car car) {
	    cars.remove(car);
	  }

<table>
<tr><td>

```
    this.cars = cars;
  }

  //...
}
```

</td><td>

```
public Set<Car> getCars() {
   //use factory method from the Collections
   return Collections.unmodifiableSet (cars);
  }
}
```

</td></tr>
</table>

- **Avoid storing unrelated or different types of objects into same collection**: CO This is analogous to storing items in pigeonholes without any labeling. To store items use **value objects** or **data objects** (as opposed to storing every attribute in an ArrayList or HashMap). Provide wrapper classes around your collections API classes like ArrayList, HashMap etc as shown in better approach column. Also where applicable consider using **composite design pattern**, where an object may represent a single object or a collection of objects. Refer **Q61** in Java section for UML diagram of a composite design pattern. If you are using J2SE 5.0 then make use of "**generics**". Refer **Q55** in Java section for generics.

Avoid where possible	Better approach

The code below is hard to maintain and understand by others. Also gets more complicated as the requirements grow in the future because we are throwing different types of objects like Integer, String etc into a list just based on the indices and it is easy to make mistakes while casting the objects back during retrieval.
 	
List **myOrder** = new ArrayList()
 	
ResultSet rs = …
 	
While (rs.hasNext()) {
 	
   List lineItem = new ArrayList();
 	
   lineItem.add (new Integer(rs.getInt("itemId")));
   lineItem.add (rs.getString("description"));
   ….
   myOrder.add(lineItem**)**;
}
 	
return **myOrder**;
 	
Example 2:
 	
List myOrder = new ArrayList(10);
 	
//create an order
OrderVO header = new OrderVO();
header.setOrderId(1001);
…
//add all the line items
LineItemVO line1 = new LineItemVO();
line1.setLineItemId(1);
LineItemVO line2 = new LineItemVO();
Line2.setLineItemId(2);
 	
List lineItems = new ArrayList();
lineItems.add(line1);
lineItems.add(line2);
 	
//to store objects
myOrder.add(order);// index 0 is an OrderVO object
myOrder.add(lineItems);//index 1 is a List of line items
 	
//to retrieve objects
myOrder.get(0);
myOrder.get(1);
 	
Above approaches are bad because disparate objects are stored in the **lineItem** collection in example-1 and example-2 relies on indices to store disparate objects. The indices based approach and storing disparate objects are hard to maintain and understand because indices are hard coded and get scattered across the
	When storing items into a collection define value objects as shown below: (**VO** is an acronym for **V**alue **O**bject).
	
	public class **LineItemVO** {
	   private int itemId;
	   private String productName;
	
	   public int getLineItemId(){return accountId ;}
	   public int getAccountName(){return accountName;}
	
	   public void setLineItemId(int accountId){
	     this.accountId = accountId
	   }
	   //implement other getter & setter methods
	}
	
	Now let's define our base wrapper class, which represents an order:
	
	public abstract class Order {
	     int orderId;
	     List lineItems = null;
	
	     public abstract int countLineItems();
	     public abstract boolean add(**LineItemVO** itemToAdd);
	     public abstract boolean remove(**LineItemVO** itemToAdd);
	     public abstract Iterator getIterator();
	     public int getOrderId(){return this.orderId; }
	}
	
	Now a specific implementation of our wrapper class:
	
	public class OverseasOrder extends Order {
	     public OverseasOrder(int inOrderId) {
	        this.lineItems = new ArrayList(10);
	        this.orderId = inOrderId;
	     }
	
	     public int countLineItems() { //logic to count }
	
	     public boolean add(**LineItemVO** itemToAdd){
	       …//additional logic or checks
	       return lineItems.add(itemToAdd);
	     }
	
	     public boolean remove(**LineItemVO** itemToAdd){
	       return lineItems.remove(itemToAdd);
	     }
	
	     public ListIterator getIterator(){ return lineItems.Iterator();}
	}
	
	Now to use:
	
	Order myOrder = new OverseasOrder(1234) ;

code. If an index position changes for some reason, then you will have to change every occurrence, otherwise it breaks your application.
 	
The above coding approaches are analogous to storing disparate items in a storage system without proper labeling and just relying on its grid position.
	LineItemVO item1 = new LineItemVO();
	Item1.setItemId(1);
	Item1.setProductName("BBQ");
	
	LineItemVO item2 = new LineItemVO();
	Item1.setItemId(2);
	Item1.setProductName("Outdoor chair");
	
	//to add line items to order
	myOrder.add(item1);
	myOrder.add(item2);
	…

Q. How can you code better without nested loops? CO Avoid nested loops where possible (e.g. for loop within another for loop etc) and instead make use of an appropriate java collection.

How to avoid nested loops with Java collection classes

Code to test if there are duplicate values in an array.

Avoid where possible -- nested loops

```java
public class NestedLoops {
  private static String[] strArray = {"Cat", "Dog", "Tiger", "Lion", "Lion"};

  public static boolean isThereDuplicateUsingLoop() {
    boolean duplicateFound = false;
    int loopCounter = 0;
    for (int i = 0; i < strArray.length; i++) {
      String str = strArray[i];
      int countDuplicate = 0;
      for (int j = 0; j < strArray.length; j++) {
        String str2 = strArray[j];
        if(str.equalsIgnoreCase(str2)) {
            countDuplicate++;
        }

        if(countDuplicate > 1) {
            duplicateFound = true;
            System.out.println("duplicate found for " + str);
        }
        loopCounter++;
      }//end of inner nested for loop

      if(duplicateFound) {
        break;
      }
    }//end of outer for loop

    System.out.println("looped " + loopCounter + " times");
    return duplicateFound;
  }

  public static void main(String[] args) {
      isThereDuplicateUsingLoop();
  }
}
```

```
------------------------------------------
output:
duplicate found for Lion
looped 20 times
```

Better approach -- using a collections class like a Set

```java
public class NonNestedLoop {
  private static String[]  strArray = {"Cat", "Dog", "Tiger", "Lion", "Lion"};

  public static boolean isThereDuplicateUsingCollection() {
    boolean duplicateFound = false;
    int loopCounter = 0;

    Set  setValues = new HashSet(10);  // create a set

    for (int i = 0; i < strArray.length; i++) {
      String str = strArray[i];
      if(setValues.contains(str)) { // check if already has this value
          duplicateFound = true;
          System.out.println("duplicate found for " + str);
      }

      setValues.add(str); // add the value to the set

      loopCounter++;

      if(duplicateFound) {
         break;
      }
    } // end of for loop

    System.out.println("looped " + loopCounter + " times");
    return duplicateFound;
  }

  public static void main(String[] args) {
      isThereDuplicateUsingCollection();
  }
}
```

```
------------------------------------------
output:
duplicate found for Lion
looped 5 times
```

The approach using a Set is more readable and easier to maintain and performs slightly better. If you have an array with 100 items then nested loops will loop through 9900 times and utilizing a collection class will loop through only 100 times.

Q 18: What is the difference between "==" and equals(...) method? What is the difference between shallow comparison and deep comparison of objects? LF CO FAQ

A 18: The questions **Q18**, **Q19**, and **Q20** are vital for effective coding. These three questions are vital when you are using a collection of objects for Example: using a java.util.Set of persistable Hibernate objects etc. It is easy to implement these methods incorrectly and consequently your program can behave strangely and also is hard to debug. So, you can expect these questions in your interviews.

== [shallow comparison]	equals( ) [deep comparison]
The == returns **true**, if the variable reference points to the same object in memory. This is a "**shallow comparison**".	The equals() - returns the results of running the **equals() method of a user supplied class, which compares the attribute values**. The equals() method provides "**deep comparison**" by checking if two objects are logically equal as opposed to the shallow comparison provided by the operator ==. If equals() method does not exist in a user supplied class then the inherited Object class's equals() method is run which evaluates if the references point to the same object in memory. The **object**.equals() works just like the "==" operator (i.e shallow comparison). Overriding the Object class may seem simple but there are many ways to get it wrong, and consequence can be unpredictable behavior. Refer **Q19** in Java section.

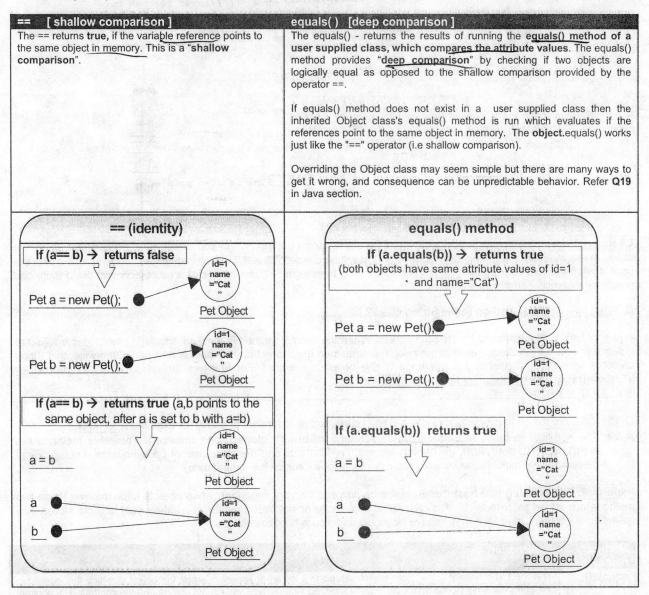

Note: String assignment with the "**new**" operator follow the same rule as == and equals( ) as mentioned above.

```
String str = new String("ABC"); //Wrong. Avoid this because a new String instance
                                 //is created each time it is executed.
```

Variation to the above rule:

The "literal" String assignment is shown below, where if the assignment value is identical to another String assignment value created then a new String object is not created. A reference to the existing String object is returned.

```
String str = "ABC";     //Right because uses a single instance rather than
                        //creating a new instance each time it is executed.
```

Let us look at an example:

```
public class StringBasics {
    public static void main(String[] args) {

        String s1 = new String("A"); //not recommended, use String s1 = "A"
        String s2 = new String("A"); //not recommended, use String s2 = "A"

        //standard: follows the == and equals() rule like plain java objects.

        if (s1 == s2) {  //shallow comparison
            System.out.println("references/identities are equal"); //never reaches here
        }
        if (s1.equals(s2)) {  //deep comparison
            System.out.println("values are equal");    // this line is printed
        }

        //variation: does not follow the == and equals rule

        String s3 = "A";  //goes into a String pool.
        String s4 = "A";  //refers to String already in the pool.

        if (s3 == s4) { //shallow comparison
            System.out.println("references/identities are equal"); //this line is printed
        }
        if (s3.equals(s4)) { //deep comparison
            System.out.println("values are equal"); //this line is also printed
        }
    }
}
```

Design pattern: String class is designed with **Flyweight** design pattern. When you create a String constant as shown above in the variation, (i.e. String s3 = "A", s4= "A"), it will be checked to see if it is already in the String pool. If it is in the pool, it will be picked up from the pool instead of creating a new one. Flyweights are shared objects and using them can result in substantial performance gains.

Q. What is an intern() method in the String class?

A pool of Strings is maintained by the String class. When the intern() method is invoked equals(...) method is invoked to determine if the String already exist in the pool. If it does then the String from the pool is returned. Otherwise, this String object is added to the pool and a reference to this object is returned. For any two Strings s1 & s2, **s1.intern() == s2.intern()** only if <u>s1.equals(s2) is true</u>.

Q 19: What are the non-final methods in Java Object class, which are meant primarily for extension? `LF` `CO`

A 19: The <u>non-final</u> methods are **equals(), hashCode(), toString(), clone()**, and **finalize()**. The other methods like **wait(), notify(), notifyAll(), getClass()** etc are <u>final</u> methods and therefore cannot be overridden. Let us look at these non-final methods, which are meant primarily for extension (i.e. inheritance).

Important: The **equals()** and **hashCode()** methods prove to be <u>very important</u>, when objects implementing these two methods are added to collections. If implemented incorrectly or not implemented at all then your objects stored in a collection like a Set, List or Map may behave strangely and also is hard to debug.

Method name	Explanation
equals() method with public access modifier	This method checks if some other object passed to it as an argument is equal the object in which this method is invoked. It is easy to implement the equals() method incorrectly, if you do not understand the <u>contract</u>. The contract can be stated in terms of 6 simple principles as follows: 1. o1.equals(o1) → which means an Object (e.g. o1) should be equal to itself. (aka **Reflexive**). 2. o1.equals(o2) **if and only** o2.equals(o1) → So it will be <u>incorrect</u> to have your own class say "MyPet" to have a equals() method that has a comparison with an Object of class "java.lang.String" class or with any other built-in Java class. (aka **Symmetric**). 3. o1.equals(o2) && o2.equals(o3) **implies that** o1.equals(o3) as well → It means that if the first object o1 equals to the second object o2 and the second object o2 is equal to the third object o3 then the first object o1 is equal to the third object o3. For example, imagine that X, Y and Z are 3 different classes. The classes X and Y both implement the equals() method in such a way that it provides comparison for objects of class X and class Y. Now if you decide to modify the equals() method of class Y so that it also provides equality comparison with class Z, then you will be violating this principle because no proper equals comparison exist for class X and class Z objects. So, if two objects agree that they are equal and follow the above mentioned symmetric principle, then

one of them cannot decide to have a similar contract with another object of different class. (aka **Transitive**)

4. o1.equals(o2) returns the same as long as **o1 and o2 are unmodified** → if two objects are equal, they must remain equal as long as they are not modified. Similarly, if they are not equal, they must remain non-equal as long as they are not modified. (aka **Consistent**)

5. !o1.equals(null) → which means that any instantiable object is not equal to null. So if you pass a null as an argument to your object o1, then it should return false. (aka **null comparison**)

6. o1.equals(o2) implies o1.hashCode() == o2.hashCode() → This is very important. If you define a equals() method then you must define a hashCode() method as well. Also it means that <u>if you have two objects that are equal then they must have the same hashCode, however the reverse is not true</u> (i.e. if two objects have the same hashCode does not mean that they are equal). <u>So, If a field is not used in equals(), then it must not be used in hashCode() method.</u> (**equals() and hashCode() relationship**)

```java
public class Pet {
  int id;
  String name;

  public boolean equals(Object obj){
     if(this == obj) return true;  // if both are referring to the same object

     if ((obj == null) || (obj.getClass() != this.getClass())) {
        return false;
     }

     Pet rhs = (Pet) obj;
      return id == rhs.id && (name == rhs.name ||
            (name != null && name.equals(rhs.name)) );
  }

  //hashCode() method must be implemented here.
  ...
}
```

hashCode() method with public access modifier	This method returns a hashCode() value as an Integer and is supported for the benefit of hashing based java.util.Collection classes like Hashtable, HashMap, HashSet etc. **If a class overrides the equals() method, it must implement the hashCode() method as well.** The general contract of the hashCode() method is that: 1. Whenever hashCode() method is invoked on the same object more than once during an execution of a Java program, this method must consistently return the <u>same integer result</u>. The integer result need not remain consistent from one execution of the program to the next execution of the same program. 2. If two objects are equal as per the equals() method, then calling the hashCode() method in each of the two objects <u>must return the same integer result</u>. So, If a field is not used in equals(), then it must not be used in hashCode() method. 3. If two objects are unequal as per the equals() method, each of the two objects can return either two different integer results or same integer results (i.e. <u>if 2 objects have the same hashCode() result does not mean that they are equal, but if two objects are equal then they must return the same hashCode() result</u>). <code>public class Pet {</code> <code> int id;</code> <code> String name;</code> <code> public boolean equals(Object obj){</code> <code> //as shown above.</code> <code> }</code> <code> //both fields id & name are used in equals(), so both fields <u>must be used in</u></code> <code> //hashCode() as well.</code> <code> public int hashCode() {</code> <code> int hash = 9;</code> <code> hash = (31 * hash) + id;</code> <code> hash = (31 * hash) + (null == name ? 0 : name.hashCode());</code> <code> return hash;</code> <code> }</code> <code>}</code>
toString()	The toString() method provided by the java.lang.Object returns a string, which consists of the class name

<table>
<tr>
<td>method with public access modifier</td>
<td>
followed by an "@" sign and then unsigned hexadecimal representation of the hashcode, for example Pet@162b91. This hexadecimal representation is not what the users of your class want to see.

Providing your toString() method makes your class much more pleasant to use and it is recommended that all subclasses override this method. The toString() method is invoked automatically when your object is passed to println(), assert() or the string concatenation operator (+).

```java
public class Pet {
        int id;
        String name;

        public boolean equals(Object obj){
                //as shown above.
        }

        public int hashCode() {
                //as shown before
        }

        public String toString() {
                StringBuffer sb = new StringBuffer();
                sb.append("id=").append(id);
                sb.append(",name=").append(name);
                return sb.toString();
        }

}
```
</td>
</tr>
<tr>
<td>clone()

method with protected access modifier</td>
<td>
You should override the clone() method very judiciously. Implementing a properly functioning clone method is complex and it is rarely necessary. You are better off providing some alternative means of object copying (refer **Q26** in Java section) or simply not providing the capability. A better approach is to provide a copy constructor or a static factory method in place of a constructor.

```java
//constructor
public Pet(Pet petToCopy){
    ...
}
```

```java
//static factory method
public static Pet newInstance(Pet petToCopy){
    ...
}
```

The clone() method can be disabled as follows:

```java
public final Object clone() throws CloneNotSupportedException {
    throw new CloneNotSupportedException();
}
```
</td>
</tr>
<tr>
<td>finalize()

method with protected access modifier</td>
<td>
Unlike C++ destructors, the finalize() method in Java is unpredictable, often dangerous and generally unnecessary. Use try{} finally{} blocks as discussed in **Q32** in Java section & **Q45** in Enterprise section. The finalize() method should only be used in rare instances as a safety net or to terminate non-critical native resources. If you do happen to call the finalize() method in some rare instances then remember to call the super.finalize() as shown below:

```java
protected void finalize() throws Throwable {
    try{
        //finalize subclass state
    }
    finally {
        super.finalize();
    }
}
```
</td>
</tr>
</table>

Q 20: When providing a user defined key class for storing objects in the HashMaps or Hashtables, what methods do you have to provide or override (i.e. **method overriding**)? LF PI CO FAQ

A 20: You should override the **equals()** and **hashCode()** methods from the *Object* class. The default implementation of the equals() and hashcode(), which are inherited from the java.lang.Object uses an object instance's memory location (e.g. MyObject@6c60f2ea). This can cause problems when two instances of the car objects have the same color but the inherited equals() will return false because it uses the memory location, which is different for the two instances. Also the **toString()** method can be overridden to provide a proper string representation of your object.

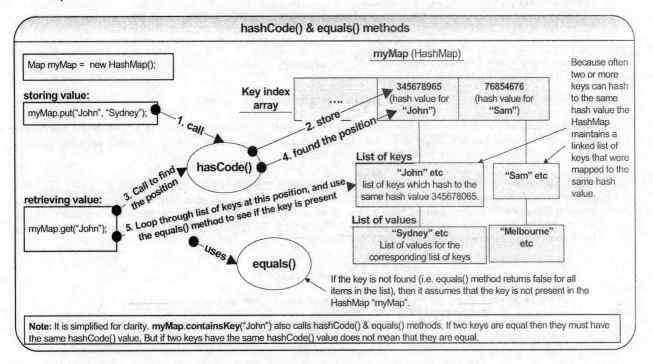

Note: It is simplified for clarity. **myMap**.containsKey("John") also calls hashCode() & equals() methods. If two keys are equal then they must have the same hashCode() value, But if two keys have the same hashCode() value does not mean that they are equal.

Q. What are the primary considerations when implementing a user defined key?

- If a class overrides **equals()**, it must override **hashCode()**.
- If 2 objects are equal, then their hashCode values must be equal as well.
- If a field is not used in equals(), then it must not be used in hashCode().
- If it is accessed often, hashCode() is a candidate for caching to enhance performance.
- It is a best practice to implement the user defined key class as an immutable (refer **Q21**) object.

Q. Why it is a best practice to implement the user defined key class as an immutable object?

Problem: As per the code snippet shown below if you use a mutable user defined class "**UserKey**" as a HashMap key and subsequently if you mutate (i.e. modify via setter method e.g. `key.setName("Sam")`) the key after the object has been added to the HashMap then you will not be able to access the object later on. The original key object will still be in the HashMap (i.e. you can iterate through your HashMap and print it – both prints as "Sam" as opposed to "John" & Sam) but you cannot access it with `map.get(key)` or querying it with `map.containsKey(key)` will return false because the key "John" becomes "Sam" in the "List of keys" at the key index "345678965" if you mutate the key after adding. These types of errors are very hard to trace and fix.

```
Map myMap = new HashMap(10);
//add the key "John"
UserKey key = new UserKey("John");   //Assume UserKey class is mutable
myMap.put(key, "Sydney");
//now to add the key "Sam"
key.setName("Sam"); // same key object is mutated instead of creating a new instance.
                    // This line modifies the key value "John" to "Sam" in the "List of keys"
                    // as shown in the diagram above. This means that the key "John" cannot be
                    // accessed. There will be two keys with "Sam" in positions with hash
                    // values 345678965 and 76854676.
myMap.put(key, "Melbourne");

myMap.get(new UserKey("John")); // key cannot be accessed. The key hashes to the same position
            // 345678965 in the "Key index array" but cannot be found in the "List of keys"
```

Solution: Generally you use a java.lang.Integer or a java.lang.String class as the key, which are immutable Java objects. If you define your own key class then it is a best practice to make the key class an immutable object (i.e. do not provide any setXXX() methods in your key class. e.g. no `setName(...)` method in the **UserKey** class). If a programmer wants to insert a new key then he/she will always have to instantiate a new object (i.e. cannot mutate the existing key because immutable key object class has no setter methods).

```
Map myMap = new HashMap(10);
//add the key "John"
UserKey key1 = new UserKey("John");   //Assume UserKey is immutable
myMap.put(key1, "Sydney");

//add the key "Sam"
UserKey key2 = new UserKey("Sam");   //Since UserKey is immutable, new instance is created.
myMap.put(key2, "Melbourne");

myMap.get(new UserKey("John"));       //Now the key can be accessed
```

Similar issues are possible with the *Set* (e.g. HashSet) as well. If you add an object to a "Set" and subsequently modify the added object and later on try to query the original object it may not be present. `mySet.contains(originalObject)` may return false.

J2SE 5.0 introduces enumerated constants, which <u>improves readability and maintainability of your code</u>. Java programming language enums are more powerful than their counterparts in other languages. Example: As shown below a class like *"Weather"* can be built on top of simple enum type *"Season"* and the class *"Weather"* can be made immutable, and only one instance of each *"Weather"* can be created, so that your *Weather* class **does not have to override equals()** and **hashCode()** methods.

```
public class Weather {
    public enum Season {WINTER, SPRING, SUMMER, FALL}
    private final Season season;
    private static final List<Weather> listWeather =  new ArrayList<Weather> ();

    private Weather (Season season) {   this.season = season;}
    public Season getSeason () { return season;}

    static {
       for (Season season : Season.values()) { //using J2SE 5.0 for each loop
            listWeather.add(new Weather(season));
       }
    }

    public static ArrayList<Weather> getWeatherList () { return  listWeather; }
    public String toString(){ return season;}  //takes advantage of toString() method of Season.
}
```

Q 21: What is the main difference between a String and a StringBuffer class? LF PI CI CO FAQ
A 21:

String	StringBuffer / StringBuilder (added in J2SE 5.0)
String is **immutable**: you can't modify a string object but can replace it by creating a new instance. Creating a new instance is rather expensive.	StringBuffer is **mutable**: use StringBuffer or StringBuilder when you want to modify the contents. *StringBuilder* was added in Java 5 and it is identical in all respects to *StringBuffer* except that it is not synchronized, which makes it slightly faster at the cost of not being thread-safe.

//Inefficient version using immutable String
String output = "Some text"
Int count = 100;
for(int i =0; i<count; i++) {
   output += i;
}
return output;
	//More efficient version using mutable StringBuffer
	StringBuffer output = new **StringBuffer**(110);// set an initial size of 110
	output.append("Some text");
	for(int i =0; i<count; i++) {
	   output.append(i);
	}
	return output.toString();

The above code would build 99 new String objects, of which 98 would be thrown away immediately. Creating new objects is not efficient.	The above code creates only two new objects, the *StringBuffer* and the final *String* that is returned. StringBuffer expands as needed, which is costly however, so it would be better to initialize the *StringBuffer* with the correct size from the start as shown.

Another important point is that creation of extra strings is not limited to overloaded mathematical operator "+" but there are several methods like **concat()**, **trim()**, **substring()**, and **replace()** in String classes that generate new string instances. So use StringBuffer or StringBuilder for computation intensive operations, which offer better performance.

Q. What is an immutable object? Immutable objects whose state (i.e. the object's data) does not change once it is instantiated (i.e. it becomes a read-only object after instantiation). Immutable classes are ideal for representing numbers (e.g. java.lang.Integer, java.lang.Float, java.lang.BigDecimal etc are immutable objects), enumerated types, colors (e.g. java.awt.Color is an immutable object), short lived objects like events, messages etc.

Q. What are the benefits of immutable objects?

- Immutable classes can greatly simplify programming by freely allowing you to cache and share the references to the immutable objects without having to defensively copy them or without having to worry about their values becoming stale or corrupted.

- Immutable classes are inherently thread-safe and you do not have to synchronize access to them to be used in a multi-threaded environment. So there is no chance of negative performance consequences.

- Eliminates the possibility of data becoming inaccessible when used as keys in HashMaps or as elements in Sets. These types of errors are hard to debug and fix. Refer **Q20** in Java section under **"Q. Why it is a best practice to implement the user defined key class as an immutable object? "**

Q. How will you write an immutable class? CO

Writing an immutable class is generally easy but there can be some tricky situations. Follow the following guidelines:

1. A class is declared final (i.e. final classes cannot be extended).
```
public final class MyImmutable { … }
```

2. All its fields are final (final fields cannot be mutated once assigned).
```
private final int[] myArray; //do not declare as → private final int[] myArray = null;
```

3. Do not provide any methods that can change the state of the immutable object in any way – not just setXXX methods, but any methods which can change the state.

4. The "this" reference is not allowed to escape during construction from the immutable class and the immutable class should have exclusive access to fields that contain references to mutable objects like arrays, collections and mutable classes like Date etc by:

    - Declaring the mutable references as private.
    - Not returning or exposing the mutable references to the caller (this can be done by defensive copying)

Wrong way to write an immutable class	Right way to write an immutable class
Wrong way to write a constructor:	Right way is to copy the array before assigning in the constructor.

`public final class MyImmutable {`
 	
  `private final int[] myArray;`
 	
  `public MyImmutable(int[] anArray) {`
    `this.myArray = anArray; // wrong`
  `}`
 	
  `public String toString() {`
    `StringBuffer sb = new StringBuffer("Numbers are: ");`
    `for (int i = 0; i < myArray.length; i++) {`
      `sb.append(myArray[i] + " ");`
    `}`
    `return sb.toString();`
  `}`
`}`
	`public final class MyImmutable {`
	
	  `private final int[] myArray;`
	
	  `public MyImmutable(int[] anArray) {`
	    `this.myArray = anArray.clone(); // defensive copy`
	  `}`
	
	  `public String toString() {`
	    `StringBuffer sb = new StringBuffer("Numbers are: ");`
	    `for (int i = 0; i < myArray.length; i++) {`
	      `sb.append(myArray[i] + " ");`
	    `}`
	    `return sb.toString();`
	  `}`
	`}`

// the caller could change the array after calling the constructor.	// the caller cannot change the array after calling the constructor.

`int[] array = {1,2};`
`MyImmutable myImmutableRef = new MyImmutable(array) ;`
`System.out.println("Before constructing " + myImmutableRef);`
`array[1] = 5; // change (i.e. mutate) the element`
`System.out.println("After constructing " + myImmutableRef);`
	`int[] array = {1,2};`
	`MyImmutable myImmutableRef = new MyImmutable(array) ;`
	`System.out.println("Before constructing " + myImmutableRef);`
	`array[1] = 5; // change (i.e. mutate)  the element`
	`System.out.println("After constructing " + myImmutableRef);`

Out put: `Before constructing Numbers are: 1 2`	**Out put**: Before constructing Numbers are: 1 2

After constructing Numbers are: 1 5	After constructing Numbers are: 1 2
As you can see in the output that the "MyImmutable" object has been mutated. This is because the object reference gets copied as discussed in **Q22** in Java section.	As you can see in the output that the "MyImmutable" object has not been mutated.
Wrong way to write an accessor. A caller could get the array reference and then change the contents: ```\npublic int[] getArray() {\n return myArray;\n}\n```	Right way to write an accessor by cloning. ```\npublic int[] getAray() {\n return (int[]) myArray.clone();\n}\n```

Important: Beware of using the clone() method on a collection like a Map, List, Set etc because they are not only difficult to implement correctly refer **Q19** in Java section but also the default behavior of an object's clone() method automatically yields a shallow copy. You have to deep copy the mutable objects referenced by your immutable class. Refer **Q26** in Java section for deep vs. shallow cloning and **Q22** in Java section for why you will be modifying the original object if you do not deep copy.

Q. How would you defensively copy a Date field in your immutable class?

```
public final class MyDiary {

    private Date myDate = null;

    public MyDiary(Date aDate){
        this.myDate = new Date(aDate.getTime());        // defensive copying by not exposing the "myDate" reference
    }

    public Date getDate() {
        return new Date(myDate.getTime);                // defensive copying by not exposing the "myDate" reference
    }
}
```

Q 22: What is the main difference between pass-by-reference and pass-by-value? `LF` `PI` `FAQ`

A 22: Other languages use **pass-by-reference** or pass-by-pointer. But in Java no matter what type of argument you pass the corresponding parameter (primitive variable or object reference) will get a copy of that data, which is exactly how **pass-by-value** (i.e. copy-by-value) works.

In Java, if a calling method passes a reference of an object as an argument to the called method then the **passed-in reference gets copied first** and then passed to the called method. Both the original reference that was passed-in and the copied reference will be <u>pointing to the same object</u>. So no matter which reference you use, <u>you will be always modifying the same original object</u>, **which is how the pass-by-reference works as well**.

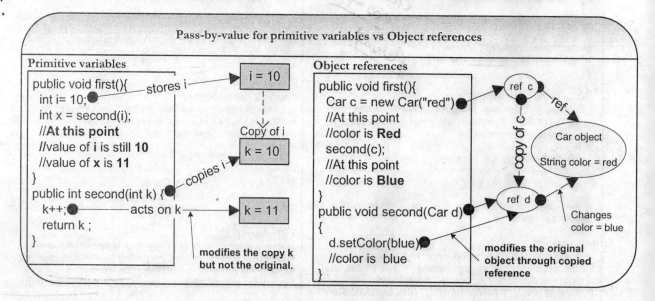

If your method call involves inter-process (e.g. between two JVMs) communication, then the reference of the calling method has a different address space to the called method sitting in a separate process (i.e. separate

JVM). Hence inter-process communication involves calling method passing objects as arguments to called method **by-value** in a serialized form, which can adversely affect performance due to marshaling and unmarshaling cost.

Note: As discussed in **Q69** in Enterprise section, EJB 2.x introduced local interfaces, where enterprise beans that can be used locally within the same JVM using Java's form of **pass-by-reference**, hence improving performance.

Q 23: What is serialization? How would you exclude a field of a class from serialization or what is a transient variable? What is the common use? What is a serial version id? LF SI PI FAQ

A 23: Serialization is a process of reading or writing an object. It is a process of saving an object's state to a sequence of bytes, as well as a process of rebuilding those bytes back into a live object at some future time. An object is marked serializable by implementing the *java.io.Serializable* interface, which is only a *marker* interface -- it simply allows the serialization mechanism to verify that the class can be persisted, typically to a file.

Transient variables cannot be serialized. The fields marked **transient** in a serializable object will not be transmitted in the byte stream. An example would be a file handle, a database connection, a system thread etc. Such objects are only meaningful locally. So they should be marked as transient in a serializable class.

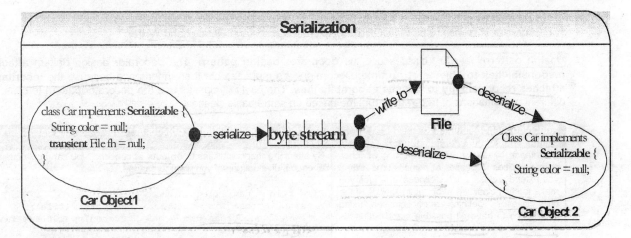

Serialization can adversely affect performance since it:

- Depends on reflection.
- Has an incredibly verbose data format.
- Is very easy to send surplus data.

Q. When to use serialization? Do not use serialization if you do not have to. A common use of serialization is to use it to send an object over the network or if the state of an object needs to be persisted to a flat file or a database. (Refer **Q57** on Enterprise section). Deep cloning or copy can be achieved through serialization. This may be fast to code but will have performance implications (Refer **Q26** in Java section).

To serialize the above "*Car*" object to a file (sample for illustration purpose only, should use try {} catch {} block):

```
Car car = new Car();    // The "Car" class implements a java.io.Serializable interface
FileOutputStream fos = new FileOutputStream(filename);
ObjectOutputStream out = new ObjectOutputStream(fos);
out.writeObject(car); // serialization mechanism happens here
out.close();
```

The **objects stored in an HTTP session should be serializable** to support in-memory replication of sessions to achieve scalability (Refer **Q20** in Enterprise section). Objects are passed in RMI (Remote Method Invocation) across network using serialization (Refer **Q57** in Enterprise section).

Q. What is Java Serial Version ID? Say you create a "Car" class, instantiate it, and write it out to an object stream. The flattened car object sits in the file system for some time. Meanwhile, if the "Car" class is modified by adding a new field. Later on, when you try to read (i.e. deserialize) the flattened "Car" object, you get the **java.io.InvalidClassException** – because all serializable classes are automatically given a unique identifier. This exception is thrown when the identifier of the class is not equal to the identifier of the flattened object. If you really think about it, the exception is thrown because of the addition of the new field. You can avoid this exception being thrown by controlling the versioning yourself by declaring an explicit **serialVersionUID**. There is also a small performance benefit in explicitly declaring your serialVersionUID (because does not have to be calculated). So, it is best practice to add your own **serialVersionUID** to your Serializable classes as soon as you create them as shown below:

```
public class Car {
    static final long serialVersionUID = 1L; //assign a long value
}
```

Note: Alternatively you can use the serialver tool comes with Sun's JDK. This tool takes a full class name on the command line and returns the serialVersionUID for that compiled class. For example:

```
static final long serialVersionUID = 10275439472837494L; //generated by serialver tool.
```

Q 24: Explain the Java I/O streaming concept and the use of the decorator design pattern in Java I/O? LF DP PI SI

A 24: Java input and output is defined in terms of an abstract concept called a "**stream**", which is a sequence of data. There are 2 kinds of streams.

- Byte streams (8 bit bytes) → Abstract classes are: **InputStream** and **OutputStream**
- Character streams (16 bit UNICODE) → Abstract classes are: **Reader** and **Writer**

Design pattern: *java.io.** classes use the **decorator design pattern**. The decorator design pattern **attaches responsibilities to objects at runtime**. Decorators are more flexible than inheritance because the **inheritance attaches responsibility to classes at compile time**. The *java.io.** classes use the decorator pattern to construct different combinations of behavior at runtime based on some basic classes.

Attaching responsibilities to classes at compile time using subclassing.	Attaching responsibilities to objects at runtime using a decorator design pattern.

Inheritance (aka subclassing) attaches responsibilities to classes at compile time. When you extend a class, each individual changes you make to child class will affect all instances of the child classes. Defining many classes using inheritance to have all possible combinations is problematic and inflexible.	By attaching responsibilities to **objects at runtime**, you can apply changes to each individual object you want to change.
	
	```File file = new File("c:/temp");```
	```FileInputStream fis = new FileInputStream(file);```
	```BufferedInputStream bis = new BufferedInputStream(fis);```
	
	Decorator
	
	Decorators decorate an object by enhancing or restricting functionality of an object it decorates. The decorators add or restrict functionality to decorated objects either before or after forwarding the request. At runtime the BufferedInputStream (bis), which is a **decorator** (aka a **wrapper** around decorated object), forwards the method call to its **decorated** object FileInputStream (fis). The "bis" will apply the additional functionality of buffering around the lower level file (i.e. fis) I/O.

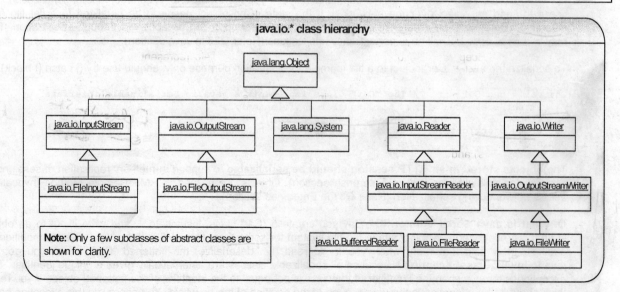

java.io.* class hierarchy

Q. How does the new I/O (NIO) offer better scalability and better performance?

Java has long been not suited for developing programs that perform a lot of I/O operations. Furthermore, commonly needed tasks such as file locking, non-blocking and asynchronous I/O operations and ability to map file to memory were not available. Non-blocking I/O operations were achieved through work around such as multithreading or using JNI. The **New I/O** API (aka **NIO**) in J2SE 1.4 has changed this situation.

A server's ability to handle several client requests effectively depends on how it uses I/O streams. When a server has to handle hundreds of clients simultaneously, it must be able to use I/O services concurrently. One way to cater for this scenario in Java is to use threads but having almost one-to-one ratio of threads (100 clients will have 100 threads) is prone to enormous **thread overhead and can result in performance and scalability problems due to consumption of memory stacks** (i.e. each thread has its own stack. Refer **Q34, Q42** in Java section) and **CPU context switching** (i.e. switching between threads as opposed to doing real computation.). To overcome this problem, a new set of non-blocking I/O classes have been introduced to the Java platform in java.nio package. The non-blocking I/O mechanism is built around *Selectors and Channels*. **Channels**, **Buffers** and **Selectors** are the core of the NIO.

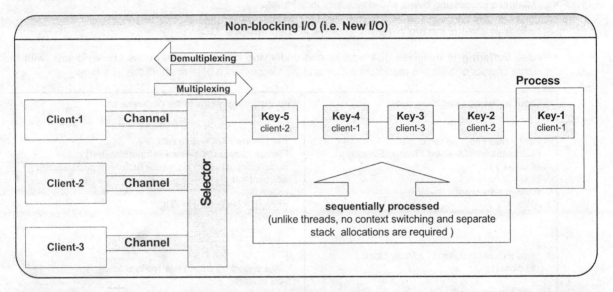

A **Channel** class represents a bi-directional communication channel (similar to *InputStream* and *OutputStream*) between datasources such as a socket, a file, or an application component, which is capable of performing one or more I/O operations such as reading or writing. Channels can be non-blocking, which means, no I/O operation will wait for data to be read or written to the network. The good thing about NIO channels is that they can be asynchronously interrupted and closed. So if a thread is blocked in an I/O operation on a channel, another thread can interrupt that blocked thread.

A **Selector** class enables multiplexing (combining multiple streams into a single stream) and demultiplexing (separating a single stream into multiple streams) I/O events and makes it possible for a single thread to efficiently manage many I/O channels. A Selector monitors selectable channels, which are registered with it for I/O events like connect, accept, read and write. The keys (i.e. Key1, Key2 etc represented by the SelectionKey class) encapsulate the relationship between a specific selectable channel and a specific selector.

Buffers hold data. Channels can fill and drain *Buffers*. Buffers replace the need for you to do your own buffer management using byte arrays. There are different types of Buffers like *ByteBuffer, CharBuffer, DoubleBuffer*, etc.

Design pattern: NIO uses a **reactor design pattern**, which demultiplexes events (separating single stream into multiple streams) and dispatches them to registered object handlers. The reactor pattern is similar to an **observer pattern** (aka publisher and subscriber design pattern), but an observer pattern handles only a single source of events (i.e. a single publisher with multiple subscribers) where a reactor pattern handles multiple event sources (i.e. multiple publishers with multiple subscribers). The intent of an observer pattern is to define a one-to-many dependency so that when one object (i.e. the publisher) changes its state, all its dependents (i.e. all its subscribers) are notified and updated correspondingly.

Another sought after functionality of NIO is its ability to **map a file to memory**. There is a specialized form of a Buffer known as "MappedByteBuffer", which represents a buffer of bytes mapped to a file. To map a file to "MappedByteBuffer", you must first get a channel for a file. Once you get a channel then you map it to a buffer and subsequently you can access it like any other "ByteBuffer". Once you map an input file to a "CharBuffer", you can do pattern matching on the file contents. This is similar to running "grep" on a UNIX file system.

Another feature of NIO is its **ability to lock and unlock files**. Locks can be exclusive or shared and can be held on a contiguous portion of a file. But file locks are subject to the control of the underlying operating system.

Q 25: How can you improve Java I/O performance? PI BP

A 25: Java applications that utilize Input/Output are excellent candidates for performance tuning. Profiling of Java applications that handle significant volumes of data will show significant time spent in I/O operations. This means substantial gains can be had from I/O performance tuning. Therefore, I/O efficiency should be a high priority for developers looking to optimally increase performance.

The basic rules for speeding up I/O performance are

- Minimize accessing the hard disk. ✓
- Minimize accessing the underlying operating system.
- Minimize processing bytes and characters individually.

Let us look at some of the techniques to improve I/O performance. CO

- Use **buffering** to minimize disk access and underlying operating system. As shown below, with buffering large chunks of a file are read from a disk and then accessed a byte or character at a time.

Without buffering : inefficient code	With Buffering: yields better performance
```try{ File f = new File("myFile.txt"); FileInputStream fis = new FileInputStream(f); int count = 0; int b = 0; while((b = fis.read()) != -1){ if(b== '\n') { count++; } } // fis should be closed in a finally block. fis.close() ; } catch(IOException io){}```	```try{ File f = new File("myFile.txt"); FileInputStream fis = new FileInputStream(f); BufferedInputStream bis = new BufferedInputStream(fis); int count = 0; int b = 0 ; while((b = bis.read()) != -1){ if(b== '\n') { count++; } } //bis should be closed in a finally block. bis.close() ; } catch(IOException io){}```
Note: fis.read() is a native method call to the underlying operating system.	**Note:** bis.read() takes the next byte from the input buffer and only rarely access the underlying operating system.

Instead of reading a character or a byte at a time, the above code with buffering can be improved further by reading one line at a time as shown below:

```
FileReader fr = new FileReader(f);
BufferedReader br = new BufferedReader(fr);
while (br.readLine() != null) count++;
```

By default the **System.out** is line buffered, which means that the output buffer is flushed when a new line character (i.e. "\n") is encountered. This is required for any interactivity between an input prompt and display of output. The line buffering can be disabled for faster I/O operation as follows:

```
FileOutputStream fos = new FileOutputStream(file);
BufferedOutputStream bos = new BufferedOutputStream(fos, 1024);
PrintStream ps  = new PrintStream(bos,false);
```

```
// To redirect standard output to a file instead of the "System" console which is the default for both "System.out" (i.e.
// standard output) and "System.err" (i.e. standard error device) variables
```

```
System.setOut(ps);
```

```
while (someConditionIsTrue)
    System.out.println("blah…blah…");
}
```

It is recommended to use logging frameworks like **Log4J** with **SLF4J** (<u>S</u>imple <u>L</u>ogging <u>F</u>açade for <u>J</u>ava), which uses buffering instead of using default behavior of **System.out.println(.....)** for better performance. Frameworks like Log4J are configurable, flexible, extensible and easy to use.

- Use the NIO package, if you are using JDK 1.4 or later, which uses performance-enhancing features like buffers to hold data, memory mapping of files, non-blocking I/O operations etc.

- I/O performance can be improved by minimizing the calls to the underlying operating systems. The Java runtime itself cannot know the length of a file, querying the file system for isDirectory(), isFile(), exists() etc must query the underlying operating system.

- Where applicable caching can be used to improve performance by reading in all the lines of a file into a Java *Collection* class like an ArrayList or a HashMap and subsequently access the data from an in-memory collection instead of the disk.

Q 26: What is the main difference between shallow cloning and deep cloning of objects? DC LF MI PI

A 26: The default behavior of an object's clone() method automatically yields a shallow copy. So to achieve a deep copy the classes must be edited or adjusted.

Shallow copy: If a shallow copy is performed on obj-1 as shown in fig-2 then it is copied but its contained objects are not. The contained objects Obj-1 and Obj-2 are affected by changes to cloned Obj-2. Java supports shallow cloning of objects by default when a class implements the *java.lang.Cloneable* interface.

Deep copy: If a deep copy is performed on obj-1 as shown in fig-3 then not only obj-1 has been copied but the objects contained within it have been copied as well. Serialization can be used to achieve deep cloning. Deep cloning through serialization is faster to develop and easier to maintain but carries a performance overhead.

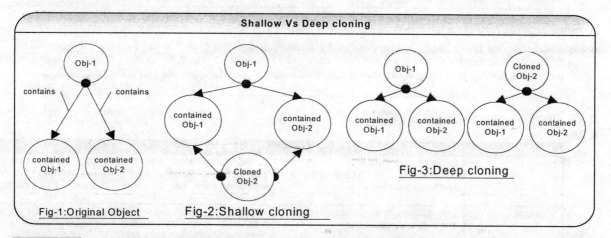

Shallow Vs Deep cloning

Fig-1:Original Object   Fig-2:Shallow cloning   Fig-3:Deep cloning

For example invoking clone() method on a collection like *HashMap, List etc* returns a <u>shallow copy of *HashMap, List,*</u> instances. This means if you clone a *HashMap,* the map instance is cloned but **the keys and values themselves are not cloned**. If you want a deep copy then a simple method is to serialize the *HashMap* to a *ByteArrayOutputSream* and then deserialize it. This creates a deep copy but <u>does require</u> that all <u>keys and values</u> in the *HashMap* are Serializable. Main advantage of this approach is that it will deep copy any arbitrary object graph. Refer **Q23** in Java section for deep copying using Serialization. Alternatively you can provide a <u>static factory method</u> to deep copy. **Example:** to deep copy a list of *Car* objects.

```
public static List deepCopy(List listCars) {
    List copiedList = new ArrayList(10);
    for (Object object : listCars) {    //JDK 1.5 for each loop
        Car original = (Car)object;
        Car carCopied = new Car();  //instantiate a new Car object
        carCopied.setColor((original.getColor()));
        copiedList.add(carCopied);
    }
    return copiedList;
}
```

Q 27: What is the difference between an instance variable and a static variable? How does a local variable compare to an instance or a static variable? Give an example where you might use a static variable? **LF FAQ**

A 27:

Static variables	Instance variables
Class variables are called static variables. There is only one occurrence of a class variable per JVM per class loader. When a class is loaded the class variables (aka static variables) are initialized.	Instance variables are non-static and there is one occurrence of an instance variable in each class instance (i.e. each object). Also known as a **member variable** or a **field**.

A static variable is used in the **singleton** pattern. (Refer **Q51** in Java section). A static variable is used with a **final** modifier to define **constants**.

Local variables	Instance and static variables
Local variables have a narrower scope than instance variables.	Instance variables have a narrower scope than static variables.
The lifetime of a local variable is determined by execution path and local variables are also known as stack variables because they live on the stack. Refer **Q34** for stack & heap.	Instance and static variables are associated with objects and therefore live in the heap. Refer **Q34** in Java section for stack & heap.
For a local variable, it is illegal for code to fail to assign it a value. It is the best practice to declare local variables only where required as opposed to declaring them upfront and cluttering up your code with some local variables that never get used.	Both the static and instance variables always have a value. If your code does not assign them a value then the run-time system will implicitly assign a default value (e.g. null/0/0.0/false).

Note: Java does not support global, universally accessible variables. You can get the same sorts of effects with classes that have static variables.

Q 28: Give an example where you might use a static method? **LF FAQ**

A 28: Static methods prove useful for creating **utility classes**, **singleton classes** and **factory methods** (Refer **Q51**, **Q52** in Java section). Utility classes are not meant to be instantiated. Improper coding of utility classes can lead to procedural coding. **java.lang.Math, java.util.Collections** etc are examples of utility classes in Java.

Q 29: What are access modifiers? **LF FAQ**

A 29:

Modifier	Used with	Description
public	Outer classes, interfaces, constructors, Inner classes, methods and field variables	A class or interface may be accessed from outside the package. Constructors, inner classes, methods and field variables may be accessed wherever their class is accessed.
protected	Constructors, inner classes, methods, and field variables. .	Accessed by other classes in the same package or any subclasses of the class in which they are referred (i.e. **same package** or **different package**).
private	Constructors, inner classes, methods and field variables,	Accessed only within the class in which they are declared
No modifier: (Package by default).	Outer classes, inner classes, interfaces, constructors, methods, and field variables	Accessed only from within the package in which they are declared.

Q 30: Where and how can you use a private constructor? **LF FAQ**

A 30: Private constructor is used if you do not want other classes to instantiate the object and to prevent subclassing. The instantiation is done by a public static method (i.e. a static factory method) within the same class.
- Used in the singleton design pattern. (Refer **Q51** in Java section).
- Used in the factory method design pattern (Refer **Q52** in Java section). e.g. java.util.Collections class (Refer **Q16** in Java section).
- Used in utility classes e.g. StringUtils etc.

Q 31: What is a final modifier? Explain other Java modifiers? **LF FAQ**

A 31: A final class can't be extended i.e. A final class can not be subclassed. A final method can't be overridden when its class is inherited. You can't change value of a final variable (i.e. it is a constant).

Modifier	Class	Method	Variable
static	A static inner class is just an inner class associated with the class, rather than with an instance of the class.	A static method is called by classname.method (e.g Math.random()), can only access static variables.	Class variables are called static variables. There is only one occurrence of a class variable per JVM per class loader.
abstract	An abstract class cannot be instantiated, must be a superclass and a class must be declared abstract whenever one or more methods are abstract.	Method is defined but contains no implementation code (implementation code is included in the subclass). If a method is abstract then the entire class must be abstract.	N/A
synchronized	N/A	Acquires a **lock on the class** for static **methods**. Acquires a **lock on the instance** for non-**static** methods.	N/A
transient	N/A	N/A	variable should not be serialized.
final	Class cannot be inherited (i.e. extended)	Method cannot be overridden.	Makes the variable immutable.
native	N/A	Platform dependent. No body, only signature.	N/A

Note: Be prepared for tricky questions on modifiers like, what is a "**volatile**"? Or what is a "**const**"? Etc. The reason it is tricky is that Java does have these keywords "const" and "volatile" as reserved, which means you can't name your variables with these names **but modifier "const" is not yet added in the language** and the **modifier "volatile" is very rarely used**.

The "volatile" modifier is used on instance variables that may be modified simultaneously by other threads. The modifier volatile only synchronizes the variable marked as volatile whereas "synchronized" modifier synchronizes all variables. Since other threads cannot see local variables, there is no need to mark local variables as volatile. **For example:**

```
volatile int number;
volatile private List listItems = null;
```

Java uses the "final" modifier to declare constants. A final variable or constant declared as "final" has a value that is immutable and cannot be modified to refer to any other objects other than one it was initialized to refer to. So the "final" modifier applies only to the value of the variable itself, and not to the object referenced by the variable. This is where the "const" modifier can come in very **useful if added to the Java language**. A reference variable or a constant marked as "const" refers to an immutable object that cannot be modified. The reference variable itself can be modified, if it is not marked as "final". The "const" modifier will be applicable only to non-primitive types. The primitive types should continue to use the modifier "final".

Q. If you want to extend the "java.lang.String" class, what methods will you override in your extending class?

You would be tempted to say equals(), hashCode() and toString() based on **Q19**, **Q20** in Java section but the "java.lang.String" class is declared final and therefore it cannot be extended.

Q 32: What is the difference between final, finally and finalize() in Java? **LF** **FAQ**
A 32:
- **final** - constant declaration. Refer **Q31** in Java section.
- **finally** - handles exception. The finally block is optional and provides a mechanism to clean up regardless of what happens within the try block (except System.exit(0) call). Use the finally block to close files or to release other system resources like database connections, statements etc. (Refer **Q45** in Enterprise section)
- **finalize()** - method helps in garbage collection. A **method** that is invoked before an object is discarded by the garbage collector, allowing it to clean up its state. Should not be used to release non-memory resources like file handles, sockets, database connections etc because Java has only a finite number of these resources and you do not know when the garbage collection is going to kick in to release these non-memory resources through the finalize() method. Refer **Q19** in Java Section.

Q 33: Why would you prefer a short circuit "&&, ||" operators over logical "& , |" operators? **LF**
A 33: Firstly *NullPointerException* is by far the most common *RuntimeException*. If you use the logical operator you can get a *NullPointerException*. This can be avoided easily by using a short circuit "&&" operator as shown below.

There are other ways to check for null but short circuit && operator can simplify your code by not having to declare separate if clauses.

```
if((obj != null) & obj.equals(newObj)) {  //can cause a NullPointerException if obj == null
    ...                                    // because obj.equals(newObj) is always executed.
}
```

Short-circuiting means that an operator only evaluates as far as it has to, not as far as it can. If the variable 'obj' equals null, it won't even try to evaluate the 'obj.equals(newObj)' clause as shown in the following example. This protects the potential *NullPointerException*.

```
if((obj != null) && obj.equals(newObj)) {  //cannot get a NullPointerException because
    ...                                     //obj.equals(newObj) is executed only if obj != null
}
```

Secondly, <u>short-circuit "&&" and "||" operators can improve performance</u> in certain situations. **For example:**

```
if((number <= 7) || (doComputeIntensiveAnalysis(number) <= 13)) { //the CPU intensive
    ....                                //computational method in bold is executed only if number > 7.
}
```

Q 34: How does Java allocate stack and heap memory? Explain re-entrant, recursive and idempotent methods/functions? **MI CI**

A 34: Each time an object is created in Java it goes into the area of memory known as **heap**. The primitive variables like int and double are allocated in the **stack** (i.e. <u>L</u>ast <u>In F</u>irst <u>O</u>ut queue), if they are local variables and in the **heap** if they are member variables (i.e. fields of a class). In Java methods and local variables are pushed into stack when a method is invoked and stack pointer is decremented when a method call is completed. In a multi-threaded application each thread will have its own stack but will share the same heap. This is why care should be taken in your code to avoid any concurrent access issues in the heap space. <u>The stack is thread-safe because each thread will have its own stack with say 1MB RAM allocated for each thread but the heap is not thread-safe unless guarded with **synchronization** through your code</u>. The stack space can be increased with the **–Xss** option.

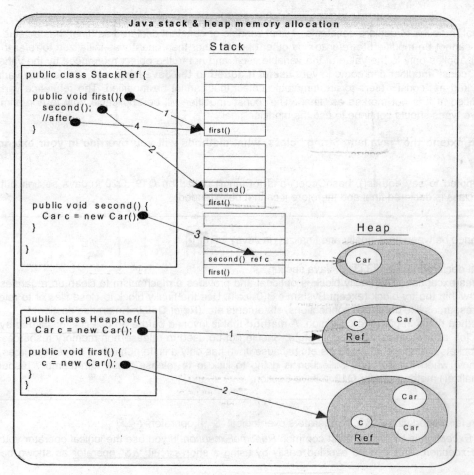

All Java methods are automatically **re-entrant**. It means that several threads can be executing the same method at once, each with its own copy of the local variables. A Java method may call itself without needing any special declarations. This is known as a **recursive** method call. Given enough stack space, recursive method calls are perfectly valid in Java though it is tough to debug. Recursive methods are useful in removing iterations from many sorts of algorithms. All recursive functions are re-entrant but not all re-entrant functions are recursive. **Idempotent** methods are methods, which are written in such a way that repeated calls to the same method with the same arguments yield same results. For example clustered EJBs, which are written with idempotent methods, can automatically recover from a server failure as long as it can reach another server (i.e. scalable).

Q 35: Explain Outer and Inner classes (or Nested classes) in Java? When will you use an Inner Class? LF SE

A 35: In Java not all classes have to be defined separate from each other. You can put the definition of one class inside the definition of another class. The inside class is called an inner class and the enclosing class is called an outer class. So when you define an inner class, it is a member of the outer class in much the same way as other members like attributes, methods and constructors.

Q. Where should you use inner classes? Code **without** inner classes **is more maintainable** and **readable**. When you access private data members of the outer class, the JDK compiler creates package-access member functions in the outer class for the inner class to access the private members. This leaves a **security hole**. In general **we should avoid using inner classes**. Use inner class only when an inner class is only relevant in the context of the outer class and/or inner class can be made private so that only outer class can access it. Inner classes are used primarily to implement helper classes like Iterators, Comparators etc which are used in the context of an outer class. CO

Member inner class	Anonymous inner class
| ```
public class MyStack {
   private Object[] items = null;
   ...
   public Iterator iterator() {
     return new StackIterator();
   }
   //inner class
   class StackIterator implements Iterator{
     ...
       public boolean hasNext(){...}
   }
}
``` | ```
public class MyStack {
   private Object[] items = null;
   ...
   public Iterator iterator() {
     return new Iterator {
       ...
       public boolean hasNext() {...}
     }
   }
}
``` |

Explain outer and inner classes?

Class Type		Description	Example + Class name
Outer class	Package member class or interface	Top level class. Only type JVM can recognize.	//package scope **class Outside{}** Outside.class

Inner class	static nested class or interface	Defined within the context of the top-level class. Must be static & can access static members of its containing class. No relationship between the instances of outside and Inside classes.	//package scope
			class Outside {
			  static class Inside{ }
			}
			
			Outside.class , Outside$Inside.class

Inner class	Member class	Defined within the context of outer class, but non-static. Until an object of Outside class has been created you can't create Inside.	class Outside{
			  class Inside(){}
			}
			
			Outside.class , Outside$Inside.class

Inner class	Local class	Defined within a block of code. Can use final local variables and final method parameters. Only visible within the block of code that defines it.	class Outside {
			  void first() {
			    final int i = 5;
			    class Inside{}
			  }
			}
			
			Outside.class , Outside1Inside.class

| Inner class | Anonymous class | Just like local class, but no name is used. Useful when only one instance is used in a method. Most commonly used in AWT/SWING event model, Spring framework hibernate call back methods etc. | //AWT example
class Outside{
  void first() {
    button.addActionListener (new ActionListener()
    {
    public void actionPerformed(ActionEvent e) {
      System.out.println("The button was pressed!");
      }
    });
  }
}

Outside.class , Outside$1.class |

Note: If you have used the **Spring** framework with the **Hibernate** framework (Both are very popular frameworks, Refer section "**Emerging Technologies/Frameworks**"), it is likely that you would have used an anonymous inner class (i.e. a class declared inside a method) as shown below:

```
//anonymous inner classes can only access local variables if they are declared as final
public Pet getPetById(final String id) {
    return (Pet) getHibernateTemplate().execute(new HibernateCallback() {
            public Object doInHibernate(Session session) {
                HibernateTemplate ht = getHibernateTemplate();
                // … can access variable "id"
                return myPet;
            }
    });
}
```

Q. Are the following valid java statements?

`Line:` `OuterClass.StaticNestedClass nestedObject = new OuterClass.StaticNestedClass();`

Yes. The above line is valid. It is an instantiation of a **static nested inner class**.

```
OuterClass outerObject = new OuterClass();
Line: OuterClass.InnerClass innerObject = outerObject.new InnerClass();
```

Yes. The above line is valid. It is an instantiation of a **member inner class**. An instance of an inner class can exist only within an instance of an outer class. The sample code for the above is shown below:

```
public class OuterClass {
    static class StaticNestedClass {
        StaticNestedClass(){
            System.out.println("StaticNestedClass");
        }
    }

    class InnerClass {
        InnerClass(){
            System.out.println("InnerClass");
        }
    }
}
```

Q 36: What is type casting? Explain up casting vs. down casting? When do you get ClassCastException? **LF** **DP** **FAQ**

A 36: Type casting means treating a variable of one type as though it is another type.

When up casting **primitives** as shown below from left to right, automatic conversion occurs. But if you go from right to left, down casting or explicit casting is required. Casting in Java is safer than in C or other languages that allow arbitrary casting. Java only lets casts occur when they make sense, such as a cast between a float and an int. However you can't cast between an int and a *String* (is an object in Java).

byte → short → int → long → float → double

```
int i = 5;
long j = i;          //Right. Up casting or implicit casting
byte b1 = i;         //Wrong. Compile time error "Type Mismatch".
byte b2 = (byte) i ; //Right. Down casting or explicit casting is required.
```

When it comes to object references you can always cast from a subclass to a superclass because a subclass object is also a superclass object. You can cast an object implicitly to a super class type (i.e. **upcasting**). If this were not the case **polymorphism wouldn't be possible**.

Upcasting vs Downcasting

```
Object
  △
  |
Vehicle
  △
  |
 ┌──────┬──────┐
Bus          Car
              △
              |
            BMW
```

```
Vehicle v1 = new Car();        //Right.upcasting or implicit casting
Vehicle v2 = new Vehicle();

Car c0 = v1;                   //Wrong. compile time error "Type Mismatch".
                               //Explicit or down casting is required
Car c1 = (Car)v1;              // Right. down casting or explicit casting.
                               // v1 has knowledge of Car due to line1

Car c2 = (Car)v2;              //Wrong. Runtime exception ClassCastException
                               //v2 has no knowledge of Car.
Bus b1 = new BMW();            //Wrong. compile time error "Type Mismatch"
Car c3 = new BMW();            //Right.upcasting or implicit casting

Car c4 = (BMW)v1;              //Wrong. Runtime exception ClassCastException
Object o = v1;                 //v1 can only be upcast to its parent or
Car c5 = (Car)v1;              //v1 can be down cast to Car due to line 1.
```

You can cast down the hierarchy as well but you must explicitly write the cast and the **object must be a legitimate instance of the class you are casting to**. The **ClassCastException** is thrown to indicate that code has attempted to cast an object to a subclass of which it is not an instance. If you are using J2SE 5.0 then "**generics**" will eliminate the need for casting (Refer **Q55** in Java section) and otherwise you can deal with the problem of incorrect casting in two ways:

- Use the exception handling mechanism to catch **ClassCastException**.

```
try{
    Object o = new Integer(1);
    System.out.println((String) o);
}
catch(ClassCastException cce) {
    logger.log("Invalid casting, String is expected…Not an Integer");
    System.out.println(((Integer) o).toString());
}
```

- Use the **instanceof** statement to guard against incorrect casting.

```
if(v2 instanceof Car) {
    Car c2 = (Car) v2;
}
```

Design pattern: The "**instanceof**" and "**typecast**" constructs are shown for the illustration purpose only. Using these constructs can be unmaintainable due to large if and elseif statements and can affect performance if used in frequently accessed methods or loops. Look at using **visitor design pattern** to avoid these constructs where applicable. (Refer **Q11** in How would you go about section…).

Points-to-ponder: You can also get a **ClassCastException** when two different class loaders load the same class because they are treated as two different classes.

Q 37: What do you know about the Java garbage collector? When does the garbage collection occur? Explain different types of references in Java? LF MI FAQ

A 37: Each time an object is created in Java, it goes into the area of memory known as heap. The Java heap is called the garbage collectable heap. The garbage collection **cannot be forced**. The garbage collector runs in low memory situations. When it runs, it releases the memory allocated by an unreachable object. The garbage collector runs on a low priority daemon (i.e. background) thread. You can **nicely ask** the garbage collector to collect garbage by calling *System.gc()* but you can't force it.

What is an unreachable object?

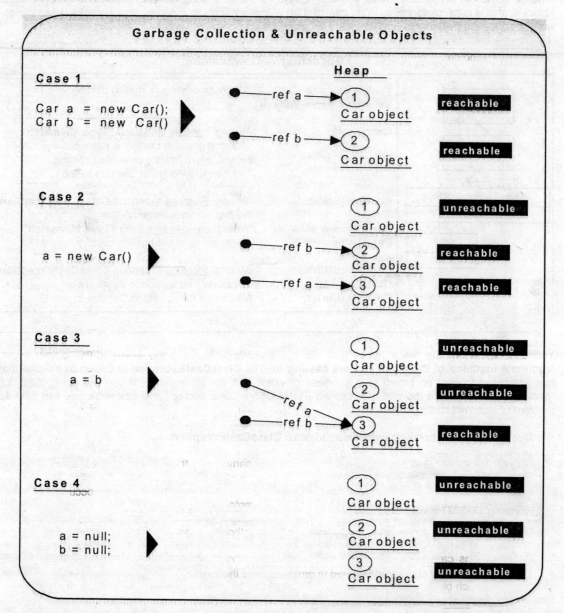

An object's life has no meaning unless something has reference to it. If you can't reach it then you can't ask it to do anything. Then the object becomes unreachable and the garbage collector will figure it out. Java automatically collects all the unreachable objects periodically and releases the memory consumed by those unreachable objects to be used by the future reachable objects.

We can use the following options with the **Java** command to enable tracing for garbage collection events.

```
java -verbose:gc  //reports on each garbage collection event.
```

Explain types of references in Java? *java.lang.ref* package can be used to declare soft, weak and phantom references.

- Garbage Collector won't remove a **strong reference**.
- A *soft reference will* only get removed if memory is low. So it is useful for implementing caches while avoiding memory leaks.
- A *weak reference* will get removed on the next garbage collection cycle. Can be used for implementing canonical maps. The **java.util.WeakHashMap** implements a *HashMap* with keys held by weak references.
- A *phantom reference* will be finalized but the memory will not be reclaimed. Can be useful when you want to be notified that an object is about to be collected.

Q 38: If you have a circular reference of objects, but you no longer reference it from an execution thread, will this object be a potential candidate for garbage collection? **LF** **MI**

A 38: Yes. Refer diagram below.

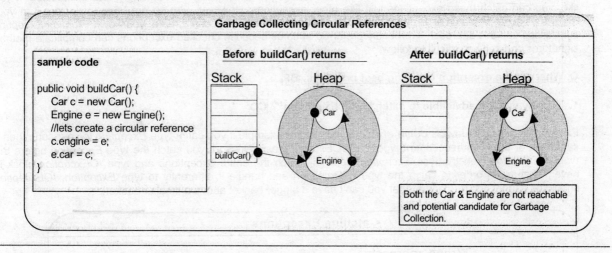

Garbage Collecting Circular References

sample code

```
public void buildCar() {
    Car c = new Car();
    Engine e = new Engine();
    //lets create a circular reference
    c.engine = e;
    e.car = c;
}
```

Before buildCar() returns

After buildCar() returns

Both the Car & Engine are not reachable and potential candidate for Garbage Collection.

Q 39: Discuss the Java error handling mechanism? What is the difference between Runtime (**unchecked**) exceptions and **checked** exceptions? What is the implication of catching all the exceptions with the type "*Exception*"? **EH** **BP** **FAQ**

A 39:

Errors: When a dynamic linking failure or some other "hard" failure in the virtual machine occurs, the virtual machine throws an Error. Typical Java programs should not catch Errors. In addition, it's unlikely that typical Java programs will ever throw Errors either.

Exceptions: Most programs throw and catch objects that derive from the Exception class. Exceptions indicate that a problem occurred but that the problem is not a serious JVM problem. An Exception class has many subclasses. These descendants indicate various types of exceptions that can occur. For example, *NegativeArraySizeException* indicates that a program attempted to create an array with a negative size. One exception subclass has special meaning in the Java language: RuntimeException. All the exceptions except RuntimeException are compiler checked exceptions. If a method is capable of throwing a checked exception it must declare it in its method header or handle it in a try/catch block. Failure to do so raises a compiler error. So checked exceptions can, at compile time, greatly reduce the occurrence of unhandled exceptions surfacing at runtime in a given application at the expense of requiring large throws declarations and encouraging use of poorly-constructed try/catch blocks. Checked exceptions are present in other languages like C++, C#, and Python.

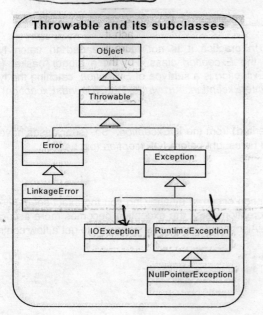

Throwable and its subclasses

Runtime Exceptions (unchecked exception)

A RuntimeException class represents exceptions that occur within the Java virtual machine (during runtime). An example of a runtime exception is NullPointerException. The cost of checking for the runtime exception often outweighs the benefit of catching it. Attempting to catch or specify all of them all the time would make your code unreadable and unmaintainable. The compiler allows runtime exceptions to go uncaught and unspecified. If you like, you can catch these exceptions just like other exceptions. However, you do not have to declare it in your "throws" clause or catch it in your catch clause. In addition, you can create your own *RuntimeException* subclasses and this approach is probably preferred at times because checked exceptions can complicate method signatures and can be difficult to follow.

Q. What are the exception handling best practices: BP

1. Q. Why is it not advisable to catch type "*Exception*"? CO

Exception handling in Java is **polymorphic** in nature. For example if you catch type *Exception* in your code then it can catch or throw its descendent types like *IOException* as well. So if you catch the type *Exception* before the type *IOException* then the type *Exception* block will catch the entire exceptions and type *IOException* block is never reached. In order to catch the type *IOException* and handle it differently to type *Exception*, *IOException* should be caught first (remember that you can't have a bigger basket above a smaller basket).

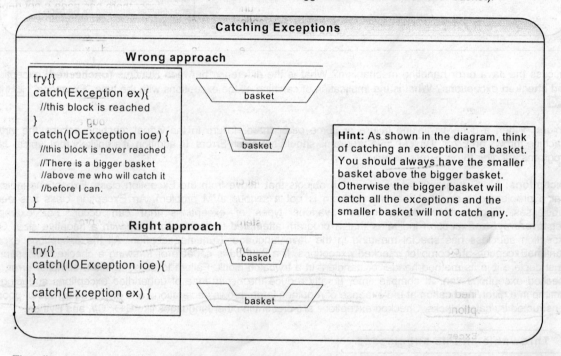

The diagram above is an example for illustration only. In practice it is not recommended to catch type "***Exception***". We should only catch specific subtypes of the *Exception* class. Having a bigger basket (i.e. *Exception*) will hide or cause problems. Since the *RunTimeException* is a subtype of *Exception*, catching the type *Exception* will catch all the run time exceptions (like *NullPointerException*, *ArrayIndexOutOfBoundsException*) as well.

Example: The *FileNotFoundException* is extended (i.e. inherited) from the *IOException*. So (subclasses have to be caught first) *FileNotFoundException* (small basket) should be caught before *IOException* (big basket).

2. Q. Why should you throw an exception early? CO

The exception stack trace helps you pinpoint where an exception occurred by showing you the exact sequence of method calls that lead to the exception. By throwing your exception early, the exception becomes more accurate and more specific. Avoid suppressing or ignoring exceptions. Also avoid using exceptions just to get a flow control.

Instead of:

```
// assume this line throws an exception because filename == null.
InputStream in = new FileInputStream(fileName);
...
```

Use the following code because you get a more accurate stack trace:

```
…
if(filename == null) {
    throw new IllegalArgumentException("file name is null");
}

InputStream in = new FileInputStream(fileName);
…
```

3. Why should you catch a checked exception late in a catch {} block?

You should not try to catch the exception before your program can handle it in an appropriate manner. The natural tendency when a compiler complains about a checked exception is to catch it so that the compiler stops reporting errors. It is a bad practice to sweep the exceptions under the carpet by catching it and not doing anything with it. The best practice is to catch the exception at the appropriate layer (e.g. an exception thrown at an integration layer can be caught at a presentation layer in a catch {} block), where your program can either meaningfully recover from the exception and continue to execute or log the exception only once in detail, so that user can identify the cause of the exception.

4. Q. When should you use a checked exception and when should you use an unchecked exception?

Due to heavy use of checked exceptions and minimal use of unchecked exceptions, there has been a hot debate in the Java community regarding true value of checked exceptions. Use checked exceptions when the client code can take some useful recovery action based on information in exception. Use unchecked exception when client code cannot do anything. For example Convert your SQLException into another checked exception if the client code can recover from it. Convert your SQLException into an unchecked (i.e. RuntimeException) exception, if the client code can not recover from it. (**Note:** Hibernate 3 & Spring uses RuntimeExceptions prevalently).

> **Important:** throw an exception early and catch an exception late but do not sweep an exception under the carpet by catching it and not doing anything with it. This will hide problems and it will be hard to debug and fix. **CO**

> **A note on key words for error handling:**
> **throw / throws** – used to pass an exception to the method that called it.
> **try** – block of code will be tried but may cause an exception.
> **catch** – declares the block of code, which handles the exception.
> **finally** – block of code, which is always executed (except System.exit(0) call) no matter what program flow, occurs when dealing with an exception.
> **assert** – Evaluates a conditional expression to verify the programmer's assumption.

Q 40: What is a user defined exception? **EH**
A 40: User defined exceptions may be implemented by defining a new exception class by extending the *Exception* class.

```
public class MyException extends Exception {

    /* class definition of constructors goes here */
    public MyException() {
        super();
    }

    public MyException (String errorMessage) {
        super (errorMessage);
    }
}
```

Throw and/or throws statement is used to signal the occurrence of an exception. To throw an exception:

```
throw new MyException("I threw my own exception.")
```

To declare an exception: `public myMethod() throws MyException {…}`

Q 41: What are the flow control statements in Java? **LF**
A 41: The flow control statements allow you to conditionally execute statements, to repeatedly execute a block of statements, or to just change the sequential flow of control.

Flow control types	Keyword

Looping	**while, do-while, for**
	
	The body of the while loop is executed only if the expression is true, so it may not be executed even once:
	
	``java
	while(i < 5){...}
	``
	
	The body of the do-while loop is executed at least once because the test expression is evaluated only after executing the loop body. Also, don't forget the ending semicolon after the while expression.
	
	``java
	do { ... } while(i < 5);
	``
	
	The for loop syntax is:
	
	``java
	for(expr1; expr2; expr3)
	{
	    // body
	}
	``
	
	expr1 → is for initialization, expr2 → is the conditional test, and expr3 → is the iteration expression. <u>Any of these three sections can be omitted and the syntax will still be legal:</u>
	
	``java
	for(; ;) {} // an endless loop
	``

Decision making	**if-else, switch-case**
	
	The if-else statement is used for decision-making -- that is, it decides which course of action needs to be taken.
	
	``java
	if (x == 5) {...} else {..}
	``
	
	The switch statement is also used for decision-making, based on an integer expression. The argument passed to the switch and case statements should be **int, short, char,** or **byte**. The argument passed to the case statement should be a literal or a final variable. If no case matches, the default statement (which is optional) is executed.
	
	``java
	int i = 1;
	switch(i)
	{
	case 0:
	  System.out.println("Zero");break; //if break; is omitted case 1: also executed
	case 1:
	  System.out.println("One");break; //if break; is omitted default: also executed
	default:
	  System.out.println("Default");break;
	}
	``

Branching	**break, continue, label:, return** The **break** statement is used to exit from a loop or switch statement, while the **continue** statement is used to skip just the current iteration and continue with the next. The **return** is used to return from a method based on a condition. The **label** statements <u>can lead to unreadable and unmaintainable spaghetti code hence should be avoided.</u>
Exception handling	**try-catch-finally, throw** Exceptions can be used to define ordinary flow control. <u>This is a misuse of the idea of exceptions, which are meant only for exceptional conditions and hence should be avoided.</u>

Q 42: What is the difference between processes and threads? **LF** **MI** **CI**

A 42: A process is an execution of a program but a thread is a single execution sequence within the process. A process can contain multiple threads. A thread is sometimes called a lightweight process.

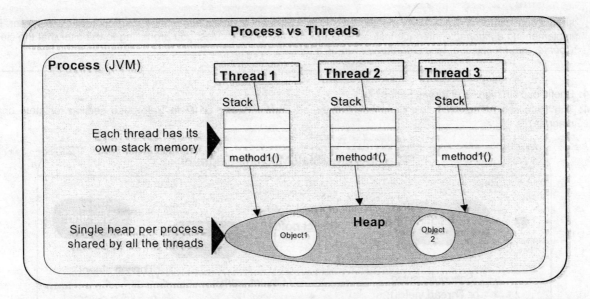

A JVM runs in a single process and threads in a JVM share the heap belonging to that process. That is why several threads may access the same object. Threads **share the heap and have their own stack space**. This is how one thread's invocation of a method and its local variables are kept thread safe from other threads. But the heap is not thread-safe and must be synchronized for thread safety.

Q 43: Explain different ways of creating a thread? **LF** **FAQ**
A 43: Threads can be used by either :

- Extending the **Thread** class
- Implementing the **Runnable** interface.

```
class Counter extends Thread {

    //method where the thread execution will start
    public void run(){
        //logic to execute in a thread
    }

    //let's see how to start the threads
    public static void main(String[] args){
        Thread t1 = new Counter();
        Thread t2 = new Counter();
        t1.start();  //start the first thread. This calls the run() method.
        t2.start(); //this starts the 2nd thread. This calls the run() method.
    }
}
```

```
class Counter extends Base implements Runnable {

    //method where the thread execution will start
    public void run(){
        //logic to execute in a thread
    }

    //let us see how to start the threads
    public static void main(String[] args){
        Thread t1 = new Thread(new Counter());
        Thread t2 = new Thread(new Counter());
        t1.start();  //start the first thread. This calls the run() method.
        t2.start(); //this starts the 2nd thread. This calls the run() method.
    }
}
```

Q. Which one would you prefer and why? The *Runnable* interface is preferred, as it does not require your object to inherit a thread because when you need multiple inheritance, only interfaces can help you. In the above example we had to extend the *Base* class so implementing *Runnable* interface is an obvious choice. Also note how the threads are started in each of the different cases as shown in the code sample. In an OO approach you

[handwritten margin note: thread shares heap but has their own stack]

should only extend a class when you want to make it different from it's superclass, and change it's behavior. By implementing a *Runnable* interface instead of extending the *Thread* class, you are telling to the user that the class *Counter* that an object of type *Counter* will run as a thread.

Q 44: Briefly explain high-level thread states? LF

A 44: The state chart diagram below describes the thread states. (Refer **Q107** in Enterprise section for state chart diagram).

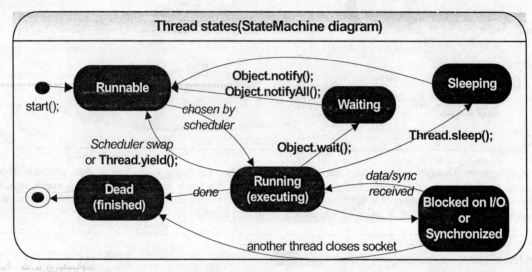

(Diagram sourced from: http://www.wilsonmar.com/1threads.htm)

- **Runnable** — waiting for its turn to be picked for execution by the thread scheduler based on thread priorities.

- **Running**: The processor is actively executing the thread code. It runs until it becomes blocked, or voluntarily gives up its turn with this static method *Thread.yield()*. Because of context switching overhead, *yield()* should not be used very frequently.

- **Waiting**: A thread is in a **blocked state** while it waits for some external processing such as file I/O to finish.

- **Sleeping**: Java threads are forcibly put to sleep (suspended) with this overloaded method: Thread.sleep(milliseconds), Thread.sleep(milliseconds, nanoseconds);

- **Blocked on I/O**: Will move to runnable after I/O condition like reading bytes of data etc changes.

- **Blocked on synchronization**: Will move to Runnable when a **lock is acquired.**

- **Dead**: The thread is finished working.

Q 45: What is the difference between yield and sleeping? What is the difference between the methods sleep() and wait()? LF FAQ

A 45: When a task invokes yield(), it changes from running state to runnable state. When a task invokes sleep(), it changes from running state to waiting/sleeping state.

The method wait(1000), causes the current thread to sleep up to one second. A thread could sleep less than 1 second if it receives the notify() or notifyAll() method call. Refer **Q48** in Java section on thread communication. The call to sleep(1000) causes the current thread to sleep for exactly 1 second.

Q 46: How does thread synchronization occurs inside a monitor? What levels of synchronization can you apply? What is the difference between synchronized method and synchronized block? LF CI PI FAQ

A 46: In Java programming, each object has a lock. A thread can acquire the lock for an object by using the **synchronized** keyword. The synchronized keyword can be applied in **method level** (coarse grained lock – can affect performance adversely) or **block level of code** (fine grained lock). Often using a lock on a method level is too coarse. Why lock up a piece of code that does not access any shared resources by locking up an entire method. Since each object has a lock, dummy objects can be created to implement block level synchronization. The block level is more efficient because it does not lock the whole method.

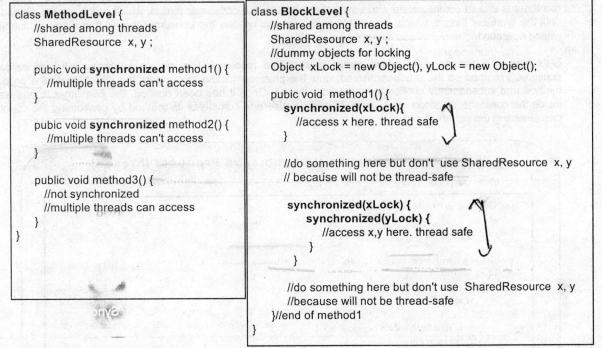

```
class MethodLevel {
    //shared among threads
    SharedResource x, y ;

    pubic void synchronized method1() {
        //multiple threads can't access
    }

    pubic void synchronized method2() {
        //multiple threads can't access
    }

    public void method3() {
        //not synchronized
        //multiple threads can access
    }
}
```

```
class BlockLevel {
    //shared among threads
    SharedResource x, y ;
    //dummy objects for locking
    Object xLock = new Object(), yLock = new Object();

    pubic void method1() {
        synchronized(xLock){
            //access x here. thread safe
        }

        //do something here but don't use SharedResource x, y
        // because will not be thread-safe

        synchronized(xLock) {
            synchronized(yLock) {
                //access x,y here. thread safe
            }
        }

        //do something here but don't use SharedResource x, y
        //because will not be thread-safe
    }//end of method1
}
```

The JVM uses locks in conjunction with monitors. A monitor is basically a guardian who watches over a sequence of synchronized code and making sure only one thread at a time executes a synchronized piece of code. Each monitor is associated with an object reference. When a thread arrives at the first instruction in a block of code it must obtain a lock on the referenced object. The thread is not allowed to execute the code until it obtains the lock. Once it has obtained the lock, the thread enters the block of protected code. When the thread leaves the block, no matter how it leaves the block, it releases the lock on the associated object.

Q. Why synchronization is important? Without synchronization, it is possible for one thread to modify a shared object while another thread is in the process of using or updating that object's value. This often causes dirty data and leads to significant errors. **The disadvantage of synchronization** is that it can cause deadlocks when two threads are waiting on each other to do something. Also synchronized code has the overhead of acquiring lock, which can adversely affect the performance.

Q. What is a ThreadLocal class?   *ThreadLocal* is a handy class for simplifying development of thread-safe concurrent programs by making the object stored in this class not sharable between threads. *ThreadLocal* class encapsulates non-thread-safe classes to be safely used in a multi-threaded environment and also allows you to create per-thread-singleton. **For *ThreadLocal* example:** Refer **Q15 (What is a Session?)** in Emerging Technologies/Frameworks section. Refer **Q51** in Java section for *singleton* design pattern.

Q 47: What is a daemon thread? LF
A 47: Daemon threads are sometimes called "service" or "background" threads. These are threads that normally run at a low priority and provide a basic service to a program when activity on a machine is reduced. An example of a daemon thread that is continuously running is the garbage collector thread. The JVM exits whenever all **non-daemon** threads have completed, which means that all daemon threads are automatically stopped. To make a thread as a daemon thread in Java → `myThread.setDaemon(true);`

Q 48: How can threads communicate with each other? How would you implement a producer (one thread) and a consumer (another thread) passing data (via stack)? LF FAQ
A 48: The **wait()**, **notify()**, and **notifyAll()** methods are used to provide an efficient way for threads to communicate with each other. This communication solves the '**consumer-producer problem**'. This problem occurs when the producer thread is completing work that the other thread (consumer thread) will use.

Example: If you imagine an application in which one thread (the producer) writes data to a file while a second thread (the consumer) reads data from the same file. In this example the concurrent threads share the same resource file. Because these threads share the common resource file they should be synchronized. Also these two threads should communicate with each other because the consumer thread, which reads the file, should wait until the producer thread, which writes data to the file and notifies the consumer thread that it has completed its writing operation.

Let's look at a sample code where **count** is a shared resource. The consumer thread will wait inside the consume() method on the producer thread, until the producer thread increments the count inside the produce() method and subsequently notifies the consumer thread. Once it has been notified, the consumer thread waiting inside the consume() method will give up its waiting state and completes its method by consuming the count (i.e. decrementing the count).

Thread communication (Consumer vs Producer threads)

```
Class ConsumerProducer {

    private int count;

    public synchronized void consume(){
        while(count == 0) {
            try{
                wait()
            }
            catch(InterruptedException ie) {
                //keep trying
            }
        }
        count --; //consumed
    }

    private synchronized void produce(){
        count++;
        notify(); // notify the consumer that count has been incremented.
    }
}
```

Note: For regular classes you can use the *Observer* interface and the *Observable* class to implement the consumer/producer communications with a model/view/controller architecture. The Java programming language provides support for the Model/View/Controller architecture with two classes:

- **Observer** -- any object that wishes to be notified when the state of another object changes.
- **Observable** -- any object whose state may be of interest, and in whom another object may register an interest.

They are suitable for any system wherein objects need to be automatically notified of changes that occur in other objects. **E.g.** Your *ConfigMgr* class can be notified to reload resource properties on change to *.properties file(s).

Q. What does join() method do? t.join() allows the current thread to wait indefinitely until thread "t" is finished. t.join (5000) allows the current thread to wait for thread "t" to finish but does not wait longer than 5 seconds.

```
try {
  t.join(5000); //current thread waits for thread "t" to complete but does not wait more than 5 sec
  if(t.isAlive()){
      //timeout occurred. Thread "t" has not finished
  }
  else {
      //thread "t" has finished
  }
}
```

Q 49: If 2 different threads hit 2 different synchronized methods in an object at the same time will they both continue? **LF**

A 49: No. Only one method can acquire the lock.

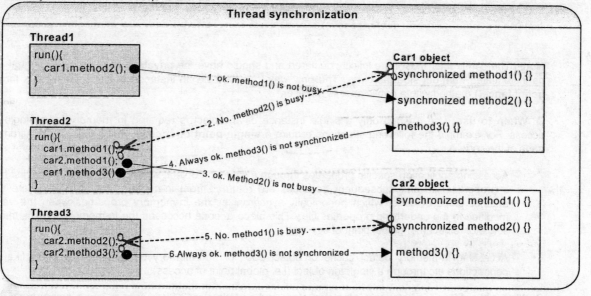

Note: If your job requires deeper understanding of threads then please refer to the following articles by Allen Holub at http://www.javaworld.com. There are number of parts (part 1 – Part - 8) to the article entitled **"Programming Java threads in the real world"**. URLs for some of the parts are: http://www.javaworld.com/javaworld/jw-09-1998/jw-09-threads.html, http://www.javaworld.com/javaworld/jw-10-1998/jw-10-toolbox.html, etc.

Q 50: Explain threads blocking on I/O? **LF**

A 50: Occasionally threads have to block on conditions other than object locks. I/O is the best example of this. Threads block on I/O (i.e. enters the waiting state) so that other threads may execute while the I/O operation is performed. When threads are blocked (say due to time consuming reads or writes) on an I/O call inside an object's synchronized method and also if the other methods of the object are also synchronized then the object is essentially frozen while the thread is blocked.

Be sure to not synchronize code that makes blocking calls, or make sure that a non-synchronized method exists on an object with synchronized blocking code. Although this technique requires some care to ensure that the resulting code is still thread safe, it allows objects to be responsive to other threads when a thread holding its locks is blocked.

Note: The **java.nio.*** package was introduced in JDK1.4. The coolest addition is non-blocking I/O (aka NIO that stands for New I/O). Refer **Q24** in Java section for NIO.

Note: Q51 & Q52 in Java section are very popular questions on design patterns.

Q 51: What is a **singleton** pattern? How do you code it in Java? **DP MI CO FAQ**

A 51: A singleton is a class that can be instantiated **only one time in a JVM per class loader**. Repeated calls always return the same instance. Ensures that a class has only one instance, and provide a **global point of access**. It can be an issue if singleton class gets loaded by multiple class loaders or JVMs.

```java
public class OnlyOne {

    private static OnlyOne one = new OnlyOne();

    // private constructor. This class cannot be instantiated from outside and
    // prevents subclassing.
    private OnlyOne(){}

    public static OnlyOne getInstance() {
        return one;
    }
}
```

```
To use it:

//No matter how many times you call, you get the same instance of the object.

OnlyOne myOne = OnlyOne.getInstance();
```

Note: The constructor must be explicitly declared and should have the <u>private access modifier, so that it cannot be instantiated from out side the class</u>. The only way to instantiate an instance of class *OnlyOne* is through the **getInstance()** method with a public access modifier.

Q. When to use: Use it when only a single instance of an object is required in memory for a single point of access. For example the following situations require a **single point of access**, which gets invoked from various parts of the code.

- Accessing application specific properties through a singleton object, which reads them for the first time from a properties file and subsequent accesses are returned from in-memory objects. Also there could be another piece of code, which periodically synchronizes the in-memory properties when the values get modified in the underlying properties file. This piece of code accesses the in-memory objects through the singleton object (i.e. global point of access).

- Accessing in-memory object cache or object pool, or non-memory based resource pools like sockets, connections etc through a singleton object (i.e. global point of access).

Q. What is the difference between a singleton class and a static class? Static class is one approach to make a class singleton by declaring all the methods as static so that you can't create any instance of that class and can call the static methods directly.

Q 52: What is a factory pattern? `DP` `CO` `FAQ`

A 52: A **Factory method pattern** (aka **Factory pattern**) is a creational pattern. The creational patterns abstract the object instantiation process by hiding how the objects are created and make the system independent of the object creation process. An **Abstract factory** pattern is one level of abstraction higher than a factory method pattern, which means it returns the factory classes.

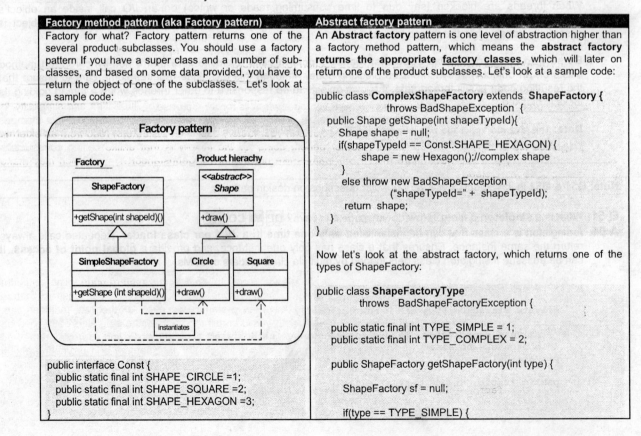

Factory method pattern (aka Factory pattern)	Abstract factory pattern
Factory for what? Factory pattern returns one of the several product subclasses. You should use a factory pattern If you have a super class and a number of sub-classes, and based on some data provided, you have to return the object of one of the subclasses. Let's look at a sample code:	An **Abstract factory** pattern is one level of abstraction higher than a factory method pattern, which means the **abstract factory returns the appropriate <u>factory classes</u>**, which will later on return one of the product subclasses. Let's look at a sample code:

Factory pattern

Factory

ShapeFactory
+getShape(int shapeId)()

SimpleShapeFactory

+getShape (int shapeId)()

Product hierachy

<> Shape
+draw()

Circle
+draw()

Square
+draw()

instantiates

```java
public interface Const {
   public static final int SHAPE_CIRCLE =1;
   public static final int SHAPE_SQUARE =2;
   public static final int SHAPE_HEXAGON =3;
}
```

```java
public class ComplexShapeFactory extends ShapeFactory {
            throws BadShapeException {
   public Shape getShape(int shapeTypeId){
     Shape shape = null;
     if(shapeTypeId == Const.SHAPE_HEXAGON) {
         shape = new Hexagon();//complex shape
     }
     else throw new BadShapeException
             ("shapeTypeId=" + shapeTypeId);
     return shape;
   }
}
```

Now let's look at the abstract factory, which returns one of the types of ShapeFactory:

```java
public class ShapeFactoryType
           throws   BadShapeFactoryException {

   public static final int TYPE_SIMPLE = 1;
   public static final int TYPE_COMPLEX = 2;

   public ShapeFactory getShapeFactory(int type) {

     ShapeFactory sf = null;

     if(type == TYPE_SIMPLE) {
```

```
public class ShapeFactory {
   public abstract Shape getShape(int shapeId);
}

public class SimpleShapeFactory extends
      ShapeFactory  throws BadShapeException {
   public Shape getShape(int shapeTypeId){
      Shape shape = null;
      if(shapeTypeId == Const.SHAPE_CIRCLE) {
         //in future can reuse or cache objects.
         shape = new Circle();
      }
      else if(shapeTypeId == Const.SHAPE_SQUARE) {
         //in future can reuse or cache objects
         shape = new Square();
      }
      else throw new BadShapeException
             ("ShapeTypeId="+ shapeTypeId);

      return shape;
   }
}
```

Now let's look at the calling code, which uses the factory:

```
ShapeFactory factory = new SimpleShapeFactory();
```

**//returns a *Shape* but whether it is a *Circle* or a
//*Square* is not known to the caller.**
```
Shape s =  factory.getShape(1);
s.draw(); // circle is drawn
```

**//returns a *Shape* but whether it is a *Circle* or a
//*Square* is not known to the caller.**
```
s = factory.getShape(2);
s.draw(); //Square is drawn
```

```
      sf = new SimpleShapeFactory();
   }
   else if (type == TYPE_COMPLEX) {
      sf = new ComplexShapeFactory();
   }
   else throw new BadShapeFactoryException("No factory!!");

   return sf;
  }
}
```

Now let's look at the calling code, which uses the factory:

```
ShapeFactoryType abFac = new  ShapeFactoryType();
ShapeFactory factory = null;
Shape s = null;
```

**//returns a *ShapeFactory* but whether it is a
//*SimpleShapeFactory* or a *ComplexShapeFactory* is not
//known to the caller.**
```
factory = abFac.getShapeFactory(1);//returns SimpleShapeFactory
```

**//returns a *Shape* but whether it is a *Circle* or a Pentagon is
//not known to the caller.**
```
s = factory.getShape(2); //returns square.
s.draw(); //draws a square
```

**//returns a *ShapeFactory* but whether it is a
//*SimpleShapeFactory* or a *ComplexShapeFactory* is not
//known to the caller.**
```
factory = abFac.getShapeFactory(2);
```

**//returns a *Shape* but whether it is a *Circle* or a *Pentagon* is
//not known to the caller.**
```
s = factory.getShape(3); //returns a pentagon.
s.draw(); //draws a pentagon
```

Q. Why use factory pattern or abstract factory pattern? Factory pattern returns an instance of several (product hierarchy) subclasses (like **Circle, Square** etc), but the calling code is unaware of the actual implementation class. The calling code invokes the method on the interface for example **Shape** and using polymorphism the correct draw() method gets invoked [Refer **Q10** in Java section for polymorphism]. So, as you can see, the factory pattern reduces the coupling or the dependencies between the calling code and called objects like *Circle, Square* etc. This is a very powerful and common feature in many frameworks. You do not have to create a new *Circle* or a new *Square* on each invocation as shown in the sample code, which is for the purpose of illustration and simplicity. In future, to conserve memory you can decide to cache objects or reuse objects in your factory with no changes required to your calling code. You can also load objects in your factory based on attribute(s) read from an external properties file or some other condition. Another benefit going for the factory is that unlike calling constructors directly, factory patterns have more meaningful names like getShape(...), getInstance(...) etc, which may make calling code more clear.

Q. Can we use the singleton pattern within our factory pattern code? Yes. Another important aspect to consider when writing your factory class is that, it does not make sense to create a new factory object for each invocation as it is shown in the sample code, which is just fine for the illustration purpose.

```
ShapeFactory factory = new SimpleShapeFactory();
```

To overcome this, you can incorporate the singleton design pattern into your factory pattern code. The singleton design pattern will create only a single instance of your *SimpleShapeFactory* class. Since an abstract factory pattern is unlike factory pattern, where you need to have an instance for each of the two factories (i.e. *SimpleShapeFactory* and ComplexShapeFactory) returned, you can still incorporate the singleton pattern as an access point and have an instance of a *HashMap,* store your instances of both factories. Now your calling method uses a static method to get the same instance of your factory, hence conserving memory and promoting object reuse:

```
ShapeFactory factory = ShapeFactory. getFactoryInstance();//returns a singleton
factory.getShape();
```

> **Note:** Since questions on singleton pattern and factory pattern are commonly asked in the interviews, they are included as part of this section. To learn more about design patterns refer **Q11, Q12** in How would you go about section…?

Q 53: What is a socket? How do you facilitate inter process communication in Java? LF

A 53: A socket is a communication channel, which facilitates **inter-process communication** (For example communicating between two JVMs, which may or may not be running on two different physical machines). A socket is an endpoint for communication. There are two kinds of sockets, depending on whether one wishes to use a connectionless or a connection-oriented protocol. The connectionless communication protocol of the Internet is called UDP. The connection-oriented communication protocol of the Internet is called TCP. UDP sockets are also called datagram sockets. Each socket is uniquely identified on the entire Internet with two numbers. The first number is a 32-bit (IPV4 or 128-bit is IPV6) integer called the Internet Address (or **IP address**). The second number is a 16-bit integer called the **port** of the socket. The IP address is the location of the machine, which you are trying to connect to and the port number is the port on which the server you are trying to connect is running. The port numbers 0 to 1023 are reserved for standard services such as e-mail, FTP, HTTP etc.

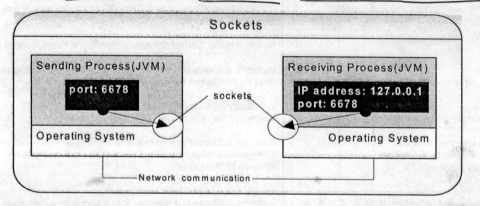

The lifetime of the socket is made of 3 phases: **Open Socket → Read and Write to Socket → Close Socket**

To make a socket connection you need to know two things: An IP address and port on which to listen/connect. In Java you can use the **Socket** (client side) and **ServerSocket** (Server side) classes.

Q 54: How will you call a Web server from a stand alone Java application/Swing client/Applet? LF

A 54: Using the **java.net.URLConnection** and its subclasses like HttpURLConnection and JarURLConnection.

URLConnection	HttpClient (i.e. a browser)
Supports HEAD, GET, POST, PUT, DELETE, TRACE and OPTIONS	Supports HEAD, GET, POST, PUT, DELETE, TRACE and OPTIONS.
Does not support cookies.	Does support cookies.
Can handle protocols other than http like ftp, gopher, mailto and file.	Handles only http.

```
public class TestServletWriter {
  public static void main(String[] args)throws Exception{
      String host = "localhost"; //i.e 127.0.0.1
      String protocol = "http"; //request/response paradigm
      int port = 18080;
      String strURL = protocol + "://" + host + ":" + port + "/myRootContext/myServlet";
      java.net.URL servletURL = new java.net.URL(strURL);

      java.net.URLConnection con = servletURL.openConnection();
      con.setDoInput(true);
      con.setDoOutput(true);
      con.setUseCaches(false);
      con.setRequestProperty("Content-Type","application/x-www-form-urlencoded");

      // Write the arguments as post data
      ObjectOutputStream out = new ObjectOutputStream(con.getOutputStream());

      out.writeObject("Hello Servlet"); //write a serializable object to the servlet.
      out.flush();
      out.close();
```

```
    ObjectInputStream ois = new ObjectInputStream(con.getInputStream());//this line is a must
    // even if you have nothing to read back from the web server because http is a
    // request/response paradigm.

    String msg = (String)ois.readObject();
    System.out.println(msg);
  }
}
```

Note: Sun provides **JSSE** (**J**ava **S**ecure **S**ocket **E**xtension) as the technology to accomplish HTTPS over the Web.

This section would not be complete without discussing some of the exciting changes in the J2SE external version 5.0 and the internal version 1.5.0 ("Tiger") release.

Q 55: Explain some of the new features in J2SE 5.0, which improves ease of development? LF FAQ

A 55: The J2SE 5.0 release is focused along the key areas of ease of development, scalability, performance, quality, etc. The new features include **generics**, **metadata** (aka **annotations**), **autoboxing** and **auto-unboxing** of primitive types, **enhanced "for" loop**, **enumerated type**, **static import**, C style **formatted output**, **formatted input**, **varargs**, etc. The following code sample depicts some of these new features. Brief explanation follows the sample code, so if you do not understand any part of the code, come back to it after reading the brief explanation.

```
package sample;

//static import
import static sample.SampleStaticValues.NUM_ZERO;

import java.util.ArrayList;
import java.util.List;
import java.util.Scanner;

public class CombinedNewFeatures {

    enum OddEven {odd,even} //use of enum keyword. An enum is a special classs.

    public static void main(String[] args) {

        //read from keyboard using the java.util.Scanner
        Scanner keyboard = new Scanner(System.in);

        System.out.println("Enter your first number?");
        int i1 = keyboard.nextInt();

        System.out.println("Enter your second number?");
        int i2 = keyboard.nextInt();

        //using generics for type safety
        List<Integer> numList = new ArrayList<Integer>();

        //using auto-boxing to convert primitive int i1,i2 to wrapper Integer object.
        numList.add(i1);
        numList.add(i2);
        //numList.add("just to prove type safety");//won't compile! Requires an Integer to be added

        //":" should be read as "foreach". So should read as, foreach "num" value in numList.
        for (Integer num : numList) {

            //using auto-unboxing feature to convert wrapper Integer object "num" to primitive.
            if(num >= 9){
                // C style printf. System.out.printf(String arg0, Object ...arg1).
                // this feature is possible due to var-args feature.
                System.out.printf("num is: %1s, list size: %2s \n", num, numList.size());
                //"%" symbol means we are using the format specifier, "1" means first arg.
                // Refer java.util.Formatter class API for the format specification details.
            }

            //need not do SampleStaticValues.NUM_ZERO due to static import feature
            if(num % 2 == NUM_ZERO){
                System.out.println("The num " + num + " is: "   + OddEven.even);
            }
            else {
```

```
                    System.out.println("The num " + num + " is: " + OddEven.odd);
            }
    }


        CombinedNewFeatures cnf = new CombinedNewFeatures();

        //invoking methods using varargs
        cnf.addNumbers(i1);
        cnf.addNumbers(i1,i2);
        cnf.addNumbers(i1,i2,5);
    }

    //method using varargs
    public void addNumbers(Object ...args){
        int sum = 0;
        for (Object object : args) {
            sum += (Integer)object;
        }
        System.out.println("sum is " + sum);
    }

    @SuppressWarnings("deprecation") //metatag (annotation)
    public static void end(){
        Thread.currentThread().stop(); //stop() is a deprecated method
    }
}


package sample;

public class SampleStaticValues {
    public static int NUM_ZERO = 0;
    public static int NUM_ONE = 0;
}


package sample;

public class ExtendedCombinedNewFeatures extends CombinedNewFeatures {

    @Override    //metatag. If you spell the methodName incorrectly, you will get a compile error.
    public void addNumbers(Object ...args) {
        //overrides baseclass methods
    }

    @Override  //metatag
    public void addValues(Object ...args) { //compile error! must override a superclass method
        //…
    }
}
```

Scanner API provide a more robust mechanism for reading in data types rather than simply parsing strings from buffered System.in calls. Prior to *Scanner* feature was introduced, to read from standard input it would be necessary to write exception handling code and wrap an InputStreamReader and a BufferedReader around *System.in*. *Scanner* class throws an unchecked exception *InputMismatchException*, which you could optionally catch. Scanner API simplifies your code as follows:

```
Scanner keyboard = new Scanner(System.in);         //no more wrapping with InputStreamReader and
                                                   //BufferedReader around System.in
System.out.println("Enter your first number?");
int i1 = keyboard.nextInt();          //no more parsing strings e.g. new Integer("5").intValue();
System.out.println("Enter your second number?");
int i2 = keyboard.nextInt();          //no more parsing strings e.g. new Integer(str).intValue();
```

Generics allow you to pass types as arguments to classes just like values are passed to methods as parameters. Generics are mainly intended for Java *Collections* API. The J2SE 5.0 compiler will check the type for you. So, the error detection has been moved to compile time as opposed to runtime and *ClassCastException* is not likely to be thrown. It is used in a typsafe manner and you do not have to cast when taking values out of the list.

```
List<Integer> numList = new ArrayList<Integer>();    //used in a typesafe way.
…
//numList.add("just to prove type safety"); //won't compile! An Integer value is required.
                            //Error detection has been moved to compile time as opposed to Runtime.
for (Integer num : numList) {        //you do not have to cast when you take values out of the list.
```

```
    ...
}
```

Auto boxing/unboxing makes a programmer's life easier by not having to write manual code for conversion between primitive types such as int, float etc and wrapper types Integer, Float etc. The J2SE-5.0 will automatically <u>box</u> and <u>unbox</u> this for you. So this is a convenience feature and is not a performance booster.

```
//using auto-boxing to convert primitive int i1,i2 to wrapper Integer object.
numList.add(i1); // no more code like -> numList.add(new Integer(i1)); autoboxed for you
numList.add(i2); // no more code like -> numList.add(new Integer(i2)); autoboxed for you
...
for (Integer num : numList) {

    //using auto-unboxing feature to convert wrapper Integer object "num" to primitive.
    if(num >= 9){ // no more code like if(num.intValue() >= 9) unboxed for you
        ...
}
```

printf method (C style) takes the arguments of a **format string** and varargs **format specifiers**. The varargs feature allows you to have as many format specifiers as you want. Refer *java.util.Formatter* API for format details. The printf() feature would not be possible if not for varargs feature, which will be discussed next.

```
// System.out.printf(String arg0, Object ...arg1).this feature is possible due to var-args feature.
System.out.printf("num is: %1s, list size: %2s \n", num, numList.size());//format specifiers in bold
//"%" symbol means we are using the format specifier, "1" means first arg.
//Refer java.util.Formatter class API for the format specification details.
```

Varargs enables the compiler to assemble the array for you based on the argument list you pass to a method. The three periods next to the parameter type (e.g. public void myMethod(Object ... args)) denotes varargs. The type must be *Object* and it must be the last argument or the only argument to the method. You can also pass primitive values due to the new Autoboxing feature.

```
    //method using varargs
    public void addNumbers(Object ...args){ //only argument to the method. ... means varargs
        int sum = 0;
        for (Object object : args) {      // compiler converts to an object array → Object[] args
            sum += (Integer)object;
        }
        System.out.println("sum is " + sum);
    }
```

The above method can be called following ways:

```
//invoking methods using varargs
cnf.addNumbers(i1);          //  one arg -> gets converted to Object[] args of size 1
cnf.addNumbers(i1,i2);       //  two arguments  -> gets converted to Object[] args of size 2
cnf.addNumbers(i1,i2,5);     //  three arguments -> gets converted to Object[] args of size 3
```

The printf() method would not be possible, if not for varargs feature.

```
// C style printf. System.out.printf(String arg0, Object ...arg1).
// this feature is possible due to var-args feature.
System.out.printf("num is: %1s, list size: %2s \n", num, numList.size()); // two arguments
```

Static imports let you avoid qualifying static members with class names. Once the static member is imported then you can use it in your code without the class name prefix.

```
//static import
import static sample.SampleStaticValues.NUM_ZERO;
...
//need not do SampleConstants.NUM_ZERO due to static import feature
if(num % 2 == NUM_ZERO){
    System.out.println("The num " + num + " is: "   + OddEven.even);
}
```

```
package sample;

public class SampleStaticValues {
    public static int NUM_ZERO = 0;
    public static int NUM_ONE = 0;
```

```
}
```

Enhanced for loop eliminates error-proneness of iterators and does not require any index variables. Also known as a "**foreach**" loop.

```
//":" should be read as "foreach". So should read as, foreach "num" value in numList.
for (Integer num : numList) { // no index variables.
    …
}
```

Enumerated types are type safe and force users of your class to use one of the acceptable values. Using static final integer values are type-unsafe and can lead to subtle bugs in your code as shown below:

```
public class PartyNeeds {
    public static final int PLATES = 1;
    public static final int CUPS = 2;
}
```

For simplicity assume that *PartyNeeds* has 2 values 1 for plates and 2 for cups, but nothing is stoping the programmer from assigning any other values like 3 or 4.

```
int  partyItem = 3; //oops not a proper value as per class PartyNeeds but can happen and go
                    //unnoticed
```

Enum will solve the above problem and it is a special type of class.

```
enum OddEven {odd,even} //use of "enum" keyword. An "enum" is a special classs.
...
if(num % 2 == NUM_ZERO){
    System.out.println("The num " + num + " is: "    + OddEven.even);
}
else {
    System.out.println("The num " + num + " is: " + OddEven.odd);
}
```

Metadata lets you avoid writing boilerplate code, by enabling tools to generate it from annotations provided by the coder. This is a declarative style programming.

```
...
public class CombinedNewFeatures {
    …
    public void addNumbers(Object ...args){
        int sum = 0;
        for (Object object : args) {
            sum += (Integer)object;
        }
        System.out.println("sum is " + sum);
    }
}
```

Now, the subclass of the above class with the @Override annotation can be written as shown below. If you misspell the overridden method name, you will get a compile error. This will safeguard your method from not being called at runtime. By adding the @Override metatag, the compiler complaints if you do not actually perform an override.

```
package sample;

public class ExtendedCombinedNewFeatures extends CombinedNewFeatures {

    @Override    //metatag. If you spell the methodName incorrectly, you will get a compile error.
    public void addNumbers(Object ...args) {
        //overrides baseclass methods
    }

    @Override  //metatag
    public void addValues(Object ...args) { //compile error! must override a superclass method
        //…
    }
}
```

Java – Swing

Q 56: What is the difference between AWT and Swing? LF DC

A 56: Swing provides a richer set of components than AWT. They are 100% Java-based. There are a few other advantages to Swing over AWT:

- Swing provides both additional components like JTable, JTree etc and added functionality to AWT-replacement components.
- Swing components can change their appearance based on the current "look and feel" library that's being used.
- Swing components follow the **Model-View-Controller** (MVC) paradigm, and thus can provide a much more flexible UI.
- Swing provides "extras" for components, such as: icons on many components, decorative borders for components, tool tips for components etc.
- Swing components are lightweight (less resource intensive than AWT).
- Swing provides built-in **double buffering** (which means an off-screen buffer [image] is used during drawing and then the resulting bits are copied onto the screen. The resulting image is smoother, less flicker and quicker than drawing directly on the screen).
- Swing provides paint debugging support for when you build your own component i.e.-slow motion rendering.

Swing also has a few disadvantages:

- If you're not very careful when programming, it can be slower than AWT (all components are drawn).
- Swing components that look like native components might not behave exactly like native components.

Q 57: How will you go about building a Swing GUI client? LF

A 57: The steps involved in building a Swing GUI are:

- Firstly, you need a container like a Frame, a Window, or an Applet to display components like panels, buttons, text areas etc. The job of a container is to hold and display components. <u>A container is also a component</u> (**note**: uses a composite design pattern). A J*Panel* is a container as well.

```
import javax.swing.JFrame;
import javax.swing.JTextArea;

public class MyFrame extends JFrame {
    public static void main(String[] args) {
        JFrame frame = new JFrame("Frame Title");
        ...// rest of the code to follow
    }
}
```

- Create some components such as panels, buttons, text areas etc.

```
//create a component to add to the frame
final JTextArea comp = new JTextArea();
JButton btn = new JButton("click");
```

- Add your components to your display area and arrange or layout your components using the *LayoutManagers*. You can use the standard layout managers like *FlowLayout*, *BorderLayout*, etc. Complex layouts can be simplified by using nested containers for example having JP*anels* within JP*anels* and each JP*anel* can use its own *LayoutManager*. You can create components and add them to whichever JP*anels* you like and JPanels can be added to the JFrame's content pane.

```
// Add the component to the frame's content pane;
// by default, the content pane has a border layout
frame.getContentPane().add(comp, BorderLayout.CENTER);
frame.getContentPane().add(btn, BorderLayout.SOUTH);
```

- Attach listeners to your components. Interacting with a *Component* causes an *Event* to occur. To associate a user action with a component, attach a listener to it. Components send events and listeners listen for events.

Different components may send different events, and require different listeners. The listeners are interfaces, not classes.

```
//Anonymous inner class registering a listener
// as well as performing the action logic.
btn.addActionListener( new ActionListener() {
    public void actionPerformed(ActionEvent ae) {
        comp.setText("Button has been clicked");
    }
});
```

- Show the frame.

```
// set the frame size and Show the frame
int width = 300;
int height = 300;
frame.setSize(width, height);
frame.setVisible(true);
```

Note: For Applets, you need to write the necessary HTML code.

Q 58: Explain the Swing *Action* architecture? **LF** **DP** **FAQ**

A 58: The Swing *Action* architecture is used to implement shared behavior between two or more user interface components. For example, the menu items and the tool bar buttons will be performing the same action no matter which one is clicked. Another distinct advantage of using actions is that when an action is disabled then all the components, which use the Action, become disabled.

Design pattern: The *javax.swing.Action* interface extends the *ActionListener* interface and is an abstraction of a command that does not have an explicit UI component bound to it. The Action architecture is an implementation of a **command design pattern**. This is a powerful design pattern because it allows the separation of controller logic of an application from its visual representation. This allows the application to be easily configured to use different UI elements without having to re-write the control or call-back logic.

Defining action classes:

```
class FileAction extends AbstractAction {
  //Constructor
  FileAction(String name) {
        super(name);
  }

  public void actionPerformed(ActionEvent ae){
        //add action logic here
  }
}
```

To add an action to a menu bar:

```
JMenu fileMenu =  new JMenu("File");
FileAction newAction = new FileAction("New");
JMenuItem item =   fileMenu.add(newAction);
item.setAccelarator(KeyStroke.getKeyStroke('N', Event.CTRL_MASK));
```

To add action to a toolbar:

```
private JToolBar toolbar = new JToolBar();
toolbar.add(newAction);
```

So, an *action* object is a listener as well as an action.

Q 59: How does Swing painting happen? How will you improve the painting performance? **LF**

A 59: If you want to create your own custom painting code or troubleshoot your Swing components, then you need to understand the basic concept of Swing painting.

- Swing GUI painting starts with the highest component that needs to be repainted and works it way down the hierarchy of components. This painting process is coordinated by the AWT painting system, but Swing repaint manager and **double-buffering code**, which means an off-screen buffer [image] is used during drawing and then the resulting bits are copied onto the screen. The resulting image is smoother, less flicker and quicker than drawing directly on the screen.

- Swing components generally repaint themselves whenever necessary. For example when you invoke the setTextt() on a component etc. This happens behind the scenes using a callback mechanism by invoking the **repaint**() method. If a component's size or position needs to change then the call to **revalidate**() method precedes the call to repaint() method.

- Like event handling code, painting code executes on the **event-dispatching thread** (Refer **Q62** in Java Section). So while an event is being handled, no painting will occur and similarly while painting is happening no events will take place.

- You can provide your own painting by overriding the **paintComponent**() method. This is one of 3 methods used by JComponents to paint themselves.

```
public class MyFramePainting extends JFrame {
    public static void main(String[] args) {
        JFrame frame = new JFrame("Frame Title");

        MyPanel panel = new MyPanel();
        panel.setOpaque(true);        //if opaque (i.e. solid) then Swing painting system
                                      //does not waste time painting behind the component.
        panel.setBackground(Color.white);
        panel.setLayout(new FlowLayout());

        ...//add to contentPane, display logic etc
    }
}
```

```
public class MyPanel extends JPanel implements MouseListener{

    Color col = Color.blue;

    public void paintComponent(Graphics gr){
        super.paintComponent(gr);

        gr.setColor(col);
        gr.drawLine(5,5, 200,200);
    }

    public MyPanel(){
        addMouseListener(this); //i.e the Panel itself
    }

    public void mouseClicked(MouseEvent ev){
        col = Color.red;
        repaint(); //invokes paintComponent(). Never invoke paintComponent() method directly
    }

    ...//other mouse events like onMousePressed etc
}
```

By default, the paintComponent() method paints the background if the component is opaque, then it performs any custom painting. The other two methods are **paintBorder**(Graphics g) and **paintChildren**(Graphics g), which tells to paint any border and paint any components contained by this component respectively. You should not invoke or override these two methods.

Q. How will you improve the painting performance?

- On components with complex output, the **repaint**() method should be invoked with arguments which define only the clip rectangle that needs updating (rectangle origin is on top left corner). Note: No **paintXXXX**() methods (including **paint**() method) should not be explicitly invoked. Only **repaint**() method can be explicitly invoked (which implicitly calls paintComponent() method) and only **paintComponent**() should be overridden if required.

```
public void mouseClicked(MouseEvent ev){
    col = Color.red;
    repaint(0,0,50,50); //invokes paintComponent with a rectangle. The origin is at top left.
}
```

- You should never turn off double buffering for any Swing components.

- The Swing painting efficiency can be optimized by the following two properties:

opaque: If the opaque (i.e. solid) property is set to true with myComponent.**setOpaque**(true) then the Swing painting system does not have to waste time trying to paint behind the component hence improves performance.

Swing containment hierarchy using JPanels within JPanels and the painting process

Top-level container paints itself → JFrame

First paints its solid grey background and then tells the JPanel to paint itself. If the content pane is not opaque then messy repaints will occur. → Content pane

We could make a JPanel a content pane by setting setOpaque(true). This will remove unnecessary painting of the container content pane. → JPanel - 1 (**opaque**) (using say BorderLayout)

If JPanel is **opaque** (e.g. JPanel -2) , it paints its background first & then the JPanel-2 asks its children JButton 1 and JButton 2 to paint themselves. If JPanel is **non-opaque** (e.g. JPanel 4), It looks up the containment hierarchy to find the closest opaque component (i.e. JPanel - 1). The opaque container JPanel -1 paints itself first and then ask its children JPanel - 4 and JLabel to paint themselves.

Opaque components like JButton 1, JButton 2 etc paint themselves when repaint() method is called.
Non-opaque components like JLabel, look up its hierarchy to find the closest opaque component, which is Jpanel-1 (because JPanel - 4 is opaque as well). The JPanel -1 paints itself first and then ask its children JPanel - 4 and JLabel to paint themselves.

Legend:
- ☐ Opaque (solid)
- ☐ Non-opaque (transparent)

JPanel - 2 (**opaque**) (using say GridLayout)

JPanel - 3 (**opaque**) (using say BorderLayout)

JPanel - 4 (**non-opaque**) (using say FlowLayout)

JButton 1 | JButton 2 | JTextField | JLabel

optimizedDrawingEnabled: This is a read only property (isOptimizedDrawingEnabled()) in *JComponent*, so the only way components can change the default value is to subclass and override this method to return the desired value. It's always possible that a non-ancestor component in the containment tree could overlap your component. In such a case the repainting of a single component within a complex hierarchy could require a lot of tree traversal to ensure 'correct' painting occurs.

- **true**: The component indicates that none of its immediate children overlap.
- **false**: The component makes no guarantees about whether or not its immediate children overlap

---

Q 60: If you add a component to the CENTER of a border layout, which directions will the component stretch? LF FAQ
A 60: The component will stretch both horizontally and vertically. It will occupy the whole space in the middle.

Q 61: What is the base class for all Swing components? LF
A 61:

Design pattern: As you can see from the diagram below, containers collect components. Sometimes you want to add a container to another container. So, a container should be a component. For example container.getPreferredSize() invokes getPreferredSize() of all contained components. **Composite design pattern** is used in GUI components to achieve this. A composite object is an object, which contains other objects. Composite design pattern manipulates composite objects just like you manipulate individual components. Refer **Q11** in How would you go about...? section.

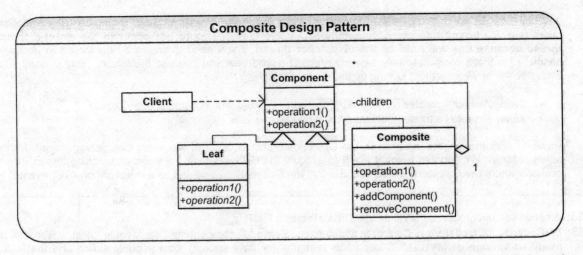

All the Swing components start with 'J'. The hierarchy diagram is shown below. **JComponent** is the base class.

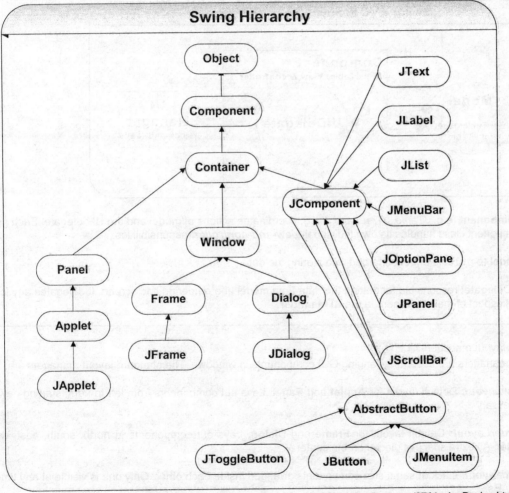

(**Diagram source**: http://www.particle.kth.se/~fmi/kurs/PhysicsSimulation/Lectures/07A/swingDesign.html)

Q 62: Explain the Swing *event dispatcher* mechanism? `LF` `CI` `PI` `FAQ`

A 62: Swing components can be accessed by the Swing **event dispatching thread**. A few operations are guaranteed to be thread-safe but most are not. Generally the Swing components should be accessed through this ***event-dispatching thread***. The *event-dispatching* thread is a thread that executes drawing of components and event-handling code. For example the paint() and actionPerformed() methods are automatically executed in the *event-dispatching thread*. Another way to execute code in the *event-dispatching thread* from outside event-handling or drawing code, is using *SwingUtilities* **invokeLater()** or **invokeAndWait()** method. **Swing lengthy initialization tasks (e.g. I/O bound and computationally expensive tasks), should not occur in the *event-dispatching thread* because this will hold up the dispatcher thread.** If you need to create a new thread for example, to handle a job that's computationally expensive or I/O bound then you can use the thread utility classes such as *SwingWorker* or *Timer* without locking up the *event-dispatching thread*.

- **SwingWorker** – creates a background thread to execute time consuming operations.
- **Timer** – creates a thread that executes at certain intervals.

However after the lengthy initialization the GUI update should occur in the event dispatching thread, for thread safety reasons. We can use **invokeLater()** to execute the GUI update in the *event-dispatching thread*. The other scenario where **invokeLater()** will be useful is that the GUI must be updated as a result of non-AWT event.

Q 63: What do you understand by MVC as used in a JTable? `LF` `DP` `FAQ`

A 63: MVC stands for **M**odel **V**iew **C**ontroller architecture. Swing "J" components (e.g. JTable, JList, JTree etc) use a **modified version of MVC**. MVC separates a model (or data source) from a presentation and the logic that manages it.

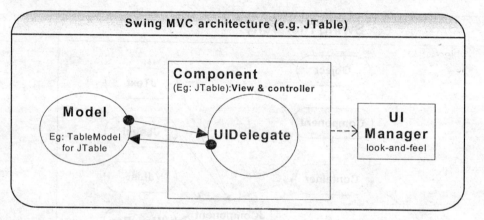

- **Component** (e.g. *JTable, JTree, and JList*): coordinates actions of model and the UI delegate. Each generic component class handles its own individual ***view-and-controller*** responsibilities.

- **Model** (e.g. *TableModel*): charged with storing the data.

- **UIDelegate**: responsible for getting the data from model and rendering it to screen. It delegates any look-and-feel aspect of the component to the **UI Manager**.

Q 64: Explain layout managers? `LF` `FAQ`

A 64: Layout managers are used for arranging GUI components in windows. The standard layout managers are:

- **FlowLayout**: Default layout for **Applet** and **Panel.** Lays out components from left to right, starting new rows if necessary.

- **BorderLayout**: Default layout for **Frame** and **Dialog.** Lays out components in north, south, east, west and center. All extra space is placed on the center.

- **CardLayout:** stack of same size components arranged inside each other. Only one is visible at any time. Used in TABs.

- **GridLayout:** Makes a bunch of components equal in size and displays them in the requested number of rows and columns.

- **GridBagLayout**: Most complicated but the most flexible. It aligns components by placing them within a grid of cells, allowing some components to span more than one cell. The rows in the grid aren't necessarily all the same height, similarly, grid columns can have different widths as well.

- *BoxLayout:* is a full-featured version of FlowLayout. It stacks the components on top of each other or places them in a row.

Complex layouts can be simplified by using nested containers for example having *panels* within *panels* and each *panel* can use its own *LayoutManager*. It is also possible to write your own layout manager or use manual positioning of the GUI components. **Note:** Further reading on each *LayoutManagers* is recommended for Swing developers.

Design pattern: The AWT containers like panels, dialog boxes, windows etc do not perform the actual laying out of the components. They delegate the layout functionality to layout managers. The layout managers make use of the **strategy design pattern**, which encapsulates family of algorithms for laying out components in the containers. If a particular layout algorithm is required other than the default algorithm, an appropriate layout manager can be instantiated and plugged into the container. For example, panels by default use the *FlowLayout* but it can be changed by executing:

```
panel.setLayout(new GridLayout(4,5));
```

This enables the layout algorithms to vary independently from the containers that use them. This is one of the key benefits of the strategy pattern.

Q 65: Explain the Swing delegation event model? LF

A 65: In this model, the objects that receive user events notify the registered listeners of the user activity. In most cases the event receiver is a component.

- **Event Types:** ActionEvent, KeyEvent, MouseEvent, WindowEvent etc.
- **Event Processors:** JButton, JList etc.
- **EventListeners:** ActionListener, ComponentListener, KeyListener etc.

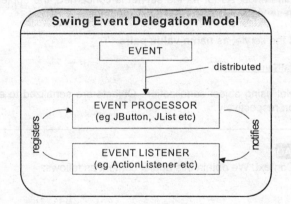

Java – Applet

Q 66: How will you initialize an applet? `LF`

A 66: By writing your initialization code in the applet's **init()** method or applet's **constructor**.

Q 67: What is the order of method invocation in an applet? `LF` `FAQ`

A 67: The Applet's life cycle methods are as follows:

- **public void init()** : Initialization method called only <u>once by the browser</u>.

- **public void start()** : Method called after init() and contains code to start processing. If the user leaves the page and returns without killing the current browser session, the start () method is called without being preceded by init ().

- **public void stop()** : Stops all processing started by start (). Done if user moves off page.

- **public void destroy()** : Called if current browser session is being terminated. Frees all resources used by the applet.

Q 68: How would you communicate between applets and servlets? `LF` `FAQ`

A 68: We can use the **java.net.URLConnection** and **java.net.URL** classes to open a standard HTTP connection and "**tunnel**" to a Web server. The server then passes this information to the servlet. Basically, the applet pretends to be a Web browser, and the servlet doesn't know the difference. As far as the servlet is concerned, the applet is just another HTTP client. Applets can communicate with servlets using GET or POST methods.

The parameters can be passed between the applet and the servlet as **name value pairs.**

    http://www.foo.com/servlet/TestServlet?LastName=Jones&FirstName=Joe).

Objects can also be passed between applet and servlet using object serialization. Objects are serialized to and from the inputstream and outputstream of the connection respectively.

Q 69: How will you communicate between two Applets? `LF` `FAQ`

A 69: All the applets on a given page share the same AppletContext. We obtain this applet context as follows:

```
AppletContext ac = getAppletContext();
```

AppletContext provides applets with methods such as getApplet(name), getApplets(), getAudioClip(url), getImage(url), showDocument(url) and showStatus(status).

Q 70: What is a signed Applet? `LF` `SE` `FAQ`

A 70: A signed Applet is a **trusted** Applet. By default, and for security reasons, Java applets are contained within a "**sandbox**". Refer to the diagram below:

This means that the applets can't do anything, which might be construed as threatening to the user's machine (e.g. reading, writing or deleting local files, putting up message windows, or querying various system parameters). Early browsers had no provisions for Java applets to reach outside of the sandbox. Recent browsers, however (Internet Explorer 4 on Windows etc), have provisions to give "**trusted**" applets the ability to work outside the sandbox. For this power to be granted to one of your applets, the applet's code must be digitally signed with your unforgeable digital ID, and then the user must state that he trusts applets signed with your ID. The untrusted applet can request to have privileges outside the sandbox but will have to request the user for privileges every time it executes. But with the trusted applet the user can choose to remember their answer to the request, which means they won't be asked again.

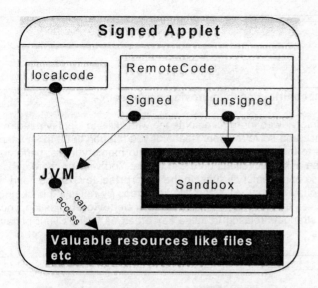

Signed Applet

Q 71: What is the difference between an applet and an application? Can you use an applet as an application? **LF** **FAQ**

A 71:

Applet	Application
Applets don't have a main method. They operate on life cycle methods init(), start(), stop(), destroy() etc.	Has a static main() method.
Applets can be embedded in HTML pages and downloaded over the Internet. Has a sandbox security model.	Has no support for embedding or downloading. Has no inherent security restriction.
Can only be executed within a Java compatible container like browser, appletviewer etc.	Applications are executed at command line by java tool.

Q. Can you use an applet as an application? Yes, by adding a main(String[] args) method to an applet.

Tech Tip #1:

-- If you want to create a new list (i.e. using java.util.List) of items from an array of objects, then it is more efficient and it is a best practice to use **Arrays.asList(…)** method as opposed to executing in a loop and copying all elements of an array one by one.

-- If you want to copy data from one array to another array then it is faster and it is a best practice to use **System.arraycopy(…)** method as opposed to executing in a loop and copying all elements of an array one by one.

Q. Which of the following approaches would you prefer and why?

Approach-1
```
if ("Peter".equals(name)) {
    //….
}
```

Approach-2
```
if (name.equals("Peter")) {
    //….
}
```

Approach-1 is preferred because the Approach-2 can throw a *java.lang.NullPointerException* if *name* is null.

Java – Performance and Memory issues

> **Q. Give me an instance where you made a significant contribution in improving performance ?**
>
> There is a good chance that the position you are being interviewed for require someone with skills to identify performance and/or memory issues and ability to optimize performance and solve memory issues. If you happen to be in an interview with an organization facing serious issues with regards to their Java application relating to memory leaks, performance problems or a crashing JVM etc then you are likely to be asked questions on these topics. You will find more questions and answers relating to these key areas (i.e. performance and memory issues) in the **Enterprise Java** section and "**How would you go about...**" sections. You could also demonstrate your skills in these key areas by reflecting back on your past experiences as discussed in **Q82** in Java section. Even though **Q82** is a **situational** or **behavioral** question, you can streamline your answer to demonstrate your technical strengths relating to these key areas as well as your behavioral ability to cope with stress.

Q 72: How would you improve performance of a Java application? PI BP FAQ
A 72:

- **Pool valuable system resources** like threads, database connections, socket connections etc. Emphasize on reuse of threads from a pool of threads. Creating new threads and discarding them after use can adversely affect performance. Also consider using multi-threading in your single-threaded applications where possible to enhance performance. Optimize the pool sizes based on system and application specifications and requirements. Having too many threads in a pool also **can result in performance and scalability problems due to consumption of memory stacks** (i.e. each thread has its own stack. Refer **Q34, Q42** in Java section) and **CPU context switching** (i.e. switching between threads as opposed to doing real computation.).

- **Minimize network overheads** by retrieving several related items simultaneously in one remote invocation if possible. Remote method invocations involve a network round-trip, marshaling and unmarshaling of parameters, which can cause huge performance problems if the remote interface is poorly designed. (Refer **Q125** in Enterprise section).

Most applications need to retrieve data from and save/update data into one or more databases. Database calls are remote calls over the network. In general data should be **lazily loaded** (i.e. load only when required as opposed to pre-loading from the database with a view that it can be used later) from a database to conserve memory but there are use cases (i.e. need to make several database calls) where **eagerly loading** data and caching can improve performance by minimizing network trips to the database. Data can be eagerly loaded with a help of SQL scripts with complex joins or stored procedures and cached using third party frameworks or building your own framework. At this point your interviewer could intercept you and ask you some pertinent questions relating to caching like:

Q: How would you refresh your cache?
A: You could say that one of the two following strategies can be used:

1. **Timed cache** strategy where the cache can be replenished periodically (i.e. every 30 minutes, every hour etc). This is a simple strategy applicable when it is acceptable to show dirty data at times and also the data in the database does not change very frequently.

2. **Dirty check** strategy where your application is the only one which can mutate (i.e. modify) the data in the database. You can set a "isDirty" flag to true when the data is modified in the database through your application and consequently your cache can be refreshed based on the "isDirty" flag.

Q: How would you refresh your cache if your database is shared by more than one application?
A: You could use one of the following strategies:

1. **Database triggers**: You could use database triggers to communicate between applications sharing the same database and write pollers which polls the database periodically to determine when the cache should be refreshed. (Refer **Q102** in Enterprise section)

2. **XML messaging** (Refer **Enterprise – JMS** subsection in Enterprise section) to communicate between other applications sharing the same database or separate databases to determine when the cache should be refreshed.

- **Optimize your I/O operations:** use buffering (Refer **Q25** in Java section) when writing to and reading from files and/or streams. Avoid writers/readers if you are dealing with only ASCII characters. You can use streams instead, which are faster. Avoid premature flushing of buffers. Also make use of the performance and scalability enhancing features such as non-blocking and asynchronous I/O, mapping of file to memory etc offered by the NIO (**New I/O**).

- **Establish whether you have a potential memory problem and manage your objects efficiently:** remove references to the short-lived objects from long-lived objects like Java collections etc (Refer **Q73** in Java section) to minimize any potential memory leaks. Also reuse objects where possible. It is cheaper to recycle objects than creating new objects each time. Avoid creating extra objects unnecessarily. For example use mutable *StringBuffer/StringBuilder* classes instead of immutable *String* objects in computation expensive loops as discussed in **Q21** in Java section and use **static factory methods** instead of constructors to recycle immutable objects as discussed in **Q16** in Java section. Automatic garbage collection is one of the most highly touted conveniences of Java. However, it comes at a price. Creating and destroying objects occupies a significant chunk of the JVM's time. Wherever possible, you should look for ways to minimize the number of objects created in your code:

  - For complex objects that are used frequently, consider creating a pool of recyclable objects rather than always instantiating new objects. This adds additional burden on the programmer to manage the pool, but in selected cases it can represent a significant performance gain. Use **flyweight** design pattern to create a pool of shared objects. Flyweights are typically instantiated by a flyweight factory that creates a limited number of flyweights based on some criteria. Invoking object does not directly instantiate flyweights. It gets it from the flyweight factory, which checks to see if it has a flyweight that fits a specific criteria (e.g. with or without GST etc) in the pool (e.g. HashMap). If the flyweight exists then return the reference to the flyweight. If it does not exist, then instantiate one for the specific criteria and add it to the pool (e.g. HashMap) and then return it to the invoking object.

  - If repeating code within a loop, avoid creating new objects for each iteration. Create objects before entering the loop (i.e. outside the loop) and reuse them if possible.

  - Use lazy initialization when you want to distribute the load of creating large amounts of objects. Use lazy initialization only when there is merit in the design.

- **Where applicable apply the following performance tips in your code:**

  - Use ArrayLists, HashMap etc as opposed to Vector, Hashtable etc where possible. This is because the methods in ArrayList, HashMap etc are not synchronized (Refer **Q15** in Java Section). Even better is to use just arrays where possible.

  - Set the initial capacity of a collection (e.g. *ArrayList*, *HashMap* etc) and *StringBuffer/StringBuilder* appropriately. This is because these classes must grow periodically to accommodate new elements. So, if you have a very large *ArrayList* or a *StringBuffer*, and you know the size in advance then you can speed things up by setting the initial size appropriately. (Refer **Q17, Q21** in Java Section).

  - Minimize the use of **casting** or runtime type checking like *instanceof* in frequently executed methods or in loops. The "casting" and "instanceof" checks for a class marked as final will be faster. Using "**instanceof**" construct is not only ugly but also unmaintainable. Look at using **visitor pattern** (Refer **Q11** in How would you go about...? section) to avoid "instanceof" constructs in frequently accessed methods.

  - Do not compute constants inside a large loop. Compute them outside the loop. For applets compute it in the init() method. Avoid nested loops (i.e. a "for" loop within another "for" loop etc) where applicable and make use of a *Collection* class as discussed in "**How can you code better without nested loops ?**" -- **Q17** in Java section.

  - Exception creation can be expensive because it has to create the full stack trace. The stack trace is obviously useful if you are planning to log or display the exception to the user. But if you are using your exception to just control the flow, which is not recommended, then throw an exception, which is pre-created. An efficient way to do this is to declare a public static final *Exception* in your exception class itself.

  - Avoid using System.out.println and use logging frameworks like Log4J etc, which uses I/O buffers (Refer **Q25** in Java section).

  - Minimize calls to Date, Calendar, etc related classes. For example:

```
//Inefficient code
public boolean isInYearCompanyWasEstablished(Date dateSupplied) {
    Calendar cal = Calendar.getInstance();
    cal.set(1998, Calendar.JAN, 01,0,0,0); //Should be read from a .proprerties file
    Date   yearStart = cal.getTime();
    cal.setTime(1998,Calendar.DECEMBER, 31,0,0,0);//Should be read from .properties.
    Date yearEnd = cal.getTime();
    return    dateSupplied.compareTo(yearStart) >=0 &&
              dateSupplied.compareTo(yearEnd) <= 0;
}
```

The above code is inefficient because every time this method is invoked 1 "Calendar" object and two "Date" objects are unnecessarily created. If this method is invoked 50 times in your application then 50 "Calendar" objects and 100 "Date" objects are created. A more efficient code can be written as shown below using a static initializer block:

//efficient code
```
private static final YEAR_START;
private static final YEAR_END;

static{
    Calendar cal = Calendar.getInstance();
    cal.set(1998, Calendar.JAN, 01,0,0,0); //Should be read from a .proprerties file
    Date   YEAR_START = cal.getTime();
    cal.setTime(1998,Calendar.DECEMBER, 31,0,0,0);//Should be read from .properties.
    Date YEAR_END = cal.getTime();

}

public boolean isInYearCompanyWasEstablished(Date dateSupplied) {
    return    dateSupplied.compareTo(YEAR_START) >=0 &&
              dateSupplied.compareTo(YEAR_END) <= 0;

}
```

No matter, how many times you invoke the method `isInYearCompanyWasEstablished(…)`, only 1 "Calendar" object 2 "Date" objects are created, since the static initializer block is executed only once when the class is loaded into the JVM.

o Minimize JNI calls in your code.

Q. When in the development process should you consider performance issues?

Set performance requirements in the specifications, include a performance focus in the analysis and design and also create a performance test environment.

Q. When designing your new code, what level of importance would you give to the following attributes?

-- Performance
-- Maintainability
-- Extendibility
-- Ease of use
-- Scalability

You should not compromise on architectural principles for just performance. You should make effort to write architecturally sound programs as opposed to writing only fast programs. If your architecture is sound enough then it would allow your program not only to scale better but also allows it to be optimized for performance if it is not fast enough. If you write applications with poor architecture but performs well for the current requirements, what will happen if the requirements grow and your architecture is not flexible enough to extend and creates a maintenance nightmare where fixing a code in one area would break your code in another area. This will cause your application to be re-written. So you should think about extendibility (i.e. ability to evolve with additional requirements), maintainability, ease of use, performance and scalability (i.e. ability to run in multiple servers or machines) during the design phase. List all possible design alternatives and pick the one which is conducive to sound design architecturally (i.e. scalable, easy to use, maintain and extend) and will allow it to be optimized later if not fast enough. You can build a vertical slice first to validate the above mentioned design attributes as discussed in **Q82** in the Java section.

> **Q. Rank the above attributes in order of importance?**
>
> There is no one correct answer for this question. **[Hint]** It can vary from application to application but typically if you write 1 - extendable, 2 - maintainable and 3 – ease of use code with some high level performance considerations, then it should allow you to optimize/tune for 4 - performance and 5 - scale. But if you write a code, which only performs fast but not flexible enough to grow with the additional requirements, then you may end up re-writing or carrying out a major revamp to your code. Refer **SOA** (Service Oriented Architecture) **Q15** in How would you go about... section.

Q 73: How would you detect and minimize memory leaks in Java? **MI** **BP** **FAQ**

A 73: In Java, memory leaks are caused by poor program design where object references are long lived and the garbage collector is unable to reclaim those objects.

Detecting memory leaks:

- Use tools like JProbe, OptimizeIt etc to detect memory leaks.

- Use operating system process monitors like task manager on NT systems, ps, vmstat, iostat, netstat etc on UNIX systems.

- Write your own utility class with the help of totalMemory() and freeMemory() methods in the Java *Runtime* class. Place these calls in your code strategically for pre and post memory recording where you suspect to be causing memory leaks. An even better approach than a utility class is using **dynamic proxies** (Refer **Q11** in How would you go about section...) or **Aspect Oriented Programming** (**AOP**) for pre and post memory recording where you have the control of activating memory measurement only when needed. (Refer **Q3 – Q5** in Emerging Technologies/Frameworks section).

Minimizing memory leaks:

> In Java, typically memory leak occurs when **an object of a longer lifecycle has a reference to objects of a short life cycle**. This prevents the objects with short life cycle being garbage collected. The developer must remember to remove the references to the short-lived objects from the long-lived objects. Objects with the same life cycle do not cause any issues because the garbage collector is smart enough to deal with the circular references (Refer **Q38** in Java section).

- Design applications with an object's life cycle in mind, instead of relying on the clever features of the JVM. Letting go of the object's reference in one's own class as soon as possible can mitigate memory problems. **Example:** myRef = null;

- Unreachable collection objects can magnify a memory leak problem. In Java it is easy to let go of an entire collection by setting the root of the collection to null. The garbage collector will reclaim all the objects (unless some objects are needed elsewhere).

- Use weak references (Refer **Q37** in Java section) if you are the only one using it. The **WeakHashMap** is a combination of *HashMap* and *WeakReference*. This class can be used for programming problems where you need to have a *HashMap* of information, but you would like that information to be garbage collected if you are the only one referencing it.

- Free native system resources like AWT frame, files, JNI etc when finished with them. **Example:** *Frame*, *Dialog*, and *Graphics* classes require that the method dispose() be called on them when they are no longer used, to free up the system resources they reserve.

Q 74: Why does the JVM crash with a core dump or a Dr.Watson error? **MI**

A 74: Any problem in pure Java code throws a Java exception or error. Java exceptions or errors will not cause a core dump (on UNIX systems) or a Dr.Watson error (on WIN32systems). Any serious Java problem will result in an *OutOfMemoryError* thrown by the JVM with the stack trace and consequently JVM will exit. These Java stack traces are very useful for identifying the cause for an abnormal exit of the JVM. So is there a way to know that *OutOfMemoryError* is about to occur? The Java J2SE 5.0 has a package called java.lang.management which has useful JMX beans that we can use to manage the JVM. One of these beans is the MemoryMXBean.

An *OutOfMemoryError* can be thrown due to one of the following 4 reasons:

- JVM may have a memory leak due to a bug in its internal heap management implementation. But this is highly unlikely because JVMs are well tested for this.

- The application may not have enough heap memory allocated for its running. You can allocate more JVM heap size (with –Xmx parameter to the JVM) or decrease the amount of memory your application takes to overcome this. To increase the heap space:

  java -Xms1024M -Xmx1024M

  Care should be taken not to make the –Xmx value too large because it can slow down your application. The secret is to make the maximum heap size value the right size.

- Another not so prevalent cause is the running out of a memory area called the **"perm"** which sits next to the heap. All the binary code of currently running classes is archived in the "perm" area. The 'perm' area is important if your application or any of the third party jar files you use <u>dynamically generate classes</u>. **For example:** "perm" space is consumed when XSLT templates are dynamically compiled into classes, J2EE application servers, JasperReports, JAXB etc use Java reflection to dynamically generate classes and/or large amount of classes in your application. To increase perm space:

  java -XX:PermSize=256M -XX:MaxPermSize=256M

- The fourth and the most common reason is that you may have a memory leak in your application as discussed in **Q73** in Java section.

[Good read/reference: "**Know your worst friend, the Garbage Collector**" http://java.sys-con.com/read/84695.htm by Romain Guy]

Q. So why does the JVM crash with a core dump or Dr.Watson error?

Both the core dump on UNIX operating system and Dr.Watson error on WIN32 systems mean the same thing. The JVM is a process like any other and when a process crashes a core dump is created. A core dump is a memory map of a running process. This can happen due to one of the following reasons:

- Using JNI (Java Native Interface) code, which has a fatal bug in its native code. **Example:** using Oracle OCI drivers, which are written partially in native code or JDBC-ODBC bridge drivers, which are written in non Java code. Using 100% pure Java drivers (communicates directly with the database instead of through client software utilizing the JNI) instead of native drivers can solve this problem. We can use Oracle thin driver, which is a 100% pure Java driver.

- The operating system on which your JVM is running might require a patch or a service pack.

- The JVM implementation you are using may have a bug in translating system resources like threads, file handles, sockets etc from the platform neutral Java byte code into platform specific operations. If this JVM's translated native code performs an illegal operation then the **operating system will instantly kill the process and mostly will generate a core dump file,** which is a hexadecimal file indicating program's state in memory at the time of error. The <u>core dump files are generated by the operating system in response to certain signals</u>. Operating system signals are responsible for notifying certain events to its threads and processes. The JVM can also intercept certain signals like **SIGQUIT** which is kill -3 < process id > from the operating system and it responds to this signal by printing out a Java stack trace and then continue to run. The JVM continues to run because the JVM has a special built-in debug routine, which will trap **the signal -3**. On the other hand signals like **SIGSTOP** (kill -23 <process id>) and **SIGKILL** (kill -9 <process id>) will cause the JVM process to stop or die. The following JVM argument will indicate JVM not to pause on **SIGQUIT** signal from the operating system.

  java –Xsqnopause

Java – Personal and Behavioral/Situational

Q 75: Did you have to use any design patterns in your Java project? `DP` `FAQ`

A 75: Yes. Refer **Q12 [Strategy]**, **Q16 [Iterator]**, **Q24 [Decorator]**, **Q36 [Visitor]**, **Q51 [Singleton]**, **Q52 [Factory]**, **Q58 [Command]**, **Q61 [Composite]**, and **Q63 [MVC-Model View Controller]** in Java section and **Q11, Q12** in How would you go about... section for a detailed discussion on design patterns with class diagrams and examples.

Resource: http://www.patterndepot.com/put/8/JavaPatterns.htm.

Why use design patterns, you may ask (Refer **Q5** in Enterprise section). Design patterns are worthy of mention in your CV and interviews. Design patterns have a number of advantages:

- Capture design experience from the past.
- Promote reuse without having to reinvent the wheel.
- Define the system structure better.
- Provide a common design vocabulary.

Some advice if you are just starting on your design pattern journey:

- If you are not familiar with UML, now is the time. UML is commonly used to describe patterns in pattern catalogues, including class diagrams, sequence diagrams etc. (Refer **Q106 - Q109** in Enterprise section).

- When using patterns, it is important to define a naming convention. It will be much easier to manage a project as it grows to identify exactly what role an object plays with the help of a naming convention e.g. AccountFacility**BusinessDelegate**, AccountFacility**Factory**, AccountFacility**ValueObject,** Account**Decorator**, Account**Visitor**, Account**TransferObject** (or AccountFacility**VO** or Account**TO**).

- Make a list of requirements that you will be addressing and then try to identify relevant patterns that are applicable. You should not just apply a pattern for the sake of learning or applying a pattern because it could become an anti-pattern.

IMPORTANT: Technical skills alone are not sufficient for you to perform well in your interviews and progress in your career. Your technical skills must be complemented with business skills (i.e. knowledge/understanding of the business, ability to communicate and interact effectively with the business users/customers, ability to look at things from the user's perspective as opposed to only technology perspective, ability to persuade/convince business with alternative solutions, which can provide a win/win solution from users' perspective as well as technology perspective), ability to communicate effectively with your fellow developers, immediate and senior management, ability to work in a team as well as independently, problem solving/analytical skills, organizational skills, ability to cope with difficult situations like stress due to work load, deadlines etc and manage or deal with difficult people, being a good listener with the right attitude (It is sometimes possible to have "**I know it all attitude**", when you have strong technical skills. This can adversely affect your ability to be a good listener, ability to look at things in a different perspective, ability to work well in a team and consequently your progression in your career) etc. Some of these aspects are covered below and should be prepared for prior to your job interview(s).

Q 76: Tell me about yourself or about some of the recent projects you have worked with? What do you consider your most significant achievement? Why do you think you are qualified for this position? Why should we hire you and what kind of contributions will you make? `FAQ`

A 76: [Hint:] Pick your recent projects and **enthusiastically** brief on it. Interviewer will be looking for how passionate you are about your past experience and achievements. Also is imperative that during your briefing, you demonstrate on a high level(without getting too technical) how you applied your skills and knowledge in some of the following key areas:

- Design concepts and design patterns: **How you understood and applied them.**
- Performance and memory issues: **How you identified and fixed them.**
- Exception handling and best practices: **How you understood and applied them.**
- Multi-threading and concurrent access: **How you identified and fixed them.**

Some of the questions in this section can help you prepare your answers by relating them to your current or past work experience. For example:

- **Design Concepts**: Refer **Q7, Q8, Q9, Q10, Q11** etc
- **Design Patterns**: Refer **Q12, Q16, Q24, Q36, Q51, Q52, Q58, Q61,** and **Q63** in Java section and **Q11, Q12** in "How would you go about…?" section for a more detailed discussion.
- **Performance issues**: Refer **Q25, Q72** etc
- **Memory issues**: Refer **Q37, Q38, Q42, Q73,** and **Q74**
- **Exception Handling**: Refer **Q39, Q40** etc
- **Multi-threading (Concurrency issues)**: Refer **Q15, Q17, Q21, Q34, Q42** and **Q46** etc

Demonstrating your knowledge in the above mentioned areas will improve your chances of being successful in your Java/J2EE interviews. 90% of the interview questions are asked based on your own resume. So in my view it is also very beneficial to mention how you demonstrated your knowledge/skills by stepping through a recent project on your resume.

The two other areas, which I have not mentioned in this section, which are also very vital, are transactions and security. These two areas will be covered in the next section, which is the Enterprise section (J2EE, JDBC, EJB, JMS, SQL, XML etc).

Even if you have not applied these skills knowingly or you have not applied them at all, just demonstrating that you have the knowledge and an appreciation will help you improve your chances in the interviews. Also mention any long hours worked to meet the deadline, working under pressure, fixing important issues like performance issues, running out of memory issues etc.

The job seekers should also ask questions to make an impression on the interviewer. Write out specific questions you want to ask and then look for opportunities to ask them during the interview. For example:

- Do you have any performance or design related issues? → Succinctly demonstrate how you would go about solving them or how you solved similar problems in your previous assignments.

- Do you follow any software development processes like agile methodology, XP, RUP etc? → Briefly demonstrate your experience, understanding and/or familiarity with the development methodology of relevance.

- Do you use any open source frameworks like Spring, Hibernate, Tapestry etc? Any build tools like Ant, Maven etc, and testing tools like JUnit etc → briefly demonstrate your experience, understanding and/or familiarity with the framework(s) of relevance.

Many interviewers end with a request to the applicant as to whether they have anything they wish to add. This is an opportunity for you to end on a positive note by making succinct statements about why you are the best person for the job by demonstrating your understanding of the key areas and how you applied them in your previous jobs.

> **Reflect back on your past jobs and pick two to five instances where you used your skills in the key areas very successfully.**

Q 77: Why are you leaving your current position? **FAQ**
A 77: [Hint]

- Do not criticize your previous employer or co-workers or sound too opportunistic.
- It is fine to mention a major problem like a buy out, budget constraints, merger or liquidation.
- You may also say that your chance to make a contribution is very low due to company wide changes or looking for a more challenging senior or designer role.

Q 78: What do you like and/or dislike most about your current and/or last position? **FAQ**
A 78: [Hint]

The interviewer is trying to find the compatibility with the open position. So

Do not say anything like:

- You dislike overtime.

- You dislike management or co-workers etc.

It is safe to say:

- You like challenges.
- Opportunity to grow into design, architecture, performance tuning etc
- Opportunity to learn and/or mentor junior developers..
- You dislike frustrating situations like identifying a memory leak problem or a complex transactional or a concurrency issue. You want to get on top of it as soon as possible.

Q 79: How do you handle pressure? Do you like or dislike these situations? **FAQ**
A 79: **[Hint]** These questions could mean that the open position is pressure-packed and may be out of control. Know what you are getting into. If you do perform well under stress then give a descriptive example. High achievers tend to perform well in pressure situations.

Q 80: What are your strengths and weaknesses? Can you describe a situation where you took initiative? Can you describe a situation where you applied your problem solving skills? **FAQ**
A 80: **[Hint]**

Strengths:

- **Taking initiatives** and **being pro-active:** You can illustrate how you took initiative to fix a transactional issue, a performance problem or a memory leak problem.

- **Design skills:** You can illustrate how you designed a particular application using OO concepts.

- **Problem solving skills:** Explain how you will break a complex problem into more manageable sub-sections and then apply brain storming and analytical skills to solve the complex problem. Illustrate how you went about identifying a scalability issue or a memory leak problem.

- **Communication skills:** Illustrate that you can communicate effectively with all the team members, business analysts, users, testers, stake holders etc.

- **Ability to work in a team environment as well as independently:** Illustrate that you are technically sound to work independently as well as have the interpersonal skills to fit into any team environment.

- **Hard working, honest,** and **conscientious etc** are the adjectives to describe you.

Weaknesses:

Select a trait and come up with a solution to overcome your weakness. Stay away from personal qualities and concentrate more on professional traits for example:

- I pride myself on being an attention to detail guy but sometimes miss small details. So I am working on applying the 80/20 principle to manage time and details. Spend 80% of my effort and time on 20% of the tasks, which are critical and important to the task at hand.

- Some times when there is a technical issue or a problem I tend to work continuously until I fix it without having a break. But what I have noticed and am trying to practice is that taking a break away from the problem and thinking outside the square will assist you in identifying the root cause of the problem sooner.

Q 81: What are your career goals? Where do you see yourself in 5-10 years? **FAQ**
A 81: **[Hint]** Be realistic. For example

- Next 2-3 years to become a senior developer or a team lead.
- Next 3-5 years to become a solution designer or an architect.

Situational questions: The open-ended questions like last two questions are asked by interviewers to identify specific characteristics like taking initiative, performance standards, accountability, adaptability, flexibility, sensitivity, communication skills, ability to cope stress etc. These questions are known as behavioral or situational questions. This behavioral technique is used to evaluate a candidate's future success from past behaviors. The answers to these questions must describe in detail a particular situation like an event, a project or an experience and how you acted on that situation and what the results were. Prepare your answers prior to the interview using the **"Situation Action Result (SAR)"** approach and avoid fabricating or memorizing your answers. You should try to relate back to your past experiences at your previous employments, community events, sporting events etc. Sample questions and answers are shown below:

Q 82: Give me an example of a time when you set a goal and were able to achieve it? Give me an example of a time you showed initiatiative and took the lead? Tell me about a difficult decision you made in the last year? Give me an example of a time you motivated others? Tell me about a most complex project you were involved in? `FAQ`

A 82:

Situation: When you were working for the ZCC Software Technology Corporation, the overnight batch process called the "Data Pacakager" was developed for a large fast food chain which has over 100 stores. This overnight batch process is responsible for performing a very database intensive search and compute changes like cost of ingredients, selling price, new menu item etc made in various retail stores and package those changes into XML files and send those XML data to the respective stores where they get uploaded into their point of sale registers to reflect the changes. This batch process had been used for the past two years, but since then the number of stores had increased and so did the size of the data in the database. The batch process, which used to take 6-8 hours to complete, had increased to 14-16 hours, which obviously started to adversely affect the daily operations of these stores. The management assigned you with the task of improving the performance of the batch process to 5-6 hours (i.e. suppose to be an overnight process).

Action: After having **analyzed the existing design** and code for the "Data Packager", **you had to take the difficult decision** to let the management know that this batch process needed to be re-designed and re-written as opposed to modifying the existing code, since it was poorly designed. It is hard to extend, maintain (i.e. making a change in one place can break the code some where else and so on) and had no object reuse through caching (makes too many unnecessary network trips to the database) etc. The management was not too impressed with this approach and concerned about the time required to rewrite this batch process since the management had promised the retail stores to provide a solution within 8-12 weeks. **You took the initiative and used your persuasive skills** to **convince the management** that you would be able to provide a re-designed and re-written solution within the 8-12 weeks with the assistance of 2-3 additional developers and two testers. You were entrusted with the task to rewrite the batch process and **you set your goal to complete the task in 8 weeks**. You decided to build the software iteratively by building individual vertical slices as opposed to the big bang waterfall approach [Refer subsection **"Enterprise – Software development process"** in Enterprise – Java section]. You redesigned and wrote the code for a typical use case from end to end (i.e. full vertical slice) within 2 weeks and subsequently carried out functional and integration testing to iron out any unforeseen errors or issues. Once the first iteration is stable, **you effectively communicated** the architecture to the management and to your fellow developers. **Motivated** and **mentored** your fellow developers to build the other iterations, based on the first iteration. At the end of iteration, it was tested by the testers, while the developers moved on to the next iteration.

Results: After having **enthusiastically** worked to your plan with **hard work**, **dedication** and **teamwork**, you were able to have the 90% of the functionality completed in 9 weeks and spent the next 3 weeks fixing bugs, tuning performance and coding rest of the functionality. The fully functional data packager was completed in 12 weeks and took only 3-4 hours to package XML data for all the stores. The team was under pressure at times but you made them believe that it is more of a **challenge as opposed to think of it as a stressful situation**. The newly designed data packager was also easier to maintain and extend. The management was impressed with the outcome and rewarded the team with an outstanding achievement award. The performance of the newly developed data packager was further improved by 20% by tuning the database (i.e. partitioning the tables, indexing etc).

Q 83: Describe a time when you were faced with a stressful situation that demonstrated your coping skills? Give me an example of a time when you used your fact finding skills to solve a problem? Describe a time when you applied your analytical and/or problem solving skills? `FAQ`

A 83:

Situation: When you were working for the Surething insurance corporation pty ltd, you were responsible for the migration of an online insurance application (i.e. external website) to a newer version of application server (i.e. the current version is no longer supported by the vendor). The migration happened smoothly and after a couple of days of going live, you started to experience "OutOfMemoryError", which forced you to restart the application server every day. This raised a red alert and the immediate and the senior management were very concerned and consequently constantly calling for meetings and updates on the progress of identifying the root cause of this issue. This has created a stressful situation.

Action: You were able to have a positive outlook by believing that this is more of a challenge as opposed to think of it as a stressful situation. You needed to be composed to get your analytical and problem solving skills to get to work. You spent some time finding facts relating to "OutOfMemoryError" (Refer **Q74** in Java section). You were tempted to increase the heap space as suggested by fellow developers but the profiling and monitoring did not indicate that was the case. The memory usage drastically increased during and after certain user operations like generating PDF reports. The generation of reports used some third party libraries, which dynamically generated classes from your templates. So you decided to increase the area of the memory known as the "perm", which sits next to the heap. This "perm" space is consumed when the classes are dynamically generated from templates during the report generation.

```
java  -XX:PermSize=256M -XX:MaxPermSize=256M
```

Results: After you have increased the "perm" size, the "OutOfMemoryError" has disappeared. You kept monitoring it for a week and everything worked well. The management was impressed with your problem solving, fact finding and analytical skills, which had contributed to the identification of the not so prevalent root cause and the effective communication with the other teams like infrastructure, production support, senior management, etc. The management also identified your ability to cope under stress and offered you a promotion to lead a small team of 4 developers.

Q 84: Describe a time when you had to work with others in the organization to accomplish the organizational goals? Describe a situation where others you worked on a project disagreed with your ideas, and what did you do? Describe a situation in which you had to collect information by asking many questions of several people? What has been your experience in giving presentations to small or large groups? How do you show considerations for others? **FAQ**

A 84:

Situation: You were working for Wealth guard Pty Ltd financial services organization. You were part of a development team responsible for enhancing an existing online web application, which enables investors and advisors view and manage their financial portfolios. The websites of the financial services organizations are periodically surveyed and rated by an independent organization for their ease of use, navigability, content, search functionality etc. Your organization was ranked 21st among 23 websites reviewed. Your chief information officer was very disappointed with this poor rating and wanted the business analysts, business owners (i.e. within the organization) and the technical staff to improve on the ratings before the next ratings, which would be done in 3 months.

Action: The business analysts and the business owners quickly got into work and came up with a requirements list of 35 items in consultation with the external business users such as advisors, investors etc. You were assigned the task of working with the business analysts, business owners (i.e internal), and project managers to provide a technical input in terms of feasibility study, time estimates, impact analysis etc. The business owners had a pre-conceived notion of how they would like things done. You had to analyze the outcome from both the business owners' perspective and technology perspective. There were times you had to use your persuasive skills to convince the business owners and analysts to take an alternative approach, which would provide a more robust solution. You managed to convince the business owners and analysts by providing visual mock-up screen shots of your proposed solution, presentation skills, ability to communicate without any technical jargons, and listening carefully to business needs and discussing your ideas with your fellow developers (i.e. being a good listener, respecting others' views and having the right attitude even if you know that you are right). You also strongly believe that good technical skills must be complemented with good interpersonal skills and the right attitude. After 2-3 weeks of constant interaction with the business owners, analysts and fellow developers, you had helped the business users to finalize the list of requirements. You also took the initiative to apply the agile development methodology to improve communication and cooperation between business owners and the developers.

Results: You and your fellow developers were not only able to effectively communicate and collaborate with the business users and analysts but also provided progressive feedback to each other due to iterative approach. The team work and hard work had resulted in a much improved and more user friendly website, which consequently improved its ratings from 21st to 13th within 3 months.

Refer **Enterprise – Personal** subsection in **Enterprise** section for more situational questions and answers.

Note: For **Q75 – Q84 tailor your answers to the job**. Also be prepared for the following questions, which ascertain how you keep your knowledge up to date, what motivates you, your ability to take initiatives, be pro-active, eagerness to work for the company, etc:

Q 85: What was the last Java related technical book or article you read? **FAQ**

A 85:

- **Mastering EJB** by Ed Roman.
- **EJB design patterns** by Floyd Marinescu.
- **Bitter Java** by Bruce Tate.
- **Thinking in Java** by Bruce Eckel.
- **Effective Java** by Joshua Bloch.

Q. What is your favorite technical book? Effective Java by Joshua Bloch

---

Q 86: Which Java related website(s) or resource(s) do you use to keep your knowledge up to date beyond Google? **FAQ**
A 86:

- http://www.theserverside.com, http://www.javaworld.com, http://www-136.ibm.com/developerworks/Java, http://www.precisejava.com, http://www.allapplabs.com, http://java.sun.com, http://www.martinfowler.com, http://www.ambysoft.com etc.

Q 87: What past accomplishments gave you satisfaction? What makes you want to work hard? **FAQ**
A 87:

- Material rewards such as salary, perks, benefits etc naturally come into play **but focus on your achievements** or **accomplishments** than on rewards.

- Explain how you took pride in fixing a complex performance issue or a concurrency issue. You could substantiate your answer with a past experience. For example while you were working for Bips telecom, you pro-actively identified a performance issue due to database connection resource leak. You subsequently took the initiative to notify your team leader and volunteered to fix it by adding finally {} blocks to close the resources. [Discussed in the **Enterprise Java** section]

- If you are being interviewed for a position, which requires your design skills then you could explain that in your previous job with an insurance company you had to design and develop a sub-system, which gave you complete satisfaction. You were responsible for designing the data model using entity relationship diagrams (E-R diagrams) and the software model using the component diagrams, class diagrams, sequence diagrams etc. [Discussed in the **Enterprise Java** section]

- If you are being interviewed for a position where you have to learn new pieces of technology/framework like dependency injection (e.g. Spring framework), component based web development frameworks like Tapestry, JSF etc, object to relational mapping frameworks like hibernate etc then you can explain with examples from your past experience where you were not only motivated to acquire new skills/knowledge but also proved that you are a quick and a pro-active learner. [Discussed in the **Emerging Technologies/Frameworks** section]

- If the job you are being interviewed for requires production support from time to time, then you could explain that it gives you satisfaction because you would like to interact with the business users and/or customers to develop your **business** and **communication** skills by getting an opportunity to understand a system from the users perspective and also gives you an opportunity to sharpen your **technical** and **problem solving** skills. If you are a type of person who enjoys more development work then you can be honest about it and indicate that you would like to have a balance between development work and support work, where you can develop different aspects of your skills/knowledge. You could also reflect an experience from a past job, where each developer was assigned a weekly roster to provide support.

- You could say that, you generally would like to work hard but would like to work even harder when there are challenges.

Q 88: Do you have any role models in software development?
A 88:

- Scott W. Ambler, Martin Fowler, Ed Roman, Floyd Marinescu, Grady Booch etc.

- Gavin King (**Hibernate** persistence framework), Rod Johnson (**Spring** framework), Howard M. Lewis Ship (**Tapestry** web framework and **Hivemind** framework), Dennis Sosnoski (**JiBX** XML binding framework) etc.

Q 89: Why do you want to work for us? What motivates you? What demotivates you? What are you looking for in your next job? What is your definition of an ideal job? **FAQ** (Research the company prior to the interview). Look at their website. Know their product lines and their competitors. Learn about their achievements or strengths.

Java – Behaving right in an interview

- Arrive 5-10 minutes before the interview. **Never arrive too late or too early**. If you are running late due to some unavoidable situation, call ahead and make sure that the interviewers know your situation. Also, be apologetic for arriving late due to unfortunate situation.

- First impressions are everything: **Firm handshake, maintain eye contact**, smile, watch your body language, be pleasant, dress neatly and **know the names of your interviewers** and **thank them by their names** for the opportunity.

- Try, not to show that you are nervous. Every body is nervous for interviews but try not to show it. [**Hint**: Just think that even if you do not get the job, it is a good learning experience and you would do better in your next interview and appreciate yourself for getting this far. You can always learn from your mistakes and do better at your next interview.]

- It is good to be confident but **do not make up your answer or try to bluff**. If you put something in your resume then better be prepared to back it up. Be honest to answer technical questions because you are not expected to remember everything (for example, you might know a few design patterns but not all of them etc). If you have not used a design pattern in question, request the interviewer, if you could describe a different design pattern. Also, try to provide brief answers, which means **not too long** and **not too short** like yes or no. Give examples of times you performed that particular task. If you would like to expand on your answer, ask the interviewer **if you could elaborate** or **go on**. It is okay to verify your answers every now and then but **avoid verifying or validating your answers too often** because the interviewer might think that you lack self-confidence or you cannot work independently. But if you do not know the answer to a particular question and keen to know the answer, you could politely request for an answer but should not request for answers too often. If you think you could find the answer(s) readily on the internet then try to remember the question and find the answer(s) soon after your interview.

- **You should also ask questions** to make an impression on the interviewer. Write out specific questions you want to ask and then look for opportunities to ask them during the interview. Many interviewers end with a request to the applicant as to whether they have anything they wish to add. This is an opportunity for you to end on a positive note by making succinct statements about why you are the best person for the job.

- **Try to be yourself**. Have a good sense of humor, a smile and a positive outlook. Be friendly but you should not tell the sagas of your personal life. If you cross your boundaries then the interviewer might feel that your personal life will interfere with your work.

- **Be confident**. I have addressed many of the popular technical questions in this book and it should improve your confidence. If you come across a question relating to a new piece of technology you have no experience with like AOP (Aspect Oriented Programming) or IoC (Inversion of Control) or a framework like Tapestry, then you can mention that you have a very basic understanding and demonstrate that you are a quick leaner by reflecting back on your past job where you had to quickly learn a new piece of a technology or a framework. Also, you can mention that you keep a good rapport with a network of talented Java/J2EE developers or mentors to discuss any design alternatives or work a rounds to a pressing problem.

- Unless asked, **do not talk about money**. Leave this topic until the interviewer brings it up or you can negotiate this with your agent once you have been offered the position. At the interview you should try to sell or **promote your technical skills, business skills, ability to adapt to changes, and interpersonal skills.** Prior to the interview find out what skills are required by thoroughly reading the job description or talking to your agent for the specific job and **be prepared to promote those skills** (Some times you would be asked why you are the best person for the job?). You should come across as you are more keen on technical challenges, learning a new piece of technology, improving your business skills etc as opposed to coming across as you are only interested in money.

- Speak clearly, firmly and with confidence but should not be aggressive and egoistical. **You should act interested in the company and the job** and **make all comments in a positive manner**. Should not speak negatively about past colleagues or employers. Should not excuse yourself halfway through the interview, even if you have to use the bathroom. Should not ask for refreshments or coffee but accept it if offered.

- At the end of the interview, **thank the interviewers by their names for their time** with a **firm handshake**, maintain **eye contact** and **ask them about the next steps** if not already mentioned to know where you are at the process and show that you are interested.

In short, arrive on time, be polite, firm hand with a smile and <u>do not act superior</u>, <u>act interested and enthusiastic</u> but not desperate, make eye contact at all times, ask questions but should not over do it by talking too much, it is okay to be nervous but try not to show it and be honest with your answers because <u>you are not expected to know the answers for all the technical questions</u>. Unless asked, do not talk about money and find every opportunity to sell your technical, business and interpersonal skills without over doing it. Finish the interview with a positive note by asking about the next steps if not already mentioned, a firm hand shake with a "thank you for the interviewer's time" with an eye contact and a smile.

General Tip #1:

- Try to find out the needs of the project in which you will be working and the needs of the people within the project.

- 80% of the interview questions are based on your own resume.

- Where possible briefly demonstrate how you applied your skills/knowledge in the key areas [design concepts, transactional issues, performance issues, memory leaks etc], business skills, and interpersonal skills as described in this book. Find the right time to raise questions and answer those questions to show your strength.

- Be honest to answer technical questions, you are not expected to remember everything (for example you might know a few design patterns but not all of them etc). If you have not used a design pattern in question, request the interviewer, if you could describe a different design pattern.

- Do not be critical, focus on what you can do. Also try to be humorous to show your smartness.

- Do not act superior. [**Technical skills must be complemented with good interpersonal skills**]

General Tip #2:

Prepare a skills/knowledge matrix in your Resume. This is very useful for someone who gained wide range of skills/knowledge in a short span by being a pro-active learner (e.g. extra reading, additional projects, outside work development projects etc). **For example:**

Java 1.3 – 5.0	18 months
Servlets / JSP	12 months
J2EE (EJB, JMS, JNDI etc)	12 months
XML, XSD, XSLT etc	6 months
Hibernate	6 months
OOA & OOD	12 months
UML	4 months
Design patterns	5 months
SQL	12 months

General Tip #3:

Unless you are applying for a position as a junior or a beginner developer, having your resume start with all the Java training and certifications may lead to a misunderstanding that you are a beginner. Your first page should concentrate on your <u>achievements</u> and <u>skills summary</u> (As in **General Tip #2**) to show that you are a skilled professional. **For example:**

- Re-designed the data packager application for the XYZ Corporation, to make it more scalable, maintainable and extendable. [**Shows that you have design skills**]

- Identified and fixed memory leak issues for the master lock application and consequently improved performance by 20% and further improved performance by introducing multi-threading and other performance tuning strategies. Identified and fixed some transactional issues for the Endeavor project, which is a web based e-commerce application. [**Shows that you are a pro-active developer with good understanding of multi-threading, transactional, performance and memory issues. Also shows that you have worked on transactional and multi-threaded systems and have an <u>eye for identifying potential failures</u>.**]

- Received an outstanding achievement award for my design and development work using Java/J2EE at the ABC Corporation. Published an article entitled "Java Tips and Tricks". [**Shows that you take pride in your achievements**]

- Mentored junior developers at JKL Corporation. [**Shows that you are an experienced developer who would like to mentor junior developers and you are not only a technology oriented person but also a people oriented person**].

Reference your achievements and accomplishments with specific examples and/or relevant paperwork (but avoid overloading the hiring manager with paperwork).

Java – Key Points

- Java is an object oriented (OO) language, which has built in support for multi-threading, socket communication, automatic memory management (i.e. garbage collection) and also has better portability than other languages across operating systems.

- Java class loaders are **hierarchical** and use a **delegation model**. The classes loaded by a child class loader have **visibility** into classes loaded by its parents up the hierarchy but the reverse is not true.

- Java packages help resolve naming conflicts when different packages have classes with the same names. This also helps you organize files within your project.

- Java does not support **multiple implementation inheritance** but supports **multiple interface inheritance**.

- **Polymorphism**, **inheritance** and **encapsulation** are the 3 pillar of an object-oriented language.

- Code reuse can be achieved through either **inheritance** ("is a" relationship) or **object composition** ("has a" relationship). Favor object composition over inheritance.

- When using **implementation inheritance**, make sure that the **subclasses depend only on the behavior of the superclass**, not the actual implementation. An **abstract** base class usually provides an implementation inheritance.

- Favor **interface inheritance** to **implementation inheritance** because it promotes the deign concept of **coding to interface** and **reduces coupling**. The interface inheritance can achieve code reuse through **object composition**.

- Design by contract specifies the obligations of a calling-method and called-method to each other using **pre-conditions**, **post-conditions** and **class invariants**.

- When using Java collections API, prefer using *ArrayList* or *HashMap* as opposed to *Vector* or *Hashtable* to **avoid any synchronization overhead**. The *ArrayList* or *HashMap* can be externally synchronized for concurrent access by multiple threads.

- Set the initial capacity of a collection appropriately and program in terms of interfaces as opposed to implementations.

- The equals() - returns the results of running the equals() method of a user supplied class, which compares the attribute values. The equals() method provides "**deep comparison**" by checking if two objects are logically equal as opposed to the shallow comparison provided by the operator ==.

- The non-final methods **equals()**, **hashCode()**, **toString()**, **clone()**, and **finalize()** are defined in the Object class and are primarily meant for extension. The equals() and hashCode() methods prove to be very important when objects implementing these two methods are added to collections.

- If a class overrides the equals() method, it must implement the hashCode() method as well. If two objects are equal as per the equals() method, then calling the hashCode() method in each of the two objects must return the same hashCode integer result but the reverse is not true (i.e. If two objects have the same hashCode does not mean that they are equal). If a field is not used in equals()method, then it must not be used in hashCode() method.

- When providing a user defined key class for storing objects in *HashMap*, you should override **equals()**, and **hashCode()** methods from the *Object* class.

- Always override the toString() method, but you should override the clone() method very judiciously. The finalize() method should only be used in rare instances as a safety net or to terminate non-critical native resources.

- *String* class is immutable and *StringBuffer* and *StringBuilder* classes are mutable. So it is more efficient to use a *StringBuffer* or a *StringBuilder* as opposed to a *String* in a computation intensive situations (i.e. in for, while loops).

- **Serialization** is a process of writing an object to a file or a stream. **Transient** variables cannot be serialized.

- Java I/O performance can be improved by using buffering, minimizing access to the underlying hard disk and operating systems. Use the NIO package for performance enhancing features like non-blocking I/O operation, buffers to hold data, and memory mapping of files.

- Each time an object is created in Java it goes into the area of memory known as **heap**. The primitive variables are allocated in the **stack** if they are local method variables and in the **heap** if they are class member variables.

- Threads **share the heap spaces** so it is **not thread-safe** and the threads have **their own stack space**, which is **thread-safe**.

- The **garbage collection cannot be forced**, but you can nicely ask the garbage collector to collect garbage.

- There two types of exceptions **checked** (i.e. compiler checked) and **unchecked** (Runtime Exceptions). It is not advisable to catch type *Exception*.

- A **process** is an execution of a program (e.g. JVM process) but a **thread** is a single execution sequence within the process.

- Threads can be created in Java by either extending the *Thread* class or implementing the *Runnable* interface.

- In Java each object has a lock and a thread can acquire a lock by using the **synchronized** key word. The synchronization key word can be applied in **method level** (coarse-grained lock) or **block level** (fine-grained lock which offers better performance) of code.

- Threads can communicate with each other using **wait()**, **notify()**, and **notifyAll()** methods. This communication solves the **consumer-producer** problem. These are non-final methods defined in the Object class.

- Sockets are communication channels, which facilitate inter-process communication.

- The J2SE 5.0 release is focused along the key areas of ease of development, scalability, performance, quality, etc. The new features include **generics**, **metadata**, **autoboxing** and **auto-unboxing** of primitive types, **enhanced for loop**, **enumerated type**, **static import**, C style formatted output with **printf()**, formatted input with the **Scanner** class, **varargs**, etc.

- Swing uses the **MVC paradigm** to provide loose coupling and action **architecture** to implement a shared behavior between two or more user interface components.

- Complex layouts can be simplified by using **nested containers** for example having panels within panels and each panel can use its own LayoutManager like **FlowLayout**, **BorderLayout**, **GridLayout**, **BoxLayout**, **CardLayout** etc. The containers like panels, dialog boxes, windows etc do not perform the actual laying out of the components. They delegate the layout functionality to layout managers. The layout managers make use of the strategy design pattern, which encapsulates family of algorithms for laying out components in the containers.

- The AWT containers like panels, dialog boxes, windows etc do not perform the actual laying out of the components. They delegate the layout functionality to layout managers. The layout managers make use of the **strategy design pattern**, which encapsulates family of algorithms for laying out components in the containers.

- Swing components should be accessed through an **event-dispatching thread**. There is a way to access the Swing event-dispatching thread from outside event-handling or drawing code, is using *SwingUtilities'* **invokeLater()** and **invokeAndWait()** methods.

- Like event handling code, painting code executes on the **event-dispatching thread**. So while an event is being handled, no painting will occur and similarly while painting is happening no events will take place.

- The paint() method should not be explicitly invoked. Only **repaint()** method can be explicitly invoked (which implicitly calls paintComponent() method) and only **paintComponent()** method should be overridden if required.

- Swing uses a **delegation event model**, in which the objects that receive user events notify the registered listeners of the user activity. In most cases the event receiver is a component.

- A signed applet can become a trusted applet, which can work outside the sandbox.

- In Java typically memory leak occurs when an object of longer life cycle has a reference to objects of a short life cycle.

- You can improve performance in Java by :

  1. Pooling your valuable resources like threads, database and socket connections.

2. Optimizing your I/O operations.
3. Minimizing network overheads, calls to *Date*, *Calendar* related classes, use of "**casting**" or runtime type checking like "**instanceof**" in frequently executed methods/loops, JNI calls, etc
4. Managing your objects efficiently by caching or recycling them without having to rely on garbage collection.
5. Using a *StringBuffer* as opposed to *String* and *ArrayList* or *HashMap* as oppose to *Vector* or *Hashtable*
6. Applying multi-threading where applicable.
7. Minimizing any potential memory leaks.

- Finally, very briefly familiarize yourself with some of the key **design patterns** like:

1. **Decorator design pattern**: used by Java I/O API. A popular design pattern.
2. **Reactor design pattern/Observer design pattern**: used by Java NIO API.
3. **Visitor design pattern**: can be used to avoid instanceof and typecast constructs.
4. **Factory method/abstract factory design pattern**: popular pattern, which gets frequently asked in interviews.
5. **Singleton pattern**: popular pattern, which gets frequently asked in interviews.
6. **Composite design pattern**: used by GUI components and also a popular design pattern
7. **MVC design pattern/architecture**: used by Swing components and also a popular pattern.
8. **Command pattern**: used by Swing action architecture and also a popular design pattern.
9. **Strategy design pattern**: A popular design pattern used by AWT layout managers.

Refer **Q11** in "**How would you go about**…" section for a detailed discussion and code samples on GoF (Gang of Four) design patterns.

Recommended reading:

- The famous Gang of Four book: Design Patterns, Eric Gamma, Richard Helm, Ralph Johnson, and John Vlissides (Addiso-Wesley Publishing Co., 1995; ISBN: 0201633612).

- Effective Java Programming Language Guide – by Joshua Bloch

---

Tech Tip #2:

Always have the Java API handy and use the standard library to take advantage of the knowledge of the experts who wrote it and the experience of those who have used it and tested it before you. Every developer should be familiar with the following key libraries: **java.lang** and **java.util** are used very often and **java.math** and **java.io** are used less often. The other libraries can be learned as and when required. If you have a specialized need then first look for a library and if you cannot find one then you can implement your own. E.g.

```
//To copy an array to another array:
String[] array1 = {"a", "b", "c"};
String[] array2 = new String[2] ;
java.lang.System.arraycopy(array1,0,array2,0,2);

//convert an array to a list
List list = java.util.Arrays.asList(array2);
System.out.println(list);//prints [a, b]

//convert the list back to an array
String[] array3 = (String[])list.toArray(new String[0]);
```

Tech Tip #3:

The data types float and double are primarily designed for engineering and scientific calculations. They are not suited for financial calculations of monetary values. Use **BigDecimal** instead. For non decimal values you could either use the primitive values such as int, long etc or wrapper classes such as Integer, Long etc. Example If you are using hibernate as your object to relational mapper and would like to map a monetary data field of "amount" with database data type numeric (10,2) then prefer using **BigDecimal** as your object data type.

SECTION TWO

Enterprise Java – Interview questions & answers

K
E
Y

A
R
E
A
S

- Specification Fundamentals SF
- Design Concepts DC
- Design Patterns DP
- Concurrency Issues CI
- Performance Issues PI
- Memory Issues MI
- Exception Handling EH
- Transactional Issues TI
- Security SE
- Scalability Issues SI
- Best Practices BP
- Coding[1] CO

FAQ - Frequently Asked Questions

---

[1] Unlike other key areas, the CO is not always shown against the question but shown above the actual content of relevance within a question.

Enterprise - J2EE Overview

Q 01: What is J2EE? What are J2EE components and services? SF FAQ

A 01: J2EE (**Java 2 Enterprise Edition**) is an environment for developing and deploying enterprise applications. The J2EE platform consists of J2EE components, services, Application Programming Interfaces (APIs) and protocols that provide the functionality for developing multi-tiered and distributed Web based applications.

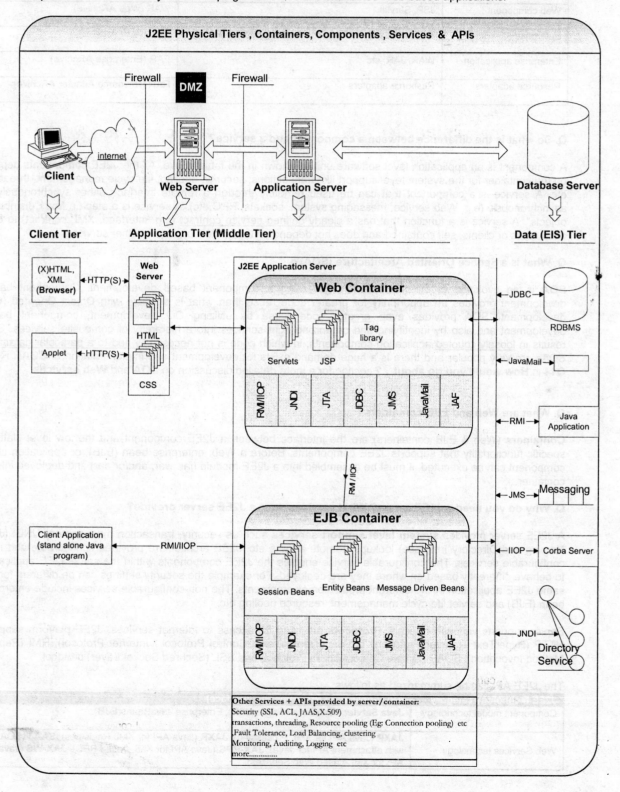

A **J2EE component** is a self-contained functional software unit that is assembled into a J2EE application with its related classes and files and communicates with other components. The J2EE specification defines the following J2EE components:

Component type	Components	Packaged as
Applet	applets	JAR (Java **AR**chive)
Application client	Client side Java codes.	JAR (Java **AR**chive)
Web component	JSP, Servlet	WAR (**Web AR**chive)
Enterprise JavaBeans	Session beans, Entity beans, Message driven beans	JAR (EJB Archive)
Enterprise application	WAR, JAR, etc	EAR (**Enterprise AR**chive)
Resource adapters	Resource adapters	RAR (**Resource Adapter AR**chive)

Q. So what is the difference between a component and a service?

A component is an application level software unit as shown in the table above. All the J2EE components depend on the container for the system level support like transactions, security, pooling, life cycle management, threading etc. A service is a component that can be used remotely through a remote interface either synchronously or asynchronously (e.g. Web service, messaging system, sockets, RPC etc). A service is a step up from "distributed objects". A service is a function that has a clearly defined service contract (e.g. interface, XML contract) to their consumers or clients, self contained and does not depend on the context or state of other services.

Q. What is a S̲ervice O̲riented A̲rchitecture (SOA)?

SOA is an evolution of the fundamentals governing a component based development. Component based development provides an opportunity for greater code reuse than what is possible with **O**bject **O**riented (**OO**) development. SOA provides even greater code reuse by utilizing OO development, component based development and also by identifying and organizing right services into a hierarchy of composite services. SOA results in loosely coupled application components, in which code is not necessarily tied to a particular database. SOAs are very popular and there is a huge demand exists for development and implementation of SOAs. Refer **Q14** in **How would you go about…?** section for a more detailed discussion on **SOA** and **Web services**.

Q. What are Web and EJB containers?

Containers (Web & EJB containers) are the interface between a J2EE component and the low level platform specific functionality that supports J2EE components. Before a Web, enterprise bean (EJB), or application client component can be executed, it must be assembled into a J2EE module (jar, war, and/or ear) and deployed into its container.

Q. Why do you need a J2EE server? What services does a J2EE server provide?

A J2EE server provides **system level support services** such us security, transaction management, JNDI (Java Naming and Directory Interface) lookups, remote access etc. J2EE architecture provides configurable and non-configurable services. The configurable service enables the J2EE components within the same J2EE application to behave differently based on where they are deployed. For example the security settings can be different for the same J2EE application in two different production environments. The non-configurable services include enterprise bean (EJB) and servlet life cycle management, resource pooling etc.

Server supports various protocols. **Protocols** are used for access to Internet services. J2EE platform supports HTTP (HyperText Transfer Protocol), TCP/IP (Transmission Control Protocol / Internet Protocol), RMI (Remote Method Invocation), SOAP (Simple Object Access Protocol) and SSL (Secured Socket Layer) protocol.

The J2EE API can be summarized as follows:

J2EE technology category	API (Application Programming Interface)
Component model technology	**Java Servlet**, JavaServer Pages(**JSP**), Enterprise JavaBeans(**EJB**).
Web Services technology	**JAXP** (Java API for XML Processing), **JAXR** (Java API for XML Registries), **SAAJ** (SOAP with attachment API for Java), **JAX-RPC** (Java API for XML-based RPC), **JAX-WS** (Java API for XML-based Web Services).

Other	JDBC (Java DataBase Connectivity), JNDI (Java Naming and Directory Interface), JMS (Java Messaging Service), JCA (J2EE Connector Architecture), JTA (Java Transaction API), JavaMail, JAF (JavaBeans Activation Framework – used by JavaMail), JAAS (Java Authentication and Authorization Service), JMX (Java Management eXtensions).

Q 02: Explain the J2EE 3-tier or n-tier architecture? SF DC FAQ

A 02: This is a very commonly asked question. Be prepared to draw some diagrams on the board. The J2EE platform is a multi-tiered system. A tier is a logical or functional partitioning of a system.

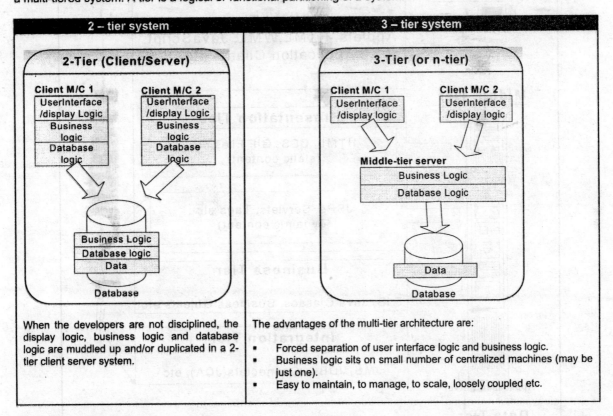

Each tier is assigned a unique responsibility in a 3-tier system. Each tier is logically separated and loosely coupled from each other, and may be distributed.

Client tier represents Web browser, a Java or other application, Applet, WAP phone etc. The client tier makes requests to the Web server who will be serving the request by either returning static content if it is present in the Web server or forwards the request to either Servlet or JSP in the application server for either static or dynamic content.

Presentation tier encapsulates the presentation logic required to serve clients. A Servlet or JSP in the presentation tier intercepts client requests, manages logons, sessions, accesses the business services, and finally constructs a response, which gets delivered to client.

Business tier provides the business services. This tier contains the business logic and the business data. All the business logic is centralized into this tier as opposed to 2-tier systems where the business logic is scattered between the front end and the backend. The benefit of having a centralized business tier is that same business logic can support different types of clients like browser, WAP (Wireless Application Protocol) client, other stand-alone applications written in Java, C++, C# etc.

Integration tier is responsible for communicating with external resources such as databases, legacy systems, ERP systems, messaging systems like MQSeries etc. The components in this tier use JDBC, JMS, J2EE Connector Architecture (JCA) and some proprietary middleware to access the resource tier.

Resource tier is the external resource such as a database, ERP system, Mainframe system etc responsible for storing the data. This tier is also known as Data Tier or EIS (Enterprise Information System) Tier.

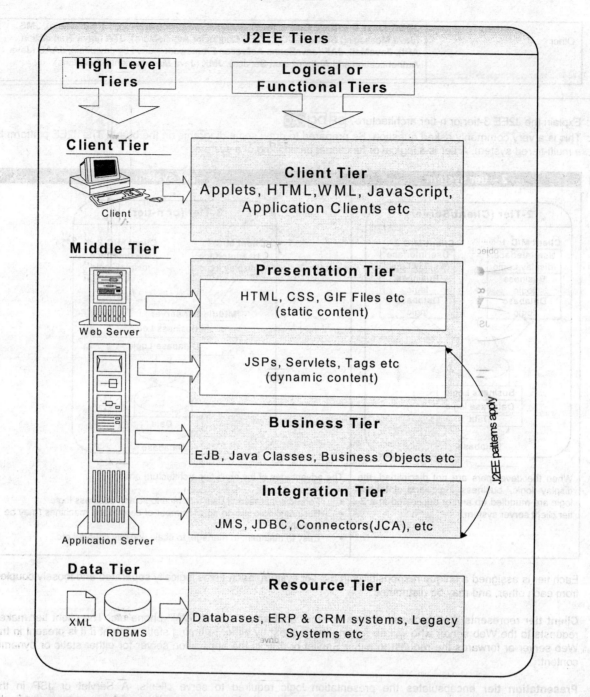

Note: On a high level J2EE can be construed as a **3-tier** system consisting of **Client Tier, Middle Tier** (or Application Tier) and **Data Tier**. But logically or functionally J2EE is a multi-tier (or n-tier) platform.

The advantages of a 3-tiered or n-tiered application: 3-tier or multi-tier architectures force separation among presentation logic, business logic and database logic. Let us look at some of the key benefits:

- **Manageability:** Each tier can be monitored, tuned and upgraded independently and different people can have clearly defined responsibilities.
- **Scalability:** More hardware can be added and allows clustering (i.e. horizontal scaling).
- **Maintainability:** Changes and upgrades can be performed without affecting other components.
- **Availability:** Clustering and load balancing can provide availability.
- **Extensibility:** Additional features can be easily added.

The following diagram gives you a bigger picture of the logical tiers and the components.

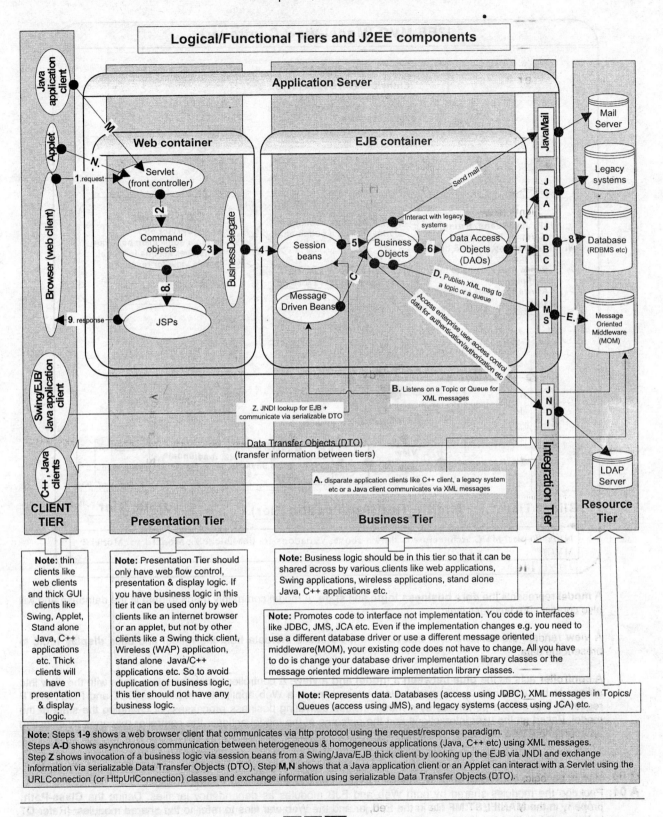

Logical/Functional Tiers and J2EE components

Note: thin clients like web clients and thick GUI clients like Swing, Applet, Stand alone Java, C++ applications etc. Thick clients will have presentation & display logic.

Note: Presentation Tier should only have web flow control, presentation & display logic. If you have business logic in this tier it can be used only by web clients like an internet browser or an applet, but not by other clients like a Swing thick client, Wireless (WAP) application, stand alone Java/C++ applications etc. So to avoid duplication of business logic, this tier should not have any business logic.

Note: Business logic should be in this tier so that it can be shared across by various clients like web applications, Swing applications, wireless applications, stand alone Java, C++ applications etc.

Note: Promotes code to interface not implementation. You code to interfaces like JDBC, JMS, JCA etc. Even if the implementation changes e.g. you need to use a different database driver or use a different message oriented middleware(MOM), your existing code does not have to change. All you have to do is change your database driver implementation library classes or the message oriented middleware implementation library classes.

Note: Represents data. Databases (access using JDBC), XML messages in Topics/Queues (access using JMS), and legacy systems (access using JCA) etc.

Note: Steps **1-9** shows a web browser client that communicates via http protocol using the request/response paradigm.
Steps **A-D** shows asynchronous communication between heterogeneous & homogeneous applications (Java, C++ etc) using XML messages.
Step **Z** shows invocation of a business logic via session beans from a Swing/Java/EJB thick client by looking up the EJB via JNDI and exchange information via serializable Data Transfer Objects (DTO). Step **M,N** shows that a Java application client or an Applet can interact with a Servlet using the URLConnection (or HttpUrlConnection) classes and exchange information using serializable Data Transfer Objects (DTO).

Q 03: Explain MVC architecture relating to J2EE? `DC` `DP` `FAQ`

A 03: This is also a very popular interview question. MVC stands for Model-View-Controller architecture. It divides the functionality of displaying and maintaining of the data to minimize the degree of coupling (i.e. promotes <u>loose coupling</u>) between components. It is often used by applications that need the ability to maintain multiple views like HTML, WML, Swing, XML based Web service etc of the <u>same data</u>. Multiple views and controllers can interface with the same model. Even new types of views and controllers can interface with a model without forcing a change in the model design.

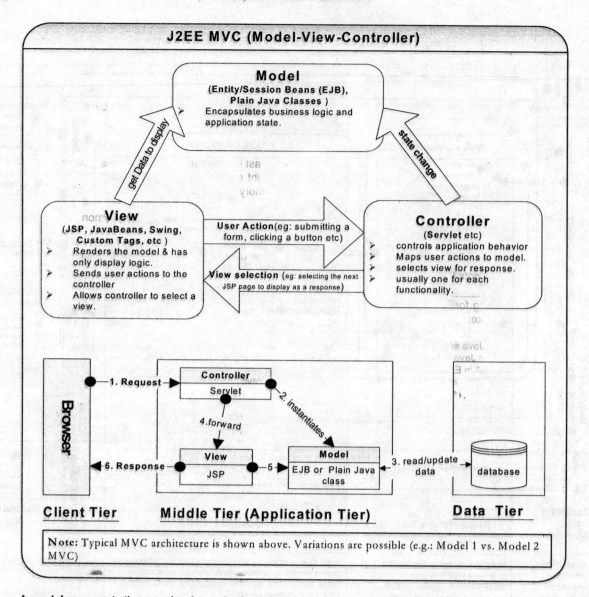

A **model** represents the **core business logic** and **state**. A model commonly maps to data in the database and will also contain core business logic.

A **view** renders the contents of a model. A view accesses the data from the model and adds **display logic** to present the data.

A **controller** acts as the **glue between a model and a view**. A controller translates interactions with the view into actions to be performed by the model. User interactions in a Web application appear as GET and POST HTTP requests. The actions performed by a model include activating business processes or changing the state of the model. Based on the user interactions and the outcome of the model actions, the controller responds by selecting an appropriate view.

Q 04: How to package a module, which is, shared by both the Web and the EJB modules? **SF**

A 04: Package the modules shared by both Web and EJB modules as dependency jar files. Define the **Class-Path:** property in the **MANIFEST.MF** file in the EJB jar and the Web war files to refer to the shared modules. [Refer **Q7** in Enterprise section for diagram: *J2EE deployment structure*].

The **MANIFEST.MF** files in the EJB jar and Web war modules should look like:

```
Manifest-Version: 1.0
Created-By: Apache Ant 1.5
Class-Path: myAppsUtil.jar
```

Q 05: Why use design patterns in a J2EE application? `DP`

A 05:

- **They have been proven.** Patterns reflect the experience and knowledge of developers who have successfully used these patterns in their own work. It lets you leverage the collective experience of the development community.

  `Example` Session facade and value object patterns evolved from performance problems experienced due to multiple network calls to the EJB tier from the Web tier. Fast lane reader and Data Access Object patterns exist for improving database access performance. The flyweight pattern improves application performance through object reuse (which minimizes the overhead such as memory allocation, garbage collection etc).

- **They provide common vocabulary.** Patterns provide software designers with a common vocabulary. Ideas can be conveyed to developers using this common vocabulary and format.

  `Example` Should we use a Data Access Object (DAO)? How about using a Business Delegate? Should we use Value Objects to reduce network overhead? Etc.

> If you are applying for a senior developer or an architect level role, you should at least know the more common design patterns like:
>
> -- Factory - **Q52** in Java section, **Q11** in How would you go about... section.
> -- Singleton - **Q51** in Java section, **Q11** in How would you go about... section.
> -- Proxy - **Q52, Q62** in Enterprise Java section, **Q11** in How would you go about... section.
> -- Command - **Q58** in Java section, **Q27, Q110, Q116** in Enterprise Java section, **Q11** in How would you go about... section.
> -- Template method - **Q110, Q116** in Enterprise Java section, **Q11** in How would you go about... section.
> -- Decorator - **Q24** in Java section, **Q11** in How would you go about... section.
> -- Strategy - **Q64** in Java section, **Q11** in How would you go about... section.
> -- Adapter - **Q110, Q116** in Enterprise Java section, **Q11** in How would you go about... section.
> -- Façade - **Q84** in Enterprise Java section, **Q11, Q12, Q15** (i.e. in **SOA**) in How would you go about... section.
> -- Business delegate – **Q83** in Enterprise Java section.
> -- MVC - **Q63** in Java section, **Q3, Q27** in Enterprise Java sections.
> -- DAO - **Q41** in Enterprise Java section.

Q 06: What is the difference between a Web server and an application server? `SF`

A 06:

Web Server	Application Server
Supports HTTP protocol. When the Web server receives an HTTP request, it responds with an HTTP response, such as sending back an HTML page (static content) or delegates the dynamic response generation to some other program such as CGI scripts or Servlets or JSPs in the application server.	Exposes **business logic** and **dynamic content** to the client through various protocols such as HTTP, TCP/IP, IIOP, JRMP etc.
Uses various scalability and fault-tolerance techniques.	Uses various scalability and fault-tolerance techniques. In addition provides resource pooling, component life cycle management, transaction management, messaging, security etc. Provides services for components like Web container for servlet components and EJB container for EJB components.

Q 07: What are ear, war and jar files? What are J2EE Deployment Descriptors? `SF` `FAQ`

A 07: The ear, war and jar are standard application deployment archive files. Since they are a standard, any application server (at least in theory) will know how to unpack and deploy them.

An EAR file is a standard JAR file with an ".ear" extension, named from **Enterprise AR**chive file. A J2EE application with all of its modules is delivered in EAR file. JAR files can't have other JAR files. But EAR and WAR (Web ARchive) files can have JAR files.

An EAR file contains all the JARs and WARs belonging to an application. JAR files contain the EJB classes and **WAR** files contain the Web components (JSPs, Servlets and static content like HTML, CSS, GIF etc). The J2EE application client's class files are also stored in a JAR file. EARs, JARs, and WARs all contain one or more XML-based deployment descriptor(s).

Deployment Descriptors

A deployment descriptor is an XML based text file with an ".xml" extension that describes a component's deployment settings. A J2EE application and each of its modules has its own deployment descriptor. Pay attention to elements marked in bold in the sample deployment descriptor files shown below.

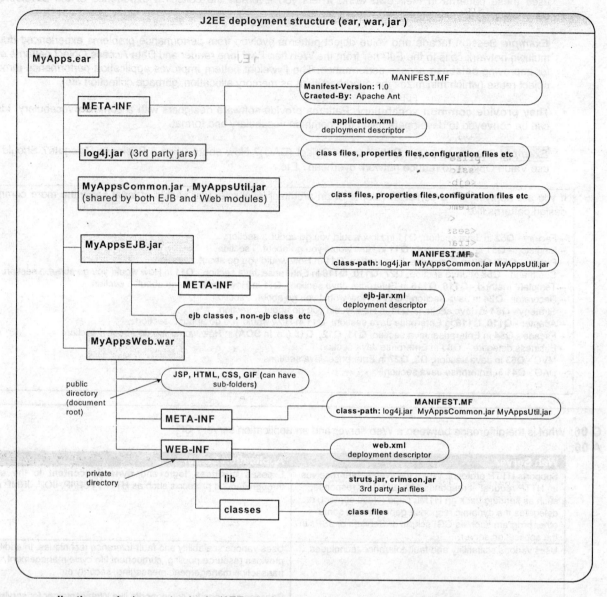

- **application.xml:** is a standard J2EE deployment descriptor, which includes the following structural information: EJB jar modules, Web war modules, <security-role> etc. Also since EJB jar modules are packaged as jars the same way dependency libraries like log4j.jar, MyAppsUtil.jar etc are packaged. The application.xml descriptor will distinguish between these two types of jar files by explicitly specifying the EJB jar modules.

```
<?xml version="1.0" encoding="UTF-8"?>
<!DOCTYPE application PUBLIC "-//Sun Microsystems, Inc.//DTD J2EE Application 1.2//EN"
                        "http://java.sun.com/j2ee/dtds/application_1_2.dtd">
<application id="Application_ID">
    <display-name>MyApps</display-name>
    <module id="EjbModule_1">
       <ejb>MyAppsEJB.jar</ejb>
    </module>

    <module id="WebModule_1">
       <web>
        <web-uri>MyAppsWeb.war</web-uri>
```

```
                <context-root>myAppsWeb</context-root>
            </web>
        </module>

        <security-role id="SecurityRole_1">
            <description>Management position</description>
            <role-name>manager</role-name>
        </security-role>
    </application>
```

- **ejb-jar.xml**: is a standard deployment descriptor for an EJB module.

```xml
<?xml version="1.0" encoding="UTF-8"?>
<!DOCTYPE ejb-jar PUBLIC "-//Sun Microsystems, Inc.//DTD Enterprise JavaBeans 1.1//EN"
                    "http://java.sun.com/j2ee/dtds/ejb-jar_1_1.dtd">
<ejb-jar id="ejb-jar_ID">
    <display-name>MyAppsEJB</display-name>

  <enterprise-beans>
      <session id="ContentService">
        <ejb-name>ContentService</ejb-name>
        <home>ejb.ContentServiceHome</home>
        <remote>ejb.ContentService</remote>
          <ejb-class>ejb.ContentServiceBean</ejb-class>
        <session-type>Stateless</session-type>
        <transaction-type>Bean</transaction-type>
      </session>

      <entity>
            <ejb-name>Bid</ejb-name>
            <home>ejb.BidHome</home>
            <remote>ejb.Bid</remote>
            <ejb-class>ejb.BidBean</ejb-class>
            <persistence-type>Container</persistence-type>
            <prim-key-class>ejb.BidPK</prim-key-class>
            <reentrant>False</reentrant>
            <cmp-field><field-name>bid</field-name></cmp-field>
            <cmp-field><field-name>bidder</field-name></cmp-field>
            <cmp-field><field-name>bidDate</field-name></cmp-field>
            <cmp-field><field-name>id</field-name></cmp-field>
      </entity>
  </enterprise-beans>

  <!-- OPTIONAL -->

  <assembly-descriptor>

      <!-- OPTIONAL, can be many -->
      <security-role>
          <description>
              Employee is allowed to ...
          </description>
          <role-name>employee</role-name>
      </security-role>

      <!-- OPTIONAL.  Can be many -->
      <method-permission>
          <!-- Define role name in "security-role" -->
          <!-- Must be one or more -->
          <role-name>employee</role-name>
          <!-- Must be one or more -->
          <method>
              <ejb-name>ContentService</ejb-name>
              <!-- * = all methods -->
              <method-name>*</method-name>
          </method>

          <method>
              <ejb-name>Bid</ejb-name>
              <method-name>findByPrimaryKey</method-name>
          </method>
      </method-permission>
      <!-- OPTIONAL, can be many.  How the container is to manage -->
      <!-- transactions when calling an EJB's business methods -->
```

```
        <container-transaction>
            <!-- Can specify many methods at once here -->
            <method>
                <ejb-name>Bid</ejb-name>
                <method-name>*</method-name>
            </method>
            <!-- NotSupported|Supports|Required|RequiresNew|Mandatory|Never -->
            <trans-attribute>Required</trans-attribute>
        </container-transaction>
    </assembly-descriptor>

</ejb-jar>
```

- **web.xml**: is a standard deployment descriptor for a Web module.

```
<?xml version="1.0" encoding="UTF-8"?>
<!DOCTYPE web-app PUBLIC "-//Sun Microsystems, Inc.//DTD Web Application 2.2//EN"
                         "http://java.sun.com/j2ee/dtds/web-app_2_2.dtd">
<web-app>
    <display-name>myWebApplication</display-name>
    <context-param>
        <param-name>GlobalContext.ClassName</param-name>
        <param-value>web.GlobalContext</param-value>
    </context-param>

    <servlet>
        <servlet-name>MyWebController</servlet-name>
        <servlet-class>web.MyWebController</servlet-class>
        <init-param>
          <param-name>config</param-name>
          <param-value>/WEB-INF/config/myConfig.xml</param-value>
        </init-param>
        <load-on-startup>1</load-on-startup>
    </servlet>

    <servlet-mapping>
        <servlet-name>MyWebController</servlet-name>
        <url-pattern>/execute/*</url-pattern>
    </servlet-mapping>

    <error-page>
        <error-code>400</error-code>
        <location>/WEB-INF/jsp/errors/myError.jsp</location>
    </error-page>

    <taglib>
        <taglib-uri>/WEB-INF/struts-bean.tld</taglib-uri>
        <taglib-location>/WEB-INF/lib/taglib/struts/struts-bean.tld</taglib-location>
    </taglib>

    <security-constraint>
        <web-resource-collection>
            <web-resource-name>Employer</web-resource-name>
            <description></description>
            <url-pattern>/execute/employ</url-pattern>
            <http-method>POST</http-method>
            <http-method>GET</http-method>
            <http-method>PUT</http-method>
        </web-resource-collection>
        <auth-constraint>
            <description></description>
            <role-name>advisor</role-name>
        </auth-constraint>
    </security-constraint>

    <login-config>
        <auth-method>FORM</auth-method>
        <realm-name>FBA</realm-name>
        <form-login-config>
          <form-login-page>/execute/MyLogon</form-login-page>
          <form-error-page>/execute/MyError</form-error-page>
        </form-login-config>
    </login-config>
```

```
<security-role>
    <description>Advisor</description>
    <role-name>advisor</role-name>
</security-role>

</web-app>
```

Q 08: Explain J2EE class loaders? SF

A 08: J2EE application server sample class loader hierarchy is shown below. (Also refer to **Q5** in Java section). As per the diagram the J2EE application specific class loaders are children of the "*System –classpath*" class loader. When the parent class loader is above the "*System –classpath*" class loader in the hierarchy as shown in the diagram (i.e. bootstrap class loader or extensions class loader) then child class loaders implicitly have visibility to the classes loaded by its parents. When a parent class loader is <u>below</u> a "*System -classpath*" class loader in the hierarchy then the <u>child class loaders will only have visibility into the classes loaded by its parents</u> **only if they are explicitly specified in a manifest file** (MANIFEST.MF) of the child class loader.

Example As per the diagram, if the EJB module *MyAppsEJB.jar* wants to refer to *MyAppsCommon.jar* and *MyAppsUtil.jar* we need to add the following entry in the MyAppsEJB.jar's manifest file MANIFEST.MF.

class-path: `MyAppsCommon.jar MyAppsUtil.jar`

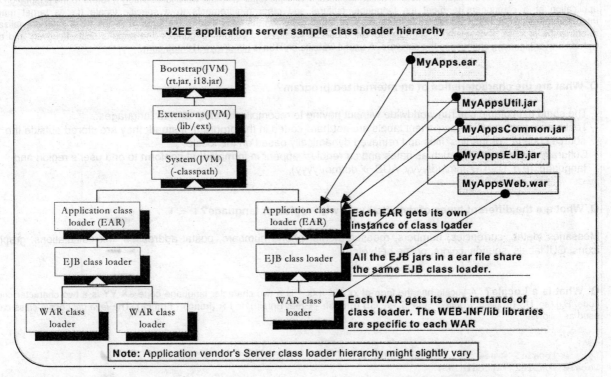

This is because the application (EAR) class loader loads the *MyAppsCommon.jar* and *MyAppsUtil*.jar. The EJB class loader loads the *MyAppsEJB.jar*, which is the child class loader of the application class loader. The WAR class loader loads the MyAppsWeb.war.

Every J2EE application or EAR gets its own instance of the application class loader. This class loader is also responsible for loading all the dependency jar files, which are shared by both Web and EJB modules. For example third party libraries like log4j, utility (e.g. MyAppsUtility.jar) and common (e.g. MyAppsCommon.jar) jars etc. Any application specific exception like *MyApplicationException* thrown by an EJB module should be caught by a Web module. So the exception class *MyApplicationException* is shared by both Web and EJB modules.

The key difference between the EJB and WAR class loader is that all the EJB jars in the application **share the same EJB class loader** whereas WAR files <u>get their own class loader</u>. This is because the EJBs have inherent relationship between one another (i.e. EJB-EJB communication between EJBs in different applications but hosted on the same JVM) but the Web modules do not. Every WAR file should be able to have its own WEB-INF/lib third party libraries and need to be able to load its own version of converted logon.jsp servlet. So each Web module is isolated in its own class loader.

So if two different Web modules want to use two different versions of the same EJB then we need to have two different ear files. As was discussed in the **Q5** in Java section the class loaders use a **delegation model** where the child class loaders delegate the loading up the hierarchy to their parent before trying to load it itself only if the parent can't load it. But with regards to WAR class loaders, some application servers provide a setting to turn this behavior off (DelegationMode=false). This delegation mode is recommended in the Servlet 2.3 specification.

> As a general rule **classes should not be deployed higher in the hierarchy than they are supposed to exist**. This is because if you move one class up the hierarchy then you will have to move other classes up the hierarchy as well. This is because classes loaded by the parent class loader can't see the classes loaded by its child class loaders (**uni-directional bottom-up visibility**).

Tech Tip #4:

Q. What do the terms internationalization(i18n) and localization(l10n) mean, and how are they related? Localization (aka **l10n**, where 10 is the number of letters between the letter 'l' and the letter 'n' in the word localization) refers to the adaptation of an application or a component to meet the language, cultural and other requirements to a specific locale (i.e. a target market). Internationalization (aka i18n, where 18 is the number of letters between the letter 'i' and the letter 'n' in the word internationalization) refers to the process of designing a software so that it can be localized to various languages and regions cost-effectively and easily without any engineering changes to the software. A useful website on i18n is http://www.i18nfaq.com.

Q. What are the characteristics of an internalized program?

-- The same executable can run worldwide without having to recompile for other or new languages.
-- Text messages and GUI component labels are not hard-coded in the program. Instead they are stored outside the source code in ".properties" files and retrieved dynamically based on the locale.
-- Culturally dependent data such as dates and currencies, appear in formats that conform to end user's region and language. (e.g. USA → mm/dd/yyyy, AUS → dd/mm/yyyy).

Q. What are the different types of data that vary with region or language?

Messages, dates, currencies, numbers, measurements, phone numbers, postal addresses, tax calculations, graphics, icons, GUI labels, sounds, colors, online help etc.

Q. What is a Locale? A Locale has the form of xx_YY (**xx** – is a two character language code **&& YY** is a two character country code. E.g. en_US (English – United States), en_GB (English - Great Britain), fr_FR (french - France). The *java.util.Locale* class can be used as follows:

```
Locale locale1 = new Locale("en", "US");
Locale locale2 = Locale.US;
Locale locale3 = new Locale("en");
Locale locale4 = new Locale("en", "US", "optional"); // to allow the possibility of more than one
                                                     // locale per language/country combination.

locale2.getDefault().toString();          //  en_US
locale2.getLanguage();                     //  "en"
locale2.getCountry();                      //  "US"
```

Resource bundles can be created using the locale to externalize the locale-specific messages:

Message_en_US.properties
```
   Greetings = Hello
```

Message_fr_FR.properties
```
   Greetings = Bonjour
```

These resource bundles reside in classpath and gets read at runtime based on the locale.

```
Locale currentLoc = new Locale("fr", "FR");
ResourceBundle messages = ResourceBundle.getBundle("Message", currentLoc);
System.out.println(messages.getString("Greetings"));  //prints Bonjour
```

Note: When paired with a locale, the closest matching file will be selected. If no match is found then the default file will be the Message.properties. In J2EE, locale is stored in HTTP session and resource bundles (stored as *.properties files under WEB-INF/classes directory) are loaded from the web.xml deployment descriptor file. Locale specific messages can be accessed via tags (e.g. Struts, JSTL etc).

The *java.text* package consists of classes and interfaces that are useful for writing internationalized programs. By default they use the default locale, but this can be overridden. E.g. *NumbeFormat*, *DateFormat*, *DecimalFormat*, *SimpleDateFormat*, *MessageFormat*, *ChoiceFormat*, *Collator* (compare strings according to the customary sorting order for a locale) etc.

DateFormat:
```
Date now = new Date();
Locale locale = Locale.US;

String s = DateFormat.getDateInstance(DateFormat.SHORT, locale).format(now);
```

NumberFormat:
```
NumberFormat usFormat = NumberFormat.getInstance(Locale.US);
String s1 = usFormat.format(1785.85);   // s1 →  1,785.85

NumberFormat germanyFormat = NumberFormat.getInstance(Locale.GERMANY);
String s2 = germanyFormat.format(1785.85);   // s2 → 1.785,85
```

To use default locale:
```
NumberFormat.getInstance();
NumberFormat.getPercentInstance();
NumberFormat.getCurrencyInstance();
```

To use specific locale:
```
NumberFormat.getInstance(Locale.US);
NumberFormat.getCurrencyInstance(myLocale);
```

Enterprise - Servlet

Desktop applications (e.g. Swing) are **presentation-centric**, which means when you click a menu item you know which window would be displayed and how it would look. Web applications are **resource-centric** as opposed to being presentation-centric. Web applications should be thought of as follows: A browser should request from a server a resource (not a page) and depending on the availability of that resource and the model state, server would generate different presentation like a regular "read-only" web page or a form with input controls, or a "page-not-found" message for the requested resource. So **think in terms of resources, not pages**.

Servlets and JSPs are **server-side** **presentation-tier** components managed by the web container within an application server. Web applications make use of http protocol, which is a **stateless** request-response based paradigm.

Q 09: What is the difference between CGI and Servlet? SF
A 09:

Traditional CGI (Common Gateway Interface)	Java Servlet
Traditional CGI creates a heavy weight process to handle each http request. N number of copies of the same traditional CGI programs is copied into memory to serve N number of requests.	Spawns a lightweight Java thread to handle each http request. Single copy of a type of servlet but N number of threads (thread sizes can be configured in an application server).

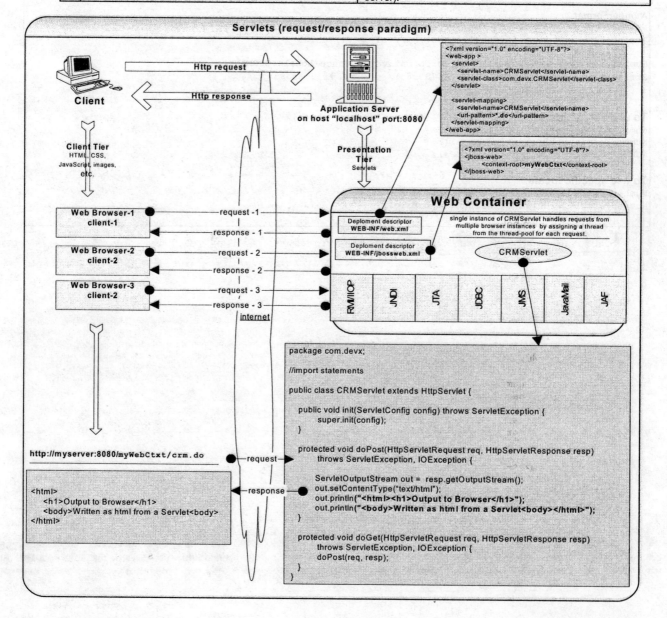

A Servlet is a Java class that **runs within a web container** in an application server, **servicing multiple client requests concurrently** forwarded through the server and the web container. The web browser establishes a socket connection to the host server in the URL , and sends the HTTP request. Servlets can forward requests to other servers and servlets and can also be used to balance load among several servers.

Q. Which protocol is used to communicate between a browser and a servlet? A browser and a servlet communicate using the **HTTP** protocol (a stateless request/response based protocol).

Q. What are the two objects a servlet receives when it accepts a call from its client? A "**ServletRequest**", which encapsulates client request from the client and the "**ServletResponse**", which encapsulates the communication from the servlet back to the client.

In addition to both HTTP request and response, HTTP headers are informational additions that convey both essential and non-essential information. For example: HTTP headers are used to convey MIME (**M**ultipurpose **I**nternet **M**ail **E**xtension) type of an HTTP request and also to set and retrieve cookies etc.

```
Content-Type: text/html
Set-Cookie:AV+USERKEY=AVSe5678f6c1tgfd;expires=Monday, 4-Jul-2006 12:00:00; path=/;domain=.lulu.com;

response.setContentType("text/html");
response.addCookie(myCookie);
```

Q. How would you get the browser to request for an updated page in 10 seconds from the server?

```
response.setHeader("Refresh", 10);
```

Refresh does not stipulate continual updates. It just specifies in how many seconds the next update should take place. So, you have to continue to supply "Refresh" in all subsequent responses. The "Refresh" header is very useful because it lets the servlet display a partial list of items or an introductory image to be displayed while the complete results or real page is displayed later (say in 10 seconds). You can also specify another page to be reloaded as follows:

```
respose.setHeader("Refresh", "10;URL=http://localhost:8080/myCtxt/crm.do");
```

The above setting can be directly set in the <HEAD> section of the HTML page as shown below as opposed to setting it in the servlet. This is useful for static HTML pages.

```
<META-HTTP-EQUIV="Refresh" CONTENT="5; URL=http://localhost:8080/myCtxt/crm.do" />
```

Q. What can you do in your Servlet/JSP code to tell browser not to cache the pages? Another useful header is the Cache-Control as shown below:

```
response.setHeader("Cache-Control","no-cache"); //document should never be cached. HTTP 1.1
response.setHeader("Pragma", "no-cache"); //HTTP 1.0
response.setDateHeader("Expires", 0);
```

Q. What is the difference between request parameters and request attributes?

Request parameters	Request attributes

Parameters are form data that are sent in the request from the HTML page. These parameters are generally form fields in an HTML form like:
 	
`<input type="text" name="param1" />`
`<input type="text" name="param2" />`
 	
`Form data can be attached to the end of the`
`URL as shown below for GET requests`
 	
`http://MyServer:8080/MyServlet?`
`param1=Peter&param2=Smith`
 	
`or sent to the sever in the request body for`
`POST requests. Sensitive form data should be`
`sent as a POST request.`
	Once a servlet gets a request, it can add additional attributes, then forward the request off to other servlets or JSPs for processing. Servlets and JSPs can communicate with each other by setting and getting attributes.
	
	`request.setAttribute("calc-value", new Float(7.0));`
	`request.getAttribute("calc-value");`

You can get them but cannot set them.
 	
`request.getParameter("param1");`
`request.getParameterNames();`
	You can both set the attribute and get the attribute. You can also get and set the attributes in session and application scopes.

Q. What are the different scopes or places where a servlet can save data for its processing? Data saved in a **request-scope** goes out of scope once a response has been sent back to the client (i.e. when the request is completed).

```
//save and get request-scoped value
request.setAttribute("calc-value", new Float(7.0));
request.getAttribute("calc-value");
```

Data saved in a **session-scope** is available across multiple requests. Data saved in the session is destroyed when the session is destroyed (not when a request completes but spans several requests).

```
//save and get session-scoped value
HttpSession  session = request.getSession(false);
If(session != null) {
    session.setAttribute("id", "DX12345");
    value = session.getAttribute("id");
}
```

Data saved in a **ServletContext** scope is shared by all servlets and JSPs in the context. The data stored in the servlet context is destroyed when the servlet context is destroyed.

```
//save and get an application-scoped value
getServletContext().setAttribute("application-value", "shopping-app");
value = getServletContext().getAttribute("application-value");
```

Q. Which code line should be set in a response object before using the PrintWriter or the OutputStream? You need to set the content type using the setContentType(…) method.

```
//to return an html
response.setContentType("text/html");
PrintWriter out = response.getWriter();
out.println("…….");

//to return an image
response.setContentType("image/gif");
```

How does a Servlet differ from an Applet?

Applet	Servlet
Applets execute on a browser.	Servlets execute within a web container in an Application Server.
Applets have a graphical user interface.	Servlets do not have a graphical user interface.

Q 10: HTTP is a stateless protocol, so, how do you maintain state? How do you store user data between requests? `SF` `PI` `BP` `FAQ`

A 10: This is a commonly asked interview question. The "http protocol" is a stateless request/response based protocol. You can retain the state information between different page requests as follows:

HTTP Sessions are the recommended approach. A session identifies the requests that originate from the same browser during the period of conversation. All the servlets can share the same session. The JSESSIONID is generated by the server and can be passed to client through cookies, URL re-writing (if cookies are turned off) or built-in SSL mechanism. Care should be taken to **minimize size of objects stored in session** and **objects stored in session should be serializable.** In a Java servlet the session can be obtained as follows: `CO`

```
HttpSession session = request.getSession(true); //returns a current session or a new session

//To put/get a value in/from the session
Name name = new Name("Peter");
session.setAttribute("Firstname", name); //session.putValue(…) is deprecated as of 2.2

session.getAttribute("Firstname");//get a value. session.getValue(…) is deprecated

//If a session is no longer required e.g. user has logged out, etc then it can be invalidated.
session.invalidate();

//you can also set the session inactivity lease period on a per session basis
session.setMaxInactiveInterval(300);//resets inactivity period for this session as 5 minutes
```

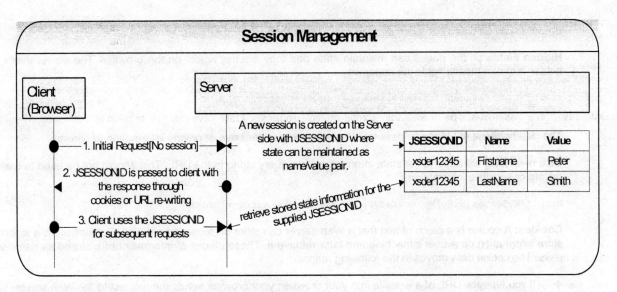

Q. Session tracking uses cookies by default. What would you do if the cookies are turned off?

If cookies are turned off, you can still enable session tracking using URL rewriting. This involves including the session ID within the link as the name/value pair as shown below.

```
http://localhost:8080/myWebCtxt/purchase.do;jsessionid=4FB61319542B5D310B243E4BDD6DC64B
```

Adding session ID to each and every link is cumbersome and hence is simplified by the following methods: **response.encodeURL**(givenURL) to associate a session ID with a given URL and if you are using redirection then **response.encodeRedirectURL**(givenURL).

```
//set a value in the session
public class CRMServlet extends HttpServlet {

    protected void doGet(HttpServletRequest req, HttpServletResponse resp) throws
                                                      ServletException, IOException {
        req.getSession().setAttribute("key", "ItemNo-1245");
        String url = resp.encodeURL("/myWebCtxt/purchase.do");

        PrintWriter pw = resp.getWriter();
        pw.println("<html>Sample encoded URL --><a href='" + url + "'>purchase</a></html>");
    }
}
```

```
//retrieve the previously set value from the session
public class PurchaseServlet extends HttpServlet {
    protected void doGet(HttpServletRequest req, HttpServletResponse resp) throws
                                                      ServletException, IOException {
        String value = (String)req.getSession().getAttribute("key");

        PrintWriter pw = resp.getWriter();
        pw.println("<html>Item to purchase is --> " + value +"</html>");
    }
}
```

When you invoke the method **encodeURL**(givenURL) with the cookies turned on, then session ID is not appended to the URL. Now turn the cookies off and restart the browser. If you invoke the encodeURL(givenURL) with the cookies turned off, the session ID is automatically added to the URL as follows:

```
http://localhost:8080/myWebCtxt/purchase.do;jsessionid=4FB61319542B5D310B243E4BDD6DC64B
```

Q. What is the difference between using getSession(<u>true</u>) and getSession(<u>false</u>) methods?

getSession(<u>true</u>): This method will check whether there is already a session exists for the user. If a session exists, it returns that session object. <u>If a session does not already exist then it creates a new session for the user.</u>

getSession(<u>false</u>): This method will check whether there is already a session exists for the user. If a session exists, it returns that session object. <u>If a session does not already exist then it returns null.</u>

Sessions can be timed out (configured in web.xml) or manually invalidated.

Hidden Fields on the pages can maintain state and they are not visible on the browser. The server treats both hidden and non-hidden fields the same way.

```
<INPUT type="hidden" name="Firstname" value="Peter">
<INPUT type="hidden" name="Lastname" value="Smith">
```

The disadvantage of hidden fields is that they may expose sensitive or private information to others.

URL re-writing will append the state information as a query string to the URL. This should not be used to maintain private or sensitive information.

```
Http://MyServer:8080/MyServlet?Firstname=Peter&Lastname=Smith
```

Cookies: A cookie is a piece of text that a Web server can store on a user's hard disk. Cookies allow a website to store information on a user's machine and later retrieve it. These pieces of information are stored as name-value pairs. The cookie data moves in the following manner:

❖ If you type the URL of a website into your browser, your browser sends the request to the Web server. When the browser does this it looks on your machine for a cookie file that URL has set. If it finds it, your browser will send all of the name-value pairs along with the URL. If it does not find a cookie file, it sends no cookie data.

❖ The URL's Web server receives the cookie data and requests for a page. If name-value pairs are received, the server can use them. If no name-value pairs are received, the server can create a new ID and then sends name-value pairs to your machine in the header for the Web page it sends. Your machine stores the name value pairs on your hard disk.

Cookies can be used to determine how many visitors visit your site. It can also determine how many are new versus repeated visitors. The way it does this is by using a database. The first time a visitor arrives; the site creates a new ID in the database and sends the ID as a cookie. The next time the same user comes back, the site can increment a counter associated with that ID in the database and know how many times that visitor returns. The sites can also store user preferences so that site can look different for each visitor.

Q. How can you set a cookie and delete a cookie from within a Servlet?

```
//to add a cookie
Cookie myCookie = new Cookie("aName", "aValue");
response.addCookie(myCookie);

//to delete a cookie
myCookie.setValue("aName", null);
myCookie.setMax(0);
myCookie.setPath("/");
response.addCookie(myCookie);
```

Q. Which mechanism to choose?

State mechanism	Description
HttpSession	• There is <u>no limit</u> on the size of the session data kept. • The performance is good. • This is the preferred way of maintaining state. If we use the HTTP session with the application server's persistence mechanism (server converts the session object into BLOB type and stores it in the Database) then the performance will be moderate to poor. Note: When using HttpSession mechanism you need to take care of the following points: • Remove session explicitly when you no longer require it. • Set the session timeout value. • Your application server may serialize session objects after crossing a certain memory limit. This is expensive and affects performance. So decide carefully what you want to store in a session.
Hidden fields	• There is <u>no limit</u> on size of the session data. • May expose sensitive or private information to others (So not good for sensitive information). • The performance is moderate.
URL rewriting	• There is a limit on the size of the session data.

	▪ Should not be used for sensitive or private information. ▪ The performance is moderate.
Cookies	▪ There is a limit for cookie size. ▪ The browser may turn off cookies. ▪ The performance is moderate. The benefit of the cookies is that state information can be stored regardless of which server the client talks to and even if all servers go down. Also, if required, state information can be retained across sessions.

Q 11: Explain the life cycle methods of a servlet? **SF** **FAQ**

A 11: The Web container is responsible for managing the servlet's life cycle. The Web container creates an instance of the servlet and then the container calls the init() method. At the completion of the init() method the servlet is in ready state to service requests from clients. The container calls the servlet's service() method for handling each request by spawning a new thread for each request from the Web container's thread pool [It is also possible to have a single threaded Servlet, refer **Q16** in Enterprise section]. Before destroying the instance the container will call the destroy() method. After destroy() the servlet becomes the potential candidate for garbage collection.

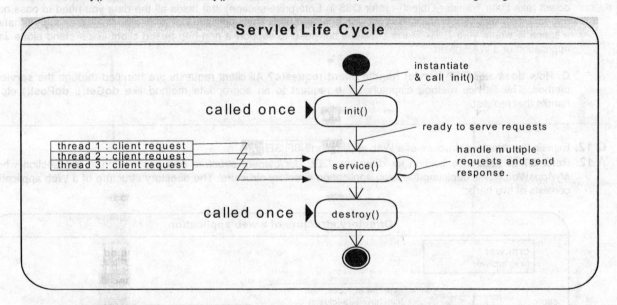

Q. What would be an effective use of the Servlet init() method? One effective use of the Servlet init() method is the creation and caching of thread-safe resource acquisition mechanisms such, as JDBC DataSources, EJB Homes, and Web Services SOAP Mapping Registry.

Q. How would you call a method in the EJB from a servlet?

```
…
MyBeanHome home = null;
…
public void init (ServletConfig config) throws ServletException {
    //1. JNDI lookup is hard coded for illustration purpose but should use a declarative
    //approach involving web.xml file and server specific deployment descriptor files because
    //if the server location changes, hardcoding may require reasonable amount of changes &
    //testing. Lookup for JBoss server is shown below:
    Properties jndiProps = new Properties();
    jndiProps.setProperty(Context.INITIAL_CONTEXT_FACTORY,
                                        "org.jnp.interfaces.NamingContextFactory");
    jndiProps.setProperty(Context.URL_PKG_PREFIXES,"org.jboss.naming:org.jnp.interfaces");
    jndiProps.setProperty(Context.PROVIDER_URL, "jnp://localhost:1099");
    Context ctx = new InitialContext(jndiProps);

    //2. lookup home(or localHome) interface. Shown for illustration. Should prefer using the
    //Service Locator pattern. Refer Q87 in Enterprise section.
    Object ref = ctx.lookup("ejb/MyBean");
    home = (MyBeanHome)PortableRemoteObject.narrow(ref, MyBeanHome.class);

}
```

```
public void doGet(HttpServletRequest req, HttpServletResponse res)throws ServletException,
                                                                    IOException
{
    ...
    //3. create a remote or a local interface
    MyBean bean = home.create();
    •//4. Now you can call business method on remote interface
    bean.invokeBusinessMethod(…);
}
```

Q. Is it possible to share an HttpSession between a Servlet/JSP and EJB? You can pass an HttpSession as a parameter to an EJB method only if all objects in session are <u>serializable</u>. This is because they are "passed-by-value" and if any values in the HttpSession are altered inside the EJB then it won't be reflected back to the HttpSession in the Servlet.

Even though it is possible to pass an HttpSession object, it is a bad practice in terms of design because you are unnecessarily coupling your presentation tier (i.e. Servlet/JSP) object with your business-tier (i.e. EJB) objects. So rather than passing the whole, large HttpSession create a class (i.e. Plain Old Java Object) that acts as a value object (aka Data Transfer Object – refer **Q85** in Enterprise section) that holds all the data you need to pass back and forth between your presentation tier and business tier. This approach would also be flexible enough to handle a scenario where your EJBs in the business tier need to support a <u>non-http based client</u> like a stand alone Java application or a WAP client.

Q. How does an HTTP Servlet handle client requests? All client requests are handled through the **service**() method. The service method dispatches the request to an appropriate method like **doGet**(), **doPost**() etc to handle that request.

Q 12: Explain the directory structure of a Web application? `SF` `SE` `FAQ`

A 12: Refer **Q7** in Enterprise section for diagram: *J2EE deployment structure* and explanation in this section where *MyAppsWeb.war* is depicting the Web application directory structure. The directory structure of a Web application consists of two parts:

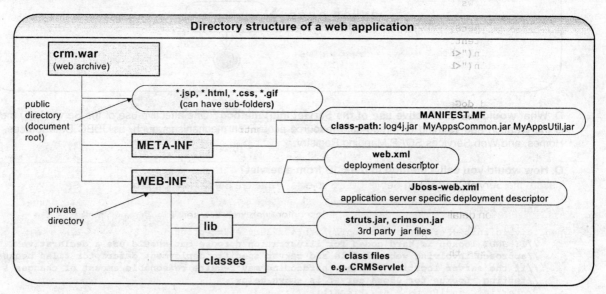

- A **public** resource directory (**document root**): The document root is where JSP pages, client-side classes and archives, and static Web resources are stored.

- A **private** directory called WEB-INF: which contains following files and directories:

  - **web.xml**: Web application deployment descriptor.
  - application server specific deployment descriptor e.g. jboss-web.xml etc.
  - ***.tld**: Tag library descriptor files.
  - **classes**: A directory that contains server side classes like servlets, utility classes, JavaBeans etc.
  - **lib**: A directory where JAR (archive files of tag libraries, utility libraries used by the server side classes) files are stored.

Note: JSP resources usually reside directly or under subdirectories of the **document root,** which **are directly accessible** to the user through the URL. If you want to protect your Web resources then hiding the JSP files behind the WEB-INF directory can protect the JSP files from direct access. Refer **Q35** in Enterprise section.

Q 13: What is the difference between doGet () and doPost () or GET and POST? **SF** **SE** **FAQ**

A 13: Prefer using doPost() because it is secured and it can send much more information to the server..

GET or doGet()	POST or doPost()
The request parameters are transmitted as a query string appended to the request. All the parameters get appended to the URL in the address bar. Allows browser bookmarks but not appropriate for transmitting private or sensitive information. http://MyServer/MyServlet?name=paul This is a security risk. In an HTML you can specify as follows: <form name="SSS" method="**GET**" >	The request parameters are passed with the body of the request. More secured. In HTML you can specify as follows: <form name="SSS" method="**POST**" >
GET was originally intended for static resource retrieval.	POST was intended for form submits where the state of the model and database are expected to change.
GET is not appropriate when large amounts of input data are being transferred. Limited to 1024 characters.	Since it sends information through a socket back to the server and it won't show up in the URL address bar, it can send much more information to the server. Unlike doGet(), it is not restricted to sending only textual data. It can also send binary data such as serialized Java objects.

Q. If you want a servlet to take the same action for both GET and POST request, what would you do? You should have doGet call doPost, or vice versa.

```
protected void doPost(HttpServletRequest req, HttpServletResponse resp)
          throws ServletException, IOException

    ServletOutputStream out =  resp.getOutputStream();
    out.setContentType("text/html");
    out.println("<html><h1>Output to Browser</h1>");
    out.println("<body>Written as html from a Servlet<body></html>");
}


protected void doGet(HttpServletRequest req, HttpServletResponse resp)
          throws ServletException, IOException
    doPost(req, resp); //call doPost() for flow control logic.
}
```

Q 14: What are the ServletContext and ServletConfig objects? What are Servlet environment objects? **SF**

A 14: The Servlet Engine uses both interfaces. The servlet engine implements the ServletConfig interface in order to pass configuration details from the deployment descriptor (web.xml) to a servlet via its init() method.

```
public class CRMServlet extends HttpServlet {
    //initializes the servlet
    public void init(ServletConfig config)throws ServletException {
        super.init(config);
    }
        ...
}
```

ServletConfig	ServletContext
The ServletConfig parameters are for **a particular Servlet**. The parameters are specified in the web.xml (i.e. deployment descriptor). It is created after a servlet is instantiated and it is used to pass initialization information to the servlet.	The ServletContext parameters are specified for the **entire Web application**. The parameters are specified in the web.xml (i.e. deployment descriptor). Servlet context is common to all Servlets. So all Servlets share information through ServletContext.

Example:

```
String strCfgPath = getServletConfig().getInitParameter("config");
String strServletName = getServletConfig().getServletName();

String strClassName = getServletContext().getAttribute("GlobalClassName");
```

Q. How can you invoke a JSP error page from a controller servlet? The following code demonstrates how an exception from a servlet can be passed to an error JSP page.

```
protected void doGet(HttpServletRequest req, HttpServletResponse resp) throws
                                                ServletException, IOException {
   try {
      //doSomething
   }
   catch(Exception ex) {
      req.setAttribute("javax.servlet.ex",ex);//store the exception as a request attribute.
      ServletConfig sConfig = getServletConfig();
      ServletContext sContext = sConfig.getServletContext();
      sContext.getRequestDispatcher("/jsp/ErrorPage.jsp").forward(req, resp);// forward the
      //request with the exception stored as an attribute to the "ErrorPage.jsp".
      ex.printStackTrace();
   }
}
```

Q. What are servlet lifecycle events? Servlet lifecycle events work like the Swing events. Any listener interested in observing the ServletContext lifecycle can implement the ServletContextListener interface and in the ServletContext attribute lifecycle can implement the ServletContextAttributesListener interface. The session listener model is similar to the ServletContext listener model (Refer Servlet spec 2.3 or later). ServletContext's and Session's listener objects are notified when servlet contexts and sessions are initialized and destroyed, as well as when attributes are added or removed from a context or session. **For example:** You can declare a listener in the web.xml deployment descriptor as follows:

```
<listener>
      <listener-class>com.MyJDBCConnectionManager </listener-class>
</listener>
```

You can create the listener class as shown below:

```
public class MyJDBCConnectionManager implements ServletContextListener {

   public void contextInitialized(ServletContextEvent event) {
      Connection con = // create a connection
      event.getServletContext().setAttribute("con", con);
   }

   public void contextDestroyed(ServletContextEvent e) {
      Connection con = (Connection) e.getServletContext().getAttribute("con");
      try { con.close(); } catch (SQLException ignored) { } // close connection
   }
}
```

The server creates an instance of the listener class to receive events and uses introspection to determine what listener interface (or interfaces) the class implements.

Q 15: What is the difference between HttpServlet and GenericServlet? SF
A 15: Both these classes are abstract but:

GenericServlet	HttpServlet
A GenericServlet has a service() method to handle requests.	The HttpServlet extends GenericServlet and adds support for HTTP protocol based methods like doGet(), doPost(), doHead() etc. All client requests are handled through the **service**() method. The service method dispatches the request to an appropriate method like **doGet**(), **doPost**() etc to handle that request. HttpServlet also has methods like doHead(), doPut(), doOptions(), doDelete(), and doTrace().
Protocol independent. GenericServlet is for servlets that might not use HTTP (for example FTP service).	Protocol dependent (i.e. HTTP).

Q 16: How do you make a Servlet thread safe? What do you need to be concerned about with storing data in Servlet instance fields? CI PI BP FAQ

A 16: As shown in the figure *Servlet Life Cycle* in **Q11** in Enterprise section, a typical (or default) Servlet life cycle creates a single instance of each servlet and creates multiple threads to handle the service() method. **The multi-threading aids efficiency but the servlet code must be coded in a thread safe manner.** The shared resources (e.g. instance variables, utility or helper objects etc) should be appropriately synchronized or should only use variables in a read-only manner. There are situations where synchronizing will not give you the expected results as shown in the diagram below and to achieve the expected results you should store your values in a user session or store them as a hidden field values. Having large chunks of code in synchronized blocks in your service or doPost() methods can adversely affect performance and makes the code more complex.

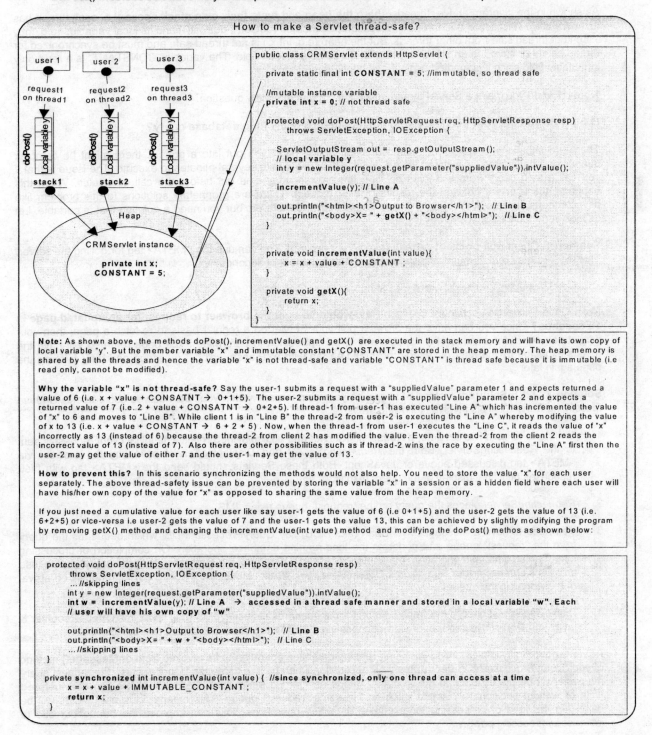

How to make a Servlet thread-safe?

```
public class CRMServlet extends HttpServlet {

    private static final int CONSTANT = 5; //immutable, so thread safe

    //mutable instance variable
    private int x = 0; // not thread safe

    protected void doPost(HttpServletRequest req, HttpServletResponse resp)
            throws ServletException, IOException {

        ServletOutputStream out = resp.getOutputStream();
        // local variable y
        int y = new Integer(request.getParameter("suppliedValue")).intValue();

        incrementValue(y); // Line A

        out.println("<html><h1>Output to Browser</h1>");  // Line B
        out.println("<body>X= " + getX() + "<body></html>");  // Line C
    }


    private void incrementValue(int value){
        x = x + value + CONSTANT ;
    }

    private void getX(){
        return x;
    }
}
```

Note: As shown above, the methods doPost(), incrementValue() and getX() are executed in the stack memory and will have its own copy of local variable "y". But the member variable "x" and immutable constant "CONSTANT" are stored in the heap memory. The heap memory is shared by all the threads and hence the variable "x" is not thread-safe and variable "CONSTANT" is thread safe because it is immutable (i.e read only, cannot be modified).

Why the variable "x" is not thread-safe? Say the user-1 submits a request with a "suppliedValue" parameter 1 and expects returned a value of 6 (i.e. x + value + CONSATNT → 0+1+5). The user-2 submits a request with a "suppliedValue" parameter 2 and expects a returned value of 7 (i.e. 2 + value + CONSATNT → 0+2+5). If thread-1 from user-1 has executed "Line A" which has incremented the value of "x" to 6 and moves to "Line B". While client 1 is in "Line B" the thread-2 from user-2 is executing the "Line A" whereby modifying the value of x to 13 (i.e. x + value + CONSTANT → 6 + 2 + 5) . Now, when the thread-1 from user-1 executes the "Line C", it reads the value of "x" incorrectly as 13 (instead of 6) because the thread-2 from client 2 has modified the value. Even the thread-2 from the client 2 reads the incorrect value of 13 (instead of 7). Also there are other possibilities such as if thread-2 wins the race by executing the "Line A" first then the user-2 may get the value of either 7 and the user-1 may get the value of 13.

How to prevent this? In this scenario synchronizing the methods would not also help. You need to store the value "x" for each user separately. The above thread-safety issue can be prevented by storing the variable "x" in a session or as a hidden field where each user will have his/her own copy of the value for "x" as opposed to sharing the same value from the heap memory.

If you just need a cumulative value for each user like say user-1 gets the value of 6 (i.e 0+1+5) and the user-2 gets the value of 13 (i.e. 6+2+5) or vice-versa i.e user-2 gets the value of 7 and the user-1 gets the value 13, this can be achieved by slightly modifying the program by removing getX() method and changing the incrementValue(int value) method and modifying the doPost() methos as shown below:

```
protected void doPost(HttpServletRequest req, HttpServletResponse resp)
        throws ServletException, IOException {
    ... //skipping lines
    int y = new Integer(request.getParameter("suppliedValue")).intValue();
    int w = incrementValue(y); // Line A  →  accessed in a thread safe manner and stored in a local variable "w". Each
    // user will have his own copy of "w"

    out.println("<html><h1>Output to Browser</h1>");  // Line B
    out.println("<body>X= " + w + "<body></html>");  // Line C
    ... //skipping lines
}

private synchronized int incrementValue(int value) { //since synchronized, only one thread can access at a time
    x = x + value + IMMUTABLE_CONSTANT ;
    return x;
}
```

Alternatively it is possible to have a **single threaded model of a servlet** by implementing the marker or null interface javax.servlet.SingleThreadedModel. The container will use one of the following approaches to ensure thread safety:

- **Instance pooling** where container maintains a pool of servlets.
- **Sequential processing** where new requests will wait while the current request is being processed.

Best practice: It is best practice to use multi-threading and stay away from the **single threaded model of the servlet** unless otherwise there is a compelling reason for it. Shared resources can be synchronized, used in read-only manner, or shared values can be stored in a session, as hidden fields or in database table. The single threaded model can adversely affect performance and hence has been deprecated in the servlet specification 2.4.

As shown in the diagram above, threads **share the heap** and **have their own stack space** (i.e. each thread has its own stack). This is how one thread's invocation of a method (doGet(), doPost()) and its local variables (e.g. int y) are kept thread safe from other threads. But the heap (e.g. int x) is not thread-safe and must be synchronized for thread safety or stored in an HTTP session or stored as a hidden field. The variable "CONSTANT" is a read only immutable field since it is marked as final and hence thread-safe.

Note: How do you make a Servlet thread safe? is a popular interview question.

Q. How do you get your servlet to stop timing out on a really long database query?

There are situations despite how much database tuning effort you put into a project, there might be complex queries or a batch process initiated via a Servlet, which might take several minutes to execute. The issue is that if you call a long query from a Servlet or JSP, the browser may time out before the call completes. When this happens, the user will not see the results of their request. There are proprietary solutions to this problem like asynchronous servlets in WebLogic, Async Beans in WebSphere etc but you need a solution that is portable. Let us look at portable solutions to this issue.

Solution 1: Client-pull or client-refresh (aka server polling): You can use the <META> tag for polling the server. This tag tells the client it must refresh the page after a number of seconds.

```
<META http-equiv="Refresh" content="10; url="newPage.html" />
```

Refer **Q9** in Enterprise section for question **How would you get the browser to request for an updated page in 10 seconds?** Once you can have the browser poll your Servlet on a regular basis to re-fetch a page, then your servlet can check for a value of a variable say in a HttpSession to determine if the page returned will have the results expected by the user or resend the <META> tag with a "Please wait ..." message and retry fetching the page again later.

Solution 2: J2EE Solution: Instead of spawning your own threads within your Servlet, you could use JMS (Java Messaging Service). This involves following steps:

1. You need to have two servlets, a *RequestingServlet* and a *DisplayingServlet*. The initial client request is sent to the RequestingServlet. Both the *RequestingServlet* and *DisplayingServlet* polled by the browser via <META> tag discussed above or JavaScript. Both these Servlets should send the <META> tag with their responses until final display of the query results.

2. *RequestingServlet* places the query on the "request" queue using JMS.

3. You need to have a MessageDrivenBean (aka MDB) say *QueryProcessorMDB*, which dequeues the query from the "request" queue and performs the long-running database operation. On completion of processing long-running database operation, the *QueryProcessorMDB* returns the query results to the "reply" queue (use javax.jms.**QueueSender** & javax.jms.**ObjectMessage**). **Note:** MDBs are invoked asynchronously on arrival of messages in the queue.

4. *DisplayingServlet* checks the "reply" queue for the query results using JMS (use javax.jms.**QueueReceiver** & javax.jms.**ObjectMessage**) every few seconds via <META> tag described above or a JavaScript.

Advantages: Firstly implementing your long-running database operation to be invoked from **onMessage()** method of your *QueryProcessorMDB* **decouples** your application whereby if a database failure occurs, the request query message will be placed back in the "request" queue and retried again later. Secondly MDBs can be **clustered** (with or without additional JVMs) to listen on the same "request" queue. This means cluster of MDBs will be balancing the load of processing long running database operations. This can improve the throughput due to increased processing power.

Q 17: What is pre-initialization of a Servlet? LF

A 17: By default the container does not initialize the servlets as soon as it starts up. It initializes a servlet when it receives a request for the first time for that servlet. This is called **lazy loading**. The servlet deployment descriptor (web.xml) defines the <load-on-startup> element, which can be configured to make the servlet container load and initialize the servlet as soon as it starts up. The process of loading a servlet before any request comes in is called **pre-loading** or **pre-initializing** a servlet. We can also specify the order in which the servlets are initialized.

```
<load-on-startup>2</load-on-startup>
```

Q 18: What is a RequestDispatcher? What object do you use to forward a request? LF CO

A 18: A Servlet can obtain its **RequestDispatcher** object from its *ServletContext*.

```
//…inside the doGet() method
ServletContext sc = getServletContext();
RequestDispatcher rd = sc.getRequestDispatcher("/nextServlet");//relative path of the resource

//forwards the control to another servlet or JSP to generate response.  This method allows one
//servlet to do preliminary processing of a request and another resource to generate the
//response.

rd.forward(request,response);

// or includes the content of the resource such as Servlet, JSP, HTML, Images etc into the
// calling Servlet's response.

rd.include(request, response);
```

What is the difference between the getRequestDispatcher(String path) method of "ServletRequest" interface and ServletContext interface?

javax.servlet.ServletRequest getRequestDispatcher(String path)	javax.servlet.ServletContext getRequestDispatcher(String path)
Accepts path parameter of the servlet or JSP to be included or forwarded <u>relative to the request of the calling servlet</u>. If the path begins with a "<u>/</u>" then it is interpreted as relative to current context root.	Does not accept relative paths and all path must start with a "<u>/</u>" and are interpreted as relative to current context root.

Q 19: What is the difference between forwarding a request and redirecting a request? LF DC FAQ

A 19: Both methods send you to a new resource like Servlet, JSP etc.

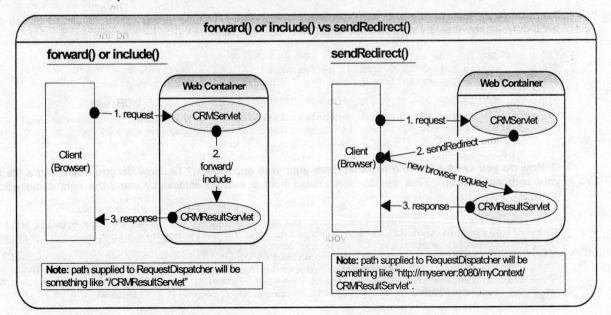

redirecting - sendRedirect()	Forward
Sends a header back to the browser, which contains the name of the resource to be redirected to. The browser will make a **fresh request from this header information**. Need to provide <u>absolute URL path</u>.	Forward action takes place within the server **without the knowledge of the browser.** Accepts relative path to the servlet or context root.
Has an overhead of extra remote trip but has the advantage of being able to refer to any resource on the same or different domain and also allows book marking of the page.	No extra network trip.

Q 20: What are the considerations for servlet clustering? `DC` `SI`

A 20: The clustering promotes high availability and scalability. The considerations for servlet clustering are:

- **Objects stored in a session should be serializable** to support in-memory replication of sessions. Also consider the overhead of serializing very large objects. Test the performance to make sure it is acceptable.
- **Design for idempotence**. Failure of a request or impatient users clicking again can result in duplicate requests being submitted. So the Servlets should be able to tolerate duplicate requests.
- **Avoid using instance and static variables in read and write mode** because different instances may exist on different JVMs. Any state should be held in an external resource such as a database.
- **Avoid storing values in a ServletContext**. A ServletContext is not serializable and also the different instances may exist in different JVMs.
- **Avoid using java.io.* because the files may not exist on all backend machines**. Instead use getResourceAsStream().

Q. How to perform I/O operations in a Servlet/JSP?

Problem: Since web applications are deployed as WAR files on the application server's web container, the full path and relative paths to these files vary for each server.

Solution -1: You can configure the file paths in web.xml using <init-param> tags and retrieve file paths in your Servlets/JSPs. But this technique requires changes to the web.xml deployment descriptor file, to point to the correct path.

Solution -2: You can overcome these configuration issues by using the features of ***java.lang.ClassLoader*** and ***javax.servlet.ServletContext*** classes. There are various ways of reading a file using the **ServletContext** API methods such as getResource(String resource),getResourceAsStream(String resource), getResourcePaths(String path) and getRealPath(String path). The getRealPath(String path) method translates virtual URL into real path refer **Q26** in Enterprise section.

```
//Get the file "products.xml" under the WEB-INF folder of  your application as inputstream
InputStream is = config.getServletContext().getResourceAsStream("/products.xml");
```

Alternatively you can use the APIs from ***ClassLoader*** as follows. The file "products.xml" should be placed under ***WEB-INF/classes*** directory where all web application classes reside.

```
//Get the URL for the file and create a stream explicitly
URL url = config.getServletContext().getResource("/products.xml");
BufferedReader br = new BufferedReader(new InputStreamReader(url.openStream));
                         OR
//use the context class loader
URL url  = Thread.currentThread().getContextClassLoader().getResource("products-out.xml");
BufferedWriter bw = new BufferedWriter(new FileWriter(url.getFile()));
```

Q. How do you send a file to a browser from your web application? I.e. how do you download a file from your web application? Files can be downloaded from a web application by using the right combination of headers.

```
//set the header to a non-standard value for attachments to be saved by the browser with the
//Save-As dialog so that it is unrecognized by the browsers because often browsers try to do
//something special when they recognize the content-type.
response.setContentType("application/x-download");
//use Content-Disposition "attachment" to invoke "Save As" dialog and "inline" for displaying
//the file content on the browser without invoking the "Save As" dialog.
response.setHeader("Content-disposition", "attachment;filename=" + fileName);
```

Q. How do you send a file from a browser to your web application? i.e. How do you upload a file to your web application?

There are better and more secured ways to upload your files instead of using using web. For example FTP, secure FTP etc. But if you need to do it via your web application then your default encoding and GET methods are not suitable for file upload and a form containing file input fields must specify the encoding type **"multipart/form-data"** and the **POST** method in the <form ..> tag as shown below:

```
<form enctype="multipart/form-data" method="POST" action="/MyServlet">
    <input type="file" name="products" />
    <input type="submit" name="Upload" value="upload" />
</form>
```

When the user clicks the "Upload" button, the client browser locates the local file and sends it to the server using HTTP POST. When it reaches your server, your implementing servlet should process the POST data in order to extract the encoded file. Unfortunately, application servers implementing the Servlet and JSP specifications are not required to handle the multipart/form-data encoding. Fortunately there are number of libraries available such as Apache Commons File Upload, which is a small Java package that lets you obtain the content of the uploaded file from the encoded form data. The API of this package is flexible enough to keep small files in memory while large files are stored on disk in a "temp" directory. You can specify a size threshold to determine when to keep in memory and when to write to disk.

Q 21: If an object is stored in a session and subsequently you change the state of the object, will this state change replicated to all the other distributed sessions in the cluster? DC SI

A 21: **No.** Session replication is the term that is used when your current service state is being replicated across multiple application instances. Session replication occurs when we replicate the information (i.e. **session attributes**) that are stored in your HttpSession. The container propagates the changes only when you call the **setAttribute(......)** method. So mutating the objects in a session and then by-passing the setAttribute(...........) will not replicate the state change. CO

Example If you have an ArrayList in the session representing shopping cart objects and if you just call **getAttribute(...)** to retrieve the ArrayList and then add or change something without calling the **setAttribute(...)** then the container may not know that you have added or changed something in the ArrayList. So the session will not be replicated.

Q 22: What is a filter, and how does it work? LF DP FAQ

A 22: A filter dynamically intercepts requests and responses to transform or use the information contained in the requests or responses but typically do not themselves create responses. Filters can also be used to transform the response from the Servlet or JSP before sending it back to client. Filters improve reusability by placing recurring tasks in the filter as a reusable unit.

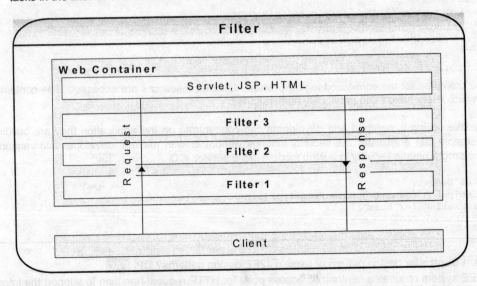

A good way to think of Servlet filters is as a chain of steps that a request and response must go through before reaching a Servlet, JSP, or static resource such as an HTML page in a Web application.

The filters can be used for caching and compressing content, logging and auditing, image conversions (scaling up or down etc), authenticating incoming requests, XSL transformation of XML content, localization of the request and the response, site hit count etc. The filters are configured through the web.xml file as follows:

```
<web-app>
   <filter>
       <filter-name>HitCounterFilter</filter-name>
       <filter-class>myPkg.HitCounterFilter</filter-class>
   </filter>

   <filter-mapping>
       <filter-name>HitCounterFilter</filter-name>
       <url-pattern>/usersection/*</url-pattern>
   </filter-mapping>
   ...
</web-app>
```

The *HitCounterFilter* will intercept the requests from the URL pattern */usersection* followed by any resource name.

Design Pattern: Servlet filters use the slightly modified version of the **chain of responsibility** design pattern. Unlike the classic (only one object in the chain handle the request) chain of responsibility where filters allow multiple objects (filters) in a chain to handle the request. If you want to modify the request or the response in the chain you can use the **decorator pattern** (Refer **Q11** in How would you go about… section).

Q 23: Explain declarative security for Web applications? **SE**

A 23: Servlet containers implement declarative security. The administration is done through the deployment descriptor web.xml file. With **declarative security** the Servlets and JSP pages will be free from any security aware code. You can protect your URLs through web.xml as shown below:

```
web-app>
  <security-constraint>
    <web-resource-collection>
        <web-resource-name>PrivateAndSensitive</web-resource-name>
        <url-pattern>/private/*</url-pattern>
    </web-resource-collection>
    <auth-constraint>
      <role-name>executive</role-name>
      <role-name>admin</role-name>
    </auth-constraint>
  </security-constraint>

  <!-- form based authorization -->
  <login-config>
     <auth-method>FORM</auth-method>
     <form-login-config>
         <form-login-page>/login.jsp</form-login-page>
         <form-error-page>/error.jsp</form-error-page>
     </form-login-config>
  </login-config>
</web-app>
```

The user will be prompted for the configured login.jsp when restricted resources are accessed. The container also keeps track of which users have been previously authenticated.

Benefits: Very little coding is required and developers can concentrate on the application they are building and system administrators can administer the security settings without or with minimal developer intervention. Let's look at a sample programmatic security in a Web module like a servlet: **CO**

```
User user = new User();
Principal principal = request.getUserPrincipal();
if (request.isUserInRole("boss"))
    user.setRole(user.BOSS_ROLE);
```

Q 24: Explain the **Front Controller** design pattern or explain J2EE design patterns? **DP** **FAQ**

A 24: **Problem**: A J2EE system requires a centralized access point for HTTP request handling to support the integration of system services like security, data validation etc, content retrieval, view management, and dispatching. When the user accesses the view directly without going through a centralized mechanism, two problems may occur:

- Each view is required to provide its own system services often resulting in **duplicate code**.
- View navigation is left to the views. This may result in shared code for view content and view navigation.
- Distributed control is **more difficult to maintain**, since changes will often need to be made in numerous places.

Solution: Generally you write specific servlets for specific request handling. These servlets are responsible for data validation, error handling, invoking business services and finally forwarding the request to a specific JSP view to display the results to the user.

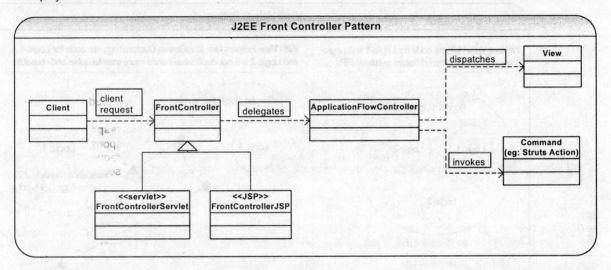

The **Front Controller** suggests that we **only have one Servlet** (instead of having specific Servlet for each specific request) centralizing the handling of all the requests and delegating the functions like validation, invoking business services etc to a command or a helper component. For example Struts framework uses the command design pattern to delegate the business services to an action class.

Benefits

- Avoid duplicating the control logic like security check, flow control etc.
- Apply the common logic, which is shared by multiple requests in the Front controller.
- Separate the system processing logic from the view processing logic.
- Provides a controlled and centralized access point for your system.

Q 25: Briefly discuss the following patterns Composite view, View helper, Dispatcher view and Service to worker? Or explain J2EE design patterns? **DP** **FAQ**

A 25:

- **Composite View:** Creates an aggregate view from atomic sub-views. The Composite view entirely focuses on the view. The view is typically a JSP page, which has the HTML, JSP Tags etc. The JSP display pages mostly have a side bar, header, footer and main content area. These are the sub-views of the view. The sub-views can be either static or dynamic. The best practice is to have these sub-views as separate JSP pages and include them in the whole view. This will enable **reuse of JSP sub-views and improves maintainability** by having to change them at one place only.

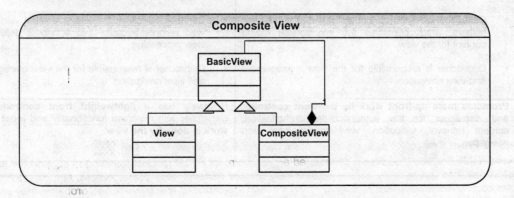

- **View Helper:** When processing logic is embedded inside the controller or view it causes code duplication in all the pages. This causes maintenance problems, as any change to piece of logic has to be done in all the views. In the view helper pattern the view delegates its processing responsibilities to its helper classes. The helper classes **JavaBeans:** used to compute and store the presentation data and **Custom Tags:** used for computation of logic and displaying them iteratively complement each other.

  Benefits Avoids embedding programming logic in the views and facilitates division of labor between Java developers and Web page designers.

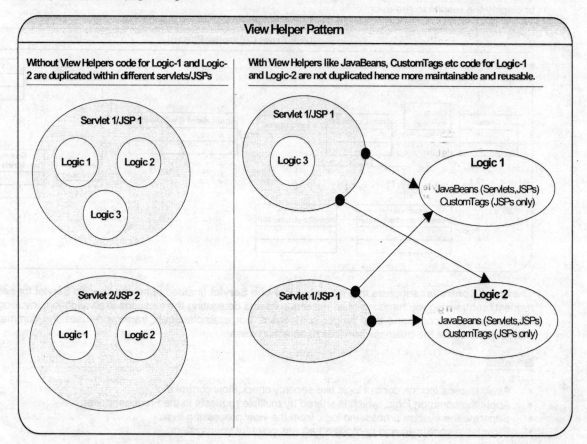

- **Service to Worker** and **Dispatcher View:** These two patterns are a combination of Front Controller and View Helper patterns with a *dispatcher* component. One of the responsibilities of a Front Controller is choosing a view and dispatching the request to an appropriate view. This behavior can be partitioned into a separate component known as a *dispatcher*. But these two patterns differ in the way they suggest different division of responsibility among the components.

Service to Worker	Dispatcher View
Combines the front controller (Refer **Q24** in Enterprise section) and dispatcher, with views and view helpers (refer **Q25** in Enterprise section) to handle client requests and dynamically prepares the response.	This pattern is structurally similar to the service to worker but the emphasis is on a different usage pattern. This combines the Front controller and the dispatcher with the view helpers but
• Controllers delegate the content retrieval to the view helpers, which populates the intermediate model content for the view.	• Controller **does not** delegate content retrieval to view helpers because this activity is deferred to view processing.
• Dispatcher is responsible for the view management and view navigation.	• Dispatcher is responsible for the view management and view navigation
Promotes more up-front work by the front controller and dispatcher for the authentication, authorization, content retrieval, validation, view management and navigation.	Relatively has a **lightweight front controller** and dispatcher with minimum functionality **and most of the work is done by the view**.

Q 26: Explain Servlet URL mapping? SF
Q 26: The "URL" denotes a <u>virtual path</u> and "File" denotes a <u>real path</u> of the resource.

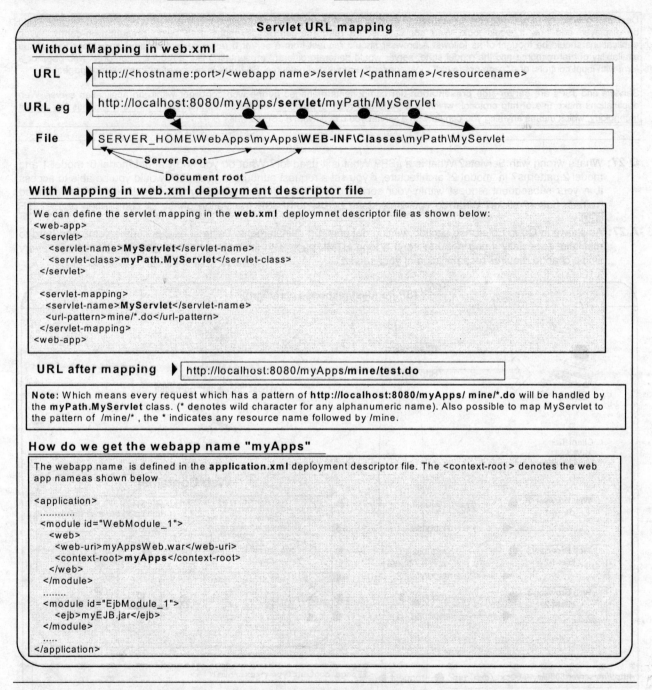

Servlet URL mapping

Without Mapping in web.xml

URL ▶ http://<hostname:port>/<webapp name>/servlet /<pathname>/<resourcename>

URL eg ▶ http://localhost:8080/myApps/**servlet**/myPath/MyServlet

File ▶ SERVER_HOME\WebApps\myApps**WEB-INF\Classes**\myPath\MyServlet

Server Root
Document root

With Mapping in web.xml deployment descriptor file

We can define the servlet mapping in the **web.xml** deploymnet descriptor file as shown below:
```
<web-app>
 <servlet>
   <servlet-name>MyServlet</servlet-name>
   <servlet-class>myPath.MyServlet</servlet-class>
 </servlet>

 <servlet-mapping>
   <servlet-name>MyServlet</servlet-name>
   <url-pattern>mine/*.do</url-pattern>
 </servlet-mapping>
<web-app>
```

URL after mapping ▶ http://localhost:8080/myApps/**mine/test.do**

Note: Which means every request which has a pattern of **http://localhost:8080/myApps/ mine/*.do** will be handled by the **myPath.MyServlet** class. (* denotes wild character for any alphanumeric name). Also possible to map MyServlet to the pattern of /mine/* , the * indicates any resource name followed by /mine.

How do we get the webapp name "myApps"

The webapp name is defined in the **application.xml** deployment descriptor file. The <context-root > denotes the web app nameas shown below
```
<application>
 ............
 <module id="WebModule_1">
   <web>
    <web-uri>myAppsWeb.war</web-uri>
    <context-root>myApps</context-root>
   </web>
 </module>
 ........
 <module id="EjbModule_1">
    <ejb>myEJB.jar</ejb>
 </module>
 .....
</application>
```

In the Model 2 MVC architecture, servlets process requests and select **JSP**s (discussed in next section) for views. So servlets act as controllers. Servlets intercept the incoming HTTP requests from the client (browser) and then dispatch the request to the business logic model (e.g. EJB, POJO - Plain Old Java Object, JavaBeans etc). Then select the next JSP view for display and deliver the view as HTML to client as the presentation (response). It is the best practice to use Web tier UI frameworks like Struts, Spring MVC, JavaServer Faces (JSF), Tapestry etc, which uses proven and tested design patterns for medium to large scale applications. Before you learn these frameworks, you should understand the web fundamentals relating to servlets, JSPs, HTTP request/response paradigm, state management, deployment structure, web container/application server services etc.

Enterprise - JSP

Desktop applications (e.g. Swing) are **presentation-centric**, which means when you click a menu item you know which window would be displayed and how it would look. Web applications are **resource-centric** as opposed to being **presentation-centric**. Web applications should be thought of as follows: A browser should request from a server a resource (not a page) and depending on the availability of that resource and the model state, server would generate different presentation like a regular "read-only" web page or a form with input controls, or a "page-not-found" message for the requested resource. So **think in terms of resources, not pages**.

Servlets and JSPs are <u>**server-side**</u> **presentation-tier** components managed by the web container within an application server. Web applications make use of http protocol, which is a <u>**stateless**</u> request-response based paradigm. <u>JSP technology extends the servlet technology</u>, which means anything you can do with a servlet you can do with a JSP as well.

Q 27: What's wrong with Servlets? What is a JSP? What is it used for? What do you know about model 0, model 1 and model 2 patterns? In "model 2" architecture, if you set a request attribute in your JSP, would you be able to access it in your subsequent request within your servlet code? How do you prevent multiple submits due to repeated "refresh button" clicks? What do you understand by the term JSP translation phase or compilation phase? **SF FAQ**

A 27: As shown in **Q9** in Enterprise section, writing out.println (...) statements using servlet is cumbersome and hard to maintain, especially if you need to send a long HTML page with little dynamic code content. Worse still, every single change requires recompilation of your servlet.

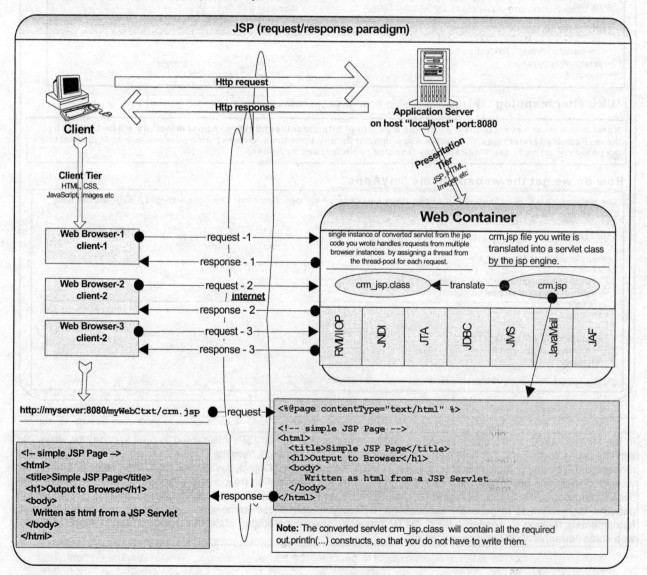

Q. Did JSPs make servlets obsolete? No. JSPs did not make Servlets obsolete. Both Servlets and JSPs are complementary technologies. You can look at the JSP technology from an HTML designer's perspective as an extension to HTML with embedded dynamic content and from a Java developer's as an extension of the Java Servlet technology. JSP is commonly used as the **presentation** layer for combining HTML and Java code. While Java Servlet technology is capable of generating HTML with **out.println**("<html>..... </html>") statements, where "*out*" is a *PrintWriter*. This **process of embedding HTML code with escape characters is cumbersome and hard to maintain**. The JSP technology solves this by providing a level of abstraction so that the developer can use custom tags and action elements, which can speed up Web development and are easier to maintain.

Q. What is a model 0 pattern (i.e. model-less pattern) and why is it not recommended? What is a model-2 or MVC architecture?

Problem: The example shown above is based on a "**model 0**" (i.e. embedding business logic within JSP) pattern. The model 0 pattern is fine for a very basic JSP page as shown above. But real web applications would have business logic, data access logic etc, which would make the above code hard to read, difficult to maintain, difficult to refactor, and untestable. It is also not recommended to embed business logic and data access logic in a JSP page since it is <u>protocol dependent</u> (i.e. HTTP protocol) and makes it unable to be reused elsewhere like a wireless application using a WAP protocol, a standalone XML based messaging application etc.

Solution: You can refactor the processing code containing business logic and data access logic into **Java classes, which adhered to certain standards**. This approach provides better testability, reuse and reduced the size of the JSP pages. This is known as the "**model 1**" pattern where JSPs retain the responsibility of a controller, and view renderer with display logic but delegates the business processing to java classes known as Java Beans. The Java Beans are Java classes, which adhere to following items:

- Implement java.io.Serializable or java.io.Externalizable interface.
- Provide a no-arguments constructor.
- Private properties must have corresponding getXXX/setXXX methods.

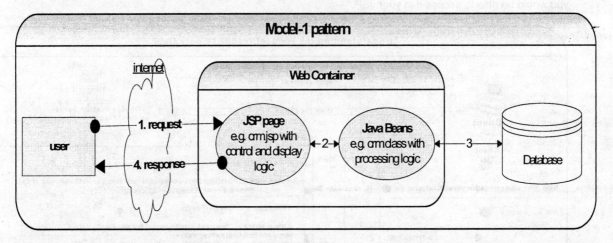

The above model provides a great improvement from the model 0 or model-less pattern, but there are still some problems and limitations.

Problem: In the model 1 architecture the JSP page is alone responsible for processing the incoming request and replying back to the user. This architecture may be suitable for simple applications, but complex applications will end up with significant amount of Java code embedded within your JSP page, especially when there is significant amount of data processing to be performed. This is a problem not only for java developers due to design ugliness but also a problem for web designers when you have large amount of Java code in your JSP pages. In many cases, the page receiving the request is not the page, which renders the response as an HTML output because decisions need to be made based on the submitted data to determine the most appropriate page to be displayed. This would require your pages to be redirected (i.e. sendRedirect (...)) or forwarded to each other resulting in a **messy flow of control** and <u>design ugliness</u> for the application. So, why should you use a JSP page as a controller, which is mainly <u>designed to be used as a template</u>?

Solution: You can use the **Model 2** architecture (**MVC – Model, View, Controller architecture**), which is a hybrid approach for serving dynamic content, since it combines the use of both Servlets and JSPs. It takes advantage of the predominant strengths of both technologies where a Servlet is the target for submitting a request and performing flow-control tasks and using JSPs to generate the presentation layer. As shown in the diagram below, the servlet acts as the controller and is responsible for request processing and the creation of any beans or objects used by the JSP as well as deciding, which JSP page to forward or redirect the request to (i.e. flow control) depending on the data submitted by the user. The JSP page is responsible for retrieving any objects or beans that may have been previously created by the servlet, and as a template for rendering the view as a response to be sent to the user as an HTML.

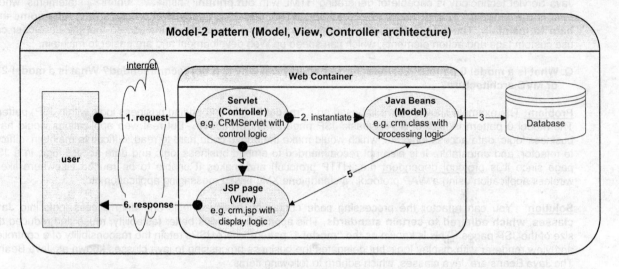

Q. If you set a request attribute in your JSP, would you be able to access it in your subsequent request within your servlet code? [This question can be asked to determine if you understand the request/response paradigm]

The answer is no because your request goes out of scope, but if you set a request attribute in your servlet then you would be able to access it in your JSP.

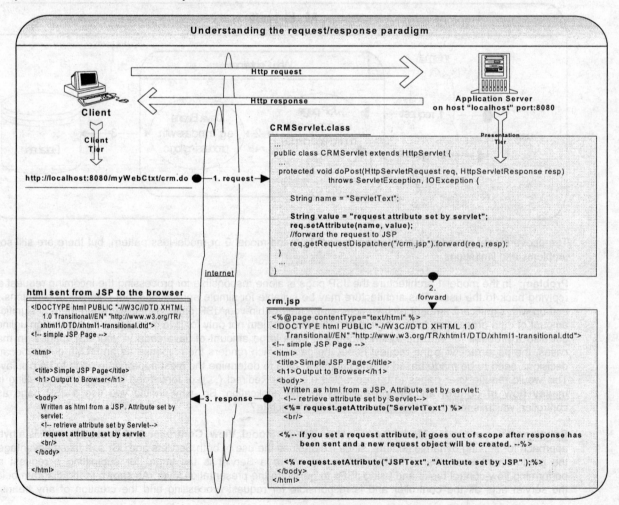

Important: Servlets and JSPs are server side technologies and it is essential to understand the HTTP request/response paradigm. A common misconception is that the Java code embedded in the HTML page is transmitted to the browser with the HTML and executed in the browser. As shown in the diagram above, this is not true. A JSP is a server side component where the page is translated into a Java servlet and executed on the server. The generated servlet (from the JSP) outputs only HTML code to the browser.

As shown above in the diagram, if you set a request attribute in your servlet code, it can be retrieved in your JSP code, since it is still in scope. Once the response has been sent back to the user (i.e. the browser) the current request goes out of scope. When the user makes another request, a new request is created and the request attribute set by the JSP code in your previous request is not available to the new request object. If you set a session attribute in your JSP, then it will be available in your subsequent request because it is still in scope. You can access it by calling **session.getAttribute("JSPText")**.

Q. How to get a pop-up window when clicking on a button?

By using Java Script in your HTML code. The following Java Script is executed in the client side within your web browser.

```
<SCRIPT type="text/javascript">
<!--
function displayWarningMessage() {

    var answer = confirm("This process may take a while, please click 'OK' to continue.");
    if (!answer){
       return false;
    }
    else{
       return disableSendBtton();
    }
}
// --></SCRIPT>
```

Q. What is client-side vs. server-side validation?

client-side validation (client-tier)	server-side validation (presentation-tier)
Java Script is used for client-side validation. Validation takes place in client-side within your browser. Java Script can be used to submit your form data after successful validation.	Form data is submitted to the server and validation is carried out in the server.
No extra network trip is required when there are validation errors because form does not have to be submitted.	Extra network round trip is required when there are validation errors because validation errors need to be reported back to the client and the form data has to be resubmitted.

Q. How do you prevent multiple submits due to repeated "refresh button" clicks?

Problem: Very often a user is completely unaware that a browser resends information to the server when a "refresh button" in Microsoft Internet Explorer or a "reload button" in Netscape/Mozilla is clicked. Even if a browser warns user, a user cannot often understand the technical meaning of the warning. This action can cause form data to be resubmitted, possibly with unexpected results such as duplicate/multiple purchases of a same item, attempting to delete the previously deleted item from the database resulting in a *SQLException* being thrown. **Non-idempotent** methods are methods that cause the state to change. But some operations like reading a list of products or customer details etc are safe because they do not alter the state of the model and the database. These methods are known as **idempotent** methods.

Solution-1: You can use a **Post/Redirect/Get** (aka **PRG**) pattern. This pattern involves the following steps:

Step-1: First a user filled form is submitted to the server (i.e. a Servlet) using a "POST" (also a "GET" method). Servlet performs a business operation by updating the state in the database and the business model.

Step-2: Servlet replies with redirect response (i.e. sendRedirect() operation as opposed to the forward() operation) for a view page.

Step-3: Browser loads a view using a "GET" where no user data is sent. This is usually a separate JSP page, which is safe from "multiple submits". For e.g. reading data from a database, a confirmation page etc.

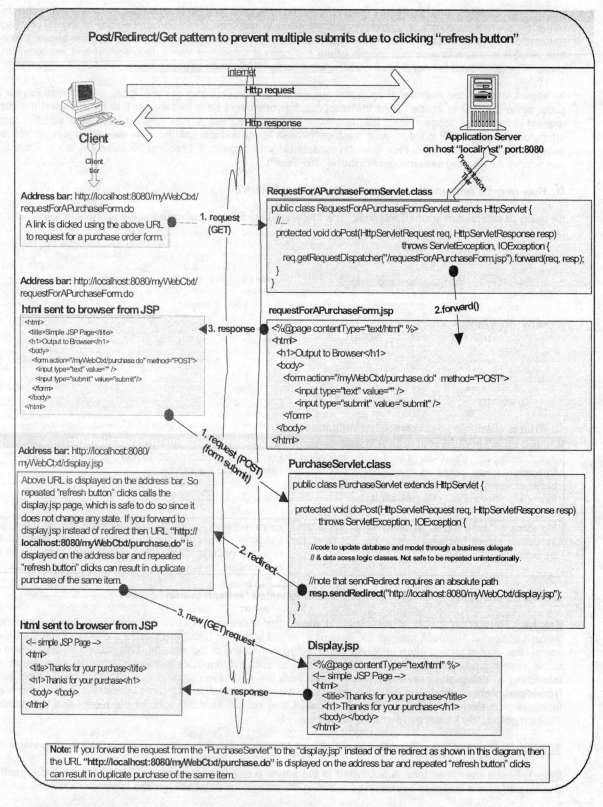

Post/Redirect/Get pattern to prevent multiple submits due to clicking "refresh button"

Advantages: Separates the view from model updates and URLs can be bookmarked.
Disadvantage: Extra network round trip.

Solution-2: The solution-1 has to make an extra network round trip. The synchronizer token pattern can be applied in conjunction with request forward (i.e. instead of redirect) to prevent multiple form submits with unexpected side effects without the extra round trip.

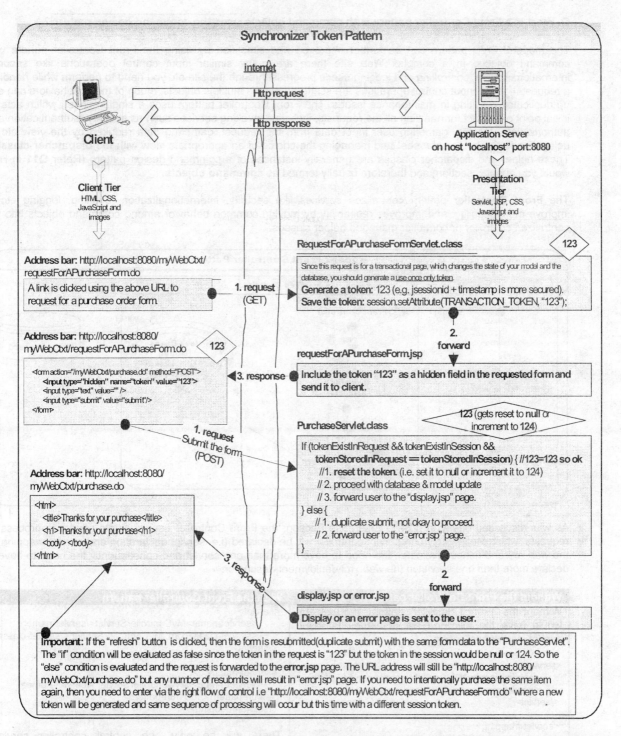

The basic idea of this pattern is to set a **use once only token** in a "session", when a form is requested and the token is stored in the form as a hidden field. When you submit the form the token in the request (i.e. due to hidden field) is compared with the token in the session. If tokens match, then reset the token in the session to null or increment it to a different value and proceed with the model & database update. If you inadvertently resubmit the form by clicking the refresh button, the request processing servlet (i.e. PurchaseServlet) first tests for the presence of a valid token in the request parameter by comparing it with the one stored in the session. Since the token was reset in the first submit, the token in the request (i.e 123) would not match with the token in the session (i.e. null or 124). Since the tokens do not match, an alternate course of action is taken like forwarding to an error.jsp page.

Note: Prohibit caching of application pages by inserting the following lines in your pages:
```
<meta HTTP-EQUIV="pragma" content="no-cache" />
<meta HTTP-EQUIV="Expires" content="-1" />
```

Q. What is a Front Controller pattern with command objects uses the command design pattern **?**

The model-2 MVC pattern can be further improved and simplified by using the Front Controller pattern with command objects. In a complex Web site there are many similar input control operations like security, internationalization, controlling and logging user's progress through the site etc you need to perform while handling a request. If these input control operations are scattered across multiple objects, much of these behaviors can end up duplicated resulting in maintenance issues. The Front Controller pattern uses a single servlet, which acts as initial point of contact for handling all the requests, including invoking services such as security (authentication and authorization), logging, gathering user input data from the request, gathering data required by the view etc by delegating to the **helper classes**, and managing the choice of an appropriate view with the **dispatcher classes**. These helper and dispatcher classes are generally instances of a command design pattern (Refer **Q11** in How would you about… section) and therefore usually termed as **command objects**.

The **Front Controller** pattern centralizes services like security, internationalization, auditing, logging etc to improve manageability, and improves reusability by moving common behavior among command objects into the centralized controller or controller managed helper classes.

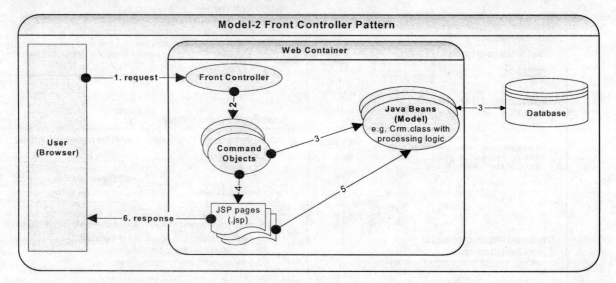

As was discussed briefly in **Q24** in Enterprise Section, the Front Controller uses a single servlet to process all requests, which means only one servlet controller will be declared (i.e. servlet declaration and servlet mapping) in the web.xml and hence eliminates the need to have more than one servlet and consequently the need to have to declare more than one servlet in the web.xml deployment descriptor.

Without the Front Controller pattern	With the Front Controller pattern

Without the "Front Controller" pattern, the web.xml would have the following set of entries for each servlet in your application.
 	
`<servlet>`
`    <servlet-name>CRMServlet</servlet-name>`
`    <servlet-class>com.CRMServlet</servlet-class>`
`</servlet>`
 	
`<servlet-mapping>`
`    <servlet-name>CRMServlet</servlet-name>`
`    <url-pattern>`**crm.do**`</url-pattern>`
`</servlet-mapping>`
 	
So, if you say you have 50 servlets in your web application, then you would have the above declarations 50 times in your web.xml file. This would make your web.xml file to be large and hard to maintain.
	`<servlet>`
	`    <servlet-name>MyControllerServlet</servlet-name>`
	`    <servlet-class>com. MyControllerServlet </servlet-class>`
	`</servlet>`
	
	`<servlet-mapping>`
	`    <servlet-name> MyControllerServlet </servlet-name>`
	`    <url-pattern>`***.do**`</url-pattern>`
	`</servlet-mapping>`
	
	There will be only one central controller servlet configured in the web.xml file.

Example of front controller pattern: The popular **request based** web framework Struts uses the Front Controller pattern, where a centralized single servlet is used for channeling all requests and creating instances of "*Action*" classes for processing user requests. The Struts "*Action*" classes are command objects.

Q. What do you understand by the term JSP translation phase or compilation phase?

As shown below in the figure the JSPs have a **translation** or a **compilation** process where the JSP engine translates and compiles a JSP file into a JSP Servlet. The translated and compiled JSP Servlet moves to the **execution phase (run time)** where they can handle requests and send responses.

Unless explicitly compiled ahead of time, JSP files are compiled the first time they are accessed. On large production sites, or in situations involving complicated JSP files, compilation may cause unacceptable delays to users first accessing the JSP page. The JSPs can be compiled ahead of time (i.e. **precompiled**) using application server tools/settings or by writing your own script.

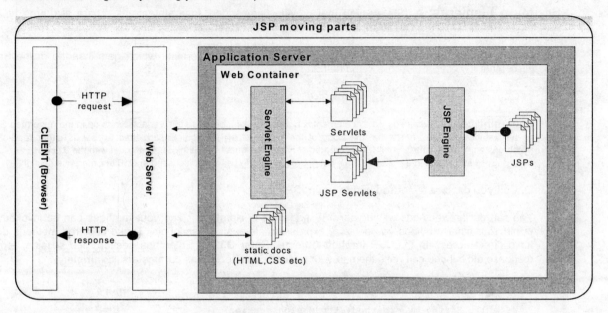

Q 28: Explain the life cycle methods of a JSP? **SF** **FAQ**
A 28:

- **Pre-translated:** Before the JSP file has been translated and compiled into the Servlet.
- **Translated:** The JSP file has been translated and compiled as a Servlet.
- **Initialized:** Prior to handling the requests in the service method the container calls the **jspInit()** to initialize the Servlet. Called only once per Servlet instance.
- **Servicing**: Services the client requests. Container calls the **_jspService()** method for each request.
- **Out of service**: The Servlet instance is out of service. The container calls the **jspDestroy()** method.

Q. Can you have your JSP-generated servlet subclass your own servlet instead of the default HttpServlet?

Your JSP generated servlet can extend your own servlet with the directive:

```
<%@ page extends="com.CRMServlet"%>
```

But, you should be very careful when having your JSP pages extend your own servlet class. By doing so you may lose any advanced optimization that may be provided by your JSP engine. If you do have a compelling reason to do so then your own superclass servlet has to fulfill the contract with the JSP engine by:

1. Implementing the **HttpJspPage** interface for HTTP protocol or **JspPage** interface. If you do not then you will have to make sure that all your super-class servlet methods are declared as final.

2. Implementing your super-class servlet methods as follows:

   - The service() method has to invoke the **_jspService()** method.
   - The init() method has to invoke the **jspInit()** method.
   - The destroy() method has invoke **jspDestroy()** method.

If the above conditions are not met, then a translation error may be thrown by your JSP engine.

Q 29: What are the main elements of JSP? What are scriptlets? What are expressions? **SF**
A 29: There are two types of data in a JSP page.

- **Static part** (i.e. HTML, CSS etc), which gets copied directly to the response by the JSP Engine.
- **Dynamic part,** which contains anything that can be translated and compiled by the JSP Engine.

There are three types of dynamic elements. (**TIP:** remember **SAD** as an abbreviation for **Scripting, Action** and **Directive** elements).

Scripting Elements: A JSP element that provides embedded Java statements. There are three types of scripting elements. They are **Declaration, Expression** and **Scriplet** elements.

1. **Declaration Element**: is the embedded Java declaration statement, which gets inserted at the Servlet class level.

    ```
    <%! Calendar c = Calendar.getInstance(); %>
    ```

    Important: declaring variables via this element is not thread-safe, because this variable ends up in the generated Servlet as an instance variable, not within the body of the _jspService() method. Ensure their access is either read-only or synchronized. You can make your JSP generated servlets implement the SingleThreadModel with the **directive** `<%@ page isThreadSafe="false" %>` but not recommended as was discussed in **Q16** in Enterprise section.

    Q. Can you declare a method within your JSP page?

    You can declare methods within your JSP pages as declarations, and your methods can be invoked from within your other methods you declare, expression elements or scriptlets. These declared methods do not have direct access to the JSP **implicit objects** (Refer **Q32** in Enterprise section) like session, request, response etc but you can pass them to your methods you declare as parameters. **Example:**

    ```
    <%!
        //JSP method where implicit session object as method argument
        public String myJspMethod(HttpSession session) {
            String str = (String)session.getAttribute("someAttrName");
            return str.substring(0,3);
        }
    %>
    ```

    Note: Declaring methods within a JSP page is a bad practice because it will make your JSP page hard to read, reuse and maintain.

    Q. If it is not a good practice to implement methods within your JSPs then can a JSP page process HTML form data?

    Yes. Unlike servlets you do not have to implement HTTP specific methods like doGet(), doPost() etc in your JSPs. In JSPs you can obtain the form data via the "request" implicit object within a scriptlet or expression as follows:

    ```
    <%
        String firstName = request.getParameter("param1");
        int  units = new Integer(request.getParameter("param2")).intValue();
    %>
    ```

2. **Expression Element**: is the embedded Java expression, which gets evaluated by the service method.

    ```
    <%= new Date() %>
    ```

3. **Scriptlet Element**: are the embedded Java statements, which get executed as part of the service method.

    ```
    <%
        String username = null;
        username = request.getParameter("userName"); //"request" is a JSP implicit object
    %>
    ```

    Important: Not recommended to use Scriptlet elements because they don't provide reusability and maintainability. Use custom tags like JSTL, JSF tags, etc or beans instead.

Q. How will you perform a browser redirection from a JSP page?

```
<% response.sendRedirect("http://www.someAbsoluteAddess.com"); %>
```

or you can alter the location HTTP header attribute as follows:

```
<%
    response.setStatus(HttpServletResponse.SC_MOVED_PERMANENTLY);
    response.setHeader("Location", "/someNewPath/index.html");
%>
```

Q. How do you prevent the HTML output of your JSP page being cached?

```
<%
        response.setHeader("Cache-Control", "no=store"); //HTTP 1.1
        response.setDateHeader("Expires", 0);
%>
```

Action Elements: A JSP element that provides information for execution phase.

```
<jsp:useBean id="object_name" class="class_name"/>
<jsp:include page="scripts/login.jsp" />
```

Q. How would you invoke a Servlet from a JSP? Or invoke a JSP form another JSP?

You can invoke a Servlet from a JSP through the **jsp:include** and **jsp:forward** action tags.

```
<jsp:include page="/servlet/MyServlet" flush="true" />
```

Refer **Q31** in Enterprise section for the difference between static include (using directive element <% @ **include** %>) and dynamic include (using action element **<jsp:include …>**).

Q. Generally you would be invoking a JSP page from a Servlet. Why would you want to invoke a Servlet from a JSP?

JSP technology is intended to simplify the programming of dynamic textual content. If you want to output any binary data (e.g. pdfs, gifs etc) then JSP pages are poor choice for the following reasons and should use Servlets instead:

- There are no methods for writing raw bytes in the JspWriter object.
- During execution, the JSP engine preserves whitespace. Whitespace is sometimes unwanted (a .gif file, for example), making JSP pages a poor choice for generating binary data. In the following example, the browser receives unnecessary newline characters in the middle or at the end of the binary data depending on the buffering of your output. "out" is a JspWriter implicit object.

```
<% out.getOutputStream().write(...some binary data...) %>
<% out.getOutputStream().write(...some more binary data...) %>
```

Q. How do you forward a request to another resource (e.g. another Servlet) from within your JSP?

```
//Without passing any parameters
<jsp:forward page="/anotherPage.jsp" />
```

Q. How does an include/forward from a JSP differ from forward/include from a servlet? How would you pass parameters between resources?

forward / include from a JSP to another JSP or a Servlet	forward / include from a Servlet to another Servlet or a JSP
<%-- forward with parameters passed --%> **<jsp:forward** page="/servlet/crm.do"> **<jsp:param** name="userName" value="Peter" /> </jsp:forward>	Refer **Q18** in Enterprise section. Get a **ServletContext** object and then the **RequestDispatcher** object. You can append a query string using "**?**" syntax with name=value pairs separated by "**&**" as shown in bold.

`<%-- include with parameters passed --%>`
`<jsp:include page="/servlet/MyServlet" flush="true" >`
  `<jsp:param name="userName" value="Peter" />`
`</jsp:include>`
 	
Alternatively you can send an appropriately scoped (request, session or application) JavaBean or instead of using `<jsp:param >` you could set attributes via the HTTP request/session objects.
 	
`<% request.setAttribute("userName", "Peter"); %>`
`<% session.setAttribute ("userName", "Peter"); %>`
 	
You can retrieve the data passed as parameters with `<jsp:param ...>` in a servlet as follows:
 	
`request.getParameter("userName");`
 	
You can retrieve the data passed as HTTP request /session attribute as follows:
 	
`request.getAttribute("userName");`
`session.getAttribute("userName");`
	`ServletContext sc = this.getServletContext()`
	`RequestDispatcher rd =`
	    `sc.getRequestDispatcher("/myPage?userName=Smith");`
	
	Invoke the include() or forward() method of the request dispatcher.
	
	`rd.include(request, response);`
	
	    or
	
	`rd.forward(request,response);`
	
	In the target Servlet or JSP, you can use the **request.getParameter("userName")** method to retrieve the parameter sent vai appended query string.
	
	You can also use the setAttribute() method of the HTTP request object.
	
	`request.setAttribute("userName", "Peter");`
	`RequestDispatcher rd =`
	    `sc.getRequestDispatcher("/myPage?userName=Smith");`
	
	In the target JSP page you can use:
	
	`<% request.getAttribute("userName"); %>`

It differs from forwarding it from a Servlet in its <u>syntax</u>. Servlets make use of a ***RequestDispatcher*** object. Refer **Q18** in Enterprise section.

Directive Elements
Directive Elements: A JSP element that provides global information for the **translation** phase. There are three types of directive elements. They are **page**, **include** and **taglib**.

```
<%-- page directives examples: --%>
<%@ page import="java.util.Date" %>    //to import
<%@ page contentType="text/html" %>    //set content type


<%-- include directive example: --%>
<%@ include file="myJSP" %>            // to include another file


<%-- taglib directive example: --%>
<%@ taglib uri="tagliburi" prefix="myTag"%>
```

Q. How does JSP handle run-time exceptions?

You can use the attribute "**errorPage**" of the "page" directive to have your uncaught RuntimeExceptions automatically forwarded to an error processing page. **Example:**

```
<%@ page errorPage="error.jsp" %>
```

Note: You must always use a relative URL as the "errorPage" attribute value.

The above code redirects the browser client to the error.jsp page. Within your error.jsp page, you need to indicate that it is an error processing page with the "**isErrorPage**" attribute of the "page" directive as shown below. "**exception**" is an implicit object <u>accessible only within error pages</u> (i.e. pages with directive `<%@ page isErrorPage="true" %>`

```
<%@ page isErrorPage="true" %>
<body>
    <%= exception.gerMessage() %>
</body>
```

Q. How will you specify a global error page as opposed to using "errorPage" and "isErrorPage" attributes?

You could specify your error page in the <u>web.xml</u> deployment descriptor as shown below:

```
// by exception type
<error-page>
      <exception-type>java.lang.Throwable</exception-type>
      <location>/error.jsp</location>
</error-page>
```

```
//or by HTTP error codes
<error-page>
      <error-code>404</error-code>
      <location>/error404.html</location>
</error-page>
```

You could retrieve the java.lang.Throwable object within your error.jsp page as follows:

```
<%= request.getAttribute("javax.servlet.error.exception")   %>
```

Note: You cannot use the **"exception"** implicit object for the global error pages. This is because of mismatch in the way servlet (uses *javax.servlet.error.exception*) and JSP (*uses javax.servlet.jsp.jspException*) let you get the java.lang.Throwable.

Q. How can you prevent the automatic creation of a session in a JSP page?

Sessions consume resources and if it is not necessary, it should not be created. By default, a JSP page will automatically create a session for the request if one does not exist. You can prevent the creation of useless sessions with the attribute "**session**" of the page directive.

```
<%@ page session="false" %>
```

Q 30: What are the different scope values or what are the different scope values for <jsp:usebean> ? **SF FAQ**
A 30:

Scope	Object	Comment
Page	PageContext	Available to the handling JSP page only.
Request	Request	Available to the handling JSP page or Servlet and forwarded JSP page or Servlet.
Session	Session	Available to any JSP Page or Servlet within the same session.
Application	Application	Available to all the JSP pages and Servlets within the same Web Application.

Q 31: What are the differences between static and a dynamic include? **SF DC FAQ**
A 31:

Static include <%@ include %>	Dynamic include <jsp:include .....>
During the translation or compilation phase all the included JSP pages are compiled into a single Servlet.	The dynamically included JSP is compiled into a separate Servlet. It is a separate resource, which gets to process the request, and the content generated by this resource is included in the JSP response.
No run time performance overhead.	Has run time performance overhead.

Which one to use: Use "static includes" when a JSP page does not change very often. For the pages, which change frequently, use dynamic includes. JVM has a 64kb limit on the size of the method and the entire JSP page is rendered as a single method (i.e. _jspService (..)). **If a JSP page is greater than 64kb, this probably indicates poor implementation**. When this method reaches its JVM limit of 64kb, the JVM throws an error. This **error can be overcome by splitting the JSP files and including them dynamically** (i.e. using <jsp:include.......>) because the dynamic includes generate a separate JSP Servlet for each included file.

Note: The "dynamic include" (jsp:include) has a **flush** attribute. This attribute indicates whether the buffer should be flushed before including the new content. In JSP 1.1 you will get an error if you omit this attribute. In JSP 1.2 you can omit this attribute because the flush attribute defaults to false.

Q 32: What are implicit objects and list them? **SF FAQ**
A 32: Implicit objects are the objects that are available for the use in JSP documents without being declared first. These objects are parsed by the JSP engine and inserted into the generated Servlet. The implicit objects are:

Implicit object	Scope	comment
request	Request	Refers to the current request from the client.
response	Page	Refers to the current response to the client.
pageContext	Page	Refers to the page's environment.

session	Session	Refers to the user's session.
application	Application	Same as ServletContext. Refers to the web application's environment.
out	Page	Refers to the outputstream.
config	Page	same as ServletConfig. Refers to the servlet's configuration.
page	Page	Refers to the page's Servlet instance.

exception	Page	exception created on this page. Used for error handling. Only available if it is an errorPage with the following directive:
		
		`<%@ page isErrorPage="true" %>`
		
		The "exception" implicit object is not available for global error pages declared through web.xml. You can retrieve the java.lang.Throwable object as follows:
		
		`<%= request.getAttribute("javax.servlet.error.exception")   %>`

```
<%
   String username = null;
   username = request.getParameter("userName"); //"request" is an implicit object
   out.print(username);                          //"out" is an implicit object
%>
```

Note: Care should be taken not to name your objects the same name as **the implicit objects**. If you have your own object with the same name, then the implicit objects take precedence over your own object.

Q. What is JSP EL (Expression Language)?

One major component of JSP 2.0 is the new expression language named EL. EL is used extensively in JSTL (**J**ava **S**tandard **T**ag **L**ibrary). However EL is a feature of JSP and not of JSTL. The EL is a language for accessing runtime data from various sources. JSP EL variables come from one of 2 ways:

1. Implicit variables as shown below:

	Implicit variable	Description	Example

Parameter values, headers and cookies for the <u>current request</u>.	param	A collection of all request parameters as a single string value for each parameter.	`<c:if test="${param.name=='peter'} " >`
			  Welcome Peter !!
			`</c:if>`

	paramValues	A collection of all request parameters as a string array value for each parameter.	
	header	A collection of all request headers as a single string value for each header.	`${header['User-Agent']}` you must use the array syntax for the header, because the name includes a dash. otherwise it would be interpreted as the value of the variable expression "header.User" minus the value of the variable named "Agent".
	headerValues	A collection of all request headers as a string array value for each header.	

	cookie	A collection of all request cookies as a single javax.servlet.http.Cookie instance value for each cookie.	`<c:if test="${ ! empty cookie.userName}">`
			  Welcome back
			  `<c:out value="${cookie.userName.value}">`
			`</c:if>`

Defined in web.xml	initParam	A collection of all application init parameters as a single string value for each parameter.	`${initParam.dataSource}`

Access to the JSP objects that represent **request, response, session, application** etc.	pageContext	An instance of the javax.servlet.jspPageContext class.	PageContext.getRequest () → `${pageContext.request}`
			PageContext.getResponse () → `${pageContext.response}`
			PageContext.getSession() → `${pageContext.session}`
			PageContext.getServletContext() →
			        `${pageContext.servletContext}`
			
			`<c:if test="${pageContext.request.method='POST'}">`
			  ....
			`</c:if>`

collections containing all objects in each specific scope. You can use these to limit the search for an object to just one scope instead of searching all scopes, which is the default if no scope is specified	pageScope	A collection of all page scope objects.	`<c:out value="${requestScope.city}" />`
	requestScope	A collection of all request scope objects.	`<c:out value="${sessionScope.city}" />`
	sessionScope	A collection of all session scope objects.	
	applicationScope	A collection of all application scope objects.	

2. **Find the first of using:** **pageContext**.findAttribute (varname) which is like getting the first of:

> **page**.getAttribute(varname);
> **request**.getAttribute(varname);
> **session**.getAttribute(varname);
> **application**.getAttribute(varname);

```
<c:out value="${city}" />
```

Q. What is the difference between a *JspWriter* denoted by the "out" implicit object and the *PrintWriter* object obtained from response.getWriter() method?

JSPs should use the JspWriter denoted by the "**out**" implicit object for sending output back to the client. A *JspWriter* is a buffered version of the *PrintWriter*. Refer JspWriter API for details. *JspWriter* also differs from a *PrintWriter* by throwing java.io.IOException, which a *PrintWriter* does not. The advantage of throwing an exception is that if your HTTP connection is broken for some reason, your JSP won't sit there trying to send characters to a broken connection.

Q 33: Explain hidden and output comments? `SF`

A 33: An output comment is a comment that is sent to the client where it is viewable in the browser's source. `CO`

```
<!-- This is a comment which is sent to the client -->
```

A hidden comment documents a JSP page but does not get sent to the client. The JSP engine ignores a hidden comment, and does not process any code within hidden comment tags.

```
<%-- This comment will not be visible to the client --%>
```

Q 34: Is JSP variable declaration thread safe? `CI` `FAQ`

A 34: No. The declaration of variables in JSP is not thread-safe, because the declared variables end up in the generated Servlet as an instance variable, not within the body of the _jspService() method.

The following declaration is not thread safe: because these declarations end up in the generated servlet as instance variables.

```
<%! int a = 5 %>
```

The following declaration is thread safe: because the variables declared inside the scriplets end up in the generated servlet within the body of the _jspService() method as local variables.

```
<% int a = 5 %>
```

Q 35: Explain JSP URL mapping? What is URL hiding or protecting the JSP page? `SF` `SE` `FAQ`

A 35: As shown in the figure, the JSP resources usually reside directly or under subdirectories (e.g. myPath) of the **document root,** which **are directly accessible** to the user through the URL. If you want to protect your Web resources then hiding the JSP files behind the WEB-INF directory can protect the JSP files, css (cascading style sheets) files, Java Script files, pdf files, image files, html files etc from direct access. The request should be made to a servlet who is responsible for authenticating and authorizing the user before returning the protected JSP page or its resources.

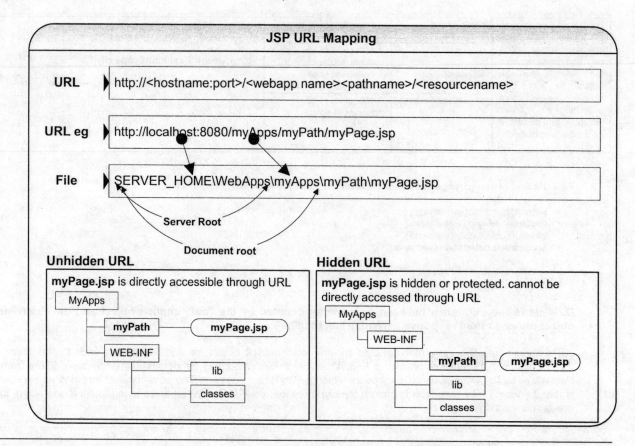

Q 36: What is JSTL? What are custom tags? Explain how to build custom tags? **SF** **FAQ**

A 36: JSTL stands for Java Standard Tag Library and is nothing more than a set of simple and standard tag libraries that encapsulates the core functionality commonly needed when writing dynamic JSP pages. JSTL was introduced to allow JSP programmers to code with tags rather than embedding Java code as scriptlets.

Using scriptlets	Using JSTL tags

``html
<html>
   <head>
   <title>simple example<title>
   </head>
<body>
      <%
       for(int i=0; i<5; i++) {
      %>
           <%= i %>
 	
      <% } %>
   </body>
</html>
``
 	
The above JSP code is hard to read and maintain.
	``html
	<%@ taglib prefix="c"
	               uri="http//java.sun.com/jstl/core">
	
	<html>
	   <head><title>simple example<title></head>
	   <body>
	     <c:forEach var="i" begin="1" end="5" step="1">
	        <c:out value="${i}">
	
	     </c:forEach>
	    </body>
	</html>
	``
	
	The above JSP code consists entirely of HTML & JSTL tags (in bold).

JSTL consists of 4 tag libraries:

Description	Tag Prefix (recommended)	Example

Core Tag Library – looping, condition evaluation, basic input, output etc.	c	`<c:out  value="${hello}" />`
		`<c:if  test="${param.name='Peter'}"> …`
		`<c:forEach items="${addresses}" var="address"> …`

Formatting/Internationalization Tag Library – parse data such as number, date, currency etc	fmt	`<fmt:formatNumber value="${now.time}" />`

XML Tag Library – tags to access XML elements.	x	`<x:forEach  select="$doc/books/book" var="n">`
		`   <x:out select="$n/title"  />`
		`</x:forEach>`

Database Tag Library – tags to	sql	`<sql:query var="emps" sql="SELECT * FROM Employee">`

access SQL databases and should be used only to create prototype programs.		

Q. What are JSP custom tags?

Custom JSP tag is a tag you define. You define how a tag, its attributes and its body are interpreted, and then group your tags into collections called tag libraries that can be used in any number of JSP files. So basically it is a reusable and extensible JSP only solution. The pre-built tags also can speed up Web development. CO

STEP: 1
Construct the Tag handler class that defines the behavior.

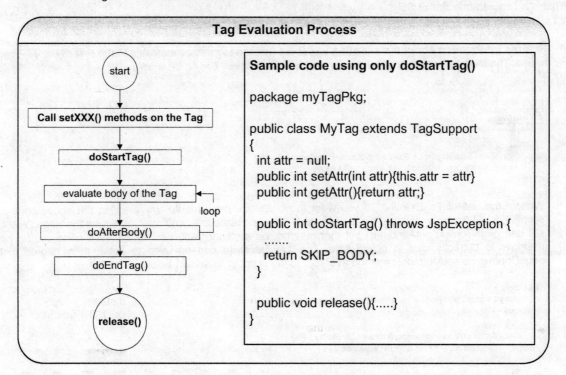

STEP: 2
The Tag library descriptor file (*.tld) maps the XML element names to the tag implementations. The code sample *MyTagDesc.tld* is shown below:

```
<taglib>
  <tag>
    <name>tag1</name>
    <tagclass>myTagPkg.MyTag</tagclass>
    <bodycontent>empty</bodycontent>
    <attribute>
       <name>attr</name>
       <required>false</required>
       <rtexprvalue>false</rtexprvalue>
    </attribute>
  </tag>
</taglib>
```

STEP: 3
The web.xml deployment descriptor maps the URI to the location of the *.tld (Tag Library Descriptor) file. The code sample web.xml file is shown below:

```
<web-app>
  <taglib>
     <taglib-uri>/WEB-INF/MyTagURI</taglib-uri>
     <taglib-location>/WEB-INF/tags/MyTagDesc.tld</taglib-location>
```

```
    </taglib>
</web-app>
```

STEP: 4
The JSP file declares and then uses the tag library as shown below:

```
<%@ taglib uri="/WEB-INF/MyTagURI" prefix="myTag" %>

<myTag:tag1 attr="abc"></myTag:tag1> or < myTag:tag1 attr="abc" />
```

Q 37: What is a TagExtraInfo class? SF

A 37: A TagExtraInfo class provides extra information about tag attributes to the JSP container at translation time.

- **Returns information about the scripting variables** that the tag makes available to the rest of the JSP page to use. The method used is:

```
VariableInfo[] getVariableInfo(TagData td)
```

Example

```
<html>
    <myTag:addObjectsToArray name="myArray" />
    <myTag:displayArray name="myArray" />
</html>
```

Without the use of TagExtraInfo, if you want to manipulate the attribute "*myArray*" in the above code in a scriptlet, it will not be possible. This is because it does not place the "*myArray*" object on the page. You can still use pageContext.getAttribute() but that may not be a cleaner approach because it relies on the page designer to correctly cast to object type. The **TagExtraInfo** can be used to make items stored in the pageContext via setAttribute() method available to the scriptlet as shown below.

```
<html>
    <myTag:addObjectsToArray name="myArray" />
    <%-- scriptlet code %>
    <%
        for(int i=0; i<myArray.length;i++){
            html +=  <LI> + myArray[i] + </LI>;
        }
    %>
</html>
```

- **Validates the attributes passed to the Tag at translation time**.

   Example It can validate the array "*myArray*" to have not more than 100 objects. The method used is:

```
boolean isValid(TagData data)
```

Q 38: What is the difference between custom JSP tags and JavaBeans? SF

A 38: In the context of a JSP page, both accomplish similar goals but the differences are:

Custom Tags	JavaBeans
Can manipulate JSP content.	Can't manipulate JSP content.
Custom tags can simplify the complex operations much better than the bean can. But require a bit more work to set up.	Easier to set up.
Used only in JSPs in a relatively self-contained manner.	Can be used in both Servlets and JSPs. You can define a bean in one Servlet and use them in another Servlet or a JSP page.

JavaBeans declaration and usage example: CO

```
<jsp:useBean id="identifier" class="packageName.className"/>
<jsp:setProperty name="identifier" property="classField" value="someValue" />
<jsp:getProperty name="identifier" property="classField" /> <%=identifier.getclassField() %>
```

Q 39: Tell me about JSP best practices? BP FAQ

A 39:

- **Separate HTML code from the Java code**: Combining HTML and Java code in the same source code can make the code less readable. Mixing HTML and scriptlet will make the code extremely difficult to read and maintain. The display or behavior logic can be implemented as a custom tags by the Java developers and Web designers can use these tags as the ordinary XHTML tags. Refer **Q36** in Enterprise section.

- **Place data access logic in JavaBeans**: The code within the JavaBean is readily accessible to other JSPs and Servlets.

- **Factor shared behavior out of Custom Tags into common JavaBeans classes**: The custom tags are not used outside JSPs. To avoid duplication of behavior or business logic, move the logic into JavaBeans and get the custom tags to utilize the beans.

- **Choose the right "*include*" mechanism**: What are the differences between static and a dynamic include? Using includes will improve code reuse and maintenance through modular design. Which one to use? Refer **Q31** in Enterprise section.

- **Use style sheets** (e.g. css), **template mechanism** (e.g. struts tiles etc) and **appropriate comments** (both hidden and output comments).

  Q. Why use style sheets? The traditional HTML approach was to "hardcode" all of the appearance information about a page. Say you want all your headings in Arial, and you have hard coded that in more than 50 pages? That is a lot of editing, and a lot of re-editing if you decide to modify the headings to courier. With all of that editing there are plenty of possibility for introducing errors. With CSS, you can decide how headings should appear, and enter that information once. Every heading in every page that is linked to this style sheet now has that appearance. Example:

  ```
  h1
  {
      font-family : arial;
      font-weight : normal;
  }
  ```

- **Use pagination for large resultsets**: If you display long lists (i.e. resultsets) in the browser, it is difficult for the user to find what he or she wants and also can prove impractical due to memory limitation, response-time limitation, page design limitation (i.e long scrollable pages are not desirable) etc. Pagination is the most common way to break up large amount of data into manageable chunks.

  Q. How do you paginate your results?

  1. Results can be read at once from the database and cached in middle-tier (e.g. HTTP session or home grown cache) for fast access in subsequent pages. This approach is memory intensive and suitable only for small-to-medium sized **recurring** queries.

  2. Results are fetched from the database on demand as the user pages. This divide and conquer approach is suitable for medium-to-large resultsets where it delivers pages on demand, direct from the database. Limiting the size of the resultsets is SQL specific. For example in MySQL/Oracle you could limit your resultsets as follows:

```
//can be user selected values or constant values
String strPageNum = request.getParameter("pageNum");
int pageNum = 0;
if(strPageNum != null){
    pageNum  = new Integer(strPageNum).intValue();
}
int maxRowsPerPage = new Integer(request.getParameter("rowsPerPage")).intValue();

//calculate
int  rowEnd = pageNum * maxRowsPerPage;
int  rowStart = (rowEnd - maxRowsPerPage) + 1;
```

In MySQL:

```
"SELECT * FROM Products p where p.category='Consumables' LIMIT " + rowStart + "," +
rowEnd
```

In Oracle:
```
"SELECT p.*, rownum as rowcount FROM  Products p where p.category='Consumables' order
by p.productNo where rowcount >= " + rowStart + " and rowcount < " + rowEnd " ;
```

Q 40: How will you avoid scriptlet code in JSP? BP FAQ
A 40: Use JavaBeans or custom tags instead.

Q. If you have to develop a web site, which has say more than 200 static & dynamic pages, how would you make sure that in future if there is any requirement for a layout change, you have to change the layout in one page not 200 or more pages?

You could use the JSP include directives for page reuse but better approach to reduce redundant code is to use frameworks like **Tiles** for page composition using template mechanism or **SiteMesh** for page decoration. SiteMesh can be used by any Java Web framework since it is a Servlet filter. SiteMesh uses the decorator design pattern.

Q. How do you connect to the database from JSP/Servlet?

A. A connection can be established to a database as shown below via scriptlet. It is not the best practice to embed data access logic in your JSP/Servlet and is shown only for illustration purpose and to create a lead up to the next section. The best practice should make use of a separate "Data Access Object (using DAO pattern)" , which gets invoked by JSP, Servlet, plain Java class, EJBs etc. The next section discusses basics and best practices relating to data access.

```
<%@ page language="java" contentTpe="text/html"
    import="java.sql.*"%>

<html>
  <title>Simple JSP Page</title>
  <h1>Output to Browser</h1>
  <body>
      <%
          //1. load the driver from specific vendor
          Class.forName("oracle.jdbc.driver.OracleDriver");

          //2. open connection to the databse by passing the URL to the database
          Connection con = DriverManager.getConnection("jdbc:oracle:thin:@hostname:1526:myDB");

          //3. create a statement object
          Statement  stmt = con.createStatement();

          //4. Create a ResultSet
          ResultSet rs = stmt.executeQuery("SELECT * FROM Employees");

          //5. you can use the ResultSet Object to read data
          while(rs.next()){
            rs.getString("firstname");
          }
      %>
  </body>
</html>
```

General Tip #4:

Every body is nervous for interviews and being a little nervous is natural. But if you are too nervous then you can overcome this by preparing for your interviews and by treating each interview as a free technical/behavioral training course. Have an attitude that even if you are not going to get the job, you are going to learn something good out of it. If you go with this attitude you will put yourself in a win/win situation and you might really get the offer. If you take this attitude you can learn a lot from your interviews. Also never think that you have to answer all the questions correctly. Do not get put off by a tricky or a difficult question. What really earns you a job is the combination of your **knowledge + experience + attitude**.

Q 41: What is JDBC? How do you connect to a database? Have you used a Data Access Object (i.e. DAO) pattern? SF DP BP FAQ

A 41: JDBC stands for **Java Database Connectivity**. It is an API which provides easy connection to a wide range of databases. To connect to a database we need to load the appropriate driver and then request for a connection object. The Class.forName(….) will load the driver and register it with the DriverManager (Refer **Q5** in Java section for dynamic class loading).

```
Class.forName("oracle.jdbc.driver.OracleDriver"); //dynamic class loading
String url = jdbc:oracle:thin:@hostname:1526:myDB;
Connection myConnection = DriverManager.getConnection(url, "username", "password");
```

The *DataSource* interface provides an alternative to the *DriverManager* for making a connection. *DataSource* makes the code more portable than DriverManager because it works with JNDI and it is created, deployed and managed separately from the application that uses it. If the DataSource location changes, then there is no need to change the code but change the configuration properties in the server. This makes your application code easier to maintain. *DataSource* allows the use of connection pooling and support for distributed transactions. A *DataSource* is not only a database but also can be a file or a spreadsheet. A *DataSource* object can be bound to JNDI and an application can retrieve and use it to make a connection to the database. J2EE application servers provide tools to define your *DataSource* with a JNDI name. When the server starts it loads all the *DataSources* into the application server's JNDI service.

DataSource configuration properties are shown below:
- **JNDI Name** → jdbc/myDataSource
- **URL** → jdbc:oracle:thin:@hostname:1526:myDB
- **UserName, Password**
- **Implementation classname** → oracle.jdbc.pool.OracleConnectionPoolDataSource
- **Classpath** → ora_jdbc.jar
- **Connection pooling** settings like → minimum pool size, maximum pool size, connection timeout, statement cache size etc.

Once the *DataSource* has been set up, then you can get the connection object as follows:
```
Context ctx = new InitialContext();
DataSource ds = (DataSource)ctx.lookup("jdbc/myDataSource");
Connection myConnection = ds.getConnection("username","password");
```

Q. Why should you prefer using DataSource?

Best practice: In a basic implementation a *Connection* obtained from a *DataSource* and a *DriverManager* are identical. But the J2EE best practice is to use **DataSource** because of its **portability, better performance due to pooling of valuable resources** and the J2EE standard requires that applications use the container's resource management facilities to obtain connections to resources. Every major web application container provides pooled database connection management as part of its resource management framework.

Design Pattern: JDBC architecture decouples an abstraction from its implementation so that the implementation can vary independent of the abstraction. This is an example of the **bridge design pattern**. The JDBC API provides the abstraction and the JDBC drivers provide the implementation. New drivers can be plugged-in to the JDBC API without changing the client code.

Q. Have you used a Data Access Object (DAO) pattern? Why is it a best practice to use a DAO pattern Design Pattern?

- A DAO class provides access to a particular data resource in the data tier (e.g. relational database, XML , mainframe etc) without coupling the resource's API to the business logic in the business tier. For example you may have a **EmployeeBO** business object class access all of its employees in the database using a DAO interface **EmployeeDAO**. If your data resource change from a database to a Mainframe system, then reimplementing **EmployeeDAO** for a different data access mechanism (to use a mainframe Connector) would have little or no impact on any classes like **EmployeeBO** that uses **EmployeeDAO** because only the implementation (e.g. **EmployeeDAOImpl**) would change but the interface remains the same. All the classes that use the DAO should code to interface not implementation. If you happen to use the popular Spring framework, then you can inject your DAO classes into your Business Object classes. Spring framework promotes the design principle of "code to interface not to implementation".

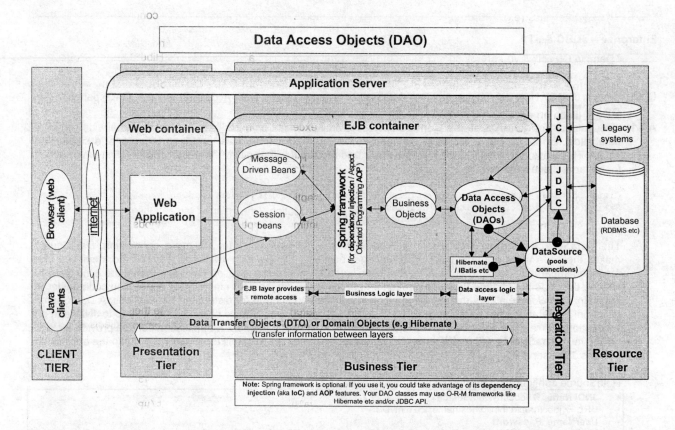

Business Objects represent the data client. They are the objects that require access to the datasource to obtain and store data. **Data Access Objects** abstract the underlying data access implementation for the business objects to enable transparent access to the datasource. The business objects also delegate data load and store operations to the Data Access Objects. A **DataSource** represents a database such as a relational database, XML repository, flat file, mainframe system etc. **Data Transfer Objects** or **Domain Objects** transfer data between client and data access objects.

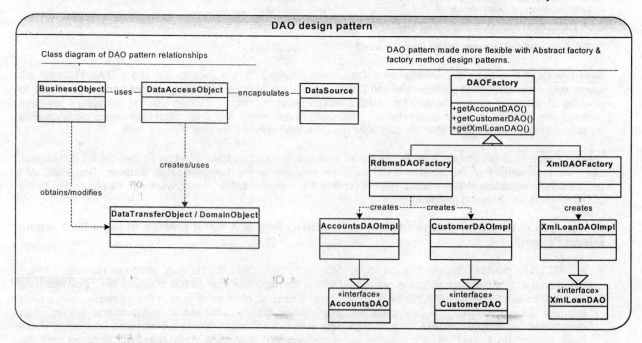

A typical DAO implementation has the following components:

- A DAO factory class (e.g. EmployeeDAOFactory) or Spring framework to inject a DAO class.
- A DAO interface (e.g. *EmployeeDAO*)

- A concrete class (e.g. **EmployeeDAOImpl**) that implements the DAO interface. Your concrete class will make use of JDBC API or open source framework API like Hibernate, IBatis etc.
- Data transfer objects (e.g. **EmployeeDTO**) transfer data between business objects and data access objects or Domain Objects if you are using any Object-to-Relational Mapping (aka ORM) tools like Hibernate.

Q. What are the best practices relating to exception handling to make your DAOs more robust and maintainable?

- If you catch an exception in your DAO code, <u>never ignore it or swallow it because ignored exceptions are hard to troubleshoot</u>. DAO class methods should throw checked exceptions only if the caller can reasonably recover from the exception or reasonably handle it (e.g. retry operations in optimistic concurrency control - Refer **Q 78** in Enterprise section etc). If the caller cannot handle the exception in a meaningful way, consider throwing a runtime (i.e. unchecked) exception. For example Hibernate 3 exceptions are all runtime exceptions.

- DAO methods should not throw low level JDBC exceptions like *java.sql.SQLException*. A DAO should encapsulate JDBC rather than expose it to rest of the application. Use chained exceptions to translate low-level exceptions into high-level checked exceptions or runtime exceptions. DAO methods should not throw *java.lang.Exception* because it is too generic and does not convey any underlying problem.

- Log your exceptions, configuration information, query parameters etc.

Q 42: What are JDBC Statements? What are different types of statements? How can you create them? **SF FAQ**

A 42: A **statement** object is responsible for sending the SQL statements to the Database. Statement objects are created from the connection object and then executed. **CO**

```
Statement stmt = myConnection.createStatement();
ResultSet rs = stmt.executeQuery("SELECT id, name FROM myTable where id =1245"); //to read
                              or
stmt.executeUpdate("INSERT INTO (field1,field2) values (1,3)");//to insert/update/delete/create
```

The types of statements are:

- **Statement** (regular statement as shown above)
- **PreparedStatement** (more efficient than statement due to pre-compilation of SQL)
- **CallableStatement** (to call stored procedures on the database)

To use prepared statement:

```
PreparedStatement prepStmt =
                myConnection.prepareStatement("SELECT id, name FROM myTable where id = ? ");
prepStmt.setInt(1, 1245);
```

Callable statements are used for calling stored procedures.

```
CallableStatement calStmt = myConnection.prepareCall("{call PROC_SHOWMYBOOKS}");
ResultSet rs = cs.executeQuery();
```

Q 43: What is a **Transaction**? What does **setAutoCommit** do? **TI PI FAQ**

A 43: A transaction is a set of operations that should be completed as a unit. If one operation fails then all the other operations fail as well. For example if you transfer funds between two accounts there will be two operations in the set

1. Withdraw money from one account.
2. Deposit money into other account.

These two operations should be completed as a single unit. Otherwise your money will get lost if the withdrawal is successful and the deposit fails. There are four characteristics (**ACID** properties) for a Transaction.

Atomicity	Consistency	Isolation	Durability
All the individual operations should either complete or fail.	The design of the transaction should update the database correctly.	Prevents data being corrupted by concurrent access by two different sources. It keeps transactions isolated or separated from each other until they are finished.	Ensures that the database is definitely updated once the Transaction is completed.

Transactions maintain data integrity. A transaction has a beginning and an end like everything else in life. The **setAutocommit(....)**, **commit()** and **rollback()** are used for marking the transactions (known as transaction demarcation). When a connection is created, it is in **auto-commit** mode. This means that each individual SQL statement is treated as a transaction and will be automatically committed immediately after it is executed. The way to allow two or more statements to be grouped into a transaction is to **disable** auto-commit mode: CO

```
try{
    Connection myConnection = dataSource.getConnection();

    // set autoCommit to false
    myConnection.setAutoCommit(false);

    withdrawMoneyFromFirstAccount(.............);     //operation 1
    depositMoneyIntoSecondAccount(.............);     //operation 2

    myConnection .commit();
}
catch(Exception sqle){
    try{
        myConnection .rollback();
    }catch( Exception e){}
}
finally{
    try{if( conn != null) {conn.close();}} catch( Exception e) {}
}
```

The above code ensures that both operation 1 and operation 2 succeed or fail as an atomic unit and consequently leaves the database in a consistent state. Also turning auto-commit off will provide better performance.

Q. What is transaction demarcation? What are the different ways of defining transactional boundaries?

Data Access Objects (DAO) are transactional objects. Each operation associated with CRUD operations like Create, Update and/or Delete operations should be associated with transactions. Transaction demarcation is the manner in which transaction boundaries are defined. There are two approaches for transaction demarcation.

Declarative transaction demarcation	Programmatic transaction demarcation
The programmer <u>declaratively</u> specifies the transaction boundaries using transaction attributes for an EJB via ejb-jar.xml deployment descriptor.	The programmer is responsible for <u>coding</u> transaction logic as shown above. The application controls the transaction via an API like JDBC API, JTA API, Hibernate API etc. JDBC transactions are controlled using the *java.sql.Connection* object. There are two modes: **auto-commit** and **manual commit**. Following methods are provided in the JDBC API via non-XA *java.sql.Connection* class for programmatically controlling transactions:
Note: Spring framework has support for declarative transaction demarcation by specifying transaction attributes via Spring config files. If you choose Spring framework to mark the transaction boundaries then you need to turn off transaction demarcation in your EJB by: `<trans-attribute>NotSupported</trans-attribute>`	

Q. How are these declarative transactions know when to rollback?	`public    void    setAutoCommit(boolean mode);`
	`public boolean getAutoCommit();`
	`public void commit();`
	`public void rollback();`

EJBs: When the EJB container manages the transaction, it is automatically rolled back when a **System Exception** occurs. This is possible because the container can intercept "SystemException". However when an **Application Exception** occurs, the container does not intercept it and therefore leaves it to the code to roll back using ctx.setRollbackOnly().	For XA-Connections use the following methods on *javax.transaction.UserTransaction*.

Refer **Q76**, **Q77** in Enterprise section to learn more about EJB exceptions and when an EJB managed transaction is rolled back.	`public void begin();`
	`public void commit();`
	`public void rollback();`
	`public int getStatus();`
	`public void setRollbackOnly();`
	`public void setTransactionTimeOut(int)`

Spring Framework: Transaction declaration format is:
 	
`PROPAGATION_NAME,ISOLATION_NAME,readOnly,timeout_NNN`
`N,+CheckedException1,-CheckedException2`	

> By default transactions are rolled-back on **java.lang.RuntimeException**. You can control when transactions are committed and rolled back with the "**+**" or "**-**" prefixes in the exception declaration. "**+**" means **commit** on exception (You can even force it on RuntimeException) and "**-**" means **rollback** on exception. You can specify multiple rules for rollback as "," separated.
>
> **For example:** Following declaration will rollback transactions on *RunTime* exceptions and *MyCheckedException*, which is a checked exception.
>
> ```
> PROPAGATION_REQUIRED,-MyCheckedException
> ```

Q. What is a distributed (aka JTA/XA) transaction? How does it differ from a local transaction? There are two types of transactions:

- **Local transaction**: Transaction is within the same database. As we have seen above, with JDBC transaction demarcation, you can combine multiple SQL statements into a single transaction, but the transactional scope is limited to a single database connection. A JDBC transaction cannot span multiple databases.

- **Distributed Transaction** (aka **Global Transaction, JTA/XA transaction**): The transactions that constitute a distributed transaction might be in the same database, but more typically are in different databases and often in different locations. **For example** A distributed transaction might consist of money being transferred from an account in one bank to an account in another bank. You would not want either transaction committed without assurance that both will complete successfully. The Java Transaction API (**JTA**) and its sibling Java Transaction Service (**JTS**), provide distributed transaction services for the J2EE platform. A distributed transaction (aka JTA/XA transaction) involves a transaction manager and one or more resource managers. A resource manager represents any kind of data store. The transaction manager is responsible for coordinating communication between your application and all the resource managers. A transaction manager decides whether to commit or rollback at the end of the transaction in a distributed system. A resource manager is responsible for controlling of accessing the common resources in the distributed system.

Q. What is two-phase commit?

A **two-phase commit** is an approach for committing a distributed transaction in 2 phases. Refer **Q73** in Enterprise section for **two-phase** commit.

Q. What do you understand by JTA and JTS?

JTA is a high level transaction interface which allows transaction demarcation in a manner that is independent of the transaction manager implementation. JTS specifies the implementation of a Transaction Manager which supports the JTA. The code developed by developers does not call the JTS methods directly, but only invokes the JTA methods. The JTA internally invokes the JTS routines.

Q. What is a XA resource?

The **XA** specification defines how an application program uses a transaction manager to coordinate distributed transactions across multiple resource managers. Any resource manager that adheres to XA specification can participate in a transaction coordinated by an XA-compliant transaction manager.

JTA transaction demarcation requires a JDBC driver that implements **XA** interfaces like javax.sql.-**XADatasource**, javax.sql.**XAConnection** and javax.sql.**XAResource**. A driver that implements these interfaces will be able to participate in JTA transactions. You will also require to set up the XADatasource using your application server specific configuration files, but once you get a handle on the DataSource via JNDI lookup, you can get a **XA connection** via javax.sql.DataSource.getConnection() in a similar manner you get a non-XA connections. XA connections are different from non-XA connections and do not support JDBC's auto-commit feature. You cannot also use the commit(), rollback() methods on the java.sql.Connection class for the XA connections. A J2EE component can begin a transaction programmatically using ***javax.transaction.UserTransaction*** interface or it can also be started declaratively by the EJB container if an EJB bean uses container managed transaction. For explicit (i.e. programmatic) JTA/XA transaction you should use the **UserTransaction**.begin(), **UserTransaction**.commit() and **UserTransaction**.rollback() methods. **For example:**
// programmatic JTA transaction

```
InitialContext ctx = new InitialContext();
UserTransaction utx = (UserTransaction)ctx.lookup("java:comp/UserTransaction");

try {
    //…
    utx.begin();
    //….
    DataSource ds = getXADatasource();
    Connection con = ds.getConnection(); // get a XAconnection.
    PreparedStatement pstmt = con.prepareStatement("UPDATE Employee emp where emp.id =?");
    pstmt.setInt(1, 12456);
    pstmt.executeUpdate();

    utx.commit();//transaction manager uses two-phase commit protocol to end transaction
}
catch(SQLException sqle){
    utx.rollback();
    throw new RuntimeException(sqle);
}
```

```
// for bean-managed EJB transaction demarcation
UserTransaction ut = ejbContext.getUserTransaction();
```

Q. Why JTA transactions are more powerful than JDBC transactions?

JTA transactions are more powerful than JDBC transaction because a JDBC transaction is limited to a single database whereas a JTA transaction can have multiple participants like:

- JDBC connections.
- JMS queues/topics.
- Enterprise JavaBeans (EJBs).
- Resource adapters that comply with J2EE Connector Architecture (**JCA**) specification.

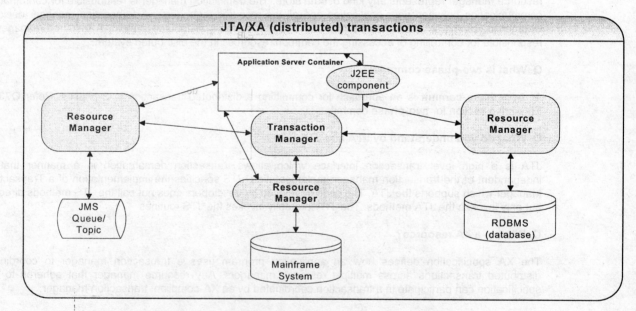

Q. What is J2EE Connector architecture (JCA)? How does it differ from JDBC?

JCA is a Java based technology solution for connecting application servers and Enterprise Information Systems (**EIS**) like Enterprise Resource Planning (**ERP**) systems, Customer Relationship Management) (**CRM**) systems etc as part of Enterprise Application Integration (**EAI**). The JCA API is used by J2EE tool developers and system integrators to create resource adapters

While JDBC is specifically used to connect J2EE applications to databases, JCA is a more generic architecture for connecting to legacy systems (including databases).

Q. How would you send a JMS message to a JMS queue/topic and update a database table within the same transaction?

Using JTA/XA transaction. A J2EE application using EJB containers can send or receive messages from one or more JMS destinations and update data in one or more databases in a single transaction. The J2EE architecture allows updates of data at multiple sites (i.e. more than one application servers) to be performed in a single transaction.

JMS messages and database updates in a single JTA/XA transaction

Same Application server: A web client invokes a method on EJB-1, which in turn sends a message to JMS Queue-1 and updates data in database-1. After that EJB-1 calls EJB-2, which updates data in database-2. The application server with its EJB container and built-in transaction manager ensures that operations A, B and C are either all committed or rolled back. If operation-B fails to update database-1 due to some error condition then operations A & B are rolled back, which means the JMS message would not be delivered to JMS Queue-1 and database-2 would not be updated.

Multiple Application servers: Both application servers with its EJB containers and built-in transaction manager ensure that opeations A, B and C are either all committed or rolled back.

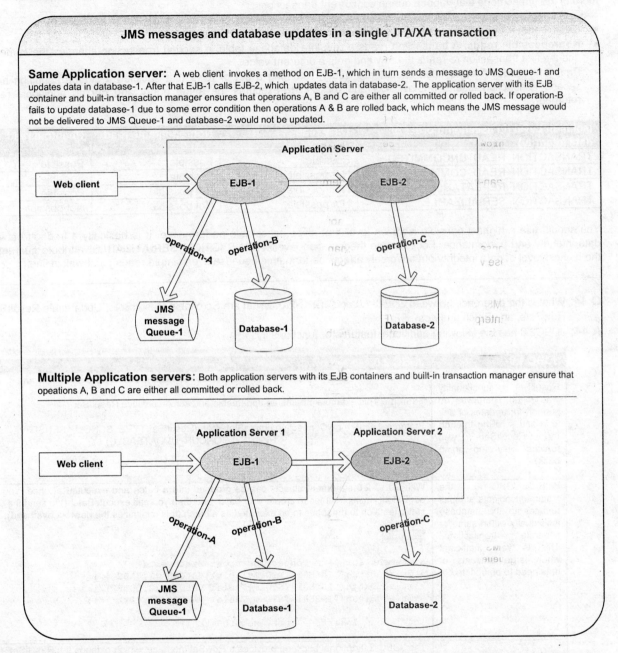

Q. What are the considerations for a programmatic transaction control within a Servlet/JSP? Can a transaction span across multiple web requests?

Web components like Servlets/JSPs may only start a transaction in its service() method and a transaction started in its service method must be completed before the service() method completes. A transaction cannot span across multiple web requests. Some of the considerations are as follows:

- JTA transactions should start and complete within the thread in which service() method is called and any additional threads created in the servlet should not try to start any JTA transaction.

- JDBC connection objects should not be stored in static fields or instance fields (for multi-threaded model). JDBC connection objects should be acquired and released within the same invocation of the service() method.

Q. How will you control two concurrent transactions accessing a database?

You can use **isolation levels**. An isolation level defines how concurrent transactions accessing a relational database are isolated from each other for read purpose. Refer **Q72** in Enterprise section. These isolation levels can prevent one or more of the phenomena that happen during concurrent transactions:

- **Dirty reads**: A transaction reads uncommitted changes from another transaction.
- **Nonrepeatable reads**: A transaction reads a row in a database table, a second transaction changes the same row and the first transaction re-reads the row and gets a different value.
- **Phantom reads**: A transaction executes a query, returning a set of rows that satisfies a search condition and a second transaction inserts another row and the first re-executes the same query and get an additional record returned.

Isolation Level (in ascending order of data integrity)	Dirty read	Nonrepeatable read	Phantom read
TRANSACTION **READ_UNCOMMITED**	Possible	Possible	Possible
TRANSACTION **READ_COMMITED**	Not possible	Possible	Possible
TRANSACTION **REPEATABLE_READ**	Not possible	Not possible	Possible
TRANSACTION **SERIALIZABLE**	Not possible	Not possible	Not possible

You should use a highest possible isolation level that gives acceptable performance. It is basically a tradeoff between data integrity and performance. For example the isolation level "TRANSACTION_**SERIALIZABLE**" attribute guarantees the highest level of data integrity but adversely affects performance because even simple reads must wait in line.

Q 44: What is the difference between JDBC-1.0 and JDBC-2.0? What are Scrollable ResultSets, Updateable ResultSets, RowSets, and Batch updates? **SF**

A 44: JDBC2.0 has the following additional features or functionality:

JDBC 1.0	JDBC 2.0
With JDBC-1.0 the ResultSet functionality was limited. There was no support for updates of any kind and scrolling through the ResultSets was forward only (no going back)	With JDBC 2.0 ResultSets are updateable and also you can move forward and backward. **Example** This example creates an updateable and scroll-sensitive ResultSet Statement stmt = myConnection.createStatement(ResultSet.TYPE_SCROLL_SENSITIVE, ResultSet.CONCUR_UPDATEABLE)

With JDBC-1.0 the statement objects submits updates to the database individually within same or separate transactions. This is very inefficient when large amounts of data need to be updated.	With JDBC-2.0 statement objects can be grouped into a batch and executed at once. You call addBatch() multiple times to create your batch and then you call executeBatch() to send the SQL statements off to database to be executed as a batch (this minimizes the network overhead).
	
	Example
	
	`Statement stmt = myConnection.createStatement();`
	`stmt.addBatch("INSERT INTO myTable1 VALUES (1,"ABC")");`
	`stmt.addBatch("INSERT INTO myTable1 VALUES (2,"DEF")");`
	`stmt.addBatch("INSERT INTO myTable1 VALUES (3,"XYZ")");`
	`...`
	`int[] countInserts = stmt.executeBatch();`

-	The JDBC-2.0 optional package provides a RowSet interface, which extends the ResultSet. One of the implementations of the RowSet is the CachedRowSet, which can be considered as a disconnected ResultSet.

Q 45: How to avoid the "running out of cursors" problem? **DC** **PI** **MI** **FAQ**

A 45: A database can run out of cursors if the connection is not closed properly or the DBA has not allocated enough cursors. In a Java code it is essential that we close all the valuable resources in a try{} and **finally**{} block. The finally{} block is always executed even if there is an exception thrown from the catch {} block. So the resources like connections and statements should be closed in a finally {} block. **CO**

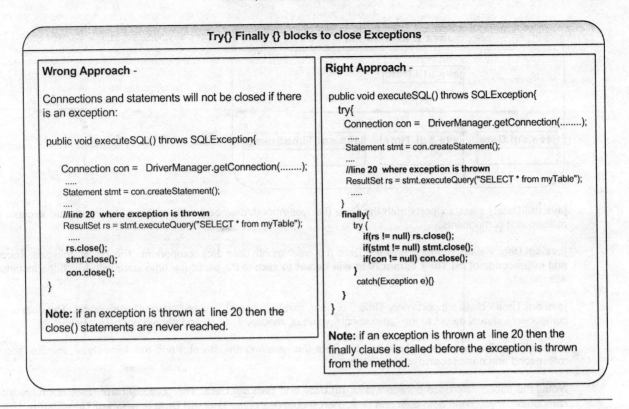

Try{} Finally {} blocks to close Exceptions

Wrong Approach -

Connections and statements will not be closed if there is an exception:

```
public void executeSQL() throws SQLException{

    Connection con =  DriverManager.getConnection(........);
    .....
    Statement stmt = con.createStatement();
    ....
    //line 20  where exception is thrown
    ResultSet rs = stmt.executeQuery("SELECT * from myTable");
     .....
     rs.close();
     stmt.close();
     con.close();
}
```

Note: if an exception is thrown at line 20 then the close() statements are never reached.

Right Approach -

```
public void executeSQL() throws SQLException{
  try{
    Connection con =  DriverManager.getConnection(........);
    .....
    Statement stmt = con.createStatement();
    ....
    //line 20  where exception is thrown
    ResultSet rs = stmt.executeQuery("SELECT * from myTable");
     .....
  }
  finally{
     try {
        if(rs != null) rs.close();
        if(stmt != null) stmt.close();
        if(con != null) con.close();
     }
      catch(Exception e){}
  }
}
```

Note: if an exception is thrown at line 20 then the finally clause is called before the exception is thrown from the method.

Q 46: What is the difference between statements and prepared statements? `SF` `PI` `SE` `BP` `FAQ`
A 46:

- Prepared statements offer better performance, as they are **pre-compiled**. Prepared statements reuse the same **execution plan** for different arguments rather than creating a new execution plan every time. Prepared statements use bind arguments, which are sent to the database engine. This allows mapping different requests with same prepared statement but different arguments to execute the same execution plan.

- Prepared statements are more secure because they use bind variables, which can prevent **SQL injection attack**.

  The most common type of SQL injection attack is SQL manipulation. The attacker attempts to modify the SQL statement by adding elements to the WHERE clause or extending the SQL with the set operators like UNION, INTERSECT etc.

  Example Let us look at the following SQL:

  ```
  SELECT * FROM users where username='bob' AND password='xyfdsw';
  ```

  The attacker can manipulate the SQL as follows

  ```
  SELECT * FROM users where username='bob' AND password='xyfdsw' OR 'a' = 'a' ;
  ```

  The above "WHERE" clause is always true because of the operator precedence. The PreparedStatement can prevent this by using **bind variables**:

  ```
  String strSQL = SELECT * FROM users where username=? AND password=?);
  PreparedStatement pstmt = myConnection.prepareStatement(strSQL);
  pstmt.setString(1,"bob");
  pstmt.setString(2, "xyfdsw");
  pstmt.execute();
  ```

Q 47: Explain differences among java.util.Date, java.sql.Date, java.sql.Time, and java.sql.Timestamp? `SF`
A 47: As shown below all the sql Date classes extend the util Date class.

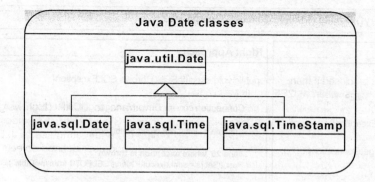

java.util.Date - class supports both the Date (i.e. year/month/date etc) and the Time (hour, minute, second, and millisecond) components.

java.sql.Date - class supports only the Date (i.e. year/month/date etc) component. The hours, minutes, seconds and milliseconds of the **Time component will be set to zero** in the particular time zone with which the instance is associated.

java.sql.Time - class supports only Time (i.e. hour, minute, second, and millisecond) component. The date components should be set to the "zero epoch" value of January 1, 1970 and should not be accessed.

java.sql.TimeStamp – class supports both Date (i.e. year/month/date etc) and the Time (hour, minute, second, millisecond and **nanosecond**) components.

Note: the subtle difference between **java.util.Date** and **java.sql.Date**. The **java.sql.Date** does not have a time component. If you need both date and time, then should use either **java.util.Date** or **java.sql.TimeStamp**.

To keep track of time Java counts the number of milliseconds from January 1, 1970 and stores it as a long value in **java.util.Date** class. The **GregorianCalendar** class provides us a way to represent an arbitrary date. The **GregorianCalendar** class also provides methods for manipulating dates (date arithmetic, date comparisons etc).

General Tip #5:

Software developers should have and demonstrate following qualities to succeed in interviews and after interviews :

Q. Tell me about yourself or about some of the recent projects you have worked with? What do you consider your most significant achievement? Why do you think you are qualified for this position? These interview questions are very common and the interviewer will be mainly looking for following qualities:

1. **Passion:** How passionate you are about your past experience and how much pride you take in your past achievements.

2. **Ability to understand potential failures**: How well you understand the key areas like concurrency issues, transactional issues, performance issues etc relating to software development and tend to avoid or know where to look for the root cause and how to go about solving it when an issue arises.

3. **Ability to see things at a high level as well as drill down when required**: Also is imperative that during your briefing, you demonstrate on a <u>high level</u> (as if you would be explaining it to a business user), how you applied your skills and knowledge. Also be prepared to drill down into detail if asked.

4. **Ability to think dynamically to deliver solutions to complex problems and ability to analyze "what if " scenarios**: What if I need to support another type of product in the future, will the current design allow me to extend? What if concurrent users access my object, will it be thread-safe? What if an exception is thrown, will my transaction get rolled back to leave the database in a consistent state? Etc.

Q. What was the last Java related technical book or article you read? Which Java related website(s) or resource(s) do you use to keep your knowledge up to date beyond Google? What do you think of some of the emerging technologies/frameworks like AOP, IoC, Spring, Tapestry etc? What recent technology trends are important to enterprise development? **Hint:** Service Oriented Architecture, component based Web frameworks, IoC, AOP (refer Emerging Technologies/Frameworks section) etc. The interviewer will be looking for your curiosity and eagerness to learn.

5. **Curiosity to learn:** How eager you are to learn new things and keep up to date with the technology.

Enterprise – JNDI & LDAP

Q 48: What is JNDI? And what are the typical uses within a J2EE application? SF FAQ

A 48: JNDI stands for **J**ava **N**aming and **D**irectory **I**nterface. It provides a generic interface to LDAP (**L**ightweight **D**irectory **A**ccess **P**rotocol) and other directory services like NDS, DNS (Domain Name System) etc. It provides a means for an application to locate components that exist in a name space according to certain attributes. A J2EE application component uses JNDI interfaces to look up and reference system-provided and user-defined objects in a component environment. JNDI is not specific to a particular naming or directory service. It can be used to access many different kinds of systems including file systems.

The JNDI API enables applications to look up objects such as DataSources, EJBs, MailSessions, JMS connection factories and destinations (Topics/Queues) by name. The Objects can be loaded into the JNDI tree using a J2EE application server's administration console. To load an object in a JNDI tree, choose a name under which you want the object to appear in a JNDI tree. J2EE deployment descriptors indicate the placement of J2EE components in a JNDI tree.

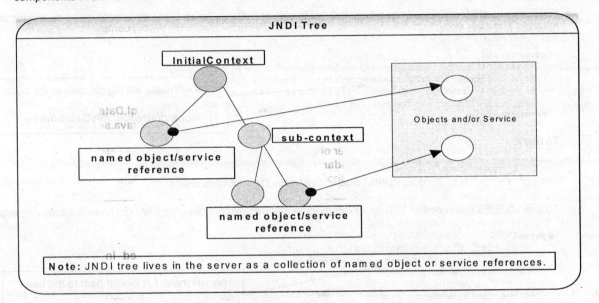

The parameters you have to define for JNDI service are as follows:

- The name service provider class name (WsnInitialContext for WebSphere application server).

```
Hashtable env = new Hashtable();
env.put(Context.INITIAL_CONTEXT_FACTORY,"com.ibm.websphere.naming.WsnInitialContextFactory");
```

- The provider URL :

    - The name service hostname.
    - The name service port number.

```
env.put(Context.PROVIDER_URL, " iiop://localhost:1050");
Context ctx = new InitialContext(env);
```

JNDI is **like** a file system or a Database.

File System	JNDI	Database
File system starts with a **mounted drive** like c:\	JNDI starts with an **InitialContext**. i.e. new InitialContext().	**Database instance**
Uses a **subdirectory**. C:\subdir1	Navigate to a **sub-context**. e.g. Subcontext1	**Tablespace**
Access a **subdirectory** c:\subdir1\subdir2	Drill down through other **sub-contexts**. e.g. subcontext1/subcontext2	**Table**
Access a **file**.	Access an **object** or a **service**.	**Data**

C:\subdir1\subdir2\myFile	new InitialContext().lookup("objectName");	
Example:	**Example:**	**Example:**
c:\subdir1\subdir2\myFile	iiop://myserver:2578/subcontext1.subcontext2.objectName	Select * from demo.myTable

Q 49: Explain the difference between the look up of "java:comp/env/ejb/MyBean" and "ejb/MyBean"? SF FAQ
A 49:

java:comp/env/ejb/MyBean	ejb/MyBean
This is a logical reference, which will be used in your code.	This is a physical reference where an object will be mapped to in a JNDI tree.

The logical reference (or alias) **java:comp/env/ejb/MyBean** is the recommended approach because you cannot guarantee that the physical JNDI location **ejb/MyBean** you specify in your code will be available. Your code will break if the physical location is changed. The deployer will not be able to modify your code. Logical references solve this problem by binding the logical name to the physical name in the application server. The logical names will be declared in the deployment descriptors (web.xml and/or ejb-jar.xml) as follows and these will be mapped to physical JNDI locations in the application server specific deployment descriptors.

To look up a JDBC resource from either Web (web.xml) or EJB (ejb-jar.xml) tier, the deployment descriptor should have the following entry:

```
<resource-ref>
    <description>The DataSource</description>
    <res-ref-name>jdbc/MyDataSource</res-ref-name>
    <res-type>javax.sql.DataSource</res-type>
    <res-auth>Container</res-auth>
</resource-ref>
```

> This will make full logical path to the bean as:
> **java:comp/env/jdbc/MyDataSource**

To use it:

```
Context ctx = new InitialContext();
Object ref = ctx.lookup(java:comp/env/jdbc/MyDataSource);
```

To look up EJBs from another EJB or a Web module, the deployment descriptor should have the following entry:

```
<ejb-ref>
    <description>myBean</description>
    <ejb-ref-name>ejb/MyBean</ejb-ref-name>
    <ejb-ref-type>Entity</ejb-ref-type>
    <ejb-link>Region</ejb-link>
    <home>com.MyBeanHome</home>
    <remote>com.MyBean</remote>
</ejb-ref>
```

> This will make full logical path to the bean as:
> **java:comp/env/ejb/MyBean**

To use it:

```
Context ctx = new InitialContext();
Object ref = ctx.lookup(java:comp/env/ejb/MyBean);
```

Q 50: What is a JNDI InitialContext? SF FAQ
A 50: All naming operations are relative to a context. The *InitalContext* implements the *Context* interface and provides an **entry point** for the resolution of names.

Q 51: What is an LDAP server? And what is it used for in an enterprise environment? SF SE
A 51: LDAP stands for **L**ightweight **D**irectory **A**ccess **P**rotocol. This is an extensible open network protocol standard that provides access to distributed directory services. LDAP is an Internet standard for directory services that run on TCP/IP. Under OpenLDAP and related servers, there are two servers – **slapd**, the LDAP daemon where the queries are sent to and **slurpd**, the replication daemon where data from one server is pushed to one or more slave servers. By having multiple servers hosting the same data, you can increase reliability, scalability, and availability.

- It defines the operations one may perform like search, add, delete, modify, change name
- It defines how operations and data are conveyed.

LDAP has the potential to consolidate all the existing application specific information like user, company phone and e-mail lists. This means that the change made on an LDAP server will take effect on every directory service based application that uses this piece of user information. The variety of information about a new user can be added through a single interface which will be made available to Unix account, NT account, e-mail server, Web Server, Job specific news groups etc. When the user leaves his account can be disabled to all the services in a single operation.

So LDAP is most useful to provide "white pages" (e.g. names, phone numbers, roles etc) and "yellow pages" (e.g. location of printers, application servers etc) like services. Typically in a J2EE application environment it will be used to authenticate and authorize users.

Q. Why use LDAP when you can do the same with relational database (RDBMS)?

In general LDAP servers and RDBMS are designed to provide different types of services. LDAP is an open standard access mechanism, so an RDBMS can talk LDAP. However the servers, which are built on LDAP, are **optimized for read access** so likely to be much faster than RDBMS in providing read access. So in a nutshell, **LDAP is more useful when the information is often searched but rarely modified**. (Another difference is that RDBMS systems store information in rows of tables whereas LDAP uses object oriented hierarchies of entries.) .

Key LDAP Terms:

DIT: **D**irectory **I**nformation **T**ree. Hierarchical structure of entries, those make up a directory.

DN: **D**istinguished **N**ame. This uniquely identifies an entry in the directory. A **DN is made up of relative DN**s of the entry and each of entry's parent entries up to the root of the tree. DN is read from right to left and commas separate these names. For example '**cn**=Peter Smith, **o**=ACME, **c**=AUS'.

objectClass: An *objectClass* is a formal definition of a specific kind of objects that can be stored in the directory. An ObjectClass is a distinct, named set of attributes that represent something concrete such as a user, a computer, or an application.

LDAP URL: This is a string that specifies the location of an LDAP resource. An LDAP URL consists of a server host and a port, search scope, **baseDN**, filter, attributes and extensions. Refer to diagram below:

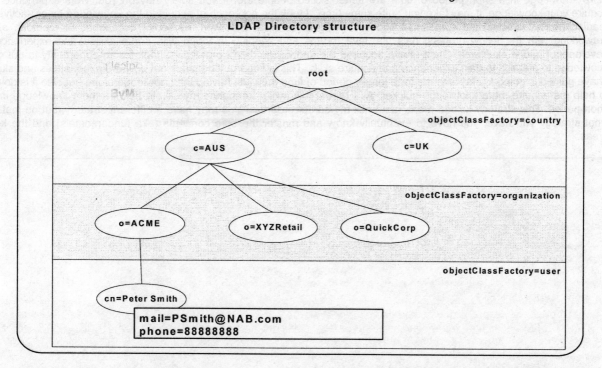

So the complete distinguished name for bottom left entry (i.e. Peter Smith) is **cn**=Peter Smith, **o**=ACME, **c**=AUS. Each entry must have at least one attribute that is used to name the entry. To manage the part of the LDAP directory you should specify the highest level parent's distinguished names in the server configuration. These distinguished names are called **suffixes**. The server can access all the objects that are below the specified suffix in the hierarchy. For example in the above diagram, to answer queries about 'Peter Smith' the server should have the **suffix** of 'o=ACME, **c**=AUS'. So we can look for "Peter Smith" by using the following distinguished name:

```
cn=Peter Smith, o=ACME, c=AUS    // where o=ACME, c=AUS is the suffix
```

LDAP schema: defines rules that specify the types of objects that a directory may contain and the required optional attributes that entries of different types should have.

Filters: In LDAP the basic way to retrieve data is done with filters. There is a wide variety of operators that can be used as follows: & (and), | (or), ! (not), ~= (approx equal), >= (greater than or equal), <= (less than or equal), * (any) etc.

```
(& (uid=a*) (uid=*l) )
```

Q. So where does JNDI fit into this LDAP? JNDI provides a standard API for interacting with naming and directory services using a service provider interface (SPI), which is analogous to JDBC driver. To connect to an LDAP server, you must obtain a reference to an object that implements the **DirContext**. In most applications, this is done by using an *InitialDirContext* object that takes a Hashtable as an argument:

```
Hashtable env = new Hashtable();
env.put(Context.INITIAL_CONTEXT_FACTORY, "com.sun.jndi.ldap.LdapCtxFactory");
env.put(Context.PROVIDER_URL, "ldap://localhost:387");
env.put(Context.SECURITY_AUTHENTICATION, "simple");
env.put(Context.SECURITY_PRINCIPAL, "cn=Directory Manager");
env.put(Context.SECURITY_CREDENTIALS, "myPassword");
DirContext ctx = new InitialDirContext(env);
```

General Tip #6:

Experience, knowledge and attitude are necessary for your career advancement. Developers with the ability to master more knowledge in a short period of time are better skilled people too. If you solely rely on your work experience to acquire your knowledge, it may take you quite some time. I took the approach of acquiring the knowledge by pro-actively reading (mainly articles and sometimes books), having a technical chat with my senior colleagues or mentors, and networking with the fellow professionals via Java forums and keeping in touch with some skilled and experienced developers I had worked with. Once I have acquired the knowledge then I pro-actively look for an opportunity to put my knowledge to practice to gain experience and acquire skills. This is important because not only the experiences and skills I have gained is going to stay with me for a longer period of time than just having the knowledge alone but also it is going to help me acquire more knowledge quicker. As I repeat this cycle, I enhance my skill to acquire more knowledge in a short period. This strategy helped me to fast track my career progress. You may have a different strategy, but no matter what strategy you have, you have to eventually know and master the core concepts (aka fundamentals) and the key areas.

Q 52: Explain the RMI architecture? SF FAQ

A 52: Java Remote Method Invocation (RMI) provides a way for a Java program on one machine to communicate with objects residing in different JVMs (i.e. different processes or address spaces). The important parts of the RMI architecture are the stub class, object serialization and the skeleton class. RMI uses a layered architecture where each of the layers can be enhanced without affecting the other layers. The layers can be summarized as follows:

- **Application Layer:** The client and server program
- **Stub & Skeleton Layer:** Intercepts method calls made by the client. Redirects these calls to a remote RMI service.
- **Remote Reference Layer**: Sets up connections to remote address spaces, manages connections, and understands how to interpret and manage references made from clients to the remote service objects.
- **Transport layer:** Based on TCP/IP connections between machines in a network. It provides basic connectivity, as well as some firewall penetration strategies.

Design pattern: RMI stub classes provide a reference to a skeleton object located in a different address space on the same or different machine. This is a typical example of a **proxy design pattern** (i.e. remote proxy), which makes an object executing in another JVM appear like a local object. In JDK 5.0 and later, the RMI facility uses **dynamic proxies** instead of generated stubs, which makes RMI easier to use. Refer **Q11** in "How would you about…" section for a more detailed discussion on proxy design pattern and dynamic proxies.

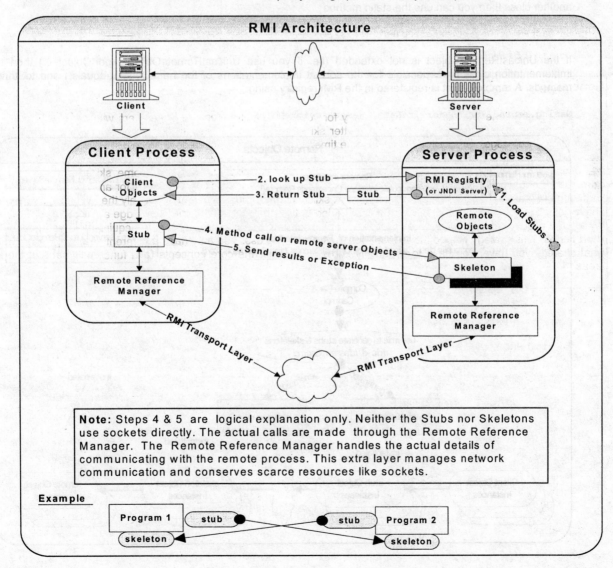

RMI Architecture

Note: Steps 4 & 5 are logical explanation only. Neither the Stubs nor Skeletons use sockets directly. The actual calls are made through the Remote Reference Manager. The Remote Reference Manager handles the actual details of communicating with the remote process. This extra layer manages network communication and conserves scarce resources like sockets.

RMI runtime steps (as shown in the diagram above) involved are:

Step 1: Start RMI registry and then the RMI server. Bind the remote objects to the RMI registry.
Step 2: The client process will look up the remote object from the RMI registry.
Step 3: The lookup will return the stub to the client process from the server process.
Step 4: The client process will invoke method calls on the stub. The stub calls the skeleton on the server process through the RMI reference manager.
Step 5: The skeleton will execute the actual method call on the remote object and return the result or an exception to the client process via the RMI reference manager and the stub.

Q 53: What is a remote object? Why should we extend *UnicastRemoteObject*? SF FAQ

A 53: A remote object is one whose methods can be invoked from another JVM (i.e. another process). A remote object class must implement the *Remote* interface. A RMI Server is an application that creates a number of remote objects.

An RMI Server is responsible for

- Creating an instance of the remote object (e.g. CarImpl instance = new CarImpl()).
- **Exporting** the remote object.
- Binding the instance of the remote object to the RMI registry.

By exporting a remote object you make it available to accept incoming calls from the client. You can export the remote object by either extending the java.rmi.server.UnicastRemoteObject or if your class is already extending another class then you can use the static method

```
UnicastRemoteObject.exportObject (this);
```

If the UnicastRemoteObject is not extended (i.e. if you use UnicastRemoteObject.exportObject(…) then the implementation class is responsible for the correct implementations of the hashCode(), equals() and toString() methods. A remote object is registered in the RMI registry using:

```
Naming.rebind(String serviceName, Remote remoteObj);
```

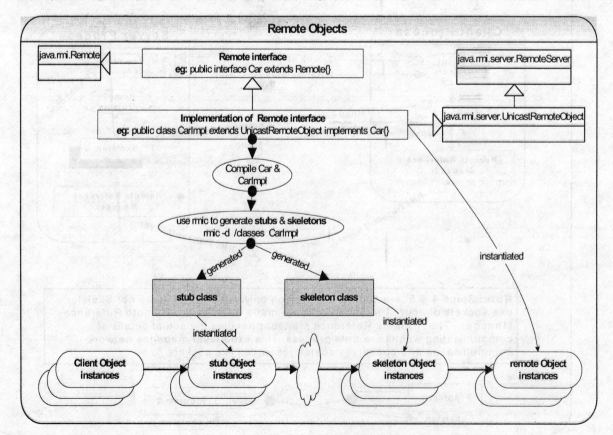

Q 54: What is the difference between RMI and CORBA? SF

A 54:

RMI	CORBA
Java only solution. The interfaces, implementations and the clients are all written in Java.	CORBA was made specifically for interoperability among various languages. For example the server could be written in C++ and the business logic can be in Java and the client can be written in COBOL.
RMI allows dynamic loading of classes at runtime.	In a CORBA environment with multi-language support it is not possible to have dynamic loading.

Q 55: What are the services provided by the RMI Object? SF

A 55: In addition to its remote object architecture, RMI provides some basic object services, which can be used in a distributed application. These services are

- **Object naming/registry service**: RMI servers can provide services to clients by registering one or more remote objects with its local RMI registry.

- **Object activation service**: It provides a way for server (i.e. remote) objects to be started on an as-needed basis. Without the remote activation service, a server object has to be registered with the RMI registry service.

- **Distributed garbage collection:** It is an automatic process where an object, which has no further remote references, becomes a candidate for garbage collection.

Q 56: What are the differences between RMI and a socket? SF

A 56:

Socket	RMI
A socket is a transport mechanism. Sockets are like applying procedural networking to object oriented environment.	RMI uses sockets. RMI is object oriented. Methods can be invoked on the remote objects running on a separate JVM.
Sockets-based network programming can be laborious.	RMI provides a convenient abstraction over raw sockets. Can send and receive any valid Java object utilizing underlying object serialization without having to worry about using data streams.

Q 57: How will you pass parameters in RMI? SF

A 57:

- Primitive types are passed by value (e.g. int, char, boolean etc).

- References to remote objects (i.e. **objects which implement the Remote interface**) are passed as remote references that allow the client process to invoke methods on the remote objects.

- Non-remote objects are passed by value using object serialization. These objects should allow them to be serialized by implementing the java.io.*Serializable* interface.

Note: The client process initiates the invocation of the remote method by calling the method on the stub. The stub (client side proxy of the remote object) has a reference to the remote object and forwards the call to the skeleton (server side proxy of the remote object) through the reference manager by **marshaling** the method arguments. During Marshaling each object is checked to determine whether it implements *java.rmi.Remote* interface. If it does then the remote reference is used as the Marshaled data otherwise the object is serialized into byte streams and sent to the remote process where it is deserialized into a copy of the local object. The skeleton converts this request from the stub into the appropriate method call on the actual remote object by **unmarshaling** the method arguments into local stubs on the server (if they are remote reference) or into local copy (if they are sent as serialized objects).

Q 58: What is HTTP tunneling or how do you make RMI calls across firewalls? SF SE

A 58: RMI transport layer generally opens direct sockets to the server. Many Intranets have firewalls that do not allow this. To get through the firewall an RMI call can be embedded within the firewall-trusted HTTP protocol. To get across firewalls, RMI makes use of HTTP **tunneling** by encapsulating RMI calls within an HTTP POST request.

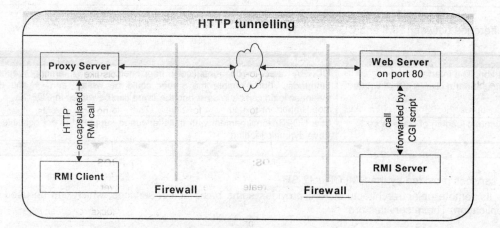

When a firewall proxy server can forward HTTP requests only to a well-known HTTP port: The firewall proxy server will forward the request to a HTTP server listening on port 80, and a CGI script will be executed to forward the call to the target RMI server port on the same machine.

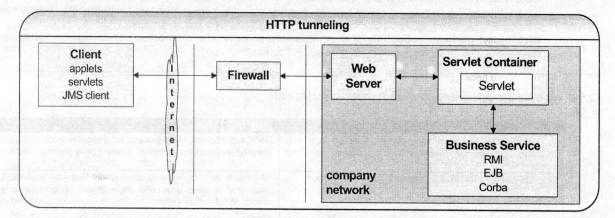

The disadvantages of HTTP tunneling are performance degradation, prevents RMI applications from using call-backs, CGI script will redirect any incoming request to any port, which is a security loophole, RMI calls cannot be multiplexed through a single connection since HTTP tunneling follows a request/response protocol etc.

Q 59: Why use RMI when we can achieve the same benefits from EJB? SF

A 59: EJBs are distributed components, which use the RMI framework for object distribution. An EJB application server provides more services like transaction management, object pooling, database connection-pooling etc, which RMI does not provide. These extra services that are provided by the EJB server simplify the programming effort at the cost of performance overhead compared to plain RMI. So if performance is important then pure RMI may be a better solution (or under extreme situations Sockets can offer better performance than RMI).

Note: The decision to go for RMI or EJB or Sockets should be based on requirements such as maintainability, ease of coding, extensibility, performance, scalability, availability of application servers, business requirements etc.

Tech Tip #5:

Q. How do you pass a parameter to your JVM?

As JVM arguments:
```
$> java MyProgram   -DallowCache=true
```

alternatively in your code:
```
System.setProperty("allowCache", Boolean.TRUE);     // to set the value
System.getProperty("allowCache");                    // to get the value
```

Enterprise – EJB 2.x

There are various persistence mechanisms available like EJB 2.x, Object-to-Relational (O/R) mapping tools like Hibernate, JDBC and EJB 3.0 (new kid on the block) etc. You will have to evaluate the products based on the application you are building because each product has its strengths and weaknesses. You will find yourself trading ease of use for scalability, standards with support for special features like stored procedures, etc. Some factors will be more important to you than for others. There is no one size fits all solution. Let's compare some of the persistence products:

EJB 2.x	EJB 3.0	Hibernate	JDBC
PROS: • Security is provided for free for accessing the EJB. • Provides declarative transactions. • EJBs are pooled and cached. EJB life cycles are managed by the container. • Has remote access capabilities and can be clustered for scalability.	**PROS:** • A lot less artifacts than EJB 2.x. Makes use of annotations or attributes based programming. • Narrows the gap between EJB 2.x and O/R mapping. • Do support OO concepts like inheritance.	**PROS:** • Simple to write CRUD (create, retrieve, update, delete) operations. • No container or application server is required and can be plugged into an existing container. • Tools are available to simplify mapping relational data to objects and quick to develop.	**PROS:** • You have complete control over the persistence because this is the building blocks of nearly all other persistence technologies in Java. • Can call Stored Procedures. • Can manipulate relatively large data sets.
Cons: • Need to understand the intricacies like rolling back a transaction, granularity etc, infrastructures like session facades, business delegates, value objects etc and strategies like lazy loading, dirty marker etc. • EJBs use lots of resources and have lots of artifacts. • Does not support OO concepts like inheritance.	**Cons:** • As of writing, It is still evolving.	**Cons:** • Little or no capabilities for remote access and distributability. • Mapping schemas can be tedious and O/R mapping has its tricks like using lazy initialization, eager loading etc. What works for one may not work for another. • Limited clustering capabilities. • Large data sets can still cause memory issues. • Support for security at a database level only and no support for role based security without any add on APIs like Aspect Oriented Programming etc.	**Cons:** • You will have to write a lot of code to perform a little. Easy to make mistakes in properly managing connections and can cause out of cursors issues. • Harder to maintain because changes in schemas can cause lot of changes to your code. • Records need to be locked manually (e.g. select for update).
As a rule of thumb, suitable for distributed and clustered applications, which is heavily transaction based. Records in use say between 1 and 50.	As a rule of thumb, suitable for distributed and clustered applications, which is heavily transaction based. Records in use say between 1 and 100.	Suitable for records in use between 100 and 5000. Watch out for memory issues, when using large data sets.	Where possible stay away from using JDBC unless you have compelling reason to use it for batch jobs where large amount of data need to be transferred, records in use greater than 5000, required to use Stored Procedures etc.

The stateless session beans and message driven beans have wider acceptance in EJB 2.x compared to stateful session beans and entity beans. Refer Emerging Technologies/Frameworks section for Hibernate and EJB 3.0.

Q 60: What is the role of EJB 2.x in J2EE? SF

A 60: EJB 2.x (Enterprise JavaBeans) is widely adopted server side component architecture for J2EE.

- EJB is a remote, distributed multi-tier system and supports protocols like JRMP, IIOP, and HTTP etc.
- It enables rapid development of reusable, versatile, and portable business components (i.e. across middleware), which are transactional and scalable.

- EJB is a specification for J2EE servers. EJB components contain only business logic and system level programming and services like transactions, security, instance pooling, multi-threading, persistence etc are managed by the EJB Container and hence simplify the programming effort.
- Message driven EJBs have support for asynchronous communication.

Note: Having said that EJB 2.x is a widely adopted server side component, **EJB 3.0** is taking ease of development very seriously and has adjusted its model to offer the POJO (Plain Old Java Object) persistence and the new **O/R mapping model based on Hibernate**. In EJB 3.0, **all kinds of enterprise beans are just POJOs**. EJB 3.0 **extensively uses Java annotations**, which replaces excessive XML based configuration files and eliminates the need for the rigid component model used in EJB 1.x, 2.x. Annotations can be used to define the bean's business interface, O/R mapping information, resource references etc. Refer **Q18** in Emerging Technologies/Frameworks section. So, for future developments look out for EJB 3.0 and/or Hibernate framework. Refer **Q14 – Q16** in Emerging Technologies/Frameworks section for discussion on Hibernate framework.

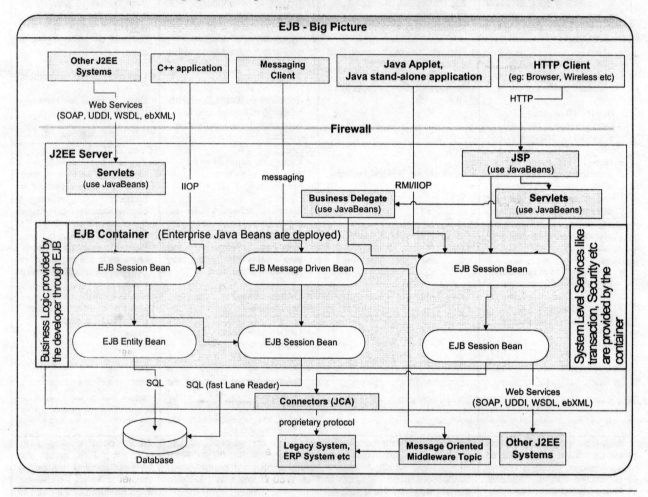

Q 61: What is the difference between EJB and JavaBeans? SF FAQ
A 61: Both EJBs and JavaBeans have very similar names but this is where the similarities end.

JavaBeans	Enterprise JavaBeans (EJB)
The components built based on JavaBeans live in a single local JVM (i.e. address space) and can be either visual (e.g. GUI components like Button, List etc) or non-visual at runtime.	The Enterprise JavaBeans are non-visual distributable components, which can live across multiple JVMs (i.e. address spaces).
No explicit support exists for services like transactions etc.	EJBs can be transactional and the EJB servers provide transactional support.
JavaBeans are fine-grained components, which can be used to assemble coarse-grained components or an application.	EJBs are coarse-grained components that can be deployed as is or assembled with other components into larger applications. EJBs must be deployed in a container that provides services like instance pooling, multi-threading, security, life-cycle management, transactions etc
Must conform to JavaBeans specification.	Must conform to EJB specification.

Q 62: Explain EJB architecture? SF
A 62:

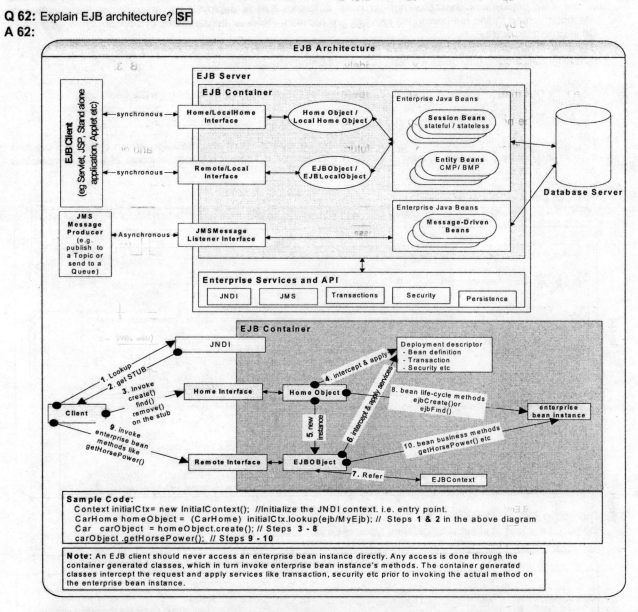

EJB Container: EJBs are software components, which run in an environment called an EJB container. An EJB cannot function outside an EJB Container. The EJB container hosts and manages an Enterprise JavaBean in a similar manner that a Web container hosts a servlet or a Web browser hosts a Java Applet. The EJB container manages the following services so that the developer can concentrate on writing the business logic:

- Transactions (refer **Q71 – Q75** in Enterprise section)
- Persistence
- EJB instance pooling
- Security (refer **Q81** in Enterprise section)
- Concurrent access (or multi-threading)
- Remote access

Design pattern: EJBs use the proxy design pattern to make remote invocation (i.e. remote proxy) and to add container managed services like security and transaction demarcation. Refer **Q11** in "How would you about…" section for a more detailed discussion on proxy design pattern and dynamic proxies.

EJBContext: Every bean obtains an <u>EJBContext</u> object, which is a reference directly to the container. The EJB can request information about its environment like the status of a transaction, a remote reference to itself (an EJB <u>cannot use</u> 'this' to reference itself) etc.

Deployment Descriptor: The container handles all the above mentioned services declaratively for an EJB based on the XML deployment descriptor (**ejb-jar.xml**). When an EJB is deployed into a container the deployment descriptor is read to find out how these services are handled. Refer to the *J2EE deployment structure* diagram in **Q6** in Enterprise section.

EJB: The EJB architecture defines 3 distinct types of Enterprise JavaBeans.

▪ Session beans.
▪ Entity beans.
▪ Message-driven beans.

The session and entity beans are invoked synchronously by the client and message driven beans are invoked asynchronously by a message container such as a Queue or a Topic. Let's look at some of the EJB container services in a bit more detail:

Instance pooling

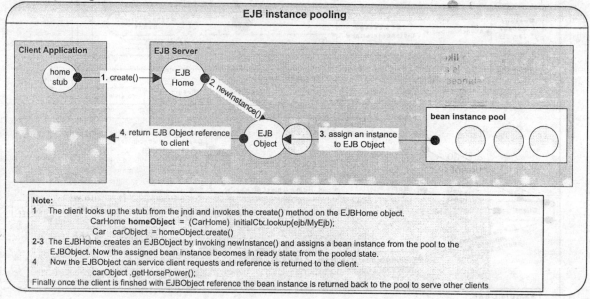

EJB instance pooling

Note:
1   The client looks up the stub from the jndi and invokes the create() method on the EJBHome object.
        CarHome **homeObject** = (CarHome) initialCtx.lookup(ejb/MyEjb);
        Car   carObject = homeObject.create()
2-3 The EJBHome creates an EJBObject by invoking newInstance() and assigns a bean instance from the pool to the
    EJBObject. Now the assigned bean instance becomes in ready state from the pooled state.
4   Now the EJBObject can service client requests and reference is returned to the client.
        carObject .getHorsePower();
Finally once the client is finshed with EJBObject reference the bean instance is returned back to the pool to serve other clients

The above diagram shows how the EJB instances are pooled and assigned to EJB Object and then returned to the pool. Let's look at in detail for different types of EJBs.

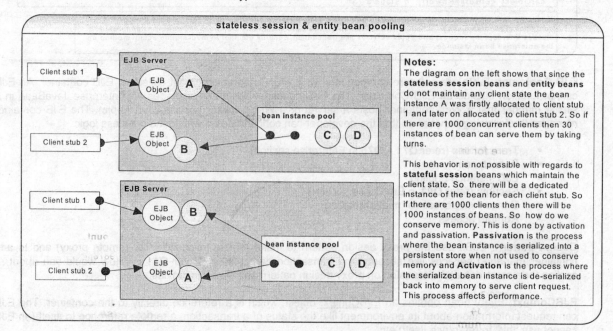

stateless session & entity bean pooling

Notes:
The diagram on the left shows that since the **stateless session beans** and **entity beans** do not maintain any client state the bean instance A was firstly allocated to client stub 1 and later on allocated to client stub 2. So if there are 1000 concurrent clients then 30 instances of bean can serve them by taking turns.

This behavior is not possible with regards to **stateful session** beans which maintain the client state. So there will be a dedicated instance of the bean for each client stub. So if there are 1000 clients then there will be 1000 instances of beans. So how do we conserve memory. This is done by activation and passivation. **Passivation** is the process where the bean instance is serialized into a persistent store when not used to conserve memory and **Activation** is the process where the serialized bean instance is de-serialized back into memory to serve client request. This process affects performance.

From the diagrams it is clear that bean instances can be reused for all the bean types except for the stateful session bean where the client state is maintained. So we need a dedicated stateful session bean for each client.

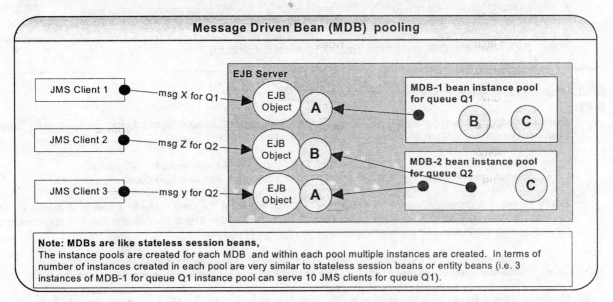

Message Driven Bean (MDB) pooling

Note: MDBs are like stateless session beans,
The instance pools are created for each MDB and within each pool multiple instances are created. In terms of number of instances created in each pool are very similar to stateless session beans or entity beans (i.e. 3 instances of MDB-1 for queue Q1 instance pool can serve 10 JMS clients for queue Q1).

Concurrent access

The session beans do not support concurrent access. The stateful session beans are exclusively for a client so there is no concurrent access. The stateless session beans do not maintain any state. It does not make any sense to have concurrent access. The entity beans represent data that is in the database table, which is shared between the clients. So to make concurrent access possible the EJB container need to protect the data while allowing many clients simultaneous access. When you try to share distributed objects you may have the following problem:

If 2 clients are using the same EJBObject, how do you keep one client from writing over the changes of the other? Say for example

```
Client-1 reads a value x= 5
Client-2 modifies the value to x=7
Now the client-1's value is invalid.
```

The entity bean addresses this by prohibiting concurrent access to bean instances. Which means several clients can be connected to one EJBObject but only one client can access the EJB instance at a time.

Persistence

Entity beans basically represent the data in a relational database. An Entity Bean is responsible for keeping its state in sync with the database.

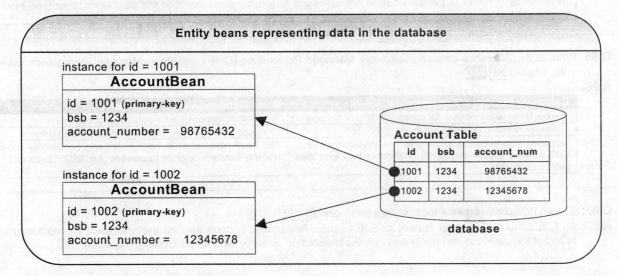

Entity beans representing data in the database

- Container-managed persistence (CMP) - The container is responsible for saving the bean's state with the help of object-relational mapping tools.
- Bean-managed persistence (BMP) – The entity bean is responsible for saving its own state.

If entity beans performance is of concern then there are other persistence technologies and frameworks like JDBC, JDO, Hibernate, OJB and Oracle TopLink (commercial product).

Q 63: What are the different kinds of enterprise beans? **SF** **FAQ**
A 63:

Session Bean: is a non-persistent object that implements some business logic running on the server. Session beans do not survive system shut down. There are two types of session beans

- Stateless session beans (i.e. each session bean can be reused by multiple EJB clients).
- Stateful session beans (i.e. each session bean is associated with one EJB client).

Entity Bean: is a persistent object that represents object views of the data, usually a row in a database. They have the primary key as a unique identifier. Multiple EJB clients can share each entity bean. Entity beans can survive system shutdowns. Entity beans can have two types of persistence

- Container-Managed Persistence (CMP) - The container is responsible for saving the bean's state.
- Bean-Managed Persistence (BMP) – The entity bean is responsible for saving its own state.

Message-driven Bean: is integrated with the Java Message Service (JMS) to provide the ability to act as a message consumer and perform asynchronous processing between the server and the message producer.

Q 64: What is the difference between session and entity beans? **SF**
A 64:

Session Beans	Entity Beans
Use session beans for application logic.	Use entity beans to develop persistent object model.
Expect little reuse of session beans.	Insist on reuse of entity beans.
Session beans control the workflow and transactions of a group of entity beans.	Domain objects with a unique identity (i.e.-primary key) shared by multiple clients.
Life is limited to the life of a particular client. Handle database access for a particular client.	Persist across multiple invocations. Handles database access for multiple clients.
Do not survive system shut downs or server crashes.	Do survive system shut downs or server crashes.

Q 65: What is the difference between stateful and stateless session beans? **SF** **FAQ**
A 65:

Stateless Session Beans	Stateful Session Bean
Do not have an internal state. Can be reused by different clients.	Do have an internal state. Reused by the same client.
Need not be activated or passivated since the beans are pooled and reused.	Need to handle activation and passivation to conserve system memory since one session bean object per client.

Q 66: What is the difference between Container Managed Persistence (CMP) and Bean Managed Persistence (BMP) entity beans? **SF** **FAQ**
A 66:

Container Managed Persistence (CMP)	Bean Managed Persistence (BMP)
The container is responsible for persisting state of the bean.	The bean is responsible for persisting its own state.
Container needs to generate database (SQL) calls.	The bean needs to code its own database (SQL) calls.
The bean persistence is independent of its database (e.g. DB2, Oracle, Sybase etc). So it is portable from one data source to another.	The bean persistence is hard coded and hence may not be portable between different databases (e.g. DB2, Oracle etc).

Q 67: Can an EJB client invoke a method on a bean directly? **SF**

A 67: An EJB client should never access an EJB directly. Any access is done through the container. The container will intercept the client call and apply services like transaction, security etc prior to invoking the actual EJB.

Q 68: How does an EJB interact with its container and what are the call-back methods in entity beans? SF

A 68: EJB interacts with its container through the following mechanisms

- **Call-back Methods:** Every EJB implements an interface (extends EnterpriseBean) which defines several methods which alert the bean to various events in its lifecycle. A container is responsible for invoking these methods. These methods notify the bean when it is about to be activated, to be persisted to the database, to end a transaction, to remove the bean from the memory, etc. For example the entity bean has the following call-back methods:

```
public interface javax.ejb.EntityBean {

    public void setEntityContext(javax.ejb.EntityContext c);
    public void unsetEntityContext();
    public void ejbLoad();
    public void ejbStore();
    public void ejbActivate();
    public void ejbPassivate();
    public void ejbRemove();
}
```

- **EJBContext:** provides methods for interacting with the container so that the bean can request information about its environment like the identity of the caller, security, status of a transaction, obtains remote reference to itself etc. e.g. isUserInRole(), getUserPrincipal(), isRollbackOnly(), etc

- **JNDI (Java Naming and Directory Interface):** allows EJB to access resources like JDBC connections, JMS topics and queues, other EJBs etc.

Q 69: What is the difference between EJB 1.1 and EJB 2.0? What is the difference between EJB 2.x and EJB 3.0? SF FAQ

A 69: EJB 2.0 has the following additional advantages over the EJB 1.1

- **Local interfaces:** These are beans that can be used locally, that means by the same Java Virtual Machine, so they do not required to be wrapped like remote beans, and arguments between those interfaces are passed directly by reference instead of by value. This improves performance.

- **ejbHome methods:** Entity beans can declare ejbHomeXXX(...) methods that perform operations related to the EJB component but that are not specific to a bean instance. The ejbHomeXXX(...) method declared in the bean class must have a matching home method XXXX(...) in the home interface.

- **Message Driven Beans (MDB):** is a completely new enterprise bean type, which is designed specifically to handle incoming JMS messages.

- **New CMP Model.** It is based on a new contract called *the abstract persistence schema*, which will allow the container to handle the persistence automatically at runtime.

- **EJB Query Language (EJB QL):** It is a SQL-based language that will allow the new persistence schema to implement and execute finder methods. EJB QL also used in new query methods ejbSelectXXX(...), which is similar to ejbFindXXXX(...) methods except that it is only for the bean class to use and not exposed to the client (i.e. it is not declared in the home interface)

Let's look at some of the new features on EJB 2.1

- **Container-managed timer service:** The timer service provides coarse-grained, transactional, time-based event notifications to enable enterprise beans to model and manage higher-level business processes.

- **Web Service support:** EJB 2.1 adds the ability of stateless session beans to implement a Web Service endpoint via a Web Service endpoint interface.

- **EJB-QL:** Enhanced EJB-QL includes support for aggregate functions and ordering of results.

Current **EJB 2.x** model is complex for a variety of reasons:

- You need to create several component interfaces and implement several unnecessary call-back methods.

- EJB deployment descriptors are complex and error prone.

- EJB components are not truly object oriented, as they have restrictions for using inheritance and polymorphism.

- EJB modules cannot be tested outside an EJB container and debugging an EJB inside a container is very difficult.

Note: EJB 3.0 is taking ease of development very seriously and has adjusted its model to offer the POJO (Plain Old Java Object) persistence and the new **O/R mapping model based on Hibernate**. In EJB 3.0, **all kinds of enterprise beans are just POJOs**. EJB 3.0 **extensively uses Java annotations**, which replaces excessive XML based configuration files and eliminate the need for rigid component model used in EJB 1.x, 2.x. Annotations can be used to define the bean's business interface, O/R mapping information, resource references etc. Refer **Q18** in Emerging Technologies/Frameworks section.

Q 70: What are the implicit services provided by an EJB container? SF FAQ
A 70:

- **Lifecycle Management:** Individual enterprise beans do not need to explicitly manage process allocation, thread management, object activation, or object destruction. The EJB container automatically manages the object lifecycle on behalf of the enterprise bean.

- **State Management:** Individual enterprise beans do not need to explicitly save or restore conversational object state between method calls. The EJB container automatically manages object state on behalf of the enterprise bean.

- **Security:** Individual enterprise beans do not need to explicitly authenticate users or check authorization levels. The EJB container automatically performs all security checking on behalf of the enterprise bean.

- **Transactions:** Individual enterprise beans do not need to explicitly specify transaction demarcation code to participate in distributed transactions. The EJB container can automatically manage the start, enrolment, commitment, and rollback of transactions on behalf of the enterprise bean.

- **Persistence:** Individual enterprise beans do not need to explicitly retrieve or store persistent object data from a database. The EJB container can automatically manage persistent data on behalf of the enterprise bean.

Q 71: What are transactional attributes? SF TI FAQ
A 71: EJB transactions are a set of mechanisms and concepts, which insures the integrity and consistency of the database when multiple clients try to read/update the database simultaneously.

Transaction attributes are defined at different levels like EJB class, a method within a class or segment of a code within a method. The attributes specified for a particular method take precedence over the attributes specified for a particular EJB class. Transaction attributes are specified *declaratively* through EJB deployment descriptors. Unless there is any compelling reason, the *declarative* approach is recommended over programmatic approach where all the transactions are handled programmatically. With the *declarative* approach, the EJB container will handle the transactions.

Transaction Attributes	Description
Required	Methods executed within a transaction. If client provides a transaction, it is used. If not, a new transaction is generated. Commit at end of method that started the transaction. Which means a method that has *Required* attribute set, but was called when the transaction has already started will not commit at the method completion. Well suited for EJB session beans.
Mandatory	Client of this EJB must create a transaction in which this method operates, otherwise an error will be reported. Well-suited for entity beans.
RequiresNew	Methods executed within a transaction. If client provides a transaction, it is suspended. If not a new transaction is generated, regardless. Commit at end of method.
Supports	Transactions are optional.
NotSupported	Transactions are not supported. If provided, ignored.
Never	Code in the EJB is responsible for explicit transaction control.

Q 72: What are isolation levels? SF TI PI FAQ
A 72: Isolation levels provide a degree of control of the effects one transaction can have on another concurrent transaction. Since concurrent effects are determined by the precise ways in which, a particular relational database

handles locks and its drivers may handle these locks differently. The semantics of isolation mechanisms based on these are not well defined. Nevertheless, certain defined or approximate properties can be specified as follows:

Isolation level	Description
TRANSACTION_SERIALIZABLE	Strongest level of isolation. Places a range lock on the data set, preventing other users from updating or inserting rows into the data set until the transaction is complete. Can produce deadlocks.
TRANSACTION_REPEATABLE_READ	Locks are placed on all data that is used in a query, preventing other users from updating the data, but new **phantom records** can be inserted into the data set by another user and are included in later reads in the current transaction.
TRANSACTION_READ_COMMITTED	Can't read uncommitted data by another transaction. Shared locks are held while the data is being read to avoid **dirty reads,** but the data can be changed before the end of the transaction resulting in **non-repeatable reads** and **phantom records.**
TRANSACTION_READ_UNCOMMITTED	Can read uncommitted data (**dirty read**) by another transaction, and **non-repeatable reads** and **phantom records** are possible. Least restrictive of all isolation levels. No shared locks are issued and no exclusive locks are honored.

Isolation levels are not part of the EJB specification. They can only be set on the resource manager either explicitly on the *Connection* (for bean managed persistence) or via the application server specific configuration. The EJB specification indicates that isolation level is part of the **Resource Manager**.

As the transaction **isolation level increases**, likely **performance degradation** follows, as additional locks are required to protect data integrity. If the underlying data does not require such a high degree of integrity, the isolation level can be lowered to improve performance.

Q 73: What is a distributed transaction? What is a 2-phase commit? `SF` `TI` `FAQ`

A 73: A **Transaction** (Refer **Q43** in Enterprise section) is a series of actions performed as a single unit of work in which either all of the actions performed as a logical unit of work in which, either all of the actions are performed or none of the actions. A transaction is often described by ACID properties (Atomic, Consistent, Isolated and Durable). A **distributed transaction** is an ACID transaction between two or more independent transactional resources like two separate databases. For the transaction to commit successfully, all of the individual resources must commit successfully. If any of them are unsuccessful, the transaction must rollback in all of the resources. A **2-phase commit** is an approach for committing a distributed transaction in 2 phases.

Phase 1 is prepare: Each of the resources votes on whether it's ready to commit – usually by going ahead and persisting the new data but not yet deleting the old data.

Phase 2 is committing: If all the resources are ready, they all commit – after which old data is deleted and transaction can no longer roll back. 2-phase commit ensures that a distributed transaction can always be committed or always rolled back if one of the databases crashes. The **XA** specification defines how an application program uses a transaction manager to coordinate distributed transactions across multiple resource managers. Any resource manager that adheres to XA specification can participate in a transaction coordinated by an XA-compliant transaction manager.

Q 74: What is dooming a transaction? `TI`

A 74: A transaction can be doomed by the following method call `CO`

```
ejbContext.setRollbackOnly();
```

The above call will force transaction to rollback. The doomed transactions decrease scalability and if a transaction is doomed why perform compute intensive operations? So you can detect a doomed transaction as shown below:
`CO`

```
public void doComputeIntensiveOperation() throws Exception {

  if ( ejbContext.getRollbackOnly() ) {
     return; // transaction is doomed so return (why unnecessarily perform compute intensive
              // operation)
  }
  else {
     performComplexOperation();
  }
}
```

Q 75: How to design transactional conversations with session beans? SF TI

A 75: A stateful session bean is a resource which has an in memory state which can be rolled back in case of any failure. It can participate in transactions by implementing SessionSynchronization. CO

SessionSynchronization

```
public class MyBean implements SessionBean, SessionSynchronization{
        public int oldVal ;   public int val ;

        public void ejbCreate(int val) throws CreateException {
                this.val=val;
                this.oldVal=val;
        }

        public void afterBegin() { this.oldVal = this.val ;}
        public void   beforeCompletion(){};
        public void afterCompletion(boolean b) {  if (b == false)  this.val = this.oldVal ; }
                .............................
}
```

```
public interface javax.ejb.SessionSynchronization {
        public void afterBegin();
        public void beforeCompletion();
        public void afterCompletion(boolean b);
}
```

The uses of SessionSynchronization are:

- Enables the bean to act as a transactional resource and undo state changes on failure.
- Enables you to cache database data to improve performance.

Q 76: Explain exception handling in EJB? SF EH CO FAQ

A 76: Java has two types of exceptions:

- **Checked exception**: derived from **java.lang.Exception** but not **java.lang.RuntimeException**.
- **Unchecked exception:** derived from **java.lang.RuntimeException** thrown by JVM.

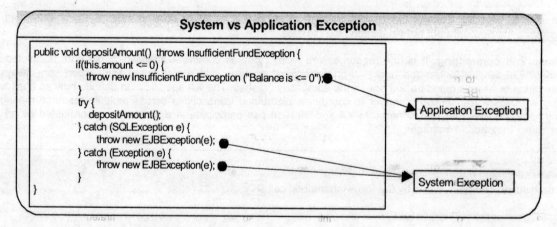

System vs Application Exception

```
public void depositAmount()  throws InsufficientFundException {
        if(this.amount <= 0) {
           throw new InsufficientFundException ("Balance is <= 0");
        }
        try {
           depositAmount();
        } catch (SQLException e) {
           throw new EJBException(e);
        } catch (Exception e) {
           throw new EJBException(e);
        }
}
```

Application Exception

System Exception

EJB has two types of exceptions:

- **System Exception**: is an **unchecked** exception derived from **java.lang.RuntimeException**. An *EJBException* is an unchecked exception, which is derived from **java.lang.RuntimeException.**

- **Application Exception**: is specific to an application and thrown because of violation of business rules (e.g. *InsufficierntFundException* etc). An Application Exception is a checked exception that is either defined by the bean developer and does not extend java.rmi.RemoteException, or is predefined in the javax.ejb package (i.e. *CreateException*, *RemoveException*, *ObjectNotFoundException* etc).

A **System Exception** is thrown by the system and is not recoverable. For example EJB container losing connection to the database server, failed remote method objects call etc. Because the System Exceptions are unpredictable, the EJB container is the only one responsible for trapping the System Exceptions. The container automatically wraps any *RuntimeException* in *RemoteException*, which subsequently gets thrown to the caller (i.e. client). In addition to intercepting System Exception the container may log the errors.

An **Application Exception** is specific to an application and is thrown because of violation of business rules. The client should be able to determine how to handle an Application Exception. If the account balance is zero then an Application Exception like **InsufficientFundException** can be thrown. If an **Application Exception** should be treated as a System Exception then it needs to be wrapped in an **EJBException,** which extends java.lang. RuntimeException so that it can be managed properly (e.g. rolling back transactions) and propagated to the client.

Q 77: How do you rollback a container managed transaction in EJB? SF TI EH FAQ
A 77: The way the exceptions are handled affects the way the transactions are managed. CO

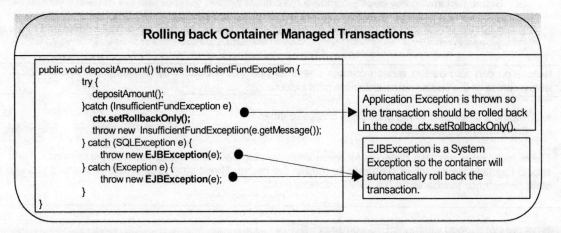

When the container manages the transaction, it is automatically rolled back when a **System Exception** occurs. This is possible because the container can intercept System Exception. However when an **Application Exception** occurs, the container does not intercept it and therefore leaves it to the code to roll back using **ctx.setRollbackOnly()**.

Be aware that handling exceptions in EJB is different from handling exceptions in Java. The Exception handling best practice tips are:

- If you cannot recover from System Exception let the container handle it.
- If a business rule is violated then throw an application exception.
- If you want to rollback a transaction on an application exception then catch the application exception and throw an *EJBException* or use `ctx.setRollbackOnly();`

Q 78: What is the difference between optimistic and pessimistic concurrency control? TI CI
A 78:

Pessimistic Concurrency	Optimistic Concurrency
A pessimistic design assumes conflicts will occur in the database tables and avoids them through exclusive locks etc.	An optimistic approach assumes conflicts won't occur, and deal with them when they do occur.
EJB (also non-EJB) locks the source data until it completes its transaction. - Provides reliable access to data. - Suitable for short transactions. - Suitable for systems where concurrent access is rare.	EJB (also non-EJB) implements a strategy to detect whether a change has occurred. Locks are placed on the database only for a small portion of the time. - Suitable for long transactions. - Suitable for systems requiring frequent concurrent accesses.
The pessimistic locking imposes high locking overheads on the server and lower concurrency.	The optimistic locking is used in the context of cursors. The optimistic locking works as follows: - No locks are acquired as rows are read. - No locks are acquired while values in the current row are changed. - When changes are saved, a copy of the row in the database is read in the locked mode. - If the data was changed after it was read into the cursor, an error

	is raised so that the transaction can be rolled back and retried. **Note: The testing for changes can be done by comparing the values, timestamp or version numbers.**

Q 79: How can we determine if the data is stale (for example when using optimistic locking)? TI

A 79: We can use the following strategy to determine if the data is stale:

- Adding version numbers

    1. Add a version number (Integer) to the underlying table.
    2. Carry the version number along with any data read into memory (through value object, entity bean etc).
    3. Before performing any update compare the current version number with the database version number.
    4. If the version numbers are equal update the data and increment the version number.
    5. If the value object or entity bean is carrying an older version number, reject the update and throw an exception.

Note: You can also do the version number check as part of the update by including the version column in the where clause of the update without doing a prior select.

- Adding a timestamp to the underlying database table.
- Comparing the data values.

These techniques are also quite useful when implementing data caching to improve performance. Data caches should regularly keep track of stale data to refresh the cache. These strategies are valid whether you use EJB or other persistence mechanisms like JDBC, Hibernate etc.

Q 80: What are not allowed within the EJB container? SF

A 80: In order to develop reliable and portable EJB components, the following restrictions apply to EJB code implementation:

- Avoid using static non-final fields. Declaring all static fields in EJB component as final is recommended. This enables the EJB container to distribute instances across multiple JVMs.

- Avoid starting a new thread (conflicts with EJB container) or using thread synchronization (allow the EJB container to distribute instances across multiple JVMs).

- Avoid using AWT or Swing functionality. EJBs are server side business components.

- Avoid using file access or java.io operations. EJB business components are meant to use resource managers such as JDBC to store and retrieve application data. But deployment descriptors can be used to store <env-entry>.

- Avoid accepting or listening to socket connections. EJB components are not meant to provide network socket functionality. However the specification lets EJB components act as socket clients or RMI clients.

- Avoid using the reflection API. This restriction enforces Java security.

- Can't use custom class loaders.

Q 81: Discuss EJB container security? SF SE

A 81: EJB components operate inside a container environment and rely heavily on the container to provide security. The four key services required for the security are:

- **Identification**: In Java security APIs this identifier is known as a **principal**.

- **Authentication**: To prove the identity one must present the credentials in the form of password, swipe card, digital certificate, finger prints etc.

- **Authorization (Access Control)**: Every secure system should limit access to particular users. The common way to enforce access control is by maintaining **security roles** and **privileges**.

- **Data Confidentiality**: This is maintained by encryption of some sort. It is no good to protect your data by authentication if someone can read the password.

The EJB specification concerns itself exclusively with **authorization** (access control). An application using EJB can specify in an abstract (declarative) and portable way that is allowed to access business methods. The EJB container handles the following actions:

- Find out the Identity of the caller of a business method.

- Check the EJB deployment descriptor to see if the identity is a member of a security role that has been granted the right to call this business method.

- Throw java.rmi.RemoteException if the access is illegal.

- Make the identity and the security role information available for a fine grained programmatic security check.

```
public  void closeAccount() {
      if (ejbContext.getCallerPrincipal().getName().equals("SMITH")) {
          //…
      }

      if (!ejbContext.isCallerInRole(CORPORATE_ACCOUNT_MANAGER)) {
          throw new SecurityException("Not authorized to close this account");
      }
}
```

- Optionally log any illegal access.

There are two types of information the EJB developer has to provide through the deployment descriptor.

- Security roles
- Method permissions

Example:

```
<security-role>
   <description>
       Allowed to open and close accounts
   </description>
   <role-name>account_manager</role-name>
</security-role>
<security-role>
   <description>
       Allowed to read only
   </description>
   <role-name>teller</role-name>
</security-role>
```

There is a many-to-many relationship between the security roles and the method permissions.

```
<method-permission>
  <role-name>teller</role-name>
  <method>
      <ejb-name>AccountProcessor</ejb-name>
      <method-name>findByPrimaryKey</method-name>
  </method>
</method-permission>
```

Just as we must declare the resources accessed in our code for other EJBs that we reference in our code we should also declare the security role we access programmatically to have a fine grained control as shown below.

```
<security-role-ref>
  <description>
      Allowed to open and close accounts
  </description>
  <role-name>account_manager</role-name>
  <role-link>executive</role-link>
</security-role-ref>
```

There is also many-to-many relationship between the EJB specific security roles that are in the deployment descriptor and the application based target security system like LDAP etc. For example there might be more than one group users and individual users that need to be mapped to a particular EJB security role 'account_manager'.

Q 82: What are EJB best practices? BP FAQ
A 82:

- Use local interfaces that are available in EJB2.0 if you deploy both the EJB client and the EJB in the same server. Use vendor specific pass-by-reference implementation to make EJB1.1 remote EJBs operate as local. [Extreme care should be taken not to affect the functionality by switching the application, which was written and tested in pass-by-reference mode to pass-by-value without analyzing the implications and re-testing the functionality.

- Wrap entity beans with session beans to reduce network calls (refer **Q84** in Enterprise section) and promote declarative transactions. Where possible use local entity beans and session beans can be either local or remote. Apply the appropriate EJB design patterns as described in **Q83 – Q87** in Enterprise section.

- Cache ejbHome references to avoid JNDI look-up overhead using service locator pattern.

- Handle exceptions appropriately (refer **Q76, Q77** in Enterprise section).

- Avoid transaction overhead for non-transactional methods of session beans by declaring transactional attribute as "Supports".

- Choose plain Java object over EJB if you do not want services like RMI/IIOP, transactions, security, persistence, thread safety etc. There are alternative frameworks such as Hibernate, Spring etc.

- Choose Servlet's **HttpSession** object rather than stateful session bean to maintain client state if you do not require component architecture of a stateful bean.

- Apply **Lazy loading** and **Dirty marker** strategies as described in **Q88** in Enterprise section.

Session Bean (stateless)	Session Bean (stateful)	Entity Bean
• Tune the pool size to avoid overhead of creation and destruction. • Use setSessionContext(..) or ejbCreate(..) method to cache any bean specific resources. • Release any acquired resources like Database connection etc in ejbRemove() method	• Tune the pool size to avoid overhead of creation and destruction. • Set proper time out to avoid resource congestion. • Remove it explicitly from client using remove() method. • Use 'transient' variable where possible to avoid serialization overhead.	• Tune the pool size to avoid overhead of creation and destruction. • Use setEntityContext(..) method to cache any bean specific resources and unsetEntityContext() method to release acquired resources. • Use lazy-loading to avoid any unnecessary loading of dependent data. Use dirty marker to avoid unchanged data update. • Commit the data after a transaction completes to reduce any database calls in between. • Where possible perform bulk updates, use CMP rather than BMP, Use direct JDBC (Fast-lane-reader) instead of entity beans, use of read-only entity beans etc.

Q 83: What is a business delegate? Why should you use a business delegate? DP PI FAQ
A 83: Questions **Q83 – Q88** are very popular EJB questions.

Problem: When presentation tier components interact directly with the business services components like EJB, the presentation components are vulnerable to changes in the implementation of business services components.

Solution: Use a **Business Delegate** to reduce the coupling between the presentation tier components and the business services tier components. Business Delegate hides the underlying implementation details of the business service, such as look-up and access details of the EJB architecture.

Business delegate **is responsible for:**

- Invoking session beans in Session Facade.

- Acting as a service locator and cache home stubs to improve performance.
- Handling exceptions from the server side. (Unchecked exceptions get wrapped into the remote exception, checked exceptions can be thrown as an application exception or wrapped in the remote exception. unchecked exceptions do not have to be caught but can be caught and should not be used in the method signature.)
- Re-trying services for the client (For example when using optimistic locking business delegate will retry the method call when there is a concurrent access.).

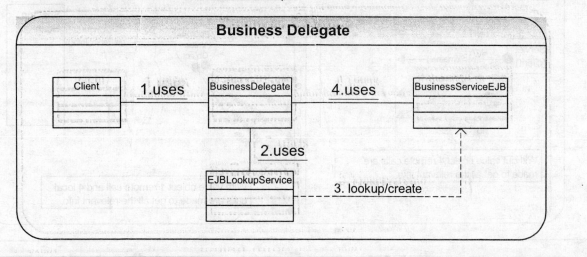

Q 84: What is a session façade? DP PI FAQ

A 84: Problem: Too many method invocations between the client and the server will lead to network overhead, tight coupling due to dependencies between the client and the server, misuse of server business methods due to fine grained access etc.

Solution: Use a **session** bean as a **façade** to encapsulate the complexities between the client and the server interactions. The Session Facade manages the business objects, and provides a uniform coarse-grained service access layer to clients.

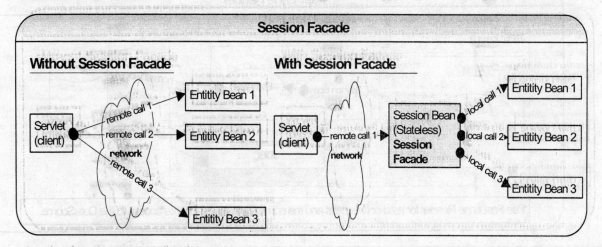

Session façade is responsible for

- Improving performance by minimizing fine-grained method calls over the network.
- Improving manageability by reducing coupling, exposing uniform interface and exposing fewer methods to clients.
- Managing transaction and security in a centralized manner.

Q 85: What is a value object pattern? DP PI FAQ

A 85: Problem: When a client makes a remote call to the server, there will be a process of network call and serialization of data involved for the remote invocation. If you make fine grained calls there will be performance degradation.

Solution: Avoid fine-grained method calls by creating a value object, which will help the client, make a coarse-grained call.

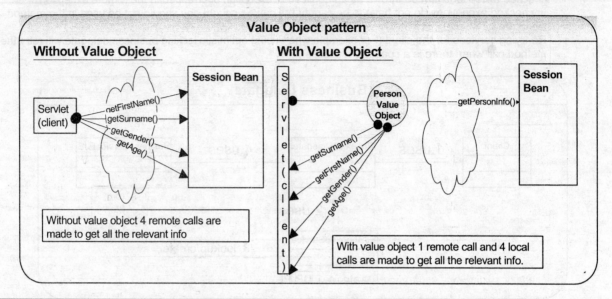

Q 86: What is a fast-lane reader? DP PI FAQ

A 86: **Problem**: Using Entity beans to represent persistent, read only tabular data incurs performance cost at no benefit (especially when large amount of data to be read).

Solution: Access the persistent data directly from the database using the DAO (Data Access Object) pattern instead of using Entity beans. The Fast lane readers commonly use JDBC, Connectors etc to access the read-only data from the data source. The main benefit of this pattern is the faster data retrieval.

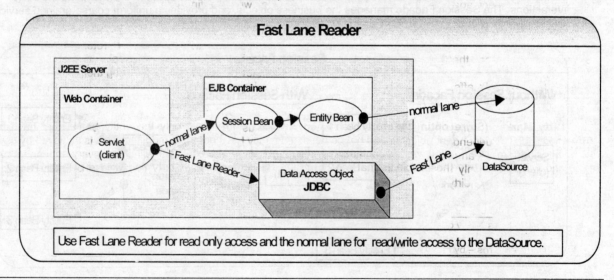

Q 87: What is a Service Locator? DP PI FAQ

A 87: **Problem**: J2EE makes use of the JNDI interface to access different resources like JDBC, JMS, EJB etc. The client looks up for these resources through the JNDI look-up. The JNDI look-up is expensive because the client needs to get a network connection to the server first. So this look-up process is expensive and redundant.

Solution: To avoid this expensive and redundant process, service objects can be cached when a client performs the JNDI look-up for the first time and reuse that service object from the cache for the subsequent look-ups. The service locator pattern implements this technique. Refer to diagram below:

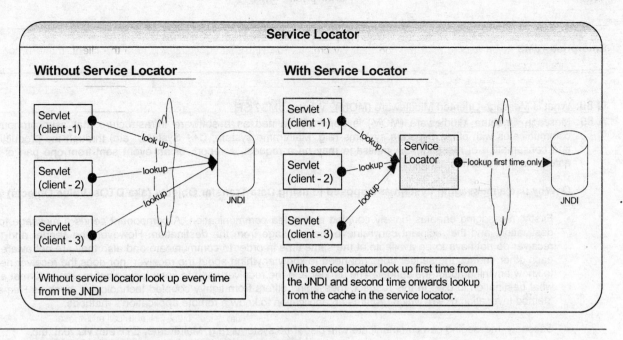

Q 88: Explain lazy loading and dirty marker strategies? `DP` `PI`

A 88: **Lazy Loading**: Lazy loading means not creating an object until the first time it is accessed. This technique is useful when you have large hierarchies of objects. You can lazy load some of the dependent objects. You only create the dependent (subordinate) objects only when you need them.

```
if ( this.data == null) {
    //lazy load data
}
```

For a CMP bean the default scenario is set to no lazy loading and the finder method will execute a single SQL select statement against the database. So, for example, with the findAllCustomers() method will retrieve all customer objects with all the CMP fields in each customer object.

If you turn on lazy loading then only the primary keys of the objects within the finder are returned. Only when you access the object, the container uploads the actual object based on the primary key. You may want to turn on the lazy loading feature if the number of objects that you are retrieving is so large that loading them all into local cache would adversely affect the performance. (**Note:** The implementation of lazy loading strategy may vary from container vendor to vendor).

Dirty Marker (Store optimization): This strategy allows us to persist only the entity beans that have been modified. The dependent objects need not be persisted if they have not been modified. This is achieved by using a dirty flag to mark an object whose contents have been modified. The container will check every dependent object and will persist only those objects that are dirty. Once it is persisted its dirty flag will be cleared. (**Note:** The implementation of dirty marker strategy may vary from container vendor to vendor).

Note: If your job requires a very good understanding of EJB 2.x then following books are recommended:
- **Mastering Enterprise JavaBeans** – by Ed Roman
- **EJB Design Patterns** – by Floyd Marinescu

Q 89: What is <u>M</u>essage <u>O</u>riented <u>M</u>iddleware (**MOM**)? What is JMS? **SF**

A 89: Message Oriented Middleware (MOM) is generally defined as a software infrastructure that asynchronously communicates with other disparate systems (e.g. Mainframe system, C++ System, etc) through the production and consumption of messages. A message may be a request, a report, or an event sent from one part of an enterprise application to another.

Q. Why use a messaging system as opposed to using Data Transfer Objects (aka DTOs, Value Objects) ?

- Firstly, messaging enables loosely coupled distributed communication. A component sends a message to a destination, and the recipient can retrieve the message from the destination. However, the sender and the receiver do not have to be available at the same time in order to communicate and also they are not aware of each other. In fact, the sender does not need to know anything about the receiver; nor does the receiver need to know anything about the sender. The sender and the receiver need to know only what message format and what destination to use. In this respect, messaging differs from tightly coupled technologies, such as Remote Method Invocation (RMI), which requires an application to know a remote application's methods.

- Secondly, messaging can communicate with disparate systems (e.g. Mainframe, C++ etc) via XML etc.

Q. How MOM is different from RPC?

Remote Procedure Call (e.g. RMI)	MOM
Remote Procedure Call (RPC) technologies like RMI attempt to mimic the behavior of system that runs in one process. When a remote procedure is invoked <u>the caller is blocked</u> until the procedure completes and returns control to the caller. This is a <u>synchronous model</u> where process is performed sequentially ensuring that tasks are completed in a predefined order. The synchronized nature of RPC <u>tightly couples</u> the client (the software making the call) to the server (the software servicing the call). The client can not proceed (its blocked) until the server responds. The tightly coupled nature of RPC creates highly interdependent systems where a failure on one system has an immediate impact on other systems.	With the use of Message Oriented Middleware (MOM), problems with the availability of subsystems are less of an issue. A fundamental concept of MOM is that communications between components is intended to be <u>asynchronous</u> in nature. Code that is written to connect the pieces together assumes that there is a one-way message that requires no immediate response. In other words, there is no blocking. Once a message is sent the sender can move on to other tasks; it doesn't have to wait for a response. This is the major difference between RPC and asynchronous messaging and is critical to understanding the advantages offered by MOM systems. In an asynchronous messaging system each subsystem (Customer, Account etc) is decoupled from the other systems. They communicate through the messaging server, so that a failure in one does not impact the operation of the others.
Client is blocked while it is being processed.	Asynchronous messages also allows for parallel processing i.e. client can continue processing while the previous request is being satisfied.

Q. Why use JMS? **FAQ** Message Oriented Middleware (MOM) systems like MQSeries, SonicMQ, etc are proprietary systems. Java Message Service (JMS) is a Java API that allows applications to create, send, receive, and read messages in a <u>standard way</u>. Designed by Sun and several partner companies, the JMS API defines a common set of interfaces and associated semantics that allow programs written in the Java programming language to communicate with other messaging implementations (e.g. SonicMQ, TIBCO etc). The JMS API minimizes the set of concepts a programmer must learn to use messaging products but provides enough features to support sophisticated messaging applications. It also strives to maximize the portability of JMS applications across JMS providers.

Many companies have spent decades developing their legacy systems. So, XML can be used in a non-proprietary way to move data from legacy systems to distributed systems like J2EE over the wire using MOM (i.e. Implementation) and JMS (i.e. Interface).

Q. What are the components of the JMS architecture?

- **Message producers:** A component that is responsible for creating a message. E.g. *QueueSender*, and *TopicPublisher*. An application can have several message producers. Each producer might be responsible for creating different types of messages and sending them to different destinations (i.e. Topic or Queue). A message producer will send messages to a destination regardless of whether or not a consumer is there to consume it.

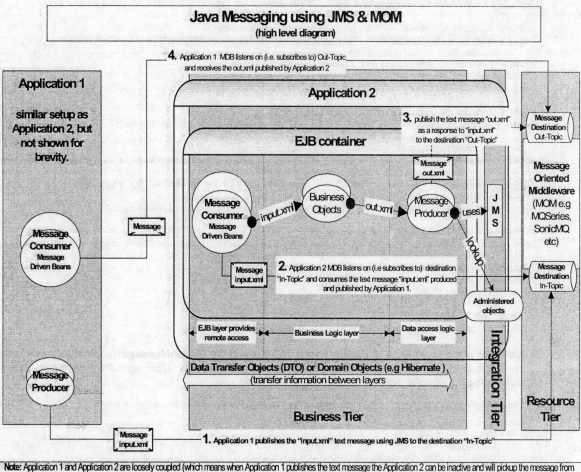

Java Messaging using JMS & MOM
(high level diagram)

Application 1

similar setup as Application 2, but not shown for brevity.

4. Application 1 MDB listens on (i.e. subscribes to) Out-Topic and receives the out.xml published by Application 2

Application 2

EJB container

3. publish the text message "out.xml" as a response to "input.xml" to the destination "Out-Topic"

Message out.xml

Message Consumer Message Driven Beans

Business Objects

input.xml → out.xml →

Message Producer · uses·

J M S

Message Oriented Middleware (MOM e.g MQSeries, SonicMQ etc)

Message Destination Out-Topic

Message Consumer Message Driven Beans

Message input.xml

2. Application 2 MDB listens on (i.e subscribes to) destination "In-Topic" and consumes the text message "input.xml" produced and published by Application 1.

lookup

Administered objects

Message Destination In-Topic

EJB layer provides remote access | Business Logic layer | Data access logic layer

Data Transfer Objects (DTO) or Domain Objects (e.g Hibernate)
(transfer information between layers)

Message Producer

Business Tier

Integration Tier

Resource Tier

Message input.xml

1. Application 1 publishes the "input.xml" text message using JMS to the destination "In-Topic"

Message

Note: Application 1 and Application 2 are loosely coupled (which means when Application 1 publishes the text message the Application 2 can be inactive and will pickup the message from the destination when it becomes active) and communicates asynchronously via Message Oriented Middleware (MOM) like MQSeries, SonicMQ etc using Java Messaging Service (i.e JMS) API and Message Driven Beans (i.e. MDBs - are asynchronous). A MDB cannot be called directly and only interface to it is by sending a JMS message to the destination like "In-Topic" of which the MDB is listening.

- **Message consumers:** A component which resides on the receiving end of a messaging application. Its responsibility is to listen for messages on a destination (i.e. Topic or Queue). E.g. *QueueReceiver*, *TopicSubscriber*, *MessageDrivenBean* (**MDB**). A MDB is simply a JMS message consumer. A client cannot access a MDB directly as you would do with Session or Entity beans. You can only interface with a MDB by sending a JMS message to a destination (i.e. Topic or Queue) on which the MDB is listening.

- **Message destinations:** A component which a client uses to specify the target of messages it sends/receives. E.g. *Topic* (publish/Subscribe domain) and *Queue* (Point-to-Point domain). Message destinations typically live on a MOM, which is remote to the clients. Message destinations are administered objects that need to be configured.

- **JMS messages:** A message is a component that contains the information (aka payload) that must be communicated to another application or component. E.g. *TextMessage* (e.g. XML message), *ObjectMessage* (e.g. serialized object) etc.

- **JMS Administered objects:** JMS administered objects are objects containing configuration information that are set up during application deployment or configuration and later used by JMS clients. They make it practical to administer the JMS API in the enterprise. These administered objects are initialized when the application server starts. When a producer or a consumer needs to get a connection to receive or send a JMS message, then you need to locate the configured administered objects *QueueConnectionFactory* or *TopicConnectionFactory*. Message destinations are administered objects that need to be configured as well. These administered objects hide provider-specific details from JMS clients.

- **JNDI naming service:** For a producer and consumer to be able to use the administered objects to send and receive messages, they must know how to locate things such as the destination and connection factories.

Example: To publish a message to a topic: (**Note:** exception handling etc are omitted for brevity)

```
String factoryJndiName = "WSMQTopicConnectionFactory";
String destinationJndiName = "wsmq/topic/ProductManagerTopic";

//JNDI lookup of administered ConnectionFactory object
Context iniCtx = new InitialContext();
TopicConnectionFactory topicCF = (TopicConnectionFactory) iniCtx.lookup(factoryJndiName);

//JNDI lookup of administered destination (i.e. Topic)
Topic topicDestination = (Topic) iniCtx.lookup(destinationJndiName);

//get a connection from the TopicConnectionFactory
TopicConnection publishConnection = topicCF.createTopicConnection();

//get a session from the connection. Session should be accessed by only one thread.
TopicSession publishSession =
                publishConnection.createTopicSession(false,TopicSession.AUTO_ACKNOWLEDGE);

//create a publisher from the session
TopicPublisher publisher = publishSession.createPublisher(topicDestination);

//create a JMS message to send
TextMessage message = publishSession.createTextMessage();
message.setText("JMS test message");

//send the message
publisher.publish(message, DeliveryMode.NON_PERSISTENT, 4, 0);
```

To consume a message, a MDB listening on a Topic executes the **onMessage**(...) method asynchronously on consumption of the message. A MDB needs to be configured via its J2EE specific deployment descriptor ejb-jar.xml and server specific deployment descriptor like jboss.xml.

```
public void onMessage(Message message) {

    String text = null;
    if (message instanceof TextMessage) {
        text = ((TextMessage)message).getText();
    }

    log.info(text);
}
```

You could also use the following code to consume messages:

```
String factoryJndiName = "WSMQTopicConnectionFactory";
String destinationJndiName = "wsmq/topic/ProductManagerTopic";

//JNDI lookup of administered ConnectionFactory object
Context iniCtx = new InitialContext();
TopicConnectionFactory topicCF = (TopicConnectionFactory) iniCtx.lookup(factoryJndiName);

//JNDI lookup of administered destination (i.e. Topic)
Topic topicDestination = (Topic) iniCtx.lookup(destinationJndiName);

//get a connection from the TopicConnectionFactory
TopicConnection subscribeConnection = topicCF.createTopicConnection();

//get a session from the connection
TopicSession subscribeSession =
                subscribeConnection.createTopicSession(false,TopicSession.AUTO_ACKNOWLEDGE);

//create a subscriber from the session
TopicSubscriber subscriber = subscribeSession.createsubscriber(topicDestination);

//look for messages every 1 second
while (true) {
    Message response = subscriber.receive();

    if (response != null && response instanceof TextMessage) {
        System.out.println (((TextMessage) response).getText());
    }
```

```
Thread.sleep(1000);
}
```

Q. Are messaging applications slow? While there is some overhead in all messaging systems, but this does not mean that the applications that are using messaging are necessarily slow. Messaging systems can achieve a throughput of 70-100 messages per second depending on the installation, messaging modes (synchronous versus asynchronous, persistent versus non-persistent), and acknowledgement options such as *auto mode*, *duplicates okay mode*, and *client mode* etc. The asynchronous mode can significantly boost performance by multi-tasking. **For example:** In an Internet based shopping cart application, while a customer is adding items to his/her shopping cart, your application can trigger an inventory checking component, and a customer data retrieval component to execute concurrently. Performance tuning comes at a cost of reliability and flexibility. Some tips on performance:

- Choose proper acknowledgement mode - AUTO_ACKNOWLEDGE or DUPS_OK_ACKNOWLEDGE give better performance than CLIENT_ACKNOWLEDGE.

- Choose non-durable (i.e. non-persistent) messages where appropriate.

- Process messages concurrently by using the server session pool. Each session in the pool can execute separate message concurrently. The JMS specification states that multi-threading a session, producer, or message method can results in non-deterministic behavior. So if your application has limited number of threads then try increasing the number of sessions. Open a connection only when required to and close it immediately after you have finished with it.

- Transactional messages are accumulated at MOM server until the transaction is committed or rolled back. This imposes significant overhead on JMS server. So divide transactional messages and non-transactional messages separately.

- Carefully set some of the configuration settings on message destinations, producer/consumer etc. This is usually a trade-off between performance and reliability. So increasing "Redelivery delay", reducing "Destination size" and "Maximum number of messages" can improve performance. The parameters "TimeToLive" and "DeliveryMode" are important from the performance and reliability perspective. Also **for example**:

```
receive();       → blocks the call until it receives the next message.
receive(long timeout); → blocks till a timeout occurs.
receiveNoWait();  → never blocks.
```

- Choose the message type carefully and compress large messages (e.g. larger than 1 MB) in a JMS application in order to reduce the amount of time required to transfer messages across the network and memory used by the JMS server at the expense of an increase in CPU usage (i.e. to compress and uncompress) of the client. Less size gives a better performance. A *ByteMessage* takes less memory than a *TextMessage*. ObjectMessage carries a serialized Java object and hence network overhead can be reduced by marking the variables that need not be sent across the network as <u>transient</u>.

- Favor using <u>JMS message header</u> fields (e.g. JMSCorrelationID, JMSMessageID, JMSReplyTo, JMSPriority, JMSTimestamp, JMSType etc) and/or the <u>message body</u> (carries main information i.e. payload as XML, Object, Stream etc) as opposed to using <u>user-defined</u> <u>message properties</u> which incur an extra cost in serialization, and are more expensive to access than standard JMS message header fields. **For example:**

```
message.setStringProperty("AccountType", "Credit" );//user-defined message property
```

Also, avoid storing large amount of data in user-defined properties or the JMS header fields because only message bodies can be compressed or paged out (i.e. freeing up virtual memory by writing it out to disk when paging is supported and enabled).

- Using a selector is expensive and it is important to consider when you are deciding where in the message to store application data that is accessed via JMS selectors. By default, a message consumer will process every message that is sent to its destination. You can modify this behavior to allow message consumers to process only the message they are interested in using message selection and filtering. There two steps involved in setting up a message filter:

  - Initialize message header fields and/or user-defined message properties.

  - Message consumers specify a query string to select certain messages based on the message header fields and user defined message properties. A message selector cannot reference the message body.

```
String selector = "salary > 30000 and age < 30";
subscribeSession.createSubscriber(responseTopic, selector, false );
```

Q. Are messaging applications reliable? What is a durable message delivery? **FAQ** This is basically a trade-off between performance and reliability. If reliability is more important then the:

- Acknowledgement mode should be set to *AUTO* where once-and-only once delivery is guaranteed.

- Message delivery mode should be set to durable (aka persistent) where the MOM writes the messages to a secure storage like a database or a file system to insure that the message is not lost in transit due to a system failure.

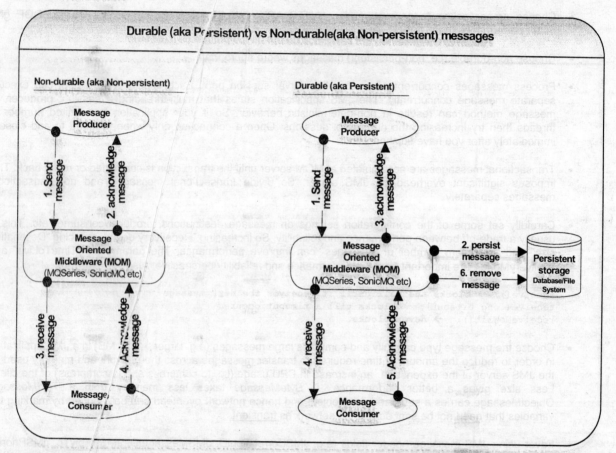

Q. What are some of the key message characteristics defined in a message header?

Characteristic	Explanation
JMSCorrelationID	Used in request/response situations where a JMS client can use the JMSCorrelationID header to associate one message with another. **For example**: a client request can be matched with a response from a server based on the JMSCorrelationID.
JMSMessageID	Uniquely identifies a message in the MOM environment.
JMSDeliveryMode	This header field contains the delivery modes: PERSISTENT or NON_PERSISTENT.
JMSExpiration	This contains the time-to-live value for a message. If it is set to zero, then a message will never expire.
JMSPriority	Sets the message priority but the actual meaning of prioritization is MOM vendor dependent.

Q. What are the different body types (aka payload types) supported for messages? All JMS messages are read-only once posted to a queue or a topic.

- **Text message**: body consists of java.lang.String (e.g. XML).
- **Map message**: body consists of key-value pairs.
- **Stream message**: body consists of streams of Java primitive values, which are accessed sequentially.
- **Object message**: body consists of a Serializable Java object.
- **Byte message**: body consists of arbitrary stream of bytes.

What is a message broker? A message broker acts as a server in a MOM. A message broker performs the following operations on a message it receives:

- Processes message header information.
- Performs security checks and encryption/decryption of a received message.
- Handles errors and exceptions.
- Routes message header and the **payload** (aka message body).
- Invokes a method with the payload contained in the incoming message (e.g. calling onMessage(..) method on a Message Driven Bean (MDB)).
- Transforms the message to some other format. For example XML payload can be converted to other formats like HTML etc with XSLT.

Q 90: What type of messaging is provided by JMS? `SF` `FAQ`

A 90: Point-to-Point: provides a traditional **queue** based mechanism where the client application sends a message through a queue to typically one receiving client that receives messages sequentially. A JMS message queue is an administered object that represents the message destination for the sender and the message source for the receiver. A Point-to-Point application has the following characteristics:

- A Point-to-Point producer is a sender (i.e. QueueSender).
- A Point-to-Point consumer is a receiver (i.e. QueueReceiver).
- A Point-to-Point destination is a queue (i.e. Queue).
- A message can only be consumed by one receiver.

Example: A call center application may use a queue based Point-to-Point domain to process all the calls where all the phone calls do not go to all the operators, but only one.

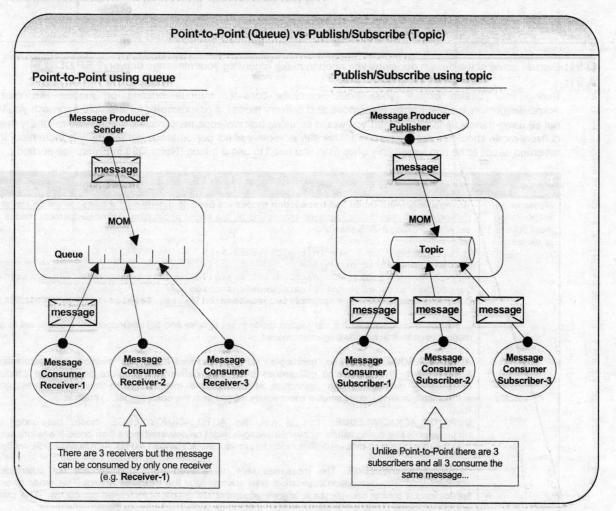

Publish/Subscribe: is a one-to-many publishing model where client applications publish messages to **topics**, which are in turn subscribed by other interested clients. All subscribed clients will receive each message. A Publish/Subscribe application has the following characteristics:

- A Publish/Subscribe producer is a publisher (i.e. TopicPublisher).
- A Publish/Subscribe consumer is a subscriber (i.e. TopicSubscriber).
- A Publish/Subscribe destination is a topic (i.e. Topic).
- A message can be consumed by multiple subscribers.

If a message publisher is also a subscriber, then a publisher can receive its own message sent to the destination. This behavior is only applicable to publish/subscribe model. This behavior can be controlled by setting the "noLocal" attribute to true when creating the publisher or the subscriber.

Example: A bulletin board application may use a topic based publish/subscribe model where everyone who is interested in particular news becomes a subscriber and when a message is published, it is sent to all its subscribers.

Q. How do you determine whether it would be better to use a Topic or Queue?

You must choose to use a *Topic* if one of the following conditions applies:

- Same message must be replicated to multiple consumers (With *Queue* a message can only be consumed by one receiver).

- A message should be dropped if there are no active consumers that would select it.

- There are many subscribers each with a unique selector.

Q 91: Discuss some of the design decisions you need to make regarding your message delivery? **SF** **DC** **FAQ**
A 91:

During your design phase, you should carefully consider various options or modes like message acknowledgement modes, transaction modes and delivery modes. **For example:** for a simple approach you would not be using transactions and instead you would be using acknowledgement modes. If you need reliability then the delivery mode should be set to persistent. This can adversely affect performance but reliability is increased. If your message needs to be consumed only once then you need to use a queue (Refer **Q90** in Enterprise section).

Design decision	Explanation
Message acknowledge ment options or modes.	**Acknowledgement mode** and **transaction** modes are used to determine if a message will be lost or re-delivered on failure during message processing by the target application. Acknowledgement modes are set when creating a JMS session. ```\nInitialContext ic = new InitialContext(…);\nQueueConnectionFactory qcf =\n (QueueConnectionFactory)ic.lookup("AccountConnectionFactory");\nQueueConnection qc = qcf.createQueueConnection();\nQueueSession session = qc.createQueueSession(false, Session.AUTO_ACKNOWLEDGE);\n``` In the above code sample, the transaction mode is set to false and acknowledgement mode is set to auto mode. Let us look at acknowledgement modes: **AUTO_ACKNOWLEDGE**: The messages sent or received from the session are automatically acknowledged. This mode also **guarantees once only delivery**. If a failure occurs while executing onMessage() method of the destination MDB, then the message is re-delivered. A message is automatically acknowledged when it successfully returns from the onMessage(…) method. **DUPS_OK_ACKNOWLEDGE**: This is just like AUTO_ACKNOWLEDGE mode, but under rare circumstances like during failure recovery messages might be delivered more than once. If a failure occurs then the message is re-delivered. This mode has fewer overheads than AUTO_ACKNOWLEDGE mode. **CLIENT_ACKNOWLEDGE**: The messages sent or received from sessions are not automatically acknowledged. The destination application must acknowledge the message receipt. This mode gives an application full control over message acknowledgement at the cost of increased complexity. This can be acknowledged by invoking the acknowledge() method on *javax.jms.Message* class.

Transactional behavior	Transactional behavior is controlled at the session level. When a session is transacted, the message oriented middleware (MOM) stages the message until the client either commits or rolls back the transaction. The completion of a session's current transaction automatically begins a new transaction.
	
	The use of transactions in messaging affects both the producers and consumers of the messages as shown below:
	
	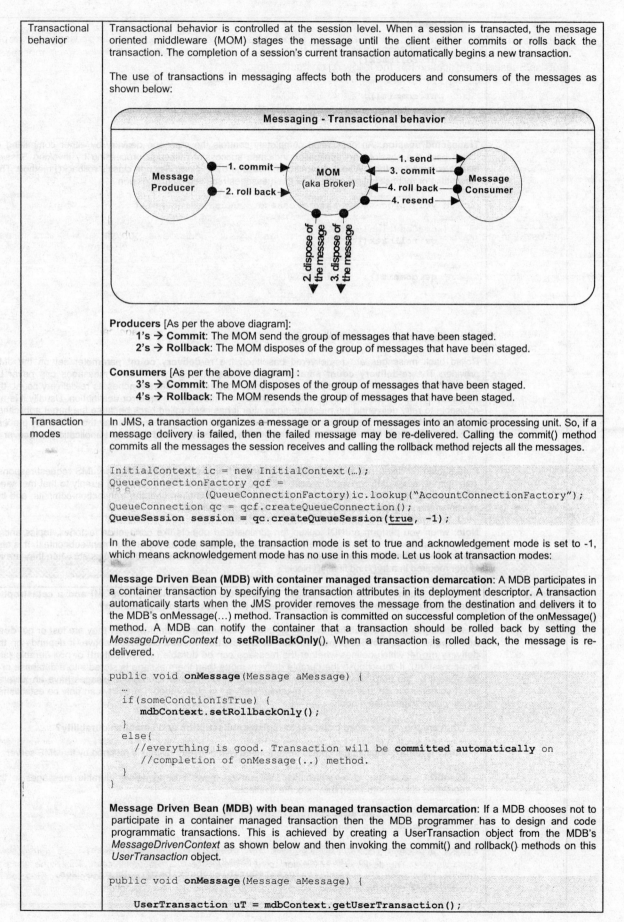
	
	Producers [As per the above diagram]:
	    1's → Commit: The MOM send the group of messages that have been staged.
	    2's → Rollback: The MOM disposes of the group of messages that have been staged.
	
	Consumers [As per the above diagram] :
	    3's → Commit: The MOM disposes of the group of messages that have been staged.
	    4's → Rollback: The MOM resends the group of messages that have been staged.

Transaction modes	In JMS, a transaction organizes a message or a group of messages into an atomic processing unit. So, if a message delivery is failed, then the failed message may be re-delivered. Calling the commit() method commits all the messages the session receives and calling the rollback method rejects all the messages.
	
	```\nInitialContext ic = new InitialContext(…);\nQueueConnectionFactory qcf =\n (QueueConnectionFactory)ic.lookup("AccountConnectionFactory");\nQueueConnection qc = qcf.createQueueConnection();\nQueueSession session = qc.createQueueSession(true, -1);\n```
	
	In the above code sample, the transaction mode is set to true and acknowledgement mode is set to -1, which means acknowledgement mode has no use in this mode. Let us look at transaction modes:
	
	Message Driven Bean (MDB) with container managed transaction demarcation: A MDB participates in a container transaction by specifying the transaction attributes in its deployment descriptor. A transaction automatically starts when the JMS provider removes the message from the destination and delivers it to the MDB's onMessage(…) method. Transaction is committed on successful completion of the onMessage() method. A MDB can notify the container that a transaction should be rolled back by setting the *MessageDrivenContext* to **setRollBackOnly**(). When a transaction is rolled back, the message is re-delivered.
	
	```\npublic void onMessage(Message aMessage) {\n …\n if(someCondtionIsTrue) {\n mdbContext.setRollbackOnly();\n }\n else{\n //everything is good. Transaction will be committed automatically on\n //completion of onMessage(..) method.\n }\n}\n```
	
	Message Driven Bean (MDB) with bean managed transaction demarcation: If a MDB chooses not to participate in a container managed transaction then the MDB programmer has to design and code programmatic transactions. This is achieved by creating a UserTransaction object from the MDB's *MessageDrivenContext* as shown below and then invoking the commit() and rollback() methods on this *UserTransaction* object.
	
	```\npublic void onMessage(Message aMessage) {\n\n UserTransaction uT = mdbContext.getUserTransaction();\n```

```
uT.begin();
….
if(someCondtionIsTrue) {
    uT.rollback();
}
else{
    uT.commit();
}
}
```

Transacted session: An application completely controls the message delivery by either committing or rolling back the session. An application indicates successful message processing by invoking *Session* class's commit() method. Also it can reject a message by invoking *Session* class's rollback() method. This committing or rollback is applicable to all the messages received by the session.

```
public void process(Message aMessage, QueueSession qs) {
    ….
    if(someCondtionIsTrue) {
        qs.rollback();
    }
    else{
        qs.commit();
    }
…
}
```

What happens to rolled-back messages?

Rolled back messages are re-delivered based on the **re-delivery count** parameter set on the JMS provider. The **re-delivery count** parameter is very important because some messages can never be successful and this can eventually crash the system. When a message reaches its re-delivery count, the JMS provider can either log the message or forward the message to an error destination. Usually it is not advisable to retry delivering the message soon after it has been rolled-back because the target application might still not be ready. So we can specify a **time to re-deliver** parameter to delay the re-delivery process by certain amount of time. This time delay allows the JMS provider and the target application to recover to a stable operational condition.

Care should be taken **not to make use of a single transaction** when using the JMS request/response paradigm where a JMS message is sent, followed by the synchronous receipt of a reply to that message. This is because a JMS message is not delivered to its destination until the transaction commits, and the receipt of the reply will never take place within the same transaction.

Note: when you perform a JNDI lookup for administered objects like connection factories, topics and/or queues, you should use the logical reference **java:comp/env/jms** as the environment subcontext. It is also vital to release the JMS resources like connection factories, sessions, queues, topics etc when they are no longer required in a try{} and finally{} block.

Message delivery options	**Q. What happens, when the messages are with the JMS provider (i.e. MOM) and a catastrophic failure occurs prior to delivering the messages to the destination application?**

The messages will be lost if they are <u>non-durable</u>. The message's state whether they are lost or not **does not depend on acknowledgement modes or transaction modes** discussed above. It depends on the **delivery mode**, which defines whether the message can be durable (aka persistent) or non-durable (aka non-persistent). If you choose the durable delivery mode then the message is stored into a database or a file system by the JMS server before delivering it to the consumer. Durable messages have an adverse effect on performance, but ensure that message delivery is guaranteed. Durability can only be established for the publish/subscribe model.

Q. What are the values need to be set to register subscription and establish durability?

• **SubscriptionID**: Subscribers should be registered with a unique ID that is retained by the JMS server.

• **ClientID**: is a unique id by which the JMS server knows how to deliver durable messages to the registered subscribers when they become available.

```
subscribeConnection.setClientID("id-123");
subscribeConnection.start();

subscribeSession = subscribeConnection.createTopicSession(false,
                TopicSession.AUTO_ACKNOWLEDGE);
subscriber = subscribeSession.createDurableSubscriber(resDestination,
   "subscription-id-123");
```

Q 92: How does XML over HTTP compare with XML using JMS? Why use XML with JMS? `SF` `SE`

A 92: XML itself does not specify a communications infrastructure. If you do not need reliable and scalable messaging then use XML over HTTP. This approach is sufficient for rudimentary applications but does not scale for distributed applications across multiple systems.

XML over HTTP	XML over JMS
Simple to implement, widely compatible and has less performance overhead but HTTP does not provide reliability in terms of guaranteed delivery because there is no message persistence, no inherent reporting facility for failed message delivery and no guaranteed once only delivery. The application programmer must build these services into the application logic to provide reliability & persistence, which is not an easy task.	This is an easy to implement, reliable, scalable and robust solution. The main disadvantage of this approach is that the JMS providers (i.e. Message Oriented Middleware) use a proprietary protocol between producer and consumer. So to communicate, you and your partners need to have the same MOM software (E.g. MQSeries). JMS allows you to toss one MOM software and plug-in another but you cannot mix providers without having to buy or build some sort of bridge.

Q. Why use XML with JMS?

- Organizations can leverage years or even decades of investment in Business-to-Business (B2B) Electronic Data Interchange (EDI) by using JMS with XML. XML is an **open standard** and it represents the data in a **non-proprietary** way.

- Sending XML messages as text <u>reduces coupling even more</u> compared to sending serializable objects. XML also solves the data representation differences with XML based technologies such as XSLT . `For example`, the way "Enterprise X" defines a purchase order will be different from the way "Enterprise Y" defines it. So the representation of XML message by "Enterprise X" can be transformed into the format understood by "Enterprise Y" using XSLT (see next section).

- Both enterprises may be using different applications to run their business. `For example` Enterprise "X" may be using Java/J2EE, while "Enterprise Y" may be using SAP. XML can solve the data formatting problems since it is an open standard with a self describing data format, which allows the design of business specific markup languages and standards like **FIXML** (Financial Information eXchange Markup Language), **FpML** (Financial products Markup Language – derivative products), **WML** (Wireles Markup Language – for wireless devices), **SAML** (Security Assertion Markup Language) etc. The structure of an XML document is similar to that of business objects with various attributes. This allows for the natural conversion of application-specific objects to XML documents and vice versa.

Q. What are the security related issues you need to consider?

- **Authentication:** Only valid applications and users are allowed to send and receive messages.

- **Data integrity:** Data should not be tampered with while in transit.

- **Encryption:** sensitive data should be encrypted while in transit to maintain confidentiality and privacy.

XML digital signature technology can be used to provide authentication, data integrity (tamper proofing) and non-repudiation. Unlike SSL, **XML encryption** can be used to encrypt and decrypt a section of a data. `For example` encrypt only the credit card information in a purchase order XML document.

You also need to consider sending messages across each organization's corporate firewall. Not every organization will open a port in the firewall other than the well-known port 80 for HTTP traffic. The solution is to make use of **HTTP tunneling**, which involves sending the data as HTTP traffic through well-known port number 80 for HTTP and then, once inside the firewall, convert this data into messages. `For example` JProxy is a J2EE based HTTP tunnel with SSL and JAAS with support for EJB, RMI, JNDI, JMS and CORBA.

Enterprise - XML

Q. What is XML? XML stands for e**X**tensible **M**arkup **L**anguage. XML is a grammatical system for constructing custom markup languages for describing business data, mathematical data, chemical data etc. **XML loosely couples disparate applications or systems utilizing JMS, Web services** etc. XML uses the same building blocks that HTML does: elements, attributes and values.

Q. Why is XML important?

- **Scalable:** Since XML is not in a binary format you can create and edit files with anything and it's also easy to debug. XML can be used to efficiently store small amounts of data like configuration files (web.xml, application.xml, struts-config.xml etc) to large company wide data with the help of XML stored in the database.

- **Fast Access**: XML documents benefit from their hierarchical structure. Hierarchical structures are generally faster to access because you can drill down to the section you are interested in.

- **Easy to identify and use**: XML not only displays the data but also tells you what kind of data you have. The mark up tags identifies and groups the information so that different information can be identified by different application.

- **Stylability**: XML is style-free and whenever different styles of output are required the same XML can be used with different style-sheets (XSL) to produce output in XHTML, PDF, TEXT, another XML format etc.

- **Linkability, in-line usability, universally accepted standard with free/inexpensive tools** etc

Q. When would you not use an XML?

XML is <u>verbose</u> and it can be 4-6 times larger in size compared to a csv or a tab delimited file. If your network lacked bandwidth and/or your content is too large and network throughput is vital to the application then you may consider using a csv or tab delimited format instead of an XML.

Q 93: What is the difference between a SAX parser and a DOM parser? **SF** **PI** **MI** **FAQ**

A 93:

SAX parser	DOM parser
A SAX (**S**imple **A**PI for **XML**) parser does not create any internal structure. Instead, it takes the occurrences of components of an input document **as events** (i.e., **event driven**), and tells the client what it reads as it reads through the input document.	A DOM (**D**ocument **O**bject **M**odel) parser **creates a tree structure in memory** from an input document and then waits for requests from client.
A SAX parser serves the client application always only with pieces of the document at any given time.	A DOM parser always serves the client application with the entire document no matter how much is actually needed by the client.
A SAX parser, however, is much more space efficient in case of a big input document (because it creates no internal structure). What's more, it runs faster and is easier to learn than DOM parser because its API is really simple. But from the functionality point of view, it provides a fewer functions, which means that the users themselves have to take care of more, such as creating their own data structures.	A DOM parser is rich in functionality. It creates a DOM tree in memory and allows you to access any part of the document repeatedly and allows you to modify the DOM tree. But it is space inefficient when the document is huge, and it takes a little bit longer to learn how to work with it.
Use SAX parser when - Input document is too big for available memory. - When only a part of the document is to be read and we create the data structures of our own. - If you use SAX, you are using much less memory and performing much less dynamic memory allocation.	Use DOM when - Your application has to access various parts of the document and using your own structure is just as complicated as the DOM tree. - Your application has to change the tree very frequently and data has to be stored for a significant amount of time.

<table>
<tr><td>

SAX Parser example: Xerces, Crimson etc

Use JAXP (**J**ava **A**PI for **X**ML **P**arsing) which enables applications to parse and transform XML documents independent of the particular XML parser. Code can be developed with one SAX parser in mind and later on can be changed to another SAX parser without changing the application code.

</td><td>

DOM Parser example: XercesDOM, SunDOM, OracleDOM etc.

Use JAXP (**J**ava **A**PI for **X**ML **P**arsing) which enables applications to parse and transform XML documents independent of the particular XML parser. Code can be developed with one DOM parser in mind and later on can be changed to another DOM parser without changing the application code.

</td></tr>
</table>

Q 94: Which is better to store data as elements or as attributes? DC

A 94: A question arising in the mind of XML/DTD designers is whether to model and encode certain information using an *element*, or alternatively, using an *attribute*. The answer to the above question is not clear-cut. But the general guideline is:

- **Using an element:** <book><title>Lord of the Rings</title>...</book>: If you consider the information in question to be part of the essential material that is being expressed or communicated in the XML, put it in an element

- **Using an attribute:** <book title=" Lord of the Rings "/>: If you consider the information to be peripheral or incidental to the main communication, or purely intended to help applications process the main communication, use attributes.

The principle is **data goes in elements** and **metadata goes in attributes.** Elements are also useful when they contain special characters like "<", ">", etc which are harder to use in attributes. The most important reason to use element is its <u>extensibility</u>. It is far easier to create child elements to reflect complex content than to break an attribute into pieces. You can use attributes along with elements to refine your understanding of that element with extra information. <u>Attributes are less verbose</u> but using attributes instead of child elements with the view of optimizing document size is a short term strategy, which can have long term consequences.

Q 95: What is XPATH? What is XSLT/XSL/XSL-FO/XSD/DTD etc? What is JAXB? What is JAXP? SF FAQ

A 95:

What is	Explanation	Example

XML	**XML** stands for eXtensible Markup Language	Sample.xml
		
		`<?xml version="1.0"?>`
		`<note>`
		` <to>Peter</to>`
		` <from>Paul</from>`
		` <title>Invite</title>`
		` <content language="English">Not Much</content>`
		`< content language="Spanish">No Mucho</content >`
		`</note>`

DTD	**DTD** stands for Document Type Definition. XML provides an application independent way of sharing data. With a DTD, independent groups of people can agree to use a common DTD for interchanging data. Your application can use a standard DTD to verify that data that you receive from the outside world is valid. You can also use a DTD to verify your own data. So the DTD is the building blocks or schema definition of the XML document.	Sample.dtd
		
		`<!ELEMENT note (to, from, title, content)>`
		`<!ELEMENT to (#PCDATA)>`
		`<!ELEMENT from (#PCDATA)>`
		`<!ELEMENT title (#PCDATA)>`
		`<!ELEMENT content (#PCDATA)>`
		`<!ATTLIST content language CDATA #Required>`

XSD	**XSD** stands for Xml Schema Definition, which is a successor of DTD. So XSD is a building block of an XML document.
	
	If you have DTD then why use XSD you may ask?
	
	XSD is more powerful and extensible than DTD. XSD has:
	
	- Support for simple and complex data types.
	- Uses XML syntax. So XSD are extensible just like
		Sample.xsd
		
		`<?xml version="1.0"?>`
		`<xs:schema xmlns:xs="http://www.w3.org/2001/XMLSchema"`
		`targetNamespace="http://www.w3schools.com"`
		`xmlns="http://www.w3schools.com"`
		`elementFormDefault="qualified">`
		
		`<xs:element name="note">`
		` <xs:complexType>`

	XML because they are written in XML.
	• Better data communication with the help of data types. For example a date like 03-04-2005 will be interpreted in some countries as 3rd of April 2005 and in some other countries as 04th March 2005.
			``xml
			<xs:sequence>
			  <xs:element name="to" type="xs:string"/>
			  <xs:element name="from" type="xs:string"/>
			  <xs:element name="title" type="xs:string"/>
			  <xs:element name="content" type="xs:string"/>
			</xs:sequence>
			</xs:complexType>
			<xs:attribute name="language" type="xs:string"
			                        use="Required" />
			</xs:element>
			
			</xs:schema>
			``

| XSL | **XSL** stands for eXtensible Stylesheet Language. The XSL consists of 3 parts:

• **XSLT**: Language for transforming XML documents from one to another.

• **XPath**: Language for defining the parts of an XML document.

• **XSL-FO**: Language for formatting XML documents. For example to convert an XML document to a PDF document etc.

XSL can be thought of as a set of languages that can :

• Define parts of an XML.
• Transform an XML document to XHTML (eXtensible Hyper Text Markup Language) document.
• Convert an XML document to a PDF document.
• Filter and sort XML data.

XSLT processor example: Xalan (from Apache).

PDF Processor example: FOP (Formatting Objects Processor from Apache) | To convert the Sample.xml file to a XHTML file let us apply the following Sample.xsl through XALAN parser.

Sample.xsl

```xml
<?xml version="1.0"?>
<xsl:stylesheet xmlns:xsl="http://www.w3.org/TR/WD-xsl">
<xsl:template match="/">
  <xsl:apply-templates select="note " />
</xsl:template>

<xsl:template match="note">
  <html>
    <head>
      <title><xsl:value-of
                   select="content/@language">
      </title>
    </head>
  </html>
</xsl:template>
</xsl:stylesheet>
```

You get the following output XHTML file:

Sample.xhtml

```xml
<html>
  <head>
    <title>English</title>
  </head>
</html>
```

Now to convert the Sample.xml into a PDF file apply the following FO (Formatting Objects) file Through the FOP processor.

Sample.fo

```xml
<?xml version="1.0" encoding="ISO-8859-1"?>
<fo:root xmlns:fo="http://www.w3.org/1999/XSL/Format">

<fo:layout-master-set>
  <fo:simple-page-master master-name="A4">
  </fo:simple-page-master>
</fo:layout-master-set>

<fo:page-sequence master-reference="A4">
  <fo:flow flow-name="xsl-region-body">
    <fo:block>
      <xsl:value-of select="content[@language='English']">
    </fo:block>
  </fo:flow>
</fo:page-sequence>
</fo:root>
```

which gives a basic Sample.pdf which has the following line

Not Much |

| XPath | Xml Path Language, a language for addressing parts of an | As per Sample.xsl |

	XML document, designed to be used by both XSLT and XPointer. We can write both the patterns (context-free) and expressions using the XPATH Syntax. XPATH is also used in XQuery.	`<xsl:template match="content[@language='English']">`
		`.........`
		`<td><xsl:value-of  select="content/@language" /></td>`

JAXP	Stands for Java API for XML Processing. This provides a common interface for creating and using SAX, DOM, and XSLT APIs in Java regardless of which vendor's implementation is actually being used (just like the JDBC, JNDI interfaces). JAXP has the following packages:
	
	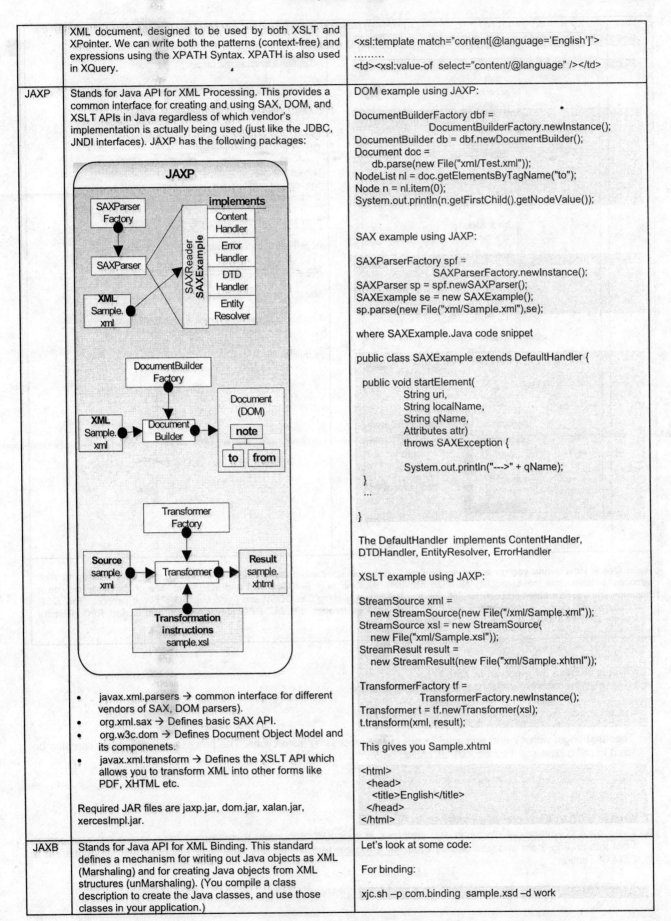
	
	• javax.xml.parsers → common interface for different vendors of SAX, DOM parsers).
	• org.xml.sax → Defines basic SAX API.
	• org.w3c.dom → Defines Document Object Model and its componenets.
	• javax.xml.transform → Defines the XSLT API which allows you to transform XML into other forms like PDF, XHTML etc.
	
	Required JAR files are jaxp.jar, dom.jar, xalan.jar, xercesImpl.jar.
		DOM example using JAXP:
		
		`DocumentBuilderFactory dbf =`
		`            DocumentBuilderFactory.newInstance();`
		`DocumentBuilder db = dbf.newDocumentBuilder();`
		`Document doc =`
		`   db.parse(new File("xml/Test.xml"));`
		`NodeList nl = doc.getElementsByTagName("to");`
		`Node n = nl.item(0);`
		`System.out.println(n.getFirstChild().getNodeValue());`
		
		SAX example using JAXP:
		
		`SAXParserFactory spf =`
		`            SAXParserFactory.newInstance();`
		`SAXParser sp = spf.newSAXParser();`
		`SAXExample se = new SAXExample();`
		`sp.parse(new File("xml/Sample.xml"),se);`
		
		where SAXExample.Java code snippet
		
		`public class SAXExample extends DefaultHandler {`
		
		`  public void startElement(`
		`        String uri,`
		`        String localName,`
		`        String qName,`
		`        Attributes attr)`
		`        throws SAXException {`
		
		`        System.out.println("--->" + qName);`
		`  }`
		`  ...`
		
		`}`
		
		The DefaultHandler implements ContentHandler, DTDHandler, EntityResolver, ErrorHandler
		
		XSLT example using JAXP:
		
		`StreamSource xml =`
		`  new StreamSource(new File("/xml/Sample.xml"));`
		`StreamSource xsl = new StreamSource(`
		`  new File("xml/Sample.xsl"));`
		`StreamResult result =`
		`  new StreamResult(new File("xml/Sample.xhtml"));`
		
		`TransformerFactory tf =`
		`            TransformerFactory.newInstance();`
		`Transformer t = tf.newTransformer(xsl);`
		`t.transform(xml, result);`
		
		This gives you Sample.xhtml
		
		`<html>`
		`  <head>`
		`    <title>English</title>`
		`  </head>`
		`</html>`

JAXB	Stands for Java API for XML Binding. This standard defines a mechanism for writing out Java objects as XML (Marshaling) and for creating Java objects from XML structures (unMarshaling). (You compile a class description to create the Java classes, and use those classes in your application.)	Let's look at some code: For binding: `xjc.sh –p com.binding  sample.xsd –d work`

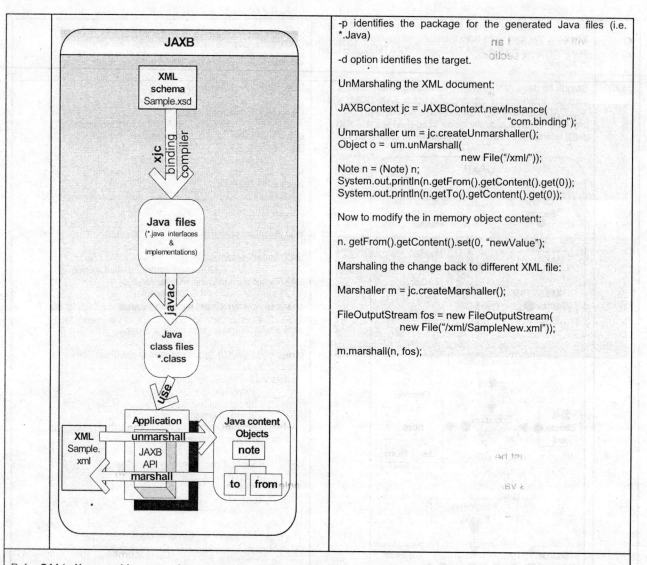

-p identifies the package for the generated Java files (i.e. *.Java)

-d option identifies the target.

UnMarshaling the XML document:

```
JAXBContext jc = JAXBContext.newInstance(
                                "com.binding");
Unmarshaller um = jc.createUnmarshaller();
Object o = um.unMarshall(
                        new File("/xml/"));
Note n = (Note) n;
System.out.println(n.getFrom().getContent().get(0));
System.out.println(n.getTo().getContent().get(0));
```

Now to modify the in memory object content:

```
n. getFrom().getContent().set(0, "newValue");
```

Marshaling the change back to different XML file:

```
Marshaller m = jc.createMarshaller();

FileOutputStream fos = new FileOutputStream(
            new File("/xml/SampleNew.xml"));

m.marshall(n, fos);
```

Refer **Q14** in **How would you go about section** for XML based standards/protocols like SOAP, WSDL, and UDDI relating to Web services, which enable interoperability between disparate systems (e.g. Between .Net and J2EE etc). These standards provide a common and interoperable approach for underlining (i.e. WSDL), publishing (i.e. UDDI) and using (i.e. SOAP) Web services. The J2EE 1.4 platform provides comprehensive support for Web services through the **JAX-RPC** (Java **API** for **XML** based **RPC** (**R**emote **P**rocedure **C**all)) and **JAXR** (Java API for XML Registries).

Q. What is version information in XML?
A. Version information in an XML is a processing instruction.

```
<?xml version="1.0" ?>
```

Tags that begin with **<?** and end with **?>** are called processing instructions. The processing instructions can also be used to call a style sheet for an XML as shown below:

```
<?xml-stylesheet type="text/css" href="MyStyle.css" ?>
```

Q. What is a CDATA section in an XML?
A. If you want to write about elements and attributes in your XML document then you will have to prevent your parser from interpreting them and just display them as a regular text. To do this, you must enclose such information in a CDATA section.

```
<![CDATA[ <customername id="123" > John </customername> ]]>
```

Q. How will you embed an XML content within an XML document?
A. By using a CDATA section.

```
<message>
       <from>LoansSystem</from>
       <to>DocumentSystem</to>
       <body>
              <![CDATA[
                     <application>
                            <number>456</number>
                            <name>Peter</name>
                            <detail>blah blah</detail>
                     </application>
              ]]>
       </body>
</message>
```

Q. How do you write comments in an XML document?
A. <!-- This is an XML comment -->

Q. How do you write an attribute value with single quotes? How do you write an element value of "> 500.00"?
A. You need to use an internal entity reference like < for <, > for >, & for &, " for ", ' for '.

```
<customer name="&quot;Mr. Smith&quot;" />
<cost> &gt; 500.00</cost>
```

Q. What is a <u>well-formed</u> XML document?
A. A well formed document adheres to the following rules for writing an XML.

- A root element is required. A root element is an element, which completely contains all the other elements.
- Closing tags are required. **<cust>**abc**</cust>** or
- Elements must be properly nested.
- XML is case sensitive. <CUSTOMER> and <Customer> elements are considered completely separate.
- An attribute's value must always be enclosed in either single or double quotes.
- Entity references must be declared in a DTD before being used except for the 5 built-in (**<, >** etc) discussed in the previous question.

Q. What is a <u>valid</u> XML document?
A. For an XML document to be valid, it must conform to the rules of the corresponding DTD (Document Type Definition – internal or external) or XSD (XML Schema Definition).

Q. How will you write an empty element?
A.
```
<name age="25"></name>
       or
<name age="25" />
```

Q. What is a namespace in an XML document?
A. Namespaces are used in XML documents to distinguish one similarly titled element from another. A namespace must have an absolutely unique and permanent name. In an XML, name space names are in the form of a URL. A default namespace for an element and all its children can be declared as follows:

```
<accounts xmlns="http://www.bank1.com/ns/account">
       …
</accounts>
```

Individual elements can be labeled as follows:

```
<accounts xmlns="http://www.bank1.com/ns/account" xmlns:bank2="http://www.bank2.com/ns/account">
       <name>FlexiDirect</name>  <!-- uses the default name space -->
       <bank2:name>Loan</bank2:name> <!-- >
       …
</accounts>
```

Q. Why use an XML document as opposed to other types of documents like a text file etc?
A.

- It is a universally accepted standard.
- Free and easy to use tools are available. Also can be stored in a database.
- Fast access due to its hierarchical structure.
- Easy to identify and use due to its markup tags.

Q. What is your favorite XML framework or a tool?
A. My favorite XML framework is **JiBX**, which unmarshals an XML document to graph of Java objects and marshals a graph of Java objects back to an XML document. It is simple to use, very flexible and fast. It can be used with existing Java classes.

Q. Explain where your project needed XML documents?
A. It is hard to find a project, which does not use XML documents.

- XML is used to communicate with disparate systems via messaging or Web Services.
- XML based protocols and standards like SOAP, ebXML, WSDL etc are used in Web Services.
- XML based deployment descriptors like web.xml, ejb-jar.xml, etc are used to configure the J2EE containers.
- XML based configuration files are used by open-source frameworks like Hibernate, Spring, Struts, and Tapestry etc.

Enterprise – SQL, Database, and O/R mapping

Q 96: Explain inner and outer joins? **SF** **FAQ**

A 96: Joins allow database users to combine data from one table with data from one or more other tables (or views, or synonyms). Tables are joined two at a time making a new table containing all possible combinations of rows from the original two tables. Lets take an example (syntax vary among RDBMS):

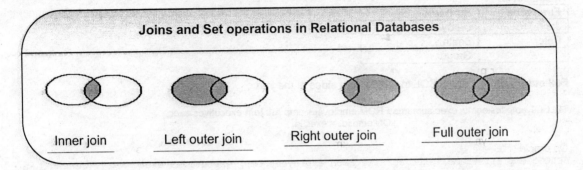

Joins and Set operations in Relational Databases

Inner join   Left outer join   Right outer join   Full outer join

Employees table

Id	Firstname	Surname	State
1001	John	Darcy	NSW
1002	Peter	Smith	NSW
1003	Paul	Gregor	NSW
1004	Sam	Darcy	VIC

Executives table

Id	Firstname	Surname	State
1001	John	Darcy	NSW
1002	Peter	Smith	NSW
1005	John	Gregor	WA

Inner joins: Chooses the join criteria using any column names that happen to match between the two tables. The example below displays only the employees who are executives as well.

```
SELECT emp.firstname, exec.surname FROM employees emp, executives exec
                      WHERE emp.id = exec.id;
```

The output is:

Firstname	Surname
John	Darcy
Peter	Smith

Left Outer joins: A problem with the inner join is that only rows that match between tables are returned. The example below will show all the employees and fill the null data for the executives.

```
SELECT emp.firstname, exec.surname FROM employees emp left join executives exec
                      ON emp.id  = exec.id;
```

On oracle
```
SELECT emp.firstname, exec.surname FROM employees emp, executives exec
                      WHERE emp.id  = exec.id(+);
```

The output is:

Firstname	Surname
John	Darcy
Peter	Smith
Paul	
Sam	

Right Outer join: A problem with the inner join is that only rows that match between tables are returned. The example below will show all the executives and fill the null data for the employees.

```
SELECT emp.firstname, exec.surname FROM employees emp right join executives exec
                              ON emp.id  = exec.id;
```

On oracle

```
SELECT emp.firstname, exec.surname FROM employees emp, executives exec
                              WHERE emp.id(+) = exec.id;
```

The output is:

Firstname	Surname
John	Darcy
Peter	Smith
	Gregor

Full outer join: To cause SQL to create both sides of the join

```
SELECT emp.firstname, exec.surname FROM employees emp full join executives exec
                              ON emp.id = exec.id;
```

On oracle

```
SELECT emp.firstname, exec.surname FROM employees emp, executives exec
                              WHERE emp.id = exec.id (+)

UNION

SELECT emp.firstname, exec.surname FROM employees emp, executives exec
                              WHERE emp.id(+) = exec.id
```

Note: Oracle9i introduced the ANSI compliant join syntax. This new join syntax uses the new keywords inner join, left outer join, right outer join, and full outer join, instead of the (+) operator.

The output is:

Firstname	Surname
John	Darcy
Paul	
Peter	Smith
Sam	
	Gregor

Self join: A self-join is a join of a table to itself. If you want to find out all the employees who live in the same city as employees whose first name starts with "Peter", then one way is to use a sub-query as shown below:

```
SELECT emp.firstname, emp.surname FROM employees emp WHERE
    city IN (SELECT city FROM employees where firstname like 'Peter')
```

The sub-queries can degrade performance. So alternatively we can use a self-join to achieve the same results.

On oracle

```
SELECT emp.firstname, emp.surname FROM employees emp, employees emp2
    WHERE emp.city = emp2.city
    AND emp2.firstname LIKE 'Peter'
```

The output is:

Firstname	Surname
John	Darcy
Peter	Smith
Paul	Gregor

Q 97: Explain a sub-query? How does a sub-query impact on performance? SF PI FAQ

A 97: It is possible to embed a SQL statement within another. When this is done on the **WHERE** or the **HAVING** statements, we have a subquery construct. What is subquery useful for? It is used to join tables and there are cases where the only way to correlate two tables is through a subquery.

```
SELECT emp.firstname, emp.surname FROM employees emp WHERE
```

```
emp.id NOT IN (SELECT id FROM executives);
```

There are performance problems with sub-queries, which may return NULL values. The above sub-query can be re-written as shown below by invoking a **correlated sub-query**:

```
SELECT emp.firstname, emp.surname FROM employees emp WHERE
emp.id NOT EXISTS (SELECT id FROM executives);
```

The above query can be re-written as an outer join for a <u>faster performance</u> as shown below:

```
SELECT emp.firstname, exec.surname FROM employees emp left join executives exec
on emp.id = exec.id AND exec.id IS NULL;
```

The above execution plan will be faster by eliminating the sub-query.

Q 98: What is normalization? When to denormalize? `DC` `PI` `FAQ`

A 98: Normalization is a design technique that is widely used as a guide in designing relational databases. Normalization is essentially a two step process that puts data into tabular form by removing repeating groups and then removes duplicated data from the relational tables (Additional reading recommended).

Redundant data wastes disk space and creates maintenance problems. If data that exists in more than one place must be changed, the data must be changed in exactly the same way in all locations which is time consuming and prone to errors. A change to a customer address is much easier to do if that data is stored only in the Customers table and nowhere else in the database.

Inconsistent dependency is a database design that makes certain assumptions about the location of data. For example, while it is intuitive for a user to look in the Customers table for the address of a particular customer, it may not make sense to look there for the salary of the employee who calls on that customer. The employee's salary is related to, or dependent on, the employee and thus should be moved to the Employees table. Inconsistent dependencies can make data difficult to access because the path to find the data may not be logical, or may be missing or broken.

First Normal Form	Second Normal Form	Third Normal Form
A database is said to be in First Normal Form when all entities have a unique identifier or key, and when every column in every table contains only a single value and doesn't contain a repeating group or composite field.	A database is in Second Normal Form when it is in First Normal Form plus every non-primary key column in the table must depend on the entire primary key, not just part of it, assuming that the primary key is made up of composite columns.	A database is in Third Normal Form when it is in Second Normal Form and each column that isn't part of the primary key doesn't depend on another column that isn't part of the primary key.

When to denormalize? Normalize for accuracy and denormalize for performance.

Typically, transactional databases are highly <u>normalized</u>. This means that redundant data is eliminated and replaced with keys in a one-to-many relationship. Data that is highly normalized is constrained by the primary key/foreign key relationship, and thus has a high degree of *data integrity*. Denormalized data, on the other hand, creates redundancies; this means that it's possible for denormalized data to lose track of some of the relationships between atomic data items. However, since all the data for a query is (usually) stored in a single row in the table, it is *much* faster to retrieve.

Q 99: How do you implement one-to-one, one-to-many and many-to-many relationships while designing tables? `SF`

A 99: **One-to-One relationship** can be implemented as a single table and rarely as two tables with primary and foreign key relationships.

One-to-Many relationships are implemented by splitting the data into two tables with primary key and foreign key relationships.

Many-to-Many relationships are implemented using join table with the keys from both the tables forming the composite primary key of the junction table.

Q 100: How can you performance tune your database? `PI` `FAQ`

A 100:

- Denormalize your tables where appropriate.
- Proper use of index columns: An index based on numeric fields is more efficient than an index based on character columns.
- Reduce the number of columns that make up a composite key.
- Proper partitioning of tablespaces and create a special tablespace for special data types like CLOB, BLOB etc.
- Data access performance can be tuned by using stored procedures to crunch data in the database server to reduce the network overhead and also caching data within your application to reduce the number of accesses.

Q 101: How will you map objects to a relational database? How will you map class inheritance to relational data model? DC FAQ

A 101: Due to impedance mismatch between object and relational technology you need to understand the process of mapping classes (objects) and their relationships to tables and relationships between them in a database. Classes represent both behavior and data whereas relational database tables just implement data. Database schemas have keys (primary keys to uniquely identify rows and foreign keys to maintain relationships between rows) whereas object schema does not have keys and instead use references to implement relationships to other objects. Let us look at some basic points on mapping:

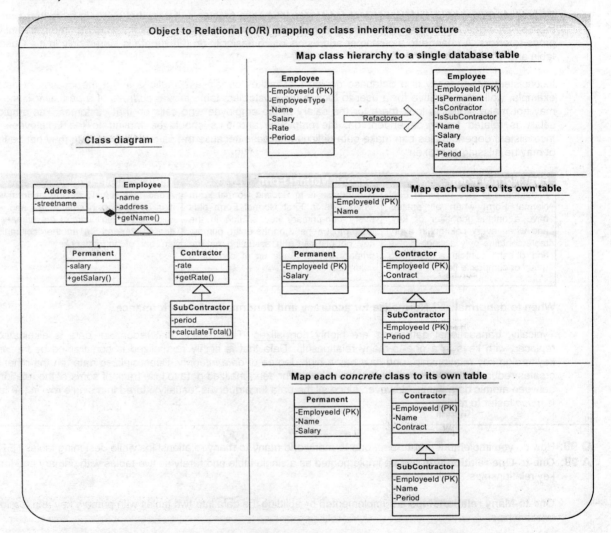

- Classes map to tables in a way but not always directly.
- An attribute of a class can be mapped to zero or more columns in a database. Not all attributes are persistent.
- Some attributes of an object are objects itself. For example an *Employee* object has an Address object as an attribute. This is basically an **association** relationship between two objects (i.e. *Employee* and

Address). This is a recursive relationship where at some point the attribute will be mapped to zero or more columns. In this example attributes of the *Address* class will be mapped zero or more columns.

- In its simple form an attribute maps to a single column whereas each has same type (i.e. attribute is a string and column is a char, or both are dates etc). When you implement mapping with different types (attribute is a currency and column is a float) then you will need to be able to convert them back and forth.

Q. How do you map inheritance class structure to relational data model? Relational databases do not support inheritance. Class inheritance can be mapped to relational tables as follows:

Map class hierarchy to single database table (aka <u>union mapping</u>): The whole class hierarchy can be stored in a single table by adding an additional column named "*EmployeeType*". The column "*EmployeeType*" will hold the values "*Permanent*", "*Contract*" and "*SubContract*". New employee types can be added as required. Although this approach is straightforward it tends to break when you have combinations like an employee is of type both "*Contractor*" and "*SubContractor*". So when you have combinations, you can use refactored table by replacing type code column "*EmployeeType*" with boolean values such as *isPermanent*, *isContractor* and *isSubContractor*.

Map each class to its own table (aka <u>vertical mapping</u>): You create one table per class (even those that are abstract). The data for a permanent employee is stored in two tables (*Employee* and *Permanent*), therefore to retrieve this data you need to join these two tables. To support additional employee type say a *Contractor*, add a new table.

Map each concrete class to its own table (aka <u>horizontal mapping</u>): You create one table per concrete class. There are tables corresponding to each class like Permanent, Contractor and SubContractor. So join is not required. To support additional employee type, add a new table.

So which approach to use? No approach is ideal for all situations. Each approach has its own pros & cons.

Map class hierarchy to single database table: <u>Advantages are:</u> no table joins are necessary to query objects in the same hierarchy and adding a new class to the hierarchy has very little overhead. <u>Disadvantages are:</u> Database constraints have to be relaxed to accommodate all attributes in the class hierarchy and also it is not easy to identify from the table schema which attributes belong to which class.

Map each class to its own table: <u>Advantages are:</u> Table schemas are separated cleanly and database constraints can be applied. <u>Disadvantages are:</u> Suffers from performance problems. If you need to query all employees then all 4 tables (i.e. *Employee*, *Permanent*, *Contractor* & *SubContractor*) need to be queried.

Map each concrete class to its own table: <u>Advantage is:</u> simplest approach. <u>Disadvantage is:</u> duplicated base class columns in each subclass table making adding an attribute to the baseclass more difficult.

Finally, No approach is ideal for all situations. The most efficient way is to "map class hierarchy to single database table" (i.e. union mapping). For dealing with complex legacy data "use map each class to its own table" (i.e. vertical mapping) which gives you more flexibility but this flexibility comes at a price of performance. The simplest way to map is to use "map each concrete class to its own table" (i.e. horizontal mapping) but this simplicity comes at a price of creating a very unnatural object model.

Note: Another option for mapping inheritance into relational database is to take a generic meta-data driven approach. This approach supports all forms of mapping. In this approach, value of a single attribute will be stored as a row in a table called "*Value*". So, to store 5 attributes you need 5 rows in "*Value*" table. You will have a table called "*Class*" where class names are stored, a table called "*Inheritance*" where subclass and superclass information is stored, a table called "*Attributes*" where class attributes are stored and an "*AttributeType*" lookup table.

Q 102: What is a view? Why will you use a view? What is an aggregate function? Etc. SF PI FAQ
A 102:

Question	Explanation
What is view? Why use a view?	View is a precompiled SQL query, which is used to select data from one or more tables. A view is like a table but it doesn't physically take any space (i.e. not materialized). Views are used for • Providing inherent security by exposing only the data that is needed to be shown to the end user. • Enabling re-use of SQL statements. • Allows changes to the underlying tables to be hidden from clients, aiding

maintenance of the database schema (i.e. encapsulation).

Views with multiple joins and filters can dramatically degrade performance because views contain no data and any retrieval needs to be processed. The solution for this is to use materialized views or create de-normalized tables to store data. This technique is quite handy in overnight batch processes where a large chunk of data needs to be processed. Normalized data can be read and inserted into some temporary de-normalized table and processed with efficiency.

| What is a database trigger? | A trigger is a fragment of code that you tell to run before or after a table is modified. There are typically three triggering EVENTS that cause trigger to 'fire': |

- **INSERT** event (as a new record is being inserted into the database).
- **UPDATE** event (as a record is being changed).
- **DELETE** event (as a record is being deleted).

Triggers can restrict access to specific data, perform logging, or audit access to data.

Q. How can you keep track of all your database changes?

If you want to keep track of all changes to a particular record, such as who modified the record, what kind of modification took place, and when the record modification occurred then you can use triggers because you can capture every action that occurred on a particular table. For example, an INSERT trigger would fire when a particular database table has a record inserted.

Q. How will you communicate between two applications sharing the same database to update one of the applications' object cache?

As shown in the diagram below, 1.→ when application 1 updates/inserts a product in the "product" table, 2. → a trigger is fired to modify the status of the "product_polling" table to "pending" from "complete" for updates and creates a new record with a pending status for inserts. 3. → Application 2 polls the "product_polling" table say every 5 minutes. If the status="pending" then application 2 reads the updated data from the product table and refreshes the cache. If the status is "complete" then the application 2 retries after 5 minutes.

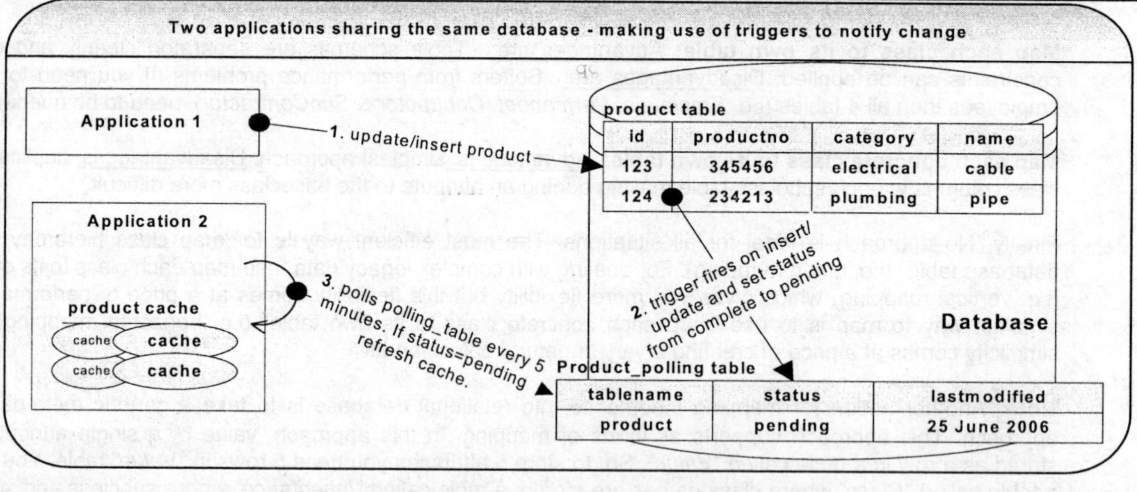

Two applications sharing the same database - making use of triggers to notify change

| Explain aggregate SQL functions? | SQL provides aggregate functions to assist with the summarization of large volumes of data. |

We'll look at functions that allow us to add and average data, count records meeting specific criteria and find the largest and smallest values in a table.

ORDERID	FIRSTNAME	SURNAME	QTY	UNITPRICE
1001	John	Darcy	25	10.5
1002	Peter	Smith	25	10.5
1003	Sam	Gregory	25	10.5

```
SELECT SUM(QTY) AS Total FROM Orders;
```

The output is: Total = 75

```
SELECT AVG(UnitPrice * QTY) As AveragePrice FROM Orders;
```

	The output is: AveragePrice = 262.50
	
	If we inserted another row to the above table:
	
	ORDERID FIRSTNAME SURNAME QTY UNITPRICE
	1004 John Darcy 20 10.50
	
	```SELECT FIRSTNAME,SUM(QTY) FROM orders```
	``` GROUP BY FIRSTNAME```
	``` HAVING SUM(QTY)>25;```
	
	The output is: John 45

Explain INSERT, UPDATE, and DELETE statements?	**INSERT** statements can be carried out several ways:
	
	```INSERT INTO ORDERS values (1004, 'John', 'Darcy', 20, 10.50);```
	
	The above statement is fine but the one below is recommended since it is less ambiguous and less prone to errors.
	
	```INSERT INTO ORDERS (orderid, firstname, surname, qty, unitprice)```
	``` values (1005, 'John', 'Darcy',```
	```20, 10.50);```
	
	We can also use INSERT with the SELECT statements as shown below
	
	```INSERT into NEW_ORDERS (orderid, firstname, surname, qty,```
	``` unitprice)```
	``` SELECT orderid, firstname, surname, qty, unitprice```
	``` FROM orders WHERE orderid = 1004;```
	
	UPDATE statement allows you to update a single or multiple statements.
	
	```UPDATE ORDERS set firstname='Peter', surname='Piper'```
	``` WHERE orderid=1004;```
	
	Also can have more complex updates like
	
	```UPDATE supplier```
	```SET supplier_name = (SELECT customer.name```
	``` FROM customers```
	``` WHERE customers.customer_id = supplier.supplier_id)```
	```WHERE EXISTS```
	``` (SELECT customer.name```
	``` FROM customers```
	``` WHERE customers.customer_id = supplier.supplier_id);```
	
	DELETE statements allow you to remove records from the database.
	
	```DELETE FROM ORDERS WHERE orderid=1004;```
	
	We can clear the entire table using
	
	```TRUNCATE TABLE employees;```
	
	When running UPDATE/DELETE care should be taken to include WHERE clause otherwise you can inadvertently modify or delete records which you do not intend to UPDATE/DELETE.

How can you compare a part of the name rather than the entire name?	You can use wild card characters like:
	
	- * (% in oracle) → Match any number of characters.
	- ? (_ in oracle) → Match a single character.
	
	To find all the employees who has "au":
	```SELECT * FROM employees emp```
	``` WHERE emp.firstname LIKE '%au%';```

How do you get distinct entries from a table?	The SELECT statement in conjunction with **DISTINCT** lets you select a set of distinct values from a table in a database. ```SELECT DISTINCT empname FROM emptable```

How can you find the total number of records in a table?	Use the **COUNT** key word: `SELECT COUNT(*) FROM emp WHERE age>25`
What's the difference between a primary key and a unique key?	Both primary key and unique key enforce uniqueness of the column on which they are defined. But by default primary key creates a **clustered index** on the column, whereas unique creates a **non-clustered index** by default. Another major difference is that, primary key doesn't allow NULLs, but unique key allows one NULL only. **Q. What is the best practice relating to primary key generation?** • A best practice in database design is to use an internally generated primary key. The database management system can normally generate a unique identifier that has no meaning outside of the database system. For example "Sequences" in Oracle, "Identity" columns in Sybase etc. • It is bad practice to use timestamps as a primary key or using it as part of your composite primary key because you can get a primary key collision when two concurrent users access the table within milliseconds. • For better performance minimize use of composite keys or use fewer columns in your composite keys. • Where possible avoid using columns with business meaning as your primary key. For example Avoid using taxfilenumber, zipcode etc as your primary key because more than one town may have the same zipcode, taxfilenumber is private and should be encrypted and stored, some people may not have a taxfile number, you may want to reuse the same taxfilenumber after an individual's death, an individual may have more than one taxfilenumber etc. Remember to choose carefully, as <u>it is difficult to change the primary key in a production table</u>. **Q. What is the best practice to generate more portable primary keys?** The approach of using database specific unique id generator like a sequence in ORACLE, identity in Sybase etc is not portable because it is database dependent. You can use an "ID table" strategy to make your unique id generation more portable. This strategy uses a separate ID table to generate unique numbers for all your tables in the database. For example, ID table may look like: ID table | name	value	minValue	maxValue
---	---	---	---
AddressID	245	0	-1
AccountID	123	0	-1	 maxValue of -1 means no max limit. You could write a EJB stateless session bean, which returns a unique id for the "name" passed in as an argument. You could use an entity bean or a stored proc to access the ID table. The ID table should be adequately isolated to prevent any dirty reads and non-repeatable reads occurring due to concurrent access to the ID table.
What are constraints? Explain different types of constraints.	Constraints enable the RDBMS enforce the integrity of the database automatically, without needing you to create triggers, rule or defaults. Types of constraints: **NOT NULL, CHECK, UNIQUE, PRIMARY KEY, FOREIGN KEY** **Q. What are the best practices relating to constraints?** • Always define referential constraints to improve referential integrity of your data. For example A "BankDetail" table can have BSB number and accountnumber as part of unique key constraint (to prevent duplicate account details), while having a generated unique identifier as the primary key. • Perform all your referential integrity checks and data validations using constraints (foreign key and constraints) instead of triggers, as constraints are faster. Limit the use of triggers only for auditing, custom tasks and validations that can not be performed using constraints. Constraints save you time as well, as you don't have to write code for these validations, allowing the RDBMS to do all the work for you.
What is an index? What are the types of indexes? How many	The books you read have indexes, which help you to go to a specific key word faster. The database indexes are similar.

| clustered indexes can be created on a table? What are the advantages and disadvantages of creating separate index on each column of a table? | Indexes are of two types. **Clustered indexes** and non-clustered indexes. When you create a clustered index on a table, all the rows in the table are stored in the order of the clustered index key. So, there can be only one clustered index per table. **Non-clustered indexes** have their own storage separate from the table data storage. The row located could be the RowID or the clustered index key, depending up on the absence or presence of clustered index on the table.

If you create an index on each column of a table, it improves the query (i.e. **SELECT**) performance, as the query optimizer can choose from all the existing indexes to come up with an efficient execution plan. At the same time, data modification operations (such as **INSERT**, UPDATE, and DELETE) will become slow, as every time data changes in the table, all the indexes need to be updated. Another disadvantage is that, indexes need disk space, the more indexes you have, more disk space is used. |

Technical Tip #6

Q. How would you build a regex (regular expression) to filter out email addresses? The reason for asking this question, is that even if you cannot answer it straight away (because regular expressions actually form a miniature language in their own right), if you know what regular expressions are, know where to and when to use them and comfortable with it then you can write any pattern with a help of a reference guide, examples (http://www.regexlib.com) and the Java regex API. You can think of regular expressions as a kind of SQL query for free flowing text.

[Hint] `String emailRegex = "(\\w+)@(\\w+\\.)(\\w+)(\\.\\w+)*";`

The above pattern will satisfy: peter@company.com , peter@company.net.au , peter@company.inet.net.au

`\w` → a word character, `.` → any character, `+` → occurring 1 or more times, `*` → occurring 0 or more times, `?` → occurring 0 or 1 time, `\.` → use \ to escape special meaning of . (which is any character), `\\` → \ to escape \ in Java because \ has a special meaning in Java.

Important: ?, *, + are _not_ wild characters. They denote occurrence of a pattern (o or 1 time etc) and also denote quantifiers like **greedy** (X? search greedily for 0 or 1 occurrence), **reluctant** (X?? search reluctantly for 0 or 1 occurrence) and **possessive** (X?+ search possessively for 0 or 1 occurrence). If you say that they are wild characters then you have not used regex before.

In Java platform (J2SE 1.4 onwards) a package called **java.util.regex** enable you to use regular expressions. E.g.

```java
public static void main(String[] args) {

    Pattern p = Pattern.compile("j",Pattern.CASE_INSENSITIVE);        // look for letter 'j'
    Matcher m = p.matcher("java Q&A, java/j2EE Q&A, j2EE Q&A ");


    boolean result = m.find();
    StringBuffer out = new StringBuffer();

    while(result) {
       m.appendReplacement(out,"J");                    // replace with uppercase letter "J"
       result = m.find();
    }

    m.appendTail(out);
    System.out.println(out.toString());

    p = Pattern.compile(",");                       // pattern to split on → comma delimited
    String[] outArray = p.split(out);               // Split based on the pattern

    for (int i = 0; i < outArray.length; i++) {
        System.out.println(i+1 + " - " + outArray[i].trim());
    }
}
```

Output is:
```
Java Q&A, Java/J2EE Q&A, J2EE Q&A
1 - Java Q&A
2 - Java/J2EE Q&A
3 - J2EE Q&A
[Java Q&A,  Java/J2EE Q&A,  J2EE Q&A ]
```

Enterprise - RUP & UML

Q 103: What is RUP? SD

A 103: Rational Unified Process (RUP) is a general framework that can be used to describe a development process. The software development cycle has got 4 phases in the following order Inception, Elaboration, Construction, and Transition.

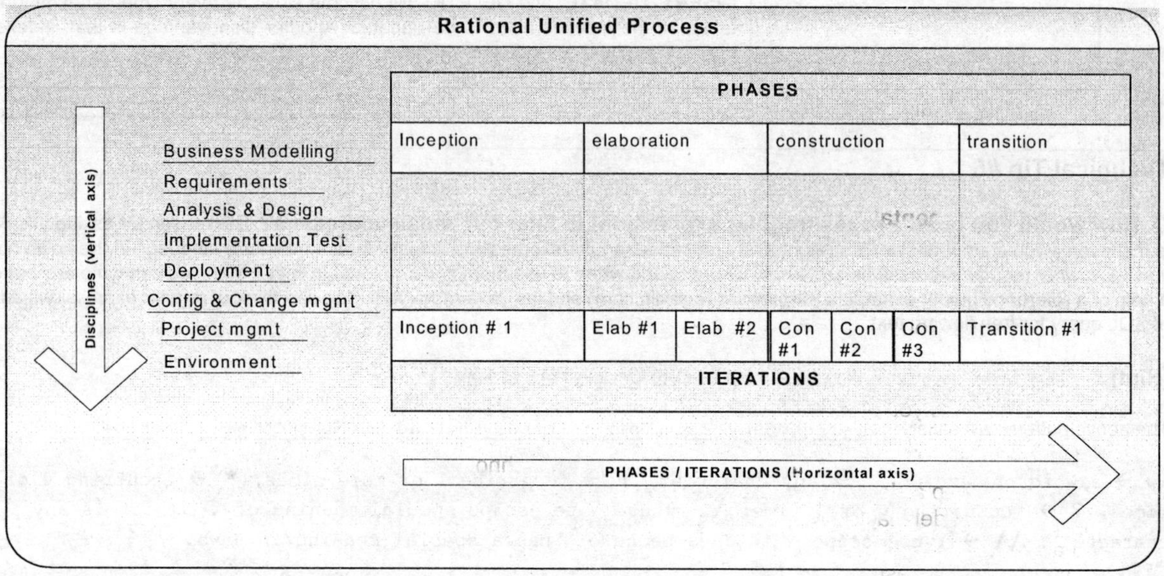

Rational Unified Process

	PHASES			
	Inception	elaboration	construction	transition
Disciplines (vertical axis): Business Modelling, Requirements, Analysis & Design, Implementation Test, Deployment, Config & Change mgmt, Project mgmt, Environment				
	Inception # 1	Elab #1 / Elab #2	Con #1 / Con #2 / Con #3	Transition #1
	ITERATIONS			

PHASES / ITERATIONS (Horizontal axis)

The core of the phases is **state-based**, and the state is determined by what fundamental questions you are trying to answer:

- **Inception** - do you and the customer have a shared understanding of the system?
- **Elaboration** - do you have baseline architecture to be able to build the system?
- **Construction** - are you developing a product?
- **Transition** - are you trying to get the customer to take ownership of the system?

RUP is based on a few important philosophies and principles:

- A software project team should **plan ahead**.
- It should know **where it is going**.
- It should capture project knowledge in a **storable** and **extensible** form.

The best practices of RUP involve the following major 5 properties:

Best practice property	Description
Use case driven	Interaction between the users and the system.
Architecture centric	Based on architecture with clear relationships between architectural components.
Iterative	The problem and the solution are divided into more manageable smaller pieces, where each iteration will be addressing one of those pieces.
Incremental	Each iteration builds incrementally on the foundation built in the previous iteration.
Controlled	Control with respect to process means you always know what to do next; control with respect to management means that all deliverables, artifacts, and code are under configuration management.

Q 104: Explain the 4 phases of RUP? SD

A 104:

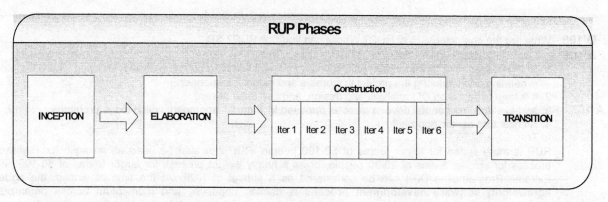

- **Inception**: During the inception phase, you work out the business case for the project. You also will be making a rough cost estimate and return on investment. You should also outline the scope and size of the project.

  The fundamental question you ask at the end of this phase: do you and the customer have a shared understanding of the system?

- **Elaboration**: At this stage you have the go ahead of the project however only have vague requirements. So at this stage you need to get a better understanding of the problem. Some of the steps involved are:

  - What is it you are actually going to build?
  - How are you going to build it?
  - What technology are you going to use?
  - Analyzing and dealing with requirement risks, technological risks, skill risks, political risks etc.
  - Develop a **domain model**, **use case model** and **a design model.** The UML techniques can be used for the model diagrams (e.g. class diagrams, sequence diagrams etc).

  An important result of the elaboration phase is that you have a **baseline architecture**. This architecture consists of:

  - A list of use cases depicting the requirements.
  - The domain model, which captures your understanding of the domain with the help of UML class diagrams.
  - Selection of key implementation technology and how they fit together. For example: Java/J2EE with JSP, Struts, EJB, XML, etc.

  The fundamental question you ask at the end of this phase: do you have a baseline architecture to be able to build the system?

- **Construction**: In this phase you will be building the system in a series of iterations. Each iteration is a mini project. You will be performing analysis, design, unit testing, coding, system testing, and integration testing for the use cases assigned to each iteration. The iterations within the construction phase are incremental and iterative. Each iteration builds on the use cases developed in the previous iterations. The each iteration will involve code rewrite, refactoring, use of design patterns etc.

  The basic documentation required during the construction phase is:

  - A **class diagram** and a **sequence diagram**.
  - Some text to pull the diagrams together.
  - If a class has complex life cycle behavior then a **state diagram** is required.
  - If a class has a complex computation then an **activity diagram** is required.

  The fundamental question you ask at the end of this phase: do you have a developed product?

- **Transition**: During this phase you will be delivering the finished code regularly. During this phase there is no coding to add functionality unless it is small and essential. There will be bug fixes, code optimization etc during this phase. An example of a transition phase is that the time between the beta release and the final release of a product.

  The fundamental question you ask at the end of this phase: are you trying to get the customer to take ownership of the developed product or system?

Q 105: What are the characteristics of RUP? Where can you use RUP? `SD`

A 105:

1. RUP is based on a few important philosophies and principles like planning ahead, knowing where the process is heading and capturing the project in storable and extensible manner.
2. It is largely based on OO analysis and design, and use case driven.
3. Iterative and incremental development as opposed to waterfall approach, which hides problems.
4. Architecture centric approach.

RUP is more suited for larger teams of 50-100 people. RUP can also be used as an agile (i.e. lightweight) process for smaller teams of 20-30 people, or as a heavy weight process for larger teams of 50-100 people. Extreme Programming (XP) can be considered as a subset of RUP. At the time of writing, the **agile (i.e lightweight) software development process** is gaining popularity and momentum across organizations. Several methodologies fit under this agile development methodology banner. All these methodologies share many characteristics like **iterative** and **incremental development**, **test driven development**, **stand up meetings to improve communication**, **automatic testing, build and continuous integration of code** etc. Refer **Q136** in Enterprise Java section.

Q 106: Why is UML important? `SD` `DC`

A 106: The more complicated the underlying system, the more critical the communication among everyone involved in developing and deploying the software. UML is a software blueprint language for analysts, designers and developers. UML provides a common vocabulary for the business analysts, architects, developers etc.

UML is applicable to the Object Oriented problem solving. UML begins with a **model**; A **model** is an abstraction of the underlying problem. The **domain** is the actual world from which the problem comes. The model consists of **objects**. The objects interact with each other by sending and receiving **messages**. The objects are characterized by **attributes** and **operations** (behaviors). The values of an object's attributes determine its **state**. The **classes** are the blueprints (or like templates) for objects. A class wraps **attributes** and **methods** into a single distinct entity. The objects are the **instances** of classes.

Q 107: What are the different types of UML diagrams? `SD` `DC` `FAQ`

A 107: **Use case diagrams**: Depicts the typical interaction between external users (i.e. actors) and the system. The emphasis is on **what** a system does rather than **how** it does it. A use case is a summary of scenarios for a single task or goal. An actor is responsible for initiating a task. The connection between actor and use case is a **communication association**.

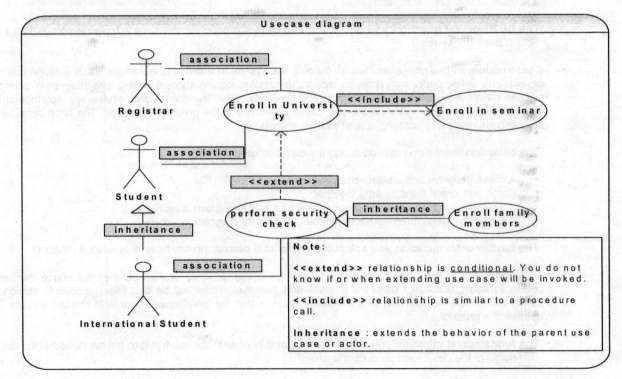

Capturing use cases is one of the primary tasks of the **elaboration phase** of RUP. In its simplest usage, you capture a use case by talking to your users and discussing the various things they might want to do with the system.

<u>When to use 'use case' diagrams?</u>

- Determining user requirements. New use cases often generate new requirements.
- Communicating with clients. The simplicity of the diagram makes use case diagrams a good way for designers and developers to communicate with clients.
- Generating test cases. Each scenario for the use case may suggest a suite of test cases.

Class diagrams: Class diagram technique is vital within **O**bject **O**riented methods. Class diagrams describe the types of objects in the system and the various static relationships among them. Class diagrams also show the attributes and the methods. Class diagrams have the following possible relationships:

- **Association**: A relationship between instances of 2 classes.

- **Aggregation**: An **association** in which one class belongs to a collection (does not always have to be a collection. You can also have cardinality of "1"). This is a **part of a whole** relationship where the **part** can exist without the **whole**. For example: A line item is whole and the products are the parts. If a line item is deleted then the products **need not be deleted**.

- **Composition**: An **association** in which one class belongs to a collection (does not always have to be a collection. You can also have cardinality of "1"). This is a **part of a whole** relationship where the **part** <u>cannot</u> exist without the **whole**. If the whole is deleted then the parts are deleted. For example: An Order is a whole and the line items are the parts. If an order is deleted then all the line items **should be deleted** as well (i.e. cascade deletes).

- **Generalization**: An inheritance link indicating that one class is a superclass of the other. The Generalization expresses the "**is a**" relationship whereas the association, aggregation and composition express the "**has a**" relationship.

- **Realization**: Implementation of an interface.

- **Dependency**: A dependency is a weak relationship where one class requires another class. The dependency expresses the "**uses**" relationship. For example: A domain model class uses a utility class like Formatter etc.

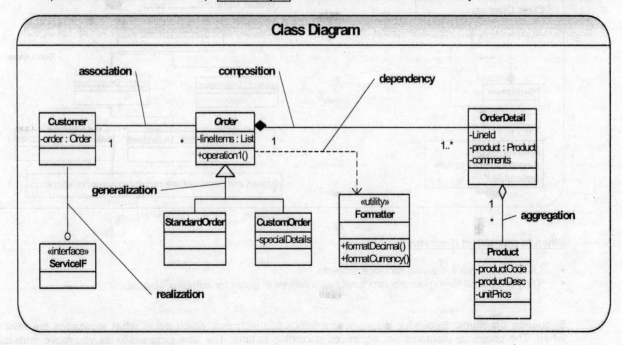

<u>When to use class diagrams?</u>

- Class diagrams are the backbone of **O**bject **O**riented methods. So they are used frequently.

- Class diagrams can have a conceptual perspective and an implementation perspective. During the analysis draw the conceptual model and during implementation draw the implementation model.

Package diagrams: To simplify complex class diagrams you can group classes into **packages**.

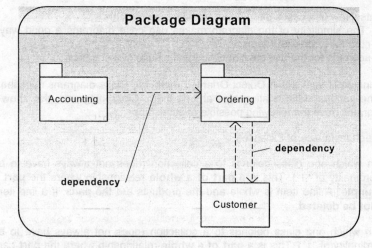

When to use package diagrams?

- Package diagrams are vital for large projects.

Object diagrams: Object diagrams show instances instead of classes. They are useful for explaining some complicated objects in detail about their recursive relationships etc.

When to use object diagrams?

- Object diagrams are a vital for large projects.
- They are useful for explaining structural relationships in detail for complex objects.

Sequence diagrams: Sequence diagrams are interaction diagrams which detail **what** messages are sent and **when**. The sequence diagrams are organized according to time. The time progresses as you move from top to bottom of the diagram. The objects involved in the diagram are shown from left to right according to **when** they take part.

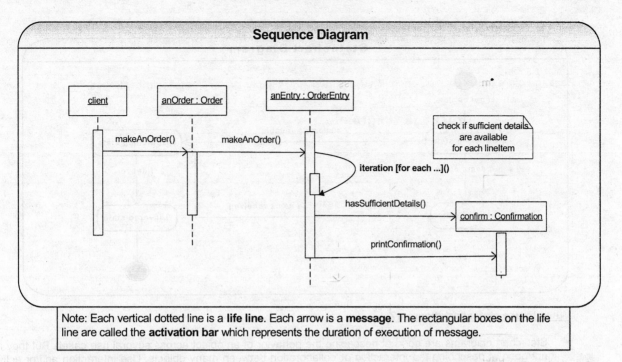

Note: Each vertical dotted line is a **life line**. Each arrow is a **message**. The rectangular boxes on the life line are called the **activation bar** which represents the duration of execution of message.

Collaboration diagrams: Collaboration diagrams are also **interaction diagrams**. Collaboration diagrams convey the same message as the sequence diagrams. But the collaboration diagrams focus on the **object roles** instead of the **times** at which the messages are sent.

The collaboration diagrams use the decimal sequence numbers as shown in the diagram below to make it clear which operation is calling which other operation, although it can be harder to see the overall sequence. The top-level message is numbered 1. The messages at the same level have the same decimal prefix but different suffixes of 1, 2 etc according to when they occur.

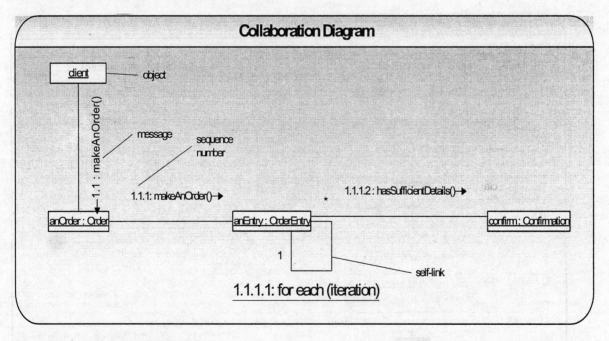

When to use interaction diagrams?

- When you want to look at behavior of several objects within a single use case. If you want to look at a single object across multiple use cases then use statechart diagram as described below.

State chart diagrams: Objects have behavior and state. The state of an object depends on its current activity or condition. This diagram shows the possible states of the object and the transitions that cause a change in its state.

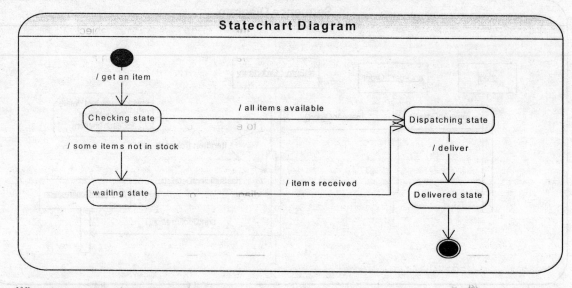

When to use statechart diagram?

- Statechart diagrams are good at describing the behavior of an object across several use cases. But they are not good at describing the interaction or collaboration between many objects. Use interaction and/or activity diagrams in conjunction with a statechart diagram.

- Use it only for classes that have complex state changes and behavior. **For example:** the User Interface (UI) control objects, Objects shared by multi-threaded programs etc.

Activity diagram: This is really a fancy flow chart. The activity diagram and statechart diagrams are related in a sense that statechart diagram focuses on object undergoing a transition process and an activity diagram focuses on the flow of activities involved in a single transition process.

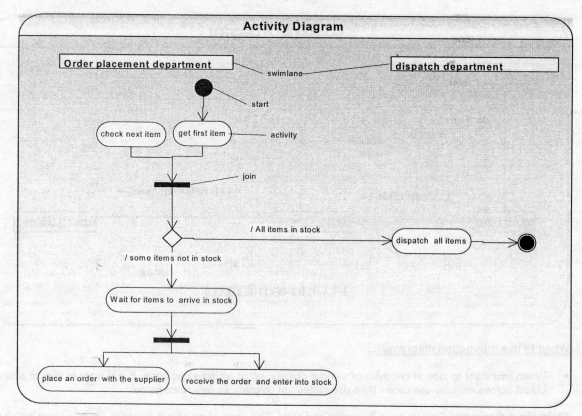

In domain modeling it is imperative that the diagram conveys which object (or class) is responsible for each activity. Activity diagrams can be divided into object **swimlanes** that determine which object is responsible for which activity. The swimlanes are quite useful because they combine the activity diagram's depiction of logic with the interaction diagram's depiction of responsibility. A single transition comes out of each **activity**, connecting to the next activity. A transition may **join** or **fork**.

When to use activity diagrams?

The **activity** and **statechart** diagrams are generally useful to express complex operations. The great strength of activity diagrams is that they support and encourage parallel behavior. The activity and statechart diagrams are beneficial for workflow modeling with multi-threaded programming.

Component and **Deployment diagrams**: A component is a code module. Component diagrams are physical diagrams analogous to a class diagram. The deployment diagrams show the physical configuration of software and hardware components. The physical hardware is made up of **nodes**. Each **component** belongs to a node.

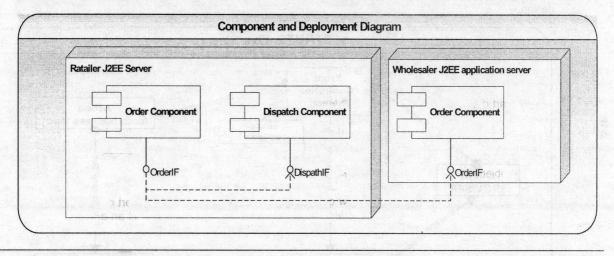

Q 108: What is the difference between aggregation and composition? SD DC FAQ

A 108:

Aggregation	Composition
Aggregation: An **association** in which one class belongs to another class or a collection. This is a **part of a whole** relationship where the **part** can exist without the **whole**. For example: A line item is whole and the products are the parts. If a line item is deleted then the products <u>need not be deleted</u>. (no cascade delete in database terms)	**Composition**: An **association** in which one class belongs to another class or a collection. This is a **part of a whole** relationship where the **part** <u>cannot</u> exist without the **whole**. If the whole is deleted then the parts are deleted. For example: An Order is a whole and the line items are the parts. If an order is deleted then all the line items <u>should be deleted</u> as well (i.e. cascade deletes in database terms).
Aggregations are not allowed to be circular.	In a garbage-collected language like Java, The **whole** has the responsibility of **preventing** the garbage collector to prematurely collect the **part** by holding reference to it.

Q 109: What is the difference between a collaboration diagram and a sequence diagram? SD DC

A 109: You can automatically generate one from the other.

Sequence Diagram	Collaboration Diagram
The emphasis is on the **sequence**.	The emphasis is on the **object roles**

Reference: The above section on RUP & UML is based on the book **UML Distilled** by Martin Fowler and Kendall Scott. If you would like to have a good understanding of UML & RUP, then this book is recommended.

Enterprise - Struts

Struts is a Web-based user interface framework, which has been around for a few years. It is a matured and proven framework, which has been used in many J2EE projects. While Struts has been demonstrating its popularity, there are emerging <u>component based</u> frameworks like **JavaServer Faces (JSF)** and **Tapestry** gaining lots of momentum and popularity. Like Struts, JSF and Tapestry provide Web application life cycle management through a controller servlet, and like Swing, JSF and Tapestry provide a <u>rich component model complete with event handling (via listeners) and component rendering</u>. So JSF and Tapestry can be considered as a combination of Struts frame work and Java Swing user interface framework. Refer **Q19 – Q20** in Emerging Technologies/Frameworks section for JSF.

Q 110: Give an overview of Struts? What is an ActionServlet? What is an Action class? What is an ActionForm? What is a Struts Validator Framework? `SF` `DP` `FAQ`

A 110: Struts is a framework with set of cooperating classes, servlets and JSP tags that make up a reusable MVC 2 design.

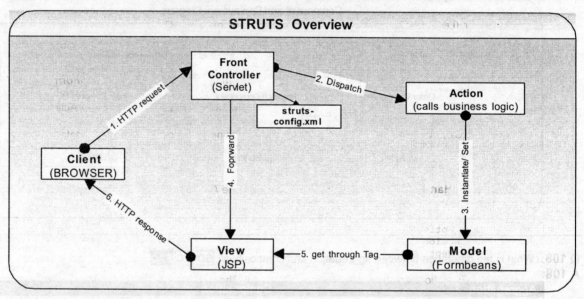

- **Client (Browser):** A request from the client browser creates an HTTP request. The Web container will respond to the request with an HTTP response, which gets displayed on the browser.

- **Controller (ActionServlet class** and **RequestProcessor class):** The controller receives the request from the browser, and makes the decision where to send the request based on the **struts-config.xml**. `Design pattern:` Struts controller uses the **command design pattern** by calling the *Action* classes based on the configuration file struts-config.xml and the *RequestProcessor* class's process() method uses **template method design pattern** (Refer **Q11** in How would you go about … section) by calling a sequence of methods like:

  - **processPath(request, response)** → read the request URI to determine path element.

  - **processMapping(request,response)** → use the path information to get the action mapping

  - **processRoles(request,respose,mapping)** → Struts Web application security which provides an authorization scheme. By default calls request.isUserInRole(). `For example` allow "/addCustomer" action if the role is executive.

    ```
    <action path="/addCustomer" roles="executive">
    ```

  - **processValidate(request,response,form,mapping)** → calls the validate() method of the ActionForm.

  - **processActionCreate(request,response,mapping)**→ gets the name of the action class from the "type" attribute of the <action> element.

- **processActionPerform(req,res,action,form,mapping)** → This method calls the execute method of the Action class which is where business logic is written.

ActionServlet class is the controller part of the MVC implementation and is the core of the framework. It processes user requests, determines what the user is trying to achieve according to the request, pulls data from the model (if necessary) to be given to the appropriate view, and selects the proper view to respond to the user. As discussed above ActionServlet class delegates the grunt of the work to the **RequestProcessor** and **Action** classes.

- **Workflow Logic (Action class):** The Servlet dispatches the request to Action classes, which act as a **thin wrapper to the business logic** (the actual business logic is carried out by either EJB session beans and/or plain Java classes). The action class helps control the **workflow** of the application. (**Note:** The Action class should only control the workflow and not the business logic of the application). The Action class uses the **Adapter design pattern** (Refer **Q11** in How would you go about ... section). The **Action** class is a wrapper around the business logic. The purpose of the Action class is to translate the HttpServletRequest to the business logic. To use the Action class, subclass and overwrite the execute() method. The actual business logic should be in a separate package or EJB to allow reuse of business logic in a protocol independent manner (i.e. the business logic should be used **not only** by HTTP clients **but also** by WAP clients, EJB clients, Applet clients etc).

- **ActionForm class:** Java representation of HTTP input data. They can carry data over from one request to another, but actually represent the data submitted with the request. The **ActionForm** class maintains the state for the Web application. ActionForm is an abstract class, which is subclassed for every input form model. The struts-config.xml file controls, which HTML form request maps to which ActionForm.

- **View (JSP):** The view is a JSP file. There is no business or flow logic and no state information. The JSP should just have tags to represent the data on the browser.

The **ExceptionHandler** can be defined to execute when the Action class's execute() method throws an Exception. For example

```
<global-exceptions>
      <exception key="my.key" type="java.io.IOException" handler="my.ExceptionHandler"/>
</global-exceptions>
```

When an IOException is thrown then it will be handled by the execute() method of the my.ExceptionHandler class.

The struts-config.xml configuration information is translated into **ActionMapping**, which are put into the **ActionMappings** collection. Further reading is recommended for a more detailed understanding.

Q. What is Struts Validator Framework?
A. Form data can be validated on the client side as well as on the server side using the Validator Framework, which was developed as a third-party add on to Struts. This framework generates the java script and it can be used to validate the form data on the client browser. Server side validation of your form can be carried out by subclassing your form class with *DynaValidatorForm* class. The Validator Framework uses 2 xml configuration files **validator-rules.xml** (defines reusable standard validation routines, which are usable in validator.xml) and **validator.xml** (defines validation applicable to a form bean).

Q. How will you display failed validation errors on JSP page?
A. Use the `<html:/errors>` tag.

Q. How will you turn on the client side validation based on validation.xml file?
A. Use the `<html:javascript />` tag.

Q 111: What is a synchronizer token pattern in Struts or how will you protect your Web against multiple submissions? **DC** **DP**

A 111: Web designers often face the situation where a form submission must be protected against duplicate or **multiple submissions**, which breaks the normal control flow sequence. This situation typically occurs when the user clicks on submit button more than once before the response is sent back or client access a page by returning to the previously book marked page or client resubmits the page by clicking the back button/refresh button .

- The simplest solution that some sites use is that displaying a warning message "Wait for a response after submitting and do not submit twice.

- In the client only strategy, a flag is set on the first submission and from then onwards the submit button is disabled based on this flag. Useful in some situations but this strategy is coupled to the browser type and version.

- For a server-based solution the J2EE pattern **synchronizer token pattern** can be applied. The basic idea is to:

1. Set a token in a session variable on the server side before sending the transactional page back to the client.

2. The token is set on the page as a hidden field. On submission of the page first check for the presence of a valid token by comparing the request parameter in the hidden field to the token stored in the session. If the token is valid continue processing otherwise take other alternative action. After testing the token must be reset to null.

Refer **Q 27** in Enterprise - JSP section under "Synchronizer token pattern". The synchronizer token pattern is implemented in Struts using the following methods:

ActionServlet.saveToken(HttpRequest) and **ActionServlet.isTokenValid**(HttpRequest) etc

---

Q 112: How do you upload a file in Struts? SF
A 112: In **JSP** page set the code as shown below: CO

```
<html:form action="upload.do" enctype="multipart/form-data" name="fileForm" type="FileForm"
        scope="session">

   Please select the file that you would like to upload:
   <html:file property="file" />
   <html:submit />

</html:form>
```

In the **FormBean** set the code as shown below:

```
public class FileForm extends ActionForm {
   private FormFile file;

   public void setFile(FormFile file){
       this.file = file;
   }

   public FormFile getFile(){
     return file;
   }
}
```

Q 113: Are Struts action classes thread-safe? SF CI FAQ
A 113: No. Struts action classes are not thread-safe. Struts action classes are cached and reused for performance optimization at the cost of having to implement the action classes in a thread-safe manner.

Q 114: How do you implement internationalization in Struts? SF
A 114: Internationalization is built into Struts framework. In the JSP page set the code as shown below: CO

```
<%@ taglib uri="/WEB-INF/struts-bean.tld" prefix="bean" %>
<%@ taglib uri="/WEB-INF/struts-html.tld" prefix="html" %>
<%@ taglib uri="/WEB-INF/struts-logic.tld" prefix="logic" %>
<html:html locale="true">
<head>
  <title>i18n</title>
</head>
```

```
<body>
  <h2><bean:message key="page.title"/></h2>
</body>
</html:html>
```

Now we need to create an application resource file named **ApplicationResource.properties**.

```
page.title=Thank you for visiting!
```

Now in Italian, create an application resource file named **ApplicationResource_it.properties**.

```
page.title=Grazie per la vostra visita!
```

Finally, add reference to the appropriate resource file in the **struts-config.xml**.

Q 115: What is an action mapping in Struts? How will you extend Struts? SF

A 115: An **action mapping** is a configuration file (struts-config.xml) entry that, in general, associates an action name with an action. An action mapping can contain a reference to **a form bean** that the action can use, and can additionally define a list of local **forwards** that is visible only to this action.

Q. How will you extend Struts?

Struts is not only a powerful framework but also very extensible. You can extend Struts in one or more of the following ways:

Plug-In: Define your own Plug-In class if you want to execute some init() and destroy() methods during the application startup and shutdown respectively. Some services like loading configuration files, initializing applications like logging, auditing, etc can be carried out in the init() method.

RequestProcessor: You can create your own *RequestProcessor* by extending the Struts RequestProcessor. For example you can override the processRoles(req, res, mapping) in your extended class if you want to query the LDAP server for the security authorization etc.

ActionServlet: You can extend the *ActionServlet* class if you want to execute your business logic at the application startup or shutdown or during individual request processing. You should take this approach only when the above mentioned approaches are not feasible.

Q 116: What design patterns are used in Struts? DP FAQ

A 116: Struts is based on model 2 MVC (Model-View-Controller) architecture. Struts controller uses the **command design pattern** (Refer **Q11** in How would you go about section) and the action classes use the **adapter design pattern**. The process() method of the RequestProcessor uses the **template method design pattern** (Refer **Q11** in How would you go about section). Struts also implement the following J2EE design patterns

- Service to Worker (Refer **Q25** in Enterprise section).
- Dispatcher View (Refer **Q25** in Enterprise section).
- Composite View (Struts Tiles) (Refer **Q25** in Enterprise section)
- Front Controller (Refer **Q24** in Enterprise section).
- View Helper (Refer **Q25** in Enterprise section).
- Synchronizer Token (Refer **Q111** in Enterprise section).

Enterprise - Web and Application servers

Q 117: What application servers, Web servers, LDAP servers, and Database servers have you used?
A 117:

Web Servers	Apache, Microsoft IIS, Netscape, Domino etc
Application Servers	IBM WebSphere, BEA WebLogic, Apache Tomcat, Borland Enterprise Server, Fujitsu Interstage, JBoss, ATG Dynamo etc
Portal servers	Websphere Portal Server, JBoss Portal Server, etc
LDAP Servers	IPlanet's directory server, SiemensDirX etc
Database Servers	IBM DB2, Oracle, SQL Server, Sybase, Informix

Q 118: What is the difference between a Web server and an application server? **SF** **FAQ**
A 118: In general, an application server prepares data for a Web server -- for example, gathering data from databases, applying relevant business rules, processing security checks, and/or storing the state of a user's session. The term application server may be misleading since the functionality isn't limited to applications. Its role is more as retriever and manager of data and processes used by anything running on a Web server. In the coming age of Web services, application servers will probably have an even more important role in managing service oriented components. One of the reasons for using an application server is to improve performance by off-loading tasks from a Web server. When heavy traffic has more users, more transactions, more data, and more security checks then more likely a Web server becomes a bottleneck.

Web Server	Application Server
Supports HTTP protocol. When a Web server receives an HTTP request, it responds with an HTTP response, such as sending back an HTML page (static content) or delegates the dynamic response generation to some other program such as CGI scripts or Servlets or JSPs in an application server.	Exposes **business logic** and **dynamic content** to a client through various protocols such as HTTP, TCP/IP, IIOP, JRMP etc.
Uses various scalability and fault-tolerance techniques.	Uses various scalability and fault-tolerance techniques. In addition provides resource pooling, component life cycle management, transaction management, messaging, security etc.

Q 119: What is a virtual host? **SF**
A 119: The term virtual host refers to the practice of maintaining **more than one server on one machine**. They are differentiated by their host names. You can have name based virtual hosts and IP address based virtual hosts. For example

A name-based "virtual host" has a **unique domain name**, but the same IP address. For example, www.company1.com and www.company2.com can have the same IP address 192.168.0.10 and share the same Web server. We can configure the Web server as follows:

```
NameVirtualHost 192.168.0.10

<VirtualHost 192.168.0.10>
    ServerName www.company1.com
    DocumentRoot /web/company1
</VirtualHost>

<VirtualHost 192.168.0.10>
    ServerName www.company2.com
    DocumentRoot /web/company2
</VirtualHost>
```

In this scenario, both www.company1.com and www.company2.com are registered with the standard **domain name service (DNS)** registry as having the IP address 192.168.0.10. A user types in the URL http://www.company1.com/hello.jsp in their browser. The user's computer resolves the name www.company1.com to the IP address 192.168.0.10. The Web server on the machine that has the IP address 192.168.0.10, so it receives the request. The Web server determines which virtual host to use by matching the request URL It gets from an HTTP header submitted by the browser with the "ServerName" parameter in the configuration file shown above.

Name-based virtual hosting is usually easier, since you have to only configure your DNS server to map each hostname to a single IP address and then configure the Web server to recognize the different hostnames as discussed in the previous paragraph. Name-based virtual hosting also eases the demand for scarce IP addresses limited by physical network connections [but modern operation systems support use of virtual interfaces, which are also known as IP aliases]. Therefore you should use name-based virtual hosting unless there is a specific reason to choose IP-based virtual hosting. Some reasons why you might consider using IP-based virtual hosting:

- Name-based virtual hosting cannot be used with SSL based secure servers because of the nature of the SSL protocol.

- Some operating systems and network equipment implement bandwidth management techniques that cannot differentiate between hosts unless they are on separate IP addresses.

- IP based virtual hosts are useful, when you want to manage more than one site (like live, demo, staging etc) on the same server where hosts inherit the characteristics defined by your main host. But when using SSL for example, a unique IP address is necessary.

For example in development environment when using the test client and the server on the same machine we can define the host file as shown below:

UNIX user: /etc/hosts
Windows user: C:\WINDOWS\SYSTEM32\DRIVERS\ETC\HOSTS

```
127.0.0.1          localhost
127.0.0.1          www.company1.com
127.0.0.1          www.company2.com
```

[Reference: http://httpd.apache.org/docs/1.3/vhosts/]

Q 120: What is application server clustering? SI

A 120: An application server cluster consists of a number of application servers loosely coupled on a network. The server cluster or server group is generally distributed over a number of machines or nodes. The important point to note is that the <u>cluster appears as a single server to its clients</u>.

The goals of application server clustering are:

- **Scalability:** should be able to add new servers on the existing node or add new additional nodes to enable the server to handle increasing loads without performance degradation, and in a manner transparent to the end users.

- **Load balancing:** Each server in the cluster should process a fair share of client load, in proportion to its processing power, to avoid overloading of some and under utilization of other server resources. Load distribution should remain balanced even as load changes with time.

- **High availability:** Clients should be able to access the server at almost all times. Server usage should be transparent to hardware and software failures. If a server or node fails, its workload should be moved over to other servers, automatically as fast as possible and the application should continue to run uninterrupted. This method provides a fair degree of application system fault-tolerance. After failure, the entire load should be redistributed equally among working servers of the system.

[Good read: Uncover the hood of J2EE clustering by Wang Yu on http://www.theserverside.com]

Q 121: Explain Java Management Extensions (**JMX**)? SF

A 121: JMX framework can improve the manageability of your application by

- Monitoring your application for performance problems, critical events, error condition statistics, etc. **For example** you can be notified if there is a sudden increase in traffic or sudden drop in performance of your website.

- Making your application more controllable and configurable at runtime by directly exposing application API and parameters. **For example** you could switch your database connection to an alternate server. You can also change the level of debugging and logging within the application without stopping the server. You could write a poller, which polls your database at a regular interval as a JMX sevice, so that you can alter the polling interval, stop and start the poller through your server console without having to stop the server.

- By interfacing JMX to your hardware, database server and application server, health checks can be performed of your infrastructure.

Q 122: Explain some of the portability issues between different application servers? **SI**
A 122: Transaction isolation levels, lazy loading and dirty marker strategies for EJB, class loading visibility etc.

If your job specification requires a basic understanding of Portals, Portlets etc or keen to learn the basics then read the following questions and answers.

Q. What is a portal?

A portal is a Web site or service that offers broad range of resources and services like e-mail, forums, search engines, on-line shopping, news, weather information, stock quotes, etc. Portal is a term generally synonymous with the terms gateway or grand entrance into the Internet for many users. E.g. www.yahoo.com, www.aol.com, www.msn.com etc. A Web portal software allows aggregation of several back-end systems, processes, sites etc brought together through a single portal page. Portals also provide additional services such as single sign-on security, customization (i.e. personalization) etc.

Q. What are the logical components to consider when building a portal to the Java Portlet specification (JSR 168)?

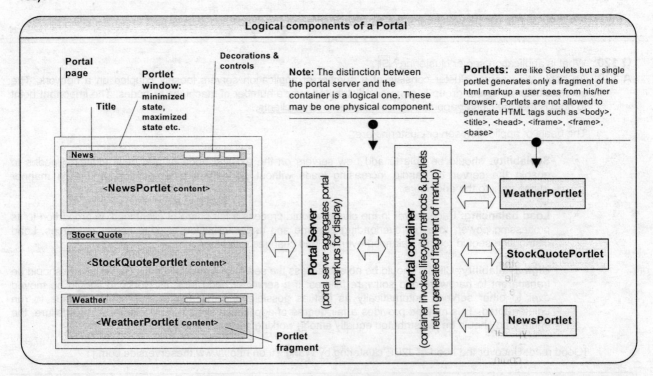

Portal server: is an application, which aggregates portlet applications together in a presentable format to the user. In addition to being a presentation layer, it allows users to customize their views including what portlet applications to show, colors, images etc. Also provides additional services like single sign-on security etc.

Portlet Container: Provides a run-time environment to portlets, much in the same way a servlet container provides the environment for servlets. The portlet container manages portlets by invoking their lifecycle methods (init(..), processAction(..), render(..), destroy() etc). The container forwards requests to an appropriate portlet. When a portlet generates a response, the container sends it to the portal server to be rendered to the user.

Portlet: provides content to its calling portal container for the purpose of being displayed on a portal page. Portlets are like servlets but portlets do not generate complete HTML documents. They only generate fragments that are included on the final portal page. Portlet applications are essentially extended Web applications (i.e. a layer on top of servlets). Portlets also share the application context with servlets and JSPs and can even include the output of another servlet or JSP as part of their content. User's actions are received within a portlet in the form of both action (to respond to user's interactions like search etc) and render methods (to paint the output of the portlet).

Note: Under the covers the GUI windows News, Stock Quote and Weather shown in the diagram are different applications, developed independently of each other and deployed as individual .war in the portal server.

Q. How do portlets differ from servlets?

The Portlet API is capable of using the existing application server infrastructure. You can call an EJB from your portlet, or you can start and participate in a global transaction controlled by your application server. In other words, portlets are Web components like servlets and can do pretty much every thing that a servlet can do except for a few important differences:

- Portlets do not generate complete HTML documents. Portlets only generate fragments of HTML that are to be included as part of the final portal page. Portlets are not allowed to generate HTML tags like <title>, <head>, <body>, <frame>, <iframe>, <base>, etc. The portal server decides where these tags should go and provides additional <table>, <tr> and <td> tags for each portlet. Portlets can access either servlets or independent JSPs by directly including their output within a portlet's rendered output, but only without these offending HTML tags.

- Portlets are not directly tied to a URL and they use methods such as createActionURL(..) or createRenderURL(..) to construct a URL that allows a user to fire actions to render currently executing portlet. You cannot send somebody URL of a portlet but you can send him/her the URL of the portal page containing a portlet.

- A Portlet can exist multiple times on the same page and the user is given the ability to control what portlets are displayed on his/her page (i.e. known as personalization). Also the user can minimize or maximize each portlet window.

Q. What are portlet window states and portlet modes?

Window states: To offer the user the ability to customize portlets, there are special window states like normal, minimized and maximized. A window state determines how much content should appear in a portlet. Normal will display the portlet's data in the amount of space defined by the portal application, maximized will display only that portlet in the whole window, and minimized may display only one or two lines of text.

Portal modes: determine what actions should be performed on a portlet. There are three standard modes like View, Edit and Help. Optional modes are possible. The *GenericPortlet* class defines three empty methods doEdit(..), doView(..) and doHelp(..). Your subclasses can implement any of these methods.

Furthermore, the portlet can use these states and modes to determine what content it needs to show the user at any given point.

Q. How do portlets provide customization in addition to window states and portlet modes?

To provide customization portlets support preferences, which are name/value pairs that can be assigned an initial value and later tailored to other values based on user preference. Preferences are initially defined within the portlet's deployment descriptor file ***portlet.xml*** and accessed through the ***PortletPreferences*** object, which provides methods to retrieve, change or store preferences. Preferences can also be read-only and also can be verified with validators.

Q. How would you achieve design flexibility in a portal to cater for different look and feel? normal Website designers know the type and amount of the initial content but portal designers have to design the portal to be flexible enough to meet diverse clients' and users' needs. Design flexibility can be achieved by using CSS (Cascading Style Sheets) to avoid hard coding colors and images into the portal so that customers can easily customize (i.e. modify) the look of their portal.

Enterprise - Best practices and performance considerations

Q 123: Give some tips on J2EE application server performance tuning? **PI** **FAQ**
A 123:

- Set the Web container threads, which will be used to process incoming HTTP requests. The minimum size should be tuned to handle the average load of the container and maximum should be tuned to handle the peak load. The maximum size should be less than or equal to the number of threads in your Web server.

- Application servers maintain a pool of JDBC resources so that a new connection does not need to be created for each transaction. Application servers can also cache your prepared statements to improve performance. So you can tune the minimum and maximum size of these pools.

- Tune your initial heap size for the JVM so that the garbage collector runs at a suitable interval so that it does not cause any unnecessary overhead. Adjust the value as required to improve performance.

- Set the session manager settings appropriately based on following guidelines:

  - Set the appropriate value for in memory session count.
  - Reduce the session size.
  - Don't enable session persistence unless required by your application.
  - Invalidate your sessions when you are finished with them by setting appropriate session timeout.

- Calls to EJB from a separate JVM are handled by ORB (Object Request Broker). ORB uses a pool of threads to handle these requests. The thread pool size should be set appropriately to handle average and peak loads.

- If a servlet or JSP file is called frequently with identical URL parameters then they can be dynamically cached to improve performance.

- Turn the application server tracing off unless required for debugging.

- Some application servers support lazy loading and dirty marker strategies with EJB to improve performance.

Q 124: Explain some of the J2EE best practices? **BP** **FAQ**
A 124:

- **Recycle your valuable resources by either pooling** or **caching**. You should create a limited number of resources and share them from a common pool (e.g. pool of threads, pool of database connections, pool of objects etc). Caching is simply another type of pooling where instead of pooling a connection or object, you are pooling remote data (database data) and placing it in the memory (using Hashtable etc).

- **Avoid embedding business logic in a protocol dependent manner** like in JSPs, HttpServlets, Struts action classes etc. This is because your business logic should be not only executed by your Web clients but also required to be shared by various GUI clients like Swing based stand alone application, WAP clients etc.

- **Automate** the build process with tools like **Ant, CruiseControl,** and **Maven** etc. In an enterprise application the build process can become quite complex and confusing.

- **Build** test cases first (i.e. Test Driven Development (TDD), refer section Emerging Technologies) using tools like **JUnit**. Automate the testing process and integrate it with build process.

- **Separate HTML code from the Java code**: Combining HTML and Java code in the same source code can make the code less readable. Mixing HTML and scriptlet will make the code extremely difficult to read and maintain. The display or behavior logic can be implemented as a custom tags by the Java developers and Web designers can use these Tags as the ordinary XHTML tags.

- It is best practice to use multi-threading and stay away from **single threaded model of the servlet** unless otherwise there is a compelling reason for it. Shared resources can be synchronized or used in read-only manner or shared values can be stored in a database table. Single threaded model can adversely affect performance.

- **Apply the following JSP best practices**:

  - **Place data access logic in JavaBeans**: The code within the JavaBean is readily accessible to other JSPs and Servlets.

  - **Factor shared behavior out of Custom Tags into common JavaBeans classes**: The custom tags are not used outside JSPs. To avoid duplication of behavior or business logic, move the logic into JavaBeans and get the custom tags to utilize the beans.

  - **Choose the right "*include*" mechanism:** What are the differences between static and a dynamic include? Using includes will improve code reuse and maintenance through modular design. Which one to use? Refer **Q31** in Enterprise section.

  - **Use style sheets** (e.g. css), **template mechanism** (e.g. struts tiles etc) and **appropriate comments** (both hidden and output comments).

- If you are using EJBs apply the EJB best practices as described in **Q82** in Enterprise section.

- Use the J2EE standard packaging specification to improve portability across Application Servers.

- Use proven frameworks like **Struts, Spring, Hibernate, JSF** etc.

- Apply appropriate proven J2EE design patterns to improve performance and minimize network communications cost (Session façade pattern, Value Object pattern etc).

- Batch database requests to improve performance. For example

```
Connection con = DriverManager.getConnection(......).
Statement stmt = con.createStatement().
stmt.addBatch("INSERT INTO  Address............");
stmt.addBatch("INSERT INTO  Contact............");
stmt.addBatch("INSERT INTO  Personal");
int[] countUpdates =  stmt.executeBatch();
```

  Use "**PreparedStatements**" instead of ordinary "Statements" for repeated reads.

- Avoid resource leaks by

  - Closing all database connections after you have used them.
  - Cleaning up the objects after you have finished with them especially when an object having a long life cycle refers to a number of objects with short life cycles, then you have the potential for memory leak.
  - Having the resource (i.e. database connections, statements, etc) clean up code in a **finally** {} block, which is always executed, even if an exception is thrown.

- Handle and propagate exceptions correctly. Decide between checked and unchecked (i.e. RunTime) exceptions.

Q 125: Explain some of the J2EE best practices to improve performance? **BP** **PI** **FAQ**

A 125: In short, manage valuable resources wisely and recycle them where possible, minimize network overheads and serialization cost, and optimize all your database operations.

- **Manage and recycle your valuable resources by either pooling or caching**. You should create a limited number of resources and share them from a common pool (e.g. pool of threads, pool of database connections, pool of objects etc). Caching is simply another type of pooling where instead of pooling a connection or object, you are pooling remote data (database data), and placing it in memory (using Hashtable etc). Unused stateful session beans must be removed explicitly and appropriate idle timeout should be set to control stateful session bean life cycle.

- **Use effective design patterns to minimize network overheads** (Session facade, Value Object etc Refer **Q84, Q85** in Enterprise section), use of fast-lane reader pattern for database access (Refer **Q86** in Enterprise section). Caching of retrieved JNDI InitialContexts, factory objects (e.g. EJB homes) etc. using the service locator design pattern, which reduces expensive JNDI access with the help of caching strategies.

- **Minimize serialization costs** by marking references (like file handles, database connections etc), which do not require serialization by declaring them '**transient**' (Refer **Q19** in Java section). Use pass-by-reference where possible as opposed to pass by value.

- **Set appropriate timeouts:** for the HttpSession objects, after which the session expires, set idle timeout for stateful session beans etc.

- Improve the **performance of database operations** with the following tips:

  - Database connections should be released when not needed anymore, otherwise there will be potential resource leakage problems.

  - Apply least restrictive but valid transaction isolation level.

  - Use JDBC prepared statements for overall database efficiency and for batching repetitive inserts and updates. Also batch database requests to improve performance.

  - When you first establish a connection with a database by default it is in auto-commit mode. For better performance turn auto-commit off by calling the connection.setAutoCommit(false) method.

  - Where appropriate (you are loading 100 objects into memory but use only 5 objects) **lazy load** your data to avoid loading the whole database into memory using the virtual proxy pattern. Virtual proxy is an object, which looks like an object but actually contain no fields until when one of its methods is called does it load the correct object from the database.

  - Where appropriate **eager load** your data to avoid frequently accessing the database every time over the network.

Tech Tip #7:

Q. How do you identify a Java process id in a UNIX machine?

```
$> ps -def | grep java
```

Q. How do you get a thread dump of a Java process in a UNIX machine?

```
$> kill -3 <process-id>
```

Q. If you have multiple java processes running in a UNIX machine, how would you identify a particular process?

```
$> /usr/ucb/bin/ps auxwww | grep java | grep <specific-process-description>
```

Q. What tools/commands do you use to help you identify an out of control Java process in a UNIX machine?

UNIX stat tools/commands like **jvmstat**, **vmstat**, **iostat** etc.

Q. How would you display the number of active established connections to localhost in a UNIX machine?

```
$> netstat -a | grep EST
```

Q. How do you find out drive statistics in a UNIX machine?

```
$> iostat -E
```

Enterprise – Logging, testing and deployment

Q 126: Give an overview of Log4J? `SF` `FAQ`

A 126: Log4j is a logging framework for Java. Log4J is designed to be fast and flexible. Log4J has 3 main components which work together to enable developers to log messages:

- Loggers [was called *Category* prior to version 1.2]
- Appenders
- Layout

Logger: The foremost advantage of any logging API like Log4J over plain System.out.println is its ability to disable certain log statements while allowing others to print unhindered. Loggers are hierarchical. The root logger exists at the top of the hierarchy. The root logger always exists and it cannot be retrieved by name. The hierarchical nature of the logger is denoted by "." notation. For example the logger "java.util" is the parent of child logger "java.util.Vector" and so on. Loggers may be assigned priorities such as DEBUG, INFO, WARN, ERROR and FATAL. If a given logger is not assigned a priority, then it inherits the priority from its closest ancestor. The logging requests are made by invoking one of the following printing methods of the logger instance: debug(), info(), warn(), error(), and fatal().

Appenders and Layouts: In addition to selectively enabling and disabling logging requests based on the logger, the Log4J allows logging requests to multiple destinations. In Log4J terms the output destination is an appender. There are appenders for console, files, remote sockets, JMS, etc. One logger can have more than one appender. A logging request for a given logger will be forwarded to all the appenders in that logger plus the other appenders higher in the hierarchy. In addition to the output destination the output format can be categorized as well. This is accomplished by associating layout with an appender. The layout is responsible for formatting the logging request according to user's settings.

Sample configuration file:

```
#set the root logger priority to DEBUG and its appender to App1
log4j.rootLogger=DEBUG, App1

#App1 is set to a console appender
log4j.appender.App1=org.apache.log4j.ConsoleAppender

#appender App1 uses a pattern layout
log4j.appender.App1.layout=org.apache.log4j.PatternLayout.
log4j.appender.App1.layout.ConversionPattern=%-4r [%t] %-5p %c %x -%m%n

# Print only messages of priority WARN or above in the package com.myapp
log4j.Logger.com.myapp=WARN
```

XML configuration for Log4j is available, and is usually the best practice. If you have both the log4j.xml and log4j.properties, then log4j.xml takes precedence.

Q 127: How do you initialize and use Log4J? `SF` `CO`

A 127:

```
public class MyApp {
    //Logger is a utility wrapper class to be written with appropriate printing methods
    static Logger log = Logger.getLogger (MyApp.class.getName());

    public void my method() {
        if(log.isDebugEnabled())
            log.debug("This line is reached............................" + var1 + "-" + var2);
        )
    }

}
```

Q 128: What is the hidden cost of parameter construction when using Log4J? `SF` `PI`

A 128:

Do not use in frequently accessed methods or loops: CO

```
log.debug ("Line number" + intVal + " is less than " + String.valueOf(array[i]));
```

The above construction has a **performance cost in frequently accessed methods and loops** in constructing the message parameter, concatenating the *String* etc regardless of whether the message will be logged or not.

Do use in frequently accessed methods or loops: CO

```
if (log.isDebugEnabled()) {
     log.debug ("Line number" + intVal + " is less than " + String.valueOf(array[i]));
}
```

The above construction will avoid the parameter construction cost by only constructing the message parameter when you are in debug mode. But it is not a best practice to place log.isDebugEnabled() around all debug code.

Q 129: What is the test phases and cycles? SD FAQ

A 129:

- **Unit tests** (e.g. JUnit etc, carried out by developers).
  There are two popular approaches to testing server-side classes: **mock objects**, which test classes by simulating the server container, and **in-container** testing, which tests classes running in the actual server container. If you are using Struts framework, *StrutsTestCase* for JUnit allows you to use either approach, with very minimal impact on your actual unit test code.

- **System tests or functional tests** (carried out by business analysts and/or testers).
- **Integration tests** (carried out by business analysts, testers, developers etc).
- **Regression tests** (carried out by business analysts and testers).
- **Stress volume tests or load tests** (carried out by technical staff).
- **User acceptance tests** (UAT – carried out by end users).

Each of the above test phases will be carried out in cycles. Refer **Q14** in How would you go about… section for JUnit, which is an open source unit-testing framework.

Q 130: Brief on deployment environments you are familiar with? FAQ

A 130: Differ from project team to project team [**Hint**] :

Application environments where "ear" files get deployed.

Development box: can have the following instances of environments in the same machine (need not be clustered).

- Development environment → used by developers.
- System testing environment → used by business analysts.

Staging box: can have the following instances of environments in the same machine (preferably clustered servers with load balancing)

- Integration testing environment → used for integration testing, user acceptance testing etc.
- Pre-prod environment → used for user acceptance testing, regression testing, and load testing or stress volume testing (SVT). [This environment should be exactly same as the production environment].

Production box:

- Production environment → live site used by actual users.

Data environments (Database)

Note: Separate boxes [not the same boxes as where applications (i.e. ear files) are deployed]

- **Development box** (database).
  Used by applications on development and system testing environments. Separate instances can be created on the same box for separate environments like development and system testing.

- **Staging Box** (database)
  Used by applications on integration testing and user acceptance testing environments. Separate instances can be created on the same box for separate environments.

- **Production Box** (database)
  Live data used by actual users of the system.

General Tip #7:

Some interviewers would like to purposely disagree with your answer or confuse you even if you are sure that you are right. If you are confident then you should not give in. You <u>should try to persuade your interviewer</u> that you are right. If you cannot persuade your interviewer then how are you going to persuade your business users or fellow developers? Once I was asked **When would you use a "const" keyword in Java?**. My answer was that even though it is a reserved word in Java, it is not yet in use in Java (as of version Java 5.0, may be added to the language in the future). The interviewer quizzed me further by saying, Are you sure? My answer was yes, and then went on to say that in Java you declare a constant with a "final" keyword.

Enterprise – Personal and Behavioral/Situational

Q 131: Tell me about yourself or about some of the recent projects you have worked with? What do you consider your most significant achievement? Why do you think you are qualified for this position? Why should we hire you and what kind of contributions will you make? **FAQ**

A 131: [Hint:] Pick your recent projects and **enthusiastically** brief on it. Interviewer will be looking for how passionate you are about your past experience and achievements. Also is imperative that during your briefing, you demonstrate on a high level(without getting too technical) how you applied your skills and knowledge in some of the following key areas:

- **Design Concepts**: Refer **Q02, Q03, Q19, Q20, Q21, Q91, Q98,** and **Q101.**
- **Design Patterns**: Refer **Q03, Q24, Q25, Q83, Q84, Q85, Q86, Q87, Q88** and **Q111.**
- **Performance issues**: Refer **Q10, Q16, Q45, Q46, Q97, Q98, Q100, Q123,** and **Q125.**
- **Memory issues**: Refer **Q45** and **Q93**
- **Multi-threading (Concurrency issues)**: Refer **Q16, Q34,** and **Q113**
- **Exception Handling**: Refer **Q76** and **Q77.**
- **Transactional issues**: Refer **Q43, Q71, Q72, Q73, Q74, Q75** and **Q77.**
- **Security issues**: Refer **Q23, Q58,** and **Q81**
- **Scalability issues**: Refer **Q20, Q21, Q120** and **Q122.**
- **Best practices**: Refer **Q10, Q16, Q39, Q40, Q46, Q82, Q124,** and **Q125**

Refer **Q75 – Q89** in Java section for frequently asked non-technical questions.

Q. Give me a high level description of your experience with the Java platform? What APIs do you have experience with?

[Hint:] Servlet, JSP, JDBC, JNDI, EJB, JMS, Swing, Applet, etc.

Q 132: Have you used any load testing tools? What source control systems have you used? What operating systems are you comfortable with? Which on-line technical resources do you use to resolve any design and/or development issues or to keep your knowledge up to date apart from Google? **SD**

A 132:

Load testing tools: Rational Robot, JMeter, LoadRunner, etc.

Source control systems: CVS, Subversion, VSS (Visual Source Safe), Rational clear case etc. Refer **Q14 in** How would you go about section…. for CVS.

Operating systems: NT, Unix, Linux, Solaris etc

Online technical resources : http://www.javaranch.com, http://www.theserverside.com, http://java.sun.com/ etc.

Q 133: Tell me a time where you had to deal with a difficult person? Why was this person difficult? How did you handle that person? **FAQ**

A 133:

Situation: When you had started a new job as a technical lead with an insurance company, where you had to manage a small team of 4-5 developers. All your team members were quite co-operative and friendly except for one member whom you would like to call Mr. X. Every time you had to talk to Mr. X you could sense some resistance to co-operate and disclose any work related information. Mr. X is also in disagreement with your views, opinion etc. **Why was this person difficult?** The root cause for this behavior was due to Mr. X was overlooked for the position of technical lead after having worked on the system for about 3 years.

Action: How did you handle that person? You had decided to be patient and tactful with Mr. X to earn his respect. After talking to a few members of the team and with your own observation you had determined that Mr. X was very technically talented but was not too popular with the business users because he always looked at things only from the technology perspective and failed to look at things from the business perspective and consequently turned a deaf year to some of the business requirements and also did not build a good rapport with the business. You always believed that having a good rapport and effective communication with the business is vital for the success of a project. So you decided to organize a two day workshop for your team and key business users on agile development methodology with the focus on building a better communication with the business. You had organized an external off-site workshop with the help of an external facilitator. You could feel during and after the workshop that Mr.X started to realize the importance of building a good rapport with the business. At early stages you minimized any contacts with Mr.X to avoid any confrontational situations and with time and patience you managed to earn his respect by being flexible and tactful, being genuinely appreciative of Mr. X's technical skills and contribution, being able to get Mr. X to realize the importance of building a good rapport with the business, giving Mr. X more responsibility and making him feel important.

Results: Mr. X became more co-operative and also endeavored to build a better rapport with the business.

Note: Some times you would be put in a difficult situation with the question, what would you do if no matter what you do, you cannot get along with a person say Mr Y? You could say that you would try to be patient and minimize or if possible avoid any contacts with Mr. Y to prevent any unpleasant situations. If that is not possible then you would have a discussion with your manager to see if he/she could improve the situation by mediating between you and Mr. Y. If none of the above approaches work then you would either move to a different team within the same organization or to another organization in the best interest of you and your organization.

Q 134: What did you like best and least about your previous company? **FAQ**

A 134: The above question reveals a lot about you. You need to make sure that what you like about your last job should be appealing to the job you are being interviewed for and what you liked least is not much importance.

Liked best: You could say that you were able to enhance your skills in problem solving, coping with stressful situations, ability to meet deadlines etc. Also can say that you acquired new technical skills and experience by learning new frameworks like Spring, Hibernate, Tapestry etc.

Liked least: You could say that you were self-motivated and worked hard to achieve your deadlines but some of your team mates slacked off from time to time and you had to pick up the extra work to achieve the team goal. **Note:** The above answer discusses a negative aspect with a positive spin. You could also say that it was not challenging enough for you, but be prepared to explain, why it was not challenging enough for you.

Q 135: Describe a situation when working as a team produced more successful results than if you had completed the project on your own? **FAQ**

A 135:

Situation: You could say that you have enjoyed working independently and as a member of the team, throughout your career and you could do both equally well. You could then say that you were involved in a project, which had a very tight deadline because it had to be completed before the end of financial year. You had to work in a team of 5 developers.

Action: You tried to get everyone involved coming up with an effective solution to meet the deadline without compromising on quality by making time for brain-storming sessions with your team members where there are no right or wrong ideas. The creativity, collective experiences and skills of a group of people were going to be greater than that of one person and this can achieve better results through co-operation and motivation.

Results: Team involvement motivated team members work smart and at times work long hours. You were able to meet the tight dead-line as a team without compromising on quality.

General Tip #8:

Some interviewers would like to ask questions that are impossible to answer to evaluate your problem solving skills. I was once asked **How many gas stations are there in Sydney?** Do not get upset. Try to solve it creatively because the interviewer is not looking for an exact answer but how well you go about solving it. My answer to the above question was looking up a Sydney street directory or ringing up Roads and Transport Authority (RTA) for number of major intersections in Sydney and multiply that by 2 (i.e. on average 2 gas stations per intersection). Alternatively you could say that there are 3 million people in Sydney of which 60% are above 18 years (i.e. 3,000,000 * 0.60 = 1.8 million) and hence hold a license. Say every 5 minutes a car pull up at a gas station (i.e. Say in 20 hours 240 cars will be serviced). So to serve 1.8 million cars you would require 1,800,000/240 = 7500 gas stations. Another possible question might be, **How many hair dressers are there in Sydney? How many liters of paint is required to paint the Sydney harbor?** [Hint: Make a replica to a reduced scale say 1:100,000 (i.e. replica:actual) and evaluate the liters of paint required by painting the replica first and then multiply the result by 100,000.]

Enterprise – Software development process

Q 136: What software development processes/principles are you familiar with? Which one have you liked the most and which one have you liked the least? **SD** **FAQ**

A 136: Agile (i.e. lightweight) software development process is gaining popularity and momentum across organizations.

Agile software development manifesto → [Good read: http://www.agilemanifesto.org/principles.html].

- Highest priority is to satisfy the customer.

- Welcome requirement changes even late in development life cycle.

- Business people and developers should work collaboratively.

- Form teams with motivated individuals who produce best designs and architectures.

- Teams should be pro-active on how to become more effective without becoming complacent.

- Quality working software is the primary measure of progress.

Why is iterative development with vertical slicing used in agile development? Your overall software quality can be improved through iterative development, which provides you with constant feedback.

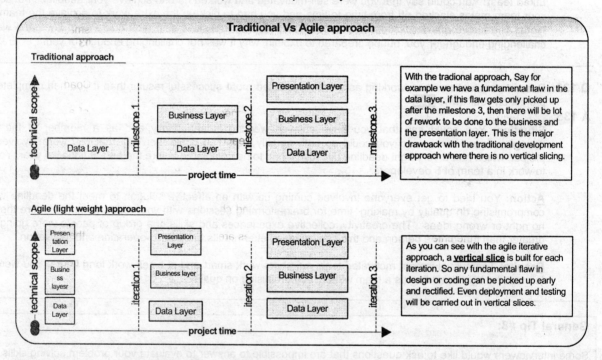

Several methodologies fit under this agile development methodology banner. All these methodologies share many characteristics like **iterative and incremental development, test driven development, stand up meetings to improve communication, automatic testing, build and continuous integration of code** etc. Among all the agile methodologies XP is the one which has got the most attention. Different companies use different flavors of agile methodologies by using different combinations of methodologies.

How does vertical slicing influence customer perception? With the iterative and incremental approach, customer will be comfortable with the progress of the development as opposed to traditional big bang approach.

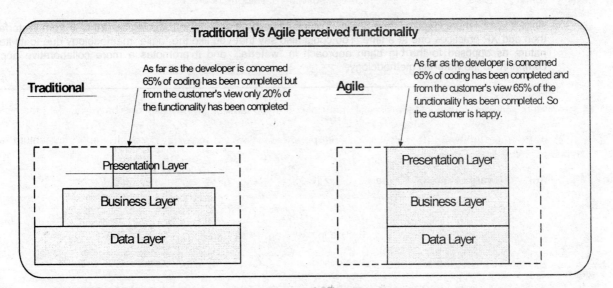

- **EXtreme Programming [XP]** → simple design, pair programming, unit testing, refactoring, collective code ownership, coding standards, etc. Refer **Q10** in "How would you go about…" section. XP has four key values: Communication, Feedback, Simplicity and Courage. It then builds up some tried and tested practices and techniques. XP has a strong emphasis on testing where tests are integrated into continuous integration and build process, which yields a highly stable platform. XP is designed for smaller teams of 20 – 30 people.

- **RUP** (Rational Unified Process) → Model driven architecture, design and development; customizable frameworks for scalable process; iterative development methodology; Re-use of architecture, code, component, framework, patterns etc. RUP can be used as an agile process for smaller teams of 20-30 people, or as a heavy weight process for larger teams of 50-100 people. Refer **Q103 – Q105** in Enterprise section.

- **Feature Driven Development [FDD]** → Jeff De Luca and long time OO guru Peter Coad developed feature Driven Development (FDD). Like the other **adaptive methodologies**, it focuses on short iterations that deliver tangible functionality. FDD was originally designed for larger project teams of around 50 people. In FDD's case the iterations are two weeks long. FDD has five processes. The first three are done at the beginning of the project. The last two are done within each iteration.

  Develop an Overall Model → Build a Features List → Plan by Feature → Design by Feature → Build by Feature

The developers come in two kinds: class owners and chief programmers. The chief programmers are the most experienced developers. They are assigned features to be built. However they don't build them alone. Instead the chief programmer identifies which classes are involved in implementing the feature and gathers their class owners together to form a feature team for developing that feature. The chief programmer acts as the coordinator, lead designer, and mentor while the class owners do much of the coding of the feature.

- **Test Driven Development [TDD]** → TDD is an iterative software development process where you **first write the test with the idea that it must fail**. Refer **Q1** in Emerging Technologies/Frameworks section…

- **Scrum** → Scrum divides a project into sprints (aka iterations) of 30 days. Before you begin a sprint you define the functionality required for that sprint and leave the team to deliver it. But every day the team holds a short (10 – 15 minute) meeting, called a scrum where the team runs through what it will achieve in the next day. Some of the questions asked in the scrum meetings are:

  - What did you do since the last scrum meetings?
  - Do you have any obstacles?
  - What will you do before next meeting?

This is very similar to stand-up meetings in XP and iterative development process in RUP.

Q. Which one have you liked the most and which one have you liked the least? You could say that liked the most is **"agile"** methodology and the least is the traditional **"waterfall"**. Many **agile** methodologies tend to go hand-in-hand (i.e. complementary). Easiest agile process to understand is Scrum. XP seems to be more popular since it is a bit more involved than Scrum. You could become agile by introducing Scrum first from Waterfall and then add XP practices one at a time. You could also say that you like the "agile" methodology due to its iterative nature as opposed to the big bang approach in "waterfall" and it promotes a more collaborative approach compared to the waterfall methodology.

Enterprise – Key Points

- J2EE is a **3-tier** (or **n-tier**) system. Each tier is logically separated and loosely coupled from each other, and may be distributed.

- J2EE applications are developed using **MVC architecture**, which divides the functionality of displaying and maintaining of the data to minimize the degree of coupling between enterprise components.

- J2EE modules are deployed as ear, war and jar files, which are standard application deployment archive files.

- HTTP is a stateless protocol and state can be maintained between client requests using HttpSession, URL rewriting, hidden fields and cookies. HttpSession is the recommended approach.

- Servlets and JSPs are by default multi-threaded, and care should be taken in declaring instance variables and accessing shared resources. It is possible to have a single threaded model of a servlet or a JSP but this can adversely affect performance.

- Clustering promotes high availability and scalability. The considerations for servlet clustering are:

  - Objects stored in the session should be serializable.
  - Design for idempotence.
  - Avoid using instance and static variables in read and write mode.
  - Avoid storing values in the *ServletContext*.
  - Avoid using java.io.* and use getResourceAsStream() instead.

- JSPs have a translation or a compilation process where the JSP engine translates and compiles a JSP file into a JSP servlet.

- JSPs have 4 different **scope** values: page, request, session and application. JSPs can be included **statically**, where all the included JSP pages are compiled into a single servlet during the translation or compilation phase or included **dynamically,** where included JSPs are compiled into separate servlets and the content generated by these servlets are included at runtime in the JSP response.

- Avoid scriptlet code in your JSPs and use **JavaBeans** or **custom tags** (e.g. Struts tags, JSTL tags, JSF tags etc) instead.

- Databases can run out of cursors if the connections are not closed properly. The valuable resources like connections and statements should be enclosed in a **try{}** and **finally{}** block.

- Prepared statements offer better performance as opposed to statements, as they are **precompiled** and **reuse the same execution plan** with different arguments. Prepared statements are also more secure because they use bind variables, which can prevent SQL injection attacks.

- JNDI provides a generic interface to LDAP and other directory services like NDS, DNS etc.

- In your code always make use of a **logical JNDI reference** (java:comp/env/ejb/MyBean) as opposed to **physical JNDI reference** (ejb/MyBean) because you cannot guarantee that the physical JNDI location you specify in your code will be available. Your code will break if the physical location is changed.

- LDAP servers are typically used in J2EE applications to authenticate and authorize users. LDAP servers are hierarchical and are **optimized for read access**, so likely to be faster than database in providing read access.

- RMI facilitates object method calls between JVMs. JVMs can be located on separate host machines, still one JVM can invoke methods belonging to an object residing in another JVM (i.e. address space). RMI uses object serialization to marshal and unmarshal parameters. The remote objects should extend the *UnicastRemoteObject*.

- To go through a firewall, the RMI protocol can be embedded within the firewall trusted HTTP protocol, which is called **HTTP tunneling**.

- EJB (i.e. 2.x) is a remote, distributed multi-tier system, which supports protocols like JRMP, IIOP, and HTTP etc. EJB components contain business logic and system level supports like security, transaction, instance pooling, multi-threading, object life-cycles etc are managed by the EJB container and hence simplify the programming effort. Having said this, there are emerging technologies like:

- Hibernate, which is an open source object-to-relational (O/R) mapping framework.
- EJB 3.0, which is taking ease of development very seriously and has adjusted its model to offer the plain old Java objects (i.e. POJOs) based persistence and the new O/R mapping model based on hibernate.

Refer **Q14 – Q18** in Emerging technologies / Frameworks section for brief discussion on hibernate and EJB 3.0.

- EJB transaction attributes (like Required, Mandatory, RequiresNew, Supports etc) are specified declaratively through EJB deployment descriptors. Isolation levels are not part of the EJB 2.x specification. So the isolation levels can be set on the resource manager either explicitly on the *Connection* or via the application server specific configuration.

- A transaction is often described by **ACID** (Atomic, Consistent, Isolated and Durable) properties. A **distributed transaction** is an ACID transaction between two or more independent transactional resources like two separate databases. A **2-phase commit** is an approach for committing a distributed transaction in 2 phases.

- EJB 2.x has two types of exceptions:

  - **System exception**: is an unchecked exception derived from *java.lang.RuntimeException*. It is thrown by the system and is not recoverable.
  - **Application exception**: is specific to an application and is thrown because of violation of business rules.

- EJB container managed transactions are automatically rolled back when a system exception occurs. This is possible because the container can intercept system exceptions. However when an application exception occurs, the container does not intercept and leaves it to the code to roll back using ctx.setRollbackOnly() method.

- EJB containers can make use of **lazy loading** (i.e. not creating an object until it is accessed) and **dirty marker** (i.e. persist only the entity beans that have bean modified) strategies to improve entity beans performance.

- Message Oriented Middleware (MOM) is a software infrastructure that asynchronously communicates with other disparate systems through the production and consumption of messages. Messaging enables loosely coupled distributed communication. Java Messaging Service (**JMS**) is a Java API that allows applications to create, send, receive read messages in a standard way, hence improves portability.

- Some of the design decisions you need to make in JMS are message acknowledgement modes, transaction modes, delivery modes etc, synchronous vs. asynchronous paradigm, message body types, setting appropriate timeouts etc.

- XML documents can be processed in your Java/J2EE application either using a SAX parser, which is event driven or a DOM parser, which creates a tree structure in memory. The other XML related technologies are DTD, XSD, XSL, XPath, etc and Java and XML based technologies are JAXP, JAXB etc.

- There is an impedance mismatch between object and relational technology. Classes represent both data and behavior whereas relational database tables just implement data. Inheritance class structure can be mapped to relational data model in one of the following ways:

  - Map class hierarchy to single database table.
  - Map each class to its own table.
  - Map each concrete class to its own table
  - Generic meta-data driven approach.

- Normalize data in your database for accuracy and denormalize data in your database for performance.

- **RUP** (Rational Unified Process) has 4 phases in the following order Inception, Elaboration, Construction, and Transition. Agile (i.e. lightweight) software development process is gaining popularity and momentum across organizations. Several methodologies like XP, RUP, Scrum, FDD, TDD etc fit under this agile development methodology banner. All these methodologies share many characteristics like iterative and incremental development, stand-up meetings to improve communication, automatic build, testing and continuous integration etc.

- UML is applicable to the object oriented (OO) problem solving. There are different types of UML diagrams like use case diagrams, class diagrams, sequence diagrams, collaboration diagrams, state chart diagrams, activity diagrams, component diagrams, deployment diagrams etc.

- Class diagrams are vital within OO methods. Class diagrams have the following possible relationships: association, aggregation, composition, generalization, realization and dependency.

- Struts is an MVC framework. Struts action classes are not thread-safe and care should be taken in declaring instance variables or accessing other shared resources. JSF is another Web UI framework like Struts gaining popularity and momentum.

- Log4j has three main components: *loggers*, *appenders* and *layouts*. Logger is a utility wrapper class. JUnit is an open source unit-testing framework.

- You can improve the performance of a J2EE application as follows :

  1. Manage and recycle your valuable resources like connections, threads etc by either pooling or caching.
  2. Use effective design patterns like session façade, value object, and fast lane reader etc to minimize network overheads.
  3. Set appropriate time-outs for HttpSession objects.
  4. Use JDBC prepared statements as opposed to statements.
  5. Release database connections in a finally {} block when finished.
  6. Apply least restrictive but valid transaction isolation level.
  7. Batch database requests.
  8. Minimize serialization costs by marking references like file handles, database connections, etc which do not require serialization by declaring them transient.

- Some of the J2EE best practices are:

  1. Recycle your valuable resources by either pooling or caching.
  2. Automate your build process with tools like Ant, CruiseControl, and Maven etc, and continuously integrate your code into your build process.
  3. Build test cases first using tools like JUnit.
  4. Use standard J2EE packaging to improve portability.
  5. Apply appropriate proven design patterns.
  6. Use proven frameworks like Struts, Spring, Hibernate, JSF, JUnit, Log4J, etc.
  7. Handle and propagate exceptions correctly.
  8. Avoid resource leaks by closing all database connections after you have used them.

- The goals of application server clustering are to achieve scalability, load balancing, and high availability.

- Java Management Extension (JMX) framework can improve the manageability of your application, for performance problems, critical events, error conditions etc and perform health checks on your hardware, database server etc. You can also configure and control your application at runtime.

- Finally get familiarized with some of the key Java & J2EE **design patterns** like:

  1. **MVC design pattern**: J2EE uses this design pattern or architecture.

  2. **Chain of responsibility design pattern**: Servlet filters use a slightly modified version of chain of responsibility design pattern.

  3. **Front controller J2EE design pattern**: provides a centralized access point for HTTP request handling to support the integration system services like security, data validation etc. This is a popular J2EE design pattern.

  4. **Composite view J2EE design pattern**: creates an aggregate view from atomic sub-views.

  5. **View helper J2EE design pattern**: avoids duplication of code. The helper classes are JavaBeans and custom tags (e.g. Struts tags, JSF tags, JSTL tags etc).

  6. **Service to worker and dispatcher view J2EE design pattern**: These two patterns are a combination of front controller and view helper patterns with a dispatcher component. These two patterns differ in the way they suggest different division of responsibility among components.

  7. **Bridge design pattern**: Java Data Base Connectivity (JDBC) uses the bridge design pattern. The JDBC API provides an abstraction and the JDBC drivers provide the implementation.

  8. **Proxy design pattern**: RMI & EJB uses the proxy design pattern. A popular design pattern.

  9. **Business delegate J2EE design pattern**: used to reduce the coupling between the presentation tier and the business services tier components.

10. **Session façade J2EE design pattern**: too many fine-grained method calls between the client and the server will lead to network overhead and tight coupling. Use a session bean as a façade to provide a coarse-grained service access layer to clients.

11. **Value object J2EE design pattern**: avoid fine-grained method calls by creating a value object, which will help the client, make a coarse-grained call.

12. **Fast-lane reader J2EE design pattern**: access the persistence layer directly using a DAO (Data Access Object) pattern instead of using entity beans.

13. **Service locator J2EE design pattern**: expensive and redundant JNDI lookups can be avoided by caching and reusing the already looked up service objects.

Recommended reading on J2EE design patterns:
- Core J2EE Patterns: Best Practices and Design Strategies, Second Edition (Hardcover) by Deepak Alur, Dan Malks, John Crupi.

Tech Tip #8:

Q. How do you list the files in current directory sorted by size in a UNIX machine?

```
$> ls -l | grep ^- | sort -nr
```

Q. How do you delete blank lines in a file in a UNIX machine ?

```
$> cat file1.txt | grep -v '^$' > file2.txt
```

Q. How would you display all the files recursively under current directory in a UNIX machine?

```
$> find . -depth -print
```

Q. How would you display disk usage in kilobytes in a UNIX machine?

```
$> du -k
```

> ## Let us put all together in
> ## the next section

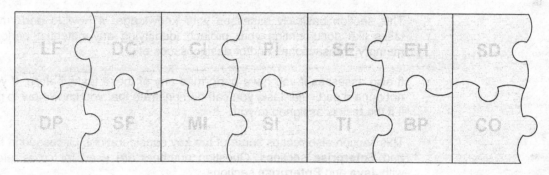

SECTION THREE

How would you go about...?

- This section basically assesses your knowledge of how to perform certain tasks like documenting your project, identifying any potential performance, memory, transactional, and/or design issues etc.

- It also assesses if you have performed any of these tasks before. If you have not done a particular task, you can demonstrate that you know how to go about it if the task is assigned to you.

- This section also recaps some of the key considerations discussed in the **Java** and **Enterprise** sections. Question numbers are used for cross-referencing with **Java** and **Enterprise** sections.

- **Q11 & Q14** are discussed in more detail and can be used as a quick reference guide in a software project. All the other questions excluding **Q11 & Q14** can be read just before an interview.

Q 01: How would you go about documenting your Java/J2EE application? FAQ

A 01: To be successful with a Java/J2EE project, proper documentation is vital.

- Before embarking on coding get the business requirements down. Build a complete list of requested features, sample screen shots (if available), use case diagrams, business rules etc as a **functional specification** document. This is the phase where business analysts and developers will be asking questions about user interface requirements, data tier integration requirements, use cases etc. Also prioritize the features based on the business goals, lead-times and iterations required for implementation.

- Prepare a **technical specification** document based on the functional specification. The technical specification document should cover:

  ❖ **Purpose of the document**: e.g. This document will emphasize the customer service functionality.

  ❖ **Overview**: This section basically covers background information, scope, any inclusions and/or exclusions, referenced documents etc.

  ❖ **Basic architecture**: discusses or references baseline architecture document. Answers questions like Will it scale? Can this performance be improved? Is it extendable and/or maintainable? Are there any security issues? Describe the vertical slices to be used in the early iterations, and the concepts to be proved by each slice. Etc. For example which MVC [model-1, model-2 etc] paradigms (Refer **Q3** in Enterprise section for MVC) should we use? Should we use Struts, JSF, and Spring MVC etc or build our own framework? Should we use a business delegate (Refer **Q83** in Enterprise section for business delegate) to decouple middle tier with the client tier? Should we use AOP (Aspect Oriented Programming) (Refer **Q3** in Emerging Technologies/Frameworks)? Should we use dependency injection? Should we use annotations? Do we require internationalization? Etc.

  ❖ **Assumptions, Dependencies, Risks** and **Issues**: highlight all the assumptions, dependencies, risks and issues. For example list all the risks you can identify.

  ❖ **Design alternatives** for each key functional requirement. Also discuss why a particular design alternative was chosen over the others. This process will encourage developers analyze the possible design alternatives without having to jump at the obvious solution, which might not always be the best one.

  ❖ **Processing logic:** discuss the processing logic for the client tier, middle tier and the data tier. Where required add process flow diagrams. Add any pre-process conditions and/or post-process conditions. (Refer **Q9** in Java section for design by contract).

  ❖ **UML diagrams** to communicate the design to the fellow developers, solution designers, architects etc. Usually class diagrams and sequence diagrams are required. The other diagrams may be added for any special cases like (Refer **Q107** in Enterprise section):

    ❖ **State chart diagram:** useful to describe behavior of an object across several use cases.

    ❖ **Activity diagram:** useful to express complex operations. Supports and encourages parallel behavior. Activity and statechart diagrams are beneficial for workflow modeling with multi threaded programming.

    ❖ **Collaboration and Sequence diagrams:** Use a collaboration or sequence diagram when you want to look at behavior of several objects within a single use case. If you want to look at a single object across multiple use cases then use statechart.

    ❖ **Object diagrams**: The Object diagrams show instances instead of classes. They are useful for explaining some complicated objects in detail such as highlighting recursive relationships.

  ❖ **List the package names, class names, database names** and **table names** with a brief description of their responsibility in a tabular form.

- Prepare a **coding standards** document for the whole team to promote consistency and efficiency. Some coding practices can degrade performance for example:

  ❖ Inappropriate use of String class. Use StringBuffer instead of String for compute intensive mutations (Refer **Q21** in Java section).

❖ Code in terms of interface. For example you might decide the LinkedList is the best choice for some application, but then later decide ArrayList might be a better choice. (Refer **Q17,Q16** in Java section)

> **Wrong approach** → ArrayList list = new ArrayList();
> **Right approach** → List list = new ArrayList(100)

❖ Set the initial capacity of a collection appropriately (e.g. ArrayList, HashMap etc). (Refer **Q17** in Java section).

❖ To promote consistency define standards for variable names, method names, use of logging, curly bracket positions etc.

▪ Prepare a **code review** document and templates for the <u>whole team</u>. Let us look at some of the elements the code review should cover:

❖ **Proper variable declaration:** e.g. instance versus static variables, constants etc.

❖ **Performance issues**: e.g. Use ArrayList, HashMap etc instead of Vector, Hashtable when there is no thread-safety issue.

❖ **Memory issues:** e.g. Improper instantiation of objects instead of object reuse and object pooling, not closing valuable resource in a finally block etc.

❖ **Thread-safety issues:** e.g. Java API classes like SimpleDateFormat, Calendar, DecimalFormat etc are not thread safe, declaring variables in JSP is not thread safe, storing state information in Struts action class or multi-threaded servlet is not thread safe.

❖ **Error handling:** e.g. Re-throwing exception without nesting original exception, EJB methods not throwing EJB exception for system exceptions, etc.

❖ **Use of coding standards:** e.g. not using frameworks, System.out is used instead of log4j etc.

❖ **Design issues:** No re-use of code, no clear separation of responsibility, invalid use of inheritance to get method reuse, servlets performing JDBC direct access instead of using DAO (Data Access Objects) classes, HTML code in Struts action or servlet classes, servlets used as utility classes rather than as a flow controller etc.

❖ **Documentation of code:** e.g. No comments, no header files etc

❖ **Bugs:** e.g. Calling *setAutoCommit* within container-managed transaction, binary OR "|" used instead of logical OR "||", relying on pass-by-reference in EJB remote calls, *ResultSet* not being closed on exceptions, EJB methods not throwing *EJBException* for system exceptions etc (Refer **Q76** & **Q77** in Enterprise section)

▪ Prepare additional optional **guideline documents** as per requirements to be shared by the team. This will promote consistency and standards. For example:

❖ Guidelines to setting up J2EE development environment.
❖ Guidelines to version control system (CVS, VSS etc).
❖ Guidelines to deployment steps, environment settings, ant targets etc.
❖ Guidelines for the data modeling (any company standards).
❖ Guidelines for error handling (Refer **Q39**, **Q40** in Java section & **Q76**, **Q77** in Enterprise section).
❖ Guidelines for user interface design.
❖ Project overview document, Software development process document etc

Some of the above mentioned documents, which are shared by the whole team, can be published in an internal website like Wiki. Wiki is a piece of server software that allows users to freely create and edit Web page content using any Web browser.

Q 02: How would you go about designing a Java/J2EE application? FAQ

A 02: Design should be specific to a problem but also should be general enough to address future requirements. Designing reusable object oriented software involves decomposing the business use cases into relevant objects and converting objects into classes.

- Create a **tiered architecture**: client tier, business tier and data tier. Each tier can be further logically divided into layers (Refer **Q2, Q3** on Enterprise section). Use MVC (**M**odel **V**iew **C**ontroller) architecture for the J2EE and Java based GUI applications.

- Create a **data model**: A data model is a detailed specification of data oriented structures. This is different from the class modeling because it focuses solely on data whereas class models allow you to define both data and behavior. **Conceptual data models** (aka domain models) are used to explore domain concepts with project stakeholders. **Logical data models** are used to explore the domain concepts, and their relationships. Logical data models depict entity types, data attributes and entity relationships (with Entity Relationship (ER) diagrams). **Physical data models** are used to design the internal schema of a database depicting the tables, columns, and the relationships between the tables. Data models can be created by performing the following tasks:

  ❖ **Identify entity types, attributes and relationships**: use entity relationship (**E-R**) diagrams.

  ❖ **Apply naming conventions (e.g. for tables, attributes, indices, constraints etc)**: Your organization should have standards and guidelines applicable to data modeling.

  ❖ **Assign keys**: surrogate keys (e.g. assigned by the database like Oracle sequences, Sybase identity columns, max()+1, universally unique identifiers UUIDs, etc), natural keys (e.g. Tax File Numbers, Social Security Numbers etc), and composite keys.

  ❖ **Normalize to reduce data redundancy and denormalize to improve performance**: Normalized data have the advantage of information being stored in one place only, reducing the possibility of inconsistent data. Furthermore, highly normalized data are loosely coupled. But normalization comes at a performance cost because to determine a piece of information you have to join multiple tables whereas in a denormalized approach the same piece of information can be retrieved from a single row of a table. Denormalization should be used only when performance testing shows that you need to improve database access time for some of your tables.

> **Note:** Creating a data model (logical, physical etc) before design model is a matter of preference, but many OO methodologies are based on creating the data model from the object **design model** (i.e. you may need to do some work to create an explicit data model but only after you have a complete OO domain and design model). In many cases when using ORM tools like Hibernate, you do not create the data model at all.

- Create a **design model**: A design model is a detailed specification of the objects and relationships between the objects as well as their behavior. (Refer **Q107** on Enterprise section)

  ❖ **Class diagram:** contains the implementation view of the entities in the design model. The design model also contains core business classes and non-core business classes like persistent storage, security management, utility classes etc. The class diagrams also describe the structural relationships between the objects.

  ❖ **Use case realizations:** are described in sequence and collaboration diagrams.

- **Design considerations when decomposing business use cases into relevant classes**: designing reusable and flexible design models requires the following considerations:

  ❖ **Granularity of the objects** (fine-grained versus coarse-grained): Can we minimize the network trip by passing a coarse-grained value object instead of making 4 network trips with fine-grained parameters? (Refer **Q85** in Enterprise section). Should we use method level (coarse-grained) or code level (fine-grained) thread synchronization? (Refer **Q46** in Java section). Should we use a page level access security or a fine-grained programmatic security?

  ❖ **Coupling between objects** (loosely coupled versus tightly coupled). Should we use business delegate pattern to loosely couple client and business tier? (Refer **Q83** in Enterprise section) Should we use dependency injection (e.g. using Spring) or factory design pattern to loosely couple the caller from the callee? (Refer **Q09** in Emerging Technologies/Frameworks).

  ❖ **Network overheads** for remote objects like EJB, RMI etc: Should we use the session façade, value object patterns? (Refer **Q84** & **Q85** in Enterprise section).
  ❖ **Definition of class interfaces** and **inheritance hierarchy:** Should we use an abstract class or an interface? Is there any common functionality that we can move to the super class (i.e. parent class)? Should we use interface inheritance with object composition for code reuse as opposed to implementation inheritance? Etc. (Refer **Q10** in Java section).

❖ **Establishing key relationships** (aggregation, composition, association etc): Should we use aggregation or composition? [composition may require cascade delete] (Refer **Q107, Q108** in Enterprise section – under class diagrams). Should we use an "**is a**" (generalization) relationship or a "**has a**" (composition) relationship? (Refer **Q9** in Java section).

❖ **Applying polymorphism** and **encapsulation**: Should we hide the member variables to improve integrity and security? (Refer **Q10** in Java section). Can we get a polymorphic behavior so that we can easily add new classes in the future? (Refer **Q8** in Java section).

❖ **Applying well-proven design patterns** (like Gang of four design patterns, J2EE design patterns, EJB design patterns etc) help designers to base new designs on prior experience. Design patterns also help you to choose design alternatives (Refer **Q11, Q12** in How would you go about...).

❖ **Scalability** of the system: **Vertical scaling** is achieved by increasing the number of servers running on a single machine. **Horizontal scaling** is achieved by increasing the number of machines in the cluster. Horizontal scaling is more reliable than the vertical scaling because there are multiple machines involved in the cluster. In vertical scaling the number of server instances that can be run on one machine are determined by the CPU usage and the JVM heap memory.

❖ **How do we replicate the session state**? Should we use stateful session beans or HTTP session? Should we serialize this object so that it can be replicated?

❖ **Internationalization** requirements for multi-language support: Should we support other languages? Should we support multi-byte characters in the database?

▪ **Vertical slicing**: Getting the reusable and flexible design the first time is impossible. By developing the initial **vertical slice** (Refer **Q136** in Enterprise section) of your design you eliminate any nasty integration issues later in your project. Also get the design patterns right early on by building the vertical slice. It will give you experience with what does work and what does not work with Java/J2EE. Once you are happy with the initial vertical slice then you can apply it across the application. The initial vertical slice should be based on a typical business use case.

▪ **Ensure the system is configurable** through property files, xml descriptor files, and annotations. This will improve flexibility and maintainability. Avoid hard coding any values. Use a constant class and/or enums (JDK 1.5+) for values, which rarely change and use property files (e.g. MyApp.properties file containing name/value pairs), xml descriptor files and/or annotations (JDK 1.5+) for values, which can change more frequently like application process flow steps etc. Use property (e.g. MyApp.properties) or xml (e.g. MyApp.xml) files for environment related configurations like server name, server port number, LDAP server location etc.

▪ **Design considerations during design, development and deployment phases:** designing a fast, secured, reliable, robust, reusable and flexible system require considerations in the following key areas:

❖ **Performance issues** (network overheads, quality of the code etc): Can I make a single coarse-grained network call to my remote object instead of 3 fine-grained calls?

❖ **Concurrency issues (multi-threading)**: What if two threads access my object simultaneously will it corrupt the state of my object?

❖ **Transactional issues (ACID properties)**: What if two clients access the same data simultaneously? What if one part of the transaction fails, do we rollback the whole transaction? Do we need a distributed (i.e. JTA) transaction? (Refer **Q43** in Enterprise section). What if the client resubmits the same transactional page again? (Refer **Q27** in Enterprise section – How do you prevent multiple submits...).

❖ **Security issues**: Are there any potential security holes for SQL injection (Refer **Q46** in Enterprise section) or URL injection (Refer **Q35** in Enterprise section) by hackers?

❖ **Memory issues**: Is there any potential memory leak problems? Have we allocated enough heap size for the JVM? Have we got enough perm space allocated since we are using 3rd party libraries, which generate classes dynamically? (e.g. JAXB, XSLT, JasperReports etc) – Refer **Q74** in Java section.

❖ **Scalability issues**: Will this application scale vertically and horizontally if the load increases? Should this object be serializable? Does this object get stored in the HttpSession?

❖ **Maintainability, reuse, extensibility etc**: How can we make the software reusable, maintainable and extensible? What design patterns can we use? How often do we have to refactor our code?

❖ **Logging and auditing** if something goes wrong can we look at the logs to determine the root cause of the problem?

❖ **Object life cycles**: Can the objects within the server be created, destroyed, activated or passivated depending on the memory usage on the server? (e.g. EJB).

❖ **Resource pooling**: Creating and destroying valuable resources like database connections, threads etc can be expensive. So if a client is not using a resource can it be returned to a pool to be reused when other clients connect? What is the optimum pool size?

❖ **Caching:** can we save network trips by storing the data in the server's memory? How often do we have to clear the cache to prevent the in memory data from becoming stale?

❖ **Load balancing**: Can we redirect the users to a server with the lightest load if the other server is overloaded?

❖ **Transparent fail over**: If one server crashes can the clients be routed to another server without any interruptions?

❖ **Clustering**: What if the server maintains a state when it crashes? Is this state replicated across the other servers?

❖ **Back-end integration**: How do we connect to the databases and/or legacy systems?

❖ **Clean shutdown**: Can we shut down the server without affecting the clients who are currently using the system?

❖ **Systems management**: In the event of a catastrophic system failure who is monitoring the system? Any alerts or alarms? Should we use JMX? Should we use any performance monitoring tools like Tivoli?

❖ **Dynamic redeployment**: How do we perform the software deployment while the site is running? (Mainly for mission critical applications 24hrs X 7days).

❖ **Portability issues**: Can I port this application to a different server 2 years from now?

Q 03: How would you go about identifying performance and/or memory issues in your Java/J2EE application? FAQ
A 03: Profiling can be used to identify any performance issues or memory leaks. Profiling can identify what lines of code the program is spending the most time in? What call or invocation paths are used to reach at these lines? What kinds of objects are sitting in the heap? Where is the memory leak? Etc.

▪ There are many tools available for the optimization of Java code like **JProfiler, Borland Optimizelt** etc. These tools are very powerful and easy to use. They also produce various reports with graphs.

Optimizeit™ Request Analyzer provides advanced profiling techniques that allow developers to analyze the performance behavior of code across J2EE application tiers. Developers can efficiently prioritize the performance of Web requests, JDBC, JMS, JNDI, JSP, RMI, and EJB so that trouble spots can be proactively isolated earlier in the development lifecycle.

Thread Debugger tools can be used to identify threading issues like thread starvation and contention issues that can lead to system crash.

Code coverage tools can assist developers with identifying and removing any dead code from the applications.

▪ **Hprof** which comes with JDK for free. Simple tool.

```
Java –Xprof myClass

java -Xrunhprof:[help]|[<option>=<value>]
java -Xrunhprof:cpu=samples, depth=6, heap=sites
```

- Use operating system process monitors like NT/XP Task Manager on PCs and commands like ps, iostat, netstat, vmstat, uptime, nfsstat etc on UNIX machines.

- Write your own wrapper MemoryLogger and/or PerformanceLogger utility classes with the help of **totalMemory()** and **freeMemory()** methods in the Java **Runtime** class for memory usage and **System.currentTimeMillis()** method for performance. You can place these MemoryLogger and PerformanceLogger calls strategically in your code. Even better approach than utility classes is using Aspect Oriented Programming (AOP – e.g. Spring AOP Refer **Q3 – Q5** in Emerging Technologies/Frameworks section) or dynamic proxies (Refer proxy design pattern in **Q11** in How would you go about...? section) for pre and post memory and/or performance recording where you have the control of activating memory/performance measurement only when needed.

Q 04: How would you go about minimizing memory leaks in your Java/J2EE application? **FAQ**

A 04: Java's memory management (i.e. Garbage Collection) prevents lost references and dangling references but it is still possible to create memory leaks in other ways. If the application runs with memory leaks for a long duration you will get the error **java.lang.OutOfMemoryError**.

In Java, typically the memory leak occurs when **an object of a longer lifecycle has a reference to the objects of a short life cycle**. This prevents the objects with short life cycle being garbage collected. The developer must remember to remove the reference to the short-lived objects from the long-lived objects. Objects with the same life cycle do not cause any problem because the garbage collector is smart enough to deal with the circular references (Refer **Q33** in Java section).

- Java *Collection* classes like Hashtable, ArrayList etc maintain references to other objects. So having a long life cycle ArrayList pointing to many short-life cycle objects can cause memory leaks.

- Commonly used **singleton design pattern** (Refer **Q51** in Java section) can cause memory leaks. Singletons typically have a long life cycle. If a singleton has an ArrayList or a Hashtable then there is a potential for memory leaks.

- Java programming language includes a finalize method that allows an object to free system resources, in other words, to clean up after itself. However using finalize doesn't guarantee that a class will clean up resources expediently. A better approach for cleaning up resources involves the finally method and an explicit close statement. So freeing up the valuable resource in the finalize method or try {} block instead of finally {} block can cause memory leaks (Refer **Q45** in Enterprise section).

Q 05: How would you go about improving performance in your Java/J2EE application? **FAQ**

A 05: The performance bottlenecks can be attributed to one or more of the following:

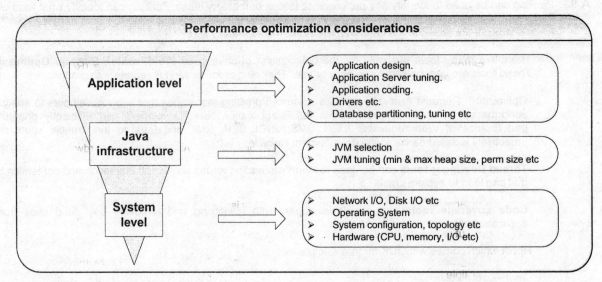

Performance optimization considerations	
Application level	➢ Application design. ➢ Application Server tuning. ➢ Application coding. ➢ Drivers etc. ➢ Database partitioning, tuning etc
Java infrastructure	➢ JVM selection ➢ JVM tuning (min & max heap size, perm size etc
System level	➢ Network I/O, Disk I/O etc ➢ Operating System ➢ System configuration, topology etc ➢ Hardware (CPU, memory, I/O etc)

Let us discuss some of the aspects in detail:

- Java/J2EE application code related performance bottlenecks:

- ❖ Refer **Q72** in Java section.
- ❖ Refer **Q123, Q125** in Enterprise section.

- ▪ Java/J2EE design related performance bottlenecks. <u>Application design</u> is one of the most important considerations for performance. A well-designed application will not only avoid many performance pitfalls but will also be easier to maintain and modify during the performance-testing phase of the project.

  - ❖ Use proper design patterns to **minimize network trips** (session facade, value object Refer etc **Q83-Q87** in Enterprise section).

  - ❖ **Minimize serialization cost** by implementing session beans with remote interfaces and entity beans with local interfaces (applicable to EJB 2.x) or even the session beans can be implemented with local interfaces sharing the same JVM with the Web tier components. For EJB1.x some EJB containers can be configured to use **pass-by-reference** instead of pass-by-value (pass-by-value requires serialization) Refer **Q69, Q82** in Enterprise section.

  - ❖ Use of multi-threading from a thread-pool (say 10 – 50 threads). Using a large number of threads adversely affects performance by consuming memory through thread stacks and CPU by context switching.

- ▪ Database related performance bottlenecks.

  - ❖ Use proper database indexes. Numeric indices are more efficient than character based indices. Minimize the number of columns in your composite keys. Performing a number of "INSERT" operations is more efficient when fewer columns are indexed and "SELECT" operations are more efficient when, adequately indexed based on columns frequently used in your "WHERE" clause. So it is a trade-off between "SELECT" and "INSERT" operations.

  - ❖ Minimize use of composite keys or use fewer columns in your composite keys.

  - ❖ Partition the database for performance based on the most frequently accessed data and least frequently accessed data.

  - ❖ Identify and optimize your SQL queries causing performance problems (Refer **Q97** in Enterprise section).

  - ❖ De-normalize your tables where necessary for performance (Refer **Q98** in Enterprise section).

  - ❖ Close database connections in your Java code in the finally block to avoid any "open cursors" problem (Refer **Q45** in Enterprise section).

  - ❖ Use **optimistic concurrency** as opposed to **pessimistic concurrency** where appropriate (Refer **Q78** in Enterprise section).

- ▪ Application Server, JVM, Operating System, and/or hardware related performance bottlenecks.

  - ❖ **Application Server**: Configure the application server for optimum performance (Refer **Q88, Q123** in Enterprise section).

  - ❖ **Operating System**: Check for any other processes clogging up the system resources, maximum number of processes it can support or connect, optimize operating system etc.

  - ❖ **Hardware**: Insufficient memory, insufficient CPU, insufficient I/O, limitation of hardware configurations, network constraints like bandwidth, message rates etc.

Q 06: How would you go about identifying any potential thread-safety issues in your Java/J2EE application? FAQ

A 06: When you are writing graphical programs like Swing or Internet programs using servlets or JSPs multi-threading is a necessity for all but some special and/or trivial programs.

An application program or a process can have multiple threads like multiple processes that can run on one computer. The multiple threads appear to be doing their work in parallel. When implemented on a multi-processor machine, they can actually work in parallel.

Unlike processes, threads share the same address space (Refer **Q42** in Java section) which means they can read and write the same variables and data structures. So care should be taken to avoid one thread disturbing the work of another thread. Let us look at some of the common situations where care should be taken:

❖ Swing components can only be accessed by one thread at a time. A few operations are guaranteed to be thread safe but the most others are not. Generally the Swing components should be accessed through an *event-dispatching thread*. (Refer **Q62** in Java section).

❖ A typical Servlet life cycle creates a single instance of each servlet and creates multiple threads to handle the service() method. **The multi-threading aids efficiency but the servlet code must be coded in a thread safe manner.** The shared resources (e.g. instance variable) should be appropriately synchronized or should only use variables in a read-only manner. (Refer **Q16** in Enterprise section).

❖ The declaration of variables in JSP is not thread-safe, because the declared variables end up in the generated servlet as an instance variable, not within the body of the _jspservice() method. (Refer **Q34** in Enterprise section).

❖ Struts framework action classes are not thread-safe. (Refer **Q113** in Enterprise section).

❖ Some Java *Collection* classes like HashMap, ArrayList etc are not thread-safe. (Refer **Q15** in Java section).

❖ Some of the Java core library classes are not thread safe. For e.g. java.util.SimpleDateFormat, java.util.Locale etc.

Q 07: How would you go about identifying any potential transactional issues in your Java/J2EE application? FAQ
A 07:

❖ When a connection is created, it is in **auto-commit** mode. This means that each individual SQL statement is treated as a transaction and will be automatically committed immediately after it is executed. The way to allow two or more statements to be grouped into a transaction is to **disable** auto-commit mode. (Refer **Q43** in Enterprise section). Disabling auto-commit mode can improve performance by minimizing number of times it accesses the database.

❖ A transaction is often described by ACID properties (Atomic, Consistent, Isolated and Durable). A **distributed transaction** is an ACID transaction between two or more independent transactional resources like two separate databases. For a transaction to commit successfully, all of the individual resources must commit successfully. If any of them are unsuccessful, the transaction must roll back all of the resources. A **2-phase commit** is an approach for committing a distributed transaction in 2 phases. Refer **Q43**, **Q73** in Enterprise section.

❖ Isolation levels provide a degree of control of the effects one transaction can have on another concurrent transaction. Concurrent effects are determined by the precise ways in which, a particular relational database handles locks and its drivers may handle these locks differently. Isolation levels are used to overcome transactional problems like lost update, uncommitted data (aka dirty reads), inconsistent data (aka. phantom update), and phantom insert. Higher isolation levels can adversely affect performance at the expense of data accuracy. Refer **Q72** in Enterprise section.

Isolation Level	Lost Update	Uncommitted Data	Inconsistent Data	Phantom Insert
Read Uncommitted	Prevented by DBMS	Can happen	Can happen	Can happen
Read Committed	Prevented by DBMS	Prevented by DBMS	Can happen	Can happen
Repeatable Read	Prevented by DBMS	Prevented by DBMS	Prevented by DBMS	Can happen
Serializable	Prevented by DBMS	Prevented by DBMS	Prevented by DBMS	Prevented by DBMS

❖ Decide between optimistic and pessimistic concurrency control. (Refer **Q78** in Enterprise section).

❖ Evaluate a strategy to determine if the data is stale when using strategies to cache data. (Refer **Q79** in Enterprise section).

EJB related transactional issues:

❖ Set the appropriate transactional attributes for the EJBs. (Refer **Q71** in Enterprise section).

❖ Set the appropriate isolation level for the EJB. The isolation level should not be any more restrictive than it has to be. Higher isolation levels can adversely affect performance. (Refer **Q72** in Enterprise section). Isolation levels are application server specific and not part of the standard EJB configuration.

❖ In EJB 2.x, transactions are rolled back by the container when a **system exception** is thrown. When an **application exception** is thrown then the transactions are not rolled back by the container. So the developer has to roll it back using **ctx.setRollbackOnly()** call. (Refer **Q76**, **Q77** in Enterprise section).

❖ Detect doomed transactions to avoid performing any unnecessary compute intensive operations. (Refer **Q72** in Enterprise section).

Q 08: How would you go about applying the Object Oriented (OO) design concepts in your Java/J2EE application? FAQ
A 08:

Question	Answer

What are the key characteristics of an OO language like Java?
 	
Refer **Q07 – Q10** in Java section
	A true object oriented language should support the following 3 characteristics:
	
	❖ **Encapsulation** (aka **information hiding**): implements information hiding and modularity (abstraction).
	
	❖ **Polymorphism**: The same message sent to different objects, results in behavior that is dependent on the nature of the object receiving the message.
	
	❖ **Inheritance**: Encourages code reuse and code organization by defining the new class based on the existing class.
	
	What is dynamic binding?
	
	Dynamic binding (aka **late binding**): The dynamic binding is used to implement polymorphism. Objects could come from local process or from across the network from a remote process. We should be able to send messages to objects without having to know their types at the time of writing the code. Dynamic binding provides maximum flexibility at the execution time. Usually dynamic binding or late binding takes a small performance hit.
	
	Refer **Q10** in Java section.
	
	Let us take an example to illustrate dynamic binding through polymorphic behavior:
	
	Say you have a method in Java
	
	```java\nvoid draw(Shape s) {\n s.erase();\n // ...\n s.draw();\n}\n```
	
	The above method will talk to any shape, so it is independent of the specific type of object it is erasing and drawing. Now let us look at some other program, which is making use of this draw(Shape s) method:
	
	```java\nCircle cir = new Circle();\nSquare sq = new Square();\n\ndraw(cir);\ndraw(sq);\n```
	
	So the interesting thing is that the method call to draw(Shape s) will cause different code to be executed. So you send a message to an object even though you don't know what specific type it is and the right thing happens. This is called dynamic binding, which gives you polymorphic behavior.

How will you decide whether to use an interface or an abstract class?	❖ **Abstract Class**: Often in a design, you want the base class to present *only an interface* for its derived classes. That is, you don't want anyone to actually create an object of the base class, only to upcast to it so that its interface can be used. This is accomplished by making that class *abstract* using the **abstract** key word. If anyone tries to make an object of an **abstract** class, the compiler prevents them. This is a tool to enforce a particular design. ❖ **Interface**: The **interface** key word takes the concept of an **abstract** class one step further by preventing any function definitions at all. An **interface** is a very useful and commonly used tool, as it provides the perfect separation of interface and implementation. In addition, you can combine many interfaces together, if you wish. (You cannot inherit from more than one regular **class** or **abstract class**.) Now the design decision… **When to use an Abstract Class**: Abstract classes are excellent candidates inside of application

frameworks. Abstract classes let you define some default behavior and force subclasses to provide any specific behavior.

When to use an Interface: If you need to change your design frequently, I prefer using interface to abstract. For example, the strategy pattern lets you swap new algorithms and processes into your program without altering the objects that use them. Example: **Strategy Design Pattern**.

Another justification of interfaces is that they solved the '**diamond problem**' of traditional multiple inheritance. Java does not support multiple inheritance. Java only supports **multiple interface inheritance**. Interface will solve all the ambiguities caused by this 'diamond problem'. Refer **Q12** in Java section.

Interface inheritance vs. **Implementation inheritance**: Prefer interface inheritance to implementation inheritance because it promotes the design concept of **coding to an interface** and **reduces coupling**. Interface inheritance can achieve **code reuse** with the help of **object composition**. Refer **Q10** in Java section.

Why abstraction is important in Object Oriented programming?	The software you develop should optimally cater for the current requirements and problems and also should be flexible enough to easily handle future changes. Abstraction is an important OO concept. The ability for a program to ignore some aspects of the information that it is manipulating, i.e. Ability to focus on the essential. Each object in the system serves as a model of an abstract "actor" that can perform work, report on and change its state, and "communicate" with other objects in the system, without revealing *how* these features are implemented. Abstraction is the process where ideas are distanced from the concrete implementation of the objects. The **concrete implementation will change but the abstract layer will remain the same**. **Let us look at an analogy:** When you drive your car you do not have to be concerned with the exact internal working of your car (unless you are a mechanic). What you are concerned with is interacting with your car via its interfaces like steering wheel, brake pedal, accelerator pedal etc. Over the years a car's engine has improved a lot but its basic interface has not changed (i.e. you still use steering wheel, brake pedal, accelerator pedal etc to interact with your car). This means that the **implementation** has changed over the years but the **interface** remains the same. Hence the knowledge you have of your car is abstract.
Explain black-box reuse and white-box reuse? Should you favor Inheritance (white-box reuse) or aggregation (black-box reuse)?	**Black-box reuse** is when a class uses another class without knowing the internal contents of it. The black-box reuses are: ❖ **Dependency** is the weakest type of black-box reuse. ❖ **Association** is when one object knows about or has a relationship with the other objects. ❖ **Aggregation** is the **whole part relationship** where one object contains one or more of the other objects. ❖ **Composition** is a stronger **whole part relationship** Refer **Q107, Q108** in Enterprise section **White-box reuse** is when a class knows internal contents of another class. E.g. **inheritance** is used to modify implementation for reusability.

Composition (Black-box reuse)	Inheritance (White-box reuse)
Defined <u>dynamically</u> or at <u>runtime</u> via object references. Since only interfaces are used, it has the advantage of maintaining the integrity (i.e. encapsulation).	Inheritance is defined <u>statically</u> or at <u>compile time</u>. Inheritance allows an easy way to modify implementation for reusability.
Disadvantage of aggregation is that it increases the number of objects and relationships.	A disadvantage of inheritance is that it breaks encapsulation, which implies implementation dependency. This means when you want to carry out the redesign where the super class (i.e. parent class) has to be modified or replaced, which is more likely to affect the subclasses as well. In general it will affect the whole inheritance hierarchy. **Verdict**: So the tendency is to favor composition over inheritance.

What is your understanding on Aspect Oriented Programming (AOP)?	Aspect-Oriented Programming (**AOP**) <u>complements</u> **OO** programming by allowing developers to dynamically modify the static OO model to create a system that can grow to meet new requirements. AOP allows us to dynamically modify our static model to include the code required to fulfill the secondary requirements (like auditing, logging, security, exception handling etc) without having to modify the original static model (in fact, we don't even need to have the original code). Better still, we can often keep this additional code in a single location rather than having to scatter it across the existing model, as we would have to if we were using OO on its own. (Refer **Q3 –Q5** in Emerging Technologies/Frameworks section.) For example A typical Web application will require a servlet to bind the HTTP request to an object and then passes to the business handler object to be processed and finally return the response back to the user. So initially only a minimum amount of code is required. But once you start adding all the other additional secondary requirements (aka **crosscutting concerns**) like logging, auditing, security, exception-handling etc the code will inflate to 2-4 times its original size. This is where AOP can help.

Q 09: How would you go about applying the UML diagrams in your Java/J2EE project? FAQ
A 09:

Question	Answer
Explain the key relationships in the use case diagrams?	Refer **Q107** in Enterprise section. Use case has 4 types of relationships: **Between actor and use case** ❖ **Association**: Between **actor** and **use case**. May be navigable in both directions according to the initiator of the communication between the actor and the use case. **Between use cases** ❖ **Extends**: This is an <u>optional</u> extended behavior of a use case. This behavior is executed only under certain conditions such as performing a security check etc. ❖ **Includes:** This specifies that the base use case needs an additional use case to fully describe its process. It is mainly used to show common functionality that is shared by several use cases. ❖ **Inheritance (or generalization):** Child use case inherits the behavior of its parent. The child may override or add to the behavior of the parent.

Usecase diagram

Note:

<<extend>> relationship is <u>conditional</u>. You do not know if or when extending use case will be invoked.

<<include>> relationship is similar to a procedure call.

Inheritance : extends the behavior of the parent use case or actor.

Q. What is a use case specification document? What should it cover?

A use case diagram shown above is a visual depiction of the different scenarios of interaction between an actor and a use case. A use case specification document should enable you to easily document the business flow. Information that you document in a use case specification should include what actors are involved, the steps that the use case performs, business rules, and so forth. A use case specification document should cover the following:

- **Actors**: List the actors that participate and interact in this use case.

- **Pre-conditions**: Pre-conditions that need to be satisfied for the use case to perform.

- **Post-conditions**: Define the different states in which you expect the system to be in, after the use case executes.

- **Basic Flow**: List the basic events that will occur when the use case is executed. List all primary activities that the use case will perform and describe the actions performed by the actor and the response of the use case to those actions. These will form the basis for writing the test cases for the system.

- **Alternative Flows**: Any subsidiary events that can occur in the use case should be listed separately.

- **Special requirements**: Business rules for the basic and alternative flows should be listed as special requirements. These business rules will also be used to write test cases. Both success and failure scenarios should be described here.

- **Use case relationships**: For complex systems, you need to document the relationships between use cases.

Q. What are the "Do"s and "Don't"s of a use case diagram?

- Use cases should not be used to capture all the details of a system. The granularity to which you define use cases in a diagram should be enough to keep the use case diagram uncluttered.

- Use cases are meant to capture "**what**" the system is and not "**how**" the system will be designed or built. Use cases should be free of any design characteristics.

What is the main difference between the collaboration diagram and the sequence diagram?	Refer **Q107** in Enterprise section: Collaboration diagrams convey the same message as sequence diagrams but the collaboration diagrams focus on **object roles** instead of **times in which** the messages are sent. The sequence diagram is time line driven.

When to use various UML diagrams?	Refer **Q107** in Enterprise section.
	
	❖ **Use case diagrams**:
	
	    ▪ Determining the user requirements. New use cases often generate new requirements.
	    ▪ Communicating with clients. The simplicity of the diagram makes use case diagrams a good way for designers and developers to communicate with clients.
	    ▪ Generating test cases. Each scenario for the use case may suggest a suite of test cases.
	
	❖ **Class diagrams**:
	
	    ▪ Class diagrams are the backbone of **O**bject **O**riented methods. So they are used frequently.
	    ▪ Class diagrams can have a conceptual perspective and an implementation perspective. During the analysis draw the conceptual model and during implementation draw the implementation model.
	
	❖ **Interaction diagrams (Sequence and/or Collaboration diagrams)**:
	
	    ▪ When you want to look at behavior of **several objects within a single use case**. If you want to look at a **single object across multiple use cases** then use statechart diagram as described below.
	
	❖ **State chart diagrams**:
	
	    ▪ Statechart diagrams are good at describing the **behavior of an object across several use cases**. But they are not good at describing the interaction or collaboration between many objects. Use interaction and/or activity diagrams in conjunction with the statechart diagram to communicate complex operations involving multi-threaded programs etc.
	
	    ▪ Use it only for classes that have complex state changes and behavior. **For example:** the User Interface (UI) control objects, Objects shared by multi-threaded programs etc.

	❖ **Activity diagram:** ▪ **Activity** and **Statechart** diagrams are generally useful to express complex operations. The great strength of activity diagrams is that they support and encourage parallel behavior. An activity and statechart diagrams are beneficial for workflow modeling with multi- threaded programming.

Q 10: How would you go about describing the software development processes you are familiar with? FAQ

A 10: In addition to technical questions one should also have a good understanding of the software development process.

Question	Answer

What is the key difference between the waterfall approach and the iterative approach to software development? How to decide which one to use?	Refer **Q103 – Q105** in Enterprise section
	
	Waterfall approach is sequential in nature. The **iterative** approach is non-sequential and incremental. The iterative and incremental approach has been developed based on the following:
	
	• **You can't express all your needs up front.** It is usually not feasible to define in detail (that is, before starting full-scale development) the operational capabilities and functional characteristics of the entire system. These usually evolve over time as development progresses.
	
	• **Technology changes over time.** Some development lifecycle spans a long period of time during which, given the pace at which technology evolves, significant technological shifts may occur.
	
	• **Complex systems.** This means it is difficult to cope with them adequately unless you have an approach for mastering complexity.
	
	How to decide which one to use?
	
	Waterfall approach is more suitable in the following circumstances:
	
	   • Have a small number of unknowns and risks. That is if
	      • It has a known domain.
	      • The team is experienced in current process and technology.
	      • There is no new technology.
	      • There is a pre-existing architecture baseline.
	   • Is of short duration (two to three months).
	   • Is an evolution of an existing system?
	
	The **iterative** approach is more suitable (Refer **Q136** in Enterprise Section)
	
	   • Have a large number of unknowns and risks. So it pays to design, develop and test a vertical slice iteratively and then replicate it through other iterations. That is if
	      • Integrating with new systems.
	      • New technology and/or architecture.
	      • The team is fairly keen to adapt to this new process.
	
	   • Is of large duration (longer than 3 months).
	   • Is a new system?

Have you used extreme programming techniques? Explain?	Extreme Programming (or XP) is a set of values, principles and practices for rapidly developing high-quality software that provides the highest value for the customer in the fastest way possible. **XP is a minimal instance of RUP.** XP is extreme in the sense that it takes **12 well-known software development "best practices" to their logical extremes.**
	
	The 12 core practices of XP are:
	
	1. **The Planning Game:** Business and development cooperate to produce the maximum business value as rapidly as possible. The planning game happens at various scales, but the basic rules are always the same:
	
	   ▪ Business comes up with a list of desired features for the system. Each feature is written out as a **user story** (or PowerPoint screen shots with changes highlighted), which gives the feature a name, and describes in broad strokes what is required. User stories are typically written on 4x6 cards.
	
	   ▪ Development team estimates how much effort each story will take, and how much effort the team can produce in a given time interval (i.e. the iteration).

- Business then decides which stories to implement in what order, as well as when and how often to produce production releases of the system.

2. **Small releases**: Start with the smallest useful feature set. Release early and often, adding a few features each time.

3. **System metaphor**: Each project has an organizing metaphor, which provides an easy to remember naming convention.

4. **Simple design**: Always use the simplest possible design that gets the job done. The requirements will change tomorrow, so only do what's needed to meet today's requirements.

5. **Continuous testing**: Before programmers add a feature, they write a test for it. Tests in XP come in two basic flavors.

   - **Unit tests** are automated tests written by the developers to test functionality as they write it. Each unit test typically tests only a single class, or a small cluster of classes. Unit tests are typically written using a unit-testing framework, such as **JUnit**.

   - **Customer to test that the overall system is functioning as specified, defines acceptance tests (aka functional tests)**. Acceptance tests typically test the entire system, or some large chunk of it. When all the acceptance tests pass for a given user story, that story is considered complete. At the very least, an acceptance test could consist of a script of user interface actions and expected results that a human can run. Ideally acceptance tests should be automated using frameworks like Canoo Web test, Selenium Web test etc.

6. **Refactoring**: Refactor out any duplicate code generated in a coding session. You can do this with confidence that you didn't break anything because you have the tests.

7. **Pair Programming**: All production code is written by two programmers sitting at one machine. Essentially, all code is reviewed as it is written.

8. **Collective code ownership**: No single person "owns" a module. Any developer is expected to be able to work on any part of codebase at any time.

9. **Continuous integration**: All changes are integrated into codebase at least daily. The tests have to run 100% both before and after integration. You can use tools like Ant, CruiseControl, and/or Maven to continuously build and integrate your code.

10. **40-Hour Workweek**: Programmers go home on time. In crunch mode, up to one week of overtime is allowed. But multiple consecutive weeks of overtime are treated as a sign that something is very wrong with the process.

11. **On-site customer**: Development team has continuous access to a real live customer or business owner, that is, someone who will actually be using the system. For commercial software with lots of customers, a customer proxy (usually the product manager, Business Analyst etc) is used instead.

12. **Coding standards**: Everyone codes to the same standards. Ideally, you shouldn't be able to tell by looking at it, which developer on the team has touched a specific piece of code.

A typical extreme programming project will have:

- All the programmers in a room together usually sitting around a large table.
- Fixed number of iterations where **each iteration takes 1-3 weeks**. At the beginning of each iteration get together with the customer.
- Pair-programming.
- Writing test cases first (i.e. TDD – **Test Driven Development**).
- Delivery of a functional system at the end of 1-3 week iteration.

| Have you used agile (i.e. Lightweight) software development methodologies? | **Agile (i.e. lightweight) software development process** is gaining popularity and momentum across organizations. Several methodologies fit under this agile development methodology banner. All these methodologies share many characteristics like **iterative and incremental development, test driven development** (i.e. TDD), **stand up meetings to improve communication, automatic testing, build and continuous integration of code** etc. Among all the agile methodologies XP is the one which has got the most attention. Different companies use different flavors of agile methodologies by using different combinations of methodologies (e.g. primarily XP with other methodologies like Scrum, FDD, TDD etc). Refer **Q136** in Enterprise section. |

Q 11: How would you go about applying the design patterns in your Java/J2EE application?

A 11: It is really worth reading books and articles on design patterns. It is sometimes hard to remember the design patterns, which you do not use regularly. So if you do not know a particular design pattern you can always honestly say that you have not used it and subsequently suggest that you can explain another design pattern, which you have used recently or more often. It is always challenging to decide, which design pattern to use when? How do you improve your design pattern skills? Practice, practice, practice. I have listed some of the design patterns below with scenarios and examples:

To understand design patterns you need to have a basic understanding of object-oriented concepts like:

Decomposition: The process of dividing a problem into smaller pieces (i.e. divide and conquer approach). The following examples will break different scenarios into objects, each with specific responsibilities. A good decomposition will often result in improved <u>reusability</u>.

Polymorphism, Inheritance, and Encapsulation: Refer **Q10** in Java section.

Loose coupling: The process of making objects independent of each other rather than dependent of one another. Loosely coupled objects are easier to <u>reuse</u> and <u>change</u>.

Note: To keep it simple, System.out.println(...) is used. In real practice, use logging frameworks like log4j. Also package constructs are not shown. In real practice, each class should be stored in their relevant packages like com.items etc. Feel free to try these code samples by typing them into a Java editor of your choice and run the main class *Shopping*. Also constants should be declared in a typesafe manner as shown below:

```java
/**
 * use typesafe enum pattern as shown below if you are using below J2SE 5.0 or use "enum" if you are using J2SE 5.0
 */
public class ItemType {
    private final String name;

    public static final ItemType Book = new ItemType("book");
    public static final ItemType CD = new ItemType("cd");
    public static final ItemType COSMETICS = new ItemType("cosmetics");
    public static final ItemType CD_IMPORTED = new ItemType("cd_imported");

    private ItemType(String name) {this.name = name;}
    public String toString() {return name;}
    //add compareTo(), readResolve() methods etc as required ...
}
```

Scenario: A company named XYZ Retail is in the business of selling *Books*, *CDs* and *Cosmetics*. *Books* are sales tax exempt and *CDs* and *Cosmetics* have a sales tax of 10%. CDs can be imported and attracts an import tax of 5%. Write a shopping basket program, which will calculate extended price (qty * (unitprice + tax)) inclusive of tax for each item in the basket, total taxes and grand total.

Solution: Sample code for the items (i.e. Goods) sold by XYZ Retail. Let's define an *Item* interface to follow the design principle of **code to an interface not to an implementation.** CO

```java
public interface Item {

    public static final int TYPE_BOOK = 1;
    public static final int TYPE_CD = 2;
    public static final int TYPE_COSMETICS = 3;
    public static final int TYPE_CD_IMPORTED = 4;

    public double getExtendedTax();
    public double getExtendedTaxPrice() throws ItemException;
    public void setImported(boolean b);
    public String getDescription();
}
```

The following class *Goods* cannot be instantiated (since it is **abstract**). You use this abstract class to achieve **code reuse**.

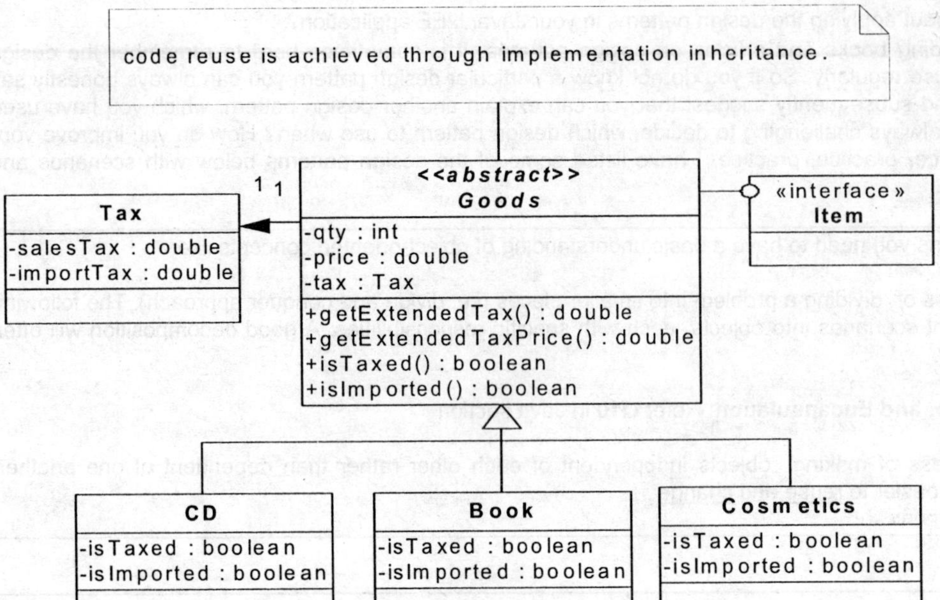

```
+-------------------------------------------------+
| code reuse is achieved through implementation inheritance. |
+-------------------------------------------------+
```

```
                     1 1    +-------------------------+         «interface»
         +----------------+  |    <<abstract>>         |O-------  +-----------+
         |      Tax       |  |       Goods             |          |   Item    |
         +----------------+  +-------------------------+          +-----------+
         |-salesTax : double|◄-|-qty : int              |
         |-importTax : double| |-price : double          |
         +----------------+  |-tax : Tax               |
                             +-------------------------+
                             |+getExtendedTax() : double|
                             |+getExtendedTaxPrice() : double|
                             |+isTaxed() : boolean      |
                             |+isImported() : boolean   |
                             +-------------------------+
                                      △
        +----------------------+----------------------+----------------------+
+------------------+   +------------------+   +------------------+
|       CD         |   |      Book        |   |    Cosmetics     |
+------------------+   +------------------+   +------------------+
|-isTaxed : boolean|   |-isTaxed : boolean|   |-isTaxed : boolean|
|-isImported : boolean| |-isImported : boolean| |-isImported : boolean|
+------------------+   +------------------+   +------------------+
```

```
/**
* abstract parent class, which promotes code reuse for all the subclasses
* like Book, CD, and Cosmetics. implements interface Item to
* promote design principle code to interface not to an implementation.
*/

public abstract class Goods implements Item {
   //define attributes
   private String description;
   private int qty;
   private double price;
   private Tax tax = new Tax();

  public Goods(String description, int qty, double price) {
     this.description = description;
     this.qty = qty;
     this.price = price;
  }

  protected abstract boolean isTaxed();
  protected abstract boolean isImported();

  public double getExtendedTax() {
      tax.calculate(isTaxed(), isImported(), price);
      return this.tax.getTotalUnitTax() * qty;
   }

public double getExtendedTaxPrice() throws ItemException {
    if (tax == null) {
        throw new ItemException("Tax should be calculated first:");
    }
    return qty * (this.tax.getTotalUnitTax() + price);
}

   //getters and setters go here for attributes like description etc
   public String getDescription() {
     return description;
   }

   public String toString() {
     return qty + " " + description + " : ";
   }

}
```

The *Book*, *CD* and *Cosmetics* classes can be written as shown below:

```
public class Book extends Goods {
    private boolean isTaxed = false;
    private boolean isImported = false;

  public Book(String description, int qty, double price) {
      super(description, qty, price);
  }

  public boolean isTaxed() {
      return isTaxed;
  }

  public boolean isImported() {
      return isImported;
  }

  public void setImported(boolean b) {
      isImported = b;
  }
}


public class CD extends Goods {
    private boolean isTaxed = true;
    private boolean isImported = false;

  public CD(String description, int qty, double price) {
      super(description, qty, price);
  }

  public boolean isTaxed() {
      return isTaxed;
  }

  public boolean isImported() {
      return isImported;
  }

  public void setImported(boolean b) {
      isImported = b;
  }
}


public class Cosmetics extends Goods {
    private boolean isTaxed = true;
    private boolean isImported = false;

  public Cosmetics(String description, int qty, double price) {
      super(description, qty, price);
  }

  public boolean isTaxed() {
      return isTaxed;
  }

  public boolean isImported() {
      return isImported;
  }

  public void setImported(boolean b) {
      isImported = b;
  }
}
```

Alternative solution: Alternatively, **instead of using inheritance, we can use object composition** to achieve code reuse as discussed in **Q10** in Java section. If you were to use object composition instead of inheritance, you would have classes *Book*, *CD* and *Cosmetics* implementing the *Item* interface directly (*Goods* class would not be required), and make use of a **GoodsHelper** class to achieve code reuse through composition.

interface inheritance where code reuse is achieved through composition [GoodsHelper]. code not shown.

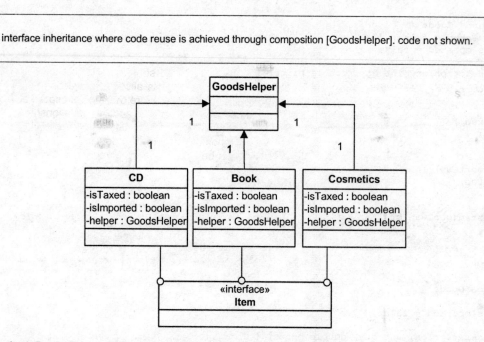

Let's define a *Tax* class, which is responsible for calculating the tax. The *Tax* class is composed in your *Goods* class, which makes use of **object composition to achieve code reuse**.

```java
public class Tax {
    //stay away from hard coding values. Define constants or read from a ".properties" file
    public static final double SALES_TAX = 0.10; //10%
    public static final double IMPORT_TAX = 0.05; //5%

    private double salesTax = 0.0;
    private double importTax = 0.0;

    public void calculate(boolean isTaxable, boolean isImported, double price) {
        if (isTaxable) {
            salesTax = price * SALES_TAX;
        }
        if (isImported) {
            importTax = price * IMPORT_TAX;
        }
    }

    public double getTotalUnitTax() {
        return this.salesTax + this.importTax;
    }
}
```

Factory method pattern: To create the items shown above we could use the **factory method pattern** as described in **Q52** in Java section. We would also implement the factory class as a singleton using the **singleton design pattern** as described in **Q51** in Java section. The factory method design pattern instantiates a class in a more flexible way than directly calling the constructor. It loosely couples your calling code from the Items it creates like *CD*, *Book*, etc. Let's look at why factory method pattern is more flexible:

- Sometimes factory methods have to return a single instance of a class instead of creating new objects each time or return an instance from a pool of objects.

- Factory methods have to return a subtype of the type requested. It also can request the caller to refer to the returned object by **its interface rather than by its implementation**, which enables objects to be created without making their implementation classes public.

- Sometimes old ways of creating objects can be replaced by new ways of creating the same objects or new classes can be added using polymorphism without changing any of the existing code which uses these objects. **For example:** Say you have a *Fruit* abstract class with *Mango* and *Orange* as its concrete subclasses, later on you can add an *Apple* subclass without breaking the code which uses these objects.

The factory method patterns consist of a **product class hierarchy** and a **creator class hierarchy**.

```
/**
 * ItemFactory is responsible for creating Item objects like CD, Book, and Cosmetics etc
 */
public abstract class ItemFactory {
    public abstract Item getItem(int itemType, String description, int qty, double price)
                                            throws  ItemException;
}
```

```
/**
 * GoodsFactory responsible for creating Item objects like CD, Book, and Cosmetics etc
 */
public class GoodsFactory extends ItemFactory {

    protected GoodsFactory() { } //protected so that only ItemFactorySelector within this package can
                                 //instantiate it to provide a single point of access
                                 //(i.e. singleton).
    /**
     * Factory method, which decides how to create Items.
     *
     * Benefits are: -- loosely-couples the client (i.e. ShoppingBasketBuilder class) from Items such
     * as CD, Book, and Cosmetics etc. In future if we need to create a Book item, which is imported,
     * we can easily incorporate this by adding a new item.TYPE_BOOK_IMPORTED and subsequently adding
     * following piece of code as shown:
     *
     * else if(itemType == TYPE_BOOK_IMPORTED){
     *      item = new Book(description, qty,price);
     *      item.setIsImported(true);
     * }
     *
     * -- It is also possible to create an object cache or object pool of our items instead of creating a new instance
     *    every time without making any changes to the calling class.
     * -- Java does not support overloaded constructors which take same parameter list. Instead, use several factory methods.
     *    E.g. getImportedItem(int itemType, String description, int qty, double price), getTaxedItem (int itemType ....) etc
     */

    public Item getItem(int itemType, String description, int qty, double price) throws ItemException
    {
        Item item = null;         //code to interface
        if (itemType == Item.TYPE_BOOK) {
            item = new Book(description, qty, price);
        } else if (itemType == Item.TYPE_CD) {
            item = new CD(description, qty, price);
        } else if (itemType == Item.TYPE_CD_IMPORTED) {
            item = new CD(description, qty, price);
            item.setImported(true);
        } else if (itemType == Item.TYPE_COSMETICS) {
            item = new Cosmetics(description, qty, price);
        } else {
            throw new ItemException("Invalid ItemType=" + itemType);
        }
        return item; //returned object is referred by its interface instead of by its implementation
    }
}
```

Let's use the abstract factory pattern to create an ItemFactory and the singleton pattern to provide a single point of access to the *ItemFactory* returned.

Abstract factory pattern: This pattern is one level of abstraction higher than the factory method pattern because you have an abstract factory (or factory interface) and have multiple concrete factories. Abstract factory pattern usually has a specific method for each concrete type being returned (e.g. createCircle(), createSquare() etc). Alternatively you can have a single method e.g. createShape(...).

Singleton pattern: Ensures that a class has only one instance and provides a global point of access to it (Refer **Q51** in Java section). E.g. a *DataSource* should have only a single instance where it will supply multiple connections from its single *DataSource* pool.

```
/**
 * Abstract factory class which creates a singleton ItemFactory dynamically based on factory name
 * supplied.
 * Benefits of singleton: -- single instance of the ItemFactory -- single point of access (global
 * access within the JVM and the class loader)
 */

public class ItemFactorySelector {
    private static ItemFactory objectFactorySingleInstance = null;
    private static final String FACTORY_NAME = "com.item.GoodsFactory"; //can use a .proprties file.

    public static ItemFactory getItemFactory() {
        try {
            if (objectFactorySingleInstance == null) {

                //Dynamically instantiate factory and factory name can also be read from a properties
                //file. in future if we need a CachedGoodsFactory which caches Items to improve memory
                //usage then we can modify the FACTORY_NAME to "com.item.CachedGoodsFactory" or
                //conditionally select one of many factories.

                Class klassFactory = Class.forName(FACTORY_NAME);
                objectFactorySingleInstance = (ItemFactory) klassFactory.newInstance();
            }
        }

        catch (ClassNotFoundException cnf) {
            throw new RuntimeException("Cannot create the ItemFactory: " + cnf.getMessage());
        }catch (IllegalAccessException iae) {
            throw new RuntimeException("Cannot create the ItemFactory: " + iae.getMessage());
        }catch (InstantiationException ie) {
            throw new RuntimeException("Cannot create the ItemFactory: " + ie.getMessage());
        }

        return objectFactorySingleInstance;
    }
}
```

Now we should build a more complex shopping basket object step-by-step, which is responsible for building a basket with items like *CD*, *Book* etc and calculating total tax for the items in the basket. The **builder design pattern** is used to define the interface *ItemBuilder* and the concrete class, which implements this interface, is named *ShoppingBasketBuilder*.

Builder pattern: The subtle difference between the builder pattern and the factory pattern is that in builder pattern, the user is given the **choice to create the type of object he/she wants but the construction process is the same**. But with the factory method pattern the **factory decides how to create one of several possible classes based on data provided to it**.

```
...//package & import statements

public interface ItemBuilder {
    public void buildBasket(int itemType, String description, int qty, double unit_price)
                                                        throws ItemException;

    public double calculateTotalTax() throws ItemException;
    public double calculateTotal() throws ItemException;
    public void printExtendedTaxedPrice() throws ItemException;
    public Iterator getIterator();
}
```

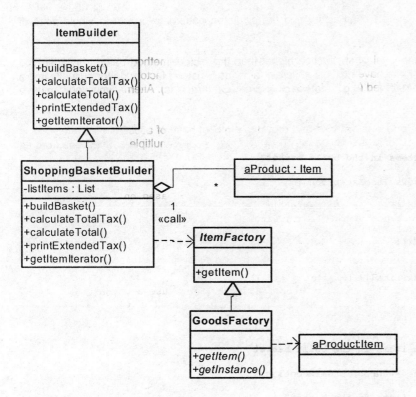

```
...//package & import statements

/**
 * Builder pattern: To simplify complex object creation by defining a class whose purpose is to
 * build instances of another class.
 * There is a subtle difference between a builder pattern and the factory pattern is that in builder
 * pattern, the user is given the choice to create the type of object he/she wants but the
 * construction process is the same. But with the factory method pattern the factory decides how to
 * create one of several possible classes based on data provided to it.
 */
public class ShoppingBasketBuilder implements ItemBuilder {

  private List listItems = null;

  private void addItem(Item item) {
    if (listItems == null) {
      listItems = new ArrayList(20);
    }
    listItems.add(item);
  }

  /**
   * builds a shopping basket
   */
  public void buildBasket(int itemType, String description, int qty, double unit_price)
                                                        throws ItemException {
    //get the single instance of GoodsFactory using the singleton pattern
    //no matter how many times you call getInstance() you get access to the same instance.
    ItemFactory factory = ItemFactorySelector.getItemFactory();

    //use factory method pattern to create item objects, based on itemType supplied to it.
    Item item = factory.getItem(itemType, description, qty, unit_price);
    this.addItem(item); //adds the item to the basket
  }

  /**
   * calculates total tax on the items in the built basket
   */
  public double calculateTotalTax()
                  throws ItemException {
    if (listItems == null) {
      throw new ItemException("No items in the basket");
```

```
    }
    double totalTax = 0.0;
    Iterator it = listItems.iterator();
    while (it.hasNext()) {
        Item item = (Item) it.next();
        totalTax += item.getExtendedTax();
    }
    return totalTax;
}


/**
 * calculates total price on the items in the built basket
 */
public double calculateTotal() throws ItemException {
    if (listItems == null) {
        throw new ItemException("No items in the basket");
    }
    double total = 0.0;
    Iterator it = listItems.iterator();
    while (it.hasNext()) {
        Item item = (Item) it.next();
        total += item.getExtendedTaxPrice();
    }
    return total;
}


/**
 * prints individual prices of the items in the built basket
 */
public void printExtendedTaxedPrice() throws ItemException {
    if (listItems == null) {
        throw new ItemException("No items in the basket");
    }
    double totalTax = 0.0;
    Iterator it = listItems.iterator();
    while (it.hasNext()) {
        Item item = (Item) it.next();
        System.out.println(item + "" + item.getExtendedTaxPrice());
    }
}

public Iterator getIterator() {
    return listItems.iterator();
}
}
```

Finally, the calling-code, which makes use of our shopping basket builder pattern to build the shopping basket step-by-step and also calculates the taxes and the grand total for the items in the shopping basket.

...//package & import statements

```
public class Shopping {
    /**
     * Class with main(String[] args) method which initially gets loaded by the
     * class loader. Subsequent classes are loaded as they are referenced in the program.
     */
    public static void main(String[] args) throws ItemException {
        process();
    }

    public static void process() throws ItemException {
        //------creational patterns: singleton, factory method and builder design patterns------
        System.out.println("----create a shopping basket with items ---");
        //Shopping basket using the builder pattern
        ItemBuilder builder = new ShoppingBasketBuilder();
        //build basket of items using a builder pattern
        builder.buildBasket(Item.TYPE_BOOK, "Book - IT", 1, 12.00);
        builder.buildBasket(Item.TYPE_CD, "CD - JAZZ", 1, 15.00);
        builder.buildBasket(Item.TYPE_COSMETICS, "Cosmetics - Lipstick", 1, 1.0);

        //let's print prices and taxes of this built basket
        double totalTax = builder.calculateTotalTax();
        builder.printExtendedTaxedPrice();
        System.out.println("Sales Taxes: " + totalTax);
```

```
    System.out.println("Grand Total:    " + builder.calculateTotal());
    System.out.println("----- After adding an imported CD to the basket ----");

    //Say now customer decides to buy an additional imported CD
    builder.buildBasket(Item.TYPE_CD_IMPORTED, "CD - JAZZ IMPORTED", 1, 15.00);

    //lets print prices and taxes of this built basket with imported CD added
    totalTax = builder.calculateTotalTax();
    builder.printExtendedTaxedPrice();
    System.out.println("Sales Taxes: " + totalTax);
    System.out.println("Grand Total:    " + builder.calculateTotal());
  }
}
```

Running the above code produces an output of:

```
----create a shopping basket with items ---
1 Book - IT : 12.0
1 CD - JAZZ : 16.5
1 Cosmetics - Lipstick : 1.1
Sales Taxes: 1.6
Grand Total:   29.6

----- After adding an imported CD to the basket ----

1 Book - IT : 12.0
1 CD - JAZZ : 16.5
1 Cosmetics - Lipstick : 1.1
1 CD - JAZZ IMPORTED : 17.25
Sales Taxes: 3.85
Grand Total:   46.85
```

Scenario: The XYZ Retail wants to evaluate a strategy to determine items with description longer than 15 characters because it won't fit in the invoice and items with description starting with "CD" to add piracy warning label.

Solution: You can implement evaluating a strategy to determine items with description longer than 15 characters and description starting with "CD" applying the **strategy design pattern** as shown below:

Strategy pattern: The Strategy pattern lets you build software as a loosely coupled collection of interchangeable parts, in contrast to a monolithic, tightly coupled system. Loose coupling makes your software much more extensible, maintainable, and reusable. The main attribute of this pattern is that each strategy encapsulates algorithms i.e. it is **not data based but algorithm based**. Refer **Q12, Q64** in Java section.

Example: You can draw borders around almost all Swing components, including panels, buttons, lists, and so on. Swing provides numerous border types for its components: bevel, etched, line, titled, and even compound. JComponent class, which acts as the base class for all Swing components by implementing functionality common to all Swing components, draws borders for Swing components, using strategy pattern.

```
public interface CheckStrategy {
   public boolean check(String word);
}
```

```
public class LongerThan15 implements CheckStrategy {
   public static final int LENGTH = 15; //constant

   public boolean check(String description) {
      if (description == null)
         return false;
      else
         return description.length() > LENGTH;
   }
}
```

```
public class StartsWithCD implements CheckStrategy {
   public static final String STARTS_WITH = "cd";

   public boolean check(String description) {
      String s = description.toLowerCase();
      if (description == null || description.length() == 0)
         return false;
      else
```

```
            return s.startsWith(STARTS_WITH);
    }
}
```

Scenario: The XYZ retail has decided to count the number of items, which satisfy the above strategies.

Solution: You can apply the **decorator design pattern** around your strategy design pattern. Refer **Q24** in Java section for the decorator design pattern used in java.io.*. The decorator acts as a **wrapper** around the *CheckStrategy* objects where by call the check(...) method on the *CheckStrategy* object and if it returns true then increment the counter. The decorator design pattern can be used to provide additional functionality to an object of some kind. The key to a decorator is that a decorator "wraps" the object decorated and looks to a client exactly the same as the object wrapped. This means that the **decorator implements the same interface as the object it decorates**.

Decorator design pattern: You can think of a decorator as a shell around the object decorated. The decorator catches any message that a client sends to the object instead. The decorator may apply some action and then pass the message it received on to the decorated object. That object probably returns a value to the decorator which may again apply an action to that result, finally sending the (perhaps-modified) result to the original client. To the client the **decorator is invisible**. It just sent a message and got a result. However the decorator had two chances to enhance the result returned.

```java
public class CountDecorator implements CheckStrategy {

    private CheckStrategy cs = null;
    private int count = 0;

    public CountDecorator(CheckStrategy cs) {
        this.cs = cs;
    }

    public boolean check(String description) {
        boolean isFound = cs.check(description);
        if (isFound)
            this.count++;
        return isFound;
    }

    public int count() {
        return this.count;
    }

    public void reset() {
        this.count = 0;
    }
}
```

There is a subtle difference between the decorator pattern and the proxy pattern is that, the main intent of the decorator pattern is to enhance the functionality of the target object whereas the main intent of the proxy pattern is to control access to the target object.

A decorator object's interface must conform to the interface of the component it decorates

Now, let's see the calling class *Shopping*:

```java
//…. package & import statements

public class Shopping {
  //...

  public static void process() throws ItemException {
      ...
    Iterator it = builder.getIterator();
    boolean bol = false;
    CheckStrategy strategy = null;

    it = builder.getIterator();
    //for starting with CD
    strategy = new StartsWithCD();
    strategy = new CountDecorator(strategy);
    while (it.hasNext()) {
        Item item = (Item) it.next();
        bol = strategy.check(item.getDescription());
        System.out.println("\n" + item.getDescription() + " --> " + bol);
    }

    System.out.println("No of descriptions starts with CD -->" +
                                        ((CountDecorator) strategy).count());


    it = builder.getIterator();
```

```
    //longer than 15 charecters
    strategy = new LongerThan15();
    strategy = new CountDecorator(strategy);
    while (it.hasNext()) {
        Item item = (Item) it.next();
        bol = strategy.check(item.getDescription());
        System.out.println("\n" + item.getDescription() + " --> " + bol);
    }

    System.out.println("No of descriptions longer than 15 characters -->" +
                                ((CountDecorator) strategy).count());
    }
}
```

Running the above code produces an output of:

```
----count item description starting with 'cd' or longer than 15 characters ---
------------------- description satarting with cd -----------------------
Book - IT --> false
CD - JAZZ --> true
Cosmetics - Lipstick --> false
CD - JAZZ IMPORTED --> true
No of descriptions starts with CD -->2
----------------- description longer than 15 characters ----------------------
Book - IT --> false
CD - JAZZ --> false
Cosmetics - Lipstick --> true
CD - JAZZ IMPORTED --> true
No of descriptions longer than 15 characters -->2
```

Scenario: So far so good, for illustration purpose if you need to adapt the strategy class to the *CountDecorator* class so that you do not have to explicitly cast your strategy classes to *CountDecorator* as shown in bold arrow in the class *Shopping*. We can overcome this by slightly rearranging the classes. The class *CountDecorator* has two additional methods count() and reset(). If you only just add these methods to the interface *CheckStrategy* then the classes *LongerThan15* and *StartsWithCD* should provide an implementation for these two methods. These two methods make no sense in these two classes.

Solution: So, to overcome this you can introduce an adapter class named *CheckStrategyAdapter*, which just provides a bare minimum default implementation. Adapter design pattern

```
public interface CheckStrategy {
    public boolean check(String word);
    public int count();
    public void reset();
}


/**
 * This is an adapter class which provides default implementations to be extended not to be used and
 * facilitates its subclasses to be adapted to each other. Throws an unchecked exception to indicate
 * improper use.
 */

public class CheckStrategyAdapter implements CheckStrategy {
   public boolean check(String word) {
        throw new RuntimeException("Improper use of CheckStrategyAdapter
                                        class method check(String word)" );
   }

   public int count() {
        throw new RuntimeException("Improper use of CheckStrategyAdapter class method count()" );
   }

   public void reset() {
        throw new RuntimeException("Improper use of CheckStrategyAdapter class method reset()" );
   }
}

public class LongerThan15 extends CheckStrategyAdapter {
   public static final int LENGTH = 15;

   public boolean check(String description) {
      if (description == null)
         return false;
```

```
        else
            return description.length() > LENGTH;
    }
}

public class StartsWithCD extends CheckStrategyAdapter {
    public static final String STARTS_WITH = "cd";

    public boolean check(String description) {
        String s = description.toLowerCase();
        if (description == null || description.length() == 0)
            return false;
        else
            return s.startsWith(STARTS_WITH);
    }
}

public class CountDecorator extends CheckStrategyAdapter {

    private CheckStrategy cs = null;
    private int count = 0;

    public CountDecorator(CheckStrategy cs) {
        this.cs = cs;
    }

    public boolean check(String description) {
        boolean isFound = cs.check(description);
        if (isFound){
            this.count++;
        }
        return isFound;
    }

    public int count() {
        return this.count;
    }

    public void reset() {
        this.count = 0;
    }
}
```

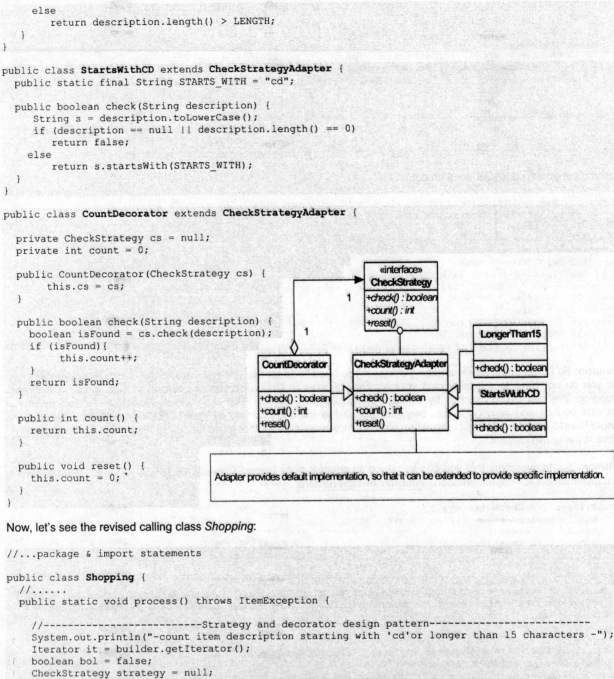

Adapter provides default implementation, so that it can be extended to provide specific implementation.

Now, let's see the revised calling class *Shopping*:

```
//...package & import statements

public class Shopping {
    //......
    public static void process() throws ItemException {

        //---------------------------Strategy and decorator design pattern--------------------------
        System.out.println("-count item description starting with 'cd'or longer than 15 characters -");
        Iterator it = builder.getIterator();
        boolean bol = false;
        CheckStrategy strategy = null;
        System.out.println("--------------- description satarting with cd -----------------");
        it = builder.getIterator();
        //for starting with CD
        strategy = new StartsWithCD();
        strategy = new CountDecorator(strategy);
        while (it.hasNext()) {
            Item item = (Item) it.next();
            bol = strategy.check(item.getDescription());
            System.out.println(item.getDescription() + " --> " + bol);
        }

        System.out.println("No of descriptions starts with CD -->" + strategy.count());

        System.out.println("-------------- description longer than 15 characters ------------------");
        it = builder.getIterator();
        //longer than 15 charecters
        strategy = new LongerThan15();
        strategy = new CountDecorator(strategy);
```

```
    while (it.hasNext()) {
        Item item = (Item) it.next();
        bol = strategy.check(item.getDescription());
        System.out.println(item.getDescription() + " --> " + bol);
    }
    System.out.println("No of descriptions longer than 15 characters -->" + strategy.count());
    }
}
```

The output is:

```
----count item description starting with 'cd'or longer than 15 characters ---
------------------- description satarting with cd -----------------------
Book - IT --> false
CD - JAZZ --> true
Cosmetics - Lipstick --> false
CD - JAZZ IMPORTED --> true
No of descriptions starts with CD -->2

------------------- description longer than 15 characters -----------------------

Book - IT --> false
CD - JAZZ --> false
Cosmetics - Lipstick --> true
CD - JAZZ IMPORTED --> true
No of descriptions longer than 15 characters -->2
```

Scenario: The XYZ Retail also requires a piece of code, which performs different operations depending on the type of item. If the item is an instance of *CD* then you call a method to print its catalog number. If the item is an instance of *Cosmetics* then you call a related but different method to print its color code. If the item is an instance of *Book* then you call a separate method to print its ISBN number. One way of implementing this is using the Java constructs **instanceof** and **explicit type casting** as shown below:

```
it = builder.getIterator();

while(it.hasNext(); ) {
    String name = null;
    Item item = (Item)iter.next();

    if(item instanceof CD) {
        ((CD) item). markWithCatalogNumber();
    } else if (item instanceof Cosmetics) {
        ((Cosmetics) item). markWithColourCode ();
    } else if (item instanceof Book) {
        ((Book) item). markWithISBNNumber();
    }
}
```

Problem: The manipulation of a collection of polymorphic objects with the constructs **typecasts** and **instanceof** as shown above can get messy and unmaintainable with large elseif constructs and these constructs in <u>frequently</u> accessed methods/ loops can adversely affect performance. **Solution**: You can apply the **visitor** design pattern to avoid using these typecast and "instanceof" constructs as shown below:

Visitor pattern: The visitor pattern makes adding new operations easy and all the related operations are localized in a visitor. The visitor pattern allows you to manipulate a collection of polymorphic objects without the messy and unmaintainable **typecasts** and **instanceof** operations. Visitor pattern allows you to add new operations, which affect a class hierarchy without having to change any of the classes in the hierarchy. **For example** we can add a *GoodsDebugVisitor* class to have the visitor just print out some debug information about each item visited etc. In fact you can write any number of visitor classes for the *Goods* hierarchy e.g. *GoodsLabellingVisitor, GoodsPackingVisitor* etc.

```
public interface Item {
    //...
    public void accept(ItemVisitor visitor);
}

public interface ItemVisitor {
    public void visit (CD  cd);
    public void visit (Cosmetics cosmetics);
    public void visit (Book book);
}
```

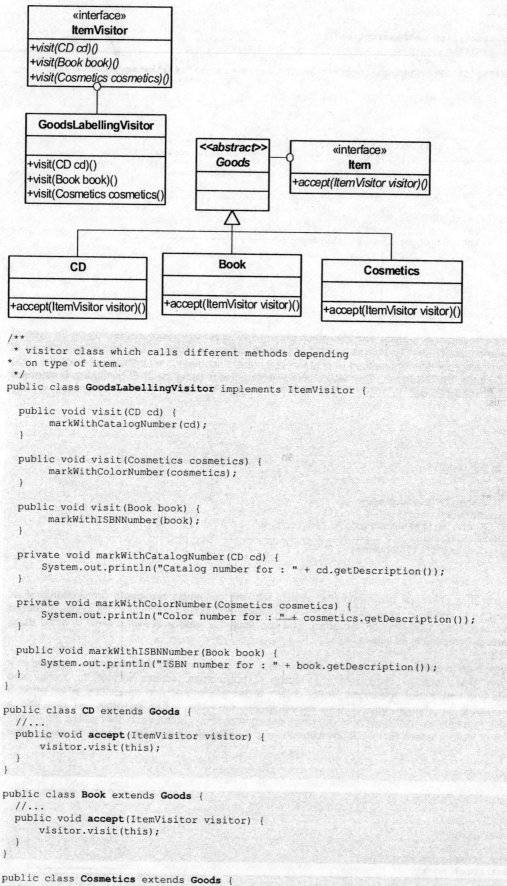

```
/**
 * visitor class which calls different methods depending
 *  on type of item.
 */
public class GoodsLabellingVisitor implements ItemVisitor {

    public void visit(CD cd) {
        markWithCatalogNumber(cd);
    }

    public void visit(Cosmetics cosmetics) {
        markWithColorNumber(cosmetics);
    }

    public void visit(Book book) {
        markWithISBNNumber(book);
    }

    private void markWithCatalogNumber(CD cd) {
        System.out.println("Catalog number for : " + cd.getDescription());
    }

    private void markWithColorNumber(Cosmetics cosmetics) {
        System.out.println("Color number for : " + cosmetics.getDescription());
    }

    public void markWithISBNNumber(Book book) {
        System.out.println("ISBN number for : " + book.getDescription());
    }
}

public class CD extends Goods {
    //...
    public void accept(ItemVisitor visitor) {
        visitor.visit(this);
    }
}

public class Book extends Goods {
    //...
    public void accept(ItemVisitor visitor) {
        visitor.visit(this);
    }
}

public class Cosmetics extends Goods {
    //...
```

```
   public void accept(ItemVisitor visitor) {
       visitor.visit(this);
   }
}
```

Now, let's see the calling code or class *Shopping*:

```
//... package and import statements

public class Shopping {

  public static void process() throws ItemException {

    //visitor pattern example, no messy instanceof and typecast constructs
    it = builder.getIterator();
    ItemVisitor visitor = new GoodsLabellingVisitor ();
    while (it.hasNext()) {
        Item item = (Item) it.next();
        item.accept(visitor);
    }
  }
}
```

The output is:

```
---- markXXXX(): avoid huge if else statements, instanceof & type casts --------
ISBN number for : Book - IT
Catalog number for : CD - JAZZ
Color number for : Cosmetics - Lipstick
Catalog number for : CD - JAZZ IMPORTED
```

Scenario: The XYZ Retail would like to have a functionality to iterate through every second or third item in the basket to randomly collect some statistics on price.

Solution: This can be implemented by applying the **iterator design pattern**.

Iterator pattern: Provides a way to access the elements of an aggregate object without exposing its underlying implementation.

```
//... package and import statements

public interface ItemBuilder {
  //..
  public com.item.Iterator getItemIterator();
}
```

```
package com.item;

public interface Iterator {
    public Item nextItem();
    public Item previousItem();
    public Item currentItem();
    public Item firstItem();
    public Item lastItem();
    public boolean isDone();
    public void setStep(int step);
}
```

```
//... package and import statements

public class ShoppingBasketBuilder
                implements ItemBuilder {

  private List listItems = null;
      |
  public Iterator getIterator() {
    return listItems.iterator();
  }

  public com.item.Iterator getItemIterator() {
    return new ItemsIterator();
  }
}
```

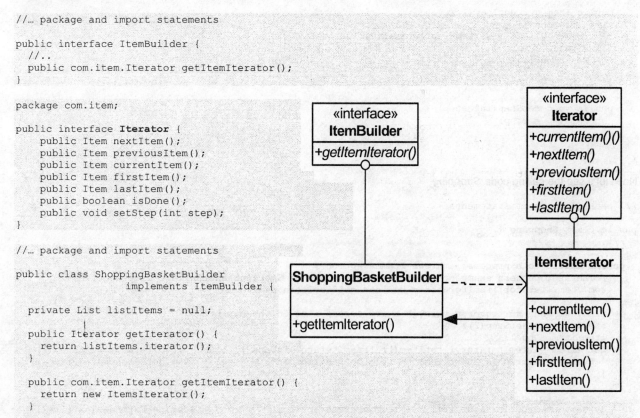

```
/**
 * inner class which iterates over basket of items
 */
class ItemsIterator implements com.item.Iterator {
  private int current = 0;

  private int step = 1;

  public Item nextItem() {
    Item item = null;
    current += step;
    if (!isDone()) {
      item = (Item) listItems.get(current);
    }
    return item;
  }

  public Item previousItem() {
    Item item = null;
    current -= step;
    if (!isDone()) {
      item = (Item) listItems.get(current);
    }
    return item;
  }

  public Item firstItem() {
    current = 0;
    return (Item) listItems.get(current);
  }

  public Item lastItem() {
    current = listItems.size() - 1;
    return (Item) listItems.get(current);
  }

  public boolean isDone() {
    return current >= listItems.size() ? true : false;
  }

  public Item currentItem() {
    if (!isDone()) {
      return (Item) listItems.get(current);
    } else {
      return null;
    }
  }

  public void setStep(int step) {
    this.step = step;
  }
}
}
```

Now, let's see the calling code *Shopping*:

```
//… package & import statements

public class Shopping {
  //..

  public static void process() throws ItemException {
    //Iterator pattern example, inner implementations of ShopingBasketBuilder is protected.
    com.item.Iterator itemIterator = builder.getItemIterator();

    //say we want to traverse through every second item in the basket
    itemIterator.setStep(2);
    Item item = null;
    for (item = itemIterator.firstItem(); !itemIterator.isDone(); item = itemIterator.nextItem()) {
      System.out.println("nextItem:" + item.getDescription() + "==>" + item.getExtendedTaxPrice());
    }

    item = itemIterator.lastItem();
    System.out.println("lastItem: " + item.getDescription() + "==> " + item.getExtendedTaxPrice());
```

```
        item = itemIterator.previousItem();
        System.out.println("previousItem:" + item.getDescription()+ "=>" + item.getExtendedTaxPrice());
    }
}
```

The output is:

```
--------------- steps through every 2nd item in the basket -----------------------
nextItem: Book - IT ====> 12.0
nextItem: Cosmetics - Lipstick ====> 1.1
lastItem: CD - JAZZ IMPORTED ====> 17.25
previousItem : CD - JAZZ====>16.5
```

Scenario: The XYZ Retail buys the items in bulk from warehouses and sells them in their retail stores. All the items sold need to be prepared for retail prior to stacking in the shelves for trade. The preparation involves 3 steps for all types of items, i.e. adding the items to stock in the database, applying barcode to each item and finally marking retail price on the item. The preparation process is common involving 3 steps but each of these individual steps is specific to type of item i.e. *Book*, *CD*, and *Cosmetics*.

Solution: The above functionality can be implemented applying the template method design pattern as shown below:

Template method pattern: When you have a sequence of steps to be processed within a method and you want to defer some of the steps to its subclass then you can use a template method pattern. So the template method lets the subclass to redefine some of the steps.

Example Good example of this is the process() method in the Struts *RequestProcessor* class, which executes a sequence of processXXXX(...) methods allowing the subclass to override some of the methods when required. Refer **Q110** in Enterprise section.

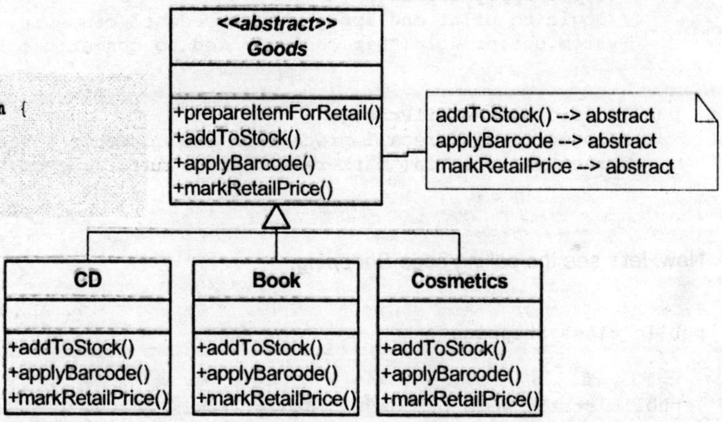

```
//...
public abstract class Goods implements Item {
    //...

    /**
     * The template method
     */
    public void prepareItemForRetail() {
        addToStock();
        applyBarcode();
        markRetailPrice();
    }

    public abstract void addToStock();
    public abstract void applyBarcode();
    public abstract void markRetailPrice();

}


//..
public class Book extends Goods {
    //..

    //following methods gets called by the template method

    public void addToStock() {
        //database call logic to store the book in stock table.
        System.out.println("Book added to stock : " + this.getDescription());
    }

    public void applyBarcode() {
        //logic to print and apply the barcode to book.
        System.out.println("Bar code applied to book : " + this.getDescription());
    }

    public void markRetailPrice() {
        //logic to read retail price from the book table and apply the retail price.
        System.out.println("Mark retail price for the book : " + this.getDescription());
    }
}
```

```
//...
public class CD extends Goods {
  //..
  //following methods gets called by the template method

  public void addToStock() {
      //database call logic to store the cd in stock table.
      System.out.println("CD added to stock : " + this.getDescription());
  }

  public void applyBarcode() {
      //logic to print and apply the barcode to cd.
      System.out.println("Bar code applied to cd : " + this.getDescription());
  }

  public void markRetailPrice() {
      //logic to read retail price from the cd table and apply the retail price.
      System.out.println("Mark retail price for the cd : " + this.getDescription());
  }
}

//...
public class Cosmetics extends Goods {
  //...

  public void addToStock() {
      //database call logic to store the cosmetic in stock table.
      System.out.println("Cosmetic added to stock : " + this.getDescription());
  }

  public void applyBarcode() {
      //logic to print and apply the barcode to cosmetic.
      System.out.println("Bar code applied to cosmetic : " + this.getDescription());
  }

  public void markRetailPrice() {
      //logic to read retail price from the cosmetic table and apply the retail price.
      System.out.println("Mark retail price for the cosmetic : " + this.getDescription());
  }
}
```

Now, let's see the calling code *Shopping*:

```
//...
public class Shopping {
  //...

  public static void process() throws ItemException {
    //...

    Item item = null;
    for (item = itemIterator.firstItem(); !itemIterator.isDone(); item = itemIterator.nextItem()) {
        item.prepareItemForRetail();
        System.out.println("-----------------------------------");
    }
  }
}
```

The output is:

```
------------------ prepareItemForRetail() --------------------------------
Book added to stock : Book - IT
Bar code applied to book : Book - IT
Mark retail price for the book : Book - IT
```

Scenario: The employees of XYZ Retail are at various levels. In a hierarchy, the general manager has subordinates, and also the sales manager has subordinates. The retail sales staffs have no subordinates and they report to their immediate manager. The company needs functionality to calculate salary at different levels of the hierarchy.

Solution: You can apply the **composite design pattern** to represent the XYZ Retail company employee hierarchy.

Composite design pattern: The composite design pattern composes objects into tree structures where individual objects like sales staff and composite objects like managers are handled uniformly. Refer **Q61** in Java section or **Q25** in Enterprise section.

```
/**
 * Base employee class
 */
public abstract class Employee {
    private String name;
    private double salary;

    public Employee(String name, double salary) {
        this.name = name;
        this.salary = salary;
    }

    public String getName() {
        return name;
    }

    public double getSalaries() {
        return salary;
    }

    public abstract boolean addEmployee(Employee emp);
    public abstract boolean removeEmployee(Employee emp);
    protected abstract boolean hasSubordinates();
}
```

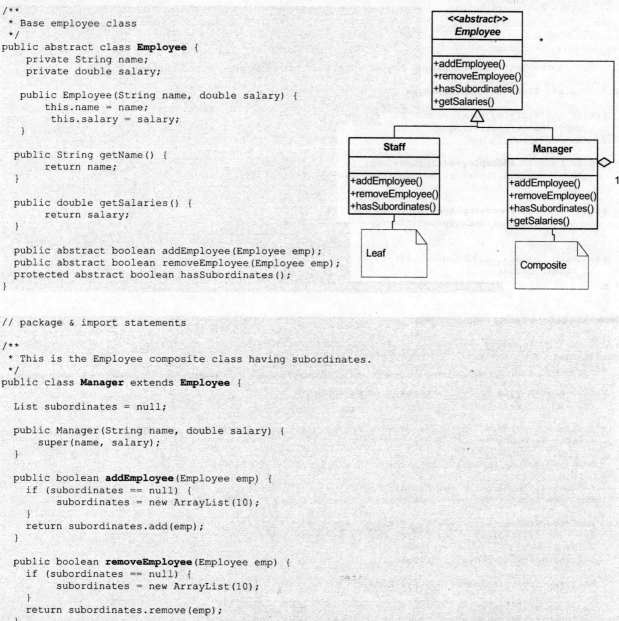

```
// package & import statements

/**
 * This is the Employee composite class having subordinates.
 */
public class Manager extends Employee {

    List subordinates = null;

    public Manager(String name, double salary) {
        super(name, salary);
    }

    public boolean addEmployee(Employee emp) {
        if (subordinates == null) {
            subordinates = new ArrayList(10);
        }
        return subordinates.add(emp);
    }

    public boolean removeEmployee(Employee emp) {
        if (subordinates == null) {
            subordinates = new ArrayList(10);
        }
        return subordinates.remove(emp);
    }

    /**
     * Recursive method call to calculate the sum of salary of a manager and his subordinates, which
     * means sum of salary of a manager on whom this method  was invoked and any employees who
     * themselves will have any subordinates and so on.
     */
    public double getSalaries() {
        double sum = super.getSalaries(); //this one's salary

        if (this.hasSubordinates()) {
        for (int i = 0; i < subordinates.size(); i++) {
            sum += ((Employee) subordinates.get(i)).getSalaries();  // recursive method call
        }
    }
    return sum;
}

public boolean hasSubordinates() {
```

```
        boolean hasSubOrdinates = false;
        if (subordinates != null && subordinates.size() > 0) {
            hasSubOrdinates = true;
        }
        return hasSubOrdinates;
    }
}

/**
 * This is the leaf staff employee object. staff do not have any subordinates.
 */
public class Staff extends Employee {

    public Staff(String name, double salary) {
        super(name, salary);
    }

    public boolean addEmployee(Employee emp) {
        throw new RuntimeException("Improper use of Staff class");
    }

    public boolean removeEmployee(Employee emp) {
        throw new RuntimeException("Improper use of Staff class");
    }

    protected boolean hasSubordinates() {
        return false;
    }
}
```

Now, let's see the calling code *Shopping*:

```
//...
public class Shopping {
    //.....

    public static void process() throws ItemException {
        //....

        System.out.println("----------------- Employee hierachy & getSalaries() recursively ---------");
        //Employee hierachy

        Employee generalManager = new Manager("John Smith", 100000.00);

        Employee salesManger = new Manager("Peter Rodgers", 80000.00);
        Employee logisticsManger = new Manager("Graham anthony", 90000.00);

        Employee staffSales1 = new Staff("Lisa john", 40000.00);
        Employee staffSales2 = new Staff("Pamela watson", 50000.00);
        salesManger.addEmployee(staffSales1);
        salesManger.addEmployee(staffSales2);

        Employee logisticsTeamLead = new Manager("Cooma kumar", 70000.00);

        Employee staffLogistics1 = new Staff("Ben Sampson", 60000.00);
        Employee staffLogistics2 = new Staff("Vincent Chou", 20000.00);
        logisticsTeamLead.addEmployee(staffLogistics1);
        logisticsTeamLead.addEmployee(staffLogistics2);

        logisticsManger.addEmployee(logisticsTeamLead);

        generalManager.addEmployee(salesManger);
        generalManager.addEmployee(logisticsManger);

        System.out.println(staffSales1.getName() + "-->" + staffSales1.getSalaries());
        System.out.println(staffSales2.getName() + "-->" + staffSales2.getSalaries());

        System.out.println("Logistics dept " + " --> " + logisticsManger.getSalaries());

        System.out.println("General Manager " + " --> " + generalManager.getSalaries());
    }
}
```

The output is:

```
-------------------- Employee hierachy & getSalaries() recursively -------------
Lisa john-->40000.0
Pamela watson-->50000.0
Logistics dept  --> 240000.0
General Manager  --> 510000.0
```

Scenario: The purchasing staffs (aka logistics staff) of the XYZ Retail Company need to **interact with other subsystems** in order to place purchase orders. They need to communicate with their stock control department to determine the stock levels, also need to communicate with their wholesale supplier to determine availability of stock and finally with their bank to determine availability of sufficient funds to make a purchase.

Solution: You can apply the façade design pattern to implement the above scenario.

Façade pattern: The façade pattern provides an interface to large subsystems of classes. A common design goal is to minimize the communication and dependencies between subsystems. One way to achieve this goal is to introduce a façade object that provides a single, simplified interface.

```java
public class StockControl {
  public boolean isBelowReorderpoint(Item item) {
    //logic to evaluate stock level for item
    return true;
  }
}
```

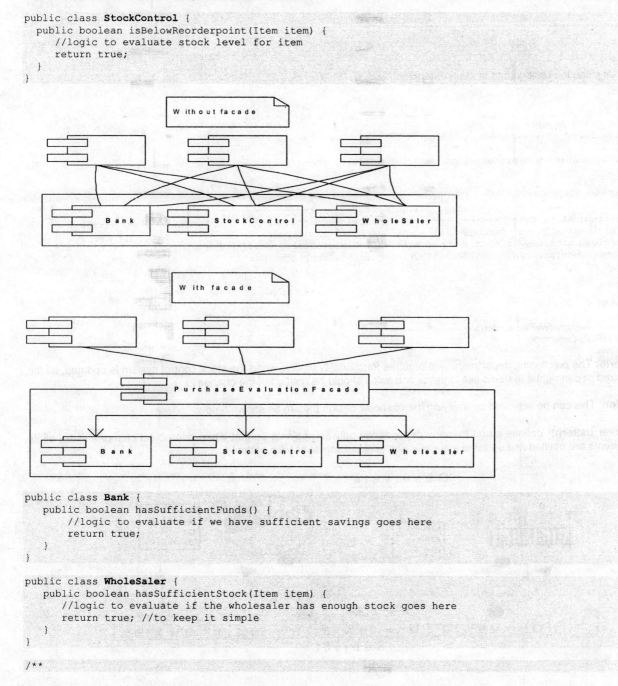

```java
public class Bank {
   public boolean hasSufficientFunds() {
      //logic to evaluate if we have sufficient savings goes here
      return true;
   }
}
```

```java
public class WholeSaler {
   public boolean hasSufficientStock(Item item) {
      //logic to evaluate if the wholesaler has enough stock goes here
      return true; //to keep it simple
   }
}
```

```
/**
```

```
 * This is the facade class
 */
public class PurchaseEvaluation {

  private StockControl stockControl = new StockControl();
  private WholeSaler wholeSaler = new WholeSaler();
  private Bank bank = new Bank();

  public boolean shouldWePlaceOrder(Item item) {
    if (!stockControl.isBelowReorderpoint(item)) {
        return false;
    }

    if (!wholeSaler.hasSufficientStock(item)) {
        return false;
    }

    if (!bank.hasSufficientFunds()) {
        return false;
    }

    return true;
  }
}
```

Now, let's see the calling code or class *Shopping*:

```
//....

public class Shopping {
  //.......

  public static void process() throws ItemException {

    //....

    //----------------------facade design pattern ---------------------------------
    System.out.println("---------------------shouldWePlaceOrder-------------------------------");
    PurchaseEvaluation purchaseEval = new PurchaseEvaluation();
    boolean shouldWePlaceOrder = purchaseEval.shouldWePlaceOrder(item);
    System.out.println("shouldWePlaceOrder=" + shouldWePlaceOrder);
  }
}
```

The output is:

```
-------------------shouldWePlaceOrder()------------------------
shouldWePlaceOrder=true
```

Scenario: The purchasing department also requires functionality where, when the stock control system is updated, all the registered departmental systems like logistics and sales should be notified of the change.

Solution: This can be achieved by applying the observer design pattern as shown below:

Observer pattern: defines a one-to-many dependency between objects so that when one object changes state, all its dependents are notified and updated automatically. (aka publish-subscribe pattern)

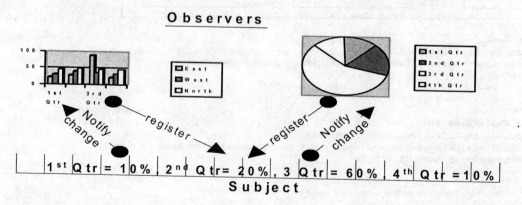

```java
/**
 * This is an observer (aka subscriber) interface. This gets notified through its update method.
 */
public interface Department {
    public void update(Item item, int qty);
}

public class LogisticsDepartment implements Department {
    public void update(Item item, int qty) {
      //logic to update department's stock goes here
      System.out.println("Logistics has updated its stock for " + item.getDescription() +
                                              " with qty=" + qty);
    }
}

public class SalesDepartment implements Department {
    public void update(Item item, int qty) {
      //logic to update department's stock goes here
      System.out.println("Sales has updated its stock for " + item.getDescription() +
                                              " with qty=" + qty);
    }
}
```

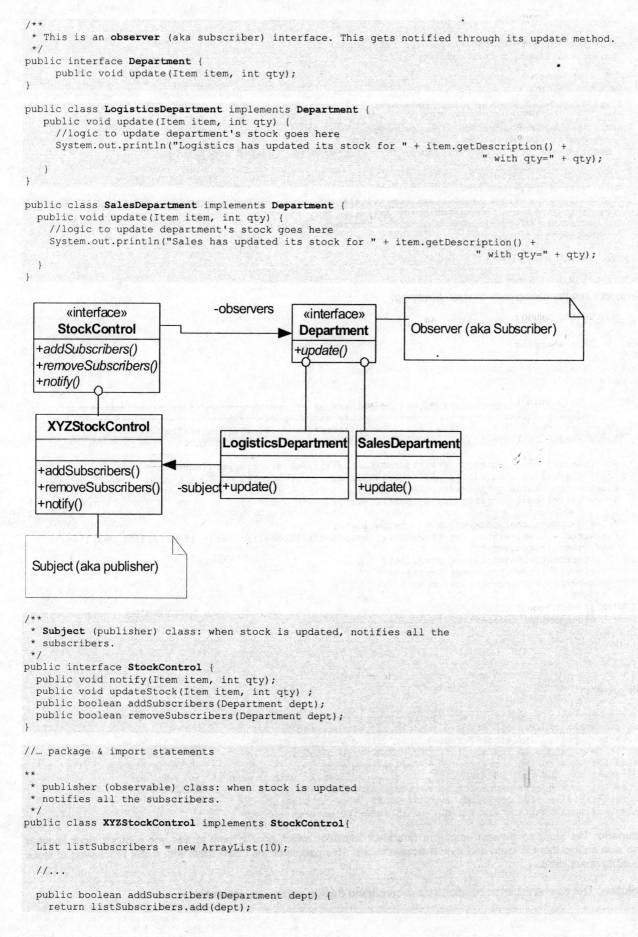

```java
/**
 * Subject (publisher) class: when stock is updated, notifies all the
 * subscribers.
 */
public interface StockControl {
  public void notify(Item item, int qty);
  public void updateStock(Item item, int qty) ;
  public boolean addSubscribers(Department dept);
  public boolean removeSubscribers(Department dept);
}

//… package & import statements

**
 * publisher (observable) class: when stock is updated
 * notifies all the subscribers.
 */
public class XYZStockControl implements StockControl{

  List listSubscribers = new ArrayList(10);

  //...

  public boolean addSubscribers(Department dept) {
    return listSubscribers.add(dept);
```

```
  }

  public boolean removeSubscribers(Department dept) {
    return listSubscribers.remove(dept);
  }

  /**
   * writes updated stock qty into databases
   */
  public void updateStock(Item item, int qty) {
    //logic to update an item's stock goes here
    notify(item, qty); //notify subscribers that with the updated stock info.
  }

  public void notify(Item item, int qty) {
    int noOfsubscribers = listSubscribers.size();
    for (int i = 0; i < noOfsubscribers; i++) {
      Department dept = (Department) listSubscribers.get(i);
      dept.update(item, qty);
    }
  }
}
```

Now, let's see the calling code or class *Shopping*:

```
// package & import statements

public class Shopping {
  //..............
  public static void process() throws ItemException {
    //.........

    //----------------------observer design pattern----------------------------------------
    System.out.println("--------------------notify stock update---------------------------");
    Department deptLogistics = new LogisticsDepartment(); //observer/subscriber
    Department salesLogistics = new SalesDepartment(); //observer/subscriber

    StockControl stockControl = new XYZStockControl();//observable/publisher
    //let's register subscribers with the publisher
    stockControl.addSubscribers(deptLogistics);
    stockControl.addSubscribers(salesLogistics);

    //let's update the stock value of the publisher
    for (item = itemIterator.firstItem(); !itemIterator.isDone(); item = itemIterator.nextItem()) {
      if (item instanceof CD) {
        stockControl.updateStock(item, 25);
      } else if (item instanceof Book){
        stockControl.updateStock(item, 40);
      }
      else {
        stockControl.updateStock(item, 50);
      }
    }
  }
}
```

The output is:

```
--------------------notify stock update---------------------------
Logistics has updated its stock for Book - IT with qty=40
Sales has updated its stock for Book - IT with qty=40
Logistics has updated its stock for CD - JAZZ with qty=25
Sales has updated its stock for CD - JAZZ with qty=25
Logistics has updated its stock for Cosmetics - Lipstick with qty=50
Sales has updated its stock for Cosmetics - Lipstick with qty=50
Logistics has updated its stock for CD - JAZZ IMPORTED with qty=25
Sales has updated its stock for CD - JAZZ IMPORTED with qty=25
```

Scenario: The stock control staff require a simplified calculator, which enable them to add and subtract stock counted and also enable them to undo and redo their operations. This calculator will assist them with faster processing of stock counting operations.

Solution: This can be achieved by applying the **command design pattern** as shown below:

Command pattern: The *Command* *pattern* is an object behavioral pattern that allows you to achieve complete decoupling between the sender and the receiver. A *sender* is an object that invokes an operation, and a *receiver* is an object that receives the request to execute a certain operation. With *decoupling,* the sender has no knowledge of the Receiver's interface. The term *request* here refers to the command that is to be executed. The Command pattern also allows you to vary when and how a request is fulfilled. At times it is necessary to issue requests to objects without knowing anything about the operation being requested or the receiver of the request. In procedural languages, this type of communication is accomplished via a call-back: a function that is registered somewhere to be called at a later point. Commands are the object-oriented equivalent of call-backs and encapsulate the call-back function.

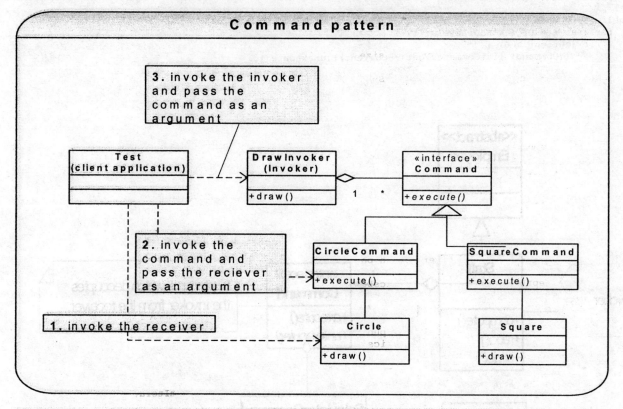

```
// package & import statements

/**
 * Invoker
 */
public class Staff extends Employee {

  private Calculator calc = new Calculator();
  private List listCommands = new ArrayList(15);
  private int current = 0;

  public Staff(String name) {
      super(name);
  }

  //...
  /**
   * make use of command.
   */
  public void compute(char operator, int operand) {
      Command command = new CalculatorCommand(calc, operator, operand);//initialise the calculator
      command.execute();
      //add commands to the list so that undo operation can be performed
      listCommands.add(command);
      current++;
  }

  /**
   * perform redo operations
   */
```

```
public void redo(int noOfLevels) {
    int noOfCommands = listCommands.size();
    for (int i = 0; i < noOfLevels; i++) {
        if (current < noOfCommands) {
            ((Command) listCommands.get(current++)).execute();
        }
    }
}

/**
 * perform undo operations
 */
public void undo(int noOfLevels) {
    for (int i = 0; i < noOfLevels; i++) {
        if (current > 0) {
            ((Command) listCommands.get(--current)).unexecute();
        }
    }
}
}
```

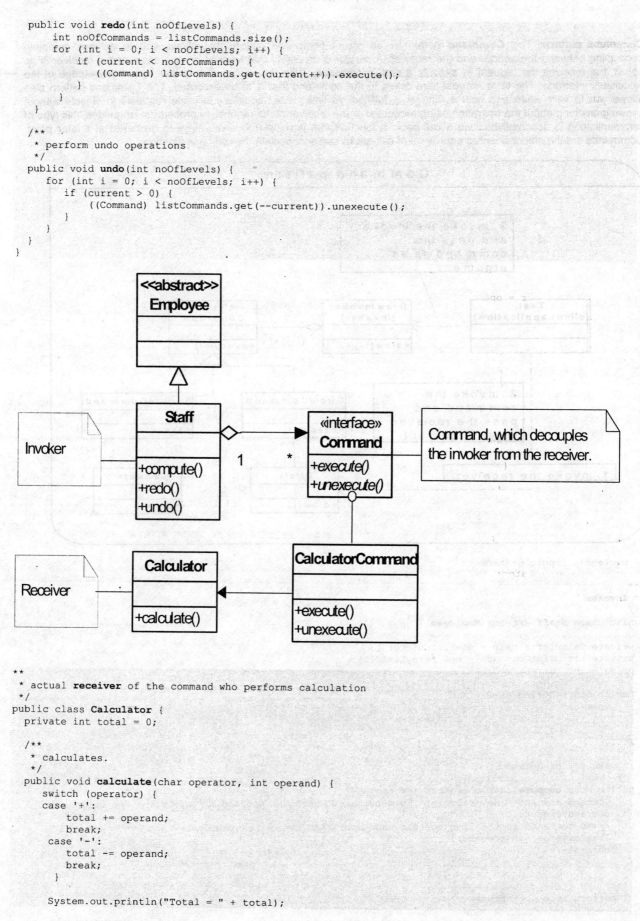

```
**
 * actual receiver of the command who performs calculation
 */
public class Calculator {
  private int total = 0;

  /**
   * calculates.
   */
  public void calculate(char operator, int operand) {
      switch (operator) {
      case '+':
          total += operand;
          break;
      case '-':
          total -= operand;
          break;
      }

      System.out.println("Total = " + total);
```

```
    }
}

/**
 * command interface
 */
public interface Command {
    public void execute();
    public void unexecute();
}


/**
 * calculator command, which decouples the receiver Calculator from the invoker Staff
 */

public class CalculatorCommand implements Command {
    private Calculator calc = null;
    private char operator;
    private int operand;

    public CalculatorCommand(Calculator calc, char operator, int operand) {
        this.calc = calc;
        this.operator = operator;
        this.operand = operand;
    }

    public void execute() {
        calc.calculate(operator, operand);
    }

    public void unexecute() {
        calc.calculate(undoOperand(operator), operand);
    }

    private char undoOperand(char operator) {
        char undoOperator = ' ';
        switch (operator) {
        case '+':
          undoOperator = '-';
          break;

        case '-':
          undoOperator = '+';
          break;
        }
        return undoOperator;
    }
}
```

Now, let's see the calling code class *Shopping*:

```
//..............
public class Shopping {
  //...........
  public static void process() throws ItemException {

      //----------------------------command design pattern----------------------------
      System.out.println("------------Calculator with redo & undo operations----------------------");
      Staff stockControlStaff = new Staff("Vincent Chou");

      stockControlStaff.compute('+',10);//10
      stockControlStaff.compute('-',5);//5
      stockControlStaff.compute('+',10);//15
      stockControlStaff.compute('-',2);//13

      //lets try our undo operations
      System.out.println("---------------undo operation : 1 level--------------------------");
      stockControlStaff.undo(1);
      System.out.println("---------------undo operation : 2 levels--------------------------");
      stockControlStaff.undo(2);

      //lets try our redo operations
      System.out.println("---------------redo operation : 2 levels--------------------------");
      stockControlStaff.redo(2);
```

```
    System.out.println("--------------redo operation : 1 level-------------------------");
    stockControlStaff.redo(1);
  }
}
```

The output is:

```
--------------Calculator with redo & undo operations----------------------
Total = 10
Total = 5
Total = 15
Total = 13
--------------undo operation : 1 level--------------------------
Total = 15
--------------undo operation :2 levels--------------------------
Total = 5
Total = 10
--------------redo operation : 2 levels--------------------------
Total = 5
Total = 15
--------------redo operation : 1 level--------------------------
Total = 13
```

Scenario: The XYZ Retail has a 3rd party software component called *XYZPriceList*, which implements an interface PriceList. This 3rd party software component is not thread-safe. So far it performed a decent job since only the sales manager had access to this software component. The XYZ Retail now wants to provide read and write access to all the managers. The source code is not available and only the API is available, so modifying the existing component is not viable. This will cause a dirty read problem if two managers try to concurrently access this component. For example, if the sales manager tries to access an item's price while the logistics manger is modifying the price (say modification takes 1 second), then the sales manager will be reading the wrong value. Let's look at this with a code sample:

```
public interface PriceList {
    public  double getPrice(int itemId) ;
    public void setPrice(int itemId,double newPrice) ;
}

//...
public class XYZPriceList implements PriceList{

    private static final Map mapPrices = new HashMap(30,.075f);
    public static PriceList singleInstance =  new XYZPriceList();//only one instance

    /**
     * static initializer block
     */
    static {
      //only one item is added to keep it simple
      mapPrices.put(new Integer(1), new Double(12.00));//Book - IT
      //... add more items to price list
    }

    public static PriceList getInstance() {
      return singleInstance;
    }

    public  double getPrice(int itemId) {
      double price = ((Double)mapPrices.get(new Integer(itemId))).doubleValue();
      System.out.println("The price of the itemId " + itemId + " = "+ price);
      return price;
    }

    public  void setPrice(int itemId,double newPrice) {
        System.out.println("wait while mutating price from 12.0 to 15.00 ...........");
        try {
            // transient value while updating with a proper value, just to illustrate the effect
            // of concurrent access
            mapPrices.put(new Integer(itemId),new Double(-1));
            Thread.sleep(1000);//assume update/set operation takes 1 second
            mapPrices.put(new Integer(itemId),new Double(newPrice));

        } catch (InterruptedException ie) {}
    }
}
```

```
«interface»
PriceList
+getPrice()
+setPrice()
        △
        |
XYZPriceList

+getPrice()
+setPrice()
```

The multi-threaded access class:

```java
public class PriceListUser implements Runnable {

  int itemId;
  double price;
  static int count = 0;

  public PriceListUser(int itemId) {
    this.itemId = itemId;
  }

  /**
   * runnable code where multi-threads are executed
   */
  public void run() {
    String name = Thread.currentThread().getName();

    if (name.equals("accessor")) {
        price = XYZPriceList.getInstance().getPrice(itemId); //using 3rd party commponent

    } else if (name.equals("mutator")) {
        XYZPriceList.getInstance().setPrice(itemId, 15.00); //using 3rd party commponent
    }
  }
}
```

Now, let's see the calling code or class *Shopping*:

```java
//....
public class Shopping {
  //....
  public static void process() throws ItemException {
    //..........

    //------------------------------------proxy design pattern--------------------------------
    System.out.println("---------------Accessing the price list---------------------------");

    PriceListUser user1 = new PriceListUser(1);//accessing same itemId=1
    PriceListUser user2 = new PriceListUser(1);//accessing same itemId=1

    Thread t1 = new Thread(user1);
    Thread t2 = new Thread(user2);
    Thread t3 = new Thread(user1);

    t1.setName("accessor");//user 1 reads the price
    t2.setName("mutator");//user 2 modifies the price
    t3.setName("accessor");//user 1 reads the price

    t1.start(); // accessor user-1 reads before mutator user-2 modifies the price as 12.00
    t2.start(); // mutator user-2 sets the price to 15.00
    t3.start(); // while the user-2 is setting the price to 15.00 user-1 reads again and gets the
                // price as 12.00
    //user-2 gets the wrong price i.e gets 12.0 again instead of 15.00
  }
}
```

The output is:

```
---------------Accessing the price list---------------------------
The price of the itemId 1 = 12.0
wait while mutating price from 12.0 to 15.00 ...........
The price of the itemId 1 = -1.0
                        OR
---------------Accessing the price list---------------------------
wait while mutating price from 12.0 to 15.00 ...........
The price of the itemId 1 = -1.0
The price of the itemId 1 = -1.0
```

Problem: You get one of the two outputs shown above depending on how the threads initialized by the operating system. The first value of 12.0 is okay and the second value of 12.0 again is a **dirty read** because the value should have been modified to 15.0 by the user-2. So the user-1 reading the value for the second time should get the value of 15.0 after it has been modified.

Solution: This threading issue and inability to modify the existing component can be solved by applying the **proxy design pattern**. You will be writing a proxy class, which will apply the locking for the entries in the *XYZPriceList*. This proxy class internally will be making use of the *XYZPriceList* in a synchronized fashion as shown below:

Proxy pattern: Provides a surrogate or placeholder for another object to control access to it. Proxy object acts as an intermediary between the client and the target object. The proxy object has the same interface as the target object. The proxy object holds reference to the target object. There are different types of proxies:

- **Remote Proxy**: provides a reference to an object, which resides in a separate address space. e.g. EJB, RMI, CORBA etc (RMI stubs acts as a proxy for the skeleton objects.)

- **Virtual Proxy**: Allows the creation of memory intensive objects on demand. The target object will not be created until it is really needed.

- **Access Proxy**: Provides different clients with different access rights to the target object.

Example In Hibernate framework (Refer **Q15 - Q16** in Emerging Technologies/Frameworks section) lazy loading of persistent objects are facilitated by virtual proxy pattern. Say you have a *Department* object, which has a collection of *Employee* objects. Let's say that *Employee* objects are lazy loaded. If you make a call department.getEmployees() then Hibernate will load only the employeeIDs and the version numbers of the *Employee* objects, thus saving loading of individual objects until later. So what you really have is a collection of proxies not the real objects. The reason being, if you have hundreds of employees for a particular department then chances are good that you will only deal with only a few of them. So, why unnecessarily instantiate all the *Employee* objects? This can be a big performance issue in some situations. So when you make a call on a particular employee i.e. employee.getName() then the proxy loads up the real object from the database.

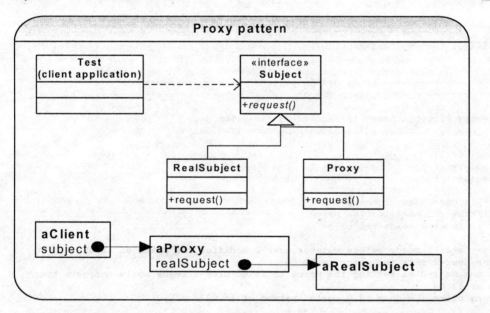

```
/**
 * synchronized proxy class for XYZPriceList
 */
public class XYZPriceListProxy implements PriceList {
//assume that we only have two items in the pricelist
Integer[] locks = { new Integer(1), new Integer(2) };//locks for each item in the price list

public static PriceList singleInstance = new XYZPriceListProxy();//single instance of XYZPriceListProxy

PriceList realPriceList = XYZPriceList.getInstance(); // real object

public static PriceList getInstance() {
    return singleInstance;
}

public double getPrice(int itemId) {
    synchronized (locks[itemId]) {
        return realPriceList.getPrice(itemId);
    }
}
```

```
}
public void setPrice(int itemId, double newPrice) {
    synchronized (locks[itemId]) {
        realPriceList.setPrice(itemId, newPrice);
    }
}
}
```

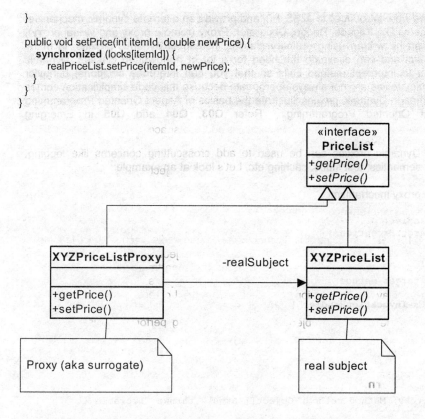

You should make a slight modification to the *PriceListUser* class as shown below in bold.

```
public class PriceListUser implements Runnable {

    int itemId;
    double price;
    static int count = 0;

    public PriceListUser(int itemId) {
        this.itemId = itemId;
    }

    /**
     * runnable code where multi-threads are executed
     */
    public void run() {
        String name = Thread.currentThread().getName();

        if (name.equals("accessor")) {
            price = XYZPriceListProxy.getInstance().getPrice(itemId);

        } else if (name.equals("mutator")) {
            XYZPriceListProxy.getInstance().setPrice(itemId, 15.00);
        }
    }
}
```

Running the same calling code *Shopping* will render the following correct results by preventing dirty reads:

```
---------------Accessing the price list----------------------------
The price of the itemId 1 = 12.0
wait while mutating price from 12.0 to 15.00 ...........
The price of the itemId 1 = 15.0
                    OR
---------+------Accessing the price list----------------------------
wait while mutating price from 12.0 to 15.00 ...........
The price of the itemId 1 = 15.0
The price of the itemId 1 = 15.0
```

What is a dynamic proxy? Dynamic proxies were introduced in J2SE 1.3, and provide an alternate dynamic mechanism for implementing many common design patterns like Façade, Bridge, Decorator, Proxy (remote proxy and virtual proxy), and Adapter. While all of these patterns can be written using ordinary classes instead of dynamic proxies, in many situations dynamic proxies are more compact and can eliminate the need for a lot of handwritten classes. Dynamic proxies are reflection-based and allow you to intercept method calls so that you can interpose additional behavior between a class caller and its callee. Dynamic proxies are not always appropriate because this code simplification comes at a performance cost due to reflection overhead. Dynamic proxies illustrate the basics of Aspect Oriented Programming (AOP) which complements your Object Oriented Programming. Refer **Q03, Q04** and **Q05** in Emerging Technologies/Frameworks section.

Where can you use dynamic proxies? Dynamic proxies can be used to add crosscutting concerns like logging, performance metrics, memory logging, retry semantics, test stubs, caching etc. Let's look at an example:

InvocationHandler interface is the heart of a proxy mechanism.

```java
import java.lang.reflect.InvocationHandler;
import java.lang.reflect.InvocationTargetException;
import java.lang.reflect.Method;

/**
 * Handles logging and invocation of target method
 */
public class LoggingHandler implements InvocationHandler {

        protected Object actual;

        public LoggingHandler(Object actual) {
                this.actual = actual;
        }

        public Object invoke(Object proxy, Method method, Object[] args)  throws Throwable {
                try {
                        System.out.println(">>>>>>start executing method: " + method.getName());
                        Object result = method.invoke(actual, args);
                        return result;
                } catch (InvocationTargetException ite) {
                        throw new RuntimeException(ite.getMessage());
                } finally {
                        System.out.println("<<<<<<finished executing method: " + method.getName());
                }
        }
}
```

Let's define the actual interface and the implementation class which adds up two integers.

```java
public interface Calculator {
     public int add(int i1, int i2);
}
```

```java
public class CalculatorImpl implements Calculator {

        public int add(int i1, int i2) {
                final int sum = i1 + i2;
                System.out.println("Sum is : " + sum);
                return sum;
        }
}
```

Factory method class *CalculatorFactory*, which uses the dynamic proxies when logging, is required.

```java
import java.lang.reflect.InvocationHandler;
import java.lang.reflect.Proxy;

/**
 * singleton factory
 */
public class CalculatorFactory {

        private static CalculatorFactory singleInstance = null;
        private CalculatorFactory() {}

        public static CalculatorFactory getInstance() {
```

```
        if (singleInstance == null) {
            singleInstance = new CalculatorFactory();
        }
        return singleInstance;
    }

    public Calculator getCalculator(boolean withLogging) {

        Calculator c = new CalculatorImpl();

        //use dynamic proxy if logging is required, which logs your method calls
        if (withLogging) {
            //invoke the handler, which logs and invokes the target method on the Calculator
            InvocationHandler handler = new LoggingHandler(c);

            //create a proxy
            c = (Calculator) Proxy.newProxyInstance(c.getClass().getClassLoader(),
                                            c.getClass().getInterfaces(), handler);
        }

        return c;
    }
}
```

Finally the test class:

```
import java.lang.reflect.InvocationHandler;
import java.lang.reflect.Proxy;

public class TestProxy {

    public static void main(String[] args) {
        System.out.println("===============Without dynamic proxy=============");
        Calculator calc = CalculatorFactory.getInstance().getCalculator(false);
        calc.add(3, 2);

        System.out.println("===============With dynamic proxy===============");
        calc = CalculatorFactory.getInstance().getCalculator(true);
        calc.add(3, 2);
    }
}
```

The output is:

```
===============Without dynamic proxy=============
Sum is : 5
===============With dynamic proxy===============
>>>>>>start executing method: add
Sum is : 5
<<<<<<finished executing method: add
```

Pattern	Description
Adapter pattern	Sometimes a library cannot be used because its interface is not compatible with the interface required by an application. Also it is possible that you may not have the source code for the library interface. Even if you had the source code, it is not a good idea to change the source code of the library for each domain specific application. This is where you can use an adapter design pattern. Adapter lets classes work together that could not otherwise because of incompatible interfaces. This pattern is also known as a wrapper.
Bridge pattern	Refer **Q41** in Enterprise section.
Chain of responsibility pattern	Refer **Q22** in Enterprise section

Useful links:

- http://www.allapplabs.com/Java_design_patterns/creational_patterns.htm
- http://www.patterndepot.com/put/8/JavaPatterns.htm
- http://www.javaworld.com/columns/jw-Java-design-patterns-index.shtml
- http://www.onjava.com/pub/a/onjava/2002/01/16/patterns.html?page=1
- http://www.corej2eepatterns.com/index.htm
- http://www.theserverside.com/books/wiley/EJBDesignPatterns/index.tss

▪   http://www.martinfowler.com/eaaCatalog/

Q 12: How would you go about designing a Web application where the business tier is on a separate machine from the presentation tier. The business tier should talk to 2 different databases and your design should point out the different design patterns? FAQ

A 12: The following diagram shows the various components at different tiers.

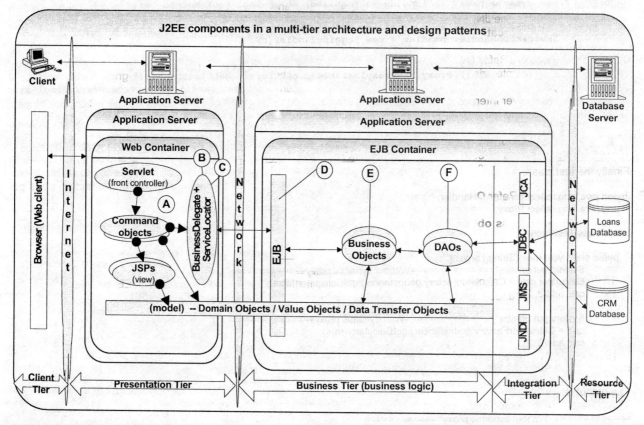

Design patterns:

A → denotes Web tier design patterns:

Model-View-Controller (MVC) design pattern: MVC stands for Model-View-Controller architecture. It divides the functionality of displaying and maintaining of the data to minimize the degree of coupling (i.e. promotes loose coupling) between components. It is often used by applications that need the ability to maintain multiple views like html, wml, JFC/Swing, XML based Web service etc of the same data. Multiple views and controllers can interface with the same model. Even new types of views and controllers can interface with a model without forcing a change in the model design. Refer **Q 03** in Enterprise section.

Front controller design pattern: The MVC pattern can be further improved and simplified by using the Front Controller pattern with command objects. The Front Controller pattern uses a single servlet, which acts as initial point of contact for handling all the requests, including invoking services such as security (authentication and authorization), logging, gathering user input data from the request, gathering data required by the view etc by delegating to the **helper classes**, and managing the choice of an appropriate view with the **dispatcher classes**. These helper and dispatcher classes are generally instances of a command design pattern (Refer **Q11** in How would you about... section) and therefore usually termed as **command objects**. The **Front Controller** pattern improves manageability, and improves reusability by moving common behavior among command objects into the centralized controller or controller managed helper classes. Also refer **Q 24** in Enterprise section.

Composite view design pattern: This will enable reuse of JSP sub-views and improves maintainability by having to change them at one place only. Refer **Q25** in Enterprise section.

View Helper: When processing logic is embedded inside the controller or view it causes code duplication in all the pages. This causes maintenance problems, as any change to piece of logic has to be done in all the views. In the view helper pattern the view delegates its processing responsibilities to its helper classes. Refer **Q25** in Enterprise section.

Service to Worker and **Dispatcher View:** Refer **Q25** in Enterprise section.

B → Use a **Business Delegate** design pattern to reduce the coupling between the presentation tier components and the business services tier components. Refer **Q83** in Enterprise sections.

C → The JNDI look-up is expensive because the client needs to get a network connection to the server first. So this look-up process is expensive and redundant. To avoid this expensive and redundant process, service objects can be cached when a client performs the JNDI look-up for the first time and reuse that service object from the cache for the subsequent look-ups. The **service locator** pattern implements this technique. Refer **Q87** in Enterprise section.

D → EJBs use **proxy** (Refer **Q62** in Java section) design pattern. Avoid fine-grained method calls by creating a **value object** (Refer **Q85** in Enterprise section) design pattern, which will help the client, make a coarse-grained call. Also use a **session façade** (Refer **Q84** in Enterprise section) design pattern to minimize network overheads and complexities between the client server interactions. For faster data access for read-only data of large resultsets use a **fast-lane reader** (Refer **Q86** in Enterprise section) design pattern.

D, E, F → Use **factory pattern** to reduce the coupling or the dependencies between the calling code (e.g. EJB etc) and called code like business objects, handler objects, data access objects etc. This is a very powerful and common feature in many frameworks. Refer **Q52** in Java section. When writing your factory class, it does not make sense to create a new factory object for each invocation. So use a **singleton** design pattern to have a single instance of the factory class per JVM per class loader. Refer **Q51** in Java section.

F → Use the **data access object** design pattern to promote the design concept of code to interface not implementation, so that the implementation can change without affecting the calling code.

Q 13: How would you go about determining the enterprise security requirements for your Java/J2EE application?
A 13: It really pays to understand basic security terminology and J2EE security features. Let's look at them:

Some of the key security concepts are:

- ❑ Authentication
- ❑ Authorization (J2EE declarative & programmatic)
- ❑ Data Integrity
- ❑ Confidentiality and privacy
- ❑ Non-repudiation and auditing

Terminology	Description
Authentication	Authentication is basically an identification process. Do I know who you are? **Terminology used for J2EE security:** **Principal:** An entity that can be identified and authenticated. For example an initiator of the request like a user. **Principal name:** Identity of a principal like user id. **Credential:** Information like password or certificate, which can authenticate a principal. **Subject:** A set of principals and their credentials associated with a thread of execution. **Authentication:** The process by which a server verifies the identity presented by a user through username/userid and password or certificate. For example the username and password supplied by the user can be validated against an LDAP server or a database server to verify he is whom he claims to be. **Authentication methods:** ❑ **Basic/Digest authentication:** Browser specific and password is encoded using Base-64 encoding. Digest is similar to basic but protects the password through encryption. This is a simple **challenge-response** scheme where the client is challenged for a user id and password. The Internet is divided into *realms*. A realm is supposed to have one user repository (e.g. LDAP or Database) so a combination of user id and password is unique to that realm. The user challenge has the name of the realm so that users with different user ids and password on different systems know which one to apply. Lets look at a HTTP user challenge format

```
WWW-Authenticate: Basic realm="realm_name"
```

The user-agent (i.e. Web browser) returns the following HTTP header field

```
Authorization: Basic userid:password
```
With **Basic authentication** the user id and password string, which is base64 encoded. The purpose of base64 is to avoid sending possibly unprintable or control characters over an interface that expects text characters. It does not provide any security because the clear text can be readily restored (i.e. decoded).

With **Digest authentication** the server challenges the user with a "nonce", which is an unencrypted random value. The user responds with a **checksum** (typically MD5 hash) of the user id, password, the "nonce" and some other data. The server creates the same checksum from the user parameters like userid, password, the nonce etc available in the user registry. If both the checksums match then it is assumed that the user knows the correct password.

❑   **Form-based authentication**: Most Web applications use the form-based authentication since it allows applications to customize the authentication interface. Uses base64 encoding, which can expose username and password unless all connections are over SSL. (Since this is the most common let us look at in greater detail under Authorization).

❑   **Certificate based authentication**: Uses PKI and SSL. This is by far the most secured authentication method. A user must provide x.509 certificate to authenticate with the server.

Authorization	Authorization is the process by which a program determines whether a given identity is permitted to access a resource such as a file or an application component. **Now that you are authenticated, I know who you are?** But <u>Are you allowed to access the resource or component you are requesting</u>?
	
	Terminology used for J2EE security:
	
	Authorization: Process of determining what type of access (if any) the security policy allows to a resource by a principal.
	
	Security role: A logical grouping of users who share a level of access permissions.
	
	Security domain: A scope that defines where a set of security policies are maintained and enforced. Also known as security policy domain or realm.
	
	J2EE uses the concept of **security roles** for both declarative and programmatic access controls. This is different from the traditional model, which is **permission-based** (for example UNIX file system security where resources like files are associated with a user or group who might have permission to read the file but not execute).
	
	Let us look at some differences between permission based and role based authorization
	
	Permission-based authorization: Typically in **permission-based** security both users and resources are defined in a registry (e.g. LDAP or Database) and the association of users and groups with the resources takes place through **Access Control Lists** (ACL). The maintenance of registry and ACLs requires a security administrator.
	
	Role based authorization: In J2EE role based model, the users and groups of users are still stored in a user registry (e.g. LDAP or Database). A mapping must also be provided between **users and groups** to the **security constraints**. This can exist in a registry or **J2EE applications themselves can have their own role based security constraints** defined through deployment descriptors like web.xml, ejb-jar.xml, and/or application.xml. So the applications themselves do not have to be defined by a security administrator.
	
	Now let's look at **role based authorization** in a bit more detail:
	
	J2EE has both a **declarative** and **programmatic** way of <u>protecting individual method of each component</u> (Web or EJB) by specifying, which security role can execute it.
	
	❑ Refer **Q23** in Enterprise section.
	❑ Refer **Q81** in Enterprise section
	❑ Also refer **Q7** in Enterprise section for the *deployment descriptors* where **<security-role>** are defined.
	
	Let's look at the commonly used form-based authentication and authorization in a bit more detail.
	
	STEP:1 The **web.xml** defines the type of authentication mechanism
	
	<code><login-config>
	  <auth-method>FORM</auth-method>
	    <realm-name>FBA</realm-name></code>

```
        <form-login-config>
            <form-login-page>myLogon</form-login-page>
            <form-error-page>myError</form-error-page>
        </form-login-config>
</login-config>
```

STEP: 2 The user creates a form that must contain fields for username, password etc as shown below. The names should be as shown for fields in bold:

```
<form method="POST" action="j_security_check">
    <input type="text" name="j_username">
    <input type="text" name="j_password">
</form>
```

STEP: 3 Set up a security realm to be used by the container. Since LDAP or database provide flexibility and ease of maintenance, Web containers have support for different types of security realms like LDAP, Database etc.

For example Tomcat Web container uses the server.xml to set up the database as the security realm.

```
<realm classname="org.apache.catalina.realm.JDBCRealm" debug="99"
    drivername="org.gjt.mm.mysql.Driver"
    connectionurl="jdbc:mysql://localhost/tomcatusers?user=test;password=test"
    usertable="users" usernamecol="user_name" usercredcol="user_pass"
    userroletable="user_roles" rolenamecol="role_name"/>
```

You have to create necessary tables and columns created in the database.

STEP: 4 Set up the security constraints in the web.xml for authorization.

```
<security-constraint>
    <web-resource-collection>
        <web-resource-name>PrivateAndSensitive</web-resource-name>
        <url-pattern>/private/*</url-pattern>
    </web-resource-collection>
    <auth-constraint>
        <role-name>executive</role-name>
        <role-name>admin</role-name>
    </auth-constraint>
</security-constraint>
```

The Web containers perform the following steps to implement security when a protected Web resource is accessed:

Step 1: Determine whether the user has been authenticated.

Step 2: If the user has not been already authenticated, request the user to provide security credentials by redirecting the user to the login page defined in the web.xml as per Step-1 & Step-2 described above.

Step 3: Validate the user credentials against the **security realm** set up for the container.

Step 4: Determine whether the authenticated user is **authorized** to access the Web resource defined in the deployment descriptor web.xml. Web containers enforce authorization on a page level. For fine grained control programmatic security can be employed using

    request.getRemoteUser(), request.isUserInRole(), request.getUserPrincipal() etc

Note: Web containers can also propagate the authentication information to EJB containers.

Data integrity	Data integrity helps to make sure if something is **intact and not tampered with** during transmission.

Checksums: Simply adds up the bytes within a file or a request message. If the checksums match the integrity is maintained. The weakness with the simplest form of checksum is that some times junks can be added to make sums equal like

```
ABCDE == EDCBA
```

There are more sophisticated checksums like **Adler-32**, **CRC-32** (refer java.util.zip package), which are designed to address the above weakness by considering not only the value of each byte but also its position.

Cryptography hashes: This uses a mathematical function to create a small result called **message digest** from the input message. Difficult to create false positives. Common hash functions are **MD5, SHA** etc.

	Data [e.g. Name is Peter]→**MD5 iterative hash function** →**Digest** [e.g. f31d120d3] It is <u>not possible to change the message digest back to its original data</u>. You can only compare two message digests i.e. one came with the client's message and the other is recomputed by the server from sent message. If both the message digests are equal then the message is intact and has not been tampered with.
Confidentiality and Privacy	The confidentiality and privacy can be accomplished through encryption. Encryption can be: **Symmetric or private-key:** This is based on a single key. This requires the sender and the receiver to share the same key. Both must have the key. The sender encrypts his message with a private key and the receiver decrypts the message with his own private key. This system is not suitable for large number of users because it requires a key for every pair of individuals who need to communicate privately. As the number of participants increases then number of private keys required also increases. So a company which wants to talk to 1000 of its customers should have 1000 private keys. Also the private keys need to be transmitted to all the participants, which has the vulnerability to theft. **The advantages of the symmetric encryption are its computational efficiency and its security.** **Asymmetric or public-key infrastructure (PKI):** This is based on a pair of mathematically related keys. One is a public key, which is distributed to all the users, and the other key is a private key, which is kept secretly on the server. So this requires only two keys to talk to 1000 customers. This is also called Asymmetric encryption because **the message encrypted by public key can only be decrypted by the private key** and the message encrypted by the private key can only be decrypted by the public key. In a public key encryption anybody can create a key pair and publish the public key. So we need to verify the owner of the public key is who you think it is. So the creator of this false public key can intercept the messages intended for someone else and decrypt it. To protect this public key systems provide mechanisms for validating the public keys using **digital signatures** and **digital certificates.** **Digital signature:** A digital signature is a stamp on the data, which is unique and very difficult to forge. A **digital signature has 2 steps** and establishes 2 things from the security perspective. **STEP 1:** To sign a document means hashing software (e.g. MD5, SHA) will crunch the data into just a few lines by the process called '**hashing**'. These few lines are called **message digest**. <u>It is not possible to change the message digest back to its original data.</u> Same as what we saw above in cryptography hashes. **This establishes whether the message has been modified between the time it was digitally signed and sent and time it was received by the recipient.** **STEP 2:** Computing the digest can verify the integrity of the message but does not stop from someone intercepting it or **verifying the identity of the signer.** This is where encryption comes into picture. Signing the message with the private key will be useful for proving that the message must have come from the user who claims to have signed it. **The second step in creating a digital signature involves encrypting the digest code created in STEP 1 with the sender's private key.** When the message is received by the recipient the following steps take place: 1. Recipient recomputes the digest code for the message. 2. Recipient decrypts the signature by using the sender's public key. This will yield the original digest code of the sender. 3. Compare the original and the recomputed digest codes. If they match then the message is both intact and signed by the user who claims to have signed it (i.e. authentic). **Digital Certificates:** A certificate represents an organization in an official digital form. This is equivalent to an electronic identity card which serves the purpose of ❑ Identifying the owner of the certificate. This is done with authenticating the owner through trusted 3rd parties called the certificate authorities (CA) e.g. Verisign etc. The CA digitally signs these certificates. When the user presents the certificate the recipient validates it by using the digital signature. ❑ Distributing the owner's public key to his/her users (or recipients of the message). The **server certificates** let visitors to your website exchange personal information like credit card number etc with the server with the confidence that they are communicating with intended site and not the rogue site impersonating the intended site. Server certificates are must for e-commerce sites. **Personal certificate**s let you authenticate a visitor's identity and restrict access to specified content to particular visitors. Personal certificates are ideal for business-to business communication where offering partners and suppliers have special access to your website. A certificate includes details about the owner of the certificate and the issuing CA. A certificate includes: ❑ Distinguished name (DN) of the owner, which is a unique identifier. You need the following for the DN:

	<ul><li>Country Name (C)</li><li>State (ST)</li><li>Locality (L)</li><li>Organization Name (O)</li><li>Organization Unit (OU)</li><li>Common Name (CN)</li><li>Email Address.</li></ul>
	❑ Public key of the owner.
	❑ The issue date of the certificate.
	❑ The expiry date of the certificate.
	❑ The distinguished name of the issuing CA.
	❑ The digital signature of the issuing CA.
	
	Now lets look at the core concept of the certificates:
	
	STEP 1: The owner makes a request to the CA by submitting a certificate request with the above mentioned details. The certificate request can be generated with tool like OpenSSL REQ, Java keytool etc. This creates a certreq.perm file, which can be transferred to CA via FTP.
	
	```-----BEGIN NEW CERTIFICATE REQUEST-----```
	```MIIBJTCB0AIBADBtMQswCQYDVQQGEwJVUzEQMA4GA1UEChs4lBMHQXJpem9uYTEN```
	```A1UEBxMETWVzYTEfMB0GA1UEChMWTWVs3XbnzYSBDb21tdW5pdHkgQ29sbGVnZTE```
	```A1UEAxMTd3d3Lm1jLm1hcmljjb3BhLmVkdTBaMA0GCSqGSIb3DQEBAQUAA0kAMEYC```
	```------END NEW CERTIFICATE REQUEST-----```
	
	STEP 2: The CA takes the owner's certificate request and creates a message 'm' from the request and signs the message 'm' with CA's private key to create a separate signature 'sig'. The message 'm' and the signature 'sig' form the certificate, which gets sent to the owner.
	
	STEP 3: The owner then distributes both parts of the certificate (message 'm' and signature 'sig') to his customers (or recipients) after signing the certificate with owner's private key.
	
	STEP 4: The recipient of the certificate (i.e. the client) extracts the certificate with owner's public key and subsequently verifies the signature 'sig' using CA's public-key. If the signature proves valid, then the recipient accepts the public key in the certificate as the owner's key.

Non-repudiation and auditing	Proof that the sender actually sent the message. It also prohibits the author of the message from falsely denying that he sent the message. This is achieved by record keeping the exact time of the message transmission, the public key used to decrypt the message, and the encrypted message itself. Record keeping can be complicated but critical for non-repudiation.
Secure Socket Layer (SSL)	Secure Socket Layer (SSL) uses a combination of symmetric and asymmetric (public-key) encryption to accomplish confidentiality, integrity, authentication and non-repudiation for Internet communication. In a nutshell SSL uses public key encryption to confidentially transmit a session key which can be used to conduct symmetric encryption. SSL uses the public key technology to negotiate a shared session key between the client and the server. The public key is stored in an X.509 certificate that usually has a digital signature from a trusted 3rd party like Verisign. Lets look at the handshake sequence where the server and the client negotiate the cipher suite to be used, establish a shared session key and authenticate server to the client and optionally client to the server. ❑ Client requests a document from a secure server https://www.myapp.com.au. ❑ The server sends its X.509 certificate to the client with its public key stored in the certificate. ❑ The client checks whether the certificate has been issued by a CA it trusts. ❑ The client compares the information in the certificate with the site's public key and domain name. ❑ Client tells the server what cipher suites it has available. ❑ The server picks the strongest mutually available ciphers suite and notifies the client. ❑ The client generates a **session key** (symmetric key or private key) and encrypts it using the server's public key and sends it to the server. ❑ The server receives the encrypted session key and decrypts it using its private key. ❑ The client and server use the session key to encrypt and decrypt the data they send to each other.

Q. What advise would you give a server side Web developer wanting to ensure that his/her code was secure from external attacks?

Security flaws in Web applications easily bypass firewalls and other basic security measures. In addition to using some of the security measures discussed above like authentication, authorization, encryption and certificates with HTTPS (i.e. HTTP + SSL) etc, it is possible to unwittingly create a Web application that allows outside access. Attackers can easily tamper any part of the HTTP request like URL, cookies, form fields, hidden fields, headers etc before submitting the request. There are some common names like **cross site scripting**, **SQL injection**, **hidden field manipulation**, **cookie poisoning**, etc for input tampering attacks.

- **Use HTTP post as opposed to HTTP get:** HTTP get sends sensitive information as a query string appended to your URL, which can be easily tampered with to determine any security holes in your web application. HTTP post is more secured due to hiding sensitive information from your URL query string.
- **Strip any unwanted special characters and tags.** Cross site scripting is by far the most common vulnerability in Web applications. This occurs when a hacker changes your URL, form fields, hidden fields, or cookie parameters to create an error or to view unauthorized information. There are dangers like:

  - Having special meta characters such as "&, >, !, $" in your browser input data have special meaning to many operating systems (e.g. "<" means read input from a file) .

  - Some applications allow users to format their input with HTML tags such as <B></B> etc. This also allows users to insert JavaScript and DHTML tags. These user created HTML can have malicious scripts, applet references, and other techniques to access files, delete files, steal information etc.

  The best practice to prevent the above mentioned security vulnerability is to strip any unwanted characters and HTML tags from user input.

  - Perform rigorous positive input data validation. Positive input validation means checking the input data against a list of valid characters like A-Z and 0-9 etc as opposed to checking for any invalid characters because it is too difficult to determine all possible malicious characters. Each input parameter should be checked against a strict format that specifies exactly what input will be allowed like data type (e.g. String, int etc), allowed character set (e.g. A-Z 0-9 etc), minimum and maximum lengths, numeric range, specific legal values (enumeration), specific patterns (regular expressions), null is allowed or not, duplicate values, required parameter or not, etc.

  - Perform server-side validation because client side validation can be easily by passed by the attacker. Client side validation should be used mainly for quick user responsiveness. Any client side validation should be revalidated on the server side.

  - Have a centralized code for input validation because scattered code is hard to maintain.

- **Handle your exceptions properly without revealing any sensitive information about your datasources, table names etc,** which could help them create a SQL injection attack (Refer **Q46** in Enterprise section). Catch all your exceptions and display harmless error messages to users and hackers alike.

- **Protect your Web resources like JSP files, HTML files, pdfs, css, script files etc behind the WEB-INF directory.** Refer **Q35** in Enterprise section.

- **Avoid using hidden fields, cookies etc to store sensitive state information.** Refer **Q10** in Enterprise section. HTML hidden fields are not hidden and not secure. Users can see them by simply viewing the HTML source of your form in their browser and also easy for a hacker to change the hidden fields and resubmit the edited form.

- Prefer prepared statements over statements to prevent any **SQL injection attacks**. Refer **Q46** in Enterprise section.

Q 14: How would you go about describing the open source projects like JUnit (unit testing), Ant (build tool), CVS (version control system) and log4J (logging tool) which are integral part of most Java/J2EE projects?

A 14: JUnit, ANT and CVS are integral part of most Java/J2EE projects. JUnit for <u>unit testing</u>, ANT for <u>build and deployment</u>, and CVS for <u>source control</u>. Let's look at each, one by one. I will be covering only the key concepts, which can be used as a reference guide in addition to being handy in interviews.

JUnit

This is a regression testing framework, which is used by developers who write unit tests in Java. **Unit testing** is relatively inexpensive and easy way to produce better code faster. Unit testing exercises testing of a very small specific functionality. To run JUnit you should have JUnit.jar in your classpath.

```
Unix:  CLASSPATH=$CLASSPATH:/usr/Java/packages/junit3.8.1/JUnit.jar
Dos:  CLASSPATH=%CLASSPATH%;C:\junit3.8.1/JUnit.jar
```

JUnit can be coded to run in two different modes as shown below:

Per test mode	Per suite setup (more common)

Per test mode

The per test mode will call the setUp() method before executing every test case and tearDown() method after executing every test case. Let's look at an example: CO

```java
import junit.framework.TestCase;
public class SampleTest extends TestCase {

  Object o = null;

  public SampleTest(String method) {
    super(method);
  }

  protected void setUp() {
    System.out.println("running setUp()");
    //Any database access code
    //Any set up code
    o = new Object();
  }

  protected void tearDown() {
    System.out.println("running tearDown()");
    //Any clean up code
    o = null;
  }

  public void testCustomer() {
    System.out.println("running testCustomer()");
    assertNotNull("check if it is null", o);
  }

  public void testAccount() {
    System.out.println("running testAccount()");
    if (someCondition == false)
      fail( "failed condition …. ");
  }

  public static Test suite() {
    TestSuite suite = new TestSuite();
    // in order of test execution
    suite.addTest(new SampleTest("testCustomer"));
    suite.addTest(new SampleTest("testAccount"));

    return suite;
  }

}
```

as per the above example the execution sequence is as follows:

```
running setUp()
running testAccount()
running tearDown()
running setUp()
running testCustomer()
running tearDown()
```

Per suite setup (more common)

In this mode the setUp() and tearDown() will be executed only once: CO

```java
import junit.framework.*;
import junit.extensions.*;
public class SampleTest2 extends TestCase {

  Object o = null;

  public SampleTest2(String method) {
    super(method);
  }

  public void testCustomer() {
    System.out.println("running testCustomer()");
    assertNotNull("check if it is null", o);
  }

  public void testAccount() {
    System.out.println("running testAccount()");
  }

  public static Test suite() {
    TestSuite suite = new TestSuite();

    suite.addTest(new SampleTest2("testCustomer"));
    suite.addTest(new SampleTest2("testAccount"));

    TestSetup wrapper = new TestSetup(suite) {

      protected void setUp() {
        oneTimeSetUp();
      }

      protected void tearDown() {
        oneTimeTearDown();
      }
    };
    return wrapper;
  }

  public static void oneTimeSetUp() {          // runs only once
    System.out.println("running setUp()");
  }

  public static void oneTimeTearDown () {       // runs only once
    System.out.println("running tearDown ()");
  }
}
```

as per the above example the execution sequence is as follows:

```
running setUp()
running testCustomer()
running testAccount()
running tearDown()
```

Q. How do you handle exceptions in JUnit? CO

Wrong approach	Right approach

```java
public void testUser( ) throws DelegateException { // bad
  try {
    executeSomeMethodThatCanThrowAnException (….);
  }
  catch(DelegateException ex) {
    ex.printStackTrace ( … );
  }
}
```

```java
public void testUser( ) {
  try {
    executeSomeMethodThatCanThrowAnException (….);
  }
  catch(DelegateException ex) {
    ex.printStackTrace ( … );
    fail (ex.getMessage ( )) ;  // good
  }
}
```

How to run JUnit?

```
Text mode: java -cp <junit.jar path> junit.textui.TestRunner
Graphics mode: java -cp <junit.jar path> junit.swingui.TestRunner
```

The smallest groupings of test expressions are the **methods** that you put them in. Whether you use JUnit or not, you need to put your test expressions into Java methods, so you might as well group the expressions, according to any criteria you want, into methods. An object that you can run with the JUnit infrastructure is a *Test*. But you can't just implement **Test** and run that object. You can only *run* specially created instances of **TestCase**. A **TestSuite** is just an object that contains an ordered list of runnable **Test** objects. **TestSuites** also implement **Test** and are runnable. **TestRunners** execute **Tests**, **TestSuites** and **TestCases**.

ANT (Another Niche Tool)

Ant is a tool which helps you build, test, and deploy (Java or other) applications. ANT is a command-line program that uses a XML file (i.e. build.xml) to describe the build process. The build.xml file describes the various tasks ant has to complete. ANT is a very powerful, portable, flexible and easy to use tool. Ant has the following command syntax:

```
ant [ant-options] [target 1] [target 2]  [....target n]
```

Some ant options are:

```
-help, -h              : print list of available ant-options (i.e. prints this message)
-verbose               : be extra verbose
-quiet                 : be extra quiet
-projecthelp , -p      : print project help information
-buildfile  <file>         : use given build file
-logger <classname>    : class which is to perform logging
-D<property=value>     : use value for given property
-propertyfile <name>   : load all properties from file with -D properties taking precedence.
-keep-going, -k        : execute all targets that do not depend on failed targets
... and more
```

Let's look at a simple build.xml file:

```
?xml version="1.0" encoding="UTF-8"?>
<project name="MyProject" default="compile" basedir=".">

 <property name="src" value=".\src\" />
 <property name="build" value=".\classes\" />

 <target name="init">
  <mkdir dir="${build}" />
 </target>

 <target name="compile" description="compiles the packages" depends="init">
  <javac srcdir="${src}" destdir="${build}" optimize="on" debug="on">
    <classpath>
       <pathelement location="${build}" />
    </classpath>
   </javac>
 </target>

 <target name="clean" description="cleans the build directory">
   <delete dir="${build}" />
 </target>

</project>
```

We can run the above with one of the following commands

```
$ ant compile
$ ant clean compile
$ ant -b build.xml compile
```

Now lets look at some of the key concepts:

Concept	Explanation with example
Ant Targets	An Ant build file contains one **project**, which itself contains multiple **targets**. Each target contains **tasks**. Targets can depend on each other, so building one target may cause others to be built first. From the above build.xml file example

name: Name of the target to run.

description: A target determines whether the target defined as internal or public based on description. If the description attribute is defined then it is public and otherwise it is internal. In the above example targets compile and clean are public. The target init is internal. When you run the following command option, only the public targets are displayed.

```
ant -projecthelp
```

depends: The target "compile" depends on the target "init". So the target init will be run before target compile is run.

If: If the given property has been defined then the target will be executed.

```
<target name="A" if="somePropertyName1">
    <echo message="I am in target A">
</target>
```

unless: If the given property is **not defined** then the target will be executed.

```
<target name="B" unless="somePropertyName2">
    <echo message="I am in target B">
</target>
```

Ant delegates work to other targets as follows:

```
<target name="build" depends="prepare">
    <antcall target="compile"  />
    <antcall target="jar"  />
</target>
```

Ant tasks

Ant task is where real work is done. A task can take any number of attributes. Ant tasks can be categorized as follows:

- ❑ **Core tasks**: Tasks that are shipped with core distribution like <javac ...>, <jar ...> etc
- ❑ **Optional tasks**: Tasks that require additional jar files to be executed like <ftp ....> etc
- ❑ **User defined tasks**: Tasks that are to be developed by users by extending Ant framework.

For example <javac > is a task.

```
<javac srcdir="${src}" destdir="${build}" optimize="on" debug="on">
    <classpath>
        <pathelement location="${build}" />
    </classpath>
</javac>
```

Ant data types

Ant data types are different to the ones in other programming languages. Lets look at some of the ant data types.

description:

```
<project default="deploy" basedir=".">
    <description> This is my project</description>
</project>
```

patternset:

? → matches a single character
* → matches 0 or more characters
** → matches 0 or more directory recursively

```
<patternset id="classfile">
  <include name="**/*.class" />
  <exclude name="**/*Test*.class" />
</patternset>
```

dirset:

```
<dirset dir="${build.dir}">
  <patternset id="classfile">
    <include name="**/classes" />
    <exclude name="**/*Test*" />
  </patternset>
</dirset>
```

fileset:

```
<fileset dir="${build.dir}">
  <include name="**/*.Java" />
  <exclude name="**/*Test*" />
</fileset>
```

filelist, filemapper,filterchain,filterreader, selectors, xmlcatalogs etc

---

Let's look at some key tasks where:

Ant updates data from repository.

Carries out unit tests with JUnit.

Builds a jar file if JUnit is success.

Email the results with the help of Ant loggers and listeners.

Fetch code updates from CVS:

```
<target name="cvsupdate" depends="prepare">
  <cvspass cvsroot="${CVSROOT}" passwd="${rep.passwd}" />
  <cvs cvsRoot="${CVSROOT}" command="update -p -d"  failOnError="true" />
</target>
```

Run unit tests with JUnit:

```
<target name="test" depnds="compile">
   <junit failureproperty="${testsFailed}" >
     <classpath>
          <pathelement path="${classpath}" />
          <pathelement path="${build.dir.class}" />
     </classpath>
     <formatter type="xml"/>
     <test name="mytests.testall" todir="${reports.dir}" />
   </junit>
</target>
```

Creating a jar file:

```
<target name="jar" depnds="test" unless="testsFailed">
    <jar destfile="${build.dir}/${name}.jar" basedir="${build.dir}"
                                       include="**/*.class" />
</target>
```

Email the results with the help of loggers:

Now let's look at how we can e-mail the run results. Ant has **listeners** and **loggers**. A listener is a component that is alerted to certain events during the life of a build. A logger is built on top of the listener and is the component that is responsible for logging details about the build. The listeners are alerted to 7 different events like build started, build finished, target started, target finished, task started, task finished and message logged.

The loggers are more useful and interesting. You are always using a logger when you run ant (i.e. DefaultLogger). You can specify the logger as shown below:

```
ant -logger org.apache.tools.ant.listener.MailLogger
```

You can also specify other loggers like XmlLogger, Log4Jlistener etc.

The MailLogger logs whatever information comes its way and then sends e-mail. A group of properties must be set for a MailLogger which can be passed on to ant as a standard commandline Java option <i.e. – DmailLogger.mailhost="blah.com" > or the <property ...> statements in the init target. Let's look at some of the properties to be set:

```
MailLogger.mailhost
MailLogger.from
MailLogger.failure.notify → whether to send an e-mail on build failure.
MailLogger.success.notify → whether to send an e-mail on build success.
MailLogger.fail.to
MailLogger.success.to
```

Note: Maven is a software project management and comprehension tool, which is gaining popularity. Maven is based on the concept of project object model (**POM**), and it can manage a project's build process, reporting and documentation from a centralized piece of information. Maven provides a uniform build system where by requiring a single set of Ant build files that can be shared by all projects using Maven. Maven provides following information about your project: Change logs from your repository information, cross referenced sources, source metrics, mailing lists, developer lists, dependency lists, unit test reports including coverage etc.

CVS

CVS is a version control or tracking system. It maintains records of files through their development and allows retrieval of any stored version of a file, and supports production of multiple versions.

```
cvs [cvs-options] command [command-options-arguments]
```
CVS allows you to split the development into 2 or more parts called a trunk (MAIN) and a branch. You can create 1 or more branches. Typically a branch is used for bug fixes and trunk is used for future development. Both the trunk and branches are stored in the same repository. This allows the change from branch (i.e. bug fixes) to ultimately or periodically be merged into the main trunk ensuring that all bug fixes get rolled into next release.

Unlike some other version control systems, CVS instead of locking files to prevent conflicts (i.e. when 2 developers modifying the same file) it simply allows multiple developers to work on the same file. Subsequently with the aid of cvs file merging feature it allows you to merge all the changes into one file. The benefits of version control systems like CVS include:

- Any stored revision of a file can be retrieved to be viewed or changed.
- Differences between 2 revisions can be displayed.
- Patches can be created automatically.
- Multiple developers can simultaneously work on the same file.
- Project can be branched into multiple streams for varied tasks and then branches can be merged back into trunk (aka **MAIN**).
- Also supports distributed development and can be configured to record commit messages into a bug tracking system.

Let's look at some of the key concepts and commands.

Concept	Explanation with examples

Building a repository	The repository should be built on a partition that is backed up and won't shut down. The repositories are stored under '**cvsroot**' i.e. /var/lib/cvsroot or /cvsroot. The command to set up the chosen directory as a CVS repository:
	
	`$ cvs -d /var/lib/cvsroot`
	
	Let's look at some command line examples:
	
	`$ mkdir /var/lib/cvsroot`
	`$ chgrp team /var/lib/cvsroot`
	`$ chmod g+srwx /var/lib/cvsroot`
	`$ cvs -d /var/lib/cvsroot`

Importing projects	After creating a repository you can import a project or a related collection of files stored under a single directory by using the following command:
	
	`cvs [-d <repository-path>] import <project_name> <vendor_tag> <related_tag>`
	
	Let's look at some command line examples:
	
	`$ cd /tmp`
	`$ mkdir ProjectX`
	`$ touch ProjectX/File1.Java`
	`$ touch ProjectX/File2.Java`
	`$ touch ProjectX/File3.Java`
	`$ cd ProjectX`
	`$ cvs -d /var/lib/cvsroot import ProjectX INITIAL start`

Creating a **sandbox**, checking out and updating files from cvs repository into a **sandbox**	Copy of the files, which gets checked out by the client from the cvs repository, is called a **sandbox**. The user can manipulate the files within the sandbox and when the files have been modified they can be resubmitted into the repository with the changes. Let's look at how to create a sandbox (i.e. a client working copy):
	
	`$ cd /myLocalCopy`
	`$ cvs -d /var/lib/cvsroot checkout ProjectX`
	
	The above command will result in creating a subdirectory called ProjectX under the present working directory "/myLocalCopy".

	Subsequently to keep the sandbox in sync with the repository, an update command can be executed. The update command checks your checked-out cvs sandbox against the cvs repository and down loads any changed files into the sandbox from the repository. `cvs  update -d`

Adding files into cvs repository from a sandbox.	To add file from sandbox into cvs repository you should create a file first.
	
	`$ touch file3`
	`$ cvs add file3`
	`$ cvs commit`
	
	To add directories and files
	
	`$ cvs add design plan design/*.rtf  plan/*.rtf`

Checking file stats and help	`$ cvs [cvs-options] stats [command-option] <filename>`
	`$ cvs -help`
	`$ cvs rlog ProjectX`

Removing a file from the cvs repository.	To remove a file from the repository, first remove the file from the sandbox directory and then run the cvs command.
	
	`$ rm file3`
	`$ cvs remove file3`
	`$ cvs commit`

Moving or renaming files	To move or rename files:
	
	`$ mv file1 file101`
	`$ cvs remove file1`
	`$ cvs add file101`
	`$ cvs commit`

Releasing a sandbox	CVS release should be used before deleting a sandbox. CVS first checks whether there are any files with uncommitted changes. `$ cvs release`

Tagging files	Tagging is a way of marking a group of file revisions as belong together. If you want to look at all the file revisions belonging to a tag the cvs will use the tag string to locate all the files.
	
	To tag files in the repository
	
	`$ cvs -d /var/lib/cvsroot rtag -r HEAD  release_1 ProjectX`
	
	To tag files in the sandbox
	
	`$ cvs tag release_1`

Removing tags	To remove a tag from sandbox.
	
	`$ cvs tag -d release_1 file1`
	
	To remove a tag from repository.
	
	`$ cvs rtag -d release_1 file1`

Retrieving files based on past revisions instead of the latest files.	We have already looked at how to checkout latest code. What if we want to checkout by a revision?
	
	`$ cvs checkout -r Tagname  ProjectX`
	
	To update by revision
	
	`$ cvs update -d  -r release_1`

Creating branches	Branches can be added to the repository tree in order to allow different development paths to be tried, or to add parallel development of code to different base versions.

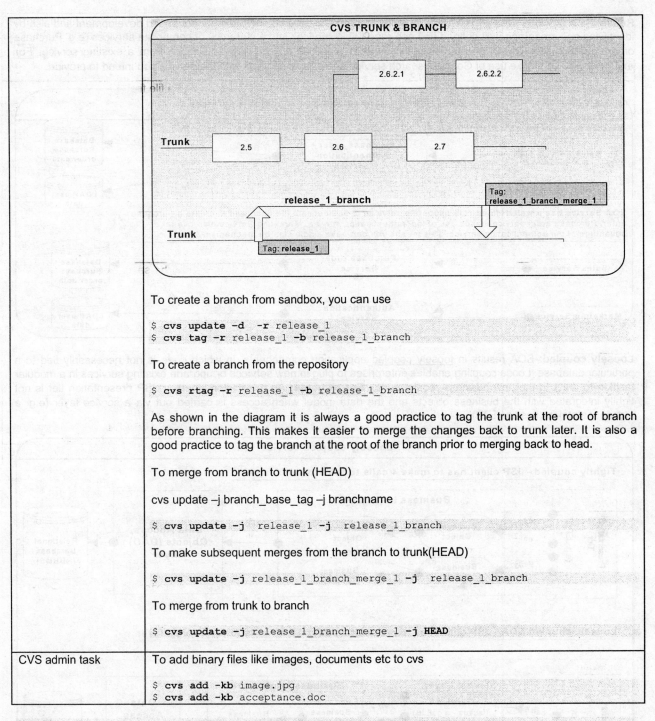

To create a branch from sandbox, you can use

```
$ cvs update -d  -r release_1
$ cvs tag -r release_1 -b release_1_branch
```

To create a branch from the repository

```
$ cvs rtag -r release_1 -b release_1_branch
```

As shown in the diagram it is always a good practice to tag the trunk at the root of branch before branching. This makes it easier to merge the changes back to trunk later. It is also a good practice to tag the branch at the root of the branch prior to merging back to head.

To merge from branch to trunk (HEAD)

cvs update –j branch_base_tag –j branchname

```
$ cvs update -j  release_1 -j  release_1_branch
```

To make subsequent merges from the branch to trunk(HEAD)

```
$ cvs update -j release_1_branch_merge_1 -j  release_1_branch
```

To merge from trunk to branch

```
$ cvs update -j release_1_branch_merge_1 -j HEAD
```

CVS admin task	To add binary files like images, documents etc to cvs
	
	`$ cvs add -kb image.jpg`
	`$ cvs add -kb acceptance.doc`

Log4J

Refer **Q126** in Enterprise section.

Q 15: How would you go about describing Service Oriented Architecture (**SOA**) and Web services? FAQ
A 15: This book would not be complete without mentioning **SOA** and **Web services**.

Q. What is a Service Oriented Architecture (SOA)? SOA is an evolution of the fundamentals governing a component based development. Component based development provides an opportunity for greater code reuse than what is possible with Object Oriented (**OO**) development.

Reuse: SOA provides even <u>greater code reuse</u> by utilizing OO development, component based development and also by identifying and organizing <u>well-defined</u> and <u>non-repeatable</u> services into a hierarchy of composite services (e.g. Purchase order service makes use of an authentication service). You can build a new application from a existing service. For example: you can make use of Google's search service and eBay's services with the service you intend to provide.

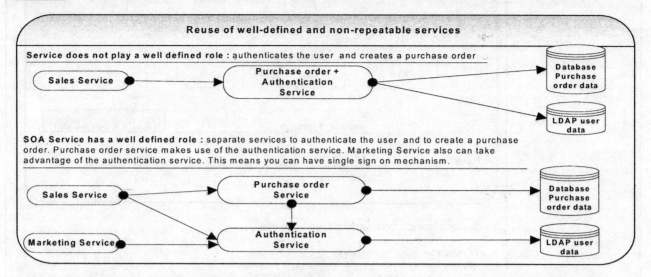

Loosely coupled: SOA results in <u>loosely coupled</u> application components, in which code is not necessarily tied to a particular database. Loose coupling enables enterprises to plug in new services or upgrade existing services in a modular fashion to react to the new business requirements. For example: An application where a JSP presentation tier is not tightly integrated with the business objects and the data model when access is carried out via a service layer (e.g. a façade -- stateless session EJB).

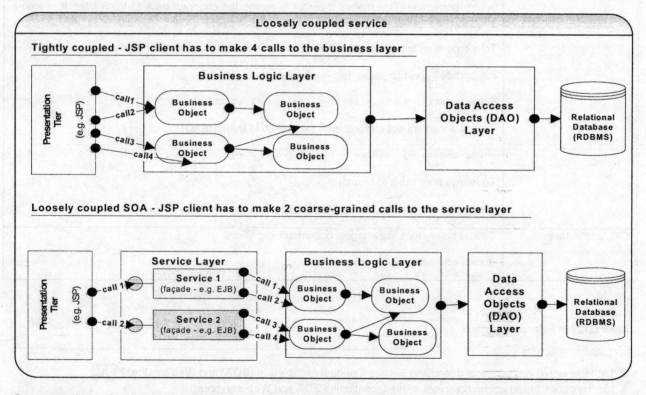

Coarse grained: Services are also should be <u>coarse grained</u> (i.e. should be a business level service. fine grained services can not only adversely affect performance but also result in tight coupling). For example: You may have a *purchase* component with individual methods to create a purchase order, add line items, and a customer component to set the customer information etc. Invoking these individual methods locally would not cause any problem but if you use remote service calls then performance problems can be evident. The solution is for the service to provide a single method call to create an order, add line items and set the customer details using a **façade design pattern** by receiving a single DTO (Data Transfer Object) or an XML containing the full data structure for the entire order.

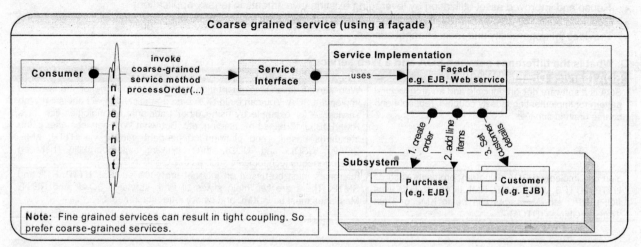

Note: SOAs are very popular and there is a huge demand exists for development and implementation of SOAs. Also examine topics such as **BPM** (Business Process Management) and **BPEL** (Business Process Execution Language).

Q. What are the best practices to follow when building applications based on SOA?

- Choose your implementation technologies carefully. Carefully consider if Web services are suitable. Sometimes using traditional technologies such as Java RMI, EJB and/or JMS may be more appropriate for your use cases than using Web services.

- Build coarse grained services as opposed to fine grained services. Fine grained services can not only adversely affect performance but also can result in tightly coupled services.

- Services need to have well-defined interfaces (i.e. contract) that are implementation independent. An important aspect of SOA is the separation of the service interface (i.e. the what) from its implementation (i.e. the how). This allows you to change implementation without breaking the contract. The same interface can be shared by many implementations.

- XML document should be preferred over Data Transfer Objects (DTOs). Data Transfer Objects (DTOs or aka Value Objects) must respect some of the rules such as:

  - They must be serializable into XML. Ability to serialize into XML guarantees platform independence.
  - They must be independent of the data source. Do not include any persistence code. SOA does not go well with Object-Relational mapping tools.

Q. What are the key advantages offered by SOA?

- Breaks down the silos of data, applications, and functionalities into enterprise services.

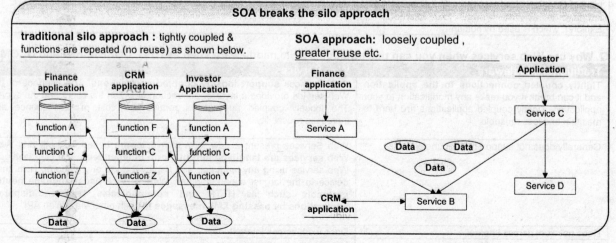

- Adapts an application to changing business needs and technological changes due to well-defined interfaces.
- Easily integrates applications with other systems in a loosely coupled manner.
- Reuse and improved asset utilization by leveraging existing investments in legacy applications.
- Business agility by quickly and easily creating a business process by leveraging on existing services.
- Provides interoperability and multi channel access.

Q. What is the difference between SOA and a Web service?

SOA (Service Oriented Architecture)	Web services
SOA is a software <u>design principle</u> and an <u>architectural pattern</u> for implementing loosely coupled, reusable and coarse grained services.	Web service is an <u>implementation technology</u> and <u>one</u> of the ways to implement SOA. You can build SOA based applications without using Web services – for example by using other traditional technologies like Java RMI, EJB, JMS based messaging, etc. But what Web services offer is the standards based and platform-independent service via HTTP, XML, SOAP, WSDL and UDDI, thus allowing interoperability between heterogeneous technologies such as J2EE and .NET.
You can implement SOA using any protocols such as HTTP, HTTPS, JMS, SMTP, RMI, IIOP (i.e. EJB uses IIOP), RPC etc. Messages can be in XML or Data Transfer Objects (DTOs).	Interfaces must be based on Internet protocols such as **HTTP**, FTP and SMTP. There are two main styles of Web services: **SOAP** and REST. Messages must be in **XML** and binary data attachments.

Q. What is the difference between a Web (website) and a Web service?

Web (website)	Web Service
A **Web** is a scalable information space with interconnected resources. A Web interconnects resources like Web pages, images, an application, word document, e-mail etc.	A **Web service** is a **service**, which lives on the **Web.** A Web service posses both the characteristics of a **Web** and a **service**. We know what a Web is; let's look at what a service is? A service is an application that exposes its functionality through an API (Application Programming Interface). So what is a component you may ask? A **service** is a **component** that can be used remotely through a remote interface either synchronously or asynchronously. The term service also implies something special about the application design, which is called a **service-oriented architecture (SOA)**. One of the most important features of SOA is the **separation of interface from implementation**. A service exposes its functionality through interface and interface hides the inner workings of the implementation. The client application (i.e. user of the service) only needs to know how to use the interface. The client does not have to understand actually how the service does its work. For example: There are so many different models of cars like MAZDA, HONDA, TOYOTA etc using different types of engines, motors etc but as a user or driver of the car you do not have to be concerned about the internals. You only need to know how to start the car, use the steering wheel etc, which is the interface to you. Usually a service runs on a server, waiting for the client application to call it and ask to do some work? These services are often run on application servers, which manage scalability, availability, reliability, multi-threading, transactions, security etc.
Designed to be consumed by humans (i.e. users, clients, business partners etc). For example: www.google.com is a Web search engine that contains index to more than 8 billion of other Web pages. The normal interface is a Web browser like Internet Explorer, which is used by human.	Designed to be consumed by software (i.e. other applications). For example: Google also provides a Web service interface through the Google API to query their search engine from an application rather than a browser. Refer http://www.google.com/apis/ for Google Web API

Q. Why use Web services when you can use traditional style middleware such as RPC, CORBA, RMI and DCOM?

Traditional middleware	Web Services
Tightly coupled connections to the application and it can break if you make any modification to your application. Tightly coupled applications are hard to maintain and less reusable.	Web Services **support loosely coupled connections**. The interface of the Web service provides a layer of abstraction between the client and the server. The loosely coupled applications reduce the cost of maintenance and increases reusability.
Generally does not support heterogeneity.	Web Services present a new form of middleware based on XML and Web. **Web services are language and platform independent**. You can develop a Web service using any language and deploy it on to any platform, from small device to the largest supercomputer. **Web service uses language neutral protocols such as HTTP and communicates between disparate applications by passing XML messages** to each other via a Web API.
Does not work across Internet.	Does work across Internet.
More expensive and hard to use.	Less expensive and easier to use.

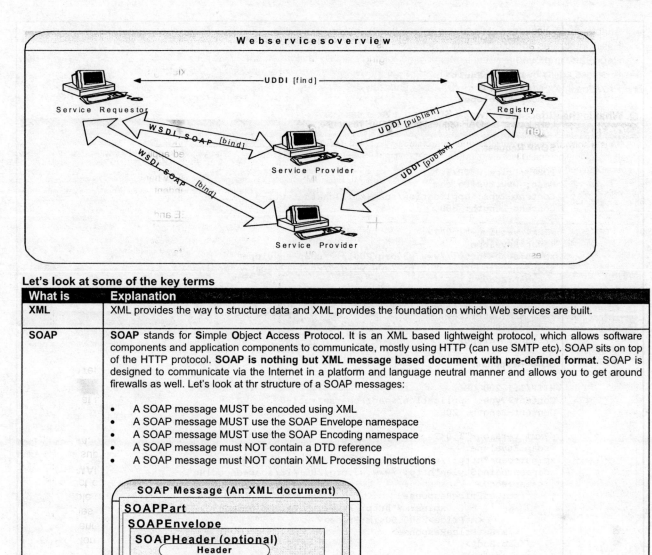

Let's look at some of the key terms

What is	Explanation
XML	XML provides the way to structure data and XML provides the foundation on which Web services are built.
SOAP	**SOAP** stands for **S**imple **O**bject **A**ccess **P**rotocol. It is an XML based lightweight protocol, which allows software components and application components to communicate, mostly using HTTP (can use SMTP etc). SOAP sits on top of the HTTP protocol. **SOAP is nothing but XML message based document with pre-defined format.** SOAP is designed to communicate via the Internet in a platform and language neutral manner and allows you to get around firewalls as well. Let's look at thr structure of a SOAP messages: • A SOAP message MUST be encoded using XML • A SOAP message MUST use the SOAP Envelope namespace • A SOAP message MUST use the SOAP Encoding namespace • A SOAP message must NOT contain a DTD reference • A SOAP message must NOT contain XML Processing Instructions

```
SOAP Message (An XML document)
  SOAPPart
    SOAPEnvelope
      SOAPHeader (optional)
          Header
          Header

      SOAPBody
          XML Content or SOAP fault

    AttachmentPart
          MIME Headers
          Content (XML, Image etc)

    AttachmentPart
          MIME Headers
          Content (XML, Image etc)
```

```
<?xml version="1.0"?>
<soap:Envelope
xmlns:soap="http://www.w3.org/2001/12/soap-envelope"
soap:encodingStyle="http://www.w3.org/2001/12/soap-encoding">
   <soap:Header>
     ...
   </soap:Header>
   <soap:Body>
     ...
```

```
        ...
      <soap:Fault>
          ...
          ...
        </soap:Fault>
      </soap:Body>
  </soap:Envelope>
```

Let's look at a SOAP request and a SOAP response:

SOAP Request:

```
POST /Price HTTP/1.1
Host: www.mysite.com
Content-Type: application/soap+xml; charset=utf-8
Content-Length: 300

<?xml version="1.0"?>
<soap:Envelope
xmlns:soap="http://www.w3.org/2001/12/soap-envelope"
soap:encodingStyle="http://www.w3.org/2001/12/soap-encoding">
  <soap:Body>
      <m:GetPrice xmlns:m="http://www.mysite.com/prices">
          <m:Item>PlasmaTV</m:Item>
      </m:GetPrice>
  </soap:Body>
</soap:Envelope>
```

SOAP Response:

```
HTTP/1.1 200 OK
Content-Type: application/soap; charset=utf-8
Content-Length: 200

<?xml version="1.0"?>
<soap:Envelope
xmlns:soap="http://www.w3.org/2001/12/soap-envelope"
soap:encodingStyle="http://www.w3.org/2001/12/soap-encoding">
  <soap:Body>
      <m:GetPriceResponse
                  xmlns:m="http://www.mysite.com/prices">
          <m:Price>3500.00</m:Price>
      </m:GetPriceResponse>
    </soap:Body>
</soap:Envelope>
```

Let's look at a HTTP header:

```
POST /Price HTTP/1.1
Host: www.mysite.com
Content-Type: text/plain
Content-Length: 200
```

SOAP HTTP Binding

A SOAP method is an HTTP request/response that complies with the SOAP encoding rules.

```
HTTP + XML = SOAP
```

Let's look at a HTTP header containing a soap message:

```
POST /Price HTTP/1.1
Host: www.mysite.com
Content-Type: application/soap+xml; charset=utf-8
Content-Length: 200
```

WSDL (Web Services Description Language)	WSDL stands for **W**eb **S**ervices **D**escription **L**anguage. A WSDL document is an XML document that describes how the messages are exchanged. Let's say we have created a Web service. Who is going to use that and how does the client know which method to invoke and what parameters to pass? There are tools that can generate WSDL from the Web service. Also there are tools that can read a WSDL document and create the necessary code to invoke the Web service. So the WSDL is the Interface Definition Language (IDL) for Web services.
UDDI (Universal	UDDI stands for **U**niversal **D**escription **D**iscovery and **I**ntegration. UDDI provides a way to publish and discover information about Web services. UDDI is like a registry rather than a repository. A registry contains only reference

Description Discovery and Integration)	information like the JNDI, which stores the EJB stub references. UDDI has white pages, yellow pages and green pages. If the retail industry published a UDDI for a price check standard then all the retailers can register their services into this UDDI directory. Shoppers will search the UDDI directory to find the retailer interface. Once the interface is found then the shoppers can communicate with the services immediately. The Web services can be registered for public use at http://www.uddi.org. Once the Web service is selected through the UDDI then it can be located using the discovery process. Before UDDI, there was no Internet standard for businesses to reach their customers and partners with information about their products and services. Neither was there a method of how to integrate businesses into each other's systems and processes. UDDI uses WSDL to describe interfaces to Web services.

So far we have looked at some open standards/protocols relating to Web services, which enable interoperability between disparate systems (e.g. Between .Net and J2EE etc). These standards provide a common and interoperable approach for <u>defining</u> (WSDL), <u>publishing</u> (UDDI) and <u>using</u> (SOAP) Web services. Now we will look at some of the Java related APIs for Web services. The J2EE 1.4 platform provides comprehensive support for Web services through the **JAX-RPC** (**J**ava **A**PI for **X**ML based **RPC** (**R**emote **P**rocedure **C**all)) and **JAXR** (**J**ava **A**PI for **X**ML **R**egistries). In the J2EE 1.4 platform you can build Web services without knowing anything about the above mentioned XML based standards and protocols. A Web service client accesses the service through the Web container or the EJB container.

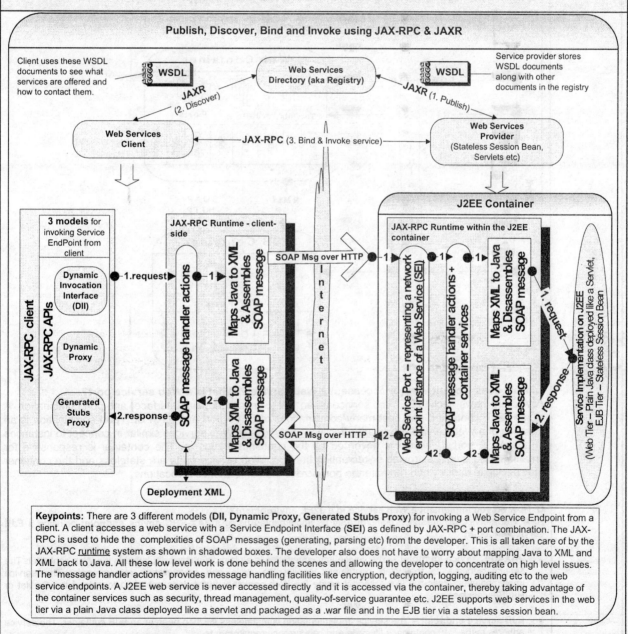

Keypoints: There are 3 different models (**DII, Dynamic Proxy, Generated Stubs Proxy**) for invoking a Web Service Endpoint from a client. A client accesses a web service with a Service Endpoint Interface (**SEI**) as defined by JAX-RPC + port combination. The JAX-RPC is used to hide the complexities of SOAP messages (generating, parsing etc) from the developer. This is all taken care of by the JAX-RPC <u>runtime</u> system as shown in shadowed boxes. The developer also does not have to worry about mapping Java to XML and XML back to Java. All these low level work is done behind the scenes and allowing the developer to concentrate on high level issues. The "message handler actions" provides message handling facilities like encryption, decryption, logging, auditing etc to the web service endpoints. A J2EE web service is never accessed directly and it is accessed via the container, thereby taking advantage of the container services such as security, thread management, quality-of-service guarantee etc. J2EE supports web services in the web tier via a plain Java class deployed like a servlet and packaged as a .war file and in the EJB tier via a stateless session bean.

| **JAX-RPC** | JAX-RPC (Java **A**PI for **X**ML based **RPC**) supports XML based RPC for Java and J2EE platforms. JAX-RPC provides an easy to develop programming model to develop Web services. As shown in the diagram above, a JAX-RPC runtime system and API abstracts the complexities of SOAP protocol by : |

- Providing a standard way of marshalling Java to XML and Java to WSDL and unmarshalling XML to Java and WSDL to Java.

- Standardizing the creation of SOAP requests and responses.

- Supporting and dispatching SOAP requests to methods on JAX-RPC Service Endpoint classes in the Web Container.

- Specifying a standard way to plug in SOAP message handlers, allowing both pre and post processing of SOAP requests and responses.

Q. What are JAX-RPC message handlers?
A. The JAX-RPC message handlers are similar to servlet filters. They provide additional message-handling facilities to Web service endpoints (both client and server) as extensions to the basic service implementation logic by providing logging, auditing, encryption, decryption etc.

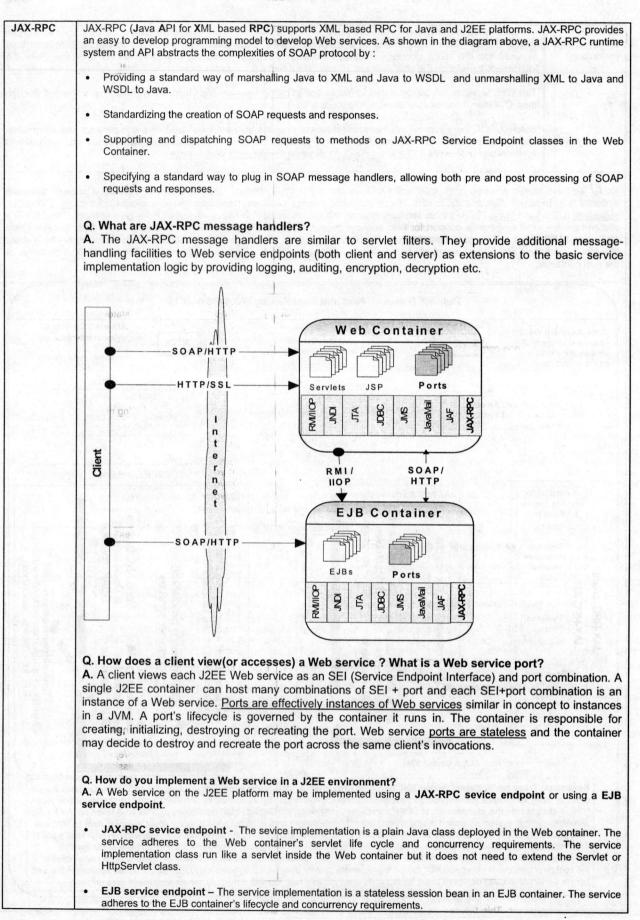

Q. How does a client view(or accesses) a Web service ? What is a Web service port?
A. A client views each J2EE Web service as an SEI (Service Endpoint Interface) and port combination. A single J2EE container can host many combinations of SEI + port and each SEI+port combination is an instance of a Web service. Ports are effectively instances of Web services similar in concept to instances in a JVM. A port's lifecycle is governed by the container it runs in. The container is responsible for creating, initializing, destroying or recreating the port. Web service ports are stateless and the container may decide to destroy and recreate the port across the same client's invocations.

Q. How do you implement a Web service in a J2EE environment?
A. A Web service on the J2EE platform may be implemented using a **JAX-RPC sevice endpoint** or using a **EJB service endpoint**.

- **JAX-RPC sevice endpoint -** The sevice implementation is a plain Java class deployed in the Web container. The service adheres to the Web container's servlet life cycle and concurrency requirements. The service implementation class run like a servlet inside the Web container but it does not need to extend the Servlet or HttpServlet class.

- **EJB service endpoint –** The service implementation is a stateless session bean in an EJB container. The service adheres to the EJB container's lifecycle and concurrency requirements.

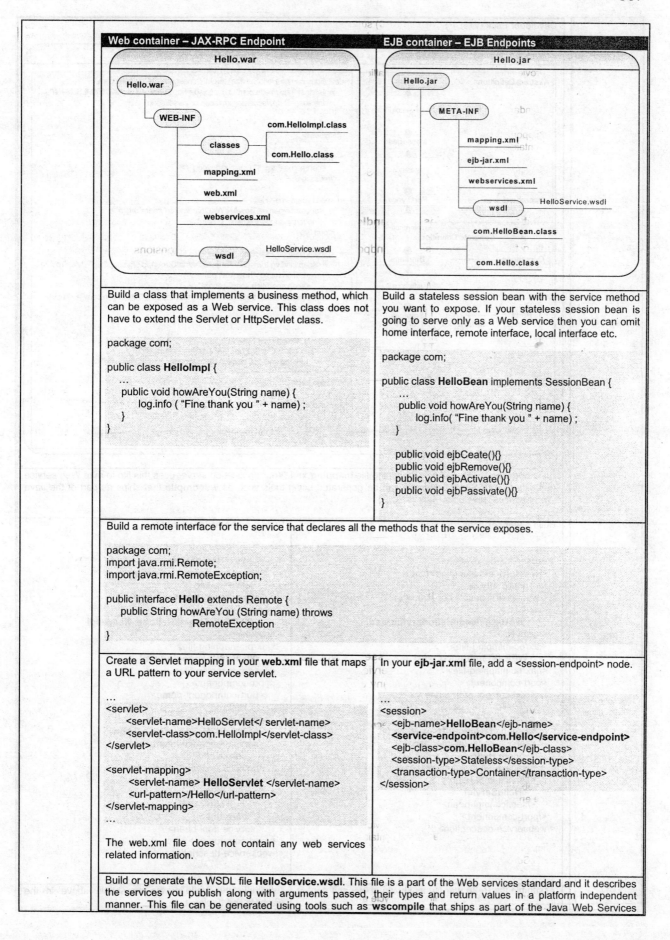

Web container – JAX-RPC Endpoint	EJB container – EJB Endpoints

Build a class that implements a business method, which can be exposed as a Web service. This class does not have to extend the Servlet or HttpServlet class.

```
package com;

public class HelloImpl {
    ...
    public void howAreYou(String name) {
        log.info ( "Fine thank you " + name) ;
    }
}
```

Build a stateless session bean with the service method you want to expose. If your stateless session bean is going to serve only as a Web service then you can omit home interface, remote interface, local interface etc.

```
package com;

public class HelloBean implements SessionBean {
    ...
    public void howAreYou(String name) {
        log.info( "Fine thank you " + name) ;
    }

    public void ejbCeate(){}
    public void ejbRemove(){}
    public void ejbActivate(){}
    public void ejbPassivate(){}
}
```

Build a remote interface for the service that declares all the methods that the service exposes.

```
package com;
import java.rmi.Remote;
import java.rmi.RemoteException;

public interface Hello extends Remote {
    public String howAreYou (String name) throws
            RemoteException
}
```

Create a Servlet mapping in your **web.xml** file that maps a URL pattern to your service servlet.	In your **ejb-jar.xml** file, add a <session-endpoint> node.

```
...
<servlet>
    <servlet-name>HelloServlet</ servlet-name>
    <servlet-class>com.HelloImpl</servlet-class>
</servlet>

<servlet-mapping>
    <servlet-name> HelloServlet </servlet-name>
    <url-pattern>/Hello</url-pattern>
</servlet-mapping>
...
```

The web.xml file does not contain any web services related information.

```
...
<session>
    <ejb-name>HelloBean</ejb-name>
    <service-endpoint>com.Hello</service-endpoint>
    <ejb-class>com.HelloBean</ejb-class>
    <session-type>Stateless</session-type>
    <transaction-type>Container</transaction-type>
</session>
```

Build or generate the WSDL file **HelloService.wsdl**. This file is a part of the Web services standard and it describes the services you publish along with arguments passed, their types and return values in a platform independent manner. This file can be generated using tools such as **wscompile** that ships as part of the Java Web Services

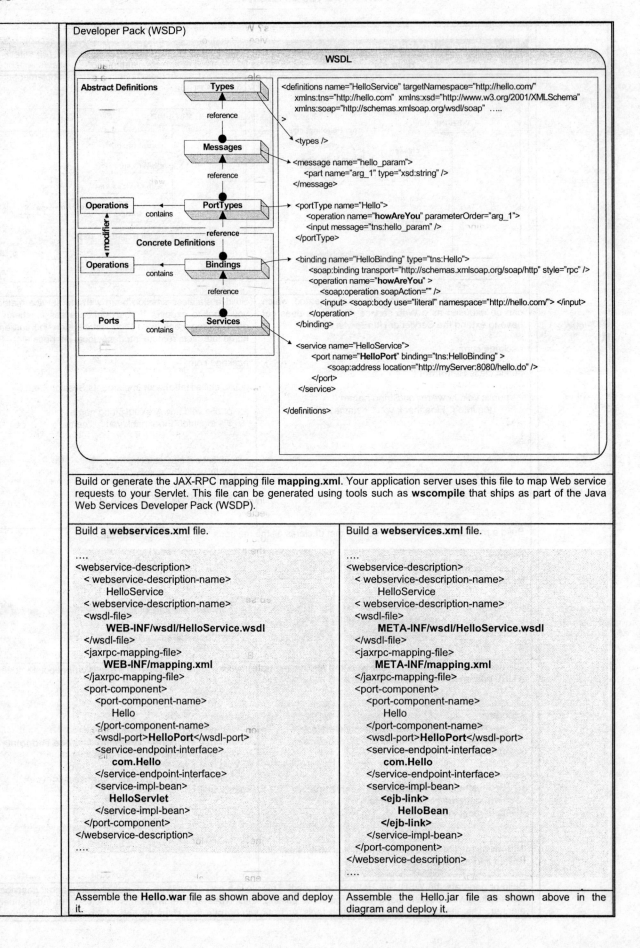

Developer Pack (WSDP)

Build or generate the JAX-RPC mapping file **mapping.xml**. Your application server uses this file to map Web service requests to your Servlet. This file can be generated using tools such as **wscompile** that ships as part of the Java Web Services Developer Pack (WSDP).

Build a **webservices.xml** file.	Build a **webservices.xml** file.
…. \<webservice-description> 　\< webservice-description-name> 　　HelloService 　\< webservice-description-name> 　\<wsdl-file> 　　**WEB-INF/wsdl/HelloService.wsdl** 　\</wsdl-file> 　\<jaxrpc-mapping-file> 　　**WEB-INF/mapping.xml** 　\</jaxrpc-mapping-file> 　\<port-component> 　　\<port-component-name> 　　　Hello 　　\</port-component-name> 　　\<wsdl-port>**HelloPort**\</wsdl-port> 　　\<service-endpoint-interface> 　　　**com.Hello** 　　\</service-endpoint-interface> 　　\<service-impl-bean> 　　　**HelloServlet** 　　\</service-impl-bean> 　\</port-component> \</webservice-description> ….	…. \<webservice-description> 　\< webservice-description-name> 　　HelloService 　\< webservice-description-name> 　\<wsdl-file> 　　**META-INF/wsdl/HelloService.wsdl** 　\</wsdl-file> 　\<jaxrpc-mapping-file> 　　**META-INF/mapping.xml** 　\</jaxrpc-mapping-file> 　\<port-component> 　　\<port-component-name> 　　　Hello 　　\</port-component-name> 　　\<wsdl-port>**HelloPort**\</wsdl-port> 　　\<service-endpoint-interface> 　　　**com.Hello** 　　\</service-endpoint-interface> 　　\<service-impl-bean> 　　　**\<ejb-link>** 　　　　**HelloBean** 　　　**\</ejb-link>** 　　\</service-impl-bean> 　\</port-component> \</webservice-description> ….
Assemble the **Hello.war** file as shown above and deploy it.	Assemble the Hello.jar file as shown above in the diagram and deploy it.

Q. How would you publish and find WSDL descriptions? What are the 4 primary UDDI data types?
A. UDDI provides a method for publishing and finding service descriptions. A complete WSDL service description is a combination of service interface and service implementation document. Since the service interface represents a reusable definition of a service, it is published in a UDDI as a tModel. The service implementation describes instances of a service. Each instance is defined using WSDL service element. Each service element in a service implementation document is used to publish a UDDI business service.

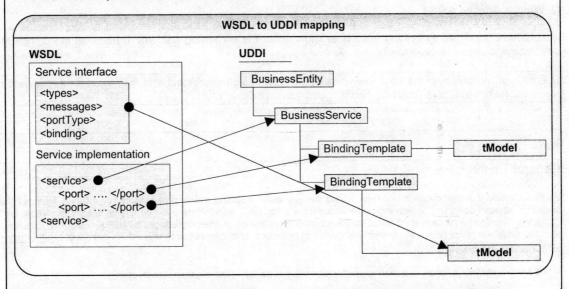

There are 4 primary UDDI data types: ***businessEntity***, ***businessService***, ***bindingTemplate***, and ***tModel***.

Q. What are the modes of operations supported by the JAX-RPC?
A. The JAX-RPC supports following 3 modes of operation:

* **Synchronous request/response mode** – After a remote method is invoked, the client's thread blocks until a return value is returned or an exception is thrown.

* **Fire and forget mode** – After a remote method is invoked, the client's thread is not blocked and it continues processing. A return value or an exception is <u>not</u> expected.

* **Non-blocking RPC invocation mode** -- After a remote method is invoked, the client's thread is not blocked and it continues processing. Later, the client processes the remote method return by performing a blocked receive call or by polling for the return value.

Q. How can a client application make a request to a Web service?
A. A client application can make use of one of the following 3 ways (Refer diagram "Publish, Discover, Bind and Invoke using JAX-RPC & JAXR"):

* **Invoking methods on a generated static stubs** - Based on the contents of a WSDL file description of a service, tools (WSDL2Java) can be used to generate stubs. The client application uses the stubs to invoke remote methods available as a Web service.

* **Using a Dynamic Proxy** - The client runtime creates a dynamic proxy that supports a Web service endpoint.

* **Using a Dynamic Invocation Interface (DII)** - Operations on target service endpoints are accessed dynamically based on an in-memory model of the WSDL file description of the service. This eliminates the need for clients to know in advance a service's exact name and parameters. A DII client can discover this at runtime by using a service broker that can look up the service's information.

All the above modes are passed through the JAX-RPC client side runtime.

JAXR	Stands for **J**ava **A**PI for **X**ML **R**egistries (JAXR). JAXR provides a uniform way (just like JDBC, JMS, JNDI etc) to use business registries based on open standards like UDDI, ebXML etc in Java programming language. Businesses can use registries to register themselves or discover other businesses in a loosely coupled manner. A business can use JAXR to search a registry for other businesses.
SAAJ	Stands for **S**OAP with **A**ttachments **A**PI for **J**ava. SAAJ enables developers to produce and consume messages conforming to SOAP specifications and provides an abstraction for handling SOAP messages with attachments.

| | Attachments can be complete XML messages, parts of XML, or MIME multipart/related (e.g. image/gif) type attachments. SAAJ supports synchronous request/response and fire and forget modes. |

Note: JAX-RPC 2.0 has been renamed to JAX-WS 2.0 (**Java API** for **XML W**eb **Se**rvices).

Q. What is Apache AXIS?
A. Apache AXIS is a Web services tool kit, which enables you to expose a functionality you have as a Web service without having to learn everything there is to know about the underlying platform. It hides all the complexities from the developer and improves productivity.

Speaking of toolkits, over the past few years some new design paradigms and frameworks have gained popularity to make you more productive. The next section gives you an overview.

General Tip #9:

If you are asked a design question like **How would you go about building a ticketing system for a travel agency?** then you should not jump into start designing by drawing some boxes for a 3 tier J2EE architecture etc. Any design should involve proper requirements gathering. The design process is all about trade-offs among performance, memory usage, reliability, scalability, coupling, maintenance etc. You could ask some relevant requirements gathering questions as shown below to show that you always gather requirements prior to designing a software system.:

-- Is it a ticketing system for an air travel only or for all modes of transport like air, train, coach etc?

-- Should this system be linked to the relevant airline systems? (This would require messaging or Web services).

-- Does this system require the services of an online payment gateway?

Q. A customer has asked you to write a function to convert a given text to uppercase. What question(s) do you need to ask to flesh out the requirements?

[Hint]

-- Do you require multilingual support? When you add more languages there are more things to consider and sometimes uppercase/lowercase classification doesn't make sense in other languages [i.e. InternationalizatioN → I18N].

-- How would you like the input text captured? GUI based or command line?

Next section very briefly covers some of the popular emerging technologies & frameworks. Some organizations might be considering or already started using these technologies. All these have emerged over the past 3 years. So it is vital that you have at least a basic understanding of these new paradigms and frameworks because these new paradigms and frameworks can offer great benefits such as ease of maintenance, reduction in code size, elimination of duplication of code, ease of unit testing, loose coupling among components, light weight and fine grained objects etc. **A few years ago, developers with EJB experience were well sought after and well paid and now a days I believe that this has changed and you need to have experience in Spring, Hibernate, and one or more component based Web frameworks like JSF and Tapestry.**

Emerging Technologies/Frameworks...

This section covers some of the popular emerging technologies you need to be at least aware of, if you have not already used them. If there are two or more interview candidates with similar skills and experience then awareness or experience with some of the emerging technologies can play a role in the decision making. Some organizations might be considering or already started using these technologies. So it is well worth your effort to demonstrate that you understand the basic concepts or have an appreciation for the following technologies/frameworks and an eagerness to learn.

- Test Driven Development (**TDD**).

- Aspect Oriented Programming (**AOP**).

- Inversion of Control (**IoC**) (Also known as **Dependency Injection**).

- Annotation or attribute based programming (xdoclet etc).

- Spring framework.

- Hibernate framework.

- EJB 3.0

- Component based Web frameworks like (**JSF, Tapestry etc**)

Note: It is out of scope for this book to cover all of these technologies/frameworks in detail. Important and popular technologies (TDD, AOP, IoC, and Annotations) and frameworks (Hibernate, Spring, EJB 3.0) are discussed with examples. If you hire smart people with a good understanding of Java/J2EE core concepts and key areas with some basic understanding of emerging technologies and frameworks then their current skills are not as important as their ability to learn quickly, eagerness to learn, and be productive.

Q. What is the hot trend in Enterprise apps these days?

This section covers some of the recent and popular design paradigms such as Plain Old Java Objects (**POJOs**) and Plain Old Java Interfaces (**POJI**) based services and interceptors, Aspect Oriented Programming (**AOP**), Dependency Injection (aka **IoC**), attributes or annotations oriented programming, etc and tools and frameworks which apply these new paradigms such as **Spring** (IoC and AOP), **Hibernate** (O/R mapping), **EJB 3.0** (POJO, POJI, and annotations), **XDoclet** (attributes oriented programming) , **JSF** (component based Web framework), **Tapestry** (component based Web framework) etc. All these have emerged over the past 2-4 years.

Q. Why should you seriously consider these technologies?

These new paradigms and frameworks can offer great benefits such as ease of maintenance, reduction in code size, elimination of duplication of code, ease of unit testing, loose coupling among components, light weight and fine grained objects, and developer productivity.

Q. How would you convince a development team to use these new paradigms/frameworks?

Build a vertical slice with some code for a business use case to demonstrate the above mentioned benefits.

Q 01: What is Test Driven Development (TDD)? FAQ

A 01: TDD is an iterative software development process where you **first write the test with the idea that it must fail**. This is a different approach to the traditional development where you write the application functionality first and then write test cases. The major benefit of this approach is that the code becomes thoroughly unit tested (you can use **JUnit** or other unit testing frameworks). For JUnit refer **Q14** on "How would you go about..." section. TDD is based on two important principles preached by its originator Kent Beck:

- **Write new business code only if an automated unit test has failed:** Business application requirements drive the tests and tests drive the actual functional code. Each test should test only one business concept, which means avoid writing a single test which tests withdrawing money from an account and depositing money into an account. Any change in the business requirements will impact pre and post conditions of the test. Talking about pre and post conditions, following **design by contract** methodology (Refer **Q11** in Java section) helps achieving TDD. In design by contract, you specify the pre and post conditions that act as contracts of a method, which provides a specification to write your tests against.

- **Eliminate duplication from the code:** A particular business concept should be implemented only once within the application code. Code for checking an account balance should be centralized to only one place within the application code. This makes your code decoupled, more maintainable and reusable.

I can hear some of you all saying how can we write the unit test code without the actual application code. Let's look at how it works in steps. The following steps are applied iteratively for business requirements.

STEP: 1 write some tests for a specific business requirement.

STEP: 2 write some basic structural code so that your **test compiles but the test should fail** (failures are the pillars of success). For example just create the necessary classes and corresponding methods with skeletal code.

STEP: 3 write the required business code to pass the tests which you wrote in step 1.

STEP: 4 finally refactor the code you just wrote to make it is as simple as it can be. You can refactor your code with confidence that if it breaks the business logic then you have unit test cases that can quickly detect it.

STEP: 5 run your tests to make sure that your refactored code still passes the tests.

STEP: 6 Repeat steps 1-5 for another business requirement.

To write tests efficiently some basic guidelines need to be followed:

- You should be able to run each test in isolation and in any order.
- The test code should not have any duplicate business logic.
- You should test for all the pre and post conditions as well as exceptions.
- Each test should concentrate on one business requirement as mentioned earlier.
- There are many ways to write test conditions so proper care and attention should be taken. In some cases pair programming can help by allowing two brains to work in collaboration. You should have strategies to overcome issues around state of data in RDBMS (Should you persist sample test data, which is a snapshot of your actual data prior to running your tests? Or should you hard code data? Or Should you combine both strategies? Etc).

Q 02: What is the point of Test Driven Development (TDD)? What do you think of TDD?

A 02: TDD process improves your confidence in the delivered code for the following reasons.

- TDD can eliminate duplication of code and also disciplines the developer to focus his mind on delivering what is absolutely necessary. This means the system you develop only does what it is supposed to do because you first write test cases for the business requirements and then write the required functionality to satisfy the test cases and no more.

- These unit tests can be repeatedly run to alert the development team immediately if someone breaks any existing functionality. All the unit tests can be run overnight as part of the deployment process and test results can be emailed to the development team.

- TDD ensures that code becomes thoroughly unit tested. It is not possible to write thorough unit tests if you leave it to the end due to deadline pressures, lack of motivation etc.

- TDD complements design by contract methodology and gets the developer thinking in terms of pre and post conditions as well as exceptions.

- When using TDD, tests drive your code and to some extent they assist you in validating your design at an earlier stage.

- TDD also helps you refactor your code with confidence that if it breaks the business logic it gets picked up when you run your unit tests next time.

- TDD promotes **design to interface not implementation** design concept. For example: when your code has to take input from an external source or device which is not present at the time of writing your unit tests, you need to create an interface, which takes input from another source in order for your tests to work.

Q. What in your own view is the worst part of Java development ? How would you go about fixing it? [Hint]

- Excessive use of checked exceptions and try {} catch {} and finally {} blocks. How to fix: Make use of frameworks like Spring, which makes use of unchecked exceptions and templates (e.g. JdbcTemplate, JndiTemplate, JmsTemplate) etc to solve the above issue in a non-intrusive and consistent manner.

- Repetition of code for example singleton factories, Data Transfer Objects (DTOs), resource management code like opening and closing resources etc. How to fix: Make use of Hibernate detached objects to avoid or minimize DTOs, Spring DAO support and templates to minimize resource management code, Spring dependency injection to avoid or minimize the number of singleton factories and use Aspect Oriented Programming (AOP – e.g. Spring AOP) to implement secondary requirements like auditing, logging, transaction management, security etc to improve productivity.

- Too many XML based configuration files. How to fix: Use Java annotations (i.e. From JDK 1.5 onwards) where applicable to have a right balance between XML configuration files and annotations.

Let us look at some of these in a bit more detail in this section.

Q 03: What is aspect oriented programming (AOP)? Do you have any experience with AOP?

A 03: Aspect-Oriented Programming (**AOP**) complements OOP (Object Oriented Programming) by allowing the developer to dynamically modify the static OO model to create a system that can grow to meet new requirements.

AOP allows you to dynamically modify your static model consisting mainly of business logic to include the code required to fulfill the secondary requirements or in AOP terminology called **cross-cutting concerns** (i.e. secondary requirements) like auditing, logging, security, exception handling etc without having to modify the original static model (in fact, we don't even need to have the original code). Better still, we can often keep this additional code in a single location rather than having to scatter it across the existing model, as we would have to if we were using OOP on its own.

For example: A typical Web application will require a servlet to bind the HTTP request to an object and then pass it to the business handler object to be processed and finally return the response back to the user. So only a minimum amount of code is initially required. But once you start adding all the other additional secondary requirements or cross-cutting concerns like logging, auditing, security, exception-handling, transaction demarcation, etc the code will inflate to 2-4 times its original size. This is where AOP can assist by separately modularizing these cross-cutting concerns and integrating theses concerns at runtime or compile time through aspect weaving. AOP allows rapid development of an evolutionary prototype using OOP by focusing only on the business logic by omitting concerns such as security, auditing, logging etc. Once the prototype is accepted, additional concerns like security, logging, auditing etc can be weaved into the prototype code to transfer it into a production standard application.

AOP nomenclature is different from OOP and can be described as shown below:

Join points: represents the point at which a cross-cutting concern like logging, auditing etc intersects with a main concern like the core business logic. Join points are locations in programs' execution path like method & constructor call, method & constructor execution, field access, class & object initialization, exception handling execution etc.

pointcut: is a language construct that identifies specific join points within the program. A pointcut defines a collection of join points and also provides a context for the join point.

Advice: is an implementation of a cross-cutting concern which is a piece of code that is executed upon reaching a pointcut within a program.

Aspect: encapsulates join points, pointcuts and advice into a reusable module for the cross-cutting concerns which is equivalent to Java classes for the core concerns in OOP. Classes and aspects are independent of one another. **Classes are unaware of the presence of aspects, which is an important AOP concept.** Only pointcut declaration binds classes and aspects.

Weaving is the process for interleaving separate cross-cutting concerns such as logging into core concerns such as business logic code to complete the system. AOP weaving composes different implementations of aspects into a cohesive system based on weaving rules. The weaving process (aka injection of aspects into Java classes) can happen at:

- **Compile-time:** Weaving occurs during compilation process.
- **Load-time:** Weaving occurs at the byte-code level at class loading time.
- **Runtime:** Similar to load-time where weaving occurs at byte-code level during runtime as join points are reached in the executing application.

So which approach to use? Load-time and runtime weaving have the advantages of being highly dynamic and enabling changes on the fly without having to rebuild and redeploy. But Load-time and runtime weaving adversely affect system performance. Compile time weaving offers better performance but requires rebuilding and redeployment to effect changes.

Q. Do you have any experience with AOP?

Two of the most interesting modules of the Spring framework are **AOP** (Aspect Oriented Programming) and Inversion Of Control (**IoC**) container (aka Dependency Injection). Let us look at a simple AOP example.

STEP 1: Define the interface and the implementation classes. Spring promotes the <u>code to interface design concept</u>.

```
public interface Hello {
    public void hello();
}
```

```
public class HelloImpl implements Hello{
    public void hello() {
        System.out.println("Printing hello. ");
    }
}
```

STEP 2: Configure the Spring runtime via the **SpringConfig.xml** file. Beans can be configured and subsequently injected into the calling *Test* class.

```
<?xml version="1.0" encoding="UTF-8"?>
<!DOCTYPE beans PUBLIC "-//SPRING//DTD BEAN//EN" "http://www.springframework.org/dtd/spring-beans.dtd">

<beans>
    <!-- bean configuration which enables dependency injection -->
    <bean id="helloBean" class="org.springframework.aop.framework.ProxyFactoryBean">
        <property name="target">
```

```
                     <bean class="HelloImpl" singleton="false" />
          </property>
     </bean>

</beans>
```

STEP 3: Write your *Test* class. The "**SpringConfig.xml**" configuration file should be in the classpath.

```java
import org.springframework.context.ApplicationContext;
import org.springframework.context.support.FileSystemXmlApplicationContext;

public class Test {

  public static void main(String[] args) {
    ApplicationContext ctx = new FileSystemXmlApplicationContext("SpringConfig.xml");

    Hello h = (Hello)ctx.getBean("helloBean");
    h.hello();
  }

}
```

If you run the **Test** class, you should get an output of :

```
Printing hello.
```

Now, if you want to trace your methods like **hello()** *before* and *after* in your **Hello** class, then you can make use of the Spring AOP.

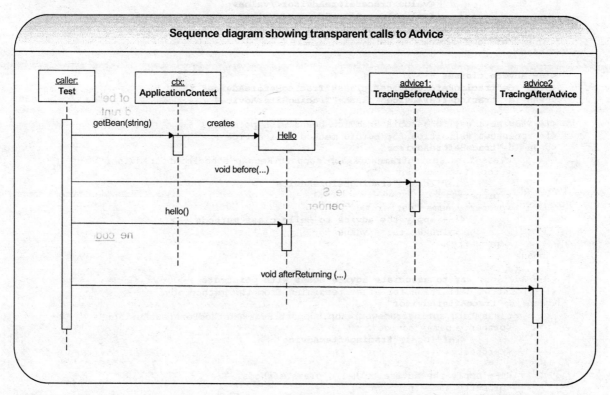

STEP 4: Firstly you need to define the classes for the *before* and *after* advice for the method tracing as follows:

```java
import java.lang.reflect.Method;
import org.springframework.aop.MethodBeforeAdvice;

public class TracingBeforeAdvice implements MethodBeforeAdvice {

  public void before(Method arg0, Object[] arg1, Object arg2) throws Throwable {
    System.out.println("Just before method call...");
  }
}
```

```
import java.lang.reflect.Method;
import org.springframework.aop.AfterReturningAdvice;

public class TracingAfterAdvice implements AfterReturningAdvice {

  public void afterReturning(Object arg0, Method arg1, Object[] arg2, Object arg3)
                                                             throws Throwable {
    System.out.println("Just after returning from the method call...");
  }
}
```

STEP 5: In order to attach the advice to the appropriate joint points, you must make a few amendments to the **SpringConfig.xml** file as shown below in bold:

```
<?xml version="1.0" encoding="UTF-8"?>
<!DOCTYPE beans PUBLIC "-//SPRING//DTD BEAN//EN" "http://www.springframework.org/dtd/spring-
beans.dtd">

<beans>
  <!-- bean configuration which enables dependency injection -->
  <bean id="helloBean"
        class="org.springframework.aop.framework.ProxyFactoryBean">
        <property name="target">
              <bean class="HelloImpl" singleton="false" />
        </property>

        <property name="interceptorNames">
              <list>
                    <value>traceBeforeAdvisor</value>
                    <value>traceAfterAdvisor</value>
              </list>
        </property>
  </bean>

  <!-- Advice classes -->
  <bean id="tracingBeforeAdvice" class="TracingBeforeAdvice" />
  <bean id="tracingAfterAdvice" class="TracingAfterAdvice" />

  <!-- Advisor: way to associate advice beans with pointcuts -->
  <!-- pointcut definition for before method call advice -->
  <bean id="traceBeforeAdvisor"
        class="org.springframework.aop.support.RegexpMethodPointcutAdvisor">
        <property name="advice">
              <ref local="tracingBeforeAdvice" />
        </property>
        <property name="pattern">
              <!-- apply the advice to Hello class methods -->
              <value>Hello.*</value>
        </property>
  </bean>

  <!-- Advisor: way to associate advice beans with pointcuts -->
  <!-- pointcut definition for after returning from the method advice -->
  <bean id="traceAfterAdvisor"
        class="org.springframework.aop.support.RegexpMethodPointcutAdvisor">
        <property name="advice">
              <ref local="tracingAfterAdvice" />
        </property>

        <!-- apply the advice to Hello class methods -->
        <property name="pattern">
              <value>Hello.*</value>
        </property>
  </bean>

</beans>
```

If you run the *Test* class again, you should get an output with AOP in action:

Just before method call...
Printing hello.
Just after returning from the method call...

As was briefly discussed in **Q43** in **Enterprise - Java** section, Spring offers <u>declarative transaction management</u>. This is enabled by Spring AOP. Declarative transaction management should be preferred over programmatic transaction management since it is non-invasive and has least impact on your application code. Not only transaction management but also other system level services like security, logging, auditing etc should be implemented declaratively with the AOP feature.

Q 04: What are the differences between OOP and AOP?
A 04:

Object Oriented Programming (OOP)	Aspect Oriented Programming (AOP)
OOP looks at an application as a set of collaborating objects. OOP code scatters system level code like logging, security etc with the business logic code.	AOP looks at the complex software system as combined implementation of multiple concerns like business logic, data persistence, logging, security, multithread safety, error handling, and so on. Separates business logic code from the system level code. In fact one concern remains unaware of other concerns.
OOP nomenclature has classes, objects, interfaces etc.	AOP nomenclature has join points, point cuts, advice, and aspects.
Provides benefits such as code reuse, flexibility, improved maintainability, modular architecture, reduced development time etc with the help of polymorphism, inheritance and encapsulation.	AOP implementation coexists with the OOP by choosing OOP as the base language. For example: AspectJ uses Java as the base language. AOP provides benefits provided by OOP plus some additional benefits which are discussed in the next question.

Q 05: What are the benefits of AOP?
A 05:

- OOP can cause the system level code like logging, transaction management, security etc to scatter throughout the business logic. AOP helps overcome this problem by centralizing these cross-cutting concerns.

- AOP addresses each aspect separately in a modular fashion with minimal coupling and duplication of code. This modular approach also promotes code reuse by using a business logic concern with a separate logger aspect.

- It is also easier to add newer functionalities by adding new aspects and weaving rules and subsequently regenerating the final code. This ability to add newer functionality as separate aspects enable application designers to delay or defer some design decisions without the dilemma of over designing the application.

- Promotes rapid development of evolutionary prototypes using OOP by focusing only on the business logic by omitting cross-cutting concerns such as security, auditing, logging etc. Once the prototype is accepted, additional concerns like security, logging, auditing etc can be weaved into the prototype code to transfer it into a production standard application.

- Developers can concentrate on one aspect at a time rather than having to think simultaneously about business logic, security, logging, performance, multithread safety etc. Different aspects can be developed by different developers based on their key strengths. For example: A security aspect can be developed by a security expert or a senior developer who understands security.

Q 06: What is attribute or annotation oriented programming? FAQ
A 06: Before looking at attribute oriented programming let's look at code generation processes. There are two kinds of code generation processes.

Passive code generation: is template driven. Input wizards are used in modern IDEs like eclipse, WebSphere Studio Application Developer (WSAD) etc where parameters are supplied and the code generator carries out the process of parameter substitution and source code generation. For example: in WSAD or eclipse you can create a new class by supplying the "New Java class" wizard appropriate input parameters like class name, package name, modifiers, superclass name, interface name etc to generate the source code. Another example would be *Velocity* template engine, which is a powerful Java based generation tool from the Apache Software Foundation.
Active code generation: Unlike passive code generators the active code generators can inject code directly into the application as and when required.

Attribute/Annotation oriented programming languages leverages active code generation with the use of declarative tags embedded within the application source code to generate any other kind of source code, configuration files, deployment descriptors etc. These declarative metadata tags are called **attributes** or **annotations**. The purpose of these *attributes* is to extend the functionality of the base language like Java, with the help of custom attributes provided by other providers like Hibernate framework, Spring framework, XDoclet etc. The attributes or annotations are specified with the symbol "**@<label>**". J2SE 5.0 has a built-in runtime support for attributes.

Let's look at an example. Say we have a container managed entity bean called Account. Using attribute oriented programming we can generate the deployment descriptor file ejb-jar.xml by embedding some attributes within the bean implementation code.

```
/**
 *  @ejb.bean
 *  name="Account"
 *  jndi-name ="ejb/Account"
 */
public abstract class AccountBean implements EntityBean {
    ….
}
```

The above-embedded attributes can generate the ejb-jar.xml as shown below using XDoclet (use an Ant script):

```
<ejb-jar>
   <entity>
      <ejb-name>Account</ejb-name>
      <home>com.AccountHome</home>
      <remote>com.Account</remote>
      <ejb-class>com.AccountBean</ejb-class>
   ….

   </entity>
</ejb-jar>
```

Q 07: What are the pros and cons of annotations over XML based deployment descriptors? FAQ

A 07: Service related attributes in your application can be configured through a XML based deployment descriptor files or annotations. XML based deployment descriptor files are processed separately from the code, often at runtime, while annotations are compiled with your source code and checked by the compiler.

XML	Annotations
More verbose because has to duplicate a lot of information like class names and method names from your code.	Less verbose since class names and method names are part of your code.
Less robust due to duplication of information which introduces multiple points for failure. If you misspell a method name then the application will fail.	More robust because annotations are processed with your code and checked by the compiler for any discrepancies and inaccuracies.

More flexible since processed separately from the code. Since it is not hard-coded can be changed later. Your deployment team has a greater flexibility to inspect and modify the configuration.	Less flexible since annotations are embedded in Java comment style within your code.
	
	 For example, to define a stateless session EJB 3.0 with annotations, which can serve both local and remote clients:
	
	 @Stateless
	 @Local ({LocalCounter.class})
	 @Remote ({RemoteCounter.class})
	
	 public class CounterBean implements LocalCounter, RemoteCounter {
	 …
	 }

XML files can express complex relationships and hierarchical structures at the expense of being verbose.	Annotations can hold only a small amount of configuration information and most of the plumbing has to be done in the framework.

Q. Which one to use?

Annotations are suitable for most application needs. XML files are more complex and can be used to address more advanced issues. XML files can be used to override default annotation values. Annotations cannot be used if you do not have access to source-code. The decision to go with annotation or XML depends upon the architecture behind the framework. For example Spring is primarily based on XML and EJB 3.0 is primarily based on annotations, but both support annotations and XML to some degree. EJB 3.0 uses XML configuration files as an optional overriding mechanism and Spring uses annotations to configure some Spring services.

Q 08: What is XDoclet?

A 08: **XDoclet** is an open source code generation engine for **attribute oriented programming** from SourceForge.net (http://xdoclet.sourceforge.net/xdoclet/index.html). So you add attributes (i.e. metadata) in JavaDoc style tags (@ejb.bean) and XDoclet will parse your source files and JavaDoc style attributes provided in the Java comment with @ symbol to generate required artifacts like XML based deployment descriptors, EJB interfaces etc. XDoclet can generate all the artifacts of an EJB component, such as remote & local interfaces as well as deployment descriptors. You place the required attributes on the relevant classes and methods that you want to process.

Q 09: What is inversion of control (**IoC**) (also known more specifically as **dependency injection**)? FAQ

A 09: Inversion of control or dependency injection (which is a <u>specific type of IoC</u>) is a term used to resolve object dependencies by injecting an instantiated object to satisfy dependency as opposed to explicitly requesting an object. So objects will not be explicitly requested but objects are provided as needed with the help of an Inversion Of Controller container (e.g. Spring, Hivemind etc). This is analogous to the Hollywood principal where the servicing objects say to the requesting client code (i.e. the caller) "don't call us, we'll call you". Hence it is called inversion of control.

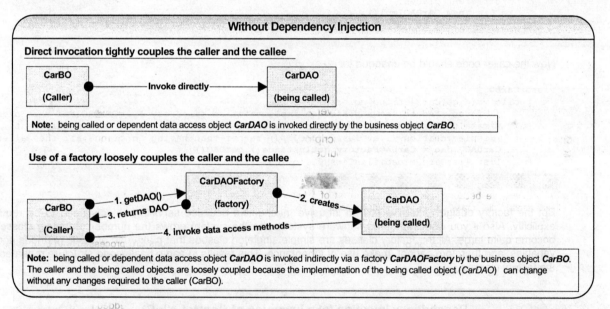

Most of you all are familiar with the software development context where client code (requesting code) collaborates with other dependent objects (or servicing objects) by knowing which objects to talk to, where to locate them and how to talk with them. This is achieved by embedding the code required for locating and instantiating the requested components within the client code. The above approach will <u>tightly couple the dependent components with the client code</u>.

Caller code:
```
class CarBO {
    public void getCars(String color) {
        //if you need to use a different implementation class say FastCarDAOImpl then need to
        //make a change to the caller here (i.e. CarDAO dao = new FastCarDAOImpl()). so the
        //caller is tightly coupled. If this line is called by 10 different callers then you
        //need to make changes in 10 places.
        CarDAO  dao = new CarDAOImpl();
        List listCars = dao.findCarsByColor(color);
    }
}
```

Being called code:

```
interface CarDAO (){
    public abstract List findCarsByColor(color);
}


interface CarDAOImpl extends CarDAO (){
    public List findCarsByColor(color) {
        //data access logic goes here
    }
}
```

This tight coupling can be resolved by applying the **factory design pattern** and **program to interfaces not to implementations driven development**.

Simplified factory class implemented with a singleton design pattern:

```
class CarDAOFactory {
    private static final  CarDAOFactory onlyInstance = new CarDAOFactory();

    private CarDAOFactory(){}//private so that cannot be instantiated from outside the class

    public CarDAOFactory getInstance(){
        return onlyInstance;
    }

    public CarDAO getDAO(){
        //if the implementation changes to FastCarDAOImpl then change here only instead of 10
        //different places.
        return  new CarDAOImpl();
    }
}
```

Now the caller code should be changed to:

```
class CarBO {
    public void getCars(String color) {
        //if you need to use a different implementation class say FastCarDAOImpl then need to
        //make one change only to the factory class CarDAOFactory to return a different
        //implementation (i.e. FastCarDAOImpl) rather than having to change all the callers.
        CarDAO  dao = CarDAOFactory.getInstance().getDAO();
        List listCars = dao.findCarsByColor(color);
    }
}
```

But the factory design pattern is still an intrusive mechanism because servicing objects need to be requested explicitly. Also if you work with large software systems, as the system grows the number of factory classes can become quite large. All the factory classes are simple singleton classes that make use of static methods and field variables, and therefore cannot make use of inheritance. This results in same basic code structure repeated in all the factory classes.

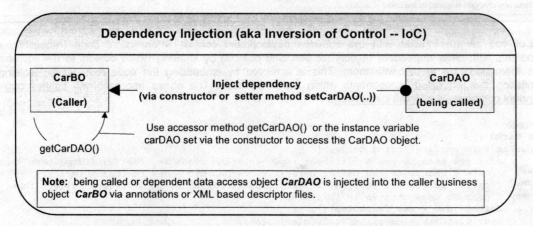

Let us look at how dependency injection comes to our rescue. It takes the approach that clients declare their dependency on servicing objects through a configuration file (like spring-config.xml) and some external piece of code (e.g. Spring) assumes the responsibility of locating and instantiating these servicing components and supplying the relevant references when needed to the client code whereby acting as the factory objects. This external piece of code is often referred to as IoC (specifically known as dependency injection) container or framework.

SpringConfig.xml

```xml
<beans>

    <bean id="car" class="CarBO" singleton="false" >
       <constructor-arg>
                <ref bean="carDao" />
        </constructor-arg>
    </bean>

    <bean id="carDao" class="CarDAOImpl" singleton="false" />

</beans>
```

Now your *CarBO* code changes to:
```java
class CarBO {
    private CarDAO dao = null;

    public CarBO(CarDAO dao) {
        this.dao = dao;
    }
    public void getCars(String color) {
        //if you need to use a different implementation class say FastCarDAOImpl then need to
        //make one change only to the SpringConfig.xml file to use a different implementation
        //class(i.e. class"FastCarDAOImpl") rather than having to change all the callers.
        List listCars = dao.findCarsByColor(color);
    }
}
```

Your calling code would be (e.g. from a Web client or EJB client):
```java
ApplicationContext ctx = new FileSystemXmlApplicationContext("SpringConfig.xml");

//lookup "car" in your caller where "carDao" is dependency injected using the constructor.
CarBO bo = (CarBO)ctx.getBean("car"); //Spring creates an instance of the CarBO object with
                                      //an instance of CarDAO object as the constructor arg.

String color = red;
bo.getCars(color)
```

You can use IoC containers like Spring framework to inject your business objects and DAOs into your calling classes. Dependencies can be wired by either using annotations or using XML as shown above. Tapestry 4.0 makes use of the Hivemind IoC container for injecting application state objects, pages etc.

IoC or dependency injection containers generally control creation of objects (by calling "new") and resolve dependencies between objects it manages. Spring framework, Pico containers, Hivemind etc are IoC containers to name a few. IoC containers support **eager instantiation**, which is quite useful if you want self-starting services that "come up" on their own when the server starts. They also support **lazy loading**, which is useful when you have many services which may only be sparsely used.

Q 10: What are the different types of dependency injections? FAQ
A 10: There are three types of dependency injections.

- Constructor Injection (e.g. Pico container, Spring etc): Injection is done through constructors.
- Setter Injection (e.g. Spring): Injection is done through setter methods.
- Interface Injection (e.g. Avalon): Injection is done through an interface.

Spring supports both constructor-based injection and setter-based injection. The above example on **Q9** is based on the constructor-based injection. Here is the same example using the Spring's setter-based injection.

SpringConfig.xml

```xml
<beans>

  <bean id="car" class="CarBO" singleton="false" >
```

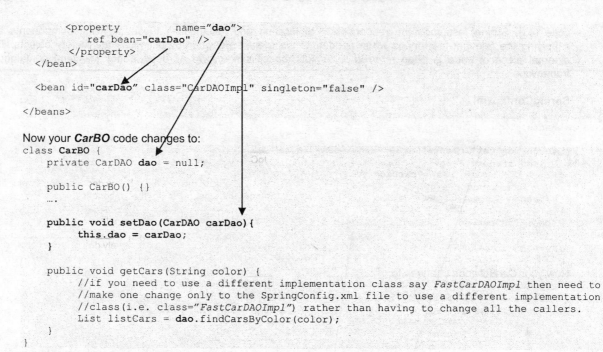

```
          <property              name="dao">
             ref bean="carDao" />
          </property>
    </bean>

    <bean id="carDao" class="CarDAOImpl" singleton="false" />

</beans>
```

Now your **CarBO** code changes to:

```
class CarBO {
    private CarDAO dao = null;

    public CarBO() {}
    ....

    public void setDao(CarDAO carDao){
        this.dao = carDao;
    }

    public void getCars(String color) {
        //if you need to use a different implementation class say FastCarDAOImpl then need to
        //make one change only to the SpringConfig.xml file to use a different implementation
        //class(i.e. class="FastCarDAOImpl") rather than having to change all the callers.
        List listCars = dao.findCarsByColor(color);
    }
}
```

The above SpringConfig.xml code creates an instance of *CarBO* object and *CarDAO* object and calls the **setDao**(*CarDAO* carDao) method, passing in the reference to the *CarDAO* object.

Your caller code would be (e.g. from a Web client or EJB client) same as above:

```
ApplicationContext ctx = new FileSystemXmlApplicationContext("SpringConfig.xml");

//lookup "car" in your caller where "carDao" is dependency injected using the setter method.
CarBO bo = (CarBO)ctx.getBean("car"); //Spring creates an instance of the CarBO object with
                                      //an instance of CarDAO object and then invokes the
                                      //setter method setDao(CarDAO carDao) on CarBO.

String color = red;
bo.getCars(color)
```

Q. Which one to use?

The choice between constructor-based injection and setter-based injection goes back to OO programming question – Should you fill fields in a constructor or setter methods?. There is no clear cut answer for this question. It is a good practice to start with constructor-based injection since it permits immutability (i.e. if your classes are meant to be immutable) and also constructors with parameters give you a clear statement of what is required to create a valid object. If there is more than one way to create a valid object then provide multiple constructors. But if you have a lot of constructor parameters then your constructors can look messy and also if you have many string based parameters then setter-based injection will be more descriptive because each setter name will indicate what the string is supposed to do (e.g. setFirstName(...), setLastName(...) etc)

Q 11: What are the benefits of IoC (aka Dependency Injection)? **FAQ**
A 11:

- Minimizes the amount of code in your application. With IoC containers you do not care about how services are created and how you get references to the ones you need. You can also easily add additional services by adding a new constructor or a setter method with little or no extra configuration.

- Makes your application more testable by not requiring any singletons or JNDI lookup mechanisms in your unit test cases. IoC containers make unit testing and switching implementations very easy by manually allowing you to inject your own objects into the object under test.

- Loose coupling is promoted with minimal effort and least intrusive mechanism. The factory design pattern is more intrusive because components or services need to be requested explicitly whereas in IoC the dependency is injected into the requesting code. Also some containers promote the design to interfaces not to implementations design concept by encouraging managed objects to implement a well-defined service interface of your own.

- IoC containers support eager instantiation and lazy loading of services. Containers also provide support for instantiation of managed objects, cyclical dependencies, life cycle management, and dependency resolution between managed objects etc.

Q 12: What is the difference between a service locator pattern and an inversion of control pattern?

A 12:

Service locator	Inversion Of Control (IoC)
The calling class which needs the dependent classes needs to tell the service locator which classes are needed. Also the calling classes have the responsibility of finding these dependent classes and invoking them. This makes the classes tightly coupled with each other.	In IoC (aka Dependency Injection) pattern the responsibility is shifted to the IoC containers to locate and load the dependent classes based on the information provided in the descriptor files. Changes can be made to the dependent classes by simply modifying the descriptor files. This approach makes the dependent classes loosely coupled with the calling class.
Difficult to unit test the classes separately due to tight coupling.	Easy to unit test the classes separately due to loose coupling.

Q 13: Why dependency injection is more elegant than a JNDI lookup to decouple client and the service?

A 13: Here are a few reasons why a JNDI look up is not elegant:

- The client and the service being looked up must agree on a string based name, which is a contract not enforced by the compiler or any deployment-time checks. You will have to wait until runtime to discover any discrepancies in the string based name between the lookup code and the JNDI registry.

- The JNDI lookup code is verbose with its own try-catch block, which is repeated across the application.

- The retrieved service objects are not type checked at compile-time and could result in a casting error at runtime.

Dependency injection is more elegant because it promotes loose coupling with minimal effort and is the least intrusive mechanism. Dependency is injected into requesting piece of code by the IoC containers like Spring etc. With IoC containers you do not care about how services are created and how you get references to the ones you need. You can also easily add additional services by adding a new constructor or a setter method with little or extra configuration.

Q 14: Explain Object-to-Relational (O/R) mapping?

A 14: There are several ways to persist data and the persistence layer is one of the most important layers in any application development. O/R mapping is a technique of mapping data representation from an object model to a SQL based relational model.

O/R mapping is well suited for read → modify → write centric applications and not suited for write centric applications (i.e. batch processes with large data sets like 5000 rows or more) where data is seldom read. Although this was generally true of many earlier O/R mapping frameworks, most today (including latest Hibernate) allow for efficient ways of performing large batch style write operations. O/R mapping tools/frameworks allow you to model **inheritance** (Refer **Q101** in Enterprise section), **association** and **composition** class relationships. O/R mapping tools work well in 80-90% of cases. Use basic database features like stored procedures, triggers etc, when O/R mapping is not appropriate. Keep in mind that no one size fits all solution. Always validate your architectural design with a vertical slice and test for performance. Some times you have to handcraft your SQL and a good O/R mapping (aka ORM) tool/framework should allow that. O/R mapping tools/frameworks allow your application to be:

- Less verbose (e.g. transparent persistence , Object Oriented query language , transitive persistence etc)
- More portable (i.e. vendor independence due to multi dialect support)
- More maintainable (i.e. transparent persistence, inheritance mapping strategies, automatic dirty checking etc).

Takes care of much of the plumbing like connection establishment, exception handling, configuration etc. You can often leverage the framework's strategies and capabilities to get efficiencies. Also provides support for eager fetching, lazy loading (i.e. using proxy objects), caching strategies and detached objects (no DTOs required). Hibernate is a popular O/R mapping (aka ORM) framework, which provides above mentioned benefits and features.

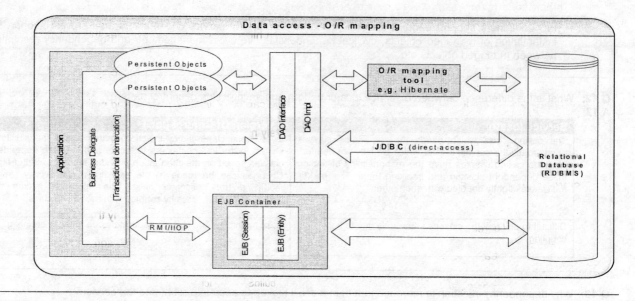

Q. Have you used any of the frameworks using paradigms like IoC, AOP, O/R mapping tool, POJO & POJI based development, component based Web frameworks etc. Where do these frameworks fit in?

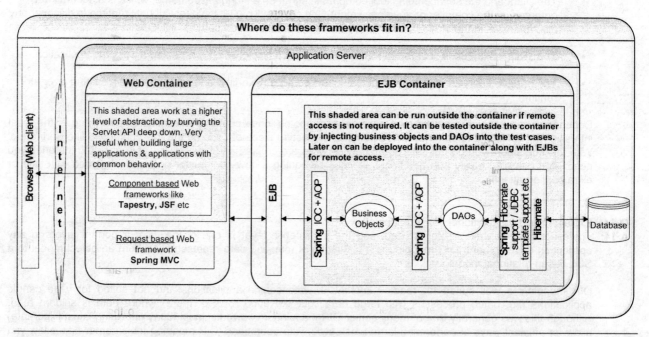

Q. What open source frameworks do you have experience with? Hibernate, IBatis, Spring, Struts, Tapestry, log4j, Ant, Quartz (scheduler, an alternative to Timer and TimerTask) etc

Q 15: Give an overview of hibernate framework? FAQ

A 15: Hibernate is a full-featured, open source Object-to-Relational (O/R) mapping framework. Unlike EJB (EJB's new persistence API can operate outside of an EJB container), Hibernate can work inside or outside of a J2EE container. Hibernate works with Plain Old Java Objects (POJOs), which is much like a JavaBean.

Q. How will you configure Hibernate?

The configuration files **hibernate.cfg.xml** (or hibernate.properties) and mapping files ***.hbm.xml** are used by the **Configuration** class to create (i.e. configure and bootstrap hibernate) the **SessionFactory**, which in turn creates the **Session** instances. *Session* instances are the primary interface for the persistence service.

- **hibernate.cfg.xml** (alternatively can use hibernate.properties): These two files are used to configure the hibernate service (connection driver class, connection URL, connection username, connection password, dialect etc). If both files are present in the classpath then hibernate.cfg.xml file overrides the settings found in the hibernate.properties file.

- **Mapping files (*.hbm.xml):** These files are used to map persistent objects to a relational database. It is the best practice to store each object in an individual mapping file (i.e. mapping file per class) because storing large numbers of persistent classes into one mapping file can be difficult to manage and maintain. The naming convention is to use the same name as the persistent (POJO) class name. For example Account.class will have a mapping file named Account.hbm.xml. Alternatively hibernate **annotations** can be used as part of your persistent class code instead of the *.hbm.xml files.

Q. What is a SessionFactory? Is it a thread-safe object?

SessionFactory is Hibernate's concept of a single datastore and is threadsafe so that many threads can access it concurrently and request for sessions and immutable cache of compiled mappings for a single database. A SessionFactory is usually only built once at startup. SessionFactory should be wrapped in some kind of singleton so that it can be easily accessed in an application code.

SessionFactory **sessionFactory** = new Configuration().configure().buildSessionfactory();

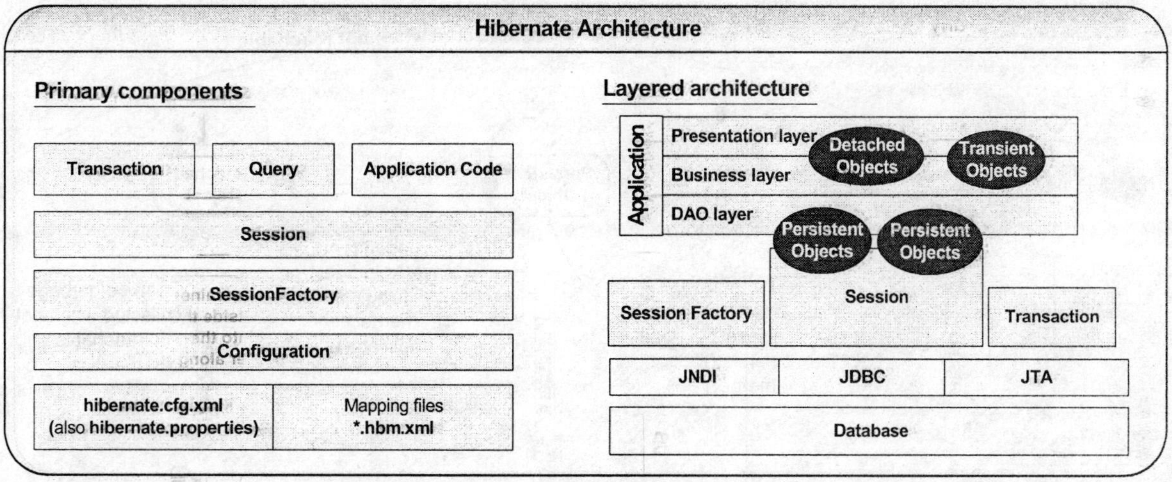

Q. What is a Session? Can you share a session object between different threads?

Session is a light weight and a non-threadsafe object (No, you cannot share it between threads) that represents a single unit-of-work with the database. Sessions are opened by a SessionFactory and then are closed when all work is complete. Session is the primary interface for the persistence service. A session obtains a database connection lazily (i.e. only when required). To avoid creating too many sessions, *ThreadLocal* class can be used as shown below to get the current session no matter how many times you make a call to the *currentSession()* method.

```
...
public class HibernateUtil {
    ...
    public static final ThreadLocal local = new ThreadLocal();

    public static Session currentSession() throws HibernateException {
        Session session = (Session) local.get();
        //open a new session if this thread has no session
        if(session == null) {
            session = sessionFactory.openSession();
            local.set(session);
        }
        return session;
    }
}
```

It is also vital that you close your session after your unit of work completes. **Note:** Keep your Hibernate Session API handy.

Q. Explain hibernate object states? Explain hibernate objects lifecycle?

Persistent	Detached	Transient
Persistent objects and collections are short lived single threaded objects, which store the persistent state. These objects synchronize their state with the database depending on your <u>flush strategy</u> (i.e. **auto-flush** where as soon as setXXX() method is called or an item is removed from a *Set, List* etc or <u>define your own synchronization points</u> with **session.flush(), transaction.commit()** calls). If you remove an item from a persistent collection like a *Set*, it will be removed from the database either immediately or when flush() or commit() is called depending on your flush strategy. They are Plain Old Java Objects (POJOs) and are <u>currently associated with a session</u>. As soon as the associated session is closed, persistent objects <u>become detached objects</u> and are free to use directly as data transfer objects in any application layers like business layer, presentation layer etc.	Detached objects and collections are instances of persistent objects that were associated with a session but currently not associated with a session. These objects can be freely used as Data Transfer Objects <u>without having any impact on your database</u>. Detached objects can be later on attached to another session by calling methods like session.update(), session.saveOrUpdate() etc. and become persistent objects.	Transient objects and collections are instances of persistent objects that were never associated with a session. These objects can be freely used as Data Transfer Objects without having any impact on your database. Transient objects become persistent objects when associated to a session by calling methods like session.save(), session.persist() etc.

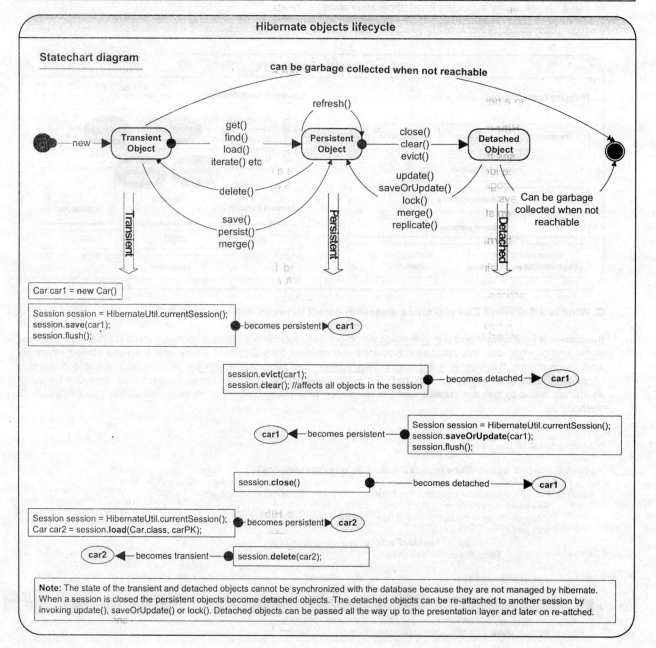

Q. What are the benefits of detached objects?

- Detached objects can be passed across layers all the way up to the presentation layer without having to use any DTOs (Data Transfer Objects). You can later on re-attach the detached objects to another session.

```
Session session1 = sessionFactory.openSession();
Car myCar = session1.get(Car.class, carId); //"myCar" is a persistent object at this stage.
session1.close();        //once the session is closed "myCar" becomes a detached object
```

  you can now pass the "myCar" object all the way upto the presentation tier. It can be modified without any effect to your database table.

```
myCar.setColor("Red");     //no effect on the database
```

  When you are ready to persist this change to the database, it can be reattached to another session as shown below:

```
Session session2 = sessionFactory.openSession();
Transaction tx = session2.beginTransaction();
session2.update(myCar);    //detached object "myCar" gets re-attached
tx.commit();               //change is synchronized with the database.
session2.close()
```

- When long transactions are required due to user think-time, it is the best practice to break the long transaction up into two or more transactions. You can use **detached objects** from the first transaction to carry data all the way up to the presentation layer. These detached objects get modified outside a transaction and later on **re-attached** to a new transaction via another session.

Q. How does Hibernate distinguish between transient (i.e. newly instantiated) and detached objects?

- Hibernate uses the "version" property, if there is one.
- If not uses the identifier value. No identifier value means a new object. This does work only for Hibernate managed surrogate keys. Does not work for natural keys and assigned (i.e. not managed by Hibernate) surrogate keys.
- Write your own strategy with Interceptor.isUnsaved().

Q. What is a Hibernate transaction object?

Transaction is a single threaded, short lived object used by the application to specify atomicity. Transaction abstracts your application code from underlying JDBC, JTA or CORBA transactions. At times a session can span several transactions. When long transactions are required due to user think-time, it is the best practice to break the long transaction up into two or more transactions. You can use **detached objects** from the first transaction to carry data all the way up to the presentation layer. These detached objects get modified outside a transaction and later on **re-attached** to a new transaction via another session.

```
Transaction tx = session.beginTransaction();
Employee emp = new Employee();
emp.setName("Brian");
emp.setSalary(1000.00);

session.save(emp);
tx.commit();
//close session
```

Q. How do you query the database with Hibernate?

Hibernate provides a very robust querying API that supports query strings, named queries and queries built as aggregate expressions. The most flexible way is using the **Hibernate Query Language syntax (HQL)**, which is easy to understand and is an <u>Object Oriented extension to SQL</u>, which supports <u>inheritance</u> and <u>polymorphism</u>.

```
Query query = session.createQuery("Select car from Car as car  where car.color = :color");
query.setString("color","black");
List list = query.list();
```

HQL	SQL
HQL uses classes and properties instead of tables and columns. HQL is less verbose than SQL and supports automatic association	SQL uses tables and columns and is more verbose.

joining. ``` Select car from Car as car join car.parts as part where car.color = 'black' and part.cost > 100"); ```	``` Select car.* from Car as car join Part part on car.part_id = part.id where car.color = 'black' and part.cost > 100"); ```

Type-safe queries can be handled by the object oriented **query by criteria** approach.

```
String color = "black";
Criteria criteria = session.createCriteria(Car.class);
criteria.add(Expression.eq("color", color));
Collection col = criteria.list();
```

You can also use Hibernate's **direct SQL** query feature. If none of the above meets your requirements then you can get a plain JDBC connection from a Hibernate session.

Q. How does hibernate support legacy applications?

You can use **user defined data types** and **composite primary keys** to get additional flexibility to support legacy applications. It is best practice to use wrapper classes like Boolean, Integer, Long etc instead of primitive types in your persistent classes. For example If you have a legacy application, which has the value of null for a *Boolean* property in its legacy table, then hibernate will throw a *PropertyAccessException* if you use the primitive type *boolean* since it cannot take the null value.

Q. Explain some of the following attributes used in *.hbm.xml mapping file?

Attribute	Description and possible values	Example

cascade	Lets you control your graph of objects as to how automatically any associated objects gets saved, updated or deleted. It is also known as <u>transitive persistence</u>.
	
	none (default): no automatic action.
	
	save-update: save or update actions are automatically passed to the child entities.
	
	delete: Delete actions are automatically passed to child entities.
	
	delete-orphan: When a child is removed from the parent, then the child is automatically deleted.
	
	all: save, update and delete actions are passed to child entities but not delete-orphan.
	
	all-delete-orphan: save, update, delete and delete-orphan actions are passed to child entities.
	
	There are other cascade values such as **merge**, **replicate**, **persist**, **lock** etc.
	
	If you have a true composition relationship, where if the parent gets deleted then the children should also be deleted, then you should set the cascade attribute to all-delete-orphan. For example if an *Order* object is deleted then all its *LineItem* objects (i.e. children) should also be deleted as well.
		``
		<hibernate-mapping>
		  <class name="Car" table="car">
		    ....
		    <set name="parts" cascade="all" lazy="true">
		      <key column="part_id" />
		      <one-to-many class="com.Part" />
		    </set>
		    ....
		  </class>
		</hibernate-mapping>
		``

inverse	This attribute is used when you use the one-to-many and many-to-one bidirectional association to indicate that many-to-one side controls the association as opposed to one-to-many side.
	
	If you do not have the inverse flag or if it is set to false then the one-to-many side will control the association, which means if you have the following scenario:
	
	Car car1 = new Car("blue");
		``
		//one-to-many side
		<hibernate-mapping>
		  <class name="Car" table="car">
		    ....
		    <set name="parts" cascade="all" inverse="true">
		      <key column="part_id" />
		      <one-to-many class="com.Part" />
		    </set>
		    ....
		  </class>
		``

	car1.getParts().add(new Part("Steering"));
	car1.getParts().add(new Part("Brake"));
	session.save(car1);
	
	This will result in 3 INSERT SQL calls (1 for the parent *Car* object and 2 times for the *Part* objects). Since the association is controlled by the *Car* object (i.e. one-to-many side), inserting the *part* objects will not set the foreign key value (i.e. car_id) into the *Part* objects. There will be <u>two additional UPDATE SQL calls</u> to add the *Car* object's foreign key value into the *Part* records. So this is not only inefficient but also will cause errors during INSERT SQL calls to *Part* objects if every part should have a car (i.e. foreign-key column car_id in *Part* is a not-null column).
	
	The solution to overcome the above issue is to set the attribute inverse="true" on the *Car* object (i.e. one-to-many side) to indicate that the ownership of the association should be given to the *Part* objects (i.e., many-to-one side). Since the association belongs to the *Part* objects there will never be an INSERT SQL call to the *Part* record with a null car_id.
		``xml
		</hibernate-mapping>
		
		//many-to-one side
		<hibernate-mapping>
		  <class name="Part" table="part">
		    ....
		    <many-to-one name="car" column="car_id" / >
		    ....
		  </class>
		</hibernate-mapping>
		``

lazy	This property is used to determine if all the associated graph of objects should be "**eagerly**" fetched or "**lazily**" loaded when methods like session.get(...), session.load(...), session.find(...), etc are executed. The lazy loading uses proxy objects.
	
	lazy= true (default on hibernate 3.0 onwards) means load associated objects lazily.
	
	lazy=false means load associated objects eagerly.
	
	It is the best practice to set the lazy attribute to true in the mapping file and make it a conscious choice to eagerly join in your HQL or eagerly fetch in your criteria query for specific use cases. For e.g.
	
	String hqlQuery = " FROM Car c OUTER JOIN FETCH c.parts WHERE c.color=?";
	
	If you want to access a lazily initialized collection, you must make sure that the <u>session is open</u>, otherwise an exception will be thrown.
	
	You could also optimize your lazy loading strategy by specifying the batch-size attribute as discussed next.
		``xml
		<hibernate-mapping>
		  <class name="Car" table="car">
		    ....
		    <set name="parts" cascade="all" lazy="true">
		      <key column="part_id" />
		      <one-to-many class="com.Part" />
		    </set>
		    ....
		  </class>
		</hibernate-mapping>
		``
		
		//session should be open to access a proxy object
		
		``java
		Session session= sessionFactory.openSession();
		Car car = session.load(Car.class, 12);// id =12
		Set parts = car.getParts();
		session.close(); //session is closed.
		Part part1 = (Part)parts.get(0); //exception is thrown
		                                //because the session is closed
		``

batch-size	This is used as an optimization strategy for loading objects lazily. Hibernate can load several uninitialized proxy objects if one proxy object or collection is accessed.
	
	For example, say you have 50 *Car* objects loaded into a session with a session.find(....) query operation. Say each car object has an association with a collection of 10 *Part* objects. So if you iterate through all your *Car* objects, there will be 50 SQL SELECT calls to the database for every invocation of *car.getParts()* method. If you set your batch-size attribute to 20, then there will be only 3 SQL SELECTs to the database. Hibernate will load 20,20,10 collections in just 3 SELECT calls.
		``xml
		<hibernate-mapping>
		  <class name="Car" table="car">
		    ....
		    <set name="parts" batch-size="20">
		      <key column="part_id" />
		      <one-to-many class="com.Part" />
		    </set>
		    ....
		  </class>
		</hibernate-mapping>
		``

unsaved-value	unsaved-value attribute comes into play when you use the **saveOrUpdate**(...) method.
	
	null is the default value. Other values supported are **any**, **none**, and **id-value**.
	
	If the unsaved-value is set to null or not set at all (default value is null) and if the *primary-key* property value is null then hibernate assumes that the object is transient and
		``xml
		<hibernate-mapping>
		  <class name="Car" table="car">
		    <id name="id" column="car_id" type="long"
		                         unsaved-value="null">
		      <generator class="native" />
		    </id>
		    <set name="parts" cascade="all" lazy="true">
		      <key column="part_id" />
		      <one-to-many class="com.Part" />
		``

assigns a new *primary-key id* value before <u>saving</u>. If the *primary-key* property value is not-null then hibernate assumes that the object is already persistent and <u>updates</u> the object in the database without inserting.
 	
If you use a long primitive value instead of a *Long* wrapper object (best practice is to use wrapper objects) to store the primary key then the unsaved-value attribute value should be set to 0 because primitive values cannot be null.
	```</set>```
	 ```....```
	 ```</class>```
	 ```</hibernate-mapping>```

Q. What is the difference between the session.get() method and the session.load() method?

Both the **session.get(..)** and **session.load()** methods create a persistent object by loading the required object from the database. But if there was not such object in the database then the method session.load(..) throws an exception whereas session.get(...) returns null.

Q. What is the difference between the session.update() method and the session.lock() method?

Both of these methods and **saveOrUpdate()** method are intended for reattaching a detached object. The session.lock() method simply reattaches the object to the session without checking or updating the database on the assumption that the database in sync with the detached object. It is the best practice to use either session.update(..) or session.saveOrUpdate(). Use session.lock() only if you are absolutely sure that the detached object is in sync with your detached object or if it does not matter because you will be overwriting all the columns that would have changed later on within the same transaction.

Note: When you reattach detached objects you need to make sure that the dependent objects are reattached as well.

Q. How would you reattach detached objects to a session when the same object has already been loaded into the session?

You can use the **session.merge()** method call.

Q. What are the general considerations or best practices for defining your Hibernate persistent classes?

A Hibernate persistent class is a Plain Old Java Object (POJO), which has not interfaces to be implemented and no persistent superclass to be extended. The following are the requirements and best practices (all are not strict requirements) to consider for your Hibernate persistent classes:

1. You must have a default no-argument constructor for your persistent classes and there should be getXXX() (i.e accessor/getter) and setXXX(i.e. mutator/setter) methods for all your persistable instance variables.

2. You should implement the **equals()** and **hashCode()** methods based on your business key and it is important <u>not to use the *id* field in your equals() and hashCode() definition if the *id* field is a surrogate key</u> (i.e. Hibernate managed identifier). This is because the Hibernate only generates and sets the field when saving the object.

```
Car car = session.load(Car.class, carId);
car.getParts().add(new Part("Steering")); // adds a new entity with id = null (if Integer)
                                           // or id = 0 (if primitive int)
car.getParts().add(new Part("Accelerator"));// has id = null too so overwrites last added
                                           // object in the Set.
```

Alternatively if you use manually assigned *id* fields then you can use your *id* field in your equals() and hashCode() methods but <u>you must make sure to set the *id* field prior to adding the object to the *Set*</u> and it is quite difficult to guarantee this in most applications.

```
Car car = session.load(Car.class, carId);
Part part1 = new Part("Steering");
part1.setId(1001);
car.getParts().add(part1));                 //adds a new part entity with id=1001
Part part2 = new Part("Accelerator");
part1.setId(1002);
car.getParts().add(part2);           //has the id=1002 so adds a new part entity with id=1002
```

So to avoid the problem of inadvertently not setting the *id* prior to adding the object to the *Set*, it is recommended to use the "semi" unique business key (i.e natural key) to implement equals() and hashCode() methods.

3. It is recommended to implement the *Serializable* interface. This is potentially useful if you want to migrate around a multi-processor cluster.

4. The persistent class should not be final because if it is final then lazy loading cannot be used by creating proxy objects.

5. Use XDoclet tags for generating your *.hbm.xml files or Annotations (JDK 1.5 onwards), which are less verbose than *.hbm.xml files.

Q. What is the difference between an object identity and a database identity?

Object	Database
Identity: `car1 == car2` (i.e. car1 & car 2 are pointing to the same object).	**Identity:** `car1.getId().equals(car2.getId())`
Equality: `car1.equals(car2)` → Refer **Q18** in Java section.	Where "id" is the primary key. If the ids are equal then both the car objects are referring to the same row in the database.

Q. What are the important considerations in writing your equals() & hashCode() methods?

1. Use your semi unique business keys. **For example** you can use the following immutable fields (i.e. instance variables) as your business keys in your *Car* persistence class: ***name***, ***model*** and ***createddate***. You need to make sure that the fields used in your equals() method must be used in your hashCode() method as well.

2. If two objects are equal i.e. car1.equals(car2) returns "true" then car1.hashCode() == car2.hashCode() must return "true" as well. But if two objects are not equal i.e. car1.equals(car2) returns "false" then car1.hashCode() == car2.hashCode() can return either "true" or "false". Refer **Q19, Q20** in Java section for a discussion on equals() and hashCode() contract.

3. When referring to fields (i.e. instance variables) of the argument object, always use the accessor methods rather than directly using the instance variables because your supplied argument object might be a proxy object rather than the actual object. **For example:**

```
public boolean equals(Object supplied) {
    if (this == supplied){
        return true;          //same objects
    }
    if (other == null) {
        return false;
    }

    if(! (other instanceOf  Car) ) {
        return false;
    }

    final Car car2 = (Car) supplied;

    if( this.name.equals (car2.getName()) &&
        this.model.equals (car2.getModel()) &&
        this.createdDate.equals (car2.getCreatedDate()) )  {

        return true;
    }
    else {
        return false;
    }
}

Need to make sure that all the three fields used in equals() method are used in hashCode() method
as well.

public int hashCode() {
    int hashCode = name.hashCode() * 11;
    hashCode =  hashCode + model.hashCode() * 17;
    hashCode =  hashCode + createdDate.hashCode() * 29;
    return hashCode;
```

Q. What are the different types of persistent objects defined by Hibernate?

- **Entity objects** (aka first rank class): These objects have a persistent identity. Usually an identifier field (e.g. id), which is managed by Hibernate. These are typically central business objects like Investor, Customer, Order etc

- **Value objects** (aka second rank class): These objects do not have an identity and only exist in a relationship to an entity object (aka first rank class). These are typically supporting objects such as Address, Name etc.

Q. How would you map a composition relationship in Hibernate?

A Hibernate component (not an architectural level component like EJB etc) is a contained **value object**, which refers to the Object Oriented notion of composition. A standard example is that of an *Address* **value object** stored as a property of an *Investor* **entity object**. *Address* value object depends on an *Investor* entity object.

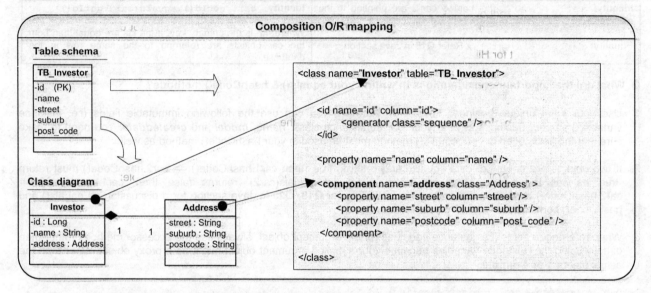

As you can see above in the fine-grained persistence diagram, there are more classes (i.e. 2 classes) than table (i.e. 1 table). Fine grained persistence object models have greater code reuse and easier to understand. Collections of components are also possible by using a <composite-element> tag. You can also define a composition relationship with a one-to-many entity association relationship with the <u>cascade attribute set to "all-delete-orphan"</u>.

Q. What association or aggregation relationships can be mapped with Hibernate?

Database relationships are typically defined in terms of cardinality and direction. From an OO perspective, relationships are defined as association or aggregation. These relationships for objects can be viewed as either unidirectional (i.e. when one object knows about the other but not vice versa) or bidirectional (i.e. both objects would know about each other). Cardinality can be defined as **one-to-one** (i.e. both on primary key as well as foreign key with a unique constraint), **one-to-many**, **many-to-one** and **many-to-many**. Hibernate managed entity objects can be mapped for all the above mentioned cardinality and direction.

Q. How would you map inheritance relationships in Hibernate? Also refer **Q101** in Enterprise section.

There are number of ways Hibernate can handle inheritance among entity objects. The simplest is to use **one table for the whole hierarchy**. Only one table is required. With this design strategy, each row of the table can hold an object of any type from the entity object inheritance hierarchy. You should assign one column as the "**discriminator**" property of an entity class, which contains a value used to tell which actual type of object is stored in that particular row.

Another strategy to map inheritance relationship is to use **table per subclass** strategy. Say you have a table called *Vehicle* and three subclass tables called *Car*, *Van* and *Bus*. These 3 subclass tables will have primary key associations to the superclass table Vehicle. So this relational model is actually a one-to-one association on a primary key. The entity object model will have a superclass representing the *Vehicle* table and 3 entity subclasses representing the *Car*, *Van* and *Bus* tables.

Another strategy to map inheritance relationship is to use **table per concrete class** strategy. There will only be 3 tables (i.e. *Car*, *Van* and *Bus*) involved for the subclasses. The entity object model will have a superclass representing the

Vehicle table and 3 entity subclasses representing the *Car*, *Van* and *Bus* tables. If your superclass *Vehicle* is abstract, then map it with abstract="true".

Finally, you could also mix **table per class hierarchy** strategy with **table per subclass** strategy.

Q 16: Explain some of the pitfalls of Hibernate and explain how to avoid them? Give some tips on Hibernate best practices? FAQ

A 16:

Pitfalls on Hibernate and how to avoid them:

- O/R mapping framework like Hibernate is well suited for read → modify → write centric applications and not suited for write centric applications (i.e. batch processes with large data sets like 5000 rows or more) where data is seldom read.

- Use the ThreadLocal session pattern when obtaining Hibernate session objects (Refer **Q15** in Emerging Technologies/Frameworks). This is important because Hibernate's native API does not use the current thread to maintain associations between session and transaction or between session and application thread. Spring ORM support for Hibernate can not only take care of the above pitfall but also can improve productivity.

- Handle resources properly by making sure you properly flush and commit each session object when persisting information and also make sure you release or close the session object when you are finished working with it. Most developers fall into this pitfall. If you pass a connection object to your session object then remember to issue **session.close().close ()** which will first release the connection back to the pool and then will close the session. If you do not pass a connection object then issue **session.close()** to close the session.

- Use **lazy associations** when you use relationships otherwise you can unwittingly fall into the trap of executing unnecessary SQL statements in your Hibernate applications. Let us look at an example: Suppose we have a class *Employee* with many-to-one relationship with class *Department*. So one department can have many employees. Suppose we want to list the name of the employees then we will construct the query as follows:

```
Query query = session.createQuery("from Employee emp");
List list =  query.list();
```

Hibernate will generate the following SQL query:

```
SELECT <fields> from Employee;
```

If it only generates the query above then it is okay and it serves our purpose, but we get another set of SQL queries without asking it to do anything. One for each of the referenced departments in *Department* table. If you had 5 departments then the following query will be executed 5 times with corresponding department id. This is the N+1 selects problem. In our example it is 5 + 1. Employee table is queried once and Department table is queried 5 times.

```
SELECT <fields> from Department where DEPARTMENT.id=?
```

Solution is to make the *Department* class lazy (in Hibernate 3.0 the default value for lazy attribute is "true"), simply by enabling the lazy attribute in the Department's hbm.xml mapping definition file, which will result in executing only the first statement from the *Employee* table and not the 5 queries from the *Department* table.

```
<class name="com.Department"  table="Department" lazy="true" > …. </class>
```

Only one query is required to return an employee object with its department initialized. In Hibernate, lazy loading of persistent objects are facilitated by proxies (i.e. virtual proxy design pattern). In the above example you have a *Department* object, which has a collection of *Employee* objects. Let's say that *Employee* objects are lazy loaded. If you make a call department.getEmployees() then Hibernate will load only the employeeIDs and the version numbers of the *Employee* objects, thus saving loading of individual objects until later. So what you really have is a collection of proxies not the real objects. The reason being, if you have hundreds of employees for a particular department then chances are good that you will only deal with only a few of them. So, why unnecessarily instantiate all the *Employee* objects? This can be a big performance issue in some situations.

- **Avoid N+1 selects problem:** Having looked at the N+1 problem occurring inadvertently due to not having a lazy association in the previous example, now what if we need the Departmental information in addition to the Employee details. It is not a good idea to execute N+1 times.

```
<class name="com.Department"  table="Department" lazy="true" > .... </class>
```

Now to retrieve *Departmental* info you would:

```
Query query = session.createQuery("from Employee emp");
List list = query.list();
Iterator it = list.iterator();

while(iter.hasNext()) {
    Employee emp = (Employee) it.next();
    emp.getDepartment().getName(); //N+1 problem. Since Department is not already loaded so
                                   //additional query is required for each department.
}
```

The solution is to make sure that the initial query retrieves all the data needed to load the objects by issuing a HQL fetch join (**eager loading**) as shown below:

```
"from Employee emp join fetch emp.Department dept"
```

The above HQL results in an inner join SQL as shown below:

```
SELECT <fields from Employee & Department> FROM employee
               inner join department on employee.departmentId = department.id.
```

Alternatively you can use a criteria query as follows:

```
Criteria crit = session.createCriteria(Employee.class);
crit.setFetchMode("department", FetchMode.EAGER);
```

The above approach creates the following SQL:

```
SELECT <fields from Employee & Department> FROM employee
            left outer join department on employee.departmentId = department.id where 1=1;
```

Tips on Hibernate best practices:

- Define equals() and hashCode() methods with the semi unique business key attributes (should not use the indentifier property) for the entity objects that are stored in a collection like a Set. Follow the equals() & hashCode() contracts.

- Leave all your associations by default as lazy and also specify an appropriate batch-size for performance. Also make it a conscious choice to eagerly fetch data only for specific use cases.

- Define your session management (i.e. use of detached objects etc), caching (both 1st level & 2nd level cache) and flush (i.e. auto-flush vs defining your own synchronization points etc) strategies early in your project.

- Prefer using bi-directional associations for a one-to-many association with an inverse="true" attribute for efficiency. Also use batch updates/inserts for bulk inserts/updates (may even consider using Stored Procedures directly for large data).

- Where possible use surrogate key as your identifier as opposed to using composite keys.

- Keep your database transactions as short as possible with the use of detached objects and also understand the Hibernate object life cycles and states.

- Use Spring ORM support for hibernate, which reduces the code size by almost a half and provides additional benefits such as easier testing, consistent exception hierarchy and management of Hibernate resources. Spring exceptions are unchecked and hence you do not have to write any try{} catch{} and finally{} semantics and also you can manage the transactions declaratively via Spring transaction management (Refer **Q43** in Enterprise section) using Spring AOP (Refer **Q3** in Emerging Technologies/Frameworks section).

Q 17: Give an overview of the Spring framework? What are the benefits of Spring framework? FAQ
A 17: The Spring framework is the leading full-stack Java/J2EE application framework. Unlike other frameworks, Spring does not impose itself on the design of a project due to its modular nature and, it has been divided logically into

independent packages, which can function independently. It provides a light weight container and a non-invasive programming model enabled by the use of **dependency injection** (aka **IoC**), **AOP** (**A**spect **O**riented **P**rogramming), and portable service abstractions (JdbcTemplate, JmsTemplate etc).

It includes abstraction layers for transactions, persistence frameworks (e.g. HibernateTemplate support for Hibernate), Web development, a JDBC integration framework, an AOP integration framework, email support, Web Services (i.e. JAX-RPC) support etc. It also provides integration modules for popular Object-to-Relational (O/R) mapping tools like Hibernate, JDO etc. The designers of an application can feel free to use just a few Spring packages and leave out the rest. The other spring packages can be introduced into an existing application in a phased manner. Spring is based on the IoC pattern (aka Dependency Injection pattern) and also complements OOP (Object Oriented Programming) with AOP (Aspect Oriented Programming). You do not have to use AOP if you do not want to and AOP complements Spring IoC to provide a better middleware solution.

As shown in the diagram below the Spring modules are built on top of the core container, which defines how beans are configured, created and managed.

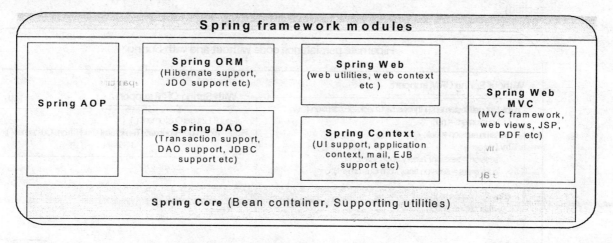

Q. Where does Spring fit in your J2EE architecture?

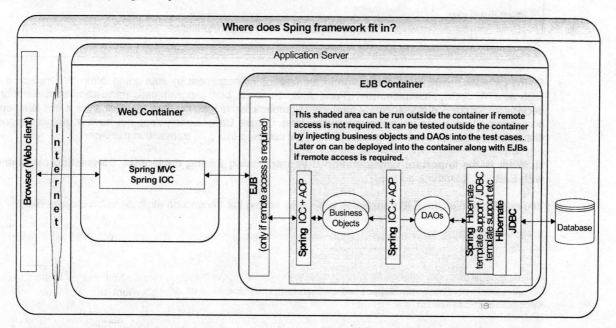

Benefits of Spring framework:

- Spring can effectively organize your middle tier objects as shown in the diagram above, whether or not you choose to use EJB. Applications built using Spring are easy to test. **For example:** As shown in the diagram above with the shaded area, your business logic and data access logic can be easily tested outside the container by injecting (i.e. **dependency injection.** Spring supports <u>constructor and setter dependency</u>

injections) business objects and DAO objects into your JUnit test cases and later on if remote access is required, can be deployed inside the EJB container with a thin layer (i.e. no business logic) of EJBs (i.e. stateless session beans for remote access). Spring also provides support for proxying remote calls via RMI, JAX-RPC etc.

- Spring can facilitate good programming practice by encouraging programming to interfaces rather than to implementation.

- Spring provides a consistent framework for data access, whether using JDBC or O/R mapping frameworks like Hibernate, TopLink or JDO. Spring ORM support for hibernate reduces the code size by almost a half and provides additional benefits such as easier testing, consistent exception hierarchy (Spring folds your SQLException to a common set of unchecked exceptions) and management of Hibernate resources like SessionFactory. Spring exceptions are unchecked and hence you do not have to write any try{} catch{} and finally{} semantics and also you can manage the transactions declaratively via Spring transaction management (Refer **Q43** in Enterprise section) using Spring AOP (Refer **Q3** in Emerging Technologies/Frameworks section).

Hibernate persistence code without and with Spring

Without Spring ORM support

```
publi List getCustomers() throws MyCheckedException {
    List customers = null;
    Session session = null;
    try {
        session = sessionFactory.openSession();
        customers = session.find("from Customer ");
    }
    catch(Exception ex){
        //handle exception
    }

    finally{
        session.close();
    }
    return customers;
}
```

With Spring ORM support

```
publi List getCustomers ( ) {
    return getHibernateTemplate().find ("from Customer ");
}
```

- Spring provides a consistent abstraction for transaction management by supporting different transaction APIs such as JTA, JDBC, Hibernate, iBATIS and JDO. Supports both programmatic transaction management and declarative transaction management (preferred approach for transaction management since it has least impact on application code due to its non-invasive nature). Unlike EJB, Spring does not have a default support for distributed transactions (i.e. XA transactions -) but can plug-in a JTA transaction manager.

Q. What is the important consideration if you are using Spring declarative transaction management with EJB (i.e. for remote access)?

You need to turn off the EJB transaction support by setting the transaction attribute to "NotSupported"

```
<container-transaction >
    <method >
        <ejb-name>CRMService</ejb-name>
        <method-name>*</method-name>
    </method>
    <trans-attribute>NotSupported</trans-attribute>
</container-transaction>
```

- JDBC applications are verbose with try{}, catch{} and finally blocks and very tedious to write. A good abstraction layer like Spring lets you customize a default JDBC with a query and anonymous inner class (Refer **Q35** in Java section) to eliminate much of the code. You do not have to worry about managing the resources like *DataSource*, *Connection*, *Statement* and *ResultSet*, configuring your *DataSource*, managing transactions and SQLExceptions. Spring IoC + AOP (for declarative transaction) will take care of all these.

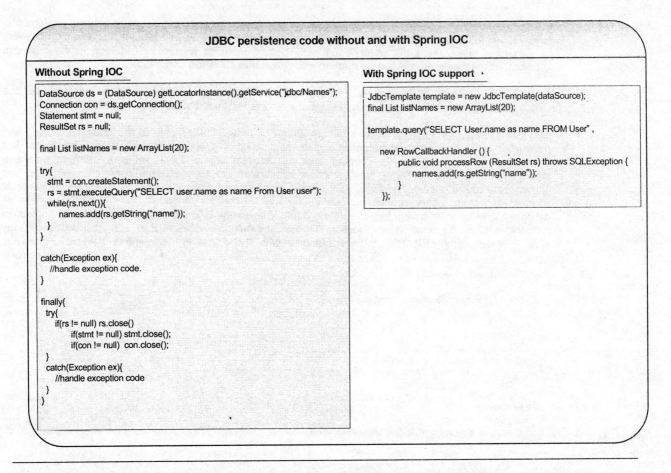

JDBC persistence code without and with Spring IOC

Without Spring IOC

```
DataSource ds = (DataSource) getLocatorInstance().getService("jdbc/Names");
Connection con = ds.getConnection();
Statement stmt = null;
ResultSet rs = null;

final List listNames = new ArrayList(20);

try{
  stmt = con.createStatement();
  rs = stmt.executeQuery("SELECT user.name as name From User user");
  while(rs.next()){
     names.add(rs.getString("name"));
  }
}

catch(Exception ex){
  //handle exception code.
}

finally{
  try{
    if(rs != null) rs.close()
        if(stmt != null) stmt.close();
        if(con != null)  con.close();
  }
  catch(Exception ex){
    //handle exception code
  }
}
```

With Spring IOC support

```
JdbcTemplate template = new JdbcTemplate(dataSource);
final List listNames = new ArrayList(20);

template.query("SELECT User.name as name FROM User" ,

    new RowCallbackHandler () {
        public void processRow (ResultSet rs) throws SQLException {
            names.add(rs.getString("name"));
        }
});
```

Q 18: How would EJB 3.0 simplify your Java development compared to EJB 1.x, 2.x ? FAQ

A 18: EJB 3.0 is taking ease of development very seriously and has adjusted its model to offer the POJO (Plain Old Java Object) persistence and the new **O/R mapping model inspired by and based on Hibernate** (a less intrusive model). In EJB 3.0, **all kinds of enterprise beans are just POJOs**. EJB 3.0 **extensively uses Java annotations**, which replace excessive XML based configuration files and eliminate the need for rigid component model used in EJB 1.x, 2.x. Annotations can be used to define a bean's business interface, O/R mapping information, resource references etc. EJB 3.0 also supports XML files for overriding default values and configuring external resources such as database connections.

- In EJB 1.x, 2.x the container manages the behavior and internal state of the bean instances at runtime. All the EJB 1.x, 2.x beans must adhere to a rigid specification. In EJB 3.0, all container services can be configured and delivered to any POJO in the application via annotations. **You can build complex object structures with POJOs. Java objects can inherit from each other.** EJB 3.0 components are only coupled via their published business interfaces hence the implementation classes can be changed without affecting rest of the application. This makes the application more robust, easier to test, more portable and makes it easier to build loosely coupled business components in POJO.

The business interface:
```
public interface Account  {
    public void deposit(double amount);
}
```

The bean implementation class:
```
@Stateless
@Remote({Account.class})
public class AccountBean implements Account {
    public void deposit(double amount){
        //....
    }
}
```

you can also specify multiple interfaces for a session bean. One for local clients and one for remote clients.

- EJB 3.0 unlike EJB 1.x, 2.x **does not have a home interface**. The bean class may or may not implement a business interface. If the bean class does not implement any business interface, a business interface will be generated using the public methods. If only certain methods should be exposed in the business interface, all of those methods can be marked with **@BusinessMethod** annotation.

- EJB 3.0 defines smart default values. For example by default all generated interfaces are local, but the @Remote annotation can be used to indicate that a remote interface should be generated.

- The EJB 3.0 (i.e, Inversion Of Control design pattern) container takes care of the creation, pooling and destruction of the session bean instances and the application only works with the business interfaces. But if the application needs a finer control over the session beans, for example to perform database initialization when the container creates the session bean or close external connection etc, you can implement lifecycle callback methods in the bean class. These methods are called by the container at various stages(e.g. bean creation and destruction) of the bean's lifecycle. Unlike EJB 2.1, where all callback methods must be implemented even if they are empty, EJB 3.0 beans can have any number of callback methods (i.e. even no methods at all) with any method name. In EJB 3.0, you can specify any bean method as a callback by annotating it with the following annotations `@PostConstruct`, `@PreDestroy`, `@PrePassivate`, `@PostPassivate`, `@PostActivate`, `@Init`, `@Remove` (only for stateful session beans) and `@PostConstruct`.

```
public class AccountBean implements Account {

    //...

    @PostConstruct
    public void initialize(){
        //initialize data from the database
    }

    @PreDestroy
    public void exit(){
        //save data back to the database
    }
}
```

- An MDB (Message Driven Bean) class must implement the *MessageListener* interface.

- EJB 3.0 makes use of dependency injection to make decoupled service objects and resources like queue factories, queues etc available to any POJO. Using the @EJB annotation, you can inject an EJB stub into any POJO managed by the EJB 3.0 container and using @Resource annotation you can inject any resource from the JNDI.

```
public class AccountMDB implements MessageListener {

    @EJB Account account;

    //use the "account" variable
    // … …
}
```

- EJB 3.0 wires runtime services such as transaction management, security, logging, profiling etc to applications at runtime. Since those services are not directly related to application's business logic they are not managed by the application itself. Instead, the services are transparently applied by the container utilizing AOP (Aspect Oriented Programming). To apply a transaction attribute to a POJO method using annotation:

```
public class Account {

    @TransactionAttribute(TransactionAttributeType.REQUIRED)
    public getAccountDetails(){
        //…
    }
}
```

- In EJB 3.0, you can extend the container services by writing your own interceptors using the `@AroundInvoke` annotation. You can specify any bean method as the interceptor method that will execute before and after any other bean method runs.

```
@Stateful
public class AccountBean implements Account {

    // bean methods that are to be intercepted by the log() method
    // … …

    @AroundInvoke
    public Object log(InvocationContext ctx) throws Exception {
        //…
    }
}
```

- EJB 3.0 supports both unidirectional and bidirectional relationships between entity beans. To create an entity bean, you only need to code a bean class and annotate it with appropriate metadata annotations. The bean class is a POJO.

```
@Entity
public class AccountEntityBean {
    private Integer accountNumber;
    private String accountName;

    @id (generate=AUTO)
    public Integer getUserId() {
        return this.accountNumber;
    }

    //getters & setters
    //… …

}
```

- EJB QL queries can be defined through the @NamedQuery annotation. You can also create regular JDBC style queries using the *EntityManager*. POJOs are not persistent by birth and become persistent once it is associated with an *EntityManager*.

Q. What recent technology trends are vital to enterprise Web development?

- Component based Web frameworks like JSF and Tapestry.
- Ajax (Asynchronous JavaScript and XML).

Q. What is a component based and event-driven Web framewok? How do they differ from request based frameworks like Struts?

Struts and many other MVC Web frameworks are request based and to achieve reusability you typically develop JSP tag libraries and/or include files with common functionality. This approach of reusability is not only ugly but also difficult to achieve code reuse. Component based and event-driven Web frameworks have emerged to provide better code reuse and improve ease of development. These component based frameworks provide an API for developing reusable features that are easily packaged and reused across applications. These frameworks are very useful when developing large Web applications or many Web applications with common functionality. The leading contenders in this space of **component based** and **event-driven** frameworks are JavaServer Faces (**JSF**) and **Tapestry**. These frameworks

- bury the Servlet API deep down and shield the developer from having to work directly with the Servlet API.
- bind Web display controls directly to Java object properties and user interactions like button click etc are mapped directly Java event handling methods in these Java objects (just like Swing).
- allow you to group and package chunks of functionality into components to be reused in different contexts or applications. The standard framework ships with the core components, enabling the most commonly required functionality and you can make use of these components to build more reusable components more specific to your application or industry.

Both the JSF and Tapestry address the above mentioned fundamentals but they differ greatly the way they implement these fundamentals.

Q 19: Briefly explain key features of the JavaServer Faces (JSF) framework?
A 19: JavaServer Faces is a new framework for building Web applications using Java. JSF provides you with the following main features:

- Basic user interface components like buttons, input fields, links etc. and custom components like tree/table viewer, query builder etc. JSF was built with a **component model** in mind to allow tool developers to support Rapid Application Development (RAD). User interfaces can be created from these reusable server-side components.

- Provides a set of JSP tags to access interface components. Also provides a framework for implementing custom components.

- Supports mark up languages other than HTML like WML (Wireless Markup Language) by encapsulating event handling and component rendering. There is a single controller servlet every request goes through where the job of the controller servlet is to receive a faces page with components and then fire off events for each component to render the components using a render tool kit.

- Uses a declarative navigation model by defining the navigation rules inside the XML configuration file faces-config.xml . This configuration file also defines bean resources used by JSF.

- JSF can hook into your model, which means the model is loosely coupled from JSF.

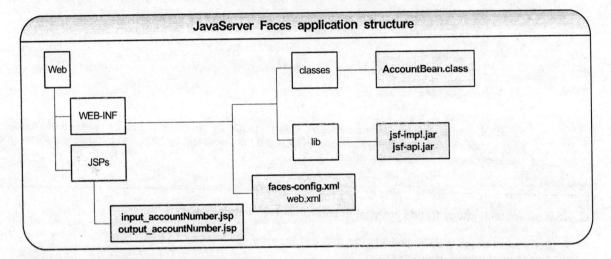

Let's look at some code snippets. Texts are stored in a properties file called **message.properties** so that this properties file can be quickly modified without having to modify the JSPs and also more maintainable because multiple JSP pages can use the same property.

```
account_nuber = Account number
account_button = Get account details
account_message=Processing account number :
```

input_accountNumber.jsp

```
<%@ taglib uri="http://java.sun.com.jsf/html" prefix="h" %>
<%@ taglib uri="http://java.sun.com.jsf/core" prefix="f" %>
<f:loadBundle basename="messages" var="msg"/>

<html>
  ...
  <body>
    <f:view>
      <h:form id="accountForm">
          <h:outputText value="#{msg.account_number}" />
          <h:inputText value="#{accountBean.accountNumber}" />
          <h:commandButton action="getAccount" value="#{msg.account_button}" />
      </h:form>
    </f:view>
  </body>
</html>
```

AccountBean.Java

```
public class AccountBean {
  String accountNumber;
```

```
public String getAccountNumber() {
    return accountNumber;
}

public void setAccountNumber(String accountNumber) {
    this.accountNumber = accountNumber;
}

}
```

faces-config.xml

```
...
<faces-config>

  <navigation-rule>
    <form-view-id>/jsps/input_accountNumber.jsp</form-view-id>
    <navigation-case>
      <from-outcome>getAccount</from-outcome>
      <to-view-id>/jsps/output_accountNumber.jsp</to-view-id>
    </navigation-case>
  </navigation-rule>
  ...

  <managed-bean>
    <managed-bean-name>accountBean</managed-bean-name>
    <managed-bean-class>AccountBean</managed-bean-class>
    <managed-bean-scope>request</managed-bean-scope>
  </managed-bean>

</faces-config>
```

output_accountNumber.jsp

```
<html>
  ...
  <body>
    <f:view>
      <h3>
        <h:outputText value="#{msg.account_message}" />
        <h:outputText value="#{accountBean.accountNumber}" />
      </h3>
    </f:view>
  </body>
</html>
```

Q 20: How would the JSF framework compare with the Struts framework? How would a Spring MVC framework compare with Struts framework?

A 20:

Struts framework	JavaServer Faces
More matured since Struts has been around for a few years. It has got several successful implementations.	Less matured than Struts.
The heart of Struts framework is the controller, which uses the front controller design pattern and the command design pattern. Struts framework has got **only single event handler** for the HTTP request.	The heart of JSF framework is the Page Controller Pattern where there is a front controller servlet where all the faces request go through with the UI components and then <u>fire off events for each component</u> and render the components using a render toolkit. So JSF can have **several event handlers on a page**. Also JSF loosely couples your model, where it can hook into your model (i.e unlike Struts your model does not have to extend JSF classes).
Struts does not have the vision of Rapid Application Development (RAD).	JSF was built with a component model in mind to allow RAD. JSF can be thought of as a combination of Struts framework for thin clients and the Java Swing user interface framework for thick clients.
Has got flexible page navigation using navigation rules inside the struts-config.xml file and Action classes using mapping.findForward (...) .	JSF allows for more flexible navigation and a better design because the navigation rule (specified in **faces-config.xml**) is decoupled from the Action whereas Struts forces you to hook navigation into your Action classes.

Struts is a sturdy frame work which is extensible and flexible. The existing Struts applications can be migrated to use JSF component tags instead of the original Struts HTML tags because Struts tags are superseded and also not undergoing any active development. You can also use the **Struts-Faces Integration** library to migrate your pages one page at a time to using JSF component tags.	JSF is more flexible than Struts because it was able to learn from Struts and other Web frameworks. JSF is also more extensible and can integrate with RAD tools etc. So JSF will be a good choice for new applications.

Struts framework	Spring MVC framework
Both are request based MVC frameworks.	
Struts addresses only the presentation aspects of application development.	Spring MVC is an integral part of the Spring framework, which fully integrates Spring with the rest of the framework that manage business components as well as other aspects of Spring enterprise development. Spring Controllers are configured via IoC like any other objects and this makes Spring MVC easier to test compared to Struts. Spring, like WebWork, provides <u>interceptors</u> as well as controllers, making it easy to factor out behavior common to the handling of many requests.
In Struts, Actions are core "processing" objects of the framework. They play the role of controllers in the MVC pattern.	Spring uses the Controller interface. In other words, Controllers process user input and dispatch to view components in Spring. The most significant difference between the Struts Action and the Spring Controller is that <u>Actions are abstract classes and Controllers are interfaces</u>. This design based on "code to interface" principle gives Spring MVC greater flexibility by minimizing the coupling between the application and the framework itself.

Struts actions are configured as "mappings" in struts-config.xml. Struts uses its own *ActionServlet* class mapped in the web.xml file.	Spring Controllers are configured as "beans" in <servlet-name>-servlet.xml. e.g. action-servlet.xml where "action" is the servlet name configured in web.xml file.
	
	`<servlet>`
	  `<servlet-name>`**action**`</servlet-name>`
	  `<servlet-class>`org.springframework.web.servlet.**DispatcherServlet**`</servlet-class>`
	  `<load-on-startup>`1`</load-on-startup>`
	`</servlet>`

Struts has specialized *ActionForm* objects to map request parameters.	The Spring MVC framework support mapping request parameters directly into POJOs (Plain Old Java Objects). This feature greatly simplifies application maintenance by limiting the number of classes to create and maintain.
Struts uses *ActionMapping* objects to represent resources such as Actions, JSPs, HTML files, Tiles etc.	This is a bit similar to *ModelAndView* interface in Spring. Spring also offers better integration with different view technologies like Velocity, XSLT etc and also enables you to integrate your own templating language into Spring with the *View* interface.
Struts uses its own tag library. E.g. html, bean and logic tag prefixes.	Spring leverages JSTL and JSP expression language (EL). Spring MVC only offers a small tag library for binding of command objects into Web form.
Pages can be composed using tiles (template) framework or decorated using SIteMesh (Servlet filter) framework.	
Validation can be supported by using the Commons validator framework consisting of validation.xml and validator-rule.xml files.	

Note: Recently a new type of Web programming has challenged the other Web frameworks called the **R**ich **I**nternet **A**pplication (**RIA**). These applications are typically use technologies such as **Ajax** which involves JavaScript to communicate with the server without reloading a Web page.

Q. What is Ajax ?

There is a lot of hype surrounding the latest Web development Ajax (Asynchronous JavaScript And XML). The intent of Ajax is to make Web pages more responsive and interactive by exchanging small amounts of data with the server behind the scenes without refreshing the page, so that the entire Web page does not have to be reloaded each time the user makes a change. Ajax technique uses a combination of JavaScript, XHTML (or HTML) and XMLHttp.

Q. Where to use Ajax ? What is the benefit of Ajax ?

In an application that requires a lot of interactivity with a business or service layer sitting on the server, where the user must reload the entire page many times. This will offer the benefits of reducing the load on the server and improving the productivity of the user due to faster response (unlike the traditional architecture where the user must wait for the entire Web page to reload to see the new results from the server, Ajax brings down JavaScript calls and the actual data. So Ajax pages appear to load quickly since the payload coming down from the server is much smaller in size than bringing down the entire HTML page in the traditional architecture).

General Tip #10:

Some interviewers would like to ask **brain teaser questions** to evaluate your mental agility. It is even more vital for the entry level positions. These brain teaser questions can help evaluate your aptitude to learn new things faster.

Questions:

Q1: If you are given a two-armed scale and 8 balls of which one is heavier than the other 7 balls. How would you go about determining the heavier ball by using the scale only twice?

Q2: If you have two containers, one holds 5 liters of milk and the other holds 3 liters of milk. How will you measure exactly 4 liters into the five liter container? (It is okay to waste milk and you can have as much milk as you like).

Q3: If you have 6 pairs of blue gloves and 4 pairs of black gloves are in a box. If you are blind folded, then how many gloves do you have to pull out before you have got a match?

Q4: If your clock shows 9:45 pm, then calculate the angle between the hour hand and the minute hand?

Q5: If you need to take a tiger, a cow and a pile of hay from one side of a river to another side by boat. You can only take one thing at a time and care should be taken what two things you leave behind together. For example if you decide to take the pile of hay first to the other side then you will be leaving behind the tiger and the cow this side, which can result in tiger eating the cow. [**HINT**: The cow can eat the pile of hay but not the tiger]

Answers:

A1: Put 3 balls on each side of the scale. **Measure 1** → If the arms are equal, then you know that the heavier ball is one of the two remaining. **Measure 2** → So weigh these two remaining balls and you will find out which is heavier.

Measure 1 → If the arms are unequal when you weighed three balls in each arm then take the three balls on the heavier side and pick any two balls out of those three **Measure 2** → and weigh them against each other to find which is heavier. If they are equal then the remaining ball is the heavy one.

A2: Fill up the 3 liter container with milk and pour it into the 5 liter container. Fill up the 3 liter container again with milk and pour it into the 5 liter container on top of the 3 liter which is already there. So you will be left with 1 liter in the 3 liter container and 5 liters in the 5 liter container. Now, empty the 5 liter container and pour the 1 liter from the 3 liter container into the 5 liter container. Fill up the 3 liter container again and pour into the 5 liter container on top of the 1 liter already there to get 4 liters.

A3: To get matching gloves you need to pick three gloves because there are only 2 colors. i.e blue, blue, black (you have a match on blue) or blue, black, black (you have a match on black) or black, blue, black (you have a match on black) and so on.

A4: When the minute hand is in 45 minutes (that is pointing against 9) the hour hand would have moved three-fourth of an hour (that is ¾ of the way to 10). Each hour division is 360 degrees / 12 hours = 30 degrees. So three-fourth of an hour is 30*(3/4) = 22.5 degrees.

A5: Firstly take the cow across to the other side of the river and leave behind the tiger with the pile of hay on this side because the tiger would not eat the hay. Come back and take the pile of hay to the other side of the river and bring back the cow with you to this side because you cannot leave behind the cow and the hay together. Take the tiger to the other side. Now you can leave behind the tiger and the hay on the other side. Come back again and finally take the cow to the other side.

So far you have briefly looked at some of the emerging paradigms like Dependency Injection (aka IoC -- Inversion Of Control), AOP (Aspect Oriented Programming), annotations, O/R mapping, component based Web technology and some of the frameworks, which are based on these paradigms like Spring (IoC & AOP), Java 5.0 annotations, Hibernate (O/R mapping), JSF (component based web framework) etc. These paradigms and frameworks simplify your programming model by hiding the complexities behind the framework and minimizing the amount of code an application developer has to write.

SECTION FIVE

Sample interview questions...

Tips:

- Try to find out the needs of the project in which you will be working and the needs of the people within the project.

- 80% of the interview questions are based on your own resume.

- Where possible briefly demonstrate how you applied your skills/knowledge in the key areas as described in this book. Find the right time to raise questions and answer those questions to show your strength.

- Be honest to answer technical questions, you are not expected to know everything (for example you might know a few design patterns but not all of them etc).

- Do not be critical, focus on what you can do. Also try to be humorous.

- Do not act in superior way.

General Tip #11:

There is a difference between looking excited about a job or a job offer and looking desperate for one. Do not immediately jump at the opportunity. If you have any impending interviews ask the interviewer for some time to respond to the offer. Never give into the pressure (e.g. this is the best job and if you do not take it right now you might miss out etc) from the job agencies. Interviewers are generally happy to wait for the right candidate. Give yourself attention to all the aspects on offer like salary, type of industry (finance, telecom, consulting etc), opportunity for growth, type of project (large scale mission critical, medium sized etc), type of role (design, development and design, team lead, architect etc), type of technology used and opportunity to learn new things (e.g. Spring, Hibernate, Tapestry, JSF, Web services, messaging etc) to keep you motivated at your job as well as improve your future job prospects. Never think of salary aspect alone. You should have a long term plan. Sometimes it is worth your while to compromise on a few quid to acquire most sought after skills (at the time of writing Spring, Hibernate, JSF, Tapestry etc) and/or valuable skills (design skills, leadership skills etc). So for each interview you attend keep a checklist of aspects on offer and always act calmly and professionally to make the right decision for you.

Java

Questions	Hint
Multi-threading	
What language features are available to allow shared access to data in a multi-threading environment?	Synchronized block, Synchronized method, wait, notify
What is the difference between synchronized method and synchronized block? When would you use?	Block on subset of data. Smaller code segment.
What Java language features would you use to implement a producer (one thread) and a consumer (another thread) passing data via a stack?	wait, notify
Data Types	
What Java classes are provided for date manipulation?	Calendar, Date
What is the difference between String and StringBuffer?	mutable, efficient
How do you ensure a class is Serializable?	Implement Serializable
What is the difference between static and instance field of a class	Per class vs. Per Object
What method do you need to implement to store class in Hashtable or HashMap?	hashCode(), equals()
How do you exclude a field of the class from serialization?	transient
Inheritance	
What is the difference between an Interface and an abstract base class?	interface inheritance, implementation inheritance.
What does overriding a method mean? (What about overloading?)	inheritance (different signature)
Memory	
What is the Java heap, and what is the stack?	dynamic, program thread execution.
Why does garbage collection occur and when can it occur?	To recover memory, as heap gets full.
If I have a circular reference of objects, but I no longer reference any of them from any executing thread, will these cause garbage collection problems?	no
Exceptions	
What is the problem or benefits of catching or throwing type "java.lang.Exception"?	Hides all subsequent exceptions.
What is the difference between a runtime exception and a checked exception?	Must catch or throw checked exceptions.

Web components

Questions	HINT
JSP	
What is the best practice regarding the use of scriptlets in JSP pages? (Why?)	Avoid
How can you avoid scriptlet code?	custom tags, Java beans
What do you understand by the term JSP compilation?	compiles to servlet code
Servlets	
What does Servlet API provide to store user data between requests?	HttpSession
What is the difference between forwarding a request and redirecting?	redirect return to browser
What object do you use to forward a request?	RequestDispatcher
What do you need to be concerned about with storing data in a servlet instance fields?	Multi-threaded.
What's the requirement on data stored in HttpSession in a clustered (distributable) environment?	Serializable
If I store an object in session, then change its state, is the state replicated to distributed Session?	No, only on setAttribute() call.
How does URL-pattern for servlet work in the web.xml?	/ddd/* or *.jsp
What is a filter, and how does it work?	Before/after request, chain.

Enterprise

Questions	Hint
JDBC	
What form of statement would you use to include user-supplied values?	PreparedStatement
Why might a preparedStatement be more efficient than a statement?	Execution plan cache.
How would you prevent an SQL injection attack in JDBC?	PreparsedStatement
What is the performance impact of testing against NULL in WHERE clause on Oracle?	Full table scan.
List advantages and disadvantages in using stored procedures?	Pro: integration with existing dbase, reduced network traffic Con: not portable, mutliple language

	knowledge required
What is the difference between sql.Date, sql.Time, and sql.Timestamp?	Date only, time only, date and time
If you had a missing int value how do you indicate this to PreparedStatement?	setNull(pos, TYPE)
How can I perform multiple inserts in one database interaction?	executeBatch
Given this problem: Program reads 100,000 rows, converts to Java class in list, then converts list to XML file using reflection. Runs out of program memory. How would you fix?	Read one row at time, limit select, allocate more heap (result set = cursor)
How might you model object inheritance in database tables?	Table per hierarchy, table per class, table per concrete class
JNDI	
What are typical uses for the JNDI API within an enterprise application	Resource management, LDAP access
Explain the difference between a lookup of these "java:comp/env/ejb/MyBean" and "ejb/MyBean"?	logical mapping performed for java:comp/env
What is the difference between new InitialContext() from servlet or from an EJB?	Different JNDI environments initialized. EJB controller by ejb-jar.xml, servlet by web.xml
What is an LDAP server used for in an enterprise environment?	authentication, authorization
What is authentication, and authorization?	Confirming identity, confirming access rights
EJB	
What is the difference between Stateless and Stateful session beans (used?)	Stateful holds per client state
What is the difference between Session bean and Entity bean (when used?)	Entity used for persistence
With Stateless Session bean pooling, when would a container typically take a instance from the pool and when would it return it?	for each business method
What is the difference between "Required", "Supports", "RequiresNew" "NotSupported", "Mandatory", "Never"	Needs transaction, existing OK but doesn't need, must start new one, suspends transaction, must already be started, error if transaction
What is "pass-by-reference" and "pass-by-value", and how does it affect J2EE applications?	Reference to actual object versus copy of object. RMI pass by value
What EJB patterns, best practices are you aware of? Describe at least two.	Façade, delegate, value list, DAO, value object
How do you define finder methods for a CMP?	Home, XML
If I reference an EJB from another EJB what can I cache to improve performance, and where should I do the caching?	Home, set it up in setSessionContext
Describe some issues/concerns you have with the J2EE specification	Get their general opinion of J2EE
Why is creating field value in setSessionContext of a performance benefit?	pooled, gc
What is the difference between System exception and application exception from an EJB method?	System exception, container will auto rollback
What do you understand by the term "offline optimistic locking" or long-lived business transaction? How might you implement this using EJB?	version number, date, field comparisons
Explain performance difference between getting a list of summary information (e.g. customer list) via finder using a BMP entity vs. Session using DAO?	BMP: n+1 database reads, n RMI calls
What is meant by a coarse-grained and a fine-grained interface?	Amount of data transferred per method call
XML/XSLT	
What is the difference between a DOM parser and a SAX parser?	DOM: reads entire model, SAX: event published during parsing
What is the difference between DTD and XML Schema?	level of detail, Schema is in XML.
What does the JAXP API do for you?	Parser independence
What is XSLT and how can it be used?	XML transformation
What would be the XPath to select any element called table with the class attribute of info?	Table[@class='info']
JMS	
How can asynchronous events be managed in J2EE?	JMS
How do transactions affect the onMessage() handling of a MDB?	Taking off queue
If you send a JMS message from an EJB, and transaction rollback, will message be sent?	yes
How do you indicate what topic or queue MDB should react to?	deployment descriptor
What is the difference between a topic and a queue?	broadcast, single
SOAP	
What is a Web service, and how does it relate to SOAP?	SOAP is the protocol
What is a common transport for SOAP messages?	HTTP
What is WSDL? How would you use a WSDL file?	XML description of Web Service: interface and how to bind to it.
With new J2EE SOAP support what is: JAXR, JAX-RPC, and SAAJ?	registry, rap, attachments
Security	
Where can container level security be applied in J2EE application?	Web Uri's, EJB methods
How can the current user be obtained in a J2EE application (Web and Enterprise)?	getUserPrincipal

	getCallerPrincipal
How can you perform role checks in a J2EE application (Web and enterprise)?	IsUserInRole() IsCallerInRole()

Design

OO

Questions	Hint
Name some type of UML diagrams.	class, sequence, activity, use case
Describe some types of relationships can you show on class diagrams?	generalization, aggregation, uses
What is the difference between association, aggregation, and generalization?	Relationship, ownership, inheritance
What is a sequence diagram used to display?	Object instance interactions via operations/signals
What design patterns do you use. Describe one you have used (not singleton)	e.g. Builder, Factory, Visitor, Chain of Command
Describe the observer pattern and an example of how it would be used	e.g. event notification when model changes to view
What are Use Cases?	Define interaction between actors and the system
What is your understanding of encapsulation?	Encapsulate data and behavior within class
What is your understanding of polymorphism?	Class hierarchy, runtime determine instance

Process

Questions	Hint
Have you heard of or used test-driven development?	e.g. XP process
What previous development process have you followed?	Rational, XP, waterfall
How do you approach capturing client requirements?	Numbered requirements, use case
What process steps would you include between the capture of requirements and when coding begins?	Architecture, Design, UML modeling
How would you go about solving performance issue in an application?	Set goals, establish bench, profile application, make changes one at a time
What developer based testing are you familiar with (before system testing?)	Unit test discussion
How might you test a business system exposed via a Web interface?	Automated script emulating browser
What is your experience with iterative development?	Multiple iteration before release

Distributed Application

Questions	Hint
Explain a typical architecture of a business system exposed via Web interface?	Explain tiers (presentation, enterprise, resource) Java technology used in each tiers, hardware distribution of Web servers, application server, database server
Describe what tiers you might use in a typical large scale (> 200 concurrent users) application and the responsibilities of each tier (where would validation, presentation, business logic, persistence occur).	Another way of asking same question as above if their answer wasn't specific enough
Describe what you understand by being able to "scale" an application? How does a J2EE environment aid scaling.	Vertical and Horizontal scaling. Thread management, clustering, split tiers
What are some security issues in Internet based applications?	authentication, authorization, data encryption, denial service, xss attacks

General

Questions	Hints
What configuration management are you familiar with?	e.g. CVS, ClearCase
What issue/tracking process have you followed?	Want details on bug recording and resolution process.
What are some key factors to working well within a team?	Gets a view on how you would work within interviewer's environment.
What attributes do you assess when considering a new job? (what makes it a good one)	Insight into what motivates you.
What was the last computing magazine you read? Last computing book? What is a regular online magazine/reference you use?	Understand how up to date you keep yourself.

GLOSSARY OF TERMS

TERM	DESCRIPTION
ACID	Atomicity, Consistency, Isolation, Durability.
Ajax	Asynchronous JavaScript And XML
aka	also known as.
AOP	Aspect Oriented Programming
API	Application Programming Interface
AWT	Abstract Window Toolkit
BLOB	Binary Large Object
BMP	Bean Managed Persistence
CGI	Common Gateway Interface
CLOB	Character Large OBject
CMP	Container Managed Persistence
CORBA	Common Object Request Broker Architecture
CRM	Customer Relationships Management
CRUD	Create, Read, Update and Delete
CSS	Cascading Style Sheets
csv	Comma Separated Value
CRC	Cyclic Redundancy Checks
DAO	Data Access Object
DNS	Domain Name Service
DOM	Document Object Model
DTD	Document Type Definition
EAR	Enterprise ARchive
EIS	Enterprise Information System
EJB	Enterprise JavaBean
EL	Expression Language
ERP	Enterprise Resource Planning
FDD	Feature Driven Development
GIF	Graphic Interchange Format
GOF	Gang Of Four
HQL	Hibernate Query Language.
HTML	Hyper Text Markup Language
HTTP	Hyper Text Transfer Protocol
I/O	Input/Output
IDE	Integrated Development Environment
IIOP	Internet Inter-ORB Protocol
IoC	Inversion of Control
IP	Internet Protocol
J2EE	Java 2 Enterprise Edition
JAAS	Java Authentication and Authorization Service
JAF	JavaBeans Activation Framework
JAR	Java ARchive
JAXB	Java API for XML Binding
JAXP	Java API for XML Parsing
JAXR	Java API for XML Registries
JAX-RPC	Java API for XML-based RPC
JAX-WS	Java API for XML-based Web Services
JCA	J2EE Connector Architecture
JDBC	Java Database Connectivity
JDK	Java Development Kit
JFC	Java Foundation Classes
JMS	Java Messaging Service
JMX	Java Management eXtensions
JNDI	Java Naming and Directory Interface
JNI	Java Native Interface
JRMP	Java Remote Method Protocol
JSF	JavaServer Faces
JSP	Java Server Pages
JSTL	Java Standard Tag Library
JTA	Java Transaction API
JVM	Java Virtual Machine
LDAP	Lightweight Directory Access Protocol

MOM	Message Oriented Middleware
MVC	Model View Controller
NDS	Novell Directory Service
NIO	New I/O
O/R mapping	Object to Relational mapping.
OO	Object Oriented
OOP	Object Oriented Programming
OOPL	Object Oriented Programming Language
ORB	Object Request Broker
ORM	Object to Relational Mapping.
POJI	Plain Old Java Interface
POJO	Plain Old Java Object
RAR	Resource adapter ARchive
RDBMS	Relational Database Management System
RMI	Remote Method Invocation
RPC	Remote Procedure Call
RUP	Rational Unified Process
SAAJ	SOAP with attachment API for Java
SAX	Simple API for XML
SOA	Service Oriented Architecture
SOAP	Simple Object Access Protocol
SQL	Structured Query Language
SSL	Secure Sockets Layer
TCP	Transmission Control Protocol
TDD	Test Driven Development
UDDI	Universal Description Discovery and Integration
UDP	User Datagram Protocol
UI	User Interface
UML	Unified Modeling Language
URI	Uniform Resource Identifier
URL	Uniform Resource Locator
UTF	
VO	Value Object which is a plain Java class which has attributes or fields and corresponding getter → getXXX() and setter → setXXX() methods .
WAR	Web ARchive
WML	Wireless Markup Language
WSDL	Web Service Description Language
XHTML	Extensible Hypertext Markup Language
XML	Extensible Markup Language
XP	Extreme Programming
XPath	XML Path
XSD	XML Schema Definition
XSL	Extensible Style Language
XSL-FO	Extensible Style Language – Formatting Objects
XSLT	Extensible Style Language Transformation

RESOURCES

Articles

- Sun Java Certified Enterprise Architect by Leo Crawford on http://www.leocrawford.org.uk/work/jcea/part1/index.html.
- Practical UML: A Hands-On Introduction for Developers by Randy Miller on http://bdn.borland.com/article/0,1410,31863,00.html
- W3 Schools on http://www.w3schools.com/default.asp.
- LDAP basics on http://publib.boulder.ibm.com/iseries/v5r2/ic2924/index.htm?info/rzahy/rzahyovrco.htm.
- Java World articles on design patterns: http://www.javaworld.com/columns/jw-Java-design-patterns-index.shtml.
- Web Servers vs. App Servers: Choosing Between the Two By Nelson King on http://www.serverwatch.com/tutorials/article.php/1355131.
- Follow the Chain of Responsibility by David Geary on Java World - http://www.javaworld.com/javaworld/jw-08-2003/jw-0829-designpatterns.html.
- J2EE Design Patterns by Sue Spielman on http://www.onjava.com/pub/a/onjava/2002/01/16/patterns.html.
- The New Methodology by Martin Fowler on http://www.martinfowler.com/articles/newMethodology.html.
- Merlin brings nonblocking I/O to the Java platform by Aruna Kalagnanam and Balu G on http://www.ibm.com/developerworks/Java/library/j-javaio.
- Hibernate Tips and Pitfalls by Phil Zoio on http://www.realsolve.co.uk/site/tech/hib-tip-pitfall-series.php.
- Hibernate Reference Documentation on http://www.hibernate.org/hib_docs/reference/en/html_single/.
- Object-relation mapping without the container by Richard Hightower on http://www-128.ibm.com/developerworks/library/j-hibern/?ca=dnt515.
- Object to Relational Mapping and Relationships with Hibernate by Mark Eagle on http://www.meagle.com:8080/hibernate.jsp.
- Mapping Objects to Relational databases: O/R Mapping In detail by Scott W. Ambler on http://www.agiledata.org/essays/mappingObjects.html.
- I want my AOP by Ramnivas Laddad on Java World.
- WebSphere Application Server 5.0 for iSeries – Performance Considerations by Jill Peterson.
- Dependency Injection using pico container by Subbu Ramanathan .
- WebSphere Application Server & Database Performance tuning by Michael S. Pallos on http://www.bizforum.org/whitepapers/candle-5.htm.
- A beginners guide to Dependency Injection by Dhananjay Nene on http://www.theserverside.com/articles/article.tss?l=IoCBeginners.
- The Spring series: Introduction to the Spring framework by Naveen Balani on http://www-128.ibm.com/developerworks/web/library/wa-spring1.
- The Spring Framework by Benoy Jose.
- Inversion of Control Containersband the Dependency Injection pattern by Martin Fowler.
- Migrate J2EE Applications for EJB 3.0 by Debu Panda on JavaPro.
- EJB 3.0 in a nutshell by Anil Sharma on JavaWorld.
- Preparing for EJB 3.0 by Mike Keith on ORACLE Technology Network.
- Simplify enterprise Java development with EJB 3.0 by Michael Juntao Yuan on JavaWorld.
- J2SE: New I/O by John Zukowski on http://java.sun.com/developer/technicalArticles/releases/nio/.
- High-Performance I/O arrives by Danniel F. Savarese on JavaPro.
- Hibernate – Proxy Visitor Pattern by Kurtis Williams.
- Best Practices for Exception Handling by Gunjan Doshi.
- Three Rules for Effective Exception Handling by Jim Cushing.
- LDAP and JNDI: Together forever – by Sameer Tyagi.
- Introduction To LDAP – by Brad Marshall.
- Java theory and practice: Decorating with dynamic proxies by Brian Goetz.
- Java Dynamic Proxies: One Step from Aspect-Oriented Programming by Lara D'Abreo.
- Java Design Patterns on http://www.allapplabs.com/java_design_patterns .
- Software Design Patterns on http://www.dofactory.com/Patterns/Patterns.aspx .
- JRun: Core Dump and Dr. Watson Errors on http://www.macromedia.com/cfusion/knowledgebase/index.cfm?id=tn_17534
- The Guerrilla Guide to Interviewing by Joel Spolsky at http://www.joelonsoftware.com/printerFriendly/articles/fog0000000073.html
- The Riddle of Job Interviews by Kate Kane at http://www.fastcompany.com/online/01/jobint_Printer_Fiendly.html
- An Introduction to Aspect-Oiented Programming with the Spring Framework, Part 1 by Russell Miles at http://www.onjava.com/lpt/a/4994
- 5 Habits Of Best Software Developers by Angusman Chakraborty at http://blog.taragana.com/index.php/archive/5-habits-of-best-doftware-developers/
- Getting started with Hibernate by Alan P Saxton at http://www.cs.bham.ac.uk/~aps/syllabi/2004_2005/issws/h03/hibernate.html
- Hibernate Tips by Jason Carreira at http://jroller.com/page/jcarreira/20050223
- Five Things I Love About Spring by Bruce A. Tate at http://www.onjava.com/lpt/a/5833
- Service-oriented modeling and architecture by Ali Arsanjani , Ph.D at http://www-128.ibm.com/developerworks/webservices/library/ws-soa-design1/
- Delving into Service-Oriented Architecture by Bernhad Borges, Kerrie Holley and Ali Arsanjani at http://www.developer.com/design/print.php/10925_3409221_1
- SOA: Are We Reinventing the Wheel? By Nick Simha at http://dev2dev.bea.com/lpt/a/435
- Getting a little closer to SOA by Fabrice Marguerie at http://madgeek.com/Articles/SOA/EN/SOA-Softly.html
- What is sevice-oriented architecture by Raghu R. Kodali at http://www.javaworld.com/javaworld/jw-06-2005/jw-0613-soa_p.html

- J2EE-Supported Web Service standards and Technologies by Vijay Ramachandran, Sean Brydon, Greg Murray. Inderjeet Singh, Beth Stearns, Thierry Violleau.
- J2EE 1.4 eases Web service development by Frank Sommers at http://www.javaworld.com/javaworld/jw-06-2003/jw-0620-webservices_p.html
- A developer's introduction to JAX-RPC, Part 1 & 2 by Joshy Joseph at http://www-128.ibm.com/developerworks/webservices/library/
- Developing Web Services with Java 2 Platform, Enterprise Edition (J2EE) 1.4 Platform by Qusay H. Mahmoud at http://java.sun.com/developer/technicalArticles/J2EE/j2ee_ws/
- Scriptless JSP Pages: The Front Man by Bear Bibeault at http://www.javaranch.com/journal/200603/Journal200603.jsp
- Advanced DAO programming by Sean Sullivan at http://www-128.ibm.com/developerworks/library/j-dao/
- Understanding JavaServer Pages Model 2 architecture by Govind Seshadri at http://www.javaworld.com/javaworld/jw-12-1999/jw-12-ssj-jspmvc_p.html
- A Fast Introduction to Basic Servlet Programming by Marty Hall at http://www.informit.com/articles/printerfriendly.asp/p=29817&r1=1
- What's new in J2Se 5.0? based on Joshua Bloch's on-line talk.
- Introducing Java 5 by Andy Grant at http://www.sitepoint.com/print/introducing-java-5
- Experiences with the New Java 5 Language Features by Jess Garms and Tim Hanson at http://dev2dev.bea.com/lpt/a/442
- Five Favorite Features from 5.0 by David Flanagan at http://www.onjava.com/lpt/a/5799
- First among equals by Kevlin Henney at http://www.regdeveloper.com/2005/12/29/first_among_equals/print.html
- Painting in AWT and Swing by Amy Fowler.
- A Hands-On Introduction for Developers by Randy Miller at http://bdn.borland.com/article/0,1410,31863,00.html
-

- www.javaworld.com articles.
- http://www-128.ibm.com/developerworks/java articles.
- http://www.devx.com/java articles.
- www.theserverside.com/tss articles.
- http://javaboutique.internet.com/articles articles.

Books

- Beginning Java 2 by Ivor Horton.
- Design Patterns by Erich Gamma, Richard Helm, Ralph Johnson, John Vlissides (GoF) .
- UML Distilled by Martin Fowler, Kendall Scott .
- Mastering Enterprise Java Beans II by Ed Roman, Scott Ambler, Tyler Jewell, Floyd Marinescu.
- EJB Design Patterns by Floyd Marinescu .
- Sun Certified Enterprise Architect for J2EE Technology Study Guide by Mark Cade and Simon Roberts.
- Professional Java Server Programming - J2EE edition by Wrox publication.
- Design Patterns Java Companion by James W. Cooper (Free download: http://www.patterndepot.com/put/8/JavaPatterns.htm).
- Test Driven Development – By Example, by Kent Beck.
- Effective Java – programming language guide by Joshua Bloch

356